5

Modern Production Management

THE WILEY SERIES IN MANAGEMENT AND ADMINISTRATION

Elwood S. Buffa, Advisory Editor
University of California, Los Angeles

Peter P. Schoderbek MANAGEMENT SYSTEMS, Second Edition

Elwood S. Buffa OPERATIONS MANAGEMENT: PROBLEMS AND MODELS, Third Edition

William R. King PROBABILITY FOR MANAGEMENT DECISIONS

Henry H. Albers PRINCIPLES OF MANAGEMENT: A MODERN APPROACH, Third Edition

Elwood S. Buffa MODERN PRODUCTION MANAGEMENT, Fourth Edition

CASES IN OPERATIONS MANAGEMENT: A SYSTEMS APPROACH
James L. McKenney and Richard S. Rosenbloom

Joseph A. Litterer ORGANIZATIONS: STRUCTURE AND BEHAVIOR, Volume I, Second Edition

Joseph A. Litterer ORGANIZATIONS: SYSTEMS, CONTROL AND ADAPTATION, Volume II

MANAGEMENT AND ORGANIZATIONAL BEHAVIOR: A MULTIDIMENSIONAL APPROACH
Billy J. Hodge and Herbert J. Johnson

Claude McMillan MATHEMATICAL PROGRAMMING: AN INTRODUCTION TO THE DESIGN AND APPLICATION OF OPTIMAL DECISION MACHINES

DECISION MAKING THROUGH OPERATIONS RESEARCH
Robert J. Thierauf and Richard A. Grosse

Elwood G. Kirkpatrick QUALITY CONTROL FOR MANAGERS & ENGINEERS

James L. Riggs PRODUCTION SYSTEMS: PLANNING, ANALYSIS AND CONTROL

Forrest P. Wyman SIMULATION MODELING: A GUIDE TO USING SIMSCRIPT

BASIC STATISTICS FOR BUSINESS AND ECONOMICS
Paul G. Hoel and Raymond J. Jessen

Richard H. Buskirk BUSINESS AND ADMINISTRATIVE POLICY

INTRODUCTION TO ELECTRONIC COMPUTING: A MANAGEMENT APPROACH
Rodney L. Boyes, Robert W. Shields and Larry G. Greenwell

COMPUTER SIMULATION OF HUMAN BEHAVIOR
John M. Dutton and William H. Starbuck

INTRODUCTION TO GAMING: MANAGEMENT DECISION SIMULATIONS
John G. H. Carlson and Michael J. Misshauk

Burt K. Scanlan PRINCIPLES OF MANAGEMENT AND ORGANIZATION

COMMUNICATION IN MODERN ORGANIZATIONS
George T. Vardaman and Patricia B. Vardaman

Joseph A. Litterer THE ANALYSIS OF ORGANIZATIONS, Second Edition

Allan Easton COMPLEX MANAGERIAL DECISIONS

To Carl

preface

The field of production and operations management continues to shift in the direction of a more analytical approach based on the continued development of management science in general. Also involved in this trend is a broadening of viewpoint so that we may properly talk about "operations management" implying a concept which transcends the manufacturing enterprise. We deal with productive activities found in many other settings than manufacturing, and activities outside the manufacturing function which interact with that function. For example, inventories in warehouse and distribution systems have a bearing on problems of programming production upstream. The recognition of this fact is forcing the adoption of the broader "systems" point of view discussed in the first three editions of this book and further developed in this edition.

The fourth edition retains the basic format of the third edition but with some major additions and deletions, as well as a general updating of material. A few of the major changes follow.

An entirely new chapter on the systems concept has been introduced in Part 1 to help lay out a general framework. These general concepts of systems and systems analysis are used in many places in the balance of the book.

The former appendices dealing with linear programming and waiting lines have been relocated in the body of the text in Part 2, "Analytical Methods."

The former two chapters on job design have been condensed into a single chapter with a new format and the elimination of the behaviorally oriented material.

The former chapter on production design of products and process planning has been divided into two chapters, absorbing some of the material dealing with automation and information systems. The two new chapters are Chapter 9, "Product Design and Processes," and Chapter 10, "Process Planning."

In Part 4, which deals with operations planning and control, the scheduling and control materials have been differentiated according to the type of system and expanded to three chapters. These three chapters deal with the scheduling and control problems in the three types of systems: high-volume systems, intermittent systems, and large project systems. Also in this section of the book, the former chapters dealing with wages and cost improvement have been eliminated.

Finally, new materials emphasizing nonmanufacturing applications have been added in a number of places and additional review questions and problems have been added at the ends of many chapters.

Pacific Palisades, California   Elwood S. Buffa

preface to the first edition

The development of knowledge in production management has been extremely rapid. The result has been that the reading material available to college survey courses in this field has reflected neither the changed conceptual framework nor the increased depth of subject matter which represents current thinking. In preparing this book, I have adopted a general outline which I believe makes possible the inclusion of much of the new material in a way that is comprehensible to the average diligent student, without placing heavy emphasis on mathematical skill. The four-part outline (Introduction, Analytical Methods in Production Management, Design of the Productive System, and Operation and Control of Production Systems) introduces a grounding in analytical method early in the book, so that the broad problem areas of system design, operation, and control can be based upon the analytical methods. In this framework, I believe that it has been possible for me to write the sections of the book that deal with the problem areas of production without great distortion or oversimplification of the new material that comes to us from management science, industrial engineering, and operations research.

In the introductory sections of the book, I recognize a broader definition of production than has been applied in comparable books of the past, although, throughout the remainder of the book, the factory model is predominant. I believe that this broader definition, which recognizes that production concepts are pervasive, is of considerable importance for the future. Our society has developed significant production systems in many kinds of activities, for example, hospitals, supermarkets, retail stores, and offices. Production really deals with the "operations" phase of any activity, regardless of its setting. The development of courses in this general field is now reflecting, and perhaps should reflect even more, that the general principles of production are applicable in all of these situations.

Finally, this book concentrates on the economics of production. Courses in the past have tended to be almost comparable to the dreaded "Introduction to Business" course, attempting to cover everything from every viewpoint. The result has often been that nothing was covered in any depth because time did not permit more than a cursory oversimplification of many challenging and important concepts. This is simply unrealistic today. The production course must recognize the existence of other important specialized areas, such as organization and general management, personnel, human relations, and industrial relations. Such a course can recognize these fields best by assuming their coverage elsewhere in the curriculum, thus allowing a more adequate coverage of the truly "hard-core" production concepts.

Elwood S. Buffa

Pacific Palisades, California
January 1961

acknowledgments

A book of this length is necessarily based on a wide variety of original sources. While I have made original contributions in some specific areas of analysis and in the conceptual framework, the bulk of the material on which the book is based comes from other contributors. I have carefully shown the sources of these materials at the points they are discussed. I hope I have made no omissions. I have benefited greatly from reviews and comments on previous editions by well known professors such as Robert Albanese of Miami University, William H. Bolen of Georgia Southern College, Robert W. Boling of the University of Tennessee, John D. Burns of DePaul University, Norbett L. Enrick of Kent State University, Warren Hausman of MIT, James L. McKenney of Harvard University, William T. Newell of the University of Washington, J. A. Sargeant of the University of Toronto, and Thomas Vollmann of the University of Rhode Island. Those who made important inputs specifically for the fourth edition are: Y. S. Chang of Boston University, George J. Gore of the University of Cincinnati, Gene J. Groff of Indiana University, S. T. Hardy of Ohio State University, Loy Housewright of Western Illinois University, and Richard J. Tersine of Old Dominion University.

Finally, I wish to acknowledge that debt I owe to my students. Working directly on an individual basis and in classes with students has been a constant source of inspiration and ideas. Some of the most notable of these students are: Jack Alcalay, Gordon Armour, Lewis Carson, Charles Holloway, Arnold Reisman, William Taubert, and Thomas Vollmann.

The manuscript was carefully prepared and proofread at several stages. It is my fondest desire that no errors remain, yet my previous experience tells me that this is virtually an impossibility.

contents

Part One   Introduction   1

1. Production & Operations Management, Past & Present   3
2. Decision Making & the Production Function   19
3. The Systems Concept   45

Part Two   Analytical Methods   65

4. Analytical Methods in Production & Operations
   Management   67
5. Cost Data for Decisions   109
6. Capital Costs & Investment Criteria   127
7. Linear Programming   147
8. Waiting Lines   193

Part Three   Design of Productive Systems   213

9. Production Design & Processes   215
10. Process Planning   251
11. Plant Location   283
12. Layout of Physical Facilities   309
13. Job Design & Man-Machine Systems   365
14. Production Standards & Work Measurement   417

Part Four   Operations Planning & Control   451

15. Production-Inventory Systems   453
16. Forecasting & Inventories   473
17. Aggregate Plans & Programs   507
18. Scheduling & Control for High-Volume Systems   547
19. Scheduling & Control for Intermittent Systems   571
20. Planning, Scheduling, & Control for Large-Scale Projects   593
21. Maintenance   621
22. Control of Quality   643

Part Five   Synthesis   671

23. Production & Operations Management—Summary   673

Part Six   Appendix—Tables   687

I. PV_{sp}, Present Value Factors for Future Single Payments   689
II. PV_a, Present Value Factors for Annuities   690
III. Factors Useful in the Construction of Control Charts   691
IV. Table of Random Digits   692

Index   693

part one

Introduction

1

Production & Operations Management, Past & Present

Some say that the postindustrial society has already been attained in the United States. The economy has the capability to produce everything needed by everyone and is indeed sometimes referred to as a surplus economy. They say that the physical production of goods and services in adequate quantities can be assumed, and therefore we must concentrate our attention on the problems of ecology, social justice, and education, as well as the problems of using leisure time effectively so that we will not be bored with the good life available for all. If the previous statements are true, then why be concerned with production

3

management? The answer is that, if we are going to allocate a substantial fraction of our national effort toward the goals alluded to above, we must either make the production machine work smoothly, effectively, and even more abundantly, or in fact we must give up some of our physical product in order to meet the objectives of some of the new goals. However, the two objectives are intertwined because an attack on social and ecological problems necessarily depends in some measure on the capabilities of the economic system. Also, some of the methods of analysis used in production and operations management and operations research are valid mechanisms to study and solve the other problems.

Most national planners seem to be assuming that we can have both a high standard of life for all as well as allocate an increasing fraction of our effort toward the solution of our social and ecological problems. Their faith is perhaps justified by the extraordinary progress and performance made in the analysis, design, and operations of productive systems in the past fifteen to twenty years. It has become clear that many phases of productive systems can be automated, that many important areas of decision can be reduced to automatic rules, and that computers can become process controllers. Yet, we cannot assume that the production machine will automatically do its job. Someone must design the productive systems as well as the information and control systems needed to operate them.

PRODUCTIVE SYSTEMS— A CRUCIAL ROLE IN MODERN SOCIETY

It would be difficult to overemphasize the crucial role effective productive systems play in modern society and in our life style. Indeed, the stamp *developed economy* carries with it the image of large, highly organized, specialized, mechanized, efficient productive systems. On the other hand, the term *underdeveloped economy* includes the image of small, handicraft, inefficient productive systems powered mainly by the muscles of men and beasts. This contrast of images is, of course, too simple an explanation for the difference between developed and underdeveloped economies. Transforming the nature of productive systems in an underdeveloped economy would not by itself create a developed one. Nevertheless, a modern society with all of its attributes of material wealth is not possible without its characteristic productive systems.

As a matter of fact, it is unfortunate that we make the association between large output per man hour and a thrifty, industrious, hardworking people with the reverse personal characteristics assigned to low output per man hour situations. Individuals in an economy typified by low output per man hour may actually work harder in a physical sense because of the absence of mechanization to accomplish the heaviest tasks.

It is also true that the high output per man hour economy is thought of as being efficient while its opposite is thought of as being inefficient. But production efficiency is a relative term meaning, essentially, "how effectively we employ the appropriate available resources (input) for a given unit of output." Thus, in developed economies costs of machinery and equipment are relatively low and labor costs are relatively high reflecting the generally high output per man hour of workers in that economy. In underdeveloped economies the reverse relative costs are generally true. (The cost of raw materials may be high or low in either situation depending on a complex of factors.) Therefore, an efficient productive system in the developed economy is one which uses mechanization to a great extent and relatively little labor to yield a minimum combined cost of capital, labor, and raw material per unit of output.

For the identical product produced in an underdeveloped economy, an efficient production system would reverse the relative amounts of capital and labor inputs in order to yield a minimum combined cost of capital, labor, and raw materials. Both systems could be efficient if they minimized the resource inputs per unit of output. This is an important point to understand about the effective design and operation of productive systems. We are not always attempting to employ the most sophisticated mechanized or automated technique known. Rather, we are attempting to employ the best balance of resources in each situation. Thus, even in the United States economy, a system designed for a relatively small output will ordinarily emphasize the use of labor as an input compared to capital. Throughout this book we retain this general viewpoint, but it is most evident in Chapters 5 and 6 where we deal with costs for managerial decisions, Chapters 9 and 10 on production design of products and process planning, Chapter 11 on plant location, Chapter 12 on layout of physical facilities, and Chapter 13 on job design and man-machine systems.

In a given production system, successful management depends on plans, an information system concerning what is actually happening, and how we react (make decisions) to changes in demand, inventory position, schedules, quality level, and product and equipment innovation. In forming plans for the operation or management of a productive system, we are attempting to allocate the available resources in the most effective way for a given forecast of demand. The resources are units of productive

Production Economics— A Problem of Cost Balance

Operating a Production System— A Problem of Information and Decision Analysis capacity such as number of man hours available at regular time and overtime, inventories available, subcontracting, as well as a negative capacity which occurs when shortages or back orders take place. In constructing production plans, each of these capacities is provided at a cost, and the best plan is one which minimizes the sum of all costs over some future time span.

In attempting to meet the objectives of a plan, certain realities interfere, such as equipment failure, human error, discrepancies in the timing of order flow, quality variation, and so on. Therefore, systems for scheduling maintenance, quality control, and cost control are invented to help retain order where otherwise the system would naturally tend toward chaos.

Productive
Systems—
Conversion to
Useful Products
or Conversion
to Pollution?

Productive systems have been commonly thought of as mechanisms for converting some sort of raw material to something useful. In the process, of course, there are normally wastes but in the past very little attention has been paid to them. The emphasis was on the useful product and wastes were disposed of in the cheapest possible way—dumped into rivers and streams or into the atmosphere. Only recently have we begun to realize that we may be fouling our own nests.

Today, socially conscious managers realize that the production function must include the processing of wastes to the point that they are benign or in themselves useful, rather than hazardous or even lethal. Waste conversion is a part of the production process and must be included in our conceptual framework.

A HISTORICAL BRIEF

The first recognized attention to production economics was paid by the great Scottish economist Adam Smith at the time the factory system was emerging. In 1776 he wrote *The Wealth of the Nations* in which he observed three basic economic advantages resulting from the division of labor. These were the development of a skill or a dexterity when a single task was performed repetitively, a saving of the time normally lost in changing from one activity to the next, and the invention of machines or tools that seemed normally to follow when men specialized their efforts on tasks of restricted scope. Smith did not deduce these ideas in a theoretical way. Instead, under the factory system, division of labor was developing as a common-sense method of production when a relatively large group of workers was brought together to produce in large quantity. Under these conditions, a cooperative approach made good sense. Smith observed this practice, noted the three advantages, and wrote about them in his book. The book was a milestone in the development of production economics, not only because Smith's observations probably accelerated the division of labor, but also because a great scholar had recognized that there existed a rationale for production. The actual development of the rationale was to take a long, long time. As we shall note, we are *now* at last in the true rapid developmental stage, where production management as a discipline is emerging from a purely descriptive phase to take on the characteristics of an applied science.

After Adam Smith, an Englishman, Charles Babbage, augmented Smith's observations and raised a number of provocative questions about production organization and economics. Basically a mathematician who became interested in manufacturing, Babbage's inquiring mind and scientific orientation led him to question many existing practices. His thoughts were summarized in the book, *On the Economy of Machinery and Manufactures* (1832). Concerning the economic advantages resulting from the division of labor, Babbage agreed with Smith, but he observed that Smith had overlooked a most important advantage. For an example, Babbage used a study of pin manufacturing (the common straight pin) as it existed at that time. The level of specialization resulted in seven basic operations for making pins.

1. *Drawing wire.* This operation consisted of drawing wire through a die to reduce it to the desired diameter.
2. *Straightening the wire.*
3. *Pointing.*
4. *Twisting and cutting heads.*
5. *Heading.*
6. *Tinning or whitening.* This operation was comparable to a modern plating process to prevent rusting of the steel wire.
7. *Papering.* This consisted of placing the completed pins in papers or cards by piercing the paper, that is, the packaging of the pins.

Babbage noted the pay scale for these different specialties in shillings and pence (s.d.) (see Table I). He then pointed out that if the shop were reorganized so that each man performed the entire sequence of operations, the wage paid to these men would be dictated by the most difficult or rarest skill required by the entire sequence. Thus the enterprise would pay for the tinning skill, even when the workman was straightening, heading, or papering. With division of labor, however,

TABLE I. Analysis of Processes and Manufacturing Costs in Pin Making English Manufacture [(178.) Pins, *"Elevens,"* 5,546 weigh one pound; *"one dozen,"* 6,932 pins weigh twenty ounces, and require six ounces of paper.]

Name of the Process	Work-men	Time of Making 1 lb of Pins, *hours*	Cost of Making 1 lb of Pins, *pence*	Work-man Earns per Day, *s.*	*d.*	Price of Making Each Part of a Single Pin, in Millionths of a Penny
1. Drawing wire (§ 170.)	Man	.3636	1.2500	3	3	225
2. Straightening the wire (§ 171.)	Woman	.3000	.2840	1	0	51
	Girl	.3000	.1420	0	6	26
3. Pointing (§ 172.)	Man	.3000	1.7750	5	3	319
4. Twisting and cutting the heads (§ 173.)	Boy	.0400	.0147	0	4½	3
	Man	.0400	.2103	5	4½	38
5. Heading (§ 174.)	Woman	4.0000	5.0000	1	3	901
6. Tinning, or whitening (§ 175.)	Man	.1071	.6666	6	0	121
	Woman	.1071	.3333	3	0	60
7. Papering (§ 176.)	Woman	2.1314	3.1973	1	6	576
		7.6892	12.8732			2320

Number of persons employed: men, 4; women, 4; children, 2; total, 10.
Reproduced from *The Economy of Machinery and Manufactures,* 1832.

just the amount of skill needed could be purchased. Therefore, in addition to the productivity advantages cited by Adam Smith, Babbage recognized the principle of limiting skills as a basis for pay.

In the years after Adam Smith's and Charles Babbage's observations, the division of labor continued and then accelerated during the first half of the twentieth century. Our great production lines represent the the principle of division of labor carried to its greatest extreme. In fact, it has been carried so far that some people are questioning the present level of application. Cost reductions, based on broadening the scope of jobs, are being reported in the literature. A name has even been coined for this new trend, "job enlargement." Perhaps the optimal level has been passed in some industries.

Frederick W. Taylor was undoubtedly the outstanding historical figure in the development of the production management field. Smith and Babbage were observers and writers, but Taylor was both a thinker and a doer. He was also an authoritarian with an indomitable will, a fact that caused him to be greatly criticized but, at the same time, may have been the source of his great contributions. The practice of the day was to allow the workmen themselves to decide the means by which production would be achieved. They determined how to produce a part, according to their skills and past experience, and the time and cost of production were guided by traditional methods. "Boondoggling" and spreading of the work were common.

Taylor was familiar with these practices because he entered the industrial system as a worker, in which capacity he refused to go along with the other workers and instead produced as much as he could. He advanced rapidly and was later in a position to experiment with some of his ideas. To comprehend the extent of Taylor's accomplishments, we must understand that he was an innovator in a managerial environment of general apathy, where strong traditions existed, giving the workmen a free rein to determine manufacturing methods and the right to hold their knowledge as trade secrets. In this static environment, Taylor set in motion a tidal wave of change in managerial philosophy which shook many organizations from top to bottom.

Essentially, Taylor's new philosophy stated that the scientific method could and should be applied to all managerial problems, and that the methods by which work was accomplished should be determined by management through scientific investigation. He listed four new duties of management which may be summarized as follows [7]*:

1. The development of a science for each element of a man's work to replace old rule-of-thumb methods.
2. The scientific selection, training, and development of workers, instead of the old practice of allowing the workman to choose his own tasks and to train himself as best as he could.
3. The development of a spirit of hearty cooperation between the workman and management to ensure that the work would be carried out in accordance with the scientifically devised procedures.
4. The division of work between the workers and the management in almost equal shares, each group taking over the work for which it was best fitted, instead of the former condition in which most work and responsibility fell on the workmen.

These four ideas, which led to much new thinking about managerial organization, are so much a part of present-day organizational practice that it is hard to believe that the situation was ever any different. Taylor's work, under the general heading of Number 1, developed into the field of methods engineering and work measurement. In more recent years, this area has expanded greatly with the help of experimental psychological and physiological researchers; now the field known as "human

---

*Numbers in brackets indicate corresponding references at the end of each chapter.

engineering" has general application in production management. From Numbers 2 and 3 has developed the field of personnel, with its techniques of personnel selection and placement, together with the organizational function of industrial relations. Number 4, the division of work between the workman and management, has had far-reaching implications. The basic managerial functions of planning and control now cover much of the work formerly done by workmen, leaving the first-line foreman and the workmen free to concentrate on the execution of carefully laid plans.

Taylor is also known for some pioneering experiments that he performed. These were in various areas including basic production organization, wage payment theory, and the development of fundamental procedures for tasks such as metal machining, pig iron handling, and shoveling which were common in the steel industry at that time. Through his metal-cutting experiments, Taylor expended thousands of pounds of metal over a period of ten years; these experiments resulted in specifications for the feeds and speeds that could be used for different metals and tool materials. Also in connection with these experiments, he discovered high-speed steel in collaboration with Maunsel White, a discovery that made him wealthy and allowed him to spend the bulk of his later life furthering his philosophy. Taylor believed that his important contributions were his general philosophy and approach to managerial problems rather than any specific discoveries. The latter were merely applications of "scientific management" to individual situations.

Taylor's uncompromising attitude in developing and installing his ideas caused much controversy, and he was strongly opposed in many quarters. In the environment in which Taylor worked, perhaps it was necessary to have a man of his hard-driving personality to change an industrial way of life.

His followers were numerous. Carl Barth, Henry L. Gantt, Harrington Emerson, Frank and Lillian Gilbreth, and others worked within Taylor's general framework and philosophy. There were others who donned his cloak without his knowledge and competence, and for a fast dollar they passed themselves off as consultants who could install the "Taylor system." Taylor disclaimed these "jackals," but they did much harm. By the bad name they gave "scientific management," they probably slowed the development of good practice in the field. Little change occurred in Taylor's basic ideas. The literature was filled with gimmicks and variants of the manifest products of Taylor's thinking, such as the wage payment plans, time study methods, and charts and mechanical control boards. But the science of production management, in the spirit Taylor envisioned it, was very slow to evolve.

There were perhaps many reasons for this slow development. Appropriate knowledge and tools were not yet available, and the misapplications of the post-Taylor period had to be lived down. Measurements in production systems commonly display great variation. For example, how much output can we expect from an operation? Output depends on the man on the job and the job conditions. But even for a given man on the job, we can expect great variation from hour to hour, day to day, week to week, etc. To describe such a system we need probability concepts and a knowledge of statistical methods. For years men tried to approach such problems by representing the output of a man or a man-machine system by a single number, as was common in most engineering problems; this method simply did not fit the situation. In fields such as mechanical engineering, electrical engineering, and chemical engineering, variability of measurements was small and the deterministic models yielded fairly good results. In production problems, however, variability was characteristic. Today, with the general knowledge of statistics and probability concepts, and with their application to production problems increasing, our models of production systems are closer to reality than ever before.

Another great difficulty that beset serious investigators in the period after Taylor was the complexity of the large-scale problems that appeared. It seemed that all variables of any problem were completely interdependent. It was obvious that mathematical techniques were needed, but none was available to give the kinds of solutions required. Even if they had been available, the time required to develop solutions manually would have been measured in man-lifetimes. Modern high-speed digital computers were needed, but these were not to become available, even for the biggest and strongest companies, until the 1950s. An attempt at mathematical analysis was made in 1915 by F. W. Harris, who developed the first economic lot-size model for a simple situation. This was further developed by F. E. Raymond and others, but applications of the idea in industry were not general. We attempt to place these historical events in perspective in Figure 1.

THE CURRENT ERA

The present upsurge of activity in the general field of production was preceded by two developments in the 1930s which helped lay the groundwork and point the way for the future. These were the develop-

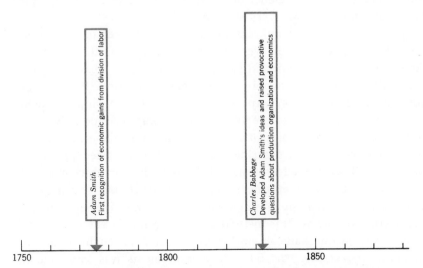

FIGURE 1. Progression of developments in production management.

ment and introduction to industry of statistical quality control by Walter Shewhart in 1931 and the development in 1934 of work sampling theory (a sampling procedure to determine standards for delays, work-time, etc.) by L. H. C. Tippett, working in England. Statistical quality control concepts grew rapidly and application of these probability concepts to the control of product quality became fairly general, especially with the onset of World War II. The acceptance of the basic concepts of sampling, control charts, etc., by workmen, foremen, and management was an important preliminary development for what was to come in the postwar period. Tippett's work-sampling procedure, however, was to lie almost completely dormant for twenty years and then finally to be dusted off by some progressive companies and put to work in the 1950s. Today it is used extensively and will very likely continue to grow in practical usefulness.

The current rate of development of production management concept, theory, and technique began shortly after World War II. Research in war operations by the armed forces produced new mathematical and computational techniques and also brought about an awareness of how to apply old techniques to war operation problems. The latter seemed to parallel problems of production operations, so the approaches to war problems began to trickle into industrial use. One significant development was the introduction of linear programming. Here at last

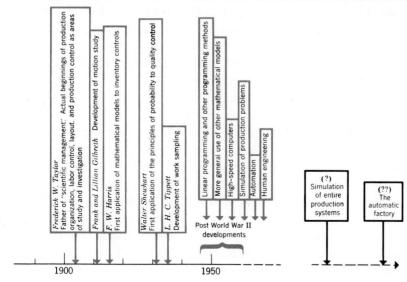

FIGURE 1. *(continued)*

was a basic mathematical tool capable of handling many of the large-scale, complex problems of scheduling and allocating the limited resources of a production system. But more important, the development of the high-speed computer made possible the solution of the large-scale linear programming problems. Linear programming without computers would have had a small field of application.

Other mathematical approaches were evolved. Waiting-line theory, which had been used for some time in the telephone industry to analyze telephone systems, found applications in production lines, tool booths, machine maintenance, etc. There developed new and more realistic inventory models that included variability and uncertainty of demand and other conditions. Models of replacement, maintenance, and competitive bidding all added to the general trend of formalizing production problems.

The computer appeared as a powerful tool in its own right, not merely as a device to perform the tedious labor of computation. With it, production systems could be simulated, modeled after fairly realistic conditions. If a complex system were simulated on a computer, the effect of alternative proposals could be determined quickly without the cost and time of actually trying the proposals in practice. On a broader scale, simulation has been done in the business decision games developed by AMA, UCLA, and others. Attempts are now being made to simulate through computer-based corporate models the actual operation of entire firms. As we shall see in Chapter 3 this is now being accomplished; in the not too distant future, progressive companies will have their operations simulated so that the probable effect of major alternative decisions can be determined before action is taken.

The computer has also contributed to the new field of automation. Here the computer is programmed to control machine tools through their entire cycle, completed parts resulting without the aid of the human hand. These developments have great future significance, both socially and economically. As technology grows in this field, computers will program systems of numerically controlled machine tools according to computer-determined schedules. An ultimate result will be the much talked of automatic factory. In some industries we are already closer to this than most people realize. For example, in the continuous chemical-processing industries, such as soap and petroleum, automatic control of processes is common and most of the labor is of an indirect or vigilance nature.

One final outgrowth of the war should be commented on, that is the attention given to human factors. This resulted from the problems that arose because of the heavy demands placed on man by radar and sonar systems, supersonic flight, high-altitude flying, etc. Research psychologists and physiologists were employed during and after the war to help design systems that more nearly matched human capabilities of sight, hearing, feeling, smell, and motor skill, as well as human tolerance of such environmental factors as heat, light, radiation, and noise. Large volumes of data were gathered. Although the human stress factors in business and industry are usually less severe than many of those experienced in war, conceptually the problems are the same, that is, to design production tasks and systems that recognize the limitations of the human operator and take advantage of man's capabilities.

The field now called human engineering, human factors, or biotechnology furnishes the basic data for job design. Standard machine tool design does not as yet take full advantage of what is known, but improvements have been made. In the factory, special machine designs reflect increasingly the fact that it is not machines that produce but man-machine systems. Human engineering is the outgrowth of motion study originally developed by the Gilbreths. It is broader in concept than motion study and accepts a broader set of criteria, such as frequency of error and psychological and physiological costs, as well as the older criteria of economy of motion and labor cost.

WHERE WE STAND TODAY

Almost two centuries have passed since Adam Smith. What have we learned about production management in that time? Where does our knowledge stand today? In assessing the past, we can say that the results speak for themselves. Productivity and total productive capacity have expanded tremendously. Life for the average man in our Western civilization has been transformed from mere existence to a scale of living undreamed of by Smith. During this period, production management has been developing largely as an *empirical* applied science. During these two hundred years, we have responded to the expanding market and to the growth of increasingly large business units by division of labor and by progressive mechanization in order to take advantage of the economies of large-scale production.

Through the years we have learned to design better work places, better material-handling equipment, and better buildings to house productive activities. We have created production lines and even automatic machines. We have learned basic principles of production economics and, thereby, have learned to employ labor, materials, and machines in a delicate balance to match the changing relative values of these basic components of production. We have learned to control the production systems that we have designed so that products or services meet quality standards and are available when needed and at a cost that may be fairly well predicted. Most of this development has been evolutionary; we improved existing systems through a process of trial and error.

Only in the last twenty years have we begun to evolve principles that make it possible to design facilities and control systems with some degree of predictability as to their performance; here is a true measure of our knowledge about production management. Today we are beginning to develop answers to problems of limited scope, knowing that the result is the best possible. That is, the result is optimal, not simply better than the previous solution. This is real progress and indicates that the applied science envisioned by Taylor is developing.

Where we stand today then, in terms of production management as an applied science, is at the threshold of the rapid developmental phase. Increased knowledge about some particular field is often related to a growth and saturation curve, where initial developments are slow and difficult. As bits of knowledge fall into place, the rate of growth acceler-

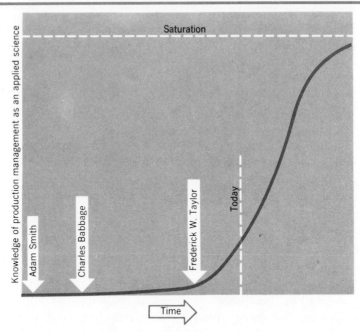

FIGURE 2.   Growth curve of knowledge of production management
as an applied science.

ates to the rapid developmental phase and finally levels off as it approaches a saturation level. We have diagrammed this growth curve in Figure 2. In the years to come the scope of the problems for which we can find provable optimal solutions will increase. The theory of production systems will be pervasive and will embrace integrated systems as a whole, not just segments of a system; our ability to design facilities and control systems with predictable characteristics will increase. The use of computers to simulate systems will become common, as will numerically controlled (computer controlled) production processes of various types.

In the past the best in production management theory was represented by its actual practice in business and industry; teaching in universities was paced by this practice. Today, theory is beginning to lead the best practice, a state of affairs that will probably continue for some time to come.

THE BIG COMPANY VERSUS THE SMALL COMPANY

The following comment is often made: "All of this talk about the new look in production management is fine for the big company—what about the small company?'' The basic principles of production economics and facility design and control are as applicable to the small organization as to the large. Implementation of these principles, however, must change with the size and financial strength of the organization. A large organization may use a high-speed computer to help generate a schedule that meets requirements with minimum inventory. The small organization may be compelled to approximate a similar solution to their schedule problems, using hand methods and graphical aids. Both organizations may be attempting to apply the same principles of scheduling. The techniques are different, but the principles are general.

We can see that production management is not a set of techniques. On the contrary, it is a set of general principles for production economics, facility design, job design, schedule design, quality control, inventory control, work measurement, and cost and budgetary control. Do we then turn our backs on technique? No. Rather, with the power of advanced technique, we evolve and refine principle. An advanced technique, such as computer simulation, may be used to develop and test various rules for scheduling to meet organization objectives. The resulting rules become principles by which we can schedule. They may be applicable in small companies as well as large ones. A mathematical technique may be used to develop decision rules for the economic amount of materials that should be purchased at one time. The resulting rules become principles by which we make certain purchasing decisions. As long as conditions are comparable, either the large or small company can use these principles. Therefore, when we study advanced analytical methods and techniques, we are not necessarily studying big company management. We are dealing with concepts and ideas that can be demonstrated by advanced methods where less powerful tools fail. The resulting concepts and ideas ordinarily have general application.

REVIEW QUESTIONS

1. What is the role of production management in a situation where society has decided to reallocate its resources in order to attack social and ecological problems?
2. Rationalize the statement that production efficiency is a relative term meaning, essentially, how effectively we employ the appropriate available resources (input) for a given unit of output.
3. Why is it that even in the United States economy, a system designed for a relatively small output will ordinarily emphasize the use of labor as an input compared to capital?

4. What is the relationship of pollution control to production management?
5. Discuss the role of Adam Smith in the origin of the formal study of production systems.
6. Discuss the contribution of Charles Babbage and the relationship of his work to that of Adam Smith.
7. What were the "four new duties of management" which were the center of Frederick Taylor's philosophy of scientific management? Relate those four new duties (or principles) to current fields of management.
8. Who was F. W. Harris and what was his contribution to the historical development of production management?
9. Relate the milestone contributions of the pioneers of production management to a time scale and appraise the current position of the field.
10. Contrast production management technique applied in large companies versus small companies.

REFERENCES

[1] Ackoff, R. L., and M. W. Sasieni. *Fundamentals of Operations Research*. John Wiley, New York, 1968.

[2] Babbage, C. *On the Economy of Machinery and Manufactures*. Knight, London, 1832.

[3] Buffa, E. S. *Operations Management: Problems and Models* (3rd ed.). John Wiley, New York, 1972.

[4] Filipetti, G. *Industrial Management in Transition*. Richard D. Irwin, Homewood, Ill., 1953.

[5] Hodge, B. J., and H. J. Johnson. *Management and Organizational Behavior*. John Wiley, New York, 1970.

[6] Litterer, J. A. *Organizations* (2nd ed.). John Wiley, New York, 1969.

[7] Taylor, F. W. *Principles of Scientific Management*. Harper & Bros., New York, 1919; reprinted in *Scientific Management*. Harper & Bros., New York, 1947.

[8] Thierauf, R. J., and R. A. Grosse. *Decision Making Through Operations Research*. John Wiley, New York, 1970.

[9] Urwick, L., and E. S. L. Brech. *The Making of Scientific Management*, Vol. 1, *Thirteen Pioneers*. Management Publications Trust, London, 1945.

2

Decision Making & the Production Function

Management's primary function is to make decisions that determine the future course of action for the organization over the short and the long term. These decisions may be directed in every conceivable physical and organizational area; they may deal with financial planning, marketing, and personnel, as well as with the operating or production phase. More often than not, decisions cut across these functional lines.

Decision theory is directed toward determining how rational decisions ought to be made. It attempts to establish a logical framework for decisions that is firmly rooted in science and mathematics as well as in the real world; in this scheme, which correlates the two areas of science and the real world for various alternative action paths, risks are assessed so that the decision maker, by his knowledge of the probable results, can decide what to do. These decisions are concerned with every factor

19

in the organization. For day-to-day operating or repetitive decisions, a set of decision rules makes possible continuity and smooth operation as for example, with industrial quality control. Large-scale decisions, such as the design capacity of a new plant, employ the same general concepts of decision theory but occur only once in a while.

NATURE OF DECISION MAKING

The obvious implication of a decision is that alternatives exist; the process of decision making selects from these alternatives the course of action to be carried out. The simplest way to make decisions is, of course, to flip a coin or let some other chance system determine the choice. Such a system is as simple-minded as it is simple, unless the outcomes of the decisions are all equally desirable. Judging desirability immediately points up the need for: (1) a purpose and (2) criteria for measuring or comparing the desirability of the alternatives in relation to the purpose. This is certainly simple enough. We have alternatives and a purpose to achieve, and we need criteria for comparison. However, the process becomes more difficult when we realize that invariably we are talking about future values and that unfortunately these future values often conflict. Each alternative may have both desirable and undesirable aspects; these conflicting values must be reconciled. Since the results expected are future results, how sure can we be of obtaining those results? What is the probability of attaining the results for each alternative? Or, turning it around, what is the risk of not attaining the forecasted result?

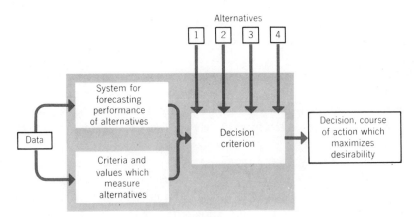

FIGURE 1.   Structure of decision making.

Actually, the final desirability of alternatives is the product of the relative benefit obtainable and the probability of attainment. Thus a "long shot" at the track that would pay $200 on a $2 ticket might have a 1 per cent chance of winning, resulting in a probability weighted payoff of $200 \times 0.01 = \$2.00$. A "favorite" paying only $2.80 but with an 80 per cent chance of winning is more desirable because the probability-weighted value of the result is greater, $2.24 versus $2.00. To be sure, *if* one wins on the "long shot," he wins much more. But the probability of winning is so small that the weighted desirability of the two alternatives makes a rational decision maker select the "favorite" in this case. Figure 1 diagrams the structure of our decision-making situation with alternatives, data from the real world, and criteria and values representing inputs to the decision maker. Inside the decision-making system are computed the predicted relative values of the alternatives based on the criteria and values. Finally, the relative desirability of the alternatives is determined by weighting the values by the probability of attainment. *The course of action that maximizes this final desirability is the rational decision.*

The sophistication of decision making for a given area depends on the level of knowledge within the area and the complexity of the decisions to be made. Sometimes we shall find that criteria and values are clear and straightforward, data are readily obtainable, future values are quite predictable, and risks are fairly clear. In these instances, decision making seems scientific, mathematical, almost automatic. In many other cases, criteria and values are vague and often take several forms whose comparability is difficult to establish. Prediction of risk and future performance may be even more difficult. Then judgment is the device by which we balance off conflicting values, assess risk, and finally select a course of action. At all times, however, decision making is the attempt to choose those courses of action that have the greatest net desirability; in this attempt we hope to use scientific methodology to the maximum and judgment to the minimum.

KINDS OF DECISIONS

There are many ways to classify decision problems. For example, one might classify the nature of the practical problems faced by the manager, the methodologies which might be used to analyze decision problems, or classify based on the amount of information available concerning the probability of occurrence of basic alternatives. The common basis for classification used in decision theory involves the latter. There are four main classes of decision problems in this context: decision making under certainty, under risk, under uncertainty, and under conflict.

When we know with certainty what will occur, given an alternative (state of nature) we have the conditions for *decision making under certainty*. In this kind of situation one need consider only one relevant payoff for each of the possible alternatives or strategies. *Decision making under risk* refers to the condition where there are a number of possible alternatives (states of nature) and the decision maker knows the probability of occurrence of each. In problems of production and operations management the probabilities of the various alternatives may be estimated based upon past experience. When the probabilities of occurrence of the various alternatives or states of nature are not known we have *decision making under uncertainty*. Such problems occur when there is no basis in past experience for estimating the probabilities of occurrence, for example, when estimating the market demand for a new untried product. Finally, *decision making under conflict* occurs when the decision maker must take account of the actions of a competitor or opponent.

Decision making in the field of production and operations management is dominated by the first two, that is, decision making under certainty and under risk. We will comment further on these two classes, giving examples.

Decision Making under Certainty. The meaning of the term certainty is that for each alternative there is one and only one value of the payoff. Given the alternative, the probability of the occurrence of the stated payoff is presumed to be 1.0. All we need do then is to find the alternative which has the best payoff and this is the alternative which should be selected. Referring to Figure 1, then, the decision criterion is simply to select the alternative with the best payoff.

Suppose, for example, that we are constructing alternate production plans to meet forecasted requirements, given a seasonal product. Several alternate schedules for meeting sales requirements could be calculated, each involving a hypothesis about the most effective way to meet requirements, using normal capacity, overtime capacity, subcontracting, and seasonal inventories. Suppose that three plans were constructed involving the use of these four sources for meeting requirements. Plan 1, level production, has no extra labor turnover cost, overtime premium, or subcontracting cost, however, the cost of carrying seasonal inventory to meet the high peak of sales is very large. Plan 2 involves some fluctuation in production level, but not so much that plant capacity with overtime work is exceeded. The result is a somewhat smaller seasonal inventory cost than for Plan 1, no subcontracting costs, and a substantial overtime premium cost. Plan 3 tends to follow the sales requirements curve quite closely, involving considerable hiring and laying off of labor. However, because of the limitations of plant capacity it is necessary to resort to maximum use of overtime as well as subcontracting. The total cost of normal and overtime labor, subcontracting, and carrying seasonal inventories for the three plans is:

Plan 1	$318,000
Plan 2	$298,000
Plan 3	$253,000

Given the payoff table it is easy to select Plan 3 as having the lowest cost. It is decision making under certainty because given the stated plan the payoff can be calculated with certainty. One should not conclude, however, that decision making under certainty is always simple. In many problems of production and operations management the models required to generate the alternatives may be very complex, involving possibly thousands of alternatives. Linear programming is a decision model of this type where the possible alternative strategies may be so numerous that it would be impossible to enumerate and compute the payoffs within the time of a human life. With the linear programming model, however, it may be possible to determine the best possible strategy within a few seconds of computer time.

Decision Making under Risk. As we noted previously, the decision maker knows the probability of occurrence of each of the possible alternatives when faced with a decision problem under risk. Normally, he depends on past experience to provide guides for the probabilities. For example, the decision to determine the optimum inventory of a replacement part to be maintained represents a decision under risk when the nature of the demand distribution is known.

Since the outcomes are associated with probabilities the decision maker will wish to make his decision in such a way that his *expected* payoff, or probability-weighted payoff, will be maximized. Again, referring to Figure 1, the decision criterion used in decision problems under risk is the expected or probability-weighted payoff.

Let us fit an example* into the framework of decision making under risk that we have discussed. Assume that you are president of a company that manufactures electrical relays. The position in which you find yourself

An Example

---

*Summarized from [3].

requires some interrelated decisions. The essential form of these problems is determined by the decisions that you make on a union dispute and on bids for two government contracts. The situation is described as follows.

Labor Dispute

You are presently involved in a labor dispute. The union has set a strike deadline of midnight tonight if you do not accept their request for a 10 per cent wage increase. You are *certain that the union will carry out their threat* and the resulting strike will cost you around $300,000. If you give in to their demand, *your total cost per relay unit will increase to $4.05, compared to the present cost of $3.80 per unit*. You feel certain that the union will be defeated if it strikes and therefore your present costs would remain fixed for the next year. You must decide:

UNION DISPUTE. Tactical Decision:
A. Give the employees the wage increase and suffer the higher cost of production.
B. Stick to the present wage scale and suffer the resulting strike loss.

Government Contract

Your union tactics are complicated by the fact that the government is letting a large contract for 10 million relay units within the next month and *you will not be in a position to bid on this contract if your employees go on strike.* However, even if you give in to the union demands and avert a strike, you still are not assured of getting the contract unless you can underbid your competitors. Possible bids and resulting probabilities of winning the contract are as follows:

GOVERNMENT CONTRACT. Tactical Decision:
      X. Not eligible to bid, company on strike. (See *B* decision above.)

	Price/Unit	Probability of Getting Contract
C.	Bid $4.15	30%
D.	Bid $4.12	50%
E.	Bid $4.10	60%
F.	Bid $4.07	80%

Test Equipment Investment

Fortunately a second major government contract is anticipated in the latter part of the year if you do not receive the lucrative contract mentioned previously. (Because of production *limitations, it will not be possible for you to assume both contracts* should you receive the first contract.) To be in a position to bid on the second contract, it is necessary at this time for you to secure adequate financial backing to guarantee the government that you can provide certain expensive testing equipment.

The larger the test facilities you can provide, the more likely it is that you will be awarded the contract. The anticipated net profit for this second project is $3 million if your unit cost is $4.05 and $4 million if your unit cost is $3.80. These figures *do not include the large investment in special test equipment* which must be written off over the life of the contract.

TEST EQUIPMENT INVESTMENT. Tactical Decision:

	Investment	Probability of Getting Contract
G.	$2,000,000	20%
H.	$2,400,000	40%
I.	$2,600,000	50%
J.	$2,900,000	60%

How Many Alternatives?   First we must see the structure of the   The Solution
various alternatives open to the decision maker. This structure is shown in Figure 2, and it may be a surprise to see that there are 20 alternatives for our example. The 20 alternatives are divided into 16 that result if the basic strategy *A* (no strike) is adopted and 4 more that are associated with the basic strategy *B* (take the strike).

We recognize that if *B* is followed, we may bid only on the second contract, so that we have only the alternatives *BXG, BXH, BXI,* and *BXJ*. Recall that *X* denotes the fact that we cannot bid on the first contract because of the strike. On the other hand, if we follow the basic strategy *A*, both contracts are open to us even though we can actually accept only one of them because of production limitations. Therefore, our strategy can combine both contracts.

FIGURE 2.   Structure of alternatives.

If we are awarded the first contract, we cannot accept the second. If we lose the first, we still have a chance for the second. Therefore, since there are 4 basic alternatives of bidding for the first contract and 4 for bidding on the second contract, there are 16 combinations (4 × 4). We shall head each of the 16 by *A* (no strike) and we have *ACG, ACH, ACI,* and *ACJ,* which are all of the combinations of *C* with the 4 basic alternatives of the second contract. The other combinations are: *ADG, ADH, ADI, ADJ, AEG, AEH, AEI, AEJ, AFG, AFH, AFI,* and *AFJ*.

How to Compute? Let us take the computations for the simpler situations first, those headed by *B* (take the strike). For each of the four alternatives, we can calculate by ordinary arithmetic how much we would make by each alternative if we actually received the contract. We have a net profit of $4 million from which we must deduct the required investment in test facilities. But the resulting figure must be tempered by the fact that we may not receive the contract. Therefore, *BXG* yields a *possible* profit of $2 million after the investment is deducted, but the probability of receiving the contract with the small investment in test facilities is very low, only 20 per cent. Therefore, the value of this alternative in relation to the others is only 20 per cent of $2 million or $400,000. From this figure we must deduct the sure loss of the strike of $300,000, so the final resulting relative value of *BXG* is only $100,000. The results for the four "strike" alternatives are given in Table I.

We see that the probability figure enters the computations directly and in a very important way. The possible return may be very high (for example, for *BXG* it is $2 million minus the strike cost), but if the probability is very low, the relative value of the alternative is low since we may have an excellent chance of actually getting the more modest returns of other alternatives.

TABLE I.	Results for Strike Alternatives					
(1)	(2)	(3)	(4)	(5)	(6)	(7)
				Proba-bility	(4) × (5)	Less the Sure Loss
	Net	Less		of	Expected	of the
	Profit	Required		Receiv-	Net	$300,000
Altern-	from	Invest-		ing	Value	Cost of
ative	Contract	ment	Equals	Contract	of Con-tract	the Strike
BXG	$4,000,000	$2,000,000	$2,000,000	20%	$400,000	$100,000
BXH	4,000,000	2,400,000	1,600,000	40%	640,000	340,000
BXI	4,000,000	2,600,000	1,400,000	50%	700,000	400,000
BXJ	4,000,000	2,900,000	1,100,000	60%	660,000	360,000

The computations for the A (no strike) alternatives are a little more complex, but the basic ideas of the possible returns, tempered by probabilities of attainment, remain the same. The slight complication comes in the fact that we cannot accept both contracts. Therefore, for each combination we must calculate:

(Possible return from first contract)
$\times$ (Probability of receiving first contract)
$+$ (Possible return from second contract)
$\times$ (Probability of receiving second contract and not receiving the first contract)

Thus we have a probability-weighted value of the first contract plus a probability-weighted value of the second contract; the latter probability allows for the fact that we might not get the first contract.

The latter probability value is easy to calculate. We may view it this way. If the probability of getting the first contract is 20 per cent, then that of not getting it is 80 per cent. If the probability of getting the second contract is 40 per cent, then the combined probability of getting the second and losing the first is 80 per cent multiplied by 40 per cent; that is, 0.80×0.40 or 32 per cent. Let us illustrate with the alternative ACG.

First contract:
  10,000,000 relay units
  Price per unit $= \$4.15$
  Cost per unit $= \$4.05$
  Probability $= 30\%$

Second contract:
  Profit from contract $= \$3,000,000$
  Required investment $= \$2,000,000$
  Probability $= 20\%$
  Probability of getting Number 2 and not Number 1 $=$
    $(1 - 0.30) \times 0.20$ or 14%

The calculation:
  $10,000,000 (4.15 - 4.05) 0.30 + (3,000,000 - 2,000,000) 0.14$
    $= 300,000 + 140,000 = \$440,000$

The results of the relative value of the entire set of "no strike" alternatives are:

ACG	\$440,000	ACI	\$440,000
ACH	\$468,000	ACJ	\$342,000

ADG	$450,000	AEG	$380,000	AFG	$200,000
ADH	$470,000	AEH	$396,000	AFH	$208,000
ADI	$450,000	AEI	$380,000	AFI	$200,000
ADJ	$380,000	AEJ	$324,000	AFJ	$172,000

We now have figures that measure the desirability of each alternative, the 16 alternatives of the *A* (no strike) series and the 4 alternatives of the *B* (strike) series. Each one is weighted by the probability of attainment. These are the important data for decision purposes.

It is important to recognize, however, that these data do not tell us actually how much we would make by each alternative. Rather, they tell us relative desirability for decision purposes. Since *ADH* gives the highest value, let us assume that we choose it. Table II tells us how much we *actually* make under the three conditions:

1. Received first contract and dropped second.
2. Lost first contract but got the second.
3. Lost both contracts.

Thus, if we adopt *ADH* as our strategy, actually we may gain a net of $700,000, $600,000, or zero. But in deciding which of the alternatives is best, it is wise to weight the possible returns by the probability. Obviously, our data will drive accountants mad and, similarly, we dare not use their data directly.

The example of the decision problem of the relay company showed that alternative courses of action are not always entirely obvious. It also showed the importance of the risks involved. We might question from where these probability values come. The probabilities for the first contract might be estimated from an analysis of the company's past bid data at various prices. Those for the second contract, involving investment in test equipment, could be estimated from an analysis of com-

TABLE II. Actual Profits under Three Conditions

	Received First Contract and Dropped Second	Lost First Contract but Got Second	Lost Both Contracts
Profit from contract	$700,000	$3,000,000	0
Invested to get second contract	—	2,400,000	0
Total profit	$700,000	$600,000	0

petitors' financial strength and past bidding behavior. Even if the probabilities were based on best guesses of the executives in the organization, we would be in a better position to make a choice than if the analysis had not been made. The element of prediction was small in the example. By the simplified structure of the example, everything could be reduced to dollar values so that the question of criteria and conflicting values was not important. By casting the problem into a structure or model, the effect of the various factors that enter the decision can be more readily ascertained. The ideas involved in predictive models are very important to us, so let us examine them more carefully.

MODELS

Models of one sort or another have been with us from childhood. The dolls, model airplanes, and toy cars we played with probably helped us learn something of value about their real world counterparts. Models are of vital importance in any intellectual attack on a problem, and we use them perhaps more frequently than we think. How often in discussion, for example, do we use analogies to explain or make a point? The professor in the classroom uses analogy and physical, graphical, and abstract models. In fact, clear thinking requires an understanding of the nature and role of models.

A model is always an abstraction to some degree of the real life thing or process for which we want to predict performance. For example, the aerodynamicist uses models and a wind tunnel to study his design. By no means does the model attempt to duplicate all characteristics of the design. Although factors of shape, weight, strength of parts, temperature, and so on are all important in determining how well the plane design may perform, the engineer is studying aerodynamic performance wherein shape is the main characteristic. Therefore, his model accurately duplicates shape and ignores other factors. The model that is used allows ease of measurement, the manipulation of variables at will, etc., and all at fairly low cost. To attempt similar studies with real planes would not only be costly and hazardous, it probably would not yield as much information. By abstracting from the real life situation, the aerodynamicist can focus his attention on something simpler and not lose much by the fact that many details have been ignored.

But the person who uses models is likely to make horrible mistakes if he stops with the model. An "armchair" model may *seem* to fit comfortably, but a model that does not accurately portray what goes on in the real world is just another model. Models must be validated—sometimes over and over again. What is needed is a model that successfully predicts what goes on in the real world situation. Certainly the first wind tunnel experiments did not do this perfectly, but by correlating results of wind tunnel tests with results of actual flight tests, the aerodynamicist has been able to improve his models so that his predictions are good. Even then, in the march of progress, new situations develop where the old models no longer can do the job as in the case of supersonic flight. Then new models must be constructed. Figure 3 shows the successive steps of forward progress in the world of models and in the real world, with intermediate evaluations used to validate a model.

Kinds of Models.   The aerodynamicist's model, which we have been discussing, is a physical model. Other physical models that many of us have seen include the astronomer's planetarium, the physicist's models of molecular structure, and the architect's model of his building design. In each case the physical model represents physically some aspect of the general problem. But there are other kinds of models, each of which abstracts further from the physical situation in order to permit study of some particular aspect of a problem. For example, *a graphic model* usually represents variables by lengths of lines in two- or three-dimensional space. For example, a graph showing how traffic density varies over the day for westbound traffic on the George Washington Bridge is a graphic model. A decision whether to drive, take a taxi, use public transportation, or stay home might be based partially on this model of traffic density.

Pictorial models often help transmit ideas and influence decisions by giving a visual picture of relationships. For example, a safety cartoon may be a pictorial model of what results from unsafe manufacturing

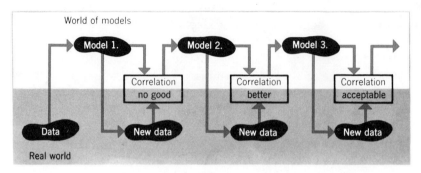

FIGURE 3.   Steps toward the development of an acceptable model.

FIGURE 4. Schematic model of an organization.

practices. Management hopes that workers will take into account this model of the forecasted effect of unsafe practices and make decisions accordingly. *Schematic models* are commonly used to show things such as information flow and current flow where the physical relationship is of lesser importance. An electrician's wiring diagram or an organization chart is a schematic model. Figure 4 is an organization chart. It is a schematic model of authority relationships within the company.

In the *mathematical model*, which represents the greatest abstraction from the real world situation, symbolism is used to depict factors in a real world situation. The symbols, rather than physical objects, can then be manipulated. Mathematical models are extremely useful in studying interrelationships of a situation. For example, the simple statement of Newton's second law of motion, $F = ma$, states a relationship between three factors: force, mass, and acceleration. Mathematical models are most common in the physical sciences and only recently have they invaded the business world. Their great advantage is that symbolic manipulation often can uncover the exact nature of interrelationships between factors that would not be obvious by other techniques.

When the complexity of the situation being studied requires mathematics that are beyond known techniques, or where the mathematics would be too complicated and time consuming to be helpful, *simulation models* can be developed and an approximation of the real life situation carried out by means of a high-speed computer. A simulation model may represent the mathematical equations that are pertinent in a way similar to the mathematical model. But instead of attempting to solve the equations for optimum answers, a series of trials is computed, thus simulating the behavior of the model under different conditions. With high-speed computers it may be possible to simulate a wide variety of conditions and simply select the decisions that perform best. There is no guarantee, of course, that the very best values or decisions have been found.

In all cases, the objective of model building is to predict some facet of performance of the system under study. That is why models are so important to decision making. Rational decision making requires forecasted performance. Models provide this link.

Models in Production Management. Production management has made use of all of the different kinds of models discussed. Physical models have been used in plant layout studies for some time. Where projects warrant their use, very detailed three-dimensional models are made so that factors of material flow, head room, access, etc., can be studied in careful detail before a new layout is actually installed. Graphic and schematic models have been common for the study of schedules, the analysis of man-machine relationships, and other aspects of the work situation. More recently, mathematical and simulation models have been developed that involve the allocation of productive resources, production programming, optimum lot sizes, and the analysis of random processes. The entire group of chapters comprising Part 2 of this book, "Analytical Methods," deals with models of various production situations that have proved useful as analytical tools.

Advantages and Disadvantages of Models. Why are models used? The most direct answer is that no better approach to forecasting performance ever has been developed. As systems for prediction, models come to us from science and represent scientific method. To build a model, whether it be physical, graphic, or mathematical, careful consideration is required of what needs to be abstracted from the real situation. When building a model, we are immediately struck by the degree of our ignorance on the subject with which we are working. What information is available? Where are the gaps in information? In its final application, a model gives insight into the problem we are solving.

The dangers of model building lie in the fact of its abstraction from the real world problem. If we keep the model in workable form, it may be oversimplified. If we attempt to be true to the real problem and not indulge in idealization, the model may be too cumbersome and expensive to construct and use. The final guide to the validity of a model is, of course, its test in the real problem situation. If it predicts performance accurately, it is a good model. If it does not, its only value is in possibly giving insight into the development of newer, improved models.

Models and Decision Making.   Why so much emphasis on models?
Can we not make decisions without them? Certainly we can. However,
without predictive models, our confidence in decisions must decline.
We again would be in the position of flipping a coin to decide which
alternatives to follow. Gambling based entirely on luck is foolish. A
professional gambler studies the odds so that he can place his bets in the
most advantageous way. What he is doing is determining models for the
games he plays so that he can predict performance. Should a business
man be any less shrewd in making his decisions?

THE PRODUCTION FUNCTION

Production is the process by which goods and services are created.
We find production processes in factories, offices, hospitals, and supermarkets. Production management deals with decision making related
to production processes, so that the resulting good or service is produced
according to the specifications, in the amounts and by the schedule
demanded, and at minimum cost. In accomplishing these objectives,
production management is associated with two broad areas of activity:
the design and the control of production systems.

For many reasons, production management is probably most often
associated with factory management rather than with the broader
definition just given. As a field of knowledge, production management
developed largely in the factory, and logically so, because the significant
problems of production first occurred in the factory. Before the factory
system came into existence, the large number of one-man shops that
produced goods presented an insignificant problem of production
management. With the factory system, however, the situation was
reversed. The question of how to organize, lay out facilities, control
quality, and meet schedules had to be answered somehow. As answers
were provided and became generalized, the field of production management began to develop.

The early steps concentrated on controlling factory labor costs, which
was logical, because, in Taylor's time the bulk of the product cost was
likely to be labor. With the continuing trend toward mechanization
and automation, the situation has changed drastically. In the factory,
indirect labor costs have increased tremendously in relation to direct
labor costs. Given the present structure of the industrial economy, a
concern finds it uneconomical to fabricate, itself, many of the components
of its products, so material costs often dominate. Therefore, in the
factory, production management has had to develop in the areas of

equipment design and selection, indirect labor cost control, production and inventory control and quality control.

But other changes have taken place since Taylor's era. While attention has been focused on the factory, the number of office workers has multiplied rapidly. Today white collar workers outnumber blue collar workers by a margin of several million. Other activities, where production management problems might have been insignificant twenty or thirty years ago, have developed into large-scale units where the operations activities cannot be ignored. For example, the corner grocery store has all but vanished, and in its place we have the high-volume supermarket. Here, the facility design is of great importance. Location, layout, and inventory control take on new significance. We all know that hospital costs have skyrocketed. Hospital administrators are recognizing operations or production problems more than ever before. Basic questions of layout, division of labor, job design, and control of errors (quality control) cannot be ignored.

This book recognizes the breadth of productive activity. Nevertheless, in the material that follows, we shall use the factory as a general model and then try to indicate how the concepts discussed apply in other situations. This method is used because practically all of the pioneering work has been done in the factory. Therefore, the most numerous examples available still come from the factory. In the coming years, this situation should change as the general principles find application in other productive activities.

A GENERALIZED DESCRIPTIVE MODEL OF PRODUCTION

In line with the thinking we have just expressed, let us construct a model of what we mean by production. According to our definition, the factory, the office, the supermarket, the hospital, etc., all represent special cases which have special characteristics. Our production system has inputs which represent the material, parts, paperwork forms, and the customers or patients, as the case may be. The inputs are processed in some way by a series of operations whose sequence and number are specified for each input. The operations may vary from one only to any number and may take on any desired characteristics; they may be mechanical, chemical, assembly, inspection and control, dispatching to the next operation, receiving, shipping, personal contact such as an interview, and paperwork operations.

The outputs of our system are completed parts, products, chemicals, service to customers or patients, completed paperwork, etc. There is provision for storage in our system after the receipt of the input and between each operation in the system. The time in storage may vary from zero to any finite value. Inputs are transported between all operations in the system. Any means of transportation may be supplied, including self-transportation in the case of clients and customers. Our model also has an information system and a decision maker. The information system interconnects all physical activities and provides a basis for management decision. These functions provide the equivalent of a "nervous system" for the model. Figure 5 represents our production system.

Systems may occur in series. For example, when completed products are shipped from the factory to a warehouse, they are leaving the factory system only to arrive at a second productive system called a warehouse. In this way, the two systems may be considered as part of one large system. Systems also may occur in parallel, such as when a number of factories produce similar products to supply several market areas. For solving some types of problems, these factories may be considered one large production system.

Now let us consider what would happen to an input to the system. After being received, the input goes into storage to take its turn in the processing. By some set of priority rules, it is drawn from storage to begin processing. These rules might be: first in—first out, time or date required for completion or delivery, urgency, or some other system of priority rules. It is then processed according to a predetermined sequence. Let us assume the sequence b, d, c, n. From initial storage it goes to operation b and is placed in temporary storage to await processing there. We assume that operation b has already some assigned work or load and, therefore, our input takes its place in line (in storage) and will be processed at b according to the priority decision rules established. After being processed at b, it is transported to d, placed in storage, drawn out according to priority rules, processed, etc. One operation may be an inspection. The operation just preceding shipment may be a packaging operation, preparing the item for shipment.

If we are speaking of a high-volume, standardized, fabricated part, the operations may be placed in sequence and interconnected by conveying equipment. The storages would take place on the conveyors themselves, and the decision rules are first in—first out. If we are speaking of the hospital, the storages may take place in waiting rooms or in hospital beds. The priority rules may be first in—first out, with urgency exceptions. Many tasks are mobile in the instance of the hospital, such as when nurses give shots or medication.

In a supermarket, products are received and stored on display shelves.

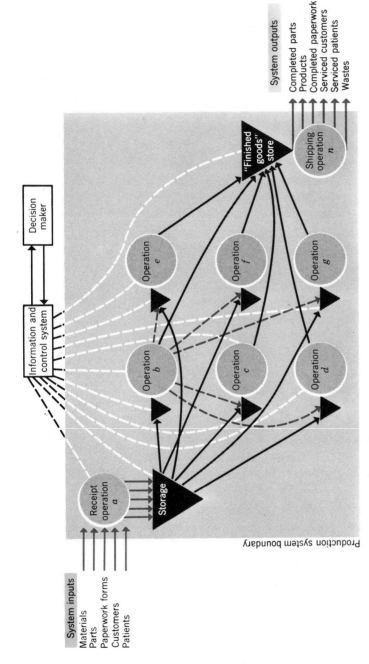

FIGURE 5. Diagram of a generalized production system. Inputs may be processed in any specified sequence of operations and are transported between operations. The number of operations may vary from one to any finite number. Storage occurs between all operations, and the time in storage may vary from essentially zero to any finite amount. *Note:* There are interconnections between all combinations of operations *b* through *f*, although only those originating at *b* are shown. The information system interconnects all activities and provides the basis for management decision.

Customer receiving is practically nonexistent as an operation. The customer picks the desired items from shelves, transports them, and takes his place in line for the single operation of check-out.

In soap manufacturing by the continuous process, materials are received and stored. Then they are taken from storage in large quantity, dissolved, and pumped through a series of chemical operations, so that transportation and storage between operations occur in the pipes. The material is chemically processed while it moves, and it emerges as soap. It is then packaged and shipped.

The job-shop manufacturing situation, where custom products are fabricated and assembled, is undoubtedly the most complex type of production system. Take a missile, for example. Thousands of individual parts must be fabricated and assembled into subassemblies and, thence, into final assemblies. This activity must be dovetailed to fit into a complex schedule, so that operation time is available when it is needed to provide parts for subassemblies and final assemblies. The pattern or flow for the multitude of parts from operation to operation is so complex that it can only be visualized by some abstract means of representation. Many parts require operation time on the same machines, but the operations occur at different times in the overall manufacturing cycle. The problem of loading the operations in such a way that the machines can be utilized effectively is obviously a difficult one.

CONTINUOUS VERSUS INTERMITTENT MODELS

Continuous flow production situations are those where the facilities are standardized as to routings and flow, since inputs are standardized. Therefore, a standard set of processes and sequence of processes can be adopted. Continuous models are represented in practice by production and assembly lines, large-scale office operations processing forms by a standard procedure, continuous flow chemical operations, etc. Intermittent production situations are those where the facilities must be flexible enough to handle a wide variety of products and sizes, or where the basic nature of the activity imposes change of important characteristics of the input (change in product design). In instances such as these, no single sequence pattern of operations is appropriate, so the relative location of the operations must be a compromise that is best for all inputs considered together.

Transportation facilities between operations also must be flexible to accommodate a wide variety of input characteristics as well as the wide variety of routes that the inputs may require. These conditions commonly define an intermittent production situation. It is intermittent because the flow is intermittent. Considerable storage between operations is required in order that individual operations can be carried on somewhat independently, resulting in ease of scheduling and in fuller utilization of men and machines. In practice, intermittent production is represented by custom or job order-type machine shops, hospitals, general offices, batch-type chemical operations, etc.

As we have shown, our generalized descriptive model in Figure 5 can be made to fit both the intermittent and continuous flow situations by the specification of some detailed characteristics. We have assumed intermittent flow in our model and defined it in general enough terms that the specification of a fixed-operation sequence, the specification of continuous flow-type transportation facilities, the assumption of low storage times between operations, and a first in—first out set of priority decision rules would all determine continuous flow conditions. The

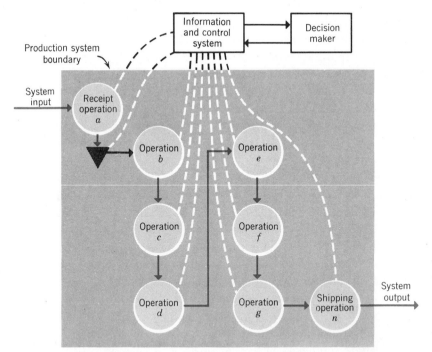

FIGURE 6. Diagram of a continuous flow production system. Input-output characteristics are standardized, allowing standardization of operations and their sequence. Minor storage of inputs occurs after receipt. Once on the transportation system, any storage between operations is combined with transportation. In the ideal situation the operations are also combined with transportation so inputs are processed while they are moved.

continuous flow situation is common enough today, however, that we tend to think in terms of the dichotomy of continuous and intermittent flow models. Therefore, we have constructed the special case of continuous flow as a separate model in Figure 6.

PROBLEMS OF PRODUCTION MANAGEMENT

Using our generalized model as a background, let us outline the nature of problems generated in a production system. These problems require two major types of decisions, one that relates to the design of the system and one that relates to the operation and control of the system (that is, both long-run and short-run decisions). The relative balance of the emphasis on such factors as cost, service, and reliability of both functional and time performance depends on the basic purposes of the total enterprise and on the general nature of the good or service being produced. Thus, in general, economic enterprises will probably emphasize cost, consistent with quality and delivery commitments. Hospitals may emphasize reliability and service, consistent with cost objectives, etc.

Long-run decisions related to the design of the production system are:

1. *Selection and design of products.* There are strong interactions between product selections and design with productive capability, and vice versa.

2. *Selection of equipment and processes.* Usually alternative equipment and processes are available for a given need. Production management must make decisions that commit capital of the enterprise and its basic approach to production in the facility design.

3. *Production design of items processed.* Production cost interacts strongly with the design of parts, products, paper work forms, etc. Design decisions often set the limiting characteristics of cost and processing for the system.

4. *Job design.* Job design is an integral part of the total system design, involving the basic organization of work as well as the integration of human engineering data to produce optimally designed jobs.

5. *Location of the system.* Location decisions can, in some cases, be important if the balance of cost factors determined by nearness to markets and material supply is critical.

6. *Facility layout.* Decisions related to design capacity, basic modes of production, shifts, use of overtime, and subcontracting must be made. In addition, operations and equipment must be located in relation to each other in a pattern that minimizes overall material-handling cost

or meets the requirements of some more complex criterion. The latter requirement is most difficult for the complex intermittent model where routes vary. Many detailed problems are associated with each other in order to specify adequately the layout of a production system. These include heating, lighting, and other utility requirements; the allocation of storage space, aisle space, etc.; and the design of the building to house the layout.

Short-run decisions related to the design of operation and control systems are:

1. *Inventory and production control.* Decisions must be made concerning how to allocate productive capacity consistent with demand and inventory policy. Feasible schedules must be worked out, and the load on men and machines and the flow of production must be controlled.

2. *Maintenance and reliability of the system.* Decisions must be made regarding maintenance effort, recognition of the random nature of equipment breakdown, and recognition that machine down-time may itself be associated with important costs or loss of sales.

3. *Quality control.* Decisions must be made to set the permissible levels of risk that bad parts are produced and shipped or that errors are made, as well as the risk that good parts are scrapped. Inspection costs must be balanced against probable losses due to passing defective material or services.

4. *Labor control.* Labor is still the major cost element in most products and services. Production planning requires an appraisal of the labor component; thus, much effort has gone into developing work measurement and wage payment systems.

5. *Cost control and improvement.* Production supervisors must make day-to-day decisions which involve the balance of labor, material, and some overhead costs.

The relative importance of these problems of production management varies considerably, depending on the nature of individual production systems. Nevertheless, every system has these problems in some degree. For example, equipment policy may occupy a dominant position in production systems where the capital investment per worker is very large, as in the petroleum industry. On the other hand, equipment policy may occupy a minor role in a production system that is represented by a large labor component or a large material component. Part of the art of production management involves the sensing of the relative importance of these various problems in a given situation.

The chapters that follow are organized into three broad sections.

Part 2 deals with general analytical methods which are of particular value in production management. These methods serve as general models for decision making which may be altered to fit specific situations. Parts 3 and 4 deal with the general problems that are faced in production.

REVIEW QUESTIONS

1. Discuss the role of decision making in the management of an enterprise.
2. Under what conditions might it be acceptable to let decisions be determined by some chance event such as the flip of a coin?
3. Discuss the structure of decision making shown in Figure 1. What is the importance of: (a) a forecasting system, (b) criteria and values, (c) alternatives, and (d) a decision criterion?
4. Discuss the four kinds of decision making and the kinds of decision problems to which each is applicable. Which approaches to decision making are most commonly used in production management?
5. How does the probability of attainment of alternatives influence their net relative desirability?
6. Develop a decision tree for the structure of alternatives of the bidding example discussed in the text.
7. What is the function of models in decision making?
8. What kinds of models are used?
9. How do we know when we have a useful model?
10. What are the advantages and pitfalls of models?
11. What kinds of models are useful in production management?
12. Define the term *production*.
13. Why is the term *production* most often associated with the factory?
14. What necessitates a broader definition of production today, than was called for in Taylor's time?
15. Show that the generalized descriptive model of production discussed in this chapter is applicable to the "operations" side of various activities.
16. Differentiate between intermittent and continuous models of production.
17. What are the short- and long-run problems of production management?

PROBLEMS

1. A processor of frozen foods must decide which crop to plant in an available tract. There are three possibilities: peas, green beans, and asparagus. Past experience gives records of yields for the three crops which depend on the weather. The probability of excellent weather is 0.30, of variable weather is 0.50, and of poor weather is 0.20. The dollar yields under the three weather conditions are shown in Table III. Determine which strategy should be selected to maximize expected yield.

TABLE III. Yields for Three Crops under Three Weather Conditions			
	Excellent Weather	Variable Weather	Poor Weather
Peas	$30,000	$20,000	$10,000
Green beans	50,000	30,000	15,000
Asparagus	60,000	20,000	5,000

2. The Electrical Equipment Company has been asked to bid on a large government order for 50,000 special relays. Three basic manufacturing methods involving varying degrees of mechanization and automation are available, all requiring investments in equipment. Table IV shows these data as well as the associated variable manufacturing costs.

TABLE IV.		
Manufacturing Method	Equipment Costs	Variable Manufacturing Costs
Low mechanization	$ 50,000	$3.00
High mechanization	150,000	2.00
Automation	200,000	1.25

The equipment costs must be fully absorbed by the contract since the relays are of special design. The probability of getting the contract depends on the bid price as shown in Table V.

TABLE V.	
Unit Price	Probability of Getting Contract
$10.00	0.25
9.50	0.50
9.00	0.75

What price should be quoted and which manufacturing method should be used to maximize expected profit?

3. Select some activity that may be familiar to you and classify it according to the intermittent-continuous classification discussed in the chapter. Identify the item being processed. Develop the structure of the network of flow of the thing being processed in the general format of a diagram similar to Figure 5 or 6 as may be appropriate.

4. For the operational system developed in problem 3, develop what you feel are the *dominant* problems of production for this particular system. Use the lists of "Production Management Problems" discussed at the end of the chapter. Discuss why these particular problems are the dominant ones for your system.

REFERENCES

[1] Albers, H. H. *Principles of Organization and Management* (3rd ed.). John Wiley, New York, 1969.

[2] Alcalay, J. A., and E. S. Buffa. "A Proposal for a General Model of a Production System." *International Journal of Production Research*, Mar. 1963.

[3] Boulden, J. B., and E. S. Buffa. "The Strategies of Interdependent Decisions." *California Management Review,* 1 (4), 94–100, 1959.

[4] Bross, I. D. F. *Design for Decision.* Macmillan, New York, 1953.

[5] Forrester, J. *Industrial Dynamics.* MIT Press, Cambridge, Mass., 1961.

[6] Groff, G. K., and J. F. Muth. *Operations Management: Analysis for Decisions.* Richard D. Irwin, Homewood, Ill., 1972.

[7] Litterer, J. A. *Organizations* (2 vols., 2nd ed.). John Wiley, New York, 1970.

[8] Litterer, J. A. *The Analysis of Organizations.* John Wiley, New York, 1965.

[9] Miller, D. W., and M. K. Starr. *Executive Decisions and Operations Research* (2nd ed.). Prentice-Hall, Englewood Cliffs, N.J., 1969.

[10] Reisman, A., and E. S. Buffa. "A General Model for Production and Operations Systems." *Management Science*, Sept. 1964.

[11] Schoderbek, P. P. *Management Systems* (2nd ed.). John Wiley, New York, 1971.

[12] Starr, M. K. "Evolving Concepts in Production Management." In: *Evolving Concepts in Management.* E. Flippo, editor. Academy of Management Proceedings, 24th Annual Meeting, Dec. 1964. Alxo reprinted as Chapter 2 in: *Readings in Production and Operations Management.* E. S. Buffa, editor. John Wiley, New York, 1966.

3

The Systems Concept

An emerging basis for unifying and relating the complexities of managerial problems is the systems concept and methodology. These concepts have been applied more to the analysis of productive systems than to other fields, but it is clear that the value of the concept in management is pervasive.

The word itself has become so commonplace in the general literature of management that one often wants to scream, for its common use almost depreciates its value. Yet the word itself is so descriptive of the general interacting nature of the myriad of elements that enter managerial problems that we can no longer talk of complex problems without using the term *systems*. Indeed, throughout this book we use the term liberally. We must learn to distinguish the general use of the term and its specific use as a mode of structuring and analyzing problems.

One of the great values of the systems concept is that it helps us to take a very complex situation and lend order and structure to it. A major contribution of the concept is the reduction of complexity in

45

managerial problems to a block diagram showing the relationship and interacting effects of the various elements which affect the problem at hand. At its present state of development and application, the systems concept is most useful in helping us gain insight into problems. At a second and very powerful level of contribution, however, systems analysis is gaining prominence as a basis for generating solutions to problems and evaluating their effects, and for designing alternate systems.

"SYSTEMS" DEFINED

But, we have been using the term *systems* without defining it. Though nearly everyone may have a general understanding of the term it may be useful to be more precise. Webster defines a system as "a regularly interacting or interdependent group of items forming a unified whole." Thus a system may have many components and objects, but they are united in the pursuit of some common goal. They are in some sense unified, organized, or coordinated. The components of a system contribute to the production of a set of outputs from given inputs which may or may not be optimal or best with respect to some appropriate measure of effectiveness. Systems are often complex although the definition does not specify that they need to be.

It is probably correct to say that some of the most interesting systems for study are complex and that a change in one variable within the system will affect many other variables of the system. Thus, in productive systems a change in production rate may affect inventories, hours worked per week, overtime hours, facility layout, and so on. Understanding and predicting these complex interactions between variables is one of our main objectives in this book.

One of the elusive aspects of the systems concept is in the definition of a specific system. The fact that we can define the system which we wish to consider and draw boundaries around it is important. We can then look inside the defined system to see what happens, but it is just as important to see how the system is affected by its environment. Thus, invariably, every system can be thought of as a part of an even larger system. One of the dangers of defining systems which are too narrow in scope is that we may fail to see broader implications. On the other hand, a broad definition of systems runs the risk of leaving out important details involved in the functioning of the system. Obviously, there is a large element of "art" in the application of systems concepts.

OPEN AND FEEDBACK SYSTEMS

A crucial part of understanding the systems concept is in seeing clearly the modules on which it is built. Forrester [8] has described open and feedback systems as follows:

> An open system is one characterized by outputs that respond to inputs but where the outputs are isolated from and have no influence on the inputs. An open system is not aware of its own performance. In an open system, past action does not control future action. An open system does not observe and react to its own performance. An automobile is an open system which by itself is not governed by where it has gone in the past nor does it have a goal of where to go in the future. A watch, taken by itself, does not observe its own inaccuracy and adjust itself—it is an open system.
>
> A feedback system, which is sometimes called a "closed" system, is influenced by its own past behavior. A feedback system has a closed loop structure that brings results from past action of the system back to control future action. One class of feedback systems—negative feedback— seeks a goal and responds as a consequence of failure to achieve the goal. A second class of feedback systems—positive feedback—generates growth processes wherein action builds a result that generates still greater action.

Both open and feedback systems have interactions with their environment so this is not the crucial distinction. An open production system, for example, might be one where the quantity and quality of the output were determined in a way which completely ignored the user environment. Such a system would continue to produce at the output rates set, regardless of finished goods inventory position and the actual demand in the marketplace. Alternately, such an open production system might continue to produce preset quality levels regardless of the marketplace acceptance of the output. As we know, however, while such systems may not observe and react directly to their own performance there is a broader level second order feedback involved which puts such enterprises out of business ultimately because they were attempting to behave like open systems where a closed system, responsive to the environment, was really appropriate. Most of the feedback systems in managerial problems are of the negative feedback type where the objective is to control a process.

Elements of Feedback Control. The elements of a basic feedback control loop are shown in Figure 1. In Figure 1, assume that the production system itself has inputs which it processes to produce outputs of

FIGURE 1. Elements of simple feedback control loop.

goods or services. In order to control the performance of the system, measurements are made on aspects of the output, perhaps in both quantity and quality terms. These measurements are compared with the desired performance and the control system interprets the difference, commanding the effector to correct performance. Thus a control system always involves some kind of measurement of what is actually happening. This information is fed into some kind of data processing system where the measurements are compared with standards which have been derived. These standards are based on managerial policies directly or indirectly.

For example, there may be a policy in a bank which states that we want to offer customer service at the windows such that the average waiting time is only one minute. If the waiting time exceeds the one minute standard by perhaps more than 10 per cent, then additional tellers' windows are opened. Alternately, one might consider a physical measurement such as a quality control on the dimension of a part or the chemical composition, or the rate of output might be the measurement to be controlled. In some instances feedback controls may require high technology and be virtually automatic and in other instances the control may require managerial intervention. Whether automatic or not, however, the same basic principles of feedback control are being used.

Combinations of Simple Feedback Systems. In Figure 2a we represent the simple subsystem module of an input-output transformation process involving information feedback to provide control of the process. These simple modules may be combined in series and in parallel as shown in Figure 2b. In Figure 2b we see that each process has its

(a) Subsytem module of an input–output transformation process

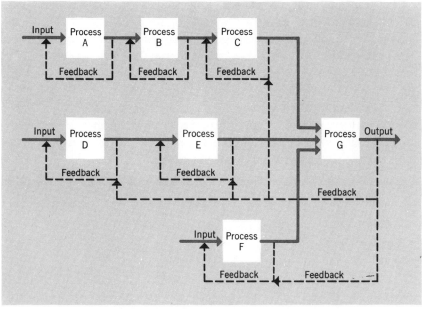

(b) Subsytem modules in series and parallel

FIGURE 2. Input-output concept of systems and subsystems with information feedback to provide the basis for control.

own feedback loop for control; however, the final output of the system of processes also provides feedback for control purposes to the critical processes upstream. These elements of managerial control might be in terms of the quality of output, the quantity of output, or some other aspect of performance.

Feedback-Time Lag Effects.   How a system under control by information feedback responds depends on a number of factors. Referring back to Figure 1, if the difference between actual and desired performance is fed back with no time lag, the effector commands the system to change settings immediately by the observed difference, and the system responds immediately, then the system would be completely responsive and presumably exhibit perfect control since any deviation is corrected immediately. Even in completely automatic, high technology, process control systems, however, this ideal is not attained. How the system responds to control depends on time lags in the feedback response system, and in the transformation process itself, on how much control action is called forth, and on the sensitivity of the system under control.

The sensitivity of the system refers to the response in the output to a change in the input. For example, in the steering mechanisms of most autos the ratio between the amount of rotation of the front wheels and a given degree of turn of the steering wheel is modest, so one does not oversteer (overcontrol). The opposite situation has been experienced by most of us in the "bumper car" autos in amusement parks where the steering ratio has been deliberately set to cause the front wheels to turn considerably for a small turn of the steering wheel. The result is a loss of control as well as some fun. Thus a system may be relatively sensitive or insensitive to control. How much control action is called for is related to the sensitivity of the system.

Another extremely important factor in the way the system output responds to control is in the time lags inherent in the feedback control system and in the process itself. If it takes substantial time for the feedback control system to respond and command an adjustment, and if the process itself is sluggish in response to changed control settings, then the system output may exhibit oscillation.

For example, if you were attempting to drive an auto with the only vision being to the rear (through the rearview mirror) the information feedback that you needed to turn would occur after you had passed the curve. To adjust you might then turn the steering wheel. But suppose it was in fact a winding road and having turned you now see that the road has subsequently turned the other way. It would require a very wide road to drive under these conditions and stay on the road, and in any case you would be oscillating back and forth over the smooth line you would drive if you could see out the windshield.

Feedback and Managerial Systems. Managerial control systems suffer from all of the unfortunate effects: time lags, sensitivity, and amount of control action. In general, long time lags and low sensitivity are the big culprits; however, there are situations where supersensitivity is difficult to deal with. For example, as we shall see in Chapter 8 on waiting lines, the number of people waiting in line at the checkout counter of a supermarket is very sensitive to utilization factors above 0.75 (ratio of arriving rate of customers to the rate at which they can be processed).

Consider the operations manager attempting to control the employment, production, and inventory levels of his operations based on month-old information feedback on the progress of retail sales. If he reacts to an increase in retail sales recorded one month ago he might increase employment and production levels at a time when sales in the field were actually decreasing. Also, retail sales might exhibit random fluctuations so that if the manager were to respond to the retail sales increase (whether the time lag was long or short) he might respond by small increases in employment and production level, taking a wait-and-see attitude, i.e., to see if the increase is permanent or only a random change in sales level.

A demonstration of the oscillatory behavior in managerial systems is shown by Forrester [8] in a simulation study of a production-distribution system for a manufactured product. The organization involved a factory, factory warehouse, distributors, and retailers, with finished goods inventory held at the three points in the distribution chain. There were information and delivery time lags throughout the system ranging from a half week for mail delivery of orders from retailers to distributors, to six weeks for the manufacture of products, given orders to produce.

An Example

With all aspects of operation stable, the system was stimulated with a simple 10 per cent increase in retail sales which remained stable at the new level from that point on. Figure 3 shows the impact on inventories at the three points in the system as well as on production and ordering behavior. The response is wild oscillation in most of the curves followed by a damping of the oscillations, rather than a smooth, stable response. With systems responding in this way to both the external environment as well as the actions which managers take, then it is somewhat easier to understand how complex and difficult it is to manage an operational system.

THE OPERATIONS FUNCTION IN CONTEXT

As we commented earlier, every system can be regarded as a part of a larger system and this is the case with the production or operations function of an enterprise. Let us now consider the operations function, with all of its internal complexities, to be one block in the much larger enterprise system. The operations function itself might be internally represented by a complex network of processes such as Figure 2b, however, we will represent it by a single block with its own inputs and

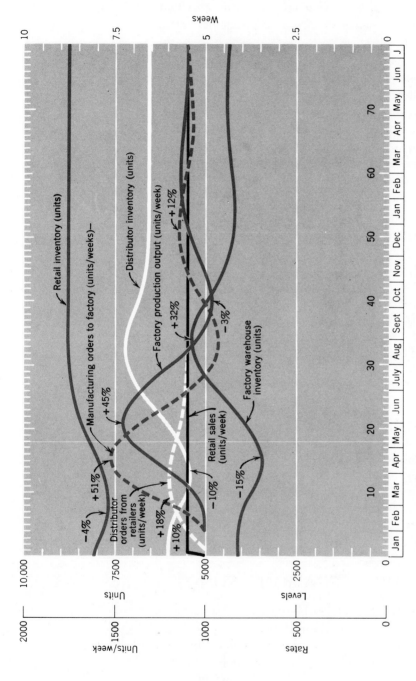

Response of production-distribution system to a sudden 10 per cent increase in retail sales. (Adapted from Forrester [8, Figure 2-2].)

FIGURE 3.

outputs. Figures 5 and 6 of Chapter 2 are also descriptive of activities going on inside the operations function.

Figure 4 is a basic schematic diagram which places the broad operations function in context. The diagram is highly aggregated both in terms of flows and in terms of functions performed. Yet it shows the nature of flow paths and the major places where transformations of one sort or another take place. Note that we have drawn certain boundaries to the system which establish pools outside the system for labor, materials and energy, equipment, external services, and financial resources. These functions are a part of the environment of the system, and there are flows between these functions external to the system and the system itself.

The flows, as indicated on the schematic diagram, are of six distinct types. The dashed line with circles represents the flow of orders. It can be seen that the orders originate in the surroundings of the system studied. They may originate in the environment as inputs to the system

FIGURE 4. General model for operational systems—basic schematic diagram. (From Reisman and Buffa [14].)

or they may be responses to information originating in and emanating from the system as might be the case where a sales organization actively solicits orders. Orders enter the system through the professional and/or service function. This is the intelligence arm of the model. Based on decisions made in this function, the incoming orders may be either routed to a sink, that is, "filed," or, after certain transformations, be sent onto the operations function, the inventory, or the proposals and/or sales function.

If the order is for proposals, it is routed to the proposals and/or sales group from which a proposal in the form of information (dashed line) is sent out. On the other hand, if the order is for goods, services, or energy which cannot be filled from inventory, the operations function fills the orders through production. If, however, the decision is made to fill the order from inventory, it is routed to that function. Where orders are sent to operations, the intelligence arm or professional and/or service function must satisfy operations with the necessary labor, materials, energy, equipment, and external services, all at the correct time and of the right kind. (Labor as referred to here may be highly professional, as in hospitals or universities.) Thus information must be sent through the employment policy and the financial and ordering policy functions so that orders may go out to the various pools.

On receipt of an order, the labor pool routes people into the system (double solid line). The population flows enter through the training function where they are processed and sent on to either operations or, perhaps, the professional function itself. Similarly, the material and energy pool routes its resources to the system through the processing delay from where they may be sent on to either the material inventory or to the operations function directly. The equipment pool sends capital equipment (solid wide line) into its processing delay and on to operations. The external services pool performs as the name implies, that is, services which cannot be performed internally within the system, owing to lack of capability, capacity limitations, and so on.

The financial pool represents the banks or the investment sector of the economy. This is the originator for all external financing. It provides the necessary capital for the system, while at the same time, being the place where surplus cash is stored (dashed lines with dollar signs). Of course, cash also enters the system from the general environment in payment for the goods produced or services rendered, and, for similar reasons, leaves the system to various pools. Notice that there is no flow of cash between segments of the internal system. The reason is, of course, that manufacturing does not pay in cash or even by check for materials coming from in-plant materials inventory since these transactions are covered by intraplant flows of information.

Information flows (dashed line) may be of several types. They may be in the form of reports or memoranda or they may be verbal; they may be requests for further information or they may be commands or instructions. In addition, information flows may contain the routine data from operations, inventory, delivery, or processing delays. Information flows may exhibit all of the characteristics of physical flows; that is, information may be generated, stored, transformed, and dissipated, and its flow may exhibit inertia.

Goods or energy may enter the professional and/or service function first. Here intelligence operations are performed and they are routed to either operations or inventory, depending on need.

Operations Function—Materials and Information Flow. The highly aggregated function blocks, of Figure 4, as well as the flows, may be broken down to any level of aggregation desired for each type

FIGURE 5. Operations function—materials flow schematic diagram. (From Reisman and Buffa [14].)

of flow through schematic diagrams such as Figure 5. Figure 5 diagrams just the materials flow for the operations function in relation to other pertinent functions. Within the operations function boundary, each small block represents either a transformation (physical, chemical, or other) or a flow element such as transportation or storage. In addition, these small blocks represent the nodes or junctions of the flow system and are the focus of much of the analysis which can be performed on the system. Note that the nodes are numbered from one to n. Figure 6 adds to the materials flow schematic diagram of Figure 5 the information flow related directly to the operations function. The interconnection of all pertinent flow diagrams such as Figures 5 and 6, according to the overall structure of Figure 4, represents the entire system for the six kinds of flow diagrams.

The value of constructing models patterned after the general form of Figures 4, 5, and 6 for specific real systems is that we may now be subjected to rigorous analysis. Such analysis may be either mathe-

FIGURE 6. Operations function—materials and information flow schematic diagram. (From Reisman and Buffa [14].)

matical in form, since we may now write equations which describe the nature of the various flows taking place, or we may simulate the operation of such a system by means of large-scale computers. The general mathematical analysis is described in [14]; an application in an electronics company of this general type of analysis is discussed in [8].

CONTROL SUBSYSTEMS

Systems concepts can be useful in understanding how the broad control subsystems function in relation to the production system itself. Figure 7 is a block diagram showing the production system in relation to control subsystems which fall within the boundaries of the dashed line. For day-to-day control of the production system we see that there is a control

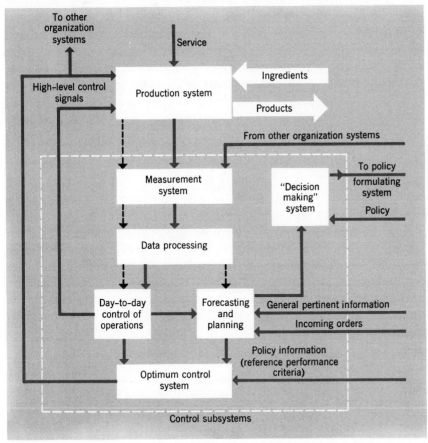

FIGURE 7. Production system in relation to control subsystems. (From Alcalay and Buffa [1].)

loop which involves measurements made on the system which are fed into data processing for interpretation and comparison with desired performance, with action taken by the day-to-day control functions. With the present capability of automatic measurement, data processing, and effector mechanisms, it is conceivable that day-to-day control can be completely automatic as it is in most petroleum refining situations.

While the day-to-day control process is going on, there is a broader control system which seeks optimum operation. The optimum control system is taking as inputs information from the day-to-day control system (short range), forecasting and planning, and policy information to create a broader range (perhaps broader horizon) criterion of performance. Such a control system might involve the alteration or correction of standards of performance. There is another type of function for the optimum control system, however, where optimum operations might not be defined on a day-to-day basis. Production scheduling is an example where a broader time horizon and broader criterion function are required to develop an optimum control system for production programs. These programs may involve complex models which balance the costs of inventories and the costs of changing production levels in anticipation of forecasted sales. The day-to-day schedule in itself may be far from optimum, but the longer range production programs may approach optimality.

EXAMPLES OF LARGE-SCALE SYSTEMS

The availability of high-speed computers has fostered the development and use of large-scale systems which have most often been used to simulate operations. These simulations provide the basis for evaluating the impact of alternate policies and plans. Since the interacting effects are so complex in such systems the analyses can provide a basis for important decisions. We shall look briefly at three such large systems: Potlatch Forests, Inc., Inland Steel Company, and VdB & J Division of Unilever.

Potlatch Forests, Inc. [3, 4]. This organization is a large forest products company having annual sales in the range of about $335 million, and employing over 12,000 individuals in 44 plants and 36 sales offices spread over the entire country. The company developed 22 interlinked computer-based models to describe various operations, groups, and subsidiary companies. The gross structure of the input-output relationships of the various divisions, groups, and subsidiaries is shown in Figure 8. Each major block in Figure 8 represents in itself

FIGURE 9. Relationships in Inland Steel model. *Courtesy Inland Steel and On-Line Decisions, Inc.*

RAW MATERIALS

FINISHED PRODUCTS

SOLD ON OPEN MARKET

Product A from Western Division
Product A from Plywood Division
Product A purchased on open market

DOD purchased on open market

From Western Lumber Division

Product AA
Product B
Product C
Product D
Other products

From Plywood Division

Product E
Product AA

From International Division

Product E
Product Z
Product Y

Other purchases
Contact purchases
Commission business

Product A from Southern Lumber Division
Product A purchased on open market
Product FF from Southern Lumber Division
Product FF purchased on open market

Financial statements,
group overhead & eliminations

From Western Lumber Division
From Plywood Division
From Marketing Division
From Southern Lumber Division

Western Lumber Division

Plywood Division

Specialty Marketing Division

Southern Lumber Division

1. Wood Products Group

Product AA
Product B
Product C
Product D
Other products

Product ABB
Product E
Product AA

Profit centers

Product AA
Product F
Product G
Product C
Other products
Product ABB

Consolidated group financial statements

Product H
Product I
COD

Specialty Marketing Division

Western Lumber Division

Lewiston Pulp & Paperboard Division

Potlatch Forests Incorporated

Product ABB fro
Product ABB
Product

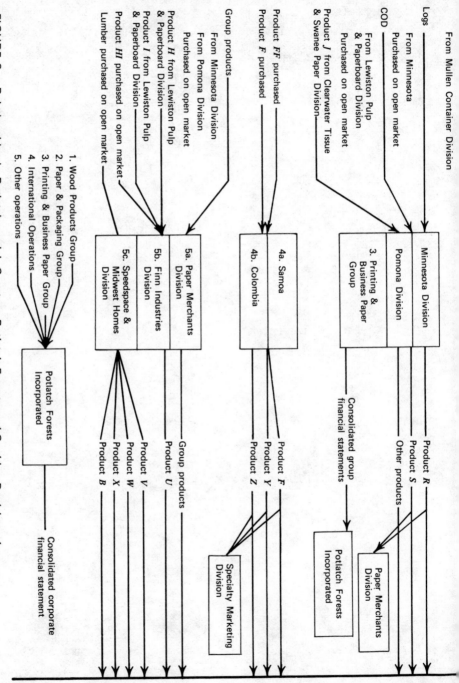

FIGURE 8. Relationships in Potlatch model. *Courtesy Potlatch Forests and On-Line Decisions, Inc.*

a system of substantial size. Prior to the existence of the corporate system models, management's assessment of the financial effects of the interactions of interplant buying and selling and changing product mixes involved long time lags. The interactive computer system, however, greatly reduced the effort needed to evaluate alternate plans because the logic of the 22 models takes into account the complex financial flows between divisions and groups.

Inland Steel [3, 4].   While the Potlatch Forests example emphasizes the successive aggregation and consolidation of financial flows, the Inland Steel Company's example shown in Figure 9 focuses first on the basic production processes and finally consolidates the financial effects in terms of standard financial statements. Given the system models, Inland Steel Management can easily raise questions such as the following:

1.   How much raw material is required to meet production forecasts?
2.   What are the cost effects of various hot metal-to-scrap ratios and the resulting yields under various assumptions of raw material costs?
3.   What are the capacity requirements for proposed levels of operation?

The management of Inland Steel used the system models in preparing contingency plans for 1971 when the company faced unusual uncertainties involving the possibility of a major automotive industry strike. The system models have also been used as a basis for its annual five-year planning cycle and for evaluating the profit sensitivity of a wide variety of input factors.

Van den Berghs & Jurgens, Ltd. (VdB & J) [3, 5].   VdB & J is a subsidiary of Unilever, Ltd., and is a major producer of white and yellow fats in the United Kingdom. Margarine sales account for 65 per cent of the total annual company's sales of about $200 million. The company devoted great effort at very substantial cost to an annual planning activity which occupied the accounting staff for approximately six months of the year. Over 7,000 values were computed as inputs for the annual plan to generate 125 reports in 12 primary formats. Data was manipulated in a number of ways by various classifications, i.e., all brands sold to bakeries, all yellow fats, etc. When an assumption was changed in one area, thousands of recalculations were necessary. With the tremendous effort necessary to undertake the creation of the plan, it was impossible for the staff to submit several alternatives to the board for consideration, and, in the event of a plan being disapproved, it was extremely difficult to generate a new one. Further, the ability to update the plan was restricted to annual or biannual exercises because of the time involved. This situation was far from effective in an environment where the raw material costs were rapidly fluctuating, a variation of over 100 per cent in some costs having been experienced in the two years just prior to the implementation of a computer-based system model called VANGUARD.

The VANGUARD system is a corporate simulator which allows one to explore the effect on the company position of changes in the whole range of variables applicable to the operation of the enterprise: for example, total market sizes and market shares, brand sales values, raw material prices, product formulations, refinery capacities, personnel costs, taxation rates, working capital requirements, etc.

The system summarized in Figure 10 consists of 15 interrelated

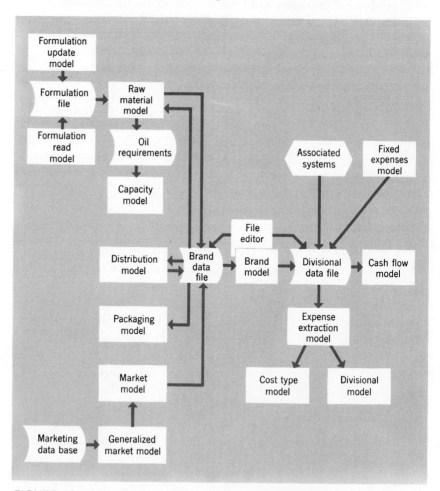

FIGURE 10. Broad relationships within the VANGUARD system. Courtesy VdB&J Division of Unilever, Ltd., and On-Line Decisions, Inc. (From Boulden and Buffa[5].)

programs, or models, each relevant to a separate aspect of company operation. The system has been used to evaluate the impact of a wide variety of important policy questions, seventeen of which are listed in references [3, 5].

IMPLICATIONS OF THE SYSTEMS CONCEPT FOR THE MANAGER

A manager who puts the systems concept to work is rewarded initially by the development of a deeper understanding of the system he manages. By developing the structure of the interacting effects of system components and the various feedback control loops in the system he can see better which "handles" to twist in order to keep himself in control of the system he manages. Indeed, with a knowledge of the system structure, he can see how he might restructure the system in order to create the most effective feedback control mechanisms.

With the availability of large-scale system models such as Potlatch Forests, Inland Steel, and VdB & J, a manager is better able to assess the effects of changes in one division component on another and on the organization as a whole. Furthermore, the manager of any one of the productive operations is better able to see how his unit fits into the whole and to understand the kinds of tradeoffs which are often made by higher level management which sometimes seemingly affect his unit adversely.

The basic systems concepts which we have discussed are applied again and again throughout the balance of the book. For example, feedback control processes are central in our discussion of automation in Chapter 9, man-machine systems in Chapter 13, the forecasting and inventory control systems of Chapter 16, the aggregate planning methods of Chapter 17 and the quality control concepts of Chapter 22. Input-output transformation processes are the basis for the entire set of chapters in Part 3 on the design of productive systems, and, in general, the kinds of tradeoffs which are required in the various decision problems throughout the book are a reflection of the systems concept.

Perhaps one of the most important contributions of systems thinking is the concept of suboptimization. Suboptimization often occurs when one views a problem narrowly. For example, one can construct mathematical formulas to determine the minimum cost (optimum) quantity of products or parts to manufacture at one time, which results in a supposedly optimum inventory level. If one broadens the definition of the system under study, however, and includes not just the inventory and reorder subsystem but the production and warehousing sub-systems as well, he may find that the inventory connected costs are a measure of only part of the problem. If the product exhibits seasonal sales, the costs of changing production levels may be significant enough to warrant carrying extra inventories to smooth production and employment. In such a situation the minimum cost inventory model would be a suboptimal policy.

Organizational suboptimization often occurs when the production and distribution functions of an enterprise are operated as essentially two different businesses. The factory manager will try to minimize his costs independently as will the sales-distribution manager. The factory manager will be faced with minimizing production cost while the sales-distribution manager will be faced mainly with an inventory management, shipping, and customer service problem. Each sub-organization attempting to optimize separately will likely result in a combined cost somewhat larger than if the attempt were made to optimize the combined system. The reasons are fairly obvious, since in minimizing the costs of inventories the sales function transmits directly to the factory most of the effects of sales fluctuations instead of absorbing these fluctuations through buffer inventories. Suboptimization is the result. By coordinating their efforts, however, it may be possible to achieve some balance between inventory costs and the costs of production fluctuation.

REVIEW QUESTIONS

1. What is a system?
2. On observing an exhibit containing an automobile, a bus, a helicopter, a train, a motorcycle, and a bicycle, a systems analyst remarked, "It's an interesting collection of ways to get around, but it's no system!" What characteristic would have had to be present to describe the exhibit as a system?
3. What are the values of the systems concept in operations management problems?
4. If every system is a part of an even larger system, how can the concept be made useful and brought to bear on specific problems?
5. How do we separate and understand the difference between the system under study and the environment in which it operates?
6. What is an open system? a closed or feedback system? What is the crucial distinction between the two kinds of systems?
7. Distinguish between a negative and a positive feedback system.
8. What are the elements which are a part of any feedback control loop?

Describe these elements in a simple thermostatic control system for a home heating plant.

9. Describe the dynamic effects of feedback control systems. What is the effect of the introduction of time lags into feedback control systems?

10. Take some specific productive system such as a bank, supermarket, hospital, or manufacturing concern, and describe the nature of the operations function. Then place the operations function into context within the overall enterprise system such as was done in Figure 4 in the text. What general kinds of flows are of particular importance in the system you have defined? Is there waste in the system? How is the waste processed? Justify the system boundary which you have drawn in relation to the environment in which the system operates. Describe the broad feedback control loops that exist in enterprises for the control of the production aspect of the enterprise. Differentiate between day-to-day control of operations and optimum system control.

11. How can the large-scale systems such as those described for Potlatch Forests, Inland Steel, and VdB & J Division of Unilever be of day-to-day value to managers? Of longer-range value?

12. What is the meaning of suboptimization? How is it related to the systems concept?

REFERENCES

[1] Alcalay, J. A., and E. S. Buffa. "A Proposal for a General Model of a Production System." *International Journal of Production Research*, Mar. 1963.

[2] Beer, S. *Management Science: The Business Use of Operations Research*. Doubleday and Co., Inc., New York, 1968.

[3] Buffa, E. S. *Operations Management: Problems and Models* (3rd ed.). John Wiley, New York, 1972.

[4] Boulden, J. B., and E. S. Buffa. "Corporate Models: On-Line, Real-Time Systems." *Harvard Business Review*, July–Aug. 1970.

[5] Boulden, J. B., and E. S. Buffa. "New Developments in On-Line Corporate Models." *On-Line Decisions*, New York, 1972.

[6] Buffa, E. S., and W. H. Taubert. *Production-Inventory Systems: Planning and Control* (2nd ed.). Richard D. Irwin, Homewood, Ill., 1972.

[7] Cleland, D. I., and W. R. King. *Systems, Organizations, Analysis, Management: A Book of Readings*. McGraw-Hill Book Co., New York, 1969.

[8] Forrester, J. *Industrial Dynamics*. MIT Press, Cambridge, Mass., 1961.

[9] Forrester, J. *Principles of Systems*. Wright-Allen Press, Inc., Cambridge, Mass., 1968.

[10] Hare, V. C., Jr. *Systems Analysis: A Diagnostic Approach*. Harcourt, Brace, and World, Inc., New York, 1967.

[11] Johnson, R. A., F. E. Kast, and J. E. Rosenzweig. *The Theory and Management of Systems* (2nd ed.). McGraw-Hill Book Co., New York, 1967.

[12] McDonough, A. M., and L. J. Garrett. *Management Systems: Working Concepts and Practices.* Richard D. Irwin, Homewood, Ill., 1965.

[13] McMillan, C., Jr., and R. F. Gonzalez. *Systems Analysis: A Computer Approach to Decision Models* (Rev. ed.). Richard D. Irwin, Homewood, Ill., 1968.

[14] Reisman, A., and E. S. Buffa. "A General Model for Production and Operations Systems." *Management Science,* 11 (1), Sept. 1964.

[15] Schoderbek, P. P. *Management Systems* (2nd ed.). John Wiley, New York, 1971.

part two

Analytical Methods

Analytical **M**ethods in **P**roduction & **O**perations **M**anagement

Perhaps the thing that distinguishes the production and operations management field at its present stage of development is the degree to which analytical methods have been applied. These analytical methods have been used both to establish a conceptual framework and to solve practical problems. Early methods of analysis represented graphic and schematic models of various aspects of a production system. Since World War II, however, there has been an increased use of more sophisticated techniques such as mathematical, statistical, and simulation models as well as the emphasis on systems and the systemic point of

67

view, discussed in Chapter 3. This increased use of analytic and systemic techniques is the most important indication that production and operations management is well on the road to becoming an applied science.

Analytical methodology in production and operations management essentially follows the basic framework of scientific method and is based on the use of various kinds of models which represent some part of the system or subsystem under study. Our general discussion of models and their place in decision making in Chapter 2 is pertinent in this regard.

A FRAMEWORK FOR ANALYSIS

This book leans heavily on the analytical approach to production and operations management and focuses at various points on both new and traditional methods of analysis. Whether new or traditional, however, the basic framework for analysis follows a pattern. The important aspect of analysis is not whether the technique used is new or traditional but whether it is the best mode of analysis available for the nature of the problem and for the practical situation surrounding the problem. It is often true that the traditional technique may be the appropriate one for a particular situation even though new and more powerful approaches exist. This might be the case where the management of the organization is just emerging into an analytical frame of mind and wishes to proceed cautiously, or where the cost of applying the newer, more sophisticated technique is not warranted. As we shall see, it is also true that some traditional approaches to analysis have not been superseded and are therefore still dominant in certain types of problems. The following outline summarizes the process of analysis for production and operations management.

Define the System under Study. This step is perhaps the most important one in the analysis of any problem in any field because it sets the horizons for analysis. If the problem is defined narrowly, the final solution is likely to be limited in application and probably wrong under certain circumstances. Recall that this is referred to as a *suboptimum* solution. Suboptimization occurs, for example, if in attempting to determine a program for the production of a seasonal product, we establish the scope of the problem as being one of minimizing labor costs. Consider a program for production to be the number of units produced in each period during a planning span of time such as a year. The program resulting in such a situation would be one of level production throughout the year even though sales vary seasonally. The reason is that to change production levels as sales vary requires the hiring and layoff of part of the labor force so that additional costs result as compared to level production.

Figure 1 shows a production program where a seasonal sales requirement is to be met by a level production plan. A broader definition of the problem reveals, of course, that other costs may be involved such as the cost of carrying inventories to absorb fluctuations in sales level. The level production program is a suboptimum solution in this instance; a solution that considers both labor and inventory costs will specify a balance between these costs rather than minimizing either of them by ignoring the other. One guide to help define the problem is then to determine what factors or variables may have an influence on the behavior of the system under study.

In general, the broader the definition or scope of the problem, the less likely is it that suboptimization will occur. This broad definition is often referred to as the "system" viewpoint; that is, we attempt to view the problem in the context of the overall system rather than narrowly. In reference to the production programming problem just discussed, the system view of the problem would suggest that we include as part of the system under study the procurement of raw materials prior to actual production as well as the distribution of finished goods to the market, since

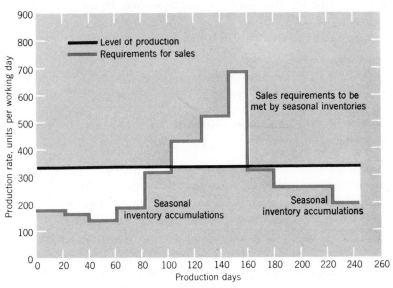

FIGURE 1. Level production program for a product having seasonal sales requirements.

the nature of the production program can affect procurement and distribution costs. Also, we should consider other ways of absorbing fluctuations in sales level such as subcontracting part of the peak requirements. The broader system view changes the nature of the apparent best solution.

It often happens, however, that the ideal of the system viewpoint cannot be achieved, either because of time and effort limitations for a practical solution or because we are as yet incapable of handling the larger problems. This inevitably results when the scope of the problem is defined as being very large. Some of the new tools of analysis which we shall discuss, such as linear programming and large-scale system simulation, have helped to improve our capability to view problems broadly. Also, rapid data processing has made the solution of some kinds of large system problems feasible, although we could not even consider them as being practical problems only a decade ago.

In defining the system to be studied, it is often of value to develop graphic, schematic, and pictorial models of the system which may help in visualizing the problem. For complex systems, the development of block diagrams that represent flow, functions, interconnections, and interactions are often helpful in this regard. Figures 4, 5, and 6 in Chapter 3, which diagram the flow aspects of generalized systems of production, are representative of schematic models.

Define a Measure of Effectiveness.   In other words, establish criteria which measure the effectiveness of alternate courses of action. Some measures might be profits, contribution, total costs, incremental costs, machine down time, machine utilization, labor costs, labor utilization, number of units processed, and flow time. Measures of effectiveness for analysis of operational systems are commonly related to some direct or indirect measure of profit, cost, quality, service or delivery time. Ordinarily then, measures of effectiveness define what it is we wish to maximize or minimize.

Construct a Model Where E, the Effect, Can Be Expressed as a Function of the Variables That Define the System.   Recall from our discussion in Chapter 2 that models are the means by which we forecast the performance of alternatives for the system under study. As we pointed out there, the validity of the model is determined by the accuracy with which it is capable of forecasting performance. In developing the model, we attempt to identify the controllable factors or variables, X_i, and those which are uncontrollable, Y_j, and attempt to formulate relationships between the measure of effectiveness E and the variables of the general form:

$$E = f(X_i, Y_j)$$

This expression merely says E, the measure of effectiveness, is a function of the controllable variables X_i and the uncontrollable variables Y_j. The specific relationships would have to be developed.

Controllable variables are those that may be manipulated pretty much at the will of management. In the production programming problem discussed previously, an example of a controllable variable is the program itself, that is, the number of units to be produced in each period. Uncontrollable variables are those that management cannot control, at least not within the limitations of the problem.

In the programming problem, consumer demand, wage rates, and inventory carrying costs are examples of uncontrollable variables. We might argue that management can influence these variables by advertising, labor negotiations, and so on. Nevertheless, management cannot change demand, wages, and carrying costs at will. In general, changes in all of these uncontrollable factors would be reflected in E, and management would respond by adjusting the production program to minimize E again. The new program would then be the best one, given the new values of the uncontrollable factors.

Generate Alternatives Based on Analysis. Evaluate these alternatives through the model, using E as a measure of effectiveness. The objective of analysis is to form a basis for problem solution; however, we should beware of becoming enthralled with "the solution." Ordinarily there are good alternate courses of action, many of which may be nearly equivalent in terms of their effectiveness as measured by E. The model constructed should make it possible to generate alternative solutions which may be appraised by the criterion E as well as other nonquantifiable factors.

At this stage, various *hypotheses* for the best solution can be stated. The model forms a basis for measuring the effect of each of these and comparing results. Of course, the informal or formal statements of logical hypotheses to be tested may have been developed prior to this step and such hypotheses may well have been the basis for undertaking the study in the first place. As a matter of fact, a large fraction of problems leading to the use of analytical methods are recognized in this way. That is, someone suggests alternate policies or procedures, and these essentially become hypotheses that must stand the tests of analytical methodology.

For the example of the production program, several alternate schedules for meeting sales requirements could be calculated, as shown in Figure 2. Each of the three alternate plans shown involves a hypothesis about the most effective way to meet requirements, using normal and overtime capacity, subcontracting, and seasonal inventories. The effects on incremental costs of the three plans is rather startling as is shown in Table I. Plan 1, level production, has no extra labor turnover cost, overtime premium, or subcontracting cost; however, the cost of carrying seasonal inventory to meet the high peak of sales in the summer is very large. Plan 2 involves some fluctuation in production level, but not so much that plant capacity with overtime work is exceeded. The result is a somewhat smaller seasonal inventory cost than for Plan 1 and a total incremental cost which is $20,000 per year less than Plan 1. Plan 3 tends to follow the sales requirement curve more closely and this involves considerable hiring and laying off of labor. Also, because of limitations of plant capacity, even with the use of overtime capacity, it is necessary to resort to subcontracting to meet the peak requirements. Nevertheless, the tremendous reduction in inventory cost makes Plan 3 the cheapest of the three plans. There are obviously other possible programs for which the total incremental costs could have been com-

FIGURE 2. Comparison of three production programs that meet requirements.

TABLE I. Comparative Incremental Costs for Three Production Programs			
	Plan 1	Plan 2	Plan 3
Inventory Requirements, units	8,000	6,885	3,691
Peak capacity required:			
(Plan 1 = 100)	100	126	165
Incremental costs:			
Seasonal stock cost*	$318,000	$239,000	$ 47,300
Labor turnover cost†	0	48,000	104,000
Overtime premium‡	0	11,000	44,000
Subcontracting cost**	0	0	57,750
	$318,000	$298,000	$253,050

*Inventory carrying cost computed at $60 per unit per year.
†A change in production rate at 20 units per day requires the employment or separation of 40 men at a cost of hiring and training an employee of $200.
‡Units produced at overtime labor rates cost $10 per unit extra.
**Units produced by subcontractors cost $15 per unit extra.

puted. For example, using a computer search programming model, we could determine a program that would approximate the minimum possible or optimum cost for the items of cost considered.

Weigh and Decide. Weight and decide what course of action to take based on a balancing of quantitative analysis and the nonquantitative factors in the situation. It might seem on the surface that the model should make this step unnecessary. After all, the measure of effectiveness is supposed to measure the effect of alternate courses of action. But does it do this completely? Usually, measures of effectiveness are not capable of reflecting all aspects of performance. There will be non-quantitative factors which must be given weight.

In the production programming example, one factor which might be given heavy weight in today's economy would be the amount of hiring and laying off to be tolerated. The organization has a social responsibility and also feels the pressure of labor, public, and community reactions. The decision maker must balance off the $65,000 per year advantage of Plan 3 over Plan 1 against the disadvantage of the labor turnover induced by Plan 3. Compared to Plan 2, which involves more moderate swings in production level, Plan 3 has an economic advantage of $45,000 per year. In addition, Plan 3 involves considerable subcontracting to meet peak sales requirements. Can quality levels be held if we work through a subcontractor? Is it worth the difference to use either Plan 1 or 2 in order to maintain closer in-house control over quality?

The generation and evaluation of alternatives are of extreme importance in the overall process because they give flexibility to the decision maker. Quite often, alternate solutions may have differences in effectiveness as measured by E which are not large, but one alternative may deal with a nonquantitative factor in a more satisfactory way. One great trap in quantitative analysis is the siren song of the "optimal solution." People are often drawn to mathematically provable optimal solutions, but we must remember that such solutions face the often severe limitations of the definition of the measure of effectiveness. If E is really all inclusive for a given situation, then judgment may not need to enter, but this is seldom the case. In the really large-scale systems with which we may deal, it is often impractical to think in terms of optimality because the system is so complex. In these situations we must think in terms of improving existing conditions rather than in terms of optimizing the overall system.

The overall framework for analysis is roughly parallel to the steps shown in Figure 3, regardless of the nature of the problem or the exact kind of analytical model used. The steps are not necessarily independent of each other in the actual solution of problems.

In Parts 3 and 4 of this book, which deal with some of the major problems that occur within the production and operations management field, we shall call attention to applications of various analytical techniques discussed generally here. These applications occur both for the analysis of problems as well as for synthesis, that is, the design of overall systems.

KINDS OF ANALYTICAL METHODS

The various kinds of models which have been shown to have applicability in one or more kinds of typical problems arising in production or operational systems are shown in Figure 3. This figure shows the overall framework for the analysis we have been discussing. They are not simply standardized models which can be "plugged" in to obtain answers; rather they are fairly general models which, when adapted to local conditions, fit a surprisingly large number of cases. We shall discuss the general characteristics and usefulness of each later in this section.

Cost Analysis   Cost analysis is still perhaps the most common of analysis methods. It takes many forms and is based on a knowledge of the behavior of cost factors. It is not simply a drawing together of cost information from

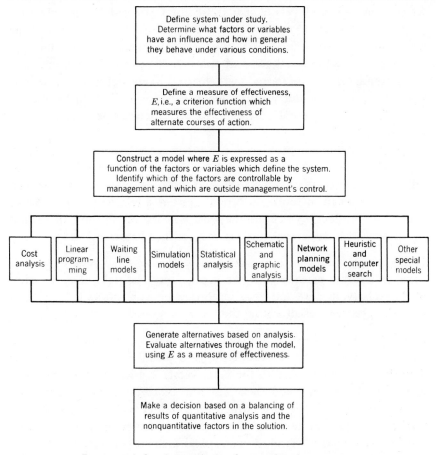

FIGURE 3. Framework for the analysis of operational systems.

accounting data because many of the accounting data have a significance only within the accounting system. Our interest is in the actual behavior of pertinent costs under the alternatives considered. *Breakeven analysis* makes use of the differences in behavior of certain costs as volume of operation varies. Breakeven analysis is useful in helping to establish a proper volume of operation, to diagnose problems, and to evaluate the appropriateness of a production process.

One of the most valuable simple techniques of analysis, *incremental cost analysis*, deals with only those costs affected by the alternate policies or actions considered. The problem of alternate production programs discussed previously in this section is an example of incremental cost analysis. Recall that we did not atempt to evaluate the alternative costs by calculating total operating costs with alternate plans. This approach would have been tedious and time consuming. Instead, we determined the levels of just those costs affected by the alternate programs, that is, inventory costs, labor turnover costs, overtime premium, and extra subcontracting costs. Incremental cost concepts are useful in virtually all areas of analysis of operational systems and occur commonly in the formal mathematical models of analysis such as linear programming and waiting line analysis as well. Both breakeven analysis and incremental cost analysis are discussed in greater detail in Chapter 5.

Another kind of cost problem occurs when capital assets are considered in the alternatives generated. The nature of cost behavior is somewhat different under these circumstances and requires special treatment. The question of when to replace a capital asset is a related problem. Since almost all production systems depend heavily on the use of capital equipment, this important topic is covered in Chapter 6.

Linear Programming

Linear programming is representative of the new methodologies that come to us from mathematics and economics. The field of application of this relatively new and very important general model is in dealing with the problems of allocating the scarce resources of an organization.

Distribution Methods. Suppose, for example, that we face a distribution problem where production of a product takes place in four factories located one each in the East, West, South, and Midwest. The market is nationwide and there are ten distribution points scattered throughout the country from which the product is shipped to the local market. Looking at just the network from factories to distribution warehouses, what is the most economical distribution system? That is, which factories should ship to which distribution warehouses and what quantities in order to minimize shipping costs? The solution is not a simple or obvious one because it is not just a matter of finding the cheapest shipping routes. The reason is that output at each of the factories is limited and the demand at each of the ten distribution warehouses is set by the market. The problem is therefore to find the most economical combination of shipments; the number of possible combinations is tremendous.

To illustrate the nature of the problem, let us take a slightly simpler but parallel situation to the distribution problem just discussed. Suppose that we have three factories located at Atlanta, Chicago, and Detroit, and that there are five distribution warehouses at Buffalo, Cincinnati, Des Moines, Milwaukee, and New York City. Figure 4 shows the general geographic relationships. Let us suppose that the capacity of each factory and the district demand at each warehouse are as shown in the far-right column

FIGURE 4.   Geographical locations of factories and distribution points.

and bottom row, respectively, of Table II. Also, the numbers in the small boxes show the shipping cost in dollars between all combinations of factories and warehouses. The shipping cost must be directly proportional to the number of units shipped or, in mathematical language, be expressible by linear equations. Table II is called a distribution matrix.

The best possible pattern of shipments is that shown in Table III where the circled numbers indicate the number of units shipped. The solution was established by distribution methods of linear programming. There are some interesting things about the solution. First, note that all conditions of supply and demand can be satisfied with just seven shipments—one less than the sum of the number of origins (factories) plus destinations (warehouses). This is always true; a solution can always be determined which has no more than this number of shipments. Sometimes a solution can be obtained with fewer shipments. Second, note in Table III that the best solution does not necessarily involve only the lowest cost routes. For example, almost half of the

TABLE II.   Distribution Matrix for Three Factories and Five Distribution Warehouses

To From	Buffalo	Cincinnati	Des Moines	Milwaukee	New York City	Factory capacity (cases)
Atlanta	50	42	49	51	55	200
Chicago	45	44	45	37	53	150
Detroit	42	43	47	42	51	180
Warehouse demand (cases)	70	90	120	50	200	530

shipments to New York City come by way of the most expensive shipment route in the entire matrix, yet there is no other combination of shipments which reduces the total shipping cost below the minimum cost of $24,610.

The example is, of course, a very simple problem, and we could establish a fairly good solution without the use of linear programming. By simply using common sense, we could assign shipments to the lower

TABLE III.   Optimum Allocation of Capacity to Demand

To From	Buffalo	Cincinnati	Des Moines	Milwaukee	New York City	Factory capacity (cases)
Atlanta	50	42 (90)	49 (20)	51	55 (90)	200
Chicago	45	44	45 (100)	37 (50)	53	150
Detroit	42 (70)	43	47	42	51 (110)	180
Warehouse demand (cases)	70	90	120	50	200	530

Total shipping cost:

Detroit–Buffalo, 70 × 42 = $2,940
Atlanta–Cincinnati, 90 × 42 =   3,780
Atlanta–Des Moines, 20 × 49 =   980
Chicago–Des Moines, 100 × 45 =   4,500
Chicago–Milwaukee, 50 × 37 =   1,850
Atlanta–New York City, 90 × 55 =   4,950
Detroit–New York City, 110 × 51 =   5,610
$24,610

cost route as far as possible, using other routes to balance off the supply and demand constraints. This is not so simply done with a problem of practical size, however. If the matrix size is increased to only 5 × 10, the problem becomes baffling. Without linear programming, we then do not know whether the solution we have developed is optimum or not, or whether it is even very good at all. With linear programming the best solution can be obtained directly, and we can prove that it is the best possible. Since there are literally thousands of possible solutions, linear programming has really accomplished something worthwhile.

Simplex Methods.   While some allocation problems can be handled in the format of the distribution methods just discussed, others require the more general simplex model. Problems to determine the optimal mix of products to produce are often approached by simplex methods of linear programming, and we shall use such a problem as an example. Suppose that an electrical equipment manufacturer makes two models of an item of test equipment and is attempting to decide how many units of each model to make for next month. The market is not the limiting factor; thus the manufacturers can sell any quantity of either model that they can produce within the limits of their capacity. Therefore, they wish to plan a mix of the two products which will maximize the total profit from the two. The profit contribution of Model 1 is $50 per unit and is $45 per unit for Model 2.

   The two units are manufactured with the same facilities involving three departments: Main Frame, Electrical Wiring, and Assembly. Assuming that the entire department capacities were used for Model 1, the capacity limits would be:

	Capacity for Model 1, Units per Month
Main Frame	400
Electrical Wiring	500
Assembly	600

On the other hand, if all capacity were turned over to Model 2, the capacity limits would be:

	Capacity for Model 2, Units per Month
Main Frame	533
Electrical Wiring	400
Assembly	800

We can visualize these capacity limits best by plotting them on a graph such as Figure 5. The axes of the graph are the numbers of units produced of the two different models. First, let us look at the limiting capacity of the Main Frame Department for the two models. If all capacity is turned over to Model 1, 400 Model 1 units can be produced (point *a* in Figure 5), and if all capacity is turned over to Model 2, 533 Model 2 units can be produced (point *b* in Figure 5), as noted before. The straight line which connects points *a* and *b* represents Main Frame Department capacities for combinations of the two models. Combinations on or below the line are all feasible, but any point falling above the line exceeds Main Frame Department capacity. Points below the line are feasible but do not use all available capacity.

Similarly, the limiting capacities of the Electrical Wiring Department for the two products are represented by points *c* and *d* and the connecting straight line represents Electrical Wiring Department capacity for combinations of the two models. Finally, the line *ef* represents the Assembly Department capacity in a similar way. Note that the line for Assembly Department capacity is entirely in the shaded portion of the graph and so places no limits on the production of the two models. The Main Frame and Wiring Departments, however, place limits on the production program which can be achieved and the maximum profit contribution occurs at a production program represented by point *g*.

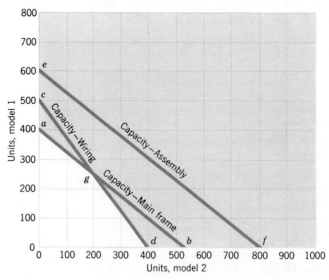

FIGURE 5. Capacities of three departments to produce two models of test equipment.

Point g represents a production program of 250 units of Model 1 and 200 units of Model 2, or a profit contribution of $50 \times 250 + 45 \times 200 = \$21,500$. There is no production program within the limits of the problem which will exceed the contribution given by this allocation of capacity to the two products. Simplex methods of linear programming can yield optimum product mix programs of this general type for extremely complex problems where the answer is not at all obvious.

With a little thought and projection, we can see that there are a large number of practical problems which are special cases of the general allocation problem. Some may be solved by distribution methods in the general format of the distribution problem discussed previously. Others require the use of the simplex method of solution and still others require other kinds of mathematical programming methods. The distribution and simplex methods of linear programming are the subjects of Chapter 7. The following is a discussion of a few typical problems where linear programming may be useful:

1. Distribution of products from a set of origin points to a number of destinations in a way that satisfies the demand at each destination and the supplies available at the origins, minimizing total transportation costs.

2. Distribution of products from factories to warehouses, similar to 1, but minimizing combined production and distribution costs. If the products have different revenues in the various marketing areas, we could maximize a function of revenue minus production-distribution costs.

3. Multiple-plant location studies where common products are produced with a decentralized complex of plants. Here we wish to evaluate various alternate locations for the construction of a new plant. Each different location considered produces a different allocation matrix of product from the factories to the distribution points because of differing production-distribution costs. The best new location is the one that minimizes total production-distribution costs for the entire system; this, of course, is not necessarily the location that seems to have the lowest production costs.

4. Locational dynamics for multiple plants. Here the problem is somewhat similar to 3 but the question is which plants to operate at what levels for a given total demand. Since additional capacity at each location can normally be obtained through overtime, and since certain overhead costs can be saved by shutting down a plant, there are conditions when total costs are minimized by shutting down a plant and supplying the total demand from the other plants, even though overtime costs are incurred. The plant to be shut down is not neces-

sarily the high production cost plant—this depends on the relative importance of production and distribution costs.

5. Redistribution of empty freight cars from their existing locations to points where they are needed in a way that minimizes transportation costs.

6. Allocation of limited raw materials used in a variety of products so that total profit is maximized, meeting market demands insofar as is possible.

7. Allocation of production facilities when alternate routings are available. Given the unit machine time for the alternate machine routes, total hours available on the different machine classes, requirements for the number of each product, and unit revenue for each product, linear programming can give a solution that maximizes some profit function, minimizes incremental costs, or meets some other management objective.

8. Blending problems. For example, a paint manufacturer may need to prepare paint vehicles that are a blend of several constituents. The constituents, such as oil and thinner, are available in limited quantity and in commercial blends of fixed proportions. Costs per gallon of the various possible raw materials are known. The problem is to determine the amount of each raw material so that required amounts for the new blends are obtained at minimum cost. Another similar problem is the blending of animal feed to provide certain minimum nutrient values at minimum cost.

9. Maximizing material utilization. Many times different stock sizes must be stamped or cut from standard raw material sizes. The problem is to determine the combination of cuts that will meet requirements for the amounts of different sizes with a minimum trim loss.

10. Developing a program for production when demand is seasonal. Here we are attempting to allocate available capacity to various production periods for the products to be produced in such a way that requirements for all products are met, and combined incremental inventory and production costs are minimized. The incremental production costs may include overtime premium, turnover costs, and extra subcontracting costs.

11. Product mix problems. Here we have a general class of problems of considerable interest. If we have production facilities that can be used to produce several different items which may have different costs, revenues, and market demands, we wish to know how best to allocate the available capacity to various products within the limitations of market demand.

12. Long-range planning. The general capacity planning problem has been treated as being met by ownership, leases, or short-term contracts. A model cast in a linear programming framework may help

in answering questions such as: (a) the effect of a given demand forecast on capacity plans, (b) the effect of changes in ownership cost, (c) the effect of changes in the costs of leased capacity, and (d) the sensitivity to forecast error of various decisions and costs.

Many production problems are related in some way to the build-up of waiting lines. In these types of problems, we have men, parts, or machines that need some sort of service at random time intervals. The activity required to service them may take a variable amount of time. Under certain conditions of arrival rates and servicing rates, a waiting line builds up. Waiting line theory provides a means of forecasting the *probable length* of the waiting line and the *probable delay or waiting time,* as well as other important data. Knowledge of these facts makes possible more intelligent decisions for questions of the following types.

Waiting Line or Queuing Models

1. How many men are needed to service a tool crib? The tool crib attendant checks out special tools to machinists and other workmen. If the number of attendants is small, they will be very busy, but a waiting line of high-paid machinists will build up. If the number of attendants is large, they will be idle much of the time, but the average waiting line will be small. A measure of effectiveness, *E,* is then the combined cost of waiting time for the attendants and the machinists. A solution indicates the number of attendants required for minimum total waiting time cost. Waiting line theory can provide the critical data required for a solution.

2. How long should a conveyor be between two stations on an assembly line? If we assume that items are not rigidly fixed to the conveyor, the length depends on the probable maximum bank that will build up between the two stations. The first station determines the arrival rate of parts. The second station determines the rate at which parts are processed and passed on. Waiting line theory can determine the probable maximum bank which, in turn, determines the length of conveyor needed to accommodate the maximum expected in-process inventory at that point.

3. How many automatic machines should one man operate? Where the machines need service, such as setup, loading, and adjusting, at random intervals, as is true with automatic looms, the optimal assignment depends on a balance between the loss of productive time from the machines and the idle time of the operator when no machines need service.

Let us take as an example the situation of the tool crib where mechanics come to obtain special tools. The attendant checks out the tool to the mechanic in exchange for a "tool check" with the mechanic's name or number on it. We assume that the mechanics arrive at random times at an average rate of 12 per hour or 1 each 5 minutes. The attendant can service the mechanics in 3 minutes

An Example

and initially we shall assume that this service time is constant for all mechanics. Table IV shows a record of the servicing of 15 mechanics. The average interval between arrivals is slightly less than 5 minutes for this sample. We see that the attendant had 32 minutes of idle time and the various mechanics waited a total of 39 minutes.

Let us see what happens if the service time is increased from 3 to 4 minutes. We assume the same schedule of arrivals and Table V results. The result is predictable. The attendant is busier now, as evidenced by the smaller idle time, but the waiting time of the mechanics is almost twice as large as before. We see immediately that the waiting time and the length of the waiting line can increase dramatically by such a change. When the average rate of arrival equals the rate at which the mechanics can be served, theoretically the length of the waiting line will increase and become infinitely long.

Now let us introduce random service times, using the same arrival schedule of the mechanics. This makes the problem a fairly realistic one, since the time required to service a mechanic should vary depending on the number of tools the mechanic needs and the size, weight, and location of the tool or tools. Table VI is a record of such a situation where the mechanics arrive at random

TABLE IV. Random Arrival Time of Mechanics, Service Time Constant at 3 Minutes

Arrival Time of Mechanics	Service Begins at	Service Ends at	Idle Time of Attendant*	Wating Time of Mechanics†	Length of Line, Exclud- ing Mechanic Being Serviced
10:00	10:00	10:03	0	0	0
10:09	10:09	10:12	6	0	0
10:13	10:13	10:16	1	0	0
10:19	10:19	10:22	3	0	0
10:34	10:34	10:37	12	0	0
10:36	10:37	10:40	0	1	1
10:37	10:40	10:43	0	3	1
10:38	10:43	10:46	0	5	2
10:39	10:46	10:49	0	7	3
10:42	10:49	10:52	0	7	3
11:02	11:02	11:05	10	0	0
11:03	11:05	11:08	0	2	1
11:05	11:08	11:11	0	3	1
11:05	11:11	11:14	0	6	2
11:09	11:14	11:17	0	5	2

*Attendants' idle time = 32 minutes.
†Mechanics' waiting time = 39 minutes.

TABLE V. Random Arrival Time of Mechanics, Service Time Constant at 4 Minutes

Arrival Time of Mechanics	Service Begins at	Service Ends at	Idle Time of Attendant*	Wating Time of Mechanics†	Length of Line, Excluding Mechanic Being Serviced
10:00	10:00	10:04	0	0	0
10:09	10:09	10:13	5	0	0
10:13	10:13	10:17	0	0	0
10:19	10:19	10:23	2	0	0
10:34	10:34	10:38	11	0	0
10:36	10:38	10:42	0	2	1
10:37	10:42	10:46	0	5	2
10:38	10:46	10:50	0	8	2
10:39	10:50	10:54	0	11	3
10:42	10:54	10:58	0	12	3
11:02	11:02	11:06	4	0	0
11:03	11:06	11:10	0	3	1
11:05	11:10	11:14	0	5	2
11:05	11:14	11:18	0	9	3
11:09	11:18	11:22	0	9	2

*Attendants' idle time = 22 minutes.
†Mechanics' waiting time = 64 minutes.

times and the service times vary randomly, averaging 3.07 minutes for the sample given. For a particular sample, the attendant's idle time and the mechanics' waiting time will depend on how well the arrivals of the mechanics match up with the longer and shorter service times. If several mechanics arrive almost simultaneously with requests requiring long service times, their waiting time will be relatively long while the attendant is continuously busy. If the long service time requests are distributed in a particular sample, their effect on the mechanics' waiting time will be smaller. Waiting line theory can forecast the *probable* waiting time and the *probable* length of the line, so management can decide what is the optimum allocation of personnel and equipment to minimize incremental costs. To do this, we must know the nature of the distributions of arrivals and of service times.

From Table VI, let us make some typical calculations, recognizing that the sample is probably too small for decision-making purposes. If the attendant is paid $2.00 per hour, then the cost of the attendant's idle time is

$$\tfrac{26}{60} \times \$2.00 = \$0.87$$

for the sample of 72 minutes, or

$$\tfrac{480}{72} \times \$0.87 = \$5.80$$

per day. If the mechanics' wages average \$3.50 per hour, the cost of their idle time is

$$\tfrac{56}{60} \times 3.50 = \$3.27$$

for the sample, or

$$\tfrac{480}{72} \times 3.27 = \$21.80$$

per day. The total cost of idle and waiting time is \$5.80 + \$21.80 = \$27.60 per day.

The question now is: Would it be economical to add a second attendant? If the second attendant were added, mechanics' waiting time would be reduced, but the total attendant's idle time would be increased. If the net effect on the cost of the combined idle plus waiting time is negative, the second attendant would be justified.

TABLE VI.   Random Arrival Time of Mechanics and Random Service Times

Arrival Time of Mechanics	Service Begins at	Service Ends at	Idle Time of Attendant*	Waiting Time of Mechanics†	Length of Line, Excluding Mechanic Being Serviced
10:00	10:00	10:01	0	0	0
10:09	10:09	10:14	8	0	0
10:13	10:14	10:15	0	1	1
10:19	10:19	10:22	4	0	0
10:34	10:34	10:40	12	0	0
10:36	10:40	10:44	0	4	1
10:37	10:44	10:51	0	7	2
10:38	10:51	10:53	0	13	3
10:39	10:53	10:57	0	14	4
10:42	10:57	11:02	0	15	4
11:02	11:02	11:03	0	0	0
11:03	11:03	11:04	0	0	0
11:05	11:05	11:07	1	0	0
11:05	11:07	11:08	0	2	1
11:09	11:09	11:12	1	0	0

*Attendants' idle time = 26 minutes.
†Mechanics' waiting time = 56 minutes.

Analytical Solutions for Waiting Line Problems. In Tables IV, V, and VI, we have simulated simple waiting line problems. In cases where the distributions of arrivals and of service times fit certain standard mathematical distributions, equations have been developed which give directly the items of data in which we are interested such as the average length of the waiting line, average waiting time, and average number of units in the system. The important restrictions are the distributions. If the actual distributions of arrivals and service times fit the standard mathematical distributions fairly well, very little work is required to determine a solution. On the other hand, if the fit is not good, a great amount of work could be needed to develop a mathematical solution. In such instances, simulation methods can be used to develop a solution, regardless of the nature of the actual distributions. These methods are discussed later in the chapter.

Poisson Arrivals. The mathematical function known as the Poisson distribution is commonly used to describe arrival rates. Figure 6 shows a Poisson distribution for arrival rates averaging 12 per hour. The simulated examples which we have been using had arrival rates that were based on this distribution. If the average arrival rate were 12 per hour and the service rate were constant at 20 per hour (3 minutes per mechanic served), as in our first simulated example (Table IV), mathematical solutions would give directly:

Average length of waiting line = 0.45 men in line excluding mechanic
being served

Average waiting time = 0.0375 hour/man or 2.25 minutes/man

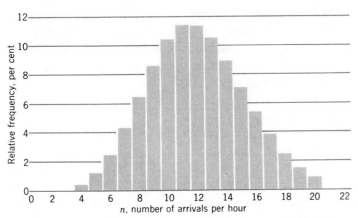

FIGURE 6. Poisson distribution of arrival rates averaging 12 per hour.

(See Chapter 8 for formulas and a more complete discussion of waiting lines.)

Our limited sample gave an average line length of 0.50 men and an average waiting time of $\frac{39}{15} = 2.6$ minutes per man. Had our sample been larger in the simulated example, we would have approached the answers given by the formulas more closely.

We mentioned earlier that, theoretically, when the mean arrival and service rates were equal, the waiting line length and, therefore, the waiting time became infinitely long. We say that this is true only theoretically, because in a practical situation several things may happen to prevent it. If people are the units involved in the waiting line, new arrivals are apt to be discouraged by an excessively long line and leave. Also, where people are involved, working hours limit the line length since it falls to zero when the work day is over. Finally, the people performing the services tend to react to the build-up of a waiting line by speeding up the rate of service. Where the units requiring service are parts or perhaps machines, some of these compensating effects do not take place.

Simulation Models

Simulation of production management problems is a rapidly growing technique. Although the fundamental ideas behind simulation can stand alone, its rapid growth actually has been paced by the high-speed electronic computer, because the arithmetic work required for practical problems is ordinarily too great for hand computation. This approach to problems sets up a simulated experiment and then carries through the experiment completely on paper (or in a computer) to see the effect of the variables of interest on the measure of effectiveness, E, which has been chosen. Simulation models follow a conceptual structure similar to that discussed under "A Framework for Analysis," except that the model is empirical. Also, the simulation model does not produce an optimum answer as with some mathematical models. Comparisons between alternatives can be made by means of the simulation model, but the analyst must set up the alternatives himself. It is a systematic trial-and-error method for solving complex problems.

Where is simulation useful? Examples might be: (a) waiting line problems where standard distributions do not approximate actual distributions for arrival and processing rates or (b) complex waiting line problems with each station having several channels, or with stations in tandem, such as on a production line. On a large scale, this technique may be used to simulate the entire production operation. Here lies the great future of simulation.

Imagine the power of such a tool for the decision maker faced constantly with a legion of alternatives regarding work scheduling, equipment, layout, methods, inventory policies, changes of work load, etc. His basic objectives are clear. He wishes to make decisions that will maximize return on investment or minimize costs—if only he could see clearly and quickly the effect of the various alternatives he faces without waiting to see how they will work out in practice. For the decision maker, the ideal situation is to be able to try out an idea without first risking or committing company funds; with a simulation model and a computer, he can try out dozens of alternatives. Also, he can learn a great deal about the interdependence of the variables in the complex system. For example, he may observe the effect of a change in inventory policy on plant capacity and labor cost. In this way he can learn to make many decisions jointly instead of separately and thereby avoid costly mistakes of suboptimization. Simulation, with the aid of high-speed computers, ultimately makes available an experimental laboratory to production management personnel.

Simulated Sampling. The sampling method, known generally as Monte Carlo, is a simulation procedure of considerable value. In the last section under waiting line theory, we spoke of distributions that did not fit the standard ones for which the theory had been worked out, and of complex waiting line situations where the mathematical complexity becomes very great. The required data can be built up through simulation of the conditions of the problem.

Let us assume that a product is being assembled by a two-station assembly line. There is one operator at each of the two stations. Operation *A* is the first of the two operations. The operator completes approximately the first half of the assembly and then sets the half-completed assembly on a section of conveyor where it rolls down to operation *B*. It takes a constant time of 0.10 minute for the part to roll down the conveyor section and be available to operator *B*. Operator *B* then completes the assembly. The average time for operation *A* is 0.52 minute per assembly and the average time for operation *B* is 0.48 minute per assembly. The simple setup is shown in Figure 7. We wish to determine the average inventory of assemblies that we may expect (average length of the waiting line of assemblies) and the average output of the assembly line. This may be done by simulated sampling as follows:

1. The distributions of assembly time for operations *A* and *B* must be known or procured. For example, these are represented by Figures 8 and 9. A study was taken for both operations and the two frequency

FIGURE 7.   Layout of two-station assembly line.

distributions resulted. For Figure 8 the value 0.25 minute occurred three times, 0.30 occurred twice, etc. The two distributions do not necessarily fit standard mathematical distributions but this is not important.

2. Convert the frequency distributions to cumulative probability distributions. This is done in Figures 10 and 11. It is done by summing the frequencies that are less than or equal to each performance time and plotting them. The cumulative frequencies are then converted to per cents by assigning the number 100 to the maximum value. As an example, let us take Figure 8 and convert it to the cumulative distribution of Figure 10. Beginning at the lowest value for performance time, 0.25 minute, there were 3 observations. Three is plotted on the cumulative chart for the time 0.25 minute. For the performance time, 0.30 minute, there were 2 observations, but there were 5 observations that measured 0.30 minute or less, so the value (5) is plotted for 0.30 minute. For the performance time, 0.35 minute, there were 10 observations recorded, but there were 15 observations that measured

FIGURE 8.   Distribution of performance times for operation A.

FIGURE 9.   Distribution of performance times for operation B.

0.35 minute or less. Figure 10 was constructed from Figure 8 by proceeding in this way. When the cumulative frequency distribution was completed, a cumulative per cent scale was constructed on the right of Figure 10 by assigning the number 100 to the maximum value, 167, and dividing the resulting scale into equal parts. This results

FIGURE 10.   Cumulative distribution of performance times for operation A.

FIGURE 11. Cumulative distribution of performance times for operation *B*.

in a cumulative probability distribution. From Figure 10 we can say that 100 per cent of the time values were 0.85 minute or less, 55.1 per cent were 0.50 minute or less, etc.

3. Sample at random from the cumulative distributions to determine specific performance times to use in simulating the operation of the assembly line. We do this by selecting numbers between 0 and 100 at random (representing probabilities or per cents). The random numbers could be selected by any random process, such as drawing numbered chips from a box. The easiest way is to use a table of random numbers such as the one in the Appendix Table IV.

The random numbers are used to enter the cumulative distributions in order to obtain time values. In the example shown in Figure 10, the random number 10 is used. A horizontal line is projected until it intersects the distribution curve; a vertical line projected to the horizontal axis gives the midpoint time value associated with the intersected point on the distribution curve, which happens to be 0.40 minute for the random number 10. Now we can see the purpose behind the conversion of the original distribution to a cumulative distribution. Only one time value can now be associated with a given random number. In the original distribution, two values would result because of the bell shape of the curve.

Sampling from the cumulative distribution in this way gives time values in random order which will occur in proportion to the original distribution, just as if assemblies were actually being produced. Table VII gives a sample of 20 time values determined in this way from the two distributions.

4. Simulate the actual operation of the assembly line. This is done in Table VIII which, of course, is very similar to the examples of waiting

TABLE VII. Simulated Sample of 20 Performance Time Values for Operations *A* and *B*

Operation *A*		Operation *B*	
Random Number	Performance Time from Figure 10	Random Number	Performance Time from Figure 11
10	0.40	79	0.60
22	0.40	69	0.50
24	0.45	33	0.40
42	0.50	52	0.45
37	0.45	13	0.35
77	0.60	16	0.35
99	0.85	19	0.35
96	0.75	4	0.30
89	0.65	14	0.35
85	0.65	6	0.30
28	0.45	30	0.40
63	0.55	25	0.35
9	0.40	38	0.40
10	0.40	0	0.25
7	0.35	92	0.70
51	0.50	82	0.60
2	0.30	20	0.35
1	0.25	40	0.40
52	0.50	44	0.45
7	0.35	25	0.35
Totals	9.75		8.20

TABLE VIII. Simulated Operation of the Two-Station Assembly Line When Operation A Precedes Operation B

Assemblies Available for Operation B at	Operation B Begins at	Operation B Ends at	Idle Time in Operation B	Waiting Time of Assemblies	Number of Parts in Line, Excluding Assembly Being Processed in Operation B
0.00	0.00	0.60	0	0	0
0.40	0.60	1.10	0	0.20	1
0.85	1.10	1.50	0	0.25	1
1.35	1.50	1.95	0	0.15	1
1.80	1.95	2.30	0	0.15	1
2.40	2.40	2.75	0.10	0	0
3.25	3.25	3.60	0.50	0	0
4.00	4.00	4.30	0.40	0	0
4.65	4.65	5.00	0.35	0	0
5.30	5.30	5.60	0.30	0	0
5.75	5.75	6.15	0.15	0	0
6.30	6.30	6.65	0.15	0	0
6.70	6.70	7.10	0.05	0	0
7.10	7.10	7.35	0	0	0
7.45	7.45	8.15	0.10	0	0
7.95	8.15	8.75	0	0.20	1
8.25	8.75	9.10	0	0.50	1
8.50	9.10	9.50	0	0.60	2
9.00	9.50	9.95	0	0.50	2
9.35	9.95	10.30	0	0.60	2

Idle time in operation B = 2.10 minutes
Waiting time of parts = 3.15 minutes
Average inventory of assemblies between A and B = 3.15/9.35
= 0.34 assemblies

Average production rate of A = $\dfrac{20 \times 60}{9.75}$ = 123 pieces/hour

Average production rate of B (while working) = $\dfrac{20 \times 60}{8.20}$ = 146 pieces/hour

Average production rate of A and B together = $\dfrac{20 \times 60}{10.30}$ = 116.5 pieces/hour

Note: In the above computations, 20 is the total number of completed assemblies; 9.75 is the total work time of operation A for 20 assemblies from Table VII; 8.20 is the total work time, exclusive of idle time, for operation B for 20 assemblies from Table VII.

line problems we used earlier. The time values for operation A (Table VII) are first used to determine when the half-completed assemblies would be available to operation B. The first assembly is completed by operator A in 0.40 minute. It takes 0.10 minute to roll down to operator B, so this point in time is selected as zero. The next assembly is available 0.40 minute later, and so on. For the first assembly, operation B begins at time zero. From the simulated sample, the first assembly requires 0.60 minute for B. At this point, there is no idle time for B and no inventory. At time 0.40 the second assembly becomes available, but B is still working on the first so the assembly must wait 0.20 minute. Operator B begins work on it at 0.60. From Table VII the second assembly requires 0.50 minute for B. We continue the simulated operation of the line in this way.

The sixth assembly becomes available to B at time 2.40, but B was ready for it at time 2.30. He therefore was forced to remain idle for 0.10 minute because of lack of work. The completed sample of 20 assemblies is progressively worked out.

The summary at the bottom of Table VIII shows the result in terms of the idle time in operation B, the waiting time of the parts, the average inventory between the two operations, and the resulting production rates. From the average times given by the original distributions, we would have guessed that A would limit the output of the line since it was the slower of the two operations. Actually, however, the line production rate is less than that dictated by A (116.5 pieces per hour compared to 123 pieces per hour for A as an individual operation.). The reason is that the interplay of performance times for A and B do not always match up very well, and sometimes B has to wait for work. B's enforced idle time plus his total work time actually determines the maximum production rate of the line.

A little thought should convince us that, if possible, it would have been better to redistribute the assembly work so that A is the faster of the two operations. Then the probability that B will run out of work is reduced. This is demonstrated by Table IX which assumes a simple reversal of the sequence of A and B. The same sample times have been used and the simulated operation of the line has been developed as before. With the faster of the two operations being first in the sequence, the output rate of the line increases and approaches the rate of the limiting operation, and the average inventory between the two operations increases. With the higher average inventory there, the second operation in the sequence is almost never idle owing to lack of work. Actually, this conclusion is a fairly general one with regard to the balance of assembly lines; that is, the best labor balance will be achieved when each succeeding operation

TABLE IX. Simulated Operation of the Two-Station Assembly Line When Operation B Precedes Operation A

Assemblies Available for Operation A at	Operation A Begins at	Operation A Ends at	Idle Time in Operation A	Waiting Time of Assemblies	Number of Parts in Line, Excluding Assembly Being Processed in Operation A
0.00	0.00	0.40	0	0	0
0.50	0.50	0.90	0.10	0	0
0.90	0.90	1.35	0	0	0
1.35	1.35	1.85	0	0	0
1.70	1.85	2.30	0	0.15	1
2.05	2.30	2.90	0	0.25	1
2.40	2.90	3.75	0	0.40	1
2.70	3.75	4.50	0	1.05	2
3.05	4.50	5.15	0	1.45	2
3.35	5.15	5.80	0	1.80	3
3.75	5.80	6.25	0	2.05	3
4.10	6.25	6.80	0	2.15	4
4.50	6.80	7.20	0	2.30	4
4.75	7.20	7.60	0	2.45	5
5.45	7.60	7.95	0	2.15	5
6.05	7.95	8.45	0	1.90	5
6.40	8.45	8.75	0	2.05	5
6.80	8.75	9.00	0	1.95	6
7.25	9.00	9.50	0	1.75	5
7.60	9.50	9.85	0	1.90	6

Idle time in operation A	= 0.10 minute
Waiting time of parts	= 25.75 minutes
Average inventory of assemblies between A and B	= 25.75/7.60
	= 3.4 assemblies

Average production rate of A (while working) $= \dfrac{20 \times 60}{9.75} = 123$ pieces/hour

Average production rate of B $= \dfrac{20 \times 60}{8.20} = 146$ pieces/hour

Average production rate of A and B together $= \dfrac{20 \times 60}{9.85} = 122$ pieces/hour

in the sequence is slightly slower than the one before it. This minimizes the idle time created when the operators run out of work because of the variable performance times of the various operations. In practical situations it is common to find safety banks of assemblies between operations in order to absorb these fluctuations in performance.

We may have wanted to build a more sophisticated model of the assembly line. Our simple model assumed that the performance times were independent of other events in the process. Perhaps in the actual situation, the second operation in the sequence would tend to speed up when the inventory began to build up. This effect could have been included if we had knowledge of how inventory affected performance time.

If we have followed this simulation example through carefully, we may be convinced that it would work but that it would be very tedious for problems of practical size. Even for our limited example, we would probably wish to have a larger run on which to base conclusions, and there would probably be other alternatives to test. For example, there may be several alternative ways to distribute the total assembly task between the two stations, or more than two stations could be considered. Which of the several alternatives would yield the smallest incremental cost of labor, inventory costs, etc.? To cope with the problem of tedium and excessive man-hours to develop a solution, the computer may be used. If a computer were programmed to simulate the operation of the assembly line, we would place the two cumulative distributions in the memory unit of the computer. Through the program, the computer would select a performance time value at random from the cumulative distribution for A in much the same fashion as we did by hand. Then it would select at random a time value from the cumulative distribution for B, make the necessary computations, and hold the data in memory. The cycle would repeat, selecting new time values at random, adding and subtracting to obtain the record that we produced by hand. A large run could be made easily and with no more effort than a small run. Various alternatives could be evaluated quickly and easily in the same manner.

A knowledge of statistics and probability provides a framework for the rigorous handling of data in such a way that we can not only draw conclusions based on the predictive model constructed but also assess the risk that the forecasts or predictions may be in error. Thus a correlation study of two factors, such as paint viscosity and paint defects, may indicate that the two factors do move together but that the probable error may be very large if we attempt to forecast the number of paint defects expected from the viscosity measured. Similarly, a statistical control chart of errors in a clerical operation, or of labor turnover, may

Statistical
Analysis

indicate that we are experiencing an abnormal situation, either above or below accepted limits of variation. In addition, however, we know that the chance that we are in error in assuming that the process is out of control is only 0.27 per cent if the usual probability control limits have been assigned.

One great contribution of modern statistics to production analysis is in the general field called statistical inference. Here we find the development of a methodology for the formal testing of hypotheses. This field in statistics is of such great value because it allows us to deal with problems that exhibit great variation in the measured values of the factors or variables that may define the system. Yet we can draw conclusions about the system, and these conclusions may be quite precise. Thus it may be possible to test the hypothesis that a new method for a clerical operation is faster or produces fewer errors. Or we may test a somewhat more complex hypothesis that of several factors which may contribute to poor quality, only one is significant.

Suppose, for example, that there are four machines used to perform an operation in the production of a part and we are experiencing difficulty with the quality of output. The foreman maintains that his four machines are not equally reliable. The plant superintendent accuses the machine operators on the theory that one simply cannot obtain qualified help these days. The workers say that the raw material is sometimes faulty, especially when it comes from a certain supplier. When the quality reports are examined, it is not at all obvious whether the machines, workers, or suppliers are at fault. It is possible, however, by resorting to a statistical inference technique, *analysis of variance*, to perform a simple experiment which will tell us with a preassigned level of confidence the contributions toward poor quality from each of the three sources.

Statistical analysis in production and operations management has a large field of application of its own. For example, techniques such as *work sampling* and *statistical quality control*, both of which are described in somewhat greater detail in Chapters 14 and 22, respectively, are based on statistical models. As a general tool of analysis, however, statistical concepts often provide help in the application of some other kinds of analytical techniques already described. For example, in attempting to determine what factors or variables are of significance in a simulation model of flow through a production system, we may test the hypothesis that the time required for flow through the system is dependent on the number of operations to be performed. Or, in studying the nature of an existing wage structure, we may wish to determine the regression line of a measure of job difficulty versus wages paid. In neither of these instances is statistical analysis the central model used; however, it contributes to the overall analysis.

The post-World War II importance of research and development and other large-scale one-time projects in our economy have called forth special planning techniques. These techniques, commonly known by the name PERT, represent the work required to be done as a network of activities which takes account of the interdependencies of timing and phasing of operations. From the basic network model, schedule statistics can be computed which make it possible to determine which activities must be done on time (are critical) and which have schedule slack. This results in a concept known as the critical path schedule. The network of activities and the schedule statistics then become a basis for plans for the deployment of resources to the project.

Network Planning Models

We shall discuss network planning methods in Chapter 20 on planning, scheduling and control for large scale projects.

It is interesting that one of the current emphases in operations management research finds considerable value in the old, perhaps arbitrary, "rules of thumb" for which management was originally criticized by management scientists. Heuristic methods, models, and programs have recently found a respectable place in analytic methodology. The term "heuristic" originally meant aiding in or guiding discovery. But in its common managerial meaning, it refers to a rigorous set of rules or guides to decision which, though not necessarily optimal, are applied consistently, are efficient, and avoid a lot of complicated problem solving. Wiest [12] gives the following simple example of a heuristic rule:

Heuristic Methods

> When the sky is cloudy, take an umbrella to work.
> The problem at hand is how to defend oneself from the potential discomforts of the weather. This simple heuristic avoids more complicated problem-solving procedures such as reading the weather reports, calling the weather bureau, analyzing barometer readings, and so forth. For many problems of this kind, we lack the time or inclination to employ more thorough problem-solving procedures. A simple (if not infallible) rule serves us best.

The difficulty in many managerial problems with using some other kinds of analysis is that the problem itself is so complex that it may be difficult or impossible to approach it mathematically. Still answers must be developed; rules of thumb which have some basis of logic may be the best methods to use. As we shall see, however, this does not mean just any rule for generating decisions but rather a logical and consistent set of rules. Within a large heuristic program, some of the individual heuristic rules used may come from the results of mathematical analysis or other research on smaller, more manageable problems.

With many problems in production and operations management, there is an extremely large number of decision points in a sequence; thus the number of possible combinations of decisions is enormous. This is illustrated by the "tree diagram" of Figure 12a. Each node represents a decision point and the lines connecting them indicate a path or sequence of decisions which lead to some particular solution. Of course, one way to find the best solution is to evaluate the end result for every combination of decision points. This we call enumeration, and it is practical only when the number of possible paths is relatively small. But the kinds of problems to which we are referring cannot be approached in this way,

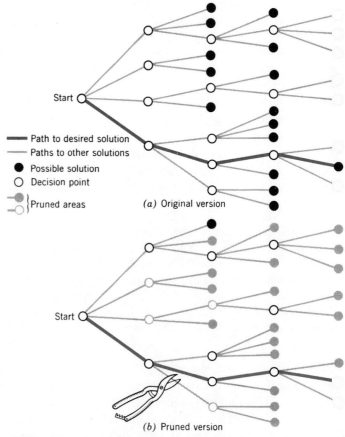

Start

━━ Path to desired solution
— Paths to other solutions
● Possible solution
○ Decision point
⎱ Pruned areas

(a) Original version

Start

(b) Pruned version

FIGURE 12.   A tree diagram representation of a problem. (From Wiest [12].)

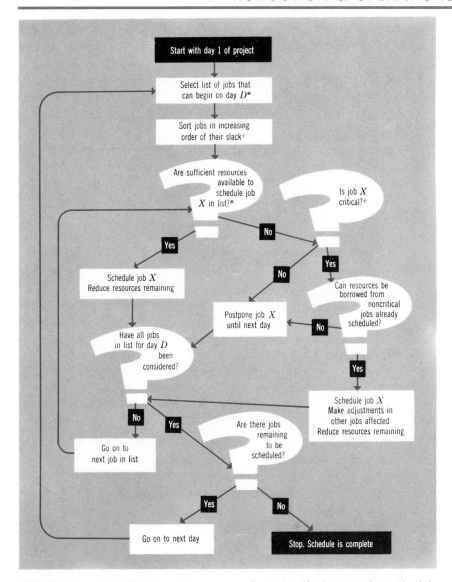

FIGURE 13.   Simplified heuristic program flow chart for large project scheduling. (From Wiest [12].)

*Day D is day under consideration; job X is job under consideration.
†Slack is a measure of the number of days a job may be delayed without delaying the project as a whole. A job is *critical* if it has no slack.

even with the aid of high-speed computers. The heuristic approach is to examine the tree diagram and to prune branches of the tree, as shown in Figure 12. Of course it is entirely possible that the pruning process may eliminate branches which could lead to excellent solutions, but this is the trade-off involved in heuristic methods. Search effort is reduced through heuristic methods at the price of possibly throwing away the very best solution.

A simplified version of a heuristic program developed by Wiest [12] as a basis for scheduling the activities in large-scale one-time projects is shown in Figure 13. The heuristic program is based largely on three heuristic rules.

1. Allocate resources serially in time. That is, start on the first day and schedule all activities possible; then do the same for the second day, and so on.

2. When several jobs compete for the same resources, give preference to the jobs with the least slack.

3. Reschedule noncritical jobs, if possible, in order to free resources for scheduling critical (nonslack) jobs.

Heuristic methods in operations management have been applied successfully in such problem areas as assembly line balancing, facilities layout, job shop scheduling, warehouse location, inventory control, and the scheduling of large-scale one-time projects.

Computer Search Methods

Another relatively new approach for obtaining excellent solutions to some very complex problems is through use of computer search methods. In the past the complexity of many operations management kinds of problems has been so serious that the model builder has had to restrict his attentions to simple models that could be solved by analytic techniques or resort to simulation or possibly heuristic methods. Today, however, the computer has made possible new quasi-analytic and heuristic search techniques. These techniques have significantly increased the probability of finding the global optimum of complex

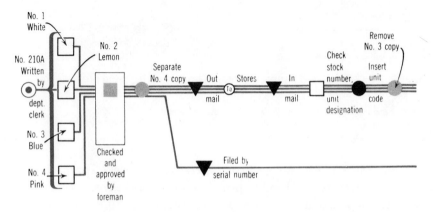

FIGURE 14. Procedure flow chart for stores requisition. (From Close [5].)

models. One such optimum seeking technique is known as a direct computer search procedure. "Direct search" methods consist of a sequential examination of a finite set of feasible trial solutions of a criterion function. A single trial evaluation is produced by specifying values for each independent variable, evaluating the criterion function, and recording the result. Each trial value is compared to the best previous value; if an improvement is observed the trial value is accepted and the previous best value rejected. The procedure continues in this way until no further improvements can be found, when a predetermined number of trial evaluations has been made, or when the computer time limit is exceeded. At this point the computer program prints out the best combination of independent variables which has been found.

The advantage of using direct search methods is in building the model of the criterion function. There are no constraints of mathematical form imposed, such as linearity. Also, to date, problems have been solved with as many as sixty independent variables, using modest computer time, and it appears that the possible number of independent variables in such programs can be expanded even more. In operations management, direct search methods have been applied to the aggregate planning and scheduling problem which we shall discuss in Chapter 17, and to the network scheduling problem with limited resources which we shall discuss in Chapter 20.

The traditional modes of analysis used in production systems have been schematic and graphic methods supplemented by incremental cost analyses. The most prominent analytical tools of this type are in the form of flow charts that show the sequence and/or timing of activities.

Schematic and Graphic Analysis

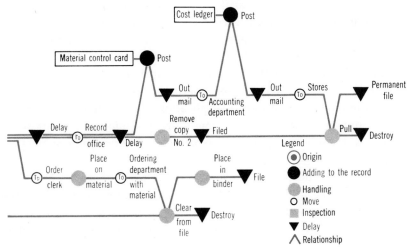

FIGURE 14. (*continued*)

For example, Figure 14 shows a procedure flow chart for a stores requisition. It shows the step-by-step activities involved in handling the four copies of the requisition by means of a system of standard symbols. The chart is in fact a schematic model of the overall system for handling stores requisitions. The flow chart can be analyzed for overlapping or duplicate functions, control, logic of flow patterns, and so on. Basically similar flow charts may follow the physical flow of material being processed through a sequence of operations as illustrated by Figure 15. Here we see a schematic diagram of the processing required by a potentiometer shaft. Here again, the flow diagram can be analyzed for the logic of flow, duplication of effort, or overlapping functions.

There are many other kinds of graphic and schematic diagrams used in the analysis of various phases of a production system, particularly in the analysis of labor utilization, production scheduling and control, and facility layout. We shall discuss these tools of analysis when we discuss the problems for which they are applicable. They are integrated as a part of our discussion of job design in Chapter 13, facility layout in Chapter 12, and scheduling and control in Chapter 19.

SUMMARY

In this chapter we have attempted to lay out a general framework for the analysis of production systems and to discuss the nature and application of some prominent modes of analysis used. In most instances the discussion of specific methods of analysis has been meant to be introductory to other sections or chapters in the book. These following sections either focus directly on an analytical methodology, such as is the case with incremental and capital cost analysis, statistical analysis, and linear programming, or are introductory to a discussion of the problems encountered in production systems. In the latter instance, the analytic techniques are discussed in relation to the problems to which they are applicable. This has been the case for waiting line models, simulation models, and schematic and graphic methods. With waiting line and simulation models, illustrations of applications are discussed at various points throughout the book. For schematic and graphic methods, most of the detailed techniques used are explained in connection with the applications.

There are some additional special analytical methods used which we have not attempted to discuss here. For example, inventory models are of great importance and are discussed within the chapter dealing with inventory control. Also, there is a wide variety of other models which

FIGURE 15.   Flow diagram for manufacture of potentiometer shafts.

have been constructed as special applications. They are discussed by other authors in many of the references given in this book.

REVIEW QUESTIONS

1. Outline a framework for analysis of production and operations management problems.
2. What is meant by a suboptimum solution?

3. What is the meaning of the term "measure of effectiveness" as it applies to managerial problems? Name some typical measures of effectiveness which might be used in production problems.
4. What are controllable and uncontrollable variables?
5. What is the nature of the general linear programming model? Name three situations where it might prove useful as a model of system behavior.
6. In a waiting line model, why is it necessary that the service rate exceed the arrival rate?
7. What are the limitations of waiting line theory?
8. How is a simulation model different from a mathematical model?
9. In simulated sampling, why are frequency distributions cumulated?
10. Discuss the application of statistical methods and statistical analysis in the general field of production and operations management.
11. What are graphic and schematic methods of analysis? For what kinds of problems are they of value in the analysis of production systems?

PROBLEMS

1. The Caribbean Tea Company is a nationwide chain of supermarkets with headquarters in Chicago, Illinois. The vice-president in charge of western operations is located in Los Angeles and controls all areas west of the Rocky Mountains. The largest portion of the western operations is centered in the greater Los Angeles metropolitan area.

Although the Los Angeles population is increasing at a rapid rate, total company sales have been leveling off. The vice-president believes that the primary cause of this condition is increased competition. Recent association publications report that the number of supermarkets is growing at a faster rate than the population.

To meet this impending crisis, the vice-president believes that the only answer lies in becoming more competitive. In pursuit of this objective, he has formed a task force to deal with the following problem areas:

(1) Product line.
(2) Pricing.
(3) Labor-saving equipment.
(4) Advertising.
(5) Improved customer service.

As part of this effort, the vice-president calls you in and says: "I want you to investigate customer service at the check-out stands and make recommendations. I don't want to influence your judgment, but it seems strange to me that when I go into a store, I frequently see long lines and about one-half of the check-out stands not being used. I think we need to do some hard thinking about how many checkers we should have. I want you to prepare a preliminary proposal of how you intend to investigate customer service at the check-out stands and submit it at the next task force meeting."

(a) Translate the vice-president's instructions into a meaningful statement of the problem as you see it.

(b) Outline a proposal to solve the problem that you have stated in question (a). Prepare your proposal in sufficient detail so that a third party could implement it with no further instructions from you.

2.   You are studying a two-station assembly line with each operator doing approximately half of the work. The distributions of assembly times are as follows:

Cycle Time (minutes)	Frequency of Cycle Times for	
	Operation A	Operation B
0.20	4	2
0.30	9	5
0.40	28	17
0.50	22	10
0.60	15	8
0.70	10	2
0.80	8	3
0.90	4	3
	100	50

(a) Construct a cumulative probability distribution which could be used in the simulation of the two-station assembly line.

(b) Simulate the assembly of 10 parts.

(c) What is the average length of the waiting line of the half-completed assemblies ahead of station B?

(d) What is the average output per hour of the assembly line?

3.   A sample of 100 customer arrivals at a check-out station of a small store is represented in the following distribution:

Time between Arrivals (minutes)	Frequency
0.5	2
1.0	6
1.5	10
2.0	25
2.5	20
3.0	14
3.5	10
4.0	7
4.5	4
5.0	2
	100

A study of the time required to service the customers by adding up the bill, receiving payment, making change, placing packages in bags, etc., yields the following distribution:

Service Time (minutes)	Frequency
0.5	12
1.0	21
1.5	36
2.0	19
2.5	7
3.0	5
	100

Set up the foregoing data in a form useful for simulation. Determine a simulation procedure which will use this revised data to furnish an estimate of the mean number of customers serviced per minute. Develop a flow chart that completely specifies the decision rules used for the simulation.

REFERENCES

[1] Anthony, R. N. *Management Accounting Principles* (Rev. ed.). Richard D. Irwin, Homewood, Ill., 1970.

[2] Barnes, R. M. *Motion and Time Study: Design and Measurement of Work* (6th ed.). John Wiley, New York, 1968.

[3] Bowman, E. H., and R. B. Fetter. *Analysis for Production and Operations Management* (3rd ed.). Richard D. Irwin, Homewood, Ill., 1967.

[4] Buffa, E. S. *Operations Management: Problems and Models* (3rd ed.). John Wiley, New York, 1972.

[5] Close, G. *Work Improvement*. John Wiley, New York, 1960.

[6] Dixon, W. J., and F. J. Massey, Jr. *Introduction to Statistical Analysis* (3rd ed.). McGraw-Hill, New York, 1969.

[7] Hoel, P. G., and R. J. Jessen. *Basic Statistics for Business and Economics*. John Wiley, New York, 1971.

[8] Nadler, G. *Work Design: A Systems Concept* (Rev. ed.). Richard D. Irwin, Homewood, Ill., 1970.

[9] Reisman, A. *Managerial and Engineering Economics*. Allyn and Bacon, Boston, 1971.

[10] Taubert, W. H. "A Computer Search Solution of the Aggregate Scheduling Problem." *Management Science*, 14 (6), Feb. 1968.

[11] Thierauf, R. J., and R. A. Grosse. *Decision Making Through Operations Research*. John Wiley, New York, 1970.

[12] Wiest, J. D. "Heuristic Programs for Decision Making." *Harvard Business Review*, Sept.–Oct. 1966.

5

Cost Data for Decisions

Is there anything significant about the term *cost data for decisions*? Why not simply talk about *cost data*? Between the two terms there are important differences; the objective of cost data resulting from the accounting function is different from the objective of cost data constructed for decision making. In general, accounting systems meet the needs of federal and state tax laws, as well as the needs of certain phases of financial management of an organization. When the end use of cost data is for decision making, however, we must be careful that average costs and allocations of fixed overhead cost items do not mask the actual behavior of costs. We shall be interested in the *net effect* on costs of each alternative being considered. As we shall see, the implications of this "net effect" criterion shift somewhat with the nature of the problem.

As a point of departure, let us recall that expense classification for a manufacturing firm follows the general structure of Figure 1. The labor and material costs at the left are considered direct since ordinarily they can be attributed to a product. Factory expense or factory overhead items are ordinarily indirect because it is often difficult to attribute

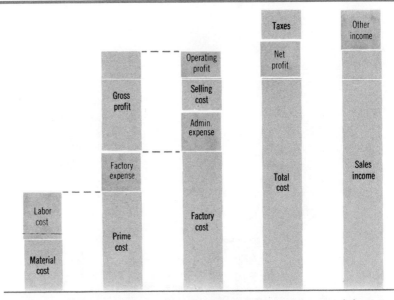

FIGURE 1. Elements of cost of manufacture. Typical items of factory expense are: indirect labor, utilities, factory supplies, maintenance and repair,
depreciation on plant and equipment, insurance, and property taxes. Typical
items of administrative expense are: salaries, office supplies, depreciation of
office property, insurance, taxes on office property, corporate income taxes,
and legal expenses. Typical items of selling expense are: sales salaries, advertising, travel, bad debts, telephone and telegraph, and office supplies.

them to a specific product without an arbitrary allocation. Administrative
and selling expenses are general overhead costs that are even more
indirect in their nature. Sometimes the costs we want to consider do not
even appear in the chart of accounts, yet our decisions may be drastically
affected by them. Sunk costs and opportunity costs are in this category.
In this chapter we want to examine the general nature and behavior
of certain kinds of costs so that we may draw on these ideas in later
chapters that deal with decision problems in specific areas.

FIXED AND VARIABLE COSTS

It is often worthwhile to consider how costs vary with the volume
produced. We think of cost items such as property taxes, indirect labor,
and building depreciation as being nonvariable, or fixed, and of items
such as direct labor, materials, and certain supplies used in the production process as being variable with volume. This dichotomy of thought

is often dangerous, however, because "fixed" costs may in some instances be thought of as varying with volume, and costs commonly thought to be variable may behave as fixed costs. Many cost items may be fixed only over short ranges of volume. Indirect labor is commonly in this class. One material handler may be adequate to a certain volume level above which we must have two handlers. To be sure, our handler is not fully utilized until we approach the critical volume, and when we add the second, both men will probably be underutilized. The semi-variable nature of such cost elements can be important in certain decision problems.

BREAKEVEN ANALYSIS

Breakeven analysis makes use of the fixed and variable nature of costs to indicate the range of volume necessary for profitable operation. If we could divide all costs into those that vary with volume and those that do not, we could compute an average total cost per unit for a given volume. Semivariable costs can be reduced to a fixed component and a variable component. This concept of average unit cost is correct only at the one volume of computation, however, since the fixed costs per unit would change as we averaged them over different volumes. Conceptually, then, it would be helpful to consider the fixed costs as a total pool of costs which must be covered by net revenue, over and above variable costs, before any profit whatever is made. This point or volume of sales where total net revenue after variable costs just equals the total pool of fixed costs is called the breakeven point. It is precisely that because it is the point in the progress of sales where the total revenue just covers the total cost, variable and fixed. Below this volume a loss is recorded; above it a profit is recorded.

Figure 2 is a diagram of the structure of a simple breakeven chart. Units of volume are plotted on the horizontal scale and dollars of sales or cost on the vertical scale. The sales line begins at the origin and is a straight line, since dollar sales are assumed to be proportional to units sold. The total cost line intersects the vertical axis at a value equal to the fixed costs and increases in proportion to the number of units sold. Above the breakeven point the ratio of profits to sales increases with each unit sold. This is because of the broadened base for the absorption of fixed costs. Contribution is at a fixed ratio, however.

Contribution.   What is contribution and how can it be used? Contribution is the difference between sales and variable costs or the

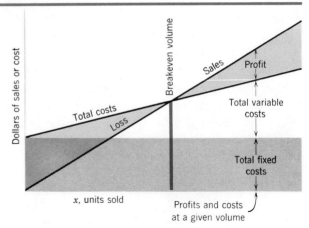

FIGURE 2. A simple breakeven chart.

contribution to fixed costs and profit; that is,

$$C = S - V \qquad (1)$$

and

$$S = F + V + P \qquad (2)$$

where

C = contribution F = fixed costs
S = sales P = profit
V = variable costs

Since both S and V vary with volume, C varies with volume also. C can then be calculated easily by knowing the percentage of the sales dollar that is V. Suppose, for example, that variable costs are 60 per cent of the sales dollar and fixed costs are $3,000,000. Then, from equation (1), C is 40 per cent. The only costs which have not yet been deducted are the fixed costs, so:

$$C = F + P \qquad (3)$$

or

$$P = C - F$$

Now we can compute profit at any level of sales. If total sales are $10,000,000, then C is 40 per cent or $4,000,000 and

$$P = C - F = \$4,000,000 - \$3,000,000 = \$1,000,000$$

If total sales are $8,000,000, C is 40 per cent or $3,200,000 and

$$P = C - F = \$3,200,000 - \$3,000,000 = \$200,000$$

The contribution concept has allowed us to compute total profit at various levels of sales rather easily. Contribution is often called a "profit pickup."

Construction of Breakeven Charts. Although the theory behind breakeven charts is simple, it is not so simple to obtain good data from which to develop the chart because the line between fixed and variable costs is not definite. We may not be safe in taking armchair classifications as valid. We deduce that certain direct labor costs ought to be variable, but are they so actually? There may be a fixed element in them. The point is this: to construct an accurate breakeven chart from cost elements, a great deal of prior work is required in order to establish the actual behavior of cost elements in relation to volume. Good breakeven charts require excellent cost accounting systems.

Another way to approach the problem is by means of the scatter diagram of costs. Data on total costs are plotted for several years and an average line drawn in. The presumption is that the different years will represent different volumes; a total cost line in relation to volume then can be inferred. The point at which the line crosses the vertical axis is an estimate of the fixed costs. Let us take the following data and plot them in Figure 3.

Year	Total Costs (dollars)	Sales (dollars)	Year	Total Costs (dollars)	Sales (dollars)
1968	1.45 million	1.75 million	1970	2.20 million	3.10 million
1969	1.70 million	2.20 million	1971	2.30 million	3.50 million

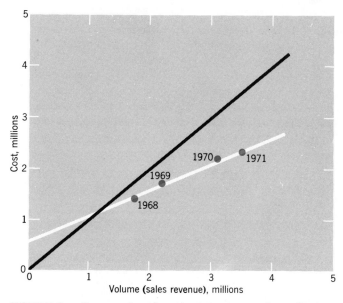

FIGURE 3.   Scatter plot of total costs versus sales volume.

The result looks good and is easy to obtain. We must question, however, whether the relation of costs to volume is perhaps more representative of inflationary tendencies during the period than it is of the way costs vary with volume. If this is a possibility, the data may be deflated to remove the effect of rising costs and prices.

It is also important that the data for the several years be fairly representative of a single set of conditions of technology, product mix, and cost performance. If major technological changes occurred during the period, we would not expect the several years to yield consistent data on which to base the construction of a breakeven chart.

Why Breakeven Points and Profits Change.   Following is a list of some items that may affect profits or both breakeven points and profits:

1. Change in volume. This has a direct effect on profits; breakeven point and contribution ratio does not change.
2. Change in product mix. Profits, breakeven point, and contribution ratio can all change. This suggests the development of breakeven charts on a product basis.
3. Performance changes of labor or of material utilization. Profits, breakeven point, and contribution ratio all change.
4. Change in fixed costs. This affects profits and breakeven point, but contribution ratio remains constant.
5. Change in selling prices. Profits, breakeven point, and contribution ratio all change.

Effect of Managerial Decisions on the Breakeven Point.   The following is a sample list of some important typical decisions:

1. Replacement of obsolete plant and equipment. Usually fixed costs will go up even though existing assets are disposed of. The most common reason for obsolescence is probably the development of new equipment that has lower variable costs. The net effect on the breakeven point is then likely to be either neutral or a decrease with resulting increased profits; this is due to the lowered variable costs (lower slope of total cost line) or to a combination of lower variable costs and lower breakeven point. Other reasons for obsolescence, such as changes of product design, would cause other patterns of change.
2. Manufacture of components previously bought. If unused capacity can be put to work, as is often the case, the net effect is on variable costs which have a direct effect on the breakeven point. If new equipment must be purchased, fixed costs go up. Then the net effect on breakeven point and gross profit will depend on the direction and magnitude of the change in variable costs.

3. Purchase of components previously manufactured. Effect depends on the actual magnitude of the costs that can be disposed of. Most fixed costs will remain, but disposal of some assets may be possible. Variable costs could change in either direction; the net effect on factory breakeven points and gross profits may be either positive or negative, depending upon the relative magnitudes of the disposals and increased variable costs.

4. Decision to retain certain labor skills at the bottom of a seasonal swing. Some variable cost has been converted to fixed. The factory breakeven point may go up.

5. Decision to utilize overtime to increase capacity. Variable costs increase, breakeven point goes up. Presumably, volume has increased and the net effect on profit will depend upon the relationships of the beginning and ending slopes of the total cost line and the magnitude of the actual volume gain.

Usefulness of Breakeven Analysis. The breakeven concept is an important one for analysis of many production and companywide problems. It is well to realize, however, that our best estimate of the breakeven "point" for a company is actually a good-sized "blob" on the chart, and the point itself lies within the blob. This is true because of the inherent difficulties of getting exact data on the ratio of fixed and variable costs and because day-to-day managerial decisions are constantly changing the breakeven point. In multiproduct, integrated organizations the meaning of the figures becomes gross and vague. The resulting gross figures for variable cost, fixed cost, and volume mask important details, so the picture that emerges of overall company operations may seem acceptable, even though serious problems exist. To measure volume for General Motors Corporation, automobiles, refrigerators, huge diesels, trucks, washing machines, spark plugs, and many other items must be included. Excellent performance in one product or department covers up poor performance in others. The use of different breakeven charts for each product makes some sense, but we must beware here. It is often very difficult to allocate many costs properly, especially if the product mix is subject to change. The most clear-cut situations are those where a fairly homogenous product is produced and volume can be measured fairly well in physical units, that is, pieces or units, tons, gallons, barrels, etc.

In spite of these difficulties, breakeven analysis is important in forming a conceptual framework for budgetary controls, profit planning, and process selection. It shows management what will happen to the breakeven point and to profits as a result of volume changes or proposed courses of action.

INCREMENTAL COSTS

Incremental costs are costs that vary with the alternative courses of action considered. They are the "net effects" that result. (The terms *incremental costs, marginal costs, out-of-pocket costs,* and *differential costs* are used somewhat interchangeably.)

We should recognize that decision making in an on-going business must always take account of the status quo. Existing conditions may favor one alternative. An example of this is the common "make-versus-buy" decision. If we are currently purchasing an item and are considering the possibility of making it instead, it will be important to note if we have capacity to do so. If we do, the incremental costs of making the item will be only the direct costs of labor and materials, plus any actual net additions to other costs such as power and supplies. The machinery, building, and supervisory and executive staffs already exist; the cost of these does not change in manufacturing the item. Therefore, we dare not use the accountant's concept of average manufacturing cost as a basis for making the decision. Only the net incremental costs need be considered. If available capacity does not exist, the net incremental costs will have to include the costs of providing the needed capacity. Conversely, if we are currently making an item which we propose to buy instead, we shall not rid ourselves of the average manufacturing cost of the item. The building, supervisory and executive staff, etc., still remain. Incremental costs that are eliminated will ordinarily be far less than the average manufacturing cost.

The concept of incremental cost often reveals a shifting line between fixed and variable costs. For example, consider the direct labor costs on a continuous production line. The sum of all labor costs for the entire line can be fairly well visualized as being variable with the number of units produced, assuming that if the line is stopped, workers are either sent home or assigned other jobs. On the other hand, if we view individual operations on the line, we find that their labor costs, in general, are not subject to managerial control. It may appear that one of these operations could be improved by the use of a better tool, better motion patterns, etc. If improvements are installed, we shall probably find that labor costs per unit on that operation do not go down (are fixed) because that operation is paced by the line. The only individual operation on the line that can have variable direct labor costs is the "bottleneck" or limiting operation. If that operation can be improved, then direct labor costs for the entire line will decrease in proportion to the improvement, but not beyond the limits imposed by the next most limiting operation.

There may be as many cost patterns within an organization as there are alternative plans. The important point to keep in mind is that incremental costs are associated with whole plans or alternatives, so average costs are almost never good estimates of the net cost effects of a decision. Following is a series of examples which illustrate incremental cost behavior in some types of problems.

A company selling about $100,000 annually has three factory employees. The company specializes in plating operations on a jobbing basis. Current conditions in the labor market make employment of part-time help difficult, and work load variations would make it undesirable anyway. One man, who is the foreman, has the essential knowledge and skill required for the various plating operations. He is paid $100 per week. The other two men are general laborers, each paid $80 per week. The three men work 40 hours per week. Production could rise considerably before a fourth man would be necessary and also must fall considerably before it would be possible to get along with only the foreman and one laborer. **Example 1**

For a certain special plating process, it has been the practice to route the work to an outside plater for a particular operation that demands special equipment. The company is now considering purchasing the special equipment so that the operation could be performed in the home plant. Cost figures are:

Cost of outside processing per piece	$0.50
Expected volume of work on special equipment next year	10,000 pieces
Estimated hours per piece spent by:	
Foreman	0.04 hour
Laborers	0.075 hour
Value of power used by new equipment per piece	$0.02
Average value of materials used	$0.02
Burden rate per hour of labor	100%

There is extra room in which to locate the new equipment, which would cost $2,000 installed. What should the company do?

In this situation, labor is a fixed cost and can be ignored. The conventional burden rate is irrelevant. The only new overhead costs are the power and the cost of the equipment itself. The only pertinent direct cost is the material. The total incremental cost of the two alternative plans for next year is:

Outside processing $5000
In-plant processing $2000 + 400 = $2400

Here the economics of the situation are obviously in favor of in-plant processing. However, note that this is not the proper way to handle the equipment cost item, for we have ignored opportunity cost of alternative investments and the fact that the equipment has a probable life greater than a year. We shall discuss these capital costs later in Chapter 6.

Example 2   A job-order tool and die shop is operating at essentially full capacity. The usual estimating procedure for new work involves an analysis of the customer's drawings and specifications to determine the materials required and the sequence and type of machining operations needed. Standard time data for the machine operations are then referred to in order to obtain estimates of the number of labor hours required. The resulting estimate of labor hours is then multiplied by $6, the total material costs are added, and finally 15 per cent is added for profit. The $6 labor rate is actually composed of an average hourly pay rate to workers of $4 per hour plus burden at 50 per cent of direct labor hours. The burden rate is commonly adjusted each six months to reflect current conditions. It includes the usual items of overhead: depreciation, supplies, *overtime premium*, administrative and selling expense, etc.

A new order is currently being considered. The estimating procedure yields $1000 for material and 1750 labor hours. The total bid including profit is then $13,225. Should the company take the order if the customer agrees to the price and delivery?

The usual accounting practice of putting overtime premium in as overhead works very well for the computation of profit and loss and for computing average costs. For evaluating this contract, however, incremental costs are needed. Since the plant is operating at full capacity, we can probably assume operation beyond the breakeven point; therefore, all fixed costs have already been covered. On the other hand, overtime labor would be required to do the job. Total out-of-pocket costs would be material plus labor plus variable overhead. Therefore, the marginal income would be $13,225 - 1000 - 1750 \times 4.00 \times 1.5 -$ variable overhead, or $1725 -$ variable overhead.

Example 3   A chemical company regularly uses a certain chemical in several end products. Some of the end products are standard items and others are made in batches on special customer order. The chemical is used at an average rate of 1000 pounds per month. The supplier is nearby and is reliable about delivery, so the company normally purchases 1000 pounds at a time and reorders when the supply dwindles to 500 pounds. With normal rates of usage and delivery time, the new order is received before the inventory falls below 200 pounds, which is considered a safe minimum.

The supplying company has now announced a change of price policy. Formerly the price was $10 per 100 pounds. The new policy includes a quantity discount schedule as follows:

0–499 pounds	$12.00 per 100 pounds
500–999 pounds	11.00 per 100 pounds

| 1000–1999 pounds | 9.50 per 100 pounds |
| More than 2000 pounds | 9.00 per 100 pounds |

Should the chemical company change its ordering policy in view of the discount schedule?

This is a complex question and cannot be answered on the basis of data already given. Other incremental costs are involved which must be considered. For example, larger orders would increase the average inventory level and the variable costs associated with inventory such as insurance, interest on working capital, and space. On the other hand, larger orders mean that fewer orders are placed in a year to satisfy needs, thereby decreasing incremental costs associated with the placing of an order, such as the labor to write up the order and the order materials themselves. The purchase plan that has the lowest total cost for all of the pertinent cost factors will be one that strikes a balance between the increasing costs of carrying inventory and the decreasing costs of preparing orders which occur as the quantity per order increases. The "price breaks," or discount schedules, tend to complicate the problem. We shall study this problem more carefully in Chapter 16, where a mathematical model of "economic lot sizes" is discussed and where the question of price breaks is considered.

Example 4

A machine shop occupies the lower floor of a two-story industrial building which is leased for three years at $1000 per month. Each floor has approximately 10,000 square feet of floor space. The shop has followed the practice of sending much of its grinding work to a production grinding shop. It is now considering whether to perform the grinding operations itself and, if so, how best to incorporate the operation. It is estimated that two additional surface grinders and one cylindrical grinder could do almost all of the work that the shop now sends out. These can be purchased for $18,000. The remaining problem is where to locate the new grinders on the floors. At present there is no open space, but the foreman says that about 300 square feet could be opened up and the grinders squeezed in at the north end of the shop if two machines are moved and some space is taken from the tool crib. The latter step will cramp the tool crib operation as well as the operation of machines in the area; nevertheless, the foreman thinks that he can manage.

There is another alternative. The lease for the company occupying the second story is about to expire, and that company is planning to move. The lessor has offered the space to the machine shop on a two-year basis, to expire at the same time as the first-floor lease, at $800 per month. This alternative provides ample room for the grinders. Which items of cost would you compare for purposes of decision making for the three alternatives?

1. Continue to send grinding out. There are the billings from the grinding company plus possible transportation costs and incremental paper work costs to do business with the grinding company.

2. Squeeze three machines into existing space. Immediate increased costs

are caused by greater congestion in other departments plus relayout costs, plus costs of operating the grinders, plus costs of owning the grinders. The space, or proportional part of the rent, is irrelevant. It is actually a sunk cost for the total lease obligation. The congestion costs are difficult to measure; they are incremental material-handling costs, the additional idle time in other departments caused by interference and waiting for materials, and increased carrying charges on larger in-process inventory caused by slower progress of materials.

3. Use second floor for grinding operations. Total incremental lease cost of $19,200 would be sunk, plus operating costs of the grinders, plus costs of owning the grinders, plus additional material handling between floors.

SUMMARY

Our viewpoint must always be: "What costs are affected by alternate action paths?" This requires that we recognize the "going concern" realities which may favor one alternative over another, for example, when idle capacity exists in a make-versus-buy comparison. The incremental cost viewpoint must be retained in reading the rest of this book. As emphasized in the next chapter, concepts of sunk costs and opportunity costs are important when evaluating alternatives that involve capital assets.

Cost data for decision-making purposes have a somewhat different function than the usual accounting reports. Accounting systems meet the needs of tax laws and are of great value in certain phases of the financial management of an organization. From the viewpoint of managerial decision making, it is of great importance to know the structure of an accounting system in order to judge whether these data will mask the true effects which we may wish to measure for a given decision-making problem.

Breakeven analysis takes advantage of a two-part classification of costs into fixed and variable components. Although the breakeven point is not easy to determine accurately, the concept is an extremely valuable one in assessing the advantageous and disadvantageous effects of many typical managerial decisions relating to plant capacity, equipment replacement, make-versus-buy decisions, and so on. As we shall see in Chapter 10, a marginal breakeven concept is of considerable value in the selection of processes. Also, we can conceive of variations of the concept of breakeven charts where revenue or cost curves or both are not linear in the operating range. We might experience decreased revenue per unit when price decreases are used to expand volume. When operating near capacity limitations, cost per unit may increase due to congestion or the use of less efficient methods or equipment. In these situations it is possible for more than one breakeven point to appear.

In the examples given under "incremental costs," we can see in every instance how we might have been misled by accepting "unit cost" figures based on ordinary cost accounting concepts. This is not to damn the accountant, because the unit cost figures that he shows are not designed particularly to help management select from the types of alternatives we have discussed. Probably the most common area of difficulty is in the burden, or burden rate, which represents an *allocation* of fixed and indirect expenses, often on an arbitrary basis. Since our thinking seems to have been structured in terms of labor, material, and overhead costs, there is a temptation to use this burden rate in all situations in order that "each product bears its fair share of these costs." Yet this view can mask important differences in alternatives. If we adopt the view of the alternative plan as a basic cost unit, instead of unit costs, it often becomes unnecessary to worry about how costs are allocated because we are concerned with the total costs associated with the plan.

Finally, we should recognize that an incremental cost analysis can take the form of a general model applicable to a class of problems. Part of the purpose of Example 3 was to point out this fact; in developing a policy for purchase quantities, we find that the pertinent incremental costs vary in a predictable way with changes in the quantity purchased, and that there is one purchase quantity which minimizes the sum of these incremental costs. The problem of how many parts to manufacture at one time can be approached in the same general way.

REVIEW QUESTIONS

1. Discuss the differences between fixed, variable, and semivariable costs.
2. Define breakeven point and contribution.
3. How can we obtain data to construct breakeven charts? Appraise these methods.
4. Discuss the effect of the following on breakeven points and profits: change in volume, change in product mix, labor performance changes, increase in fixed costs, increase in selling prices.
5. What is the effect on the breakeven point on the following typical managerial decisions: increase in plant capacity, replacement of obsolete equipment, manufacturing components previously bought, decision to retain

certain labor skills at the bottom of a seasonal swing, decision to utilize overtime to increase capacity?

6. Appraise the usefulness of breakeven analysis for a multiproduct organization.

7. Define the term *incremental costs*.

8. What is the effect of idle capacity on the incremental costs to manufacture an item instead of purchasing it?

9. Give examples of the following: direct labor cost is a fixed expense; material is a sunk cost; investment in plant and equipment is a variable cost.

PROBLEMS

1. The Stamped Metal Products Company (StaMCo) is considering the manufacture of a special item for the Air Force. After considerable analysis, the company has identified the following costs:

Material	$0.5 per unit
Tooling	20 hours
Unit direct labor	0.4 hour
Labor rate	$2 per hour
Factory burden	115% of labor
General and administrative burden	20% of factory cost
Target profit	10% of total cost

Construct a breakeven chart on a 10,000 unit basis with a unit sales price of $3.

2. A foreman in an automatic screw machine department uses screw machines of essentially two sizes for all work done. One size is for small parts and the other for larger parts, the dimensions of the part dictating when it must be run on the large machines. In general, the large machine costs more originally, uses more power, and operates more slowly than the small one. These differences are summarized below for a typical order.

	Small Screw Machine	Large Screw Machine
Original cost	$18,000	$23,000
Setup time	6 hours	6 hours
Total run time (lot of 10,000 parts)	50 hours	65 hours
Value of energy	$10	$13

Labor is paid at $3.25 per hour and the departmental burden rate is 100 per cent of labor cost.

The foreman finds that he is operating to capacity with the small machines but has additional small parts to run. These parts can also be run on the large machines but, as noted before, at higher cost. He also can schedule overtime on the small machines to accomplish the work. Assume the job in question is the typical one for which data are given. Which machine should the foreman use? Why?

3. The King Cookie Company is a baking company with headquarters on the West Coast. Sales have increased steadily during the past decade. However, the president believes that profits are not as high as they should be for the firm's sales volume. From examination of the profits of other baking companies and attendance at some AMA meetings, the president believes that the firm should be able to make a net profit before taxes of 12 per cent of sales.

The president has asked each member of the top management group to prepare a budget "request" for the coming fiscal year encompassing all activities under his control. The marketing division's forecast of $4,000,000 has been approved as the planning base for these budget requests. The president stressed that he was anxious to improve the profit margin and requested all officers to "pare the fat" off their budget requests. The marketing division's budget request for 1973 has been completed and is as follows:

Salaries	$130,000
Travel and entertainment	40,000
Advertising	120,000
Other expenses	70,000
	$360,000

The accounting department has prepared an estimated fiscal 1972 income statement by straight-line extrapolation to a full 12 months. This statement and the supporting schedules are given in Table I. The vice-president in charge

TABLE I. Estimated 1972 Income Statement

	Thousands of Dollars	Per Cent* of Sales
Sales	3600	100.00
Cost of sales:		
Material	380	10.6
Direct labor	850	23.6
Manufacturing expense (schedule 2)	1040	28.9
Total cost of sales	2270	63.1
Gross profit	1330	36.9
Expenses:		
Distribution (schedule 3)	185	5.1
Marketing (schedule 4)	340	9.4
Administration (schedule 5)	690	19.2
Total expenses	1215	33.7
Net profit before taxes	115	3.2

(*continued*)

TABLE I *(continued)*

	Thousands of Dollars	Per Cent* of Sales
Schedule 2—Estimated 1972 Manufacturing Expenses		
Indirect labor	380	10.6
Direct supplies	150	4.2
Indirect supplies	30	0.8
Repairs and maintenance	200	5.6
Utilities	30	0.8
Depreciation	250	6.9
Total manufacturing expenses	1040	28.9
Schedule 3—Estimated 1972 Distribution Expenses		
Salaries	70	1.9
Postage and freight	90	2.5
Other expenses	25	0.7
Total distribution expenses	185	5.1
Schedule 4—Estimated 1972 Marketing Expenses		
Salaries	120	3.3
Travel and entertainment	36	1.0
Advertising	120	3.3
Other expenses	64	1.8
Total marketing expenses	340	9.4
Schedule 5—Estimated 1972 Administrative Expenses		
Salaries:		
Executive	60	1.7
Staff	85	2.4
Accounting	110	3.1
Office supplies	20	0.6
Travel and entertainment	54	1.5
Telephone	71	2.0
Rent	60	1.7
Taxes (other than income)	50	1.4
Professional services	40	1.1
Other expenses	140	3.9
Total administrative expenses	690	19.2

*Some percentage figures do not add to subtotals because of rounding errors.

TABLE II. Consolidation of Grass Roots Estimates Made by Managers of Departments under the Control of the Vice-President in Charge of Operations	
Estimated 1973 Manufacturing Expenses	Thousands of Dollars
Materials	430
Direct labor	960
Indirect labor	430
Direct supplies	180
Indirect supplies	35
Repairs and maintenance	300
Utilities	35
Depreciation	240
Total	2610
Estimated 1973 Distribution Expenses	
Salaries	75
Postage and freight	100
Other expenses	30
Total	205

of operations has done "grass roots" planning by asking his subordinate managers to estimate their expenses for fiscal 1973. Table II gives the consolidation of this estimate.

Using the information given and any necessary assumptions you need:

1. Determine your best estimate of the various production and distribution expenses for the coming year.

2. Determine the budget request that you would submit if you were the vice-president in charge of operations.

3. Explain and justify your two budgets and any differences between the three sets of figures (i.e., "grass roots" consolidation, best estimate, and budget request).

Clearly state why you need to make each assumption, and estimate its soundness.

REFERENCES

[1] Anthony, R. N. *Management Accounting Principles* (Rev. ed.), Richard D. Irwin, Homewood, Ill., 1970.
[2] Goetz, B. E. *Management Planning and Control*. McGraw-Hill, New York, 1949.

[3] Grant, E. L., and W. G. Ireson. *Principles of Engineering Economy* (5th ed.). Ronald Press, New York, 1970.

[4] Keller, I. W., and W. L. Ferrara. *Management Accounting for Profit Control.* McGraw-Hill, New York, 1966.

[5] Stanbus, G. J. *Activity Costing and Input-Output Accounting.* Richard D. Irwin, Homewood, Ill., 1971.

Capital **C**osts **&** **I**nvestment **C**riteria

Capital costs affect decision problems in production management whenever a physical asset or expenditure is involved that provides a continuing benefit or return. From an accounting point of view, the original capital expenditure must be recovered through the mechanism of depreciation and must be deducted from income as an expense of doing business. The number of years over which the asset is depreciated and the allocation of the total amount to each of these years (i.e., whether straight-line or some accelerated rate of depreciation) represent alternate strategies directed toward tax policy. We must remember that all these depreciation terms and allocations are arbitrary and are not designed

127

from the point of view of cost data for decision making relative to operations. Our interest will be in capital cost data, which will aid us in deciding between alternative courses of action involving different systems of production, different degrees of mechanization, the replacement of existing assets, etc.

Let us begin our analysis with a very simple example which we shall treat in an unsophisticated way. We have just installed a piece of equipment which performs a highly specialized operation for us. The installation was a custom job which fit into our particular situation. Because of the specialized nature of the equipment and the custom installation, the equipment is of no value to anyone else; its salvage value is zero. As with many kinds of productive equipment, its useful physical life can be prolonged almost indefinitely by maintenance and repair, so it is difficult to say as yet what the life of the equipment will be. Since the equipment has no salvage value, we must face the fact that the entire $10,000 seems to go down some sort of economic sink the minute the equipment becomes ours. We say that the $10,000 is a *sunk cost*, meaning simply that it is gone forever, regardless of what we may list as the "book value" of the equipment. Since the $10,000 is "sunk," it is completely irrelevant to any future decisions because no future decision can affect it.

The cost of owing the equipment (as distinct from the costs of operating and maintaining it) is simply $10,000. We hope to spread this total over a period of time so that the *average* annual cost of ownership will not be too great. In five years the average cost of owning the equipment is only $10,000/5 = $2000 per year. In ten years the average annual cost is down to $1000 per year. This decreasing average annual cost of owning the machine is diagrammed in Figure 1. Regardless of how long we keep the equipment, this cost of owning is irrelevant because it is a past cost. The only future costs that we shall incur for this equipment are the costs of operating and maintaining it. Once the machine is installed, these are the only costs subject to managerial control by future decisions.

Let us assume that two men are required to operate the equipment at $4000 per year per man. Maintenance costs are expected to be $2000 the first year, thereafter increasing $200 per year. Figure 2 shows the total of these costs diagrammed in relation to time. We assume that there are no other pertinent costs. Since the original cost of the equipment is sunk and the only future costs are the operating and maintenance costs, we are in a position to see under what conditions we would consider this setup to be obsolete and would replace it. We would want to replace it at any time that we could find a functionally equivalent setup that

FIGURE 1.   Decreasing annual average cost of owning a machine
that cost $10,000 originally and has no salvage value at any time.

could offer a total average annual cost of owning plus operation and
maintenance that fell below the cost curve of Figure 2. Let us assume
that during the fourth year of operation of this setup (which we shall
now call the present setup), a new equipment design is developed.

This *new equipment design* has an important advantage over the old
one. Because it is more automatic, it can be operated by one man. The
more automatic features require an additional $1000 maintenance effort,
however; therefore the first-year operating and maintenance cost is
expected to be $4000 operating labor plus $3000 maintenance. This total

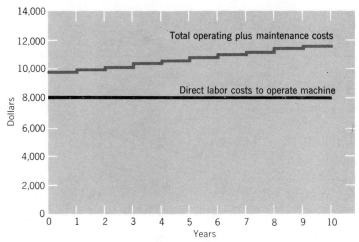

FIGURE 2.   Operating and maintenance costs, showing rising costs
of maintenance.

of $7000 is expected to increase by $200 per year as before because of mounting maintenance charges. The improved design costs $12,000 installed. Now we want to see if the average annual total of the costs of owning plus operating and maintaining the improved equipment design is less than the $10,600 current annual expense (fourth year) for the present setup. First, let us note that while we ignore the original sunk cost of the present setup, this is not true for the installed cost of the improved design. It is still a future cost. We have not bought it yet, so the installed cost must be considered.

To see the picture clearly, let us plot, on the same chart, the average annual cost of owning (capital cost) and the annual operating and maintenance costs for the improved equipment design. These costs are shown in Figure 3, where we also show the total of the two costs year by year. The total cost curve is developed simply by adding the cost of owning to the operating and maintenance costs for each year. Note that the total cost is very high during the first two years, reaches a minimum during the eighth year, and then begins to rise again. It is high in the early years because the annual average costs of owning the equipment are very high during those years. It begins to rise again, but slowly, after the eighth year because of the influence of rising maintenance costs. Now let us examine the significance of the total cost curve for this simplified example. For the present setup the total

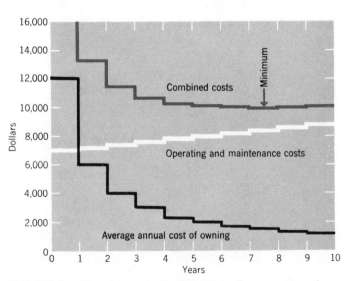

FIGURE 3. Year-by-year average costs for a proposed replacement machine costing $12,000 initially and having no salvage value at any time.

incremental cost for this year is $10,600, as we have already noted, a sum that we expect will become larger in future years. However, the total average annual cost for the proposed setup will be less than $10,600 after the fourth year. It seems clear that a decision to replace the present setup is needed.

The situation we have assumed is quite clear cut. However, we may raise the question: "What criteria for comparison are we using here?" The answer is that we are looking at the best possible future cost performance for both the present and proposed setups. The best cost performance possible for the present design is $10,600, which is this year's operating and maintenance cost. The best cost performance possible for the proposed design is achieved if it is held in service for eight years; its total cost would average only $9900 per year for the entire eight-year span. As long as the best performance of the proposed design (represented by the minimum of the total cost curve) is less than the best performance of the present design, it would be economical to make the switch. Of course, this statement must be tempered with a recognition of important intangible values and the accuracy of the cost estimates.

We have been assuming a fairly simple situation where we have chosen to ignore certain factors. Let us introduce some additional ideas. Suppose that we are discussing an asset that is used for more general purposes, such as an over-the-road semitrailer truck. Let us assume that we own such a truck and the first question before us is: "How much will it cost us to *own* this truck for one more year?" These costs of owning, or capital costs, cannot be derived from the ordinary accounting records of the organization. The cost of owning it for one more year depends on its current value. If the truck can be sold on the second-hand market for $5000, this is a measure of its economic value. Since it has value, we have two basic alternatives: we can sell it for $5000 or we can retain it. If we sell, the $5000 can earn interest or a return in an alternative investment. If we keep the truck, we forego the return, which then becomes an *opportunity cost* of holding the truck one more year. Similarly, if we keep the truck, it will be worth less a year from now, so there is a second opportunity cost measured by the fall in salvage value during the year.

The loss of opportunity to earn a return and the loss of salvage value during the year are the costs of continued ownership. They are opportunity costs rather than costs paid out; nevertheless, they can be of real importance in comparing alternatives that require different amounts of

Opportunity Costs

investment. There is one more possible component of capital cost for the next year if the truck is retained—the cost of possible renewals or "capital additions" necessary to keep the truck operating. We are not thinking of ordinary maintenance here, but major overhauls such as a new engine or an engine overhaul that extend the physical life for some time. In summary, the capital costs or costs of owning the truck for one more year are:

1. Opportunity costs:
    a. Interest on opening salvage value.
    b. Loss in salvage value during the year.
2. Capital additions or renewals required to keep the truck running for at least an additional year.

By assuming a schedule of salvage values, we can compute the year-by-year capital costs for an asset. This is done in Table I for a truck that cost $10,000 initially and has the salvage schedule indicated. The final result is the projected capital cost incurred for each year. If we determine the way operating and maintenance costs increase as the truck ages, we can plot a set of curves of yearly costs. The combined capital plus operating and maintenance cost curve will have a minimum point as before. This minimum of the combined cost curve defines the best cost-performance year in the life of the equipment. Beyond that year, the effect of rising maintenance costs more than counterbalances the declining capital costs. Note that such a plot is different from Figure 3 where we were plotting annual average costs instead of yearly costs.

TABLE I.   Year-by-Year Capital Costs for a Semitrailer Truck, Given a Salvage Schedule (interest at 10%)

Year	Year-End Salvage Value	Fall in Salvage Value during Year	Interest on Opening Salvage Value	Capital Cost, Sum of Fall in Value, and Interest
New	$10,000	—	—	—
1	8,300	$1,700	$1,000	$2,700
2	6,900	1,400	830	2,230
3	5,700	1,200	690	1,890
4	4,700	1,000	570	1,570
5	3,900	800	470	1,270
6	3,200	700	390	1,090
7	2,700	500	320	820
8	2,300	400	270	670
9	1,950	350	230	580
10	1,650	300	195	495

What is the effect of obsolescence on the cost of owning and operating a machine? By definition, when a machine is obsolete there exists an alternative machine or system that is more economical to own and operate. Clearly, the existence of the new machine does not cause any increase in the cost of operating and maintaining the present machine. Those costs are already determined by the design, installation, and condition of the present machine. However, the existence of the new machine causes the salvage value of the present setup to fall and, therefore, induces an increased capital cost. Thus, for assets in technologically dynamic classifications, the salvage value schedule falls rapidly in anticipation of typical obsolescence rates. Economic lives are very short. On the other hand, where the rate of innovation is relatively slow, salvage values hold up fairly well.

Table II compares year-by-year capital costs for two machines which cost $10,000 initially but have different salvage schedules. The value of machine 1 holds the best, machine 2 having more severe obsolescence reflected in its salvage schedule. The result is that capital costs in the initial years are greater for machine 2 than for machine 1. The average capital costs for the first five years are:

Machine 1	$1913
Machine 2	$2198

Therefore, if the schedules of operating expenses for the two machines were identical, machine 1 would seem more desirable. However, since

TABLE II. Comparison of Capital Costs for Two Machines Costing $10,000 Initially but with Different Salvage Schedules (interest at 10%)

Machine 1				Machine 2			
Year-End Salvage Value	Fall in Value During Year	Interest at 10% on Opening Value	Capital Cost	Year-End Salvage Value	Fall in Value During Year	Interest at 10% on Opening Value	Capital Cost
$10,000	—	—	—	$10,000	—	—	—
8,330	$1,670	$1,000	$2,670	7,150	$2,850	$1,000	$3,850
6,940	1,390	833	2,223	5,100	2,050	715	2,765
5,780	1,160	694	1,854	3,640	1,460	510	1,970
4,820	960	578	1,538	2,600	1,040	364	1,404
4,020	800	482	1,282	1,860	740	260	1,000
3,350	670	402	1,072	1,330	530	186	716
2,790	560	335	895	950	380	133	513
2,320	470	279	749	680	270	95	365
1,930	390	232	622	485	195	68	263
1,610	320	193	513	345	140	49	189

Present Values

the timing of the capital costs is different for the two machines, it would be better, for comparative purposes if we could adjust all figures to their equivalent present values.

Since money has a time value, future expenditures and opportunity costs will have different present or current values to us. What do we mean by the time value of money? Since money can earn interest, $1000 in hand now is equivalent to $1100 a year from now if the present sum can earn interest at 10 per cent. Similarly, if we must wait a year to receive $1000 due now, we should expect not $1000 a year hence but $1100. When the time spans involved are extended, the appropriate interest is compounded and its effect becomes much larger. The timing of payments and receipts can make an important difference in the value of various alternatives.

Let us illustrate this point briefly and more precisely before returning to the example of the two machines. We know that if a principal sum P is invested at interest rate i, it will yield a future total sum S in n years hence if all of the earnings are retained and compounded. Therefore, P in the present is entirely equivalent to S in the future by virtue of the compound amount factor. That is,

$$S = P(1 + i)^n$$

where $(1 + i)^n = $ the compound amount factor for interest rate i and n years.

Similarly, we can solve for P to determine the present worth of a sum to be paid n years hence. That is,

$$P = \frac{S}{(1 + i)^n} = S \times PV_{sp}$$

where $PV_{sp} = $ the present value of a single payment S to be made n years hence with interest rate i. Therefore, if we were to receive a payment of $10,000 in ten years, we should be willing to accept a smaller but equivalent sum now. If interest at 10 per cent were considered fair and adequate, that smaller but equivalent sum would be:

$$P = 10,000 \times 0.3855 = \$3,855$$

since

$$\frac{1}{(1 + 0.10)^{10}} = PV_{sp} = 0.3855$$

Now let us return to the example of the two machines. The capital costs for each machine occur by different schedules because of different salvage values. If all future values were adjusted to the present as a common base time, we could compare the totals to see which investment alternative was advantageous. This we have done in Table III, where we have assumed an operating cost schedule in column (2), determined combined operating and capital costs in columns (5) and (6), and listed present values in columns (8) and (9). The present value of the entire stream of expenditures and opportunity costs is $32,398 for machine 1. The net difference in present values for the two machines is shown at the bottom of Table III. Since the operating cost schedule was identical for both machines, the difference reflects differences in the present worth of capital costs. Obviously, the method allows for different operating cost schedules as well.

There are some difficulties with the methods just described. First, we have assumed that the schedule of salvage values is known, which, more often than not, is not true. Second, at some point in the life of the machines it becomes economical to replace them with identical models. Therefore, a chain of identical machines should be considered for comparative purposes; the machine is replaced in the year in which operating and capital costs are just equal to the interest on the present worth of all future costs. The essence of this latter statement is that we are seeking a balance between this year's costs (operating and capital costs) and opportunity income from disposal (interest on the present worth of all future costs). When the opportunity income from disposal is the greater of the two, replacement with the identical machine is called for. Most common criteria for comparing alternative capital investments attempt to circumvent these problems by: (a) assuming an economic life and (b) assuming some standard schedule for the decline in value of the asset. We shall now consider some of these criteria.

COMMON CRITERIA FOR COMPARING ECONOMIC ALTERNATIVES

Some of the common criteria used for evaluating proposals for capital expenditures and for comparing alternatives involving capital assets are: (a) present values, (b) average investment, (c) rate of return, and (d) payoff period.

Present value methods for comparing alternatives take the sum of present values of all future out-of-pocket expenditures and credits over the economic life of the asset. This figure is compared for each alternative. If differences in revenue are also involved, their present values must also be accounted for. Table I in the Appendix gives the present values for

Present Value Criterion

TABLE III. Present Value of Capital and Operating Costs for the Two Machines from Table II; Schedule of Operating Costs Is the Same for Both Machines (interest at 10%)

Year (1)	Operating Cost (2)	Capital Costs (from Table II)		Combined Operating and Capital Costs		Present Worth Factor for Year Indicated** (7)	Present Worth of Combined Costs for Year Indicated	
		Machine 1 (3)	Machine 2 (4)	Machine 1 (5)	Machine 2 (6)		Machine 1 (8)	Machine 2 (9)
1	$3,000	$2,670	$3,850	$5,670	$6,850	0.909	$5,154	$6,227
2	3,200	2,223	2,765	5,423	5,765	0.826	4,479	4,762
3	3,400	1,854	1,970	5,254	5,370	0.751	3,946	4,033
4	3,600	1,538	1,404	5,138	5,004	0.683	3,509	3,418
5	3,800	1,282	1,000	5,082	4,800	0.621	3,160	2,981
6	4,000	1,072	716	5,072	4,716	0.565	2,866	2,665
7	4,200	895	513	5,095	4,713	0.513	2,614	2,418
8	4,400	749	365	5,149	4,765	0.467	2,405	2,225
9	4,600	622	273	5,222	4,873	0.424	2,214	2,066
10	4,800	513	189	5,313	4,989	0.386	2,051	1,926
Totals							$32,398	$32,721

Machine 1, present worth of all future values is total of column (8) less present worth of tenth-year salvage value, i.e., $32,398 − 1610* × 0.386 = 32,398 − 621 = $31,777.

Machine 2, $32,721 − 345* × 0.386 = 32,721 − 133 = $32,588.

*Tenth-year salvage values from Table II.

**From Table I (Appendix).

single future payments or credits; Table II in the Appendix gives present values for annuities for various years and interest rates. An annuity is a sum that is received or paid annually. The factors in Table II convert the entire series of annual sums to a single sum in the present for various interest rates and years. We shall use the notation PV_a for the present value factor of an annuity.

Suppose we are considering a machine that costs $15,000 installed. We estimate that the economic life of the machine is eight years, at which time its salvage value is expected to be about $3000. For simplicity, we take the average operating and maintenance costs to be $5000 per year. At 10 per cent interest, the present value of the expenditures and credits is:

An Example

Initial investment	$15,000 \times PV_{sp} = 15,000 \times 1.000 =$	15,000
Annual operating and maintenance costs	$5,000\ PV_a = 5,000 \times 5.335 =$	26,675
		41,675
Less credit of present value of salvage to be received in eight years	$3,000 \times PV_{sp} = 3,000 \times 0.467 =$	1,401
		$40,274

The net total of $40,274 is the present value of the expenditures and credits over the eight-year expected life of the machine. The initial investment is already at present value; that is, the present value factor is 1.000. The annual costs of operation and maintenance are an eight-year annuity, so the entire stream of annual costs can be adjusted to present value by the multiplication of PV_a from Table II (Appendix). Finally, the present value of the salvage is deducted. This total could be compared with comparable figures for other alternatives over the same eight-year period. If another alternative machine is estimated to have a different economic life, perhaps four years, then to make the present value totals comparable, two cycles of the four-year machine would be compared with one cycle of the eight-year machine. If the operating and maintenance costs increased as the machine aged, the present value of the expenditure in each year would be determined separately by PV_{sp}.

Average investment methods estimate an average annual cost of owning plus operating and maintaining an asset. The average annual capital costs are approximated by average salvage loss plus interest on the average investment, assuming the decline in value of the asset is on a uniform or straight-line basis. Figure 4 shows the assumed structure for the decline in value of an asset and the calculation of average investment. Thus, if a machine cost $10,000 and was estimated to have a ten-year life with a salvage value at the end of that time of $1000, the capital costs are approximated by:

Average
Investment
Criterion

Average annual salvage loss, $\dfrac{10{,}000 - 1{,}000}{10} = \$900$

Annual interest on average investment, at 10%

$$\frac{(10{,}000 + 1{,}000)0.10}{2} = 5{,}500 \times 0.10 = \$550$$

Average annual capital cost $= \$900 + \$550 = \$1{,}450$

If operating and maintenance costs were estimated to average \$12,500 per year over the ten-year machine life, the total average annual cost for comparison would be $1{,}450 + 12{,}500 = \$13{,}950$. Differences in annual revenue between alternatives can be accounted for in the operating costs. Comparable calculations for alternative machines would form the basis for comparison. For a strictly economic comparison, the alternative presenting the lowest average annual cost would be selected.

Rate of Return
Criterion

One common method of evaluating new projects or comparing alternative courses of action is to calculate a rate of return which is then judged for adequacy. Usually no attempt is made to take account of interest costs, so the resulting figure is referred to as the "unadjusted" rate of return, that is, unadjusted for interest values. It is computed as follows:

Unadjusted rate of return

$$= \frac{100\,(\text{net monetary operating advantage} - \text{amortization})}{\text{average investment}}$$

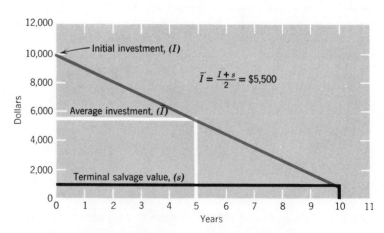

FIGURE 4. Relationship of initial investment, terminal salvage value, and average investment for "average investment methods."

The net monetary advantage reflects the algebraic sum of incremental costs of operation and maintenance and possible differences in revenue. If the rate computed is a "before-tax" rate, then the amortization

$$\left(\frac{\text{Incremental investment}}{\text{Economic life}} \right)$$

is subtracted and the result is divided by average investment and multiplied by 100 to obtain a percentage return. If an "after-tax" rate is sought, the net increase in income taxes due to the project is subtracted from the net monetary advantage and the balance of the calculation is as it was before. Obviously, the adequacy of a given rate of return changes drastically if it is being judged as an after-tax return.

Let us carry through a simple example. We assume that new methods have been proposed for the line assembly of a product which had been assembled in a central area, each assembly being completed by one individual. The new methods require the purchase and installation of conveyors and fixtures that cost $50,000 installed including the costs of relayout. The new line assembly methods require five fewer assemblers. After the increased maintenance and power costs are added in, the net monetary operating advantage is estimated as $20,000 per year. Economic life is estimated at five years. The unadjusted before-tax return is: **An Example**

$$\frac{20,000 - \dfrac{50,000}{5}}{\dfrac{50,000}{2}} \times 100 = 40\%$$

The after-tax return requires that incremental taxes be deducted. Incremental taxable income will be the operating advantage less increased allowable tax depreciation. Assuming straight-line depreciation and an allowed depreciation term of eight years, incremental taxable income is $20,000 less $50,000/8, or $20,000 − $6,250 = $13,750. Assuming an income tax rate of 50 per cent, the incremental tax due to the project is $6875. The after-tax return is therefore:

$$\frac{20,000 - 6,875 - 10,000}{25,000} \times 100 = \frac{3,125 \times 100}{25,000} = 12.5\%$$

Whether or not either the before- or after-tax rates calculated in this example are adequate is a matter to be judged in relation to the risk involved in the particular venture and the returns possible through alternate uses of the capital.

The payoff period is the time required for an investment to "pay for itself" through the net operating advantage that would result from its installation. It is calculated as follows: **Payoff Periods**

$$\text{Payoff period in years} = \frac{\text{Net investment}}{\text{Net annual operating advantage after taxes}}$$

The payoff period for the conveyor installation which we discussed previously is

$$\frac{\$50,000}{\$13,125} = 3.8 \text{ years}$$

It is the period of time for the net after-tax advantage to just equal the net total amount invested. Presumably, after that period, "it is all gravy"; the $13,125 per year is profit since the invested amount has been recovered. The question might be raised: "If the economic life of the equipment is five years and 10 per cent is regarded as an appropriate rate of after-tax return for the project, what *should* the payoff period be?" Obviously, the period for both capital recovery and return is the five-year economic life. The period that recovers capital only, but that also allows enough time left in the economic life to provide the return, will be somewhat shorter and will depend on the required rate of return. Let us note now that the payoff period is another interpretation that can be given to the present value factors for annuities, PV_a, given in Table II (Appendix). As an example, for an economic life of five years and a return rate of 10 percent, $PV_a = 3.791$ from Table II (Appendix). This indicates that capital recovery takes place in 3.791 years. The equivalent of 10 percent compound interest takes place in $5.000 - 3.791 = 1.209$ years. Therefore, any of the PV_a values in Table II (Appendix) for a given economic life in years and a given return rate indicate the shorter period in years required to return the investment. Or, more simply, they give directly the payoff period.

The proper procedure would be to estimate economic life and determine the applicable return rate. From the present value tables, determine the payoff period associated with these conditions. Then compute the actual payoff period of the project in question and compare it to the standard period from the tables. If the computed period is less than, or equal to, the standard period, the project meets the payoff and risk requirements imposed. If the computed value is greater than the table value, the project would earn less than the required rate.

SUMMARY

In this chapter we have attempted to survey the cost concepts that bear on investment decisions, such as sunk costs and opportunity costs, as well as to describe the most common investment criteria used by business and industry today. All these methods represent some approximation and idealization of the general investment problem. For example, all require an assumption of an economic life and of some standard schedule for the decline in value of the assets being analyzed. In addition, there are many less obvious conceptual ideas for which they do not account.

The various criteria are not all equivalent or interchangeable. The present value methods are the most flexible and involve the least assumptions. They can be tailored to meet specific situations involving wide variations in salvage schedules, projected cost patterns, and future periodic capital additions. The average investment criterion is basically an approximation to a variant of present value methods which expresses the data in terms of an equivalent average annual cost adjusted for interest values. The average investment criterion computes an average annual cost which assumes a uniform decline in salvage value of the assets and ignores the timing of expenditures by computing interest on average investment. The average investment, rate of return, and payoff criteria all approximate future operating costs by an average period. For simple machines, this may be a reasonable assumption; but for complex equipment and for buildings, future costs may have a pattern in relation to time which is not well represented by an average figure.

In terms of the preference of using one criterion over another, there are some reasonable guides. If the project involves long projected lives with complex patterns of future expenditures, interest values may tip the balance in favor of one alternative, and the present value criterion should be used. When future operating costs are reasonably well represented by an average figure, the choice between average investment, rate of return, and payoff period may rest on the preference for a particular way of expressing answers; that is, in terms of return on investment, annual costs, or time to pay off.

REVIEW QUESTIONS

1. Why is a sunk cost irrelevant in models for investment?
2. How are book values of equipment handled in investment analysis?
3. What is an opportunity cost?
4. What are capital costs?
5. What is the structure of capital costs incurred by retaining ownership of an asset one more year?
6. What is the meaning of the term *economic life? Physical life?*
7. How is obsolescence reflected in the actual costs of owning and operating an asset?
8. What is the compound amount factor? How is it computed?

9. What is the meaning of the reciprocal of the compound amount factor?
10. What is an annuity?
11. Define the factor PV_a. What is the meaning of its reciprocal?
12. Why is it that most common criteria for comparing alternate capital investments assume an economic life and some standard schedule for the decline in value of the asset?
13. Outline the methodology for comparing alternate investments by the present value criterion.
14. How are the capital costs approximated in the average investment criterion?
15. Compare the calculations required for the before- and after-tax rate of return.
16. Outline the payoff period criterion methodology. With what standard payoff period should the computed value be compared to determine if the investment is justified? How is the standard payoff period determined?
17. Compare and evaluate the four criteria for investment analysis discussed. Under what conditions might we use each of them?

PROBLEMS

1. The proud owner of a new automobile states that he intends to hold his car only two years in order to minimize repair costs which he feels should be near zero during the initial period. He paid $4,000 for the car new and blue book value schedules suggest that it will be worth only $2,000 two years hence. He normally drives 10,000 miles per year and he estimates that his cost of operation is $0.10 per mile. What are his projected capital costs for the first two years, if interest of 6 per cent represents a reasonable alternate investment for him?

2. Suppose we are considering the installation of a small computer to accomplish internal tasks of payroll computation, invoicing, and other routine accounting. The purchase price is quoted as $300,000 and salvage value five years later is expected to be $100,000. The operating costs are expected to be $100,000 per year, mainly for personnel to program, operate, and maintain the computer. What is the present value of the costs to own and operate the computer over its five-year economic life? The value of money in the organization is 15 per cent.

3. Using the average investment criterion as a basis for comparison, at what annual lease cost would we break even for the data on the computer in Problem 2? If the machine is leased, maintenance is furnished, reducing annual operating costs to $70,000.

4. An aggressive marketer of a new office copier has made its machine available for sale as well as lease. The idea of buying a copying machine seems revolutionary, but less so when we examine our present costs which come to

$6,500 per year for lease plus per copy charges. If we own a machine the costs of paper and maintenance is projected to be $1,500 per year. The new copier costs $10,000 installed and is assumed to have an economic life of five years and a salvage value of $2,000.

(a) What is the projected unadjusted rate of return if we install the copier?

(b) If incremental taxes for the project are $1,000, what is the adjusted rate of return?

5.   What is the actual payoff period for the office copier project discussed in Problem 4? If interest is 10 per cent what should the minimum payoff period be to make the investment economically sound? Does the office copier project meet the payoff standard?

6.   A concern is considering the purchase of two alternate machines to perform an important operation in their manufacturing process. The first machine is a standard one. The second is more expensive but has a higher degree of automation incorporated in it. Both meet capacity needs. Comparative data are as follows:

	Machine 1	Machine 2
Installed cost	$20,000	$30,000
Estimated economic life	10 years	10 years
Salvage value	$5,000	$7,000
Labor cost/year	$12,000	$6,000
Maintenance cost, first year	$1,000*	$2,000†

The value of money within the organization for investments of this kind is 10 per cent. Which machine is preferable, using the present value criterion?

7.   A trucking firm is in the shorthaul local trucking business, servicing industrial plants which require the transfer of a wide variety of parts, materials, and packages. One large local firm has established a new plant 100 miles (6-hour round trip) away and has called for bids to truck 50 tons per day of an important subassembly unit one way to the new plant (assume 20 working days per month) and would permit transfer either during the day or during the night. The contract to be let is for a year with an option for the industrial firm to renew if performance is satisfactory. The trucking firm currently owns two 10-ton trucks which service the local shorthaul business during regular daytime working hours, but they are available for service at night. Truck drivers earn $24 for an 8-hour day with 8 hours work guaranteed.

To take the contract the trucking firm would need to enlarge its capacity. It has narrowed the field to two types of 10-ton trucks, one of which is available on a lease basis and the other for purchase. The cost characteristics of the two trucks are as follows:

---

*Increases $100 per year after first year.
†Increases $200 per year after first year.

Leased diesel truck:

Lessors pays all taxes, insurance and license fees as well as maintenance. Operating costs to be absorbed by the leasee are:

Lease charges	$800 per month per truck
Fuel, oil, and tires	5¢ per mile

Purchased gasoline truck:

Purchase price is $20,000 with terminal salvage value of $4000 at the end of 6 years. Other costs are:

Fuel, oil, and tires	8¢ per mile
Maintenance	2¢ per mile
Taxes, insurance and license	$100 per month per truck

Determine the number of additional trucks required, assuming that no truck can be operated more than 16 hours per day. Using the *average* investment criterion, determine which alternative is the cheaper of the two. (Interest rate = 15 per cent.) What action do you recommend?

8. A new office duplicating machine costing $5600 will enable a company to save $0.03 per sheet. The present usage rate is approximately 9000 sheets per month. Calculate the after-tax rate of return.

Economic life	8 years
Depreciation term	10 years
Depreciation method	Straight-line
Incremental tax rate	50 per cent
Interest rate	10 per cent

9. You have been offered the popcorn concession at the Stamped Metal Products Company (StaMCo) for five years at a cost of $2000 including equipment. A preliminary analysis indicates that annual operating costs would be $4000 and mean annual sales would be $5000. You would like a 12 per cent return on your investment. (Ignore taxes; use $500 salvage value.)

(a) Determine the acceptance or rejection of this investment on the basis of the payoff period criterion.

(b) Determine the acceptance or rejection on the basis of present value criteria.

(c) If the equipment costs $1500 and will be worth $500 at the end of five years, what is the annual straight-line depreciation?

(d) What is the yearly investment in equipment?

10. A new machine costing $108,000 will give a $64,000 per year net operating advantage before taxes. Calculate the after tax rate of return.

Depreciation term	6 years
Depreciation method	Straight-line
Economic life	4 years
Tax rate	50 per cent
Interest rate	10 per cent

11.   We are considering whether or not to replace an existing machine with a new design. The existing machine has no market value, but has a book value of $2000. The new machine costs $10,000 initially and has an eight-year projected economic life with no terminal salvage value. Comparative operating costs are:

	Old	New
Direct Labor	$9500/year	$4000/year
Wasted material	500/year	400/year
Insurance and property taxes	500/year	100/year
Supplies	1000/year	900/year

The company is in the 50-per-cent tax bracket, and 10 per cent is considered a minimum interest rate. Allowed depreciation term is 10 years, straight-line. Using the "payoff period" criterion, decide if the company should install the new machine.

12.   You have been asked to analyze the economics of acquiring one of two competitive machines. Each of these machines will perform the necessary task. The following information is available on the machines.

	Machine A	Machine B
First cost	$10,000	$7,000
Estimated salvage value (10 years hence)	4,000	2,000
Estimated annual operating and maintenance cost	1,000	1,500
Interest rate—6 per cent		

Which machine would you purchase? Justify your answer by using the "present value" and "average investment" methods.

13.   A company is considering whether or not to replace an existing machine with an improved machine. The existing machine has a book value of $9000. The new machine costs $20,000 installed; the company is also offered a $2000 trade-in allowance for the existing machine. The new machine is expected to have an eight-year economic life with no terminal salvage value. Comparative costs (annual) are:

	Old	New
Direct labor	$19,500	$12,000
Wasted material	500	400
Insurance and property taxes	500	600
Depreciation	1,500	2,000
Supplies	2,000	1,000

The company is in the 50-per-cent tax bracket, and 10 per cent is considered a minimum interest rate. Allowed depreciation term is 10 years, straight-line.

Using the payoff criterion, decide if the company should install the new machine.

14. Two different fork-lift trucks are being considered for handling materials in a given plant. Both have an estimated service life of four years. However, truck A will have a first cost of $10,000 whereas the cost of truck B is $9000. Annual disbursements for such things as labor, maintenance, repairs, and power will also be different. With truck A, they are expected to be $500 per year. With truck B, they are expected to be $500 during the first year and should increase at a rate of $100 per year thereafter. The expected salvage values for trucks A and B are $1900 and $1600, respectively. If the firm's cost of capital is 10 per cent, which is the more economic alternative?

15. The Cyprus Mines Corporation sells about 20,000 tons of copper ore per month at a price of $50 per ton. Their fixed costs amount to $40,000 per month and the company accountant estimates that 10,000 tons of ore must be sold per month to break even. A group of businessmen who have acquired some surplus armored tractors have discovered that this equipment is suitable for use in open-pit copper mining and, in fact, increases the efficiency of the extraction process. Consequently, they are offering to sell the equipment to CMC. Based on the offering price, CMC management calculated that these tractors will cost $10,000 per month to own and operate. However, they would still like to make at least the same amount of profit that they are making at their present level of sales. (They do not anticipate any reduction in sales in the future.) What must be the reduction in their variable costs as a result of using these tractors in order for CMC to accept the deal?

REFERENCES

[1] Barish, N. N. *Economic Analysis for Engineering and Managerial Decision Making*. McGraw-Hill Book Co., New York, 1962.

[2] Dean, J. *Capital Budgeting*. Columbia University Press, New York, 1951.

[3] Grant, E. L., and W. G. Ireson. *Principles of Engineering Economy* (5th ed.). Ronald Press, New York, 1970.

[4] Reisman, A. *Managerial and Engineering Economics*. Allyn and Bacon, Boston, 1971.

[5] Reisman, A. and E. S. Buffa. "A General Model for Investment Policy." *Management Science*, **8** (3), Apr. 1962.

[6] Terborgh, G. *Business Investment Policy*. Machinery and Allied Products Institute, Washington, D.C., 1958.

[7] Thuesen, H. G., and W. J. Fabrycky. *Engineering Economy* (3rd ed.). Prentice-Hall, Englewood Cliffs, N.J., 1964.

7

*L*inear *P*rogramming

DISTRIBUTION METHODS OF LINEAR PROGRAMMING

Linear programming is a new mathematical technique developed about the time of World War II. Its value in relation to production management is the fact that allocation problems of great complexity, involving a large number of variables, can often be solved in this way. Before the development of linear programming, these kinds of problems could be approached only with graphic and schematic models. The work of finding solutions was on a trial-and-error basis, and no one was ever sure the best solution had been obtained. What kinds of problems are we talking about? Let us begin with an illustrative example but one which, because of its simplicity, does not require linear programming for a solution.

Let us assume that we transport parts and materials from place to place within our plant and warehouse by means of skid trucks and skids. The parts and materials are loaded on the skids. A skid truck can then pick up a load in minimum time by sliding under the skid and lifting it off the floor. It can then be transported to its destination and set down as quickly as it was picked up. (See Figure 1.) We are interested in the redistribution, for the least cost, of empty skids to locations where they are needed. In Department A we have 16 empties and in Department B we have 20. It happens that Department C needs 20 and

An Example

147

FIGURE 1. Diagram of skid truck.

Department *D* needs 16. The empty skids can be moved two at a time with a skid truck, so that essentially we have available 8 loads at *A* and 10 at *B*. We need 10 loads at *C* and 8 at *D*. We choose as our measure of effectiveness the total distance moved by the truckers to redistribute the skids. This measure fits in with the idea of linear programming; that is, 200 feet are considered twice as costly as 100 feet. Each of the four departments has a man assigned to general material handling, so in each instance the empties are either delivered by Departments *A* and *B* or picked up by Departments *C* and *D*. The distances, supplies, and demands are indicated in Figure 2.

Here it is evident that the best procedure is to move the 8 loads at *A* to *C*, and to split the 10 loads available at *B*, 2 to *C* and 8 to *D*. This satisfies our requirements and does the entire job with the minimum distance of 3080 feet. All other combinations yield a greater total distance. We can see why by inspecting Figure 2. Our best or optimum solution does not use the longest route *AD* (225 feet) at all. If we try to use that route, we must transfer one or

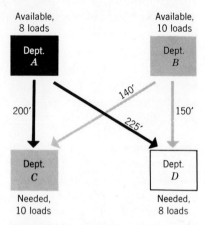

FIGURE 2. Supplies of empty skids, demands for empty skids, and move distances.

more loads from the *AC* (200 feet) route, which would cost us an extra 25 feet for each load. This is not offset by the transfer of an equivalent number of loads from route *BD* (150 feet) to *BC* (140 feet). Therefore, there is a net increase in distance of 15 feet for every load taken by the long *AD* route.

The solution for this problem is obvious, but even for this simple situation there are nine different feasible ways to accomplish the task of transferring the empty skids. If we move now to a problem of the proportions we might expect in industry (for example, 10 sources and 10 destinations or more), we can see that the answer is no longer obvious. The number of possible alternative ways of accomplishing the redistribution task is so great that we cannot consider trying to calculate exhaustively the costs of each alternative in order to find the optimum or minimum cost way. Distribution methods of linear programming provide a way of getting to the optimum solution.

DISTRIBUTION METHODS

Let us expand our problem of redistributing empty skids. We assume that we have three departments, *A*, *B*, and *C*, that have an excess of skids over and above their needs, and we have four departments, *W*, *X*, *Y*, and *Z*, that need skids. Remembering that two skids can be transported at a time, we simply tabulate in Table I the number of loads of skids available and required. Happily, skids available match skids required, although this is not a requirement for solution. In the small boxes of Table I we have also tabulated the time required to make a round trip between all combinations of departments. For example,

TABLE 1. Summary of Skids Available and Required, and Round Trip Times by Departments (distribution matrix)

From Dept. \ To Dept.	W	X	Y	Z	Empties available (loads)
A	10	22	10	20	8
B	15	20	12	8	13
C	20	12	10	15	11
Empties required (loads)	7	10	6	9	32

the round-trip time from *A* to *W* is 10 minutes. Table I is called a distribution matrix. Now, our measure of effectiveness is round-trip time, and we wish to distribute the 32 loads from Departments *A*, *B*, and *C* to Departments *W*, *X*, *Y*, and *Z* in such a way that the total time spent is at a minimum, within the restrictions imposed by skid loads available and required.

An Initial Solution
Let us make a beginning by assigning the various loads in an arbitrary way, ignoring the time values. We begin in the upper left-hand corner of the matrix (the so-called northwest corner) and we note that *A* has 8 loads available and *W* needs 7 loads. We assign the 7 from *A* to *W*. (See Table II). Circled numbers represent assigned loads. For example, 7 in box *AW* means 7 loads from *A* to *W*. We have not yet used up *A*'s supply, so we move to the right under column *X* and assign the balance of *A*'s supply, 1 load, to *X*. Looking at the bottom of *X*'s column, we note that it has a total requirement of 10, we we drop down to row *B* and assign the balance of *X*'s requirements, 9 loads, from *B*'s supply of 13. We then move to the right again and assign the balance of *B*'s

TABLE II.   Northwest Initial Solution

To Dept. / From Dept.	W	X	Y	Z	Empties available (loads)
A	10 ⑦	22 ①	10	20	8
B	15	20 ⑨	12 ④	8	13
C	20	12	10 ②	15 ⑨	11
Empties required (loads)	7	10	6	9	32

Total time required:

$$AW, \; 7 \times 10 = 70 \text{ minutes}$$
$$AX, \; 1 \times 22 = 22 \text{ minutes}$$
$$BX, \; 9 \times 20 = 180 \text{ minutes}$$
$$BY, \; 4 \times 12 = 48 \text{ minutes}$$
$$CY, \; 2 \times 10 = 20 \text{ minutes}$$
$$CZ, \; 9 \times 15 = \underline{135 \text{ minutes}}$$
$$475 \text{ minutes}$$

supply of 4 loads to *Y*. We continue in this way, stair-stepping down the matrix until all of the arbitrary assignments have been made, as in Table II. The total time required for this solution, 475 minutes, is calculated in Table II below the matrix. The general method of solution, which we shall describe, is called the stepping-stone method. The squares that have assignments are often called *stone squares*, and those without assignments, *water squares*. We shall refer to them simply as squares with assignments and squares without assignments, or *open squares*.

Is the initial northwest solution the best one? We can answer this by successively examining the squares without assignments to see if total time is reduced by shifting assignments to them. When all possible shifts in assignments of this nature have been made, we can be certain of an optimum solution. Let us see how this procedure can be done. First, we want to be sure that any shift made conforms to the restrictions of available and required loads. Let us select the first square without an assignment in the first column, square *BW*. If we were to add one load each to *BW* and *AX* and subtract one load each from *AW* and *BX*, we would still satisfy the restrictions of available and required loads. Table III shows us that such a shift would not be advantageous because

Improving the Initial Solution

TABLE III.	Evaluation of Square *BW* for Possible Improvement				
From Dept. \ To Dept.	*W*	*X*	*Y*	*Z*	Empties available (loads)
A	(−) 10 ⑦ →	22 ① (+)	10	20	8
B	(+) ← 15	20 ⑨ (−)	12 ④	8	13
C	20	12 ②	10 ⑨	15	11
Empties required (loads)	7	10	6	9	32

Evaluation of square *BW*: for one unit, change in cost is:

$$+15 - 10 + 22 - 20 = +7$$

This would result in a net increase in the total time; therefore the changes are not made.

we would be shifting from lower cost routes to higher cost routes. We would be adding a load each to routes BW and AX at a cost of $15 + 22 = 37$ minutes and subtracting a load each from AW and BX at a saving of $10 + 20 = 30$ minutes, or a net increase of $37 - 30 = 7$ minutes per load.

Each square that has no assignment may be evaluated for improvement in a similar way. The pattern is not always a rectangular one, however. In Table IV we show the pattern required to evaluate square CW for possible improvement. What we must have is a closed path starting at the square to be evaluated, with right-angle turns only at squares that already have assignments, proceeding either clockwise or counterclockwise. Squares may be skipped to get to the corners, as illustrated in Table IV. No diagonal movement is permitted. Beginning at the square being evaluated, we assign a plus sign, since we propose to add a load, and alternate with minus and plus signs as we go around the closed path. There is ordinarily only one closed path to evaluate for a given open square if the initial arbitrary solution has been established properly. We see, according to Table IV, that there is no advantage in making any shifts to square CW, so we proceed systematically to evaluate the unassigned squares in column X.

TABLE IV.	Evaluation of Square CW for Possible Improvement				
To Dept. From Dept.	W	X	Y	Z	Empties available (loads)
A	10 (−) ⑦	22 (+) ①	10	20	8
B	15	20 (−) ⑨	12 (+) ④	8	13
C	20 (+)	12	10 (−) ②	15 ⑨	11
Empties required (loads)	7	10	6	9	32

Evaluation of square CW: for one unit, change in cost is:

$$+20 - 10 + 22 - 20 + 12 - 10 = +14$$

This would also result in a net increase in the total time and, therefore, the changes are not made.

Square CX is the only open square in column X to evaluate at this time, and it is evaluated in Table V by the same procedure. Here we see that there is an advantage in making a shift, because for each load shifted to CX and BY from BX and CY there is a net decrease of 6 minutes in roundtrip time. Since we have found an advantageous shift, we want to take maximum advantage of it by increasing the assignment at CX to the maximum. The shift in assignments is limited to 2 loads, however, because that is the existing assignment at CY, and we cannot reduce it below zero. Therefore, the maximum improvement in the solution that we can effect at CX is 2 loads at a time saving of 6 minutes per load, or 12 minutes. The new total time is now reduced to 463 minutes. We make the changes in assignment indicated and the resulting assignments to the four squares affected are:

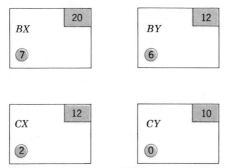

We proceed systematically through the table, evaluating each open square and making shifts in assignments when they are advantageous. Of course, we may find that squares which previously indicated no improvement possible may later yield improvement because of subsequent changes. This process is continued until all open squares show no further improvement.

An Optimal Solution

At this point, an optimal solution has been obtained and is shown in Table VI. The total time required by the optimal solution is 330 minutes, which is about 30 per cent less than the original northwest corner solution. This reduction in total time can be accomplished by the column-by-column evaluation of 13 open squares, 6 of which yield improvement. The first time through the table, no improvement is obtained from BW, CW, and CY, but squares CX, AY, AZ, and BZ, in sequence, yield improvement. The second time through the table, BW, CW, AX, and BX yield no improvement, but AY and CY do. At this point the solution is optimal, because a reevaluation of all squares without assignments shows no further improvement possible.

TABLE V. Evaluation of Square CX for Possible Improvement

From Dept. \ To Dept.	W	X	Y	Z	Empties available (loads)
A	10 — ⑦	22 — ①	10	20	8
B	15	20 (−) — ⑨	12 (+) — ④	8	13
C	20	12 (+)	10 — ②(−)	15 — ⑨	11
Empties required (loads)	7	10	6	9	32

Evaluation of square CX: for one unit, change in cost is:

$$+12 - 20 + 12 - 10 = -6$$

Since this is a net improvement, increase the assignment to CX to the maximum possible. This is limited by the assignment for CY which can be reduced by only 2. Maximum improvement at CX is, therefore, $2(-6) = -12$.

New total time = $475 - 12 = 463$ minutes.

TABLE VI. An Optimal Solution. Evaluation of All Squares without Assignments in This Table Result in no Further Improvement

From Dept. \ To Dept.	W	X	Y	Z	Empties available (loads)
A	10 — ⑦	22	10 — ①	20	8
B	15	20	12 — ④	8 — ⑨	13
C	20	12 — ⑩	10 — ①	15	11
Empties required (loads)	7	10	6	9	32

Total time required, 330 minutes.

This procedure is tedious, even for a small problem, but it must be remembered that "dog work" of this nature is very well suited to the electronic computer. Therefore, our interest in solving problems by the methods described should lie in acquiring an understanding of what is being done rather than in an attempt to develop skill in the methods. We should point out also that the initial northwest corner solution, which we used to explain the method, is definitely not the best way to begin a solution, although it is probably the easiest way to begin. We shall comment on improved starting solutions under, "Techniques for Simplifying Problem Solution."

Another aspect of the mechanics of developing a solution which we should mention is the condition known as degeneracy. Degeneracy occurs in distribution problems when, in shifting assignments to take advantage of a potential improvement, two of the existing assignments go to zero, instead of only one, as has been true in our previous examples. Examination of the problem in Table VII (which is only slightly different from the example that we have been working with) shows that this is about to happen. This problem was set up in the usual way, and an initial northwest corner solution was established. The open squares were evaluated column by column, and changes in assignments were made when they indicated improvement potential. In Table VII we are evaluating square BZ by the closed-path pattern shown. A potential improvement is indicated, since shifting one unit saves 15 minutes. We wish to press this advantage to the maximum by shifting as many

Degeneracy in Distribution Problems

TABLE VII.   Evaluation of Square *BZ* Produces Degeneracy

To Dept. From Dept.	W	X	Y	Z	Empties available (loads)
A	10 ⑤	22	10	20 ③	8
B	15	20 ⑤ (−)	12 ⑧	8 (+)	13
C	20	12 ⑥ (+)	10	15 (−) ⑤	11
Empties required (loads)	5	11	8	8	32

loads as possible. We are limited by both squares *BX* and *CZ*, each of which have 5 loads assigned to them. When the shift in assignments is made, both *BX* and *CZ* go to zero. This is shown in the resulting distribution matrix of Table VIII. Several of the open squares, *CW, AX, BX, CY,* and *CZ,* cannot be evaluated because a closed path cannot be established for them.

The degeneracy can be resolved by regarding one of the two squares where the allocations disappeared as an allocated square with zero allocation. (Think of it as an infinitesimally small allocation.) This is illustrated in Table IX. The zero allocation square is then used to complete paths in the usual way. If it happens in subsequent manipulations that the zero allocation square is the one that limits shifts in assignment, the zero allocation is shifted to the square being evaluated and the usual procedure is then continued. This is illustrated in Table X. When square *CY* is evaluated, potential improvement is indicated, but no shift in actual assignment can be made because of the limitation of the zero allocation. The zero allocation is then moved to *CY* and the procedure is continued until an optimal solution is obtained.

Unequal Supply and Demand We may now bring up the question of the handling of a problem where supply and demand are unequal. Suppose that, in our problem, the total of loads available from the three departments is 37, but the four departments state a need for a total of only 32. This situation can be handled in the problem by creating a dummy department to receive the extra 5 loads. The nonexistent department is assigned zero round-trip times,

TABLE VIII. Problem Now Degenerate, Squares *CW, AX, BX, CY* and *CZ* Cannot Be Evaluated

From Dept. \ To Dept.	W	X	Y	Z	Empties available (loads)
A	10 ⑤	22	10	20 ③	8
B	15	20	12 ⑧	8 ⑤	13
C	20	12 ⑪	10	15	11
Empties required (loads)	5	11	8	8	32

TABLE IX. Degeneracy Resolved

From Dept. \ To Dept.	W	X	Y	Z	Empties available (loads)
A	10 ⑤	22	10	20 ③	8
B	15	20	12 ⑧	8 ⑤	13
C	20	12 ⑪	10 ⓪	15	11
Empties required (loads)	5	11	8	8	32

since the loads will never be sent. The optimum solution then assigns 32 of the 37 available loads in the most economical way to the four real departments and assigns the balance to the dummy department.

First, we can simplify the arithmetic complexity considerably by two methods. A little thought about the illustrative example we used will convince us that it is the cost differences that are important in determining the optimal allocation rather than their absolute values. There-

Techniques for Simplifying Problem Solution

TABLE X. Shift of Zero Allocation When It Is the Limiting Allocation

From Dept. \ To Dept.	W	X	Y	Z	Empties available (loads)
A	10 ⑤	22	10	20 ③	8
B	15	20	12 ⑧ (−)	8 ⑤ (+)	13
C	20	12 ⑪	10 ⓪ (+)	15 ⓪ (−)	11
Empties required (loads)	5	11	8	8	32

fore, we can reduce all costs by a fixed amount, and the resulting allocations will be unchanged. In our illustrative example, we may subtract 8 from all distribution time values so that the numbers with which we must work are of such magnitude that many evaluations can be accomplished by inspection. Another simplification in the arithmetic may be accomplished by expressing the rim conditions in the simplest terms, for example, in thousands of units so that we can work with one or two digit numbers only.

Getting an Advantageous Initial Solution.   The northwest corner initial solution is actually not used a great deal in practice, since it is ordinarily a rather poor solution which will involve a number of steps to develop an optimal solution. Placing the lowest cost cell in the northwest corner gives us an advantageous start. The usual procedure is to start with some solution by inspecting the most promising routes, entering allocations which are consistent with the rim conditions. In establishing such an initial solution, the only rules to be observed are that there must be exactly $m + n - 1$ allocations, and it must be possible to evaluate all open squares by the closed path methods previously discussed. If the initial solution turns out to be degenerate, it is a simple matter to increase the allocations to the exact number required by resorting to the zero allocation. There are a number of short-cut methods which are commonly used such as row minimum, column minimum, matrix minimum, and VAM [3, 8, 12, 14].

USES FOR DISTRIBUTION METHODS

The broad problems of the relation of factories to warehouses, warehouses to distributors, etc., represent one large area in the usefulness of linear programming. This is emphasized in the multiplant situation where shipping costs to various distributors or warehouses differ. It is easy to see that this situation parallels the example of the distribution of empty skids which we have been using. The factories have capacities of products available and the warehouses or distributors have demands for the products. A minimum shipping cost solution is needed. The limits of the problem can be expanded. The cost of production at the different factories may vary because of differences in labor rates, raw material costs, etc. We can, therefore, determine an allocation that minimizes the sum of production plus shipping costs within the framework of product demands at the various warehouses. This eliminates the chance of adopting a decision that would result in suboptimization if the two decisions are made separately; that is, a given shipping schedule might be a minimum cost schedule when considered separately but not the minimum when production and shipping costs are considered together.

Other important broad problems can be evaluated within this general framework. Suppose one of the factories is a high-cost producer. What is the effect on combined production plus shipping cost of shutting down this plant and supplying solely from the others, or of supplying from the others by overtime work or additional shifts, or of building a new plant in an advantageous location? Different locations can also be evaluated. The same sort of questions could be evaluated regarding warehouses.

Within the confines of a particular factory, there are transportation problems for which linear programming methods may be used profitably; the assignment of orders to alternate machines that have different production costs may be formulated in a parallel way.

THE SIMPLEX METHOD OF LINEAR PROGRAMMING

The simplex method is more general in scope of application than are the distribution methods. Distribution-type problems, which we have just discussed, may be solved by the simplex method also, but with a greater amount of work. The simplex method, however, can be used where distribution methods cannot. We shall set up an example for simplex solution so that we may see the nature of the problems to which the simplex method is applicable. Once the model for a problem is established in terms of the simplex method, we may regard the solution more or less as a mechanical procedure. If the rules for solution are followed precisely, given the simplex model of the problem, the answers will be obtained. We shall discuss an elementary description of the mechanics of a simplex solution later in this chapter.

For simple problems we can show graphically how the restrictions in a linear programming problem limit the possible solutions and also see how the objective function is used to select the optimum solution. To do this, let us assume a simple situation for a plant which manufactures washing machines and dryers. The major manufacturing departments are the Stamping Department, the Motor and Transmission Department, and final assembly lines for the washer and dryer. The Stamping Depart-

Graphic Interpretation of the Simplex Method of Linear Programming ment fabricates a large number of the metal parts for both the washer and dryer. Monthly department capacities are:

Stamping Dept.	10,000 washers or	10,000 dryers
Motor and Transmission Dept.	16,000 washers or	7,000 dryers
Washer Assembly Dept.	9,000 washers	—
Dryer Assembly Dept.	—	5,000 dryers

In other words, the same facilities for the two products are used for stamping and for motor and transmission. The Stamping Department can produce parts for 10,000 washers per month or 10,000 dryers per month, as well as combination amounts of washers and dryers. We have a similar situation with the Motor and Transmission Department, but the final assembly lines are separate for the two products.

The contribution to fixed cost and profit (sales value less variable costs) is $90 per washer and $100 per dryer. We wish to know how many of each product to produce in order to maximize contribution, assuming that we can sell what we make.

First, let us set up the restrictions of the problem. We shall denote the number of washers by x and the number of dryers by y. The simplest

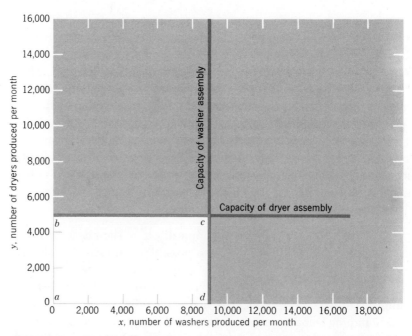

FIGURE 3. Graphic illustration of limitations imposed by the assembly line capacity of washers and dryers.

restrictions are those imposed by the two final assembly lines. They indicate that the number of washers per month must be less than or equal to 9000 and the number of dryers must be less than or equal to 5000. These are plotted in Figure 3, the shaded areas indicating those parts of the graph which are eliminated as feasible solutions to the problem by limitations of assembly line capacity. Any solution to the problem must be a combination of a number of washers and dryers which falls within area *abcd*.

The other restrictions to the problem are only slightly different. The stamping department capacity limits production to 10,000 washers per month, 10,000 dryers per month, or any comparable combination of washer and dryer production. Satisfactory combinations are 8000 washers, and 2000 dryers, 5000 each, etc. This restriction is shown in Figure 4 as a straight line which restricts further the space allowing feasible solutions. Figure 4 also shows the limitations imposed by the capacities of the Motor and Transmission Department, represented by another straight line which goes through the two points $(x = 0, y = 7000)$ and $(x = 16,000, y = 0)$. Combinations of washer and dryer production which are equivalent fall on this straight line as before;

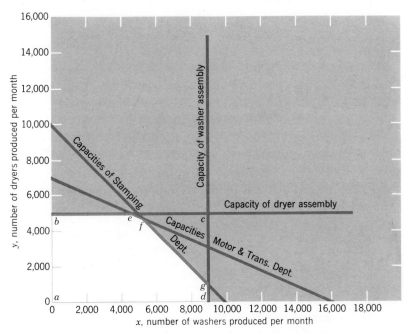

FIGURE 4. Remaining limitations imposed by capacities of the Stamping Department and the Motor and Transmission Department. The area enclosed by *abefgd* includes all feasible solutions to the problem.

for example, washers 8000, dryers 3500. We now know that the combination of washer and dryer production which we are seeking lies within the area *abefgd*. All other combinations have been eliminated by the stated restrictions of the problem. The remaining question is: Which feasible combination will maximize contribution?

We said previously that contribution was earned at the rate of $90 per washer and $100 per dryer. Our objective function is then

$$90x + 100y = \text{max}$$

We want the combination of the number of washers and dryers produced that is both feasible and maximizes contribution. Let us select arbitrarily some contribution to see how it looks graphically. At a total contribution of $450,000, for example, the objective function becomes

$$90x + 100y = 450,000$$

when

$$x = 0, \qquad y = 4500$$

and

$$y = 0, \qquad x = 5000$$

The line passing through these two points is shown as the $450,000 line in Figure 5. This line defines all combinations of washer and dryer production that yields a total contribution of $450,000.

Now let us choose a larger value of contribution, perhaps $630,000. The objective function becomes

$$90x + 100y = 630,000$$

when

$$x = 0, \qquad y = 6300$$

and

$$y = 0, \qquad x = 7000$$

The line passing through these two points is also shown in Figure 5 as the $630,000 line. It defines all combinations of washer and dryer production that yield a total contribution of $630,000. Note that it is parallel to the $450,000 line. If we increase contribution again to $900,000, we have the $900,000 line shown in Figure 5. We can see now that we shall be limited in the size of total contribution by point *f*. It defines the combination of washer and dryer production that produces the largest possible contribution within the space of feasible solutions. Reading from the graph, point *f* is approximately at the coordinates, $x = 5300$, $y = 4700$. Since point *f* is the intersection of the two lines that define

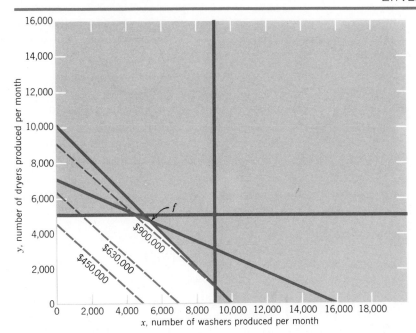

FIGURE 5. Contribution lines plotted to show the effect of larger and larger contributions. The contribution lines appear as parallel lines. The maximum possible contribution within the area of permitted solutions is defined by a line through point *f*.

stamping capacity and motor and transmission capacity, we can determine point *f* exactly by solving the equations of these two lines simultaneously. These two equations are of the form $y = mx + b$, where m is the slope of the line and b is the y intercept. The two equations are:

Stamping capacity,

$$y = 10{,}000 - x \qquad (1)$$

Motor and transmission capacity,

$$y = 7000 - \tfrac{7}{16} x \qquad (2)$$

Solving simultaneously,

$$10{,}000 - x = 7000 - \tfrac{7}{16} x$$

$$\tfrac{9}{16} x = 3000$$

$$x = 5333 \text{ washers}$$

Using $x = 5333$ in Equation 1,

$$y = 10{,}000 - 5333 = 4667 \text{ dryers}$$

Of course, this agrees with the approximate values read from the graph. Note that all the lines restricting the problem, as well as the lines representing the objective function, are straight lines. All the relationships are linear and thus the term, linear programming.

The graphical interpretation of linear programming can also be extended to three-dimensional space. For example, we could show three products, perhaps washers, dryers, and combination washer-dryers. The lines which represent restrictions on the problem become planes. Feasible solutions appear in a volume instead of an area, and optimal solutions occur at the intersections of planes instead of lines. Beyond three-dimensional problems, there is no direct geometric representation.

A SIMPLE PROBLEM FOR ALGEBRAIC SOLUTION

Let us assume a problem situation. We are bulk producers of a single plastic sheet material which we sell in three sizes, that is, thicknesses. We have two complete setups for production, both erected on the same site; we shall refer to them as plant A and plant B. Plant B is of later design and was built specifically to produce sizes 1 and 2 economically, since these two sizes had the greatest demand. However, plant B is less economical than A for size 3. The figures are summarized in Table XI. We also see in Table XI that the variable costs of operation per hour of plant A are $250 compared to $300 for plant B, and that both plants can be operated up to 100 hours per week but not more than that. The hourly variable costs include all labor, supplies, power, etc., but do not include raw material costs. These are identical for a given size run in either plant and so may be considered irrelevant for this problem.

TABLE XI. Time Requirements, Variable Hourly Costs, and Total Time Availability for Plants A and B

	Hours per 100 Pounds	
Size	Plant A	Plant B
1	0.25	0.20
2	0.40	0.25
3	0.35	0.40
Variable costs/hour	$250	$300
Maximum available hours per week	100	100

Table XII gives us sales revenue figures and maximum demands for the three sizes. In planning for production, we can assume that amounts up to and including these figures can be produced, or less than these figures if it is more economical.

The big question is: How should production be allocated to the two plants for the three sizes in order to maximize some index of profit, our ultimate objective? First, our measure of effectiveness is C, contribution: the difference between revenue and variable costs. Second, Table XI gives us incremental or variable costs and limitations on production time available. Finally, Table XII gives us data on revenue and also gives us limitations on how much we can sell. Let us try to express these ideas more precisely.

Since we have limitations on the number of hours that the two plants can operate, and since we know the time required to produce each size on each machine, we can write for plant A:

Symbolic Formulation of the Problem

> (unit hours for size 1) × (amount of size 1)
> + (unit hours for size 2) × (amount of size 2)
> + (unit hours for size 3) × (amount of size 3)
> cannot exceed 100 hours

All of the data for this word statement come from Table XI. To put it in symbolic form, we let x represent the amounts of each product. By using subscripts, x_{1A} is the amount of size 1 produced in plant A, x_{2A} the amount of size 2 in plant A, etc. The equivalent statement in symbolic form is:

$$0.25x_{1A} + 0.40x_{2A} + 0.35x_{3A} \leq 100 \qquad (3)$$

This says exactly what the word statement did. The symbol $\leq$ is read "less than or equal to." It refers only to the hours to be worked in plant A on each of the three sizes. Similarly, we may write an equivalent symbolic statement for plant B:

$$0.20x_{1B} + 0.25x_{2B} + 0.40x_{3B} \leq 100 \qquad (4)$$

TABLE XII.   Sales Revenue and Maximum Demand for Three Sizes

Size	Sales Revenue/100 Pounds	Maximum Demand per Week, 100 Pounds
1	$100	310
2	$120	300
3	$150	125

Now we have six unknowns, x_{1A}, x_{1B}, x_{2A}, x_{2B}, x_{3A}, and x_{3B}, the amounts in 100 pounds of each of the three sizes to be produced in each of the two plants.

Symbolic statements (3) and (4) are called inequalities or inequations. In essence, they state that the total time allocated to each of the three sizes might not equal 100 hours; that is, there could be some idle time. So for plant A, if we let W_A be the idle time, we have an equation with W_A taking up the slack:

$$0.25x_{1A} + 0.40x_{2A} + 0.35x_{3A} + W_A = 100 \qquad (5)$$

The idle time, W_A, could be zero, but we shall let the solution tell us what it should be in order that our profit measure may be maximum. Similarly, W_B is the idle time for plant B; therefore we have

$$0.20x_{1B} + 0.25x_{2B} + 0.40x_{3B} + W_B = 100 \qquad (6)$$

Now we turn our attention to the total amounts produced, which we know cannot exceed 310, 300, and 125 for the three sizes, respectively, because of limitations of demand. Since the x's represent the amounts produced, we know that the amount of size 1 produced in plant A plus the amount produced in plant B cannot exceed 310 or

$$x_{1A} + x_{1B} \leq 310 \qquad (7)$$

Similarly, for sizes 2 and 3:

$$x_{2A} + x_{2B} \leq 300 \qquad (8)$$

$$x_{3A} + x_{3B} \leq 125 \qquad (9)$$

As before, we know that we might not produce the maximum amount of each of the three sizes, so again we take up the slack by three new variables W_1, W_2, and W_3, and we end up with three equations instead of inequations:

$$x_{1A} + x_{1B} + W_1 = 310 \qquad (10)$$

$$x_{2A} + x_{2B} + W_2 = 300 \qquad (11)$$

$$x_{3A} + x_{3B} + W_3 = 125 \qquad (12)$$

Finally, we have one more statement to make which, when expressed symbolically, will complete the model of our problem. It is the profit function to be maximized, which we defined merely as contribution, the revenue minus incremental or variable costs, or:

$$C = \text{revenue} - \text{variable costs} = \text{maximum}$$

From Table XII we have the revenue per 100 pounds given as $100,

$120, and $150 for the three sizes, respectively. If we multiply each of these by the amounts produced and then add them up, we have the total revenue:

$$\text{Revenue} = 100(x_{1A} + x_{1B}) + 120(x_{2A} + x_{2B}) + 150(x_{3A} + x_{3B})$$

To compute the variable costs, we have the cost per hour of plant A given as $250 and plant B as $300. If we multiply the total hours worked in plant A by $250 and the total hours worked in plant B by $300 and add them, we have the total variable cost for the production plan:

$$\text{Variable cost} = 250(0.25x_{1A} + 0.40x_{2A} + 0.35x_{3A}) \\ + 300(0.20x_{1B} + 0.25x_{2B} + 0.40x_{3B})$$

Since $C =$ revenue $-$ variable costs

$$C = 100(x_{1A} + x_{1B}) + 120(x_{2A} + x_{2B}) + 150(x_{3A} + x_{3B}) \\ - 250(0.25x_{1A} + 0.40x_{2A} + 0.35x_{3A}) \\ - 300(0.20x_{1B} + 0.25x_{2B} + 0.40_{3B}) = \text{max}$$

The profit function can be simplified by multiplying through the factors and collecting like terms to obtain

$$C = 37.5x_{1A} + 40x_{1B} + 20x_{2A} + 45x_{2B} + 62.5x_{3A} + 30x_{3B} = \text{max} \quad (13)$$

Term C actually represents the sum of the difference between revenue and variable cost for each size on each machine, multiplied by the amount produced. The total, C, is the thing that we want to be as big as possible, and this is indicated by setting C equal to "max."

We now have 5 equations and 11 unknowns, plus the objective function which we wish to maximize. Let us put them all together with like variables in columns as shown *above* Table XIII. Now, if we place the variables at the heads of the columns and list only the coefficients below, we have Table XIII. In this table we assume that in each column the coefficients are zero where no number is given.

Table XIII begins to look like the simplex matrix, the tabular format used in the solution of simplex linear programming problems. In this form it can be solved by an iterative process to determine the value of each of the 11 variables. An iterative process is an arithmetic procedure which repeats itself again and again by some standard set of rules. From our previous discussion and from basic algebra, we know that with 5 equations, only 5 of the variables can have positive values and at least 6 are zero. The simplex solution tells us which variables are zero and the value of the others for the condition when C is the maximum possible. The solution for this problem is:

Equations with Like Variables in Columns

$$0.25x_{1A} + 0.40x_{2A} + 0.35x_{3A} + W_A = 100 \quad (5)$$

$$0.20x_{1B} + 0.25x_{2B} + 0.40x_{3B} + W_B = 100 \quad (6)$$

$$x_{1A} + x_{1B} + W_1 = 310 \quad (10)$$

$$x_{2A} + x_{2B} + W_2 = 300 \quad (11)$$

$$x_{3A} + x_{3B} + W_3 = 125 \quad (12)$$

$$37.5x_{1A} + 40x_{1B} + 20x_{2A} + 45x_{2B} + 62.5x_{3A} + 30x_{3B} = \max \quad (13)$$

TABLE XIII. Matrix of Coefficients of 5 Equations and 11 Variables

x_{1A}	x_{1B}	x_{2A}	x_{2B}	x	x_{3B}	W_A	W_B	$W.$	W_2	W_3	Right Side of Equation
0.25		0.40		0.35		1					100
	0.20		0.25		0.40		1				100
1	1							1			310
		1	1						1		300
				1	1					1	125
37.5	40	20	45	62.5	30						max

C is a maximum of \$33,250 when the 11 variables take on the following values: (The mechanics of the simplex solution for this problem are developed later in this chapter.)

$$x_{1A} = 185 \text{ hundred pounds} \quad \text{(size 1 in plant } A\text{)}$$
$$x_{1B} = 125 \text{ hundred pounds} \quad \text{(size 1 in plant } B\text{)}$$
$$x_{2A} = 0 \text{ hundred pounds} \quad \text{(size 2 in plant } A\text{)}$$
$$x_{2B} = 300 \text{ hundred pounds} \quad \text{(size 2 in plant } B\text{)}$$
$$x_{3A} = 125 \text{ hundred pounds} \quad \text{(size 3 in plant } A\text{)}$$
$$x_{3B} = 0 \text{ hundred pounds} \quad \text{(size 3 in plant } B\text{)}$$
$$W_A = 10 \text{ hours} \quad \text{(idle time in plant } A\text{)}$$
$$W_B = 0 \text{ hours} \quad \text{(idle time in plant } B\text{)}$$
$$W_1 = 0 \text{ hundred pounds} \quad \text{(excess demand, size 1)}$$
$$W_2 = 0 \text{ hundred pounds} \quad \text{(excess demand, size 2)}$$
$$W_3 = 0 \text{ hundred pounds} \quad \text{(excess demand, size 3)}$$

Let us see if these values check with the restrictions on capacity and demand of 310, 300, and 125 hundred pounds for the three sizes, respectively. The solution gives us:

	Produced, Hundred Pounds		
	Size 1	Size 2	Size 3
Plant A	185	0	125
Plant B	125	300	0
Totals	310	300	125

We also established 100 hours as the maximum time available per week in each plant. We convert the amounts produced of each size in each plant to equivalent hours by multiplying by the unit times required. Then we have the following:

Size	Plant A, Hours		Plant B, Hours	
1	$0.25 \times 185 =$	46.25	$0.20 \times 125 =$	25.00
2	$0.40 \times 0 =$	0	$0.25 \times 300 =$	75.00
3	$0.35 \times 125 =$	43.75	$0.40 \times 0 =$	0
Idle hours		10.00		0
		100.00		100.00

Therefore, the solution tells us that our measure of profit will be maximized if we (a) meet the demand figures, (b) keep plant A idle for 10 hours, and produce sizes 1 and 3 in the amounts shown, and (c) work plant B the full 100 hours and produce sizes 1 and 2 in the amounts shown.

This is a simple problem compared to the complexities of real-life industrial problems. Even then, the answer is not obvious. From the time requirements in plants A and B for the different sizes, we might suspect that plant B should emphasize sizes 1 and 2. After all, it was designed to produce those sizes economically. However, the distribution of productive hours is certainly not obvious, nor is the fact that plant A should be idle 10 hours.

Variations of
the Problem

We should note that the linear programming model that we have been working with can yield programs with other basic objectives. For example, a program to maximize equipment utilization would require an objective function where the sum of the two slack variables W_A and W_B is at a minimum. Alternatively, an objective of maximum tonnage could be programmed by using an objective function where the sum of all of the x's is maximized. The same five problem equations would be used in both instances.

General
Applicability

The problem we have used as an example is representative of a large class of problems where we must *allocate limited resources among competing activities or uses*. The models for specific problems may involve *restrictions* as illustrated in our sample problem. For example, we were permitted to utilize machine hours up to the maximum of 100 hours, or demand was limited to certain specific maximums. We do not mean to imply by this example that all problems involve formulations of this type. We can handle equally well *requirements, equalities,* and *approximations*. By requirements we mean that a lower limit is specified instead of an upper limit. In our previous example, we may have wanted to specify that neither plant A nor plant B could be operated less than 40 hours per week. This could have been stated in the form of two more inequalities, one each for plants A and B. Equations would have resulted had we specified that the two plants must be operated exactly 100 hours each. If we had wanted the two plants to operate *about* 100 hours each, but slight variation either way could be tolerated, we could employ approximations in our model. These different kinds of specifications can be employed alternately in the same basic problem to evaluate the effect on the profit function of different policies regarding working hours, utilization of equipment, etc.

SIMPLEX SOLUTION

We shall develop the basic simplex method of solution by means of a simplified problem. A manufacturer has two products, I and II, both of which are made in two steps by machines A and B. The process times per hundred for the two products on the two machines are (setup times are negligible):

Product	Machine A	Machine B
I	4 hours	5 hours
II	5 hours	2 hours

For the coming period, machine A has available 100 hours and B has available 80 hours.

The contribution for product I is $10 per 100 units and for product II, $5 per 100 units. The manufacturer is in a market upswing and can sell as much as he can produce of both products for the immediate period ahead. We wish to determine how much of products I and II he should produce to maximize his contribution.

We adopt a system of notation. We let x_I be the amount in 100's of product I and x_{II} the amount in 100's of product II which will be produced. We are limited only by the available hours on machines A and B, so we know that the sum of the times spent producing the two products on the two machines cannot exceed 100 hours for machine A and 80 hours for machine B. We can express this symbolically as:

Formulation of the Problem

$$\text{Machine } A \qquad 4x_I + 5x_{II} \leq 100 \qquad (14)$$

$$\text{Machine } B \qquad 5x_I + 2x_{II} \leq 80 \qquad (15)$$

Since the total contributions, which we want to be as large as possible, depends only on the amounts of the two products produced, we can state:

$$10x_I + 5x_{II} = \max \qquad (16)$$

This is our *objective function*. We want to find the combination of values for x_I and x_{II} which fits into the restrictions imposed by the manufacturing times for the two products, and the total available time, as expressed by Equations 14 and 15, and in addition makes the total contribution, as expressed by Equation 16, a maximum.

We want to recognize that it is entirely possible that machines A and B could have idle time. If W_A is the idle time on machine A and W_B the idle time on machine B, Equations 14 and 15 become:

$$4x_I + 5x_{II} + W_A = 100 \qquad (17)$$

$$5x_I + 2x_{II} + W_B = 80 \qquad (18)$$

Let us rearrange Equations 17 and 18 by placing the variables x_I, x_{II}, W_A, and W_B at the heads of columns, with only the coefficients below

Initial Solution

in columns. Also, we move the numbers on the right-hand side of the equation to the left. This is done in Table XIV.

We have two equations and four unknowns. Recall by our previous discussion that a maximum of two of these variables can have positive values and that at least two of them must be zero. This gives us the key to establishing an initial solution, which we may then use as a basis for improvement. If we start out by assuming that x_I and x_{II} are both zero, it is easy to see by Equations 17 and 18 that W_A must be 100 and W_B must be 80. Admittedly this solution is a very poor one because it says that all the available time is idle, but it fits the problem equations and allows us to start. We place this initial or trivial solution in the matrix array, as in Table XIV. Note that we have placed the coefficients of the objective function above the array in Table XV. The stub identifies the variables in the solution and shows their values. To the left in the stub, we have the contribution rates of the variables in the objective function. Neither W_A nor W_B are in the objective function, so zeros are placed in this column. This makes good sense; if the two machines are completely idle, the contribution is zero. The value of the objective function at this point is

$$10(0) + 5(0) + (0)W_A + (0)W_B = 0$$

Before proceeding, let us name the various parts of the matrix. Figure 6 shows the nomenclature of the various parts of the matrix. The solution stub will always contain three columns. The body and identity will vary in size, depending on the particular problem.

To improve the initial solution, we must have a measure of the potential improvement that we would make in the objective function by bringing some of the variables into the solution which are now zero instead of the variables that are now in the solution. We shall develop an *index row* which will be placed just below the present initial matrix. These index numbers will appear under the constant column, the body, and the identity. They are calculated from the formula:

Index number =
Σ (numbers in column) $\times$ (corresponding number in objective column)
$\quad$ $-$ (number in objective row at head of column)

For our problem, the index row numbers are:

(1) Index number for constant column

$$= (100 \times 0 + 80 \times 0) - 0 = 0$$

TABLE XIV.	Problem Equations in Matrix Form			
	x_I	x_{II}	W_A	W_B
100	4	5	1	0
80	5	2	0	1

(2) Index number for first column of body

$$= (4 \times 0 + 5 \times 0) - 10 = -10$$

(3) Index number for second column of body

$$= (5 \times 0 + 2 \times 0) - 5 = -5$$

(4) Index number for first column of identity

$$= (1 \times 0 + 0 \times 0) - 0 = 0$$

(5) Index number for second column of identity

$$= (0 \times 0 + 1 \times 0) - 0 = 0$$

We now place the index numbers in the initial simplex matrix. (See Table XVI.)

We see that the index row is merely the objective row preceded by minus signs. This occurs only when the objective column contains all zeros.

The larger the negative number, the greater is the potential improvement per unit of the new variable to be introduced. If all of the numbers under the body and identity of the index row were zero or positive,

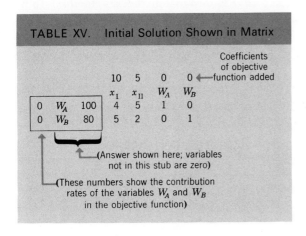

TABLE XV.   Initial Solution Shown in Matrix

FIGURE 6. Nomenclature of the simplex matrix.

no further improvement could be obtained, which would indicate that the solution presented in the stub was an optimal solution.

We see from Table XVI that the column headed by the variable x_I has the greatest improvement potential, so we select it as the *key column*. This selection means that the variable x_I will be introduced into the solution in favor of W_A or W_B. To determine whether x_I will replace W_A or W_B, we must select a *key row*. To do this, *we divide each number in the constant column by the corresponding positive nonzero number in the key column.* The resulting quotients are compared and the *key row* is selected as the row yielding the smallest nonnegative quotient. For our problem, the quotients are:

$$\text{First row} \quad \frac{100}{4} = 25$$

$$\text{Second row} \quad \frac{80}{5} = 16 \text{ (key row)}$$

The smallest nonnegative quotient is 16, computed for the second row, and it becomes the key row. The number that is common to both the key column and the key row is designated the *key number*. Table XVII shows the matrix with the key column, row, and number identified.

Let us pause for a moment to examine the rationale of what we are doing. Recall in the distribution method that when we found a square

TABLE XVI. Initial Simplex Matrix Showing Index Row

			10	5	0	0	
			x_I	x_{II}	W_A	W_B	
0	W_A	100	4	5	1	0	
0	W_B	80	5	2	0	1	
		0	−10	−5	0	0	←Index row

TABLE XVII. Initial Simplex Matrix with Key Column, Row, and Number Identified

			10	5	0	0
			x_I	x_{II}	W_A	W_B
0	W_A	100	4	5	1	0
Key row → 0	W_B	80	5	2	0	1
		0	−10	−5	0	0

*Key number   Key column

that yielded a potential improvement in total distribution costs, we wanted to transfer as many units as possible to that route in order to make the improvements as big as possible. But we were always limited by the negative square that already had the smallest allocation. This sort of situation is exactly what determines which row is the key row. We know that x_I will be introduced into the solution, and we wish to know what is its maximum value consistent with both problem equations, assuming that none of the variables can take on negative values. In the first equation, x_I would be the largest possible when x_{II} and W_A were zero; that is,

$$4x_I + 5x_{II} + W_A = 100$$

or

$$x_I = \frac{100}{4} = 25$$

In the second equation, x_I would be the largest possible when x_{II} and W_B were zero; that is,

$$5x_I + 2x_{II} + W_B = 80$$

or

$$x_I = \frac{80}{5} = 16$$

Thus the second equation is the one that limits x_I. It can be no bigger than 16, and this fact dictates the selection of the second row as the key row.

With the key column and row selected, we can prepare a new table representing an improved solution. The first step in developing the new table is to calculate the coefficients for the *main row*. This main row appears in the same relative position in the new table as the key row in the preceding table. It is computed by dividing the coefficients of the key row by the key number. Table XVIII shows this development.

TABLE XVIII.   Simplex Matrix with Main Row of New Table

		1st table	10	5	0	0
			x_I	x_{II}	W_A	W_B
0	W_A	100	4	5	1	0
0	W_B	80	5	2	0	1
		0	-10	-5	0	0

2nd table

	16	1	⅗	0	⅕	← Main row

The variable and its objective number from the head of the key column, x_I and 10, are placed in the stub of the main row replacing W_B and 0 from the previous table. The balance of the objective and variable columns in the stub is copied from the previous table; the new table, developed to this point, now appears as Table XIX.

Now all of the remaining coefficients in the new table, including the constant column, the body, the identity, and the index row, can be calculated to complete the table by the following formula:

$$\text{New number} = \text{old number} - \frac{\left(\begin{array}{c}\text{corresponding}\\\text{number of}\\\text{key row}\end{array}\right) \times \left(\begin{array}{c}\text{corresponding}\\\text{number of}\\\text{key column}\end{array}\right)}{\text{key number}}$$

(1)   First row constant column

$$\text{New number} = 100 - \frac{80 \times 4}{5} = 36$$

TABLE XIX.   Simplex Matrix with Variable and Objective Columns of Stub Completed

		1st table	10	5	0	0
			x_I	x_{II}	W_A	W_B
0	W_A	100	4	5	1	0
0	W_B	80	5	2	0	1
		0	-10	-5	0	0

2nd table

0	W_A					
10	x_I	16	1	⅖	0	⅕

(2) First row, first column of body

$$\text{New number} = 4 - \frac{5 \times 4}{5} = 0$$

(3) Index row, constant column

$$\text{New number} = 0 - \frac{80 \times (-10)}{5} = 160$$

The remaining coefficients can be calculated in the same way and the completed improved solution is shown in Table XX, with a new index row which shows any new possibilities for improvement.

We pause to note that the solution at this stage is:

$$x_{\text{I}} = 16$$

$$x_{\text{II}} = 0$$

$$W_A = 36$$

$$W_B = 0$$

The values in the constant column of the stub indicate this, x_{II} and W_B being zero since they are not in the stub at all. The value of the objective function (contribution) for this solution is \$160, given in the constant column, index row.

However, Table XX shows that the solution can still be improved since a (-1) appears in the index row under the variable x_{II}. Since it is the only negative number in the index row, it is selected as the key

TABLE XX. Simplex Matrix
with First Iteration Completed

1st table

			10	5	0	0
			x_{I}	x_{II}	W_A	W_B
0	W_A	100	4	5	1	0
0	W_B	80	5	2	0	1
		0	-10	-5	0	0

2nd table

			x_{I}	x_{II}	W_A	W_B
0	W_A	36	0	$17\frac{1}{5}$	1	$-4\frac{1}{5}$
10	x_{I}	16	1	$\frac{2}{5}$	0	$\frac{1}{5}$
		160	0	-1	0	2

column for the next iteration. The key row is selected in the same way as before. The two quotients are:

$$\text{First row} \quad \frac{36}{17/5} = \frac{180}{17} = 10.59$$

$$\text{Second row} \quad \frac{16}{2/5} = 40$$

The first row has the smallest nonnegative quotient, so it is selected as the key row. A new main row is calculated as before by dividing the coefficients in the main row by the key number. The new variable, x_{II}, and its objective number are entered in the stub, and the new numbers in the body, identity, and index row are computed as before. The remaining variable and its objective number are copied from the preceding iteration table; Table XXI shows the new solution.

The new solution in Table XXI is optimal since no further improvement is indicated in the index row. The values of the variables for the optimal solution are:

$$x_I = 200/17$$

$$x_{II} = 180/17$$

$$W_A = 0$$

$$W_B = 0$$

TABLE XXI. Simplex Matrix, Second and Final Iteration Completed

				10	5	0	0
1st table				x_I	x_{II}	W_A	W_B
	0	W_A	100	4	5	1	0
	0	W_B	80	5	2	0	1
			0	−10	−5	0	0
2nd table							
	0	W_A	36	0	$17/5$	1	$-4/5$
	10	x_I	16	1	$2/5$	0	$1/5$
			160	0	−1	0	2
3rd table							
	5	x_{II}	$180/17$	0	1	$5/17$	$-4/17$
	10	x_I	$200/17$	1	0	$-2/17$	$5/17$
			$2900/17$	0	0	$5/17$	$30/17$

If these values are inserted in Equations 17 and 18, we find that they check exactly. The solution indicates that products I and II should be produced in the amounts shown by x_I and x_{II} (in 100's) to produce a maximum contribution of $C = 2900/17 = \$170.59$. For each iteration, the value of the objective function is shown in the constant column, index row. It was $160 for the second solution and $2900/17 = \$170.59$ for the optimal solution. The solution is unique; that is, no other combination of x_I and x_{II} will yield a contribution figure that is as high as this.

1. *Formulate the problem and the objective function.*
2. *Develop the initial simplex matrix* including the initial trivial solution and the index row numbers. The index row numbers in the initial matrix are calculated by the formula:

$$\text{Index number} = \sum \begin{pmatrix} \text{numbers} \\ \text{in} \\ \text{column} \end{pmatrix} \times \begin{pmatrix} \text{corresponding} \\ \text{number in} \\ \text{objective} \\ \text{column} \end{pmatrix} - \begin{pmatrix} \text{number in} \\ \text{objective} \\ \text{row at head} \\ \text{of column} \end{pmatrix}$$

3. *Select the key column,* the column with the most negative number in the body or the identity.
4. *Select the key row,* the row with the smallest nonnegative quotient obtained by dividing each number of the constant column by the corresponding positive, nonzero number in the key column.
5. *The key number* is at the intersection of the key row and key column.
6. *Develop the main row of the new table.*

$$\text{Main row} = \frac{\text{key row of preceding table}}{\text{key number}}$$

The main row appears in the new table in the same relative position as the key row of the preceding table.

7. *Develop the balance of the new table.*
   a. The variable and its objective number at the head of the key column are entered in the stub of the new table to the left of the main row, replacing the variable and objective number from the key row of the preceding table.
   b. The remainder of the variable and objective columns are reproduced in the new table exactly as they were in the preceding table.
   c. The balance of the coefficients for the new table are calculated by the formula:

$$\text{New number} = \text{old number} - \frac{\begin{pmatrix} \text{corresponding} \\ \text{number of} \\ \text{key row} \end{pmatrix} \times \begin{pmatrix} \text{corresponding} \\ \text{number of} \\ \text{key column} \end{pmatrix}}{\text{key number}}$$

8. *Repeat (iterate) steps 3 through 7c until all the index numbers (not including the constant column) are positive. An optimal solution then results.*

The interpretation of the resulting optimum solution is as follows: The solution appears in the stub. The variables shown in the variable column have values shown in the corresponding rows of the constant column. The value of the objective function is shown in the constant column, index row. All variables not shown in the stub are equal to zero.

Checking
the Work

The simplest and most effective check of the work in progress is to establish a check column to the right of the simplex matrix. The numbers in the check column are simply the algebraic sum of all the numbers in a given row, beginning with the constant column and adding all the coefficients to the right. This check column can be established for each row, including the index row. All transformations of the numbers in the check column are the same as for any of the other numbers in the table. After transformation, the algebraic sum of the row coefficients should equal the transformed number in the check column. If it does not, an error has been made and it should be traced and corrected before proceeding. A check column is employed in the illustrative solution of the plastic sheet problem that was set up earlier in this chapter and is solved later as shown in Table XXIII.

Degeneracy in
the Simplex
Solution

Degeneracy in the simplex solution can be recognized at the time that the key row is being selected. If a tie exists between two or more rows for the smallest nonnegative quotient at that time, then the problem is degenerate. Table XXII shows this situation for a simple matrix that is slightly different from the example we have been using. Dividing the constant column by the corresponding number in the key column, we have:

Row 1 $100/4 = 25$

Row 2 $125/5 = 25$

TABLE XXII. Degeneracy in the Simplex Matrix

			10	5	0	0
			x_I	x_{II}	W_A	W_B
0	W_A	100	4	5	1	0
0	W_B	125	5	2	0	1
		0	−10	2	0	0

A tie exists and there is the possibility that if the wrong row is selected as the key row, the variable in the stub of the other row may disappear. The problem may begin to cycle at this point and an optimum solution could not be obtained. The degeneracy is resolved by the following procedure.

1. Divide each element in the tied rows by the key column number in that row.
2. Compare the resulting ratios column by column, from left to right, first in the identity and then in the body.
3. The first comparison that yields unequal ratios breaks the tie.
4. The key row is that row which has the algebraically smaller ratio.

Applying this procedure to the degenerate problem of Table XXII, we begin our paired comparison in the identity. The ratios in column W_A are:

$$\begin{array}{ll} \text{First row} & \frac{1}{4} \\ \text{Second row} & 0 \end{array}$$

The second row yields the algebraically smaller ratio; therefore, it is selected as the key row. The regular simplex procedure then is resumed. This procedure for resolving degeneracy is general and can be applied at any stage of the solution to any size matrix.

This completes the essential procedure of the simplex solution. There is a great deal more to know about the simplex method than is shown here, however. We have illustrated with a problem that involved restrictions (i.e., the hours were limited to certain maximum values). In problems involving requirements (e.g., hours must be greater than or equal to certain specified values), equalities (e.g., hours must be exactly equal to specified values), or approximations, the slack variables must be handled correctly to prepare the model for simplex solution. All of these and other topics pertinent to linear programming can be found in books devoted to the study of this subject.

The simplex solution for this problem is shown in Table XXIII. For details of the problem itself and the formulation of the problem equations and objective function, see pages 164–169. We begin with the initial trivial solution and show the iterations required without further comment.

Simplex Solution of the Plastic Sheet Problem

TABLE XXIII. Simplex Solution for the Plastic Sheet Problem Formulated and Discussed on Pages 164–169

Initial Simplex Matrix

			37.5 x_{1A}	40 x_{1B}	20 x_{2A}	45 x_{2B}	62.5 x_{3A}	30 x_{3B}	0 W_A	0 W_B	0 W_1	0 W_2	0 W_3	ck
0	W_A	100	0.25	0	0.40	0	0.35	0	1	0	0	0	0	102.00
0	W_B	100	0	0.20	0	0.25	0	0.40	0	1	0	0	0	101.85
0	W_1	310	1	1	0	0	0	0	0	0	1	0	0	313
0	W_2	300	0	0	1	1	0	0	0	0	0	1	0	303
0	W_3	125	0	0	0	0	1	1	0	0	0	0	1	128
		0	−37.5	−40	−20	−45	−62.5	−30	0	0	0	0	0	−235.0

First Iteration

			x_{1A}	x_{1B}	x_{2A}	x_{2B}	x_{3A}	x_{3B}	W_A	W_B	W_1	W_2	W_3	ck
0	W_A	56.25	0.25	0	0.40	0	0	−0.35	1	0	0	0	−0.35	57.2
0	W_B	100	0	0.20	0	0.25	0	0.40	0	1	0	0	0	101.85
0	W_1	310	1	1	0	0	0	0	0	0	1	0	0	313
0	W_2	300	0	0	1	1	0	0	0	0	0	1	0	303
62.5	x_{3A}	125	0	0	0	0	1	1	0	0	0	0	1	128
		7,812.5	−37.5	−40	−20	−45	0	32.5	0	0	0	0	62.5	7,765

Second Iteration

			x_{1A}	x_{1B}	x_{2A}	x_{2B}	x_{3A}	x_{3B}	W_A	W_B	W_1	W_2	W_3	ck
0	W_A	56.25	0.25	0	0.40	0	0	−0.35	1	0	0	0	−0.35	57.2
0	W_B	25	0	0.20	−0.25	0	0	0.40	0	1	0	−0.25	0	26.10
0	W_1	310	1	1	0	0	0	0	0	0	1	0	0	313
45	x_{2B}	300	0	0	1	1	0	0	0	0	0	1	0	303
62.5	x_{3A}	125	0	0	0	0	1	1	0	0	0	0	1	128
		21,312.5	−37.5	−40	25	0	0	32.5	0	0	0	45	62.5	21,400

Third Iteration

			x_{1A}	x_{1B}	x_{2A}	x_{2B}	x_{3A}	x_{3B}	W_A	W_B	W_1	W_2	W_3	ck
0	W_A	56.25	0.25	0	0.40	0	0	−0.35	1	0	0	0	−0.35	57.2
40	x_{1B}	125	0	1	−1.25	0	0	2	0	5	0	−1.25	0	130.5
0	W_1	185	1	0	+1.25	0	0	−2	0	−5	1	+1.25	0	182.5
45	x_{2B}	300	0	0	1	1	0	0	0	0	0	1	0	303
62.5	x_{3A}	125	0	0	0	0	1	1	0	0	0	0	1	128
		26,312.5	−37.5	0	−25	0	0	112.5	0	200	0	−5	62.5	26,620

Fourth Iteration (optimal solution)

			x_{1A}	x_{1B}	x_{2A}	x_{2B}	x_{3A}	x_{3B}	W_A	W_B	W_1	W_2	W_3	ck
0	W_A	10	0	0	0.0875	0	0	0.15	1	1.25	−0.25	−0.3125	−0.35	11.575
40	x_{1B}	125	0	1	−1.25	0	0	2	0	5	0	−1.25	0	130.5
37.5	x_{1A}	185	1	0	1.25	0	0	−2	0	−5	1	1.25	0	182.5
45	x_{2B}	300	0	0	1	1	0	0	0	0	0	1	0	303
62.5	x_{3A}	125	0	0	0	0	1	1	0	0	0	0	1	128
		33,250	0	0	21.875	0	0	37.5	0	12.5	37.5	41.875	62.5	33,463.75

RANGE OF APPLICATION FOR LINEAR PROGRAMMING

The following set of examples of linear programming applications will give an idea of the range of problems where linear programming may be used:

1. *Allocation of production facilities when alternate routings are available.* Given the unit machining time for the alternate machine routes, total hours available on the different machine classes, requirements for the number of each product, and unit revenue for each product, linear programming can give a solution which would maximize some profit function, minimize incremental cost, or meet some other management objective. This is similar to our previous example but not identical because a sequence of operations is involved here.

2. *Allocation of limited funds to various items of inventory* to minimize losses from less than optimal inventory levels.

3. *Blending problems.* For example, a paint manufacturer may need to prepare paint vehicles that are a blend of several constituents. The constituents, such as oil and thinner, are available in limited quantity and in commercial blends of fixed proportions. Costs per gallon of the various possible raw materials are known. The problem is to determine the amount of each raw material such that the required amounts for the new blends are obtained at minimum cost. Another similar problem is the blending of animal feed to provide certain minimum nutrient values at minimum cost.

4. *Procurement problems.* For example, a manufacturer wants to know which parts to make and which to buy to maximize profit within plant capacity restrictions or within basic policies to subcontract a given minimum amount. Where subcontracting with particular suppliers is limited by policy or by the supplier's capacity, competing bids may be programmed so that profit is maximized within the policy or capacity restrictions.

5. *Scheduling of production to meet a sales forecast*, using inventory fluctuations and overtime work to absorb random and seasonal variations in load.

6. *Maximizing material utilization.* Many times different stock sizes must be stamped or cut from standard raw material sizes. The question is: What combination of cuts will meet requirements for the amounts of the different sizes with a minimum of trim loss?

OTHER PROGRAMMING METHODS

The principal limitation of linear programming is that it requires all relationships to be linear. For example, if direct labor on 5 units is $10, then direct labor on 10 units is $20, or simply $2 per unit. Actually, direct labor cost per unit might change with volume, depending on pay systems and the per cent of capacity at which we are operating. In a similar way, many other measures that we might want to use in linear programming models may not actually be linear or straight-line relationships. Very often, however, a straight-line relationship is an excellent approximation to the actual situation. Or, even though the relation is not linear over its entire range, the part in which we may have interest may be approximately linear. In these instances, linearity is assumed and linear programming models used with small loss of precision.

Quadratic programming is an algebraic technique which makes it possible to approximate more closely some actual cost curves and include them in programming models.

Dynamic programming makes it possible to solve multistage programming problems where the decisions generated by stage 1 become conditions of the problem for stage 2, etc. For example, in scheduling production, the amount we plan to produce this month is dependent partially on how much we produced last month because of the possible accumulation or reduction of backlogs.

REVIEW QUESTIONS

1. What is the general nature of problems which may be approached by linear programming?
2. In distribution problems, how do we know whether or not a shift in assignments is advantageous? How do we know when an optimal solution has been obtained?
3. Is it possible to have more than one optimal allocation? What is the practical significance of this?
4. How would an objective function related to profits rather than costs affect the practical procedures of solving distribution-type problems?
5. What is the significance of degeneracy in distribution problems and how may it be resolved so that we can proceed with the solution?
6. In practical problems, it would often be true that supply and demand are not equal. How can this be handled in the distribution matrix?
7. Figure 4 shows the effect of the restrictions on the Stamping Department, Motor and Transmission Department, dryer assembly, and washer assembly capacities in limiting the feasible solutions to the problem. What other restrictions are implicit in Figure 4?
8. What is the practical result of having an objective function that is parallel to the critical line segment of the polygon of feasible solutions in the graphical representation of linear programming?
9. Are market restrictions fundamentally different from capacity restrictions in determining the polygon of feasible solutions?
10. Outline the procedure for simplex solution of linear programming programs. Express the procedure in the form of a flow chart.
11. What is the function of slack variables in the simplex procedure?

PROBLEMS

1. A company has four factories from which it ships to four warehouses which are the distribution points. The production costs and capacities in each of the four factories are:

	Cost per 100, Dollars	Capacity, Hundreds
F_1	40	140
F_2	43	260
F_3	39	360
F_4	45	220

Demands for the product in each of the four distribution points are:

	Demand, Hundreds
W_1	180
W_2	280
W_3	150
W_4	200

Transportation costs in dollars per 100 between the various combinations of factories and warehouses are:

	W_1	W_2	W_3	W_4
F_1	48	60	56	58
F_2	47	57	53	59
F_3	51	63	61	63
F_4	51	63	55	61

What is the allocation of capacity to demand which minimizes combined production and distribution costs?

2. A company with factories at A, B, C, and D supplies warehouses at E, F, G, and H. Monthly factory capacities are 100, 80, 120, and 90, respectively, for regular production. If overtime production is utilized, the capacities can be increased to 120, 110, 160, and 140, respectively. Incremental unit overtime costs are $5, $2, $3, and $4, respectively. Present incremental profits per unit excluding shipping costs are $14, $9, $16, and $27, respectively, for regular production. The current monthly warehouse requirements are 110, 70, 160, and 130, respectively. Unit shipping costs are as follows:

	To			
From	E	F	G	H
A	$3	$4	$5	$7
B	$2	$9	$6	$8
C	$4	$3	$8	$5
D	$6	$5	$4	$6

Determine the optimum distribution for this company.

3. You are the production control superintendent at Blackstone Rubber Company. On arriving at work one morning, you find the following pallet information on your desk:

Department	Pallets Available
A	18
B	27
C	21

	Pallets Required
G	14
H	12
I	23
J	17

The time to move a pallet is as follows:

From A to G	13 minutes
From A to H	25 minutes
From A to I	12 minutes
From A to J	21 minutes
From B to G	18 minutes
From B to H	23 minutes
From B to I	14 minutes
From B to J	9 minutes
From C to G	23 minutes
From C to H	15 minutes
From C to I	12 minutes
From C to J	16 minutes

(a) What is the optimum distribution plan to minimize move time?

(b) What is the worst distribution plan you could devise?

4. A company is manufacturing a product in three plants: (A)lbuquerque, (B)enton Harbor, and (C)entro. It distributes the product from three main warehouses located at (D)enver, (E)lmira, and (F)ort Worth. Prices in the three main market areas vary, and production costs in the three main plants vary. The data below summarize distribution costs, production costs, prices, capacities, and demands.

Distribution Costs, Dollars/Unit

	To		
From	D	E	F
A	0.06	0.08	0.05
B	0.10	0.03	0.10
C	0.08	0.12	0.07

Monthly Capacities and Unit Production Costs

Plant	Monthly Capacity Units	Average Unit Cost at Capacity	Unit Fixed Cost at Capacity	Unit Variable Costs
A	2000	0.30	0.10	0.20
B	2500	0.36	0.08	0.28
C	1800	0.42	0.12	0.30

Monthly Demand and Selling Prices in Market Areas

Area	Monthly Demand	Price, $/Unit
D	1600	0.45
E	2400	0.42
F	2000	0.40

Determine the optimal shipping plan.

5. A company with plants at Austin, Blythe, Cucumonga, and Dallas ships to warehouses at Eaton, Fresno, Gallup, and Hot Springs. Plant capacities, warehouse requirements, and shipping costs between the various plants and warehouses are as follows:

Plant Capacities		Warehouse Requirements	
Austin	500	Eaton	400
Blythe	900	Fresno	800
Cucumonga	800	Gallup	700
Dallas	300	Hot Springs	600

Shipping Costs (per unit)

Austin to Eaton	$10	Blythe to Eaton	$11
Austin to Fresno	14	Blythe to Fresno	18
Austin to Gallup	9	Blythe to Gallup	16
Austin to Hot Springs	6	Blythe to Hot Springs	7
Cucumonga to Eaton	$ 8	Dallas to Eaton	$15
Cucumonga to Fresno	4	Dallas to Fresno	13
Cucumonga to Gallup	12	Dallas to Gallup	17
Cucumonga to Hot Springs	5	Dallas to Hot Springs	20

What is the minimum shipping cost?

6. A company has factories at A, B, and C which supply warehouses at D, E, F, and G. Monthly factory capacities are 160, 150, and 190, respectively.

Monthly warehouse requirements are 80, 90, 110, and 160, respectively. Unit shipping costs are as follows:

	To			
From	D	E	F	G
A	$42	$48	$38	$37
B	$40	$49	$52	$51
C	$39	$38	$40	$43

Determine the minimum distribution cost.

7. Once upon a time Lucretia Borgia invited 50 enemies to dinner. The pièce de résistance was to be poison. In those crude days only two poisons were on the market, poison X and poison Y. Before preparing the menu, however, the remarkably talented young lady considered some of the restrictions placed on her scheme:

(a) If she used more than one-half pound of poison, the guests would detect it and refuse to eat.

(b) Lucretia's own private witch, a medieval version of the modern planning staff, once propounded some magic numbers for her in the following doggerel:

> One Y and X two,
> If less than half,
> Then woe to you.

(c) Poison X will kill 75 and poison Y will kill 200 people per pound.

(d) Poison X costs 100 solid gold pieces per pound, and poison Y 400 solid gold pieces per pound.

After devising a menu to cover up the taste of the poison, Lucretia found she was very short of solid gold pieces. In fact, unless she were very careful she would not be able to have another scheduled poisoning orgy that month. So she called in her alchemist, a very learned man, and told him about her problem. The alchemist had little experience in solving problems of this type, but he was able to translate the four restrictions into mathematical statements.

$$(1) \quad X + Y \leq \tfrac{1}{2}$$
$$(2) \quad 2X + Y \geq \tfrac{1}{2}$$
$$(3) \quad 75X + 200Y \geq 50$$
$$(4) \quad 100X + 400Y = \text{cost}$$

Assist the alchemist in solving this problem. The penalty for failure will be an invitation to next month's dinner.

8. A company makes three products, x, y, and z, out of three materials p_1, p_2, p_3. The three products use units of the three materials according to the following table:

Product	P_1	P_2	P_3
x	2	0	3
y	3	2	2
z	0	5	4

The unit contributions of the three products are:

Product	Contribution
x	$3
y	$5
z	$4

The availabilities of the three materials are:

Material	Amount Available, Units
P_1	8
P_2	10
P_3	15

Determine the optional product mix.

9. A company makes four products, v, x, y, and z, which flow through four departments, drill, mill, lathe, and assembly. The hours of department time required by each of the products per unit are:

Product	Drill	Mill	Lathe	Assembly
v	3	0	3	4
x	7	2	4	6
y	4	4	0	5
z	0	6	5	3

The unit contributions of the four products and hours of availability in the four departments are:

Product	Contribution
v	$9
x	$18
y	$14
z	$11

Department	Hours Available
Drill	70
Mill	80
Lathe	90
Assembly	100

Determine the optimal product mix.

10.   A mining company owns two different mines that produce a given kind of ore. After the ore is crushed, it is graded into three classes: high-grade, medium-grade, and low-grade ores. There is some demand for each grade of ore. The mining company has contracted to provide a smelting plant with 12 tons of high-grade, 8 tons of medium-grade, and 24 tons of low-grade ore per week. It costs the company $200 per day to run the first mine and $160 per day to run the second. These mines have different capacities, however. In a day's operation the first mine produces 6 tons of high-grade, 2 tons of medium-grade, and 4 tons of low-grade ore, whereas the second mine produces daily 2 tons of high-grade, 2 tons of medium-grade, and 12 tons of low-grade ore. How many days a week should each mine be operated to fulfill the company's orders most economically? (*Hint:* Let x be the number of days per week that mine 1 operates, and y the number of days per week that mine 2 operates. Solve by the graphical method.)

11.   A company sells two different products, A and B. The selling price and incremental cost information are as follows:

	Product A	Product B
Selling price	60	40
Incremental cost	30	10
Contribution	30	30

The two products are produced in a common production process and are sold in two different markets. The production process has a capacity of 30,000 man-hours. It takes three hours to produce a unit of A and one hour to produce a unit of B. The market has been surveyed and the company officials feel that the maximum number of units of A that can be sold is 8000; the maximum for B is 12,000 units. Subject to these limitations, the products can be sold in any combination.

(a) Formulate the above problem as a linear programming simplex problem; that is, write the appropriate equations.

(b) Solve this problem by graphical methods.

REFERENCES

[1] Bertoletti, M. E., J. Chapiro, and H. R. Rieznik. "Optimization of Investment—A Solution by Linear Programming." *Management Technology*, (1), 64–75, Jan. 1960.

[2] Bowman, E. H., and R. B. Fetter. *Analysis for Production and Operations Management* (3rd ed.). Richard D. Irwin, Homewood, Ill., 1967.

[3] Buffa, E. S. *Operations Management: Problems and Models* (3rd ed.). John Wiley, New York, 1972.

[4] Charnes, A., and W. W. Cooper. *Management Models and Industrial*

Applications of Linear Programming (2 vols.). John Wiley, New York, 1961.

[5] Eisemann, K., and W. N. Young. "Study of a Textile Mill with the Aid of Linear Programming." *Management Technology*, (1), 52–63, Jan. 1960.

[6] Fabian, T. "A Linear Programming Model of Integrated Iron and Steel Production." *Management Science*, **4** (4), 415–449, July 1958.

[7] Fabian, T. "Blast Furnace Production—A Linear Programming Example." *Management Science*, **14** (2), Oct. 1967.

[8] Ferguson, R. O., and L. F. Sargent. *Linear Programming*. McGraw-Hill, New York, 1958.

[9] Fetter, R. B. "A Linear Programming Model for Long-Range Capacity Planning." *Management Science*, **7** (4), 372–378, July 1961.

[10] Greene, J. H., K. Chatto, C. R. Hicks, and C. B. Cox. "Linear Programming in the Packaging Industry." *Journal of Industrial Engineering*, **10** (5), 364–372, 1959.

[11] Hanssmann, F., and S. W. Hess. "A Linear Programming Approach to Production and Employment Scheduling." *Management Technology*, (1), 46–52, Jan. 1960.

[12] Metzger, R. W. *Elementary Mathematical Programming*. John Wiley, New York, 1958.

[13] Metzer, R. W., and R. Schwarzbek. "A Linear Programming Application to Cupola Charging." *Journal of Industrial Engineering*, **12** (2), 87–93, Mar.–Apr. 1961.

[14] Thierauf, R. J., and R. A. Grosse. *Decision Making Through Operations Research*. John Wiley, New York, 1970.

[15] Vajda, S. *Readings in Linear Programming*. John Wiley, New York, 1958.

Waiting Lines

The original work in waiting line or queuing theory was done by A. K. Erlang, a Danish telephone engineer. Erlang started his work in 1905 in an attempt to determine the effect of fluctuating service demand (arrivals) on the utilization of automatic dial equipment. It has been only since the end of World War II that work on waiting line models has been extended to other kinds of problems. A wide variety of seemingly diverse problem situations are now recognized as being described by the general waiting line model. In all instances, we have an input that arrives at some facility for service or processing. The time between the arrival of individual inputs at the service facility is commonly random. Similarly, the time for service or processing is commonly a random variable. Table I shows the waiting line model elements for a number of common situations.

Four basic structures of waiting line situations describe the general conditions at the servicing facility. The simplest situation is where arriving units form a single line to be serviced by a single processing facility, for example, a one-man barber shop. This is called the single-channel, single-phase case. If the number of processing stations is increased (two or more barbers), but still draws on the one waiting line, we have a multiple-channel, single-phase case, since a customer can be serviced by any one of the barbers. A simple assembly line has a number

193

(a) Single-channel, single-phase case

(b) Multiple-channel, single-phase case

(c) Single-channel, multiple-phase case

(d) Multiple-channel, multiple-phase case

FIGURE 1.   Four basic structures of waiting line situations.

of service facilities in series or tandem and is the single-channel, multiple-phase case. Finally, we have the multiple-channel, multiple-phase case which might be illustrated by two or more parallel production lines. Figure 1 shows the four cases diagrammed and labeled. Variations in the four basic structures may be in the queue discipline; that is, the order in which inputs are taken out of the waiting line. We have implied a first come–first served queue discipline in the diagrams, but obviously priority systems could be used. Also, combinations of the basic structures could exist.

The common basic waiting line models have been developed on the assumption that *arrival rates* follow the Poisson distribution and that

TABLE I. Waiting Line Model Elements for Some Commonly Known Situations

	Unit Arriving	Service or Processing Facility	Service or Process Being Performed
Ships entering a port	Ships	Docks	Unloading and loading
Maintenance and repair of machines	Machine breaks down	Repair crew	Repair machine
Assembly line, not mechanically paced	Parts to be assembled	Individual assembly operations or entire line	Assembly
Doctor's office	Patients	Doctor, his staff, and facilities	Medical care
Purchase of groceries at a supermarket	Customers with loaded grocery carts	Checkout counter	Tabulation of bill, receipt of payment, and bagging of groceries
Auto traffic at an intersection or bridge	Automobiles	Intersection or bridge with control points such as traffic lights or toll booths	Passage through intersection or bridge
Inventory of items in a warehouse	Order for withdrawal	Warehouse	Replenishment of inventory

service times follow the negative exponential distribution. This situation is commonly referred to as the Poisson arrival—exponential holding-time case. These assumptions are often quite valid in operating situations.

POISSON ARRIVAL RATES

The Poisson distribution of arrival rates occurs frequently in the real world. Figures 2 and 3 are examples of cases that have been validated by statistical analysis. Figure 2 is based on a broad study by Nelson [7] of the distributions of arrival rates and processing times in a Los Angeles jobbing machine shop. The frequency of arrivals of job orders at 15 machine centers for a period of three months was tabulated. Table II summarizes the data on the distribution of arrival rates, and Figure 2 shows the graphs for two of the machine groups compared to the theoretical distribution of the Poisson. The distributions for the entire set of 15 machine centers were subjected to careful statistical tests in comparison to the Poisson, using the chi square goodness of fit test.

FIGURE 2. Comparison of the distribution of arrival rates at two machine centers in a jobbing machine shop with the Poisson distribution. (Adapted from [7].)

It was concluded that the distributions of arrival rates for all 15 machine centers were not significantly different from the Poisson distribution.

Figure 3 shows the comparison between the actual distribution of order rates and the Poisson distribution. This study took place at the Kodak Park Works of the Eastman Kodak Company. The distribution represented the rate at which orders for mixed chemicals needed by several production departments in the company were received at a storeroom. Statistical tests again indicated that the actual distribution was described adequately by the Poisson.

Although we cannot say with finality that distributions of arrival rates are always described adequately by the Poisson, there is much evidence to indicate that this is often the case. We might have reasoned that this should be true, because the Poisson distribution corresponds to completely random arrivals since it is assumed that an arrival is completely independent of other arrivals as well as of any condition of the waiting line.

TABLE II. Distributions of Arrival Rates of Job Orders to 15 Machine Centers in a Jobbing Machine Shop over a Three-Month Period*

Machine Group	Number of Machines in Group	Total Arrivals in Three Months	Mean Arrival Rate, Arrivals per Work Day	Distribution of Arrivals— Job Lots per Work Day								
				0	1	2	3	4	5	6	7	8
Engine lathes	7	120	1.935	11	14	21	4	9	2	1	—	—
Turret lathes	6	104	1.677	13	20	15	6	6	1	—	1	—
Automatic lathes	3	6	0.097	57	4	1	—	—	—	—	—	—
Hollow spindle lathes	1	27	0.435	40	18	3	1	—	—	—	—	—
Milling machines	6	107	1.726	14	19	12	10	4	2	—	—	1
Saws	2	77	1.242	25	14	11	9	1	2	—	—	—
Drill presses	3	95	1.532	15	18	18	6	3	1	1	—	—
Punch presses	2	37	0.597	39	12	8	3	—	—	—	—	—
Boring machines	2	33	0.532	39	16	4	3	—	—	—	—	—
Slotters	1	14	0.226	51	9	1	1	—	—	—	—	—
Hydrostatic pipe tester	1	33	0.532	37	19	5	—	1	—	—	—	—
Upsetters	2	57	0.919	25	22	10	5	—	—	—	—	—
Shapers	2	5	0.081	59	1	2	—	—	—	—	—	—
Wheelabrator	1	24	0.387	44	14	3	—	1	—	—	—	—
Pipe threading machine	1	30	0.484	37	20	5	—	—	—	—	—	—

*Adapted from [7].

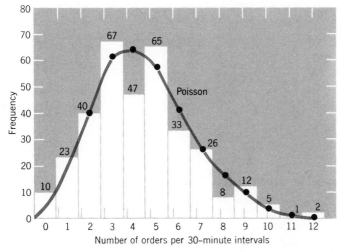

FIGURE 3. Distribution of order rates for mixed chemicals compared to the Poisson distribution. (From [4].)

The commonly used symbol for average arrival rate in waiting line models is the Greek letter lambda (λ), arrivals per time unit. It can be shown that when the arrival rates follow a Poisson process with mean arrival rate λ, the time between arrivals follows a negative exponential distribution with mean time between arrivals of $1/\lambda$. This relationship between mean arrival rate and mean time between arrivals does not necessarily hold for other distributions. The negative exponential distribution, then, is also representative of a Poisson process, but describes the time between arrivals and specifies that these time intervals are completely random. Negative exponential distributions are shown in Figures 4 and 5.

FIGURE 4. Comparison of actual and theoretical distributions for two machine groups. (From [7].)

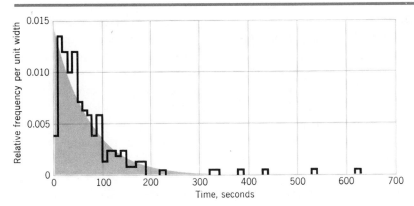

FIGURE 5. Service time at a tool crib. (From [1].)

EXPONENTIAL SERVICE TIMES

The commonly used symbol for average service rate in waiting line models is the Greek letter mu (μ), the number of services completed per time unit. As with arrivals, it can be shown that when service rates follow a Poisson process with mean service rate μ, the distribution of service times follows the negative exponential distribution with mean service time $1/\mu$. The reason for the common reference to *rates* in the discussion of arrivals and to *times* in the discussion of service is simply a matter of practice. We should hold it clearly in mind, however, for both arrivals and service, that in the general Poisson models, rates follow the Poisson distribution and times follow the negative exponential distribution.

The evidence that real-world service distributions commonly follow the Poisson process is not nearly as strong as it was for arrivals. Nevertheless, in some instances the assumption appears to be valid. Nelson's study of the distributions of arrival and service times in a Los Angeles jobbing machine shop, cited previously in our discussions of arrivals, did *not* indicate that the exponential model fit the actual distributions adequately for all machine centers. The machine centers where service time distributions seemed adequately described by the negative exponential were turret lathes, milling machines, boring machines, and the wheelabrator. In general, the instances where the exponential hypothesis was reasonable occurred in the machine centers with the largest mean processing time.

Nelson's study indicated that other mathematical distributions, such as the hyperexponential and the hyper-Erlang, were better descriptions of the actual distributions. Figure 4 shows the distributions and fitted curves for the drill presses and the upsetters. A visual comparison indicates that the negative exponential distribution does not yield the best fit; this was also indicated by statistical analysis.

Other evidence indicates that in some cases the negative exponential distribution fits. Figure 5, for example, shows that service time at a tool crib was nearly exponentially distributed. The duration of local telephone calls that are not made from a pay station has been shown to be exponential.

The net result of our discussion is that we cannot assume without a careful check that service distributions are described by a Poisson process. We may expect some instances where the negative exponential fits, but in many instances service times have been shown to be approximated by some unimodal distribution, usually somewhat positively skewed.

We might ask at this point why the interest in establishing the validity of the Poisson and negative exponential distributions. The answer is that where the assumptions hold, the resulting waiting line formulas are quite simple. The Poisson and negative exponential distributions are single-parameter distributions; that is, they are completely described by one parameter, the mean. For the Poisson distribution the standard deviation is the square root of the mean, and for the negative exponential distribution the standard deviation is equal to the mean. The result is that the mathematical derivations and resulting formulas are not complex. Where the assumptions do not hold, the mathematical development may be rather complex or we may resort to other techniques for solution, such as simulation. We shall discuss these techniques at a later point; however, our present objective is to discuss waiting line models based on the Poisson process for arrivals and service; that is, the situation commonly referred to as Poisson arrival rates and exponential holding times.

INFINITE WAITING LINE MODELS

We must now make another distinction in the classifications of waiting line models, between situations where the waiting line theoretically may become infinite and where the maximum length of the waiting line is finite. In practice, we would apply infinite waiting line models where the number in line could grow very large. The high average rate of arrivals of autos at the entrance of the Golden Gate Bridge does imply the potential of the very large waiting line. In contrast, consider the case of maintaining a bank of 10 automatic machines. The breakdown of a machine is considered to be an arrival. Obviously, the maximum possible waiting line of machines to be serviced is 10. It is finite and requires a different analysis resulting in a different model compared to the infinite waiting line problem.

We assume that the following conditions are valid: (a) Poisson arrival rates, (b) exponential service times, (c) first come–first served queue discipline, (d) the mean service rate μ is greater than the mean arrival rate λ. Under these conditions, the following equations apply:

Single-Channel, Single-Phase Case

Mean number in waiting line

$$L_q = \frac{\lambda^2}{\mu(\mu - \lambda)} \tag{1}$$

Mean number in system, including the one being serviced

$$L = \frac{\lambda}{\mu - \lambda} = L_q + \frac{\lambda}{\mu} \tag{2}$$

Mean waiting time

$$W_q = \frac{\lambda}{\mu(\mu - \lambda)} = \frac{L_q}{\lambda} \tag{3}$$

Mean time in system, including service

$$W = \frac{1}{\mu - \lambda} = W_q + \frac{1}{\mu} = \frac{L}{\lambda} \tag{4}$$

Probability of n units in the system

$$P_n = \left(1 - \frac{\lambda}{\mu}\right)\left(\frac{\lambda}{\mu}\right)^n \tag{5}$$

At first glance, it might seem that the difference between the mean number in the system and the mean number in the waiting line $(L - L_q)$ should be 1, the unit being served. A check of the formulas, however, indicates that this is not true; the difference is less than 1. A moment's reflection indicates the intuitive reason. Sometimes, because of the random nature of arrivals and service times, the service facility is idle so the average number being served per unit of time must be less than 1. Also note that the difference between the mean time in the system and the mean waiting time $(W - W_q)$ is simply the average time for service. If we take the ratio between the mean arrival rate and the mean service rate, we have an index of the utilization of the service facility. The ratio is commonly called the utilization factor and is denoted by the Greek letter rho (ρ). If the two rates are equal, $\rho = 1$, and theoretically the service facility could be used 100 per cent of the time. But let us see what actually happens to the queue as ρ varies from zero to one. Figure 6 summarizes the result of computing L_q for different values of ρ. As ρ approaches unity, the number waiting in line increases rapidly and approaches infinity. We can also see that this is true by examining Equations 1, 2, 3, and 4. In all cases, $\mu - \lambda$ appears in the denominator. When λ and μ are equal, $\mu - \lambda$ is zero and the value of L, L_q, W, or W_q becomes infinitely large. In practical situations, this never really happens because arrivals may not choose to wait if the line is already very long, or someone takes action either to reduce the arrival rate or increase the processing rate to remedy the situation.

We see now one of the requirements of any practical system: μ must always exceed λ, otherwise we cannot have a stable system. If units are arriving faster on the average than they can be processed, the waiting line will be continuously increasing and no steady state will be achieved.

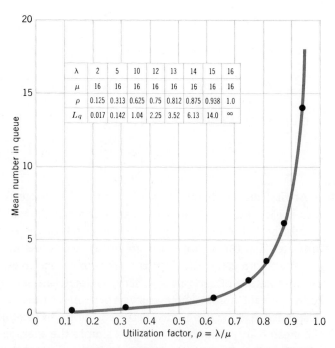

λ	2	5	10	12	13	14	15	16
μ	16	16	16	16	16	16	16	16
ρ	0.125	0.313	0.625	0.75	0.812	0.875	0.938	1.0
L_q	0.017	0.142	1.04	2.25	3.52	6.13	14.0	∞

FIGURE 6. Relationship of queue length to the utilization factor ρ.

When conditions of arrival and service rate are such that the average length of the waiting line increases, as noted in Figure 6, we can reason that the probability that the service facility will be idle must become rather small. Equation 5 allows us to calculate this probability rather easily. The probability of 0 units in the system (service facility idle), P_0, is

$$P_0 = \left(1 - \frac{\lambda}{\mu}\right)\left(\frac{\lambda}{\mu}\right)^0$$

and, since $(\lambda/\mu)^0 = 1$,

$$P_0 = \left(1 - \frac{\lambda}{\mu}\right) = (1 - \rho)$$

This is the probability that the service facility will be idle and checks our intuition that utilization of the facility plus idleness should total 100 per cent.

Constant service times modify the formulas for the mean number in the waiting line and mean waiting time only slightly. The formulas are:

Mean number in waiting line

$$L_q = \frac{\lambda^2}{2\mu(\mu - \lambda)} \tag{6}$$

Mean waiting time

$$W_q = \frac{\lambda}{2\mu(\mu - \lambda)} \tag{7}$$

Whereas constant service time does not represent a large number of real situations, it is reasonable in cases where a machine processes arriving items by a fixed cycle.

Let us illustrate the usefulness of the basic equations in a typical decision problem. Suppose that we have a tool crib in a factory where mechanics come to check out special tools needed for the completion of a particular task assigned to them. A study is made of the time between arrivals and of the time required for service. Both distributions are found to be adequately described by the negative exponential. The average time between arrivals was found to be 60 seconds and the average time for service 50 seconds. The arrival and service rates per minute are:

$$\lambda = \tfrac{1}{60} \times 60 = 1 \text{ arrival per minute}$$

$$\mu = \tfrac{1}{50} \times 60 = 1.2 \text{ services per minute}$$

Let us determine the magnitude of waiting line lengths, waiting time, and the per cent of idle time of the attendant, using Equations 1, 2, 3, 4, and 5.

An Example

$$L_q = \frac{\lambda^2}{\mu(\mu - \lambda)} = \frac{1^2}{1.2(1.2 - 1.0)} = \frac{1}{1.2 \times 0.2} = 4.17 \text{ mechanics in line}$$

$$L = \frac{\lambda}{\mu - \lambda} = \frac{1}{1.2 - 1.0}$$

$$= 5 \text{ mechanics in line, including the mechanic being served}$$

$$W_q = \frac{\lambda}{\mu(\mu - \lambda)} = \frac{1}{1.2(1.2 - 1.0)} = \frac{1}{1.2 \times 0.2}$$

$$= 4.17 \text{ minutes per mechanic}$$

$$W = \frac{1}{\mu - \lambda} = \frac{1}{1.2 - 1.0} = 5 \text{ minutes waiting time, including service}$$

$$\text{Idle time} = 1 - \rho = 1 - \frac{1}{1.2} = 0.1667, \text{ or } 16.67\% \text{ idle time of attendant}$$

If the attendant is paid $2 per hour and the mechanics are paid $4 per hour, what policy or service should be established? What cost function do we wish to minimize? If we add more attendants, the waiting line and mechanics' waiting time will be reduced, but the idle time of the attendants will be increased. Therefore, we wish to determine the number of attendants that will minimize the combined cost of attendants' idle time, plus the cost of mechanics' waiting time. For one attendant the cost of idle time is:

$$8 \times 0.1667 \times 2.00 = \$2.67 \text{ per day}$$

If mechanics arrive at the rate of 1 per minute, then 480 are served in an 8-hour day, and the daily cost of waiting time is

480 (waiting time per mechanic in hours) (hourly pay rate)

$$= 480 \times \frac{W_q}{60} \times 4.00 = 480 \times \frac{4.17}{60} \times 4.00 = \$133.50 \text{ per day}$$

Obviously, with one attendant, we are incurring a very large waiting time cost ($33\frac{1}{3}$ hours per day) in relation to the cost of the attendants' idle time, and more attendants to step up the effective service rate will be justified. But before we can proceed with our analysis, we must have information about the next most complex situation, because if we add a second, third, or fourth attendant, we are dealing with the multiple-channel, single-phase situation.

Multiple-Channel, Single-Phase Case   In the multiple-channel case, we assume the same conditions of Poisson arrivals, exponential service times, and first come–first served queue discipline. The effective service rate $M\mu$ must be greater than the arrival rate λ, where M is the number of channels. The resulting steady-state equations for the multiple-channel case are quite complex compared to the single-channel case. Derivations of equations for the multiple-channel case are available in the references [3, 9].

To show the effects of multiple channels, we have plotted Figures 7 and 8. From Figure 7 we can obtain L_q and W_q; from Figure 8 we can determine L and W. To use either Figure 7 or 8, we must compute the utilization factor $\rho = \lambda/M\mu$, where M is the number of channels and λ and μ are Poisson arrival and service rates as before. The service rate μ is the rate at each service faciiity, and the total effective service rate for the system is $M\mu$. By using Figure 7, for example, if $\lambda = 10$ per hour, $\mu = 4$ per hour, and $M = 5$, then $\rho = 10/(5 \times 4) = 0.5$. From Figure 7, $L_q = \lambda W_q = 0.14$ unit in the waiting line. Since $\lambda = 10$, $W_q = 0.14/10 = 0.014$ hour. Figure 8 would be used in a similar way to determine L and W.

FIGURE 7. L_q (mean number in queue) or λW_q for different values of M versus the utilization factor ρ. $L_q = \lambda W_q$.

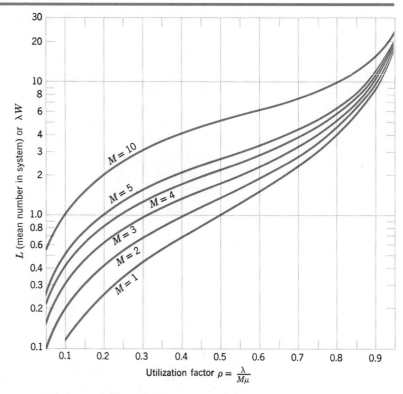

FIGURE 8. *L* (mean number in system) or λW for different values of *M* versus the utilization factor ρ. $L = \lambda W$.

The Effect of Increasing the Number of Channels. To compare the effects of increasing the numbers of channels, it is useful to plot curves for line lengths and waiting times versus the utilization factor which may now be generalized as $\rho = \lambda/M\mu$, where *M* is the number of channels. Figure 7 and 8 show line lengths and waiting times for $M = 1, 2, 3, 4, 5,$ and 10. If, for example, we are faced with a situation where $\rho = 0.9$ for the single-channel case, then L_q is approximately 8 from Figure 7. Adding a second channel reduces the utilization factor to $\rho = 0.9/2 = 0.45$, which results in $L_q = 0.23$ from Figure 7. The effects are surprisingly large; that is, we can obtain disproportionate gains in queue length and waiting time by increasing the number of channels. We can see intuitively that this might be true from Figure 6 since queue length and waiting time begin to increase very rapidly at about $\rho = 0.8$. A rather small increase in the capacity of the system (decrease in ρ) at these high loads can produce a large decrease in line length and waiting time.

Let us return now to the tool crib example. If a second tool crib attendant were added, the utilization factor becomes $\rho = 1/(2 \times 1.2) = 0.417$, whereas previously it was 0.833. Reading approximate values from the curves of Figure 7, $L_q = 0.175$ and $W_q = 0.175/\lambda = 0.175/1 = 0.175$ minute per mechanic. The cost of mechanics' waiting time is now reduced to

$$480 \times \frac{0.175}{60} \times 4 = \$5.60 \text{ per day}$$

The idle time of the attendants has increased by 8 hours. However, since there is no more work to be done than before, it is simply distributed between two attendants. The new idle time cost is then

$$\$2.67 + \$2 \times 8 = \$18.67 \text{ per day}$$

The combined cost of waiting plus idle time is much less (\$24.27) when two attendants are available than when only one was available (\$136.17). We can also see without further detailed analysis that it would not be economical to add a third attendant, since the incremental cost of doing so would be \$16.00 per day and the waiting time cost with two attendants is only \$5.60 per day with two attendants.

The Effect of Pooling Facilities.   This effect can also be seen from Figure 7. Suppose, for example, that since we find a second attendant is warranted following our previous analysis, the proposal is made to decentralize and have two separate tool cribs. What effect will this have on waiting time costs? With two separate tool cribs we shall assume that half the mechanics go to each, so the average arrival rate at each crib is now 0.5 arrival per minute. The utilization factor is then $\rho = 0.417$ and waiting time per mechanic is $L_q/\lambda = 0.3/0.5 = 0.6$ minute from Figure 7. This translates into a waiting time cost for the two tool cribs of

$$\frac{0.6}{60} \times 480 \times 4 = \$19.20 \text{ per day}$$

This compares to \$5.60 per day waiting time cost for the single facility with two attendants. The result is clear. One large facility can give better service than an equivalent number of small facilities. This, of course, accounts only for the waiting time costs. In the case of the tool crib, a centralized facility would have other economic advantages and disadvantages such as reduced total investment in tools and increased transportation time by mechanics.

FINITE WAITING LINE MODELS

Many practical waiting line problems which occur in production systems have the characteristics of finite waiting line models. This is true whenever the population of machines, men, or items which may arrive for service is limited to a relatively small finite number. The result is that we must express arrivals in terms of a unit of the population rather than as an average rate. Arrivals then are expressed as arrivals per time unit per item in the population arriving. In the infinite waiting line case the average length of the waiting line is effectively independent of the number in the arriving population, but in the finite case the number in the queue may represent a significant proportion of the arriving population; therefore the probabilities associated with arrivals are affected. The resulting mathematical formulations are somewhat more difficult computationally than for the infinite queue case. Fortunately, however, finite queuing tables [8] are available which make problem solution very simple. Although there is no definite number that we can point to as a dividing line between finite and infinite applications, the finite queuing tables have data for populations from 4 to 250 and may be taken as a general guide. The tables are based on a finite model for exponential times between arrivals and service times.

SUMMARY

Waiting line models are among the most used of quantitative methods today. The common assumptions of Poisson arrivals and exponential holding times are reasonable in quite a number of instances. In many cases where they are not appropriate, we have a nonhomogeneous situation where two or more basic conditions are mixed; for example, the service times of a punch press department that handled both repair work (very small orders) and production work (large orders). In such a case the resulting distribution of service times really reflects two basic distributions.

Note that we did not cover any of the multiple-phase cases, situations involving arrival and/or service distributions other than the Poisson, and queue disciplines other than first come–first served. It is felt that these more complex structures are best handled through the technique of computer simulation. Also, because of work done by P. M. Morse [6] and others, there is considerable information about the machine maintenance problem.

1. Outline and compare the four alternate structures of waiting line situations discussed. Suggest a physical example of each.
2. If arrival rates follow the Poisson distribution, what would be the distribution of the times between arrivals?
3. What evidence is there that arrival rates in actual situations do in fact follow the Poisson distribution?
4. What evidence is there that service times follow the negative exponential distribution in actual processing situations?
5. Contrast infinite and finite waiting line models. What is the characteristic of the situation that makes the distinction between the two kinds of waiting line models?
6. Why is it not true that the difference between the mean number in the system L and the mean number in the waiting line L_q is simply the number of items being served?
7. Explain in physical terms why the waiting line may become infinitely long when the utilization factor is 1.
8. What are the effects on waiting time costs of pooling facilities?

PROBLEMS

1. Trucks arrive at a dock in a Poisson manner at the rate of 8 per hour. Service time distribution is closely approximated by the negative exponential. The average service time is 5 minutes. Calculate:
(a) The mean number in the waiting line.
(b) The mean number in the system.
(c) The mean waiting time.
(d) The mean time in the system.
(e) The probability of six units being in the system.
(f) The utilization factor.

2. People arrive at a theater ticket booth in a Poisson-distributed arrival rate of 25 per hour. Service time is constant at 2 minutes. Calculate:
(a) The mean number in the waiting line.
(b) The mean waiting time.
(c) The utilization factor.

3. A taxi cab company has 4 taxi cabs at a particular location. Customer arrival rates and service rates are Poisson distributed. The average arrival rate is 10 per hour. The average service time is 20 minutes.
(a) Calculate the utilization factor.
(b) From Figure 7, determine the mean number in the waiting line.
(c) From Figure 8, determine the mean number in the system.
(d) Test the answers to b and c by the formula $L = L_q + \lambda/\mu$.

(e) Determine the mean waiting time.

(f) Determine the mean time in the system.

4.   Using the data in problem 3:

(a) What would the utilization factor be if the number of taxi cabs was increased from 4 to 5?

(b) What would be the effect of this change on the mean number in the waiting line as determined by Figure 7?

5.   A trucking company has docking facilities with Poisson-distributed arrival and service rates. Trucks arrive at the rate of 10 per hour and the unloading rate is 2 trucks per man-hour. The time to unload a truck is inversely proportional to the number of workers unloading. The docking facility permits either one or two trucks to be unloaded at the same time. Under the present system, the entire crew works on the same truck until unloading is completed. Each man on the dock crew is paid $2 per hour. The cost of an idle truck and driver is estimated to be $15 per hour.

(a) Determine the optimal number of workers for this docking facility and the average hourly cost.

(b) What would be the effect of a 10 per cent increase in arrival rate on the optimal number of men? On the utilization factor?

(c) What change in average hourly cost would result if the men were split into two crews?

(d) What advantages would be gained by such a split?

(e) Is such a split analogous to the facilities pooling as discussed in the chapter?

6.   A hotel beauty shop has Poisson process arrival and service rates of 3 per hour and 1.25 per hour, respectively. Beauty operators are paid $1.75 per hour plus tips, and, time and one-half for over 40 hours per week. Incremental profit averages $1 per customer; fixed expenses are $100 per week, and the shop operates on a 6 day 48 hour week. Because of competitive factors, the management does not want customers to wait more than 15 minutes on the average.

(a) Determine the optimal number of beauty operators.

(b) Determine the weekly profit.

(c) Evaluate the possibility of remaining open an extra hour each night if the average demand would be 10 per cent less than normal.

(d) How much can the shop afford to pay per week for advertising that will increase business 5 per cent?

7.   An automatic vending machine dispenses a cup of coffee in 1 minute. Customers arrive every 5 minutes according to a Poisson process.

(a) What is the average waiting time per person?

(b) What is the average number of people that will be waiting for service?

8.   Airplanes arrive at an airport at an average rate of 1 every 2 minutes (Poisson process). The average rate at which airplanes can be landed and the airstrip cleared is 1 every 90 seconds.

(a) What is the average waiting time per airplane?

(b) What is the average number of planes waiting to land?

(c) What changes in (a) and (b) would occur if the service rate were changed to 25 per hour?

9. A stenographer in a large insurance company types renewal notices to be sent to policyholders. The timing of these notices is random since they are determined by the dates of sales. As a net result, the number of notices that need to be sent during any 8-hour day is subject to considerable variation. A study reveals that the average number of renewal notices per day is 300 and the distribution follows a Poisson process. From a time study of the operation it was found that the time to process 1 renewal was fairly constant with a standard time of 1.5 minutes per renewal notice.

(a) What is the average time lag from the time a renewal comes up until it is processed?

(b) What is the average backlog of renewals waiting to be processed?

(c) What would be the effect on the answers obtained in (a) and (b) if the average number of renewal notices increased by 5 per cent?

10. Vehicles arrive at a toll gate at the rate of 10 per minute according to a Poisson process. The attendant can issue toll tickets at a rate of 12 per minute in a manner that approximates a Poisson process.

(a) What is the average length of waiting line?

(b) What is the average time that a vehicle waits at the gate?

(c) If the attendant were replaced by a machine with a constant service rate of 12 per minute, what would be the answers to (a) and (b)?

11. A doctor has more business than he can handle. He now schedules patient arrivals at an average rate of 1 every 15 minutes. The actual arrival pattern of individuals tends to follow a Poisson process. The present average service rate is 1 patient every 10 minutes (Poisson process). A proposed relayout of the consultation offices, utilizing more room and making possible less lost time, would enable the doctor to increase the average service rate to 1 patient every 6 minutes. If the average contribution to overhead and profit is $5 per visit and the doctor does not wish to increase the average waiting time per patient, what is the net change in hourly contribution to profit and overhead?

REFERENCES

[1] Brigham, F. "On a Congestion Problem in an Aircraft Factory." *Operations Research*, **3** (4), 412–428, 1955.

[2] Buffa, E. S. *Operations Management: Problems and Models* (3rd ed.). John Wiley, New York, 1972.

[3] Churchman, C. W., R. L. Ackoff, and E. L. Arnoff. *Introduction to Operations Research*. John Wiley, New York, 1957.

[4] Feorene, O. J. "The Gentle Art of Simultation." *Proceedings, Twelfth Annual Industrial Engineering Institute*, UCLA, pp. 15–18, 1960.

[5] Malcolm, D. G. "Queuing Theory in Organization Design." *Journal of Industrial Engineering*, 19–27, Nov.–Dec. 1955.

[6] Morse, P. M. *Queues, Inventories, and Maintenance.* John Wiley, New York, 1958.

[7] Nelson, R. T. "An Empirical Study of Arrival, Service Time, and Waiting Time Distributions of a Job Shop Production Process." Research Report No. 60, *Management Sciences Research Project*, UCLA, 1959.

[8] Peck, L. G., and R. N. Hazelwood. *Finite Queuing Tables.* John Wiley, New York, 1958.

[9] Saaty, T. L. *Elements of Queuing Theory.* McGraw-Hill, New York, 1961.

[10] Saaty, T. L. "Resume of Useful Formulas in Queuing Theory." *Operations Research*, 5 (2), 1957.

[11] Sasieni, M., A. Yaspan, and L. Friedman. *Operations Research.* John Wiley, New York, 1959.

part three

Design of Productive Systems

Production Design & Processes

The minimum possible cost of producing a part or product is established originally by the designer. The most clever production engineer cannot change this situation, he can only minimize the production cost within the limitations of the design. Therefore, the obvious time to start thinking about basic modes of production for parts and products is while they are still in the design stage. This conscious effort to design for low manufacturing cost is referred to as *production design*, as distinct from functional design. To be sure, the designer's first responsibility is to create something that functionally meets requirements, but once this is accomplished, ordinarily there are alternatives of design, all of which meet functional requirements. Which of these alternatives will minimize production cost? A well-conceived design has already narrowed the available alternatives and specified, for example, a sand-casting, if that is appropriate in view of both function and cost considerations.

Given the design, *process planning* for manufacture must be carried out to specify, in careful detail, the processes required and their sequence. Production design first sets the minimum possible cost that

215

can be achieved through the specification of materials, tolerances, basic configurations, methods of joining parts, etc. Final process planning then attempts to achieve that minimum through the specification of processes and their sequence which meet the exacting requirements of the design specifications. Here, the process planner may work under the limitations of available equipment in small lot manufacture (see Chapter 19 on production scheduling). But if the volume is great or the design stable or both, he may be able to consider special-purpose equipment and special-purpose layout (see Chapter 12 on layout). In performing his functions, the process planner is setting the basic design of the production system.

The strong relation between product design and production cost has long been recognized by industry; various attempts to cope with the problem have been made. In general, engineers who design products are trained in the technical aspects of their specialties, such as mechanical design, electronics, and thermodynamics, and not in manufacturing methods and costs. On the other hand, production men often simply ignore the functional requirements of a part and meet the exact specifications while they curse the designer. This lack of mutual understanding is expressed by the following little poem, credited to Mr. Kenneth Lane, a design engineer at the General Electric Company [6].

As Some Men See Us

The Designer bent across his board
Wonderful things in his head were stored
And he said as he rubbed his throbbing bean
"How can I make this thing tough to machine?
If this part here were only straight
I'm sure the thing would work first rate,
But 'twould be so easy to turn and bore
It never would make the machinists sore.
I better put in a right angle there
Then watch those babies tear their hair
Now I'll put the holes that hold the cap
Way down in here where they're hard to tap.
Now this piece won't work, I'll bet a buck
For it can't be held in a shoe or chuck
It can't be drilled or it can't be ground
In fact the design is exceedingly sound."
He looked again and cried—"At last—
Success is mine, it can't even be cast."

To combat the problem, some companies have tried to train their designers concerning basic manufacturing processes and costs. Others have had production engineers consult with designers at the time of critical decisions; still others have turned over functional designs to an entirely different group whose responsibility is production design. Lockheed Aircraft Corporation [8] has a cost analysis group within their engineering division which is used primarily in making comparative cost analyses of design proposals. A monthly control graph is kept which shows the effect of design decisions on projected manufacturing cost in relation to the limits of the possible high and low, indicated by alternative designs that meet functional requirements.

The thesis of a production design philosophy is that nearly always alternatives of design exist that still meet functional requirements. For the projected volume of the part or product, then, what differences in cost would result? Here we must broaden our thinking because the possible areas of cost which can be affected by design are likely to be more pervasive than we imagine. There are the obvious cost components of direct labor and materials, but perhaps not so obvious are the effects on equipment costs, tooling costs, indirect labor costs, and the non-manufacturing costs of engineering. Indirect costs tend to be hidden, but suppose one design required 30 different parts whereas another required only 15. There are differences in indirect costs due to the greater paperwork and the cost of ordering, storing, and controlling 30 parts instead of 15 for each completed item. Figure 1 shows a comparison for just such a situation involving alternate designs of a typical aircraft control surface. The indirect cost for each design is composed of those items necessary to process parts through the paperwork system and includes items such as planning; tool ordering; material purchasing; shop and assembly order writing; storage of material; dispatching of material, tools, and parts; order control; accounting; transportation; inspection; etc.

A typical cost breakdown showing how design affects various components is shown in Figure 2. The shaded areas of Figure 2 indicate the relative amount of the cost category under the direct control of the design engineer. The shaded areas were determined by studies at Lockheed of detailed cost estimates over a period of years. Hundreds of designs were analyzed "by taking the difference in cost between two or more designs which were functionally acceptable, the difference in cost between the least and most expensive indicating the effect the Design Engineer had in determining the cost of the product [8]."

Design I

Total parts 20
Different parts 15
Identical parts 6

Contract indirect
(paperwork) cost $484.00

Design II

Total parts 20
Different parts 20
Identical parts 0

Contract indirect
(paperwork) cost $624.00

Design III

Total parts 9
Different parts 4
Identical parts 6

Contract indirect
(paperwork) cost $218.00

FIGURE 1. Effect of alternative designs on indirect labor costs. (From [8].)

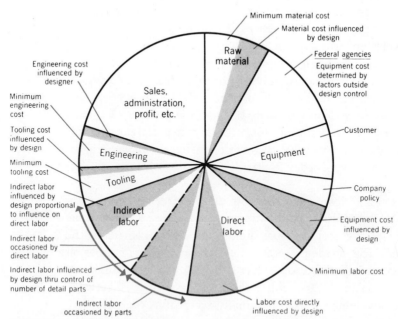

FIGURE 2. Cost breakdown of a transport airplane, showing the effect of design alternatives on various major components of cost. (From [8].)

The scope of production processes covers the entire spectrum from the completely manual task, through man-machine systems, to automated processes where labor is either indirect or of a vigilance nature. Manual tasks, usually in combination with mechanical aids, still account for a large share of productive activity. The design of these manual tasks and the manual or vigilance phases of machine operations are considered separately in Chapters 13 and 14. Manual operations, or man-machine operations that have a strong manual component, are typical of assembly work, offices, supermarkets, hospitals, and so on.

Some production processes have a considerable technological base. The metal-working industries, wood-working industries, plastics, and chemicals are representative of these.

The basic nature of processing is one of transformation, that is, something is happening which in some way transforms the thing being worked on. In general, these transformations may effect a chemical change, alter the basic shape or form, add or subtract parts as in assembly, change the location of the thing being processed as in transportation operations, provide or alter information systems as in clerical operations, or check on the accuracy of any other process as in inspection operations.

Processes Involve Transformation

Chemical Processes.   Chemical processes are common in industries such as petroleum, plastics, steel-making, and aluminum. It is, of course, impossible to generalize in a short time the nature and range of chemical processing. Industrially, these processes occur both as batch processes and continuous processes. Illustrative of batch processes is the operation of a blast furnace in the steel industry. Figure 3 is a diagram of the basic flows involved. In the operation of a blast furnace, pig iron is produced from iron ore, coke, and limestone. Skip cars running up an inclined track charge iron ore, coke, and limestone into the top hopper in alternate layers. Blasts of hot air are injected at the bottom of the furnace which serves to support the combustion of the coke. As the coke burns, the oxygen in the iron ore is absorbed. The charge gradually moves downward in the furnace into progressively higher temperature zones until the iron becomes molten and forms a pool at the bottom of the furnace. The limestone absorbs certain impurities. Periodically a batch of molten iron is drawn off into the ladle and is later poured into ingots. Continuous chemical processes might be typified by petroleum processes. Here the material being processed

FIGURE 3.   Diagram of a blast furnace for making pig iron.

moves continuously through a series of heating, pressurizing, mixing, etc.—processes of great complexity.

Processes to Change Shape or Form.   The most common processes of this general type are found in the metal-forming and machining industries, the wood-working industry, and in plastic molding and forming. In the metal industries, some of the primary forming operations may take place at the mill, such as the rolling of basic shapes in steel, aluminum, or other metals. The result of these processes are bars, sheets, billets, I-beams, and many other shapes which are standard and can be used to advantage for further processing. Alternately, some products would require beginning with some molding process such as sand-casting or die-casting to establish the basic shape or form which may or may not require further processing. Figure 4 shows four important steps in the die-casting process. Other basic forming processes are powder metallurgy, drop-forging, and stamping. Table I shows a comparison of various forming processes together with conditions for their appropriate use.

Metal machining is accomplished through basic machine tool processes which involve the generation of cylindrical surfaces, flat surfaces, complex curves, and holes. This classification seems simple enough, but the number of different types of machine tools to accomplish these tasks is multiplied by different sizes and shapes of parts to be machined, the quality of finish required, accuracy demands, and differences in output rate demanded in various manufacturing situations. Thus a shaper and a planer are both used to generate flat surfaces. For the

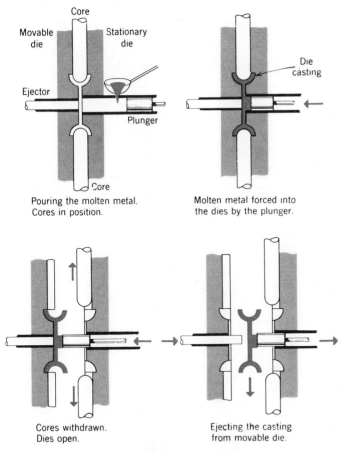

FIGURE 4. The die-casting of brass, aluminum, or magnesium in horizontal plunger cold-chamber machine. (Courtesy Reed-Prentice Corporation.)

TABLE I. Comparison of Forming Processes

Forming Processes	Tolerances Held	Setup or Tools	Run or Process Time	Finishing Required	Appropriate Volume	Other Comments
Sand-casting	Loose, 1½%/inch	Pattern, core	Long	Relatively large amount of metal to be removed	Low	Great flexibility
Die-casting	Very good, no finish machining required in many cases	Dies expensive : $1000–$10,000	Short	None to relatively small	High	In general, limited to low melting-point alloys
Powder metallurgy	Very good, ±.05%/inch	Dies, $2000 and more	Mold and sintering (intermediate)	Usually none	>5000	Very hard parts can only be made this way
Drop forge	Good	Dies, expensive	Intermediate	Relatively small	Intermediate to high	Great strength
Stamping	Good	Dies, expensive	Short	Small	High	

planer, however, the work reciprocates instead of the tool, and its reciprocating table accommodates large pieces better than does the shaper. Similarly, a grinder can produce cylindrical surfaces as does the lathe, or flat surfaces like the mill, but the big difference in application is in resulting accuracy and finish. The grinder, therefore, is largely a finishing tool, used only after other machine tools have made the rough cuts that produce the basic dimensions.

A lathe produces cylindrical surfaces, holes, threads, plain surfaces on the face of the work, and so on. But different types of lathes are adapted to different production rates. The engine lathe might be used if one or a few parts are to be produced. But if several thousand parts are to be produced, some type of automatic lathe would probably be considered. In this proliferation of machine types, we are not including special-purpose machines. The automatic lathe would still be considered a general-purpose machine, since it can be set up to run various kinds of materials and parts in its general capability class. In all of these machining operations, metal is removed from the part in small chips by the cutting action of a tool. The cutting action is accomplished by either a rotating or reciprocating action of the tool relative to the part. In combination with this motion, either the tool or the work must "feed" to produce a continuous cutting action over an entire surface. Figure 5 shows a summary of tool and work piece motion for the main machine tools. Many machine tool processes have been automated through a process which combines computer instructions with the machine. These automated processes, known as numerically controlled processes, are discussed in greater detail later in this chapter.

Assembly Processes.   Some processes used to assemble parts and materials are welding, soldering, riveting, screw-fastening, and stapling and adhesive joining. Assembly processes are common in the automotive industry, the electronics industry, the appliance industry, and many others. Indeed, they are extremely common in all mechanical-electrical industries. The usual situation prevailing for assembly operations involves a considerable proportion of manual work, usually supplemented by mechanical aids. In general, automation has not touched most assembly operations with the exception of high-volume electronics assembly. With the development of printed circuitry, the electronics industry has designed automatic equipment to assemble component parts, such as resistors and condensers, to the printed circuit boards. Much of the analysis of assembly types of operations depends on the analysis of hand motions and the relationships between the operator and his tools.

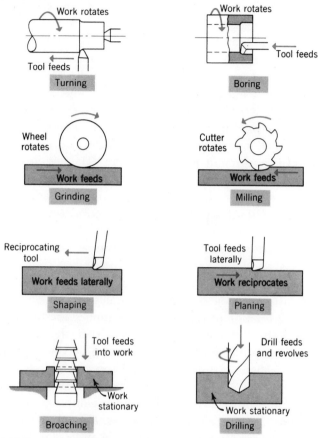

FIGURE 5. Basic processes used for machining parts to planned dimensions. (From [2].)

Transport Processes. The transformation taking place in a transport process is the transformation of place. The economist would state that by means of a transport process we have given a part or product "place utility." Whatever the rationale, transport processes are of extreme importance in most production systems. In some phases of operations management, such as distribution, the transport operation is the one of central interest. In manufacturing, internal material handling represents one of the most costly kinds of operations performed. In Chapter 12 we focus on the nature of material-handling activities for functional and line production.

Clerical Processes and Information Systems. Whereas mechanical kinds of processes tend to change shape or form, clerical processes transform information. The volume of clerical activity has grown rapidly to the point where the number of clerical workers in the United States is greater than the number of blue-collar workers. The equivalent of clerical activity is accomplished with a broad spectrum of techniques extending from the purely manual through all degrees of mechanization to the epitomy of automation, the integrated data processing system.

The design of the item being processed in information systems is dependent on the nature of the system itself and the degree of mechanization involved. Manual clerical operations exert a relatively small influence on the design of the item being processed. On the other hand a punched card system, or a computer based system virtually dictates the use of punched cards, magnetic tape, or perforated paper tape as the bases for information storage and input to the system. One punched card has 80 columns or a capacity for 80 characters (letters or numbers). A little over eight inches of perforated paper tape and about three-eighths inch of magnetic tape can contain the same number of characters. Magnetic tape input also has the advantage of speed. Data can be read at rates up to 170,000 characters per second, while cards are typically read at the rate of 250 to 300 characters per second and perforated tape is read at about 400 characters per second. By contrast, good human reading speeds are in the range of 300 to 500 words per minute of text with reading of numbers being very much slower. Perforated paper tape systems have been integrated with present methods of developing and transcribing records by incorporating tape writing units with typewriters and adding machines, etc. The perforated tape is then produced as a by-product of an operation necessary to the existing paperwork system. Figure 6 shows a typical application.

Figure 7 shows an overview of a total management information system for the Able Manufacturing Company, a hypothetical company manufacturing styled goods with manufacturing plants in various parts of the country and nationwide sale and distribution facilities. The concept of the system as a whole is based on a central information processing unit with a broad, up-to-date data base pertinent to sales, planning, control, finance, procurement, production, warehousing, and distribution. Current information from the various functional areas of the enterprise flows into the central processor as inputs. By a variety of models and/or programs, the various outputs are generated in the form of regular and special reports. With such an integrated system, different kinds of reports for different purposes and for different levels of management are relatively easy to generate. For example, a sales forecast by sales regions in gross dollars of sales may be of value

FIGURE 6. (*a*) Friden FLEXOWRITER produces a code-punched card as a by-product of writing the original document. (*b*) Friden Add-Punch machine. (Courtesy Friden, Inc.)

FIGURE 7. Overview of Able Manufacturing Company's integrated management information system. (From J. W. Konvalinka and H. G. Trentin, "Management Information Systems," *Management Services*, Sept.—Oct. 1965.)

to the sales function and to general management. But in that form it is useless to the production function which needs the information translated into products, assemblies, parts, and the equivalent demand on various classes of equipment in order to procure materials and schedule production.

General- versus Special-Purpose Machines. General-purpose machines have general use capability in their field. For example, a typewriter is a general-purpose machine. It can be used for various kinds of copy: letters, manuscripts, some kinds of charts, and figures. On the other hand, a typewriter can be made special purpose by adapting it to the special uses of accounting. The accounting machines do the accounting tasks very well, but perform poorly on many tasks demanded of a general typewriter. In the machine shop we find the general-purpose lathe, drill press, milling machine, and planers which are capable of performing their functions by generating cylindrical surfaces, holes, and flat surfaces on a wide variety of parts and materials. Yet, where the situation warrants it, we find special designs of these types of machines which are meant to produce some one part or group of parts very efficiently.

An example might be a special lathe to produce proper outside diameters for an automotive piston. It has special quick-clamping devices and special cutters, is of the right size, and runs at the proper spindle speed to machine the outside diameter surface in minimum time, yet its capability would be restricted in the machining of other parts. Since the volume of pistons is so great, this specialization of equipment design is warranted.

General-purpose machines find their field of application in an atmosphere of low volume and instability of part or product design, or of market; that is, where conditions demand flexibility. They are of fairly standard design and, therefore, first cost and obsolescence costs are likely to be lower than for an equivalent special-purpose machine. Special-purpose machines commonly have evolved from their general purpose counterparts as the volume of a particular part or product increased. By specializing designs, higher production rates can be achieved. The special design might include special fixtures, more automatic devices, and better integration of the machine design with the special conditions of the task.

Thus, incoming work might be fed automatically to the machine, instead of requiring the operator to procure a part and place it in the machine. Sometimes the special design incorporates additional machine operations which also serve to increase productivity. The more costly special-purpose design may result in lower unit production cost because of considerably lower labor costs. The economic methods of analysis of Chapters 5 and 6 may be used as a basis for decision making between general- and special-purpose machines for specific instances. The use of economic analysis, of course, assumes conditions of market stability and stability of part or product design, so that machine obsolescence is not likely to occur immediately from these sources.

AUTOMATION

No discussion of processes is complete today without reference to automation. Although automation is new in the sense that principles have only recently been applied to the mechanical and assembly types of processes, the basic ideas are not new. Such processes as the thermostatic control of room temperature have been known and used for some time. The common float valve used in toilets automatically fills the tank to a given level and then shuts off. The process industries have used the principals of automation for some time to control chemical processes.

The economics of industrial mechanization logically began with the tasks where mechanization could be justified and where machines could perform tasks that could not be accomplished manually. In the march of economic events, labor has become more expensive relative to machines and a continuous process of substitution has taken place. It is logical that the most difficult technological developments should not be the first ones applied. Even if known one hundred years ago, these ideas would not have been justified economically. Therefore, the substitution of machines to perform the *control* functions of the human operator had to wait until the present when labor rates are very high. The ultimate development in this trend is a completely integrated automatic sequence beginning with the input of raw material and ending with a final product, without human labor or control other than to design and build the original equipment and process and to maintain the system once installed.

Actually, automation has two main branches. The first is concerned with the control of processes as we have discussed, and involves the *feedback* of information to maintain control of a variable such as temperature, pressure, dimension, or chemical composition within certain predetermined limits. Here we find the field of process control and the digital or numerical control of machine tools. The second branch may or may not involve feedback of information, but it is essentially the automatic handling of parts between operations in such a way that the part is indexed and placed in the exact position to be processed by the subsequent operation or machine. The whole sequence is co-ordinated carefully so that the several operations in the sequence go through their cycles at just the right instant when all parts have been indexed in position. What we have then is one giant machine where the individual operations are components of the machine, coordinated to work as a unit.

The possible types of operations that can be included in such a sequence are limited only by economics and the imagination of the engineers. Most types of metal machining, gaging, and inspection pro-cesses have been incorporated as well as some assembly or joining operations. These developments are typical of large-volume, standard-ized product designs such as automobiles. The first type which employs feedback control is termed a *closed loop*. The second type, which we might characterize as progressive mechanization, is termed *open loop*. Both are automation since the result is automatic production. First, let us examine the nature of feedback so we can see the difference between open and closed loops.

Feedback. We can demonstrate the nature of feedback and feedback control by contrasting a simple processing situation with and without feedback. In Figure 8 we have diagrammed one station of what could be considered a series of operations. Parts are fixed to the transfer device which moves them past cutting tools such as the one shown in Figure 8. Other cuts might be sidecuts, slots, induction hardening,

FIGURE 8. Open-loop setup for milling a part to the standard dimen-sion, 1.000 ± 0.001 inch. Once set, the cutter should continue to produce parts that are in control unless something in the system changes, such as tool wear or movement from the original setting. When out-of-control dimensions are noted, the operator must determine the cause and reset the cutter. The system presumably will produce parts in control for another period of time. The system is an open loop because there are no direct means of ensuring that the finish dimension continuously will meet control standards.

grinding, lapping, or gaging. All of the tools, as well as the one illustrated, are preset to yield the desired dimensions on the output. Once set, the operations proceed automatically. Direct labor would be required only to load parts into the line series of operations, unload at the far end, and to start and stop the entire process. Depending on the part design and the relative economic advantage, the loading and unloading operations could be mechanized also. At each operation, including the one shown, established standards must be met. These standards must be related to the dimensions produced, the surface quality, hardness, etc. For the operation shown in Figure 8, the standard to be controlled is the dimension 1.000 ± 0.001 inch.

Through quality control procedures at the end of the sequence of operations or through intermediate checkpoints, we gain information about the state of control of the process. If part dimensions go out of control, the machine will be stopped, the cause determined, cutters reground, reset, or changed, and the machine started up again. Once the cutters are reset, we can assume that parts will be produced automatically again for some time until future changes or adjustments are required. This is *automation*, but we term it *open-loop* automation because there is no direct automatic means for insuring that the output of the system will meet the desired standards. How do we close the loop?

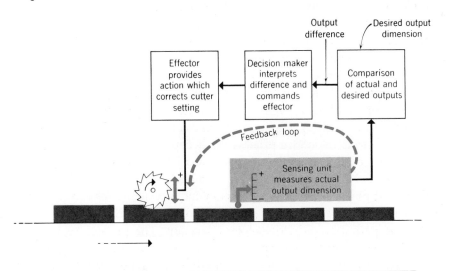

FIGURE 9. Schematic representation of closed-loop setup for milling a part. Loop is closed because a measure of output is now fed back to provide direct and automatic means for correcting cutter setting.

Figure 9 shows schematically what is required to close the loop. Closing the loop is called *feedback*. In a feedback loop we need a *sensing unit* to measure the output (in our example, a dimension) and a *means of comparison* of the actual output with the desired output. The difference, which may be either positive or negative, is then fed to a *decision maker* which interprets the error information and commands the *effector* to make a correction in the proper magnitude and direction so that the output will meet standards. In our example, this feedback loop could compensate for expected tool wear and other deviations from normal operation.

A Computer-Controlled Production Line. As mentioned earlier, the ultimate in the development of the automation trend is a completely integrated automatic sequence beginning with the input of raw material and ending with a final product, without human labor and control. This concept, applied to the manufacturing and control of carbon resistors, has been carried through by the Western Electric Company. These resistors are shown in Figure 10 and are used in immense quantities in a variety of electronic equipment. The resistors must work under extreme conditions of cold, heat, humidity, vibration, and shock. In certain defense equipment, a failure rate of no more than one per 200 million hours (23,000 years) of operation is permissible. This very high reliability requirement triggered the design and development of the automated system. In the past, individual precision components of this type have been made by manual or semiautomatic processes which invited contamination from handling and related difficulties stemming from human control.

The 110-foot long machine shown in Figure 11 has eleven machine stations on the line as well as the computer and control cabinets. In addition to controlling step by step details of manufacture, the computer which controls the entire process can accept a production schedule for a month's output and thereafter automatically issue detailed instructions to the fabricating machines to make and package any or all of four basic physical sizes of resistors in whatever quantities and resistance values desired. Feedback of processed data from three key points along the line permits rapid closed-loop operation. The process begins with the deposition of carbon on a tiny ceramic core. This core goes successively through inspection, termination, capping, establishment of resistance value, second inspection, molding of a protective case, electrical leakage inspection, final inspection, and packing. Throughout the entire sequence, the resistor is untouched by human hands.

Epoxy encapsulated resistor

Film free of any organic coatings

Protective air space

Gold sputtered terminations low contact resistance

Percussion welded lead

Epoxy effective moisture seal

Gold flashed cap

(a)

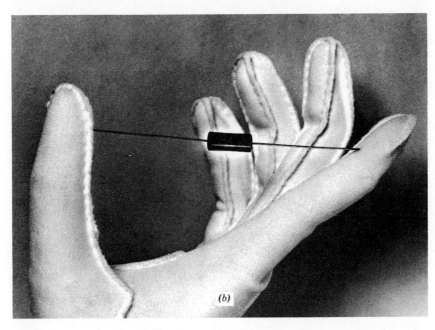

(b)

FIGURE 10. Typical resistor for which computer-controlled production line was developed. (a) Basic design and components of resistor. (b) Relative size of carbon resistors. (Courtesy Western Electric Company.)

The heart of the control equipment is a digital computer with a magnetic drum memory. Basically, the computer performs in three areas:

1. It programs production. A month's requirement can be fed into the computer at random. The computer then completely schedules and programs the work, arranging it according to the four resistor power sizes and an almost infinite number of possible resistance values.
2. Using the methods of statistical quality control, it analyzes control data plotted at three critical points in the automated process and

FIGURE 11. Machine stations in the automated production line for manufacturing deposited carbon resistors: A, computer; B, input-output control station; C, coating station; D, first inspection station; E, terminating station; F, conveyor control equipment; G, capping station; H, helixing station; J, second inspection station; K, encapsulating station; L, leak detector station; M, marking station; N, third inspection station; O, packing station; P, conveyor control equipment; Q, cap-lead welding machine; R, detail of conveyor line. (Courtesy Western Electric Company.)

applies statistical tests to determine if a trend in quality characteristics is developing.

3. It formulates quality control information to detect any drift away from the accepted manufacturing tolerances. No control action takes place while this analysis indicates normal statistical distributions around desired mean values. When a trend away from normality develops, however, the computer uses stored data to calculate new set-up information for the station that has gone out of control.

Numerically Controlled Processes

When positions and paths of cutter tools are under the control of a digital computer, we have numerical control. The feedback paths or circuits in this case do not emanate from a measurement taken on the workpiece itself, but from the basic positioning controls of the tools or tables which determine the position of cutters relative to the work. The feedback loops continually compare actual position with programmed position and applied correction when necessary.

Position Control. Position control is the simplest to achieve and is perhaps best illustrated by the drilling of holes that must be positioned accurately to meet standards. The drill tool can be moved in two dimensions to accomplish the desired position after which the tool advances into the work to produce the hole. Figure 12 shows a diagram of a position-controlled drill press. The system uses a punched paper tape

FIGURE 12.   Position-controlled drill press. (From [5].)

for instructions. The instructions are coded to indicate the beginning of a new block of data concerning the position reading for the x dimension and the y dimension. For both the x and y dimensions, the tape reads four numbers so the positions may be specified to the nearest 0.001 inch for the system diagrammed.

Let us use the x dimension as an example. If the actual reading is greater than that specified, the comparator registers a plus error which drives the x drive motor to rotate in the proper direction to correct the error. A negative error would cause the drive motor to rotate in the opposite direction. When the difference is zero, the drive motor stops. When differences for x and y dimensions are zero, the drillhead is signaled. It then drills the holes, retracts, and signals the tape unit to read in the next drill position data.

Contour Control. Contour control takes the ideas just stated one step further. Three dimensions must be controlled instead of two; in addition, it is not only position that must be specified, but the actual *path* that the cutter must take. This involves a much more complicated programming problem since complex curves and surfaces must often be specified. Such a system has great inherent flexibility in terms of part shapes that can be produced as well as in changeover from job to job. One of the system's major advantages is that the machine tool is not tied up for long periods during setup, since practically all preparation time is in programming. Thus, its big field of applicability is for parts that are produced in low volumes.

Programming Systems. Programming for numerically controlled systems has been carried to the point where the computer itself can do much of the detailed programming. It is given instructions in a special programming language similar to FORTRAN. One such programming language, called APT—Automatic Programming for Tools, includes over 300,000 instructions to a computer and is particularly pointed toward the continuous path or contour control problem. In this system the programmer works from design specifications; he gives instructions to the computer in terms of geometrical definitions of the part to be made and appropriate cutting routines. Each instruction calls forth an entire series of computer machine language instructions. The result is that an experienced part programmer using the APT language can program a complex part with relatively few instructions. Figure 13 shows an example of the instructions required to machine a "saddle surface."

The overall process is shown in Figure 14. The programming instructions prepared from the blueprint specifications are commonly called a "manuscript," as shown at (2) in Figure 14. This information is punched into control cards at (3) and read by a high-speed reader (4) into the central processing unit (5). Within the central processor the data are interpreted and processed according to the internally stored program. These results are translated into numerical control codes and simultaneously printed on a high-speed printer which produces a listing (6) of the part program instructions; control cards are printed out by a repunch unit (7). These output cards contain all of the control data necessary to guide the tool through the complete manufacture of the part in question. For tools that are guided by magnetic tape, the cards are converted. The resulting tape (8) controls the machine tool through the complete manufacturing cycle.

```
NOPOST
CUTTER/.5, 25
TOLER/.001
SOUTH=LINE/6,-6,-6,-6
RSIDE=LINE/6,-6,6,6
LSIDE=LINE/-6,-6,-6,6
PSIS/(PS=QADRIC/1,-1,0,0,0,0,0,0,0,36,-36)
FROM/(SETPT=POINT/12,-12,5)
GO/ON,RSIDE,ON,SOUTH,TO,PS
TLON,GOLFT/SOUTH,ON,LSIDE
C=3
D=.6
SWEEP=MACRO,A,B
GORGT/LSIDE
GORGT/(LINE/PARLEL,SOUTH,YLARGE,A)
GOLFT/RSIDE
GOLFT/(LINE/PARLEL,SOUTH,YLARGE,B)
TERMAC
LOOPST
MAC)    CALL/SWEEP,C,D
        IF(11.999-D)TERM,TERM,NEXT
NEXT)   C=C+.6
        D=D+.6
        JUMPTO/MAC
TERM)   GODLTA/0,0,5
        LOOPND
        GOTO/SETPT
        END
        FINI
```

FIGURE 13. Example of APT III programming instructions required for a "saddle surface." (Courtesy Dr. Gastone Chingari, Remington Rand Univac Division of Sperry Rand Corporation.)

Much of the designers latitude lies in the selection of materials and, often, the basic kind of processes. The real point is that each material and process is appropriate under certain combinations of conditions of

Basic Design
Alternatives

FIGURE 14. Overall programming system and information flow for a numerical control program system. (Courtesy Dr. Gastone Chingari, Remington Rand Univac Division of Sperry Rand Corporation.)

functional requirements and manufacturing cost. Manufacturing cost is drastically affected by the contemplated volume. Therefore, in general, sand-casting is economical for low volumes and the other methods for intermediate and high volumes. But we can give no definite number of parts that represents a breakeven volume between any pair of the materials and processes because the breakeven volume depends on the particular part.

Thus, a mere 1000 parts could justify a die-casting in preference to a sand-casting if the part were fairly simple and the resulting surfaces were of adequate finish and tolerance, since the machining and finishing costs would be somewhat less than those for sand-casting. On the other hand, a very high die cost for a more complex part might shoot the breakeven volume to 10,000. The important point is that for each design situation the functional alternatives must be compared on an incremental cost basis according to the principles discussed under economic analysis (Chapters 5 and 6). The following examples of contrasting designs and costs illustrate the kinds of cost factors that can be affected by the differences in the basic part design.

Processes and Materials.   Figure 15 shows a design contrast of a bracket for a Westinghouse electric motor. Originally it was machined

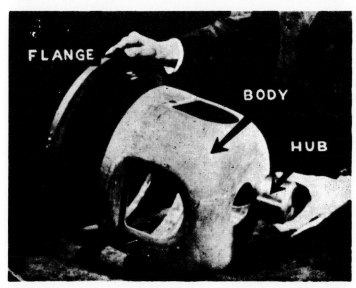

FIGURE 15.   Motor bracket designed to be formed in presses instead of from a casting resulted in a stronger, lighter design which was more economical to manufacture. (Courtesy Westinghouse Electric Corporation.)

from a casting. Analysis of functional and economic considerations revealed that it could be made in three pieces, as shown, and be stronger, lighter, and more economical to manufacture. The body and hub were designed to be drawn to shape from sheet steel, and the flange was designed to be formed in a press. The volume required of such brackets justified the expenditure of forming dies and resulted in a superior functional design as well.

Figure 16 shows two designs of a cam switch assembly. The design on the right involved a brass casting with the other parts assembled to it. The design on the left is from an extrusion and was functionally equivalent to the assembled design. The extruded design eliminated most of the machining and also cost less in raw material. The net difference was dramatic. To manufacture the extruded design cost 55 per cent of the amount needed for the assembled design.

Joining of Parts. The methods by which parts are joined together can result in important differences in cost. Figure 17 shows contrasting designs of a resistor tube. The design on the left makes it possible to spot weld the bracket at a substantially lower cost. Figure 18 makes a similar point, showing contrasting designs of a tank liner. The riveted design required that holes be made in the liners to admit the rivets and washers. The stapled design eliminated the need for the holes, and the stapling operation itself was much faster than riveting.

Tolerances. Design engineers are always accused of specifying closer tolerances than are necessary. This undoubtedly happens. It is obvious that to achieve a tolerance of ± 0.0001 inch is more expensive than to hold to only ± 0.0010 inch because of greater skill requirements, because of better equipment requirements, because of more scrap, and

FIGURE 16. The extruded design on the left cost only 55 per cent of the cast and assembled design. (Courtesy Westinghouse Electric Corporation.)

New design   Old design

FIGURE 17. The design of this resistor was functionally acceptable as either an arc-welded joint (right) or a spot-welded joint (left). However, spot welding was substantially more economical. (Courtesy Westinghouse Electric Corporation.)

because such operations as grinding may need to be added. But sometimes a closer tolerance will save adjusting and fitting time when parts are assembled. Figure 19 shows just such a case. The requirements for the assembly shown there are that the holes at the ends of the three contact arms be in line within ± 0.005 inch. These arms are mounted

Riveted   Stapled

FIGURE 18. Either riveted or stapled tank liners meet functional requirements, but stapling eliminates the need for holes to be made, rivets and washers to be positioned, and rivets to be upset. On balance, the stapled design is much more economical. (Courtesy Westinghouse Electric Corporation.)

FIGURE 19. Specification of closer tolerances reduced overall production costs on this assembly by eliminating costly adjusting operations. (Courtesy Westinghouse Electric Corporation.)

on a micarta bar with a steel center and are held in place by a part called a staple. The square bar could not be held to a tolerance closer than 0.012 inch and, as a result, the arms often fit too loosely or too tightly, with adjusting operations required. A closer tolerance specification of ± 0.002 inch for the bar eliminates the adjusting. The bar is molded oversized and broached to the closer tolerance. A special assembly fixture permits the broaching to be accomplished as a part of the assembly operation.

Simplified Designs. When two or more parts are finally assembled rigidly together, it raises the question of whether or not the assembled unit could be designed as one piece. This is often feasible when a single material will meet service requirements for all surfaces and cross sections of the part. Figure 20 shows such an example for a contact arm of a circuit breaker. The design on the left is made of two parts, a casting and a punching. The parts are machined separately and then joined together with two screws. The one-piece design shown on the right involves a precision casting which eliminates all but the very close machining. The one-piece design requires 74 per cent as much machining time, 50 per cent as much assembly time, and a substantial decrease in material cost. Because of very high volume, the one-piece design is $50,000 cheaper over a two and one-half year period.

Reduced Machining. Figure 21 shows a contrasting design for a cam subassembly of a limit switch, the difference being based on a substitution of raw materials. In the original design the shaft was machined from a solid bar. The large-diameter middle section of the shaft centered

FIGURE 20. The simplified design on the right involves a precision casting which requires only 74 per cent as much machining time, 50 per cent as much assembly time, and a substantial decrease in material cost compared to the design on the left. (Courtesy Westinghouse Electric Corporation.)

FIGURE 21. New and old designs for a cam subassembly of a limit switch. (Courtesy Westinghouse Electric Corporation.)

the spring and separated the two cams. A square was milled on each side to key with the square holes of the cams. The new design used square raw stock, with the size of the raw stock matching that of the square that was formerly milled. A sleeve was provided as a spacer for the cams which slipped over the square of the shaft. The milling operation was eliminated and the amount of material to be removed was greatly reduced; the savings more than offset the cost of manufacturing the new sleeve.

SUMMARY

In effect, the product designer establishes the constraints within which the production system designer must function. A broad knowledge of processes and their capabilities provides the basis for the rational consideration of basic alternatives available. These processes involve all types of transformations including physical, chemical, place, information content, etc. Processes also involves a complete range of the mode of execution from purely manual to completely automatic.

REVIEW QUESTIONS

1. Discuss the relationship of functional design and production design in determining a product design that meets functional requirements, cost considerations, and the limitations of available processes.
2. Discuss the nature of costs that can be affected by alternate designs.
3. What are the areas of applicability of molded plastics, sand-castings, die-castings, drop-forgings, stamped and formed parts, and machined parts? What kinds of considerations affect the choice?
4. Contrast the conceptual differences between mechanization and automation.
5. What are the elements of feedback control?
6. Describe automation with and without feedback control.
7. What is unique and different about the feedback control loops used with numerically controlled machine tools and the feedback control illustrated by Figure 9?
8. What is position control? Contour control?
9. Select a consumer or industrial product and critically analyze its design in terms of:
   (a) production design and producibility
   (b) its use by the consumer
   (c) its maintainability
10. Discuss the statement, "close tolerances in part manufacture result in high costs."

11. Select some nonmanufacturing activity and survey the nature of trans-
     formation operations which you find in the operations phase. Classify
     these operations in terms of the classification given in the text, for example,
     chemical, processes to change shape or form, assembly, transport, and
     clerical. Classify the equipment used in the operations activity in terms
     of its general or special-purpose nature.
12. Discuss the level and sophistication of automated activity in offices,
     banks, hospitals, warehousing, supermarkets, and department stores.

PROBLEM

The Precision Aerospace Manufacturing Company (PAMCo) is considering the
installation of its first numerically controlled machine tool. The machine being
considered is a highly flexible numerically controlled (N/C) milling machine
capable of handling a wide variety of machining tasks. The machine could be
purchased for $150,000. Since the machine would be PAMCo's first N/C
machine, the manufacturing engineer held that it was justified as *manufacturing
research* and need not meet the same rigid justification requirements normally
established for conventional equipment. This view found small support when
presented to the manufacturing manager. The frustrated engineer, now determined to make his point, decided to dig deeply to show the far-reaching effects
that numerical control methods could have on manufacturing costs. He felt
that the direct cost reductions were relatively obvious, but that the indirect
cost reductions were not properly understood and were perhaps more important than the direct cost reduction for N/C. To make the contrast a specific
one, the engineer selected one particular part which he felt was typical (see
Figure 22) and based all calculations on that part.

Direct Cost Reductions

The engineer obtained actual data for the manufacture of the part by conventional means and supplemented these data with estimates for part programming and the expected production cycle for the N/C machine. Table II
is a summary of the time requirements for the two contrasting technologies.
The engineer then projected his figures to an annual basis by assuming two-
shift operation (4000 hours per year) for the N/C machine and the equivalent
man-machine hours required by conventional methods, $\frac{0.895}{0.405} \times (4000) =$
8840 hours. The reduction in man-hours by use of the N/C machine was then
4840 hours per year. He then took the average hourly machine shop wage of
$2.75 per hour. To this he added 30 per cent for fringe benefits to cover retire-
ment, vacations and holidays, social security, insurance, and so on. In addition,
the factory overhead was computed at the rate of 25 per cent of direct labor
cost so the resulting effective hourly labor cost was $4.26 per hour. The com-
puted direct labor cost reduction was then 4840 × $4.26 = $20,618 per year.

FIGURE 22. Casting to be machined by N/C methods at PAMCo.

TABLE II. Estimated Time Requirements, Conventional versus N/C Machining Methods

	Conventional Machining				N/C Machining		
	Hours per 20-Part Lot				Hours per 20-Part Lot		
Operation	Setup	Run	Total	Operation	Part Programming and Setup	Run	Total
Mill boss	0.70	0.80	1.50	All operations	1.70	6.40	8.10
Drill, ream, and center bore boss hole	1.70	4.20	5.90				
Straddle mill 2 bosses	0.90	0.75	1.65				
Drill, bore, and ream 1½″ hole	1.20	4.00	5.20				
Drill, bore, and ream ½″ hole	1.05	2.60	3.65				
Totals	5.55	12.35	17.90	Totals	1.70	6.40	8.10
Total time per part, hours, 0.895				Total time per part, hours, 0.405			

Some of the indirect effects the enginer found were in the category of tooling costs, inventories, intraplant material handling, and inspection.

Tooling Costs. On investigation the engineer found two kinds of tooling cost reductions. The first was a one-time savings which would occur initially as new jobs were tooled up for the N/C machine to the point where the machine was operating at full load. He felt that these were not annual savings in tooling costs but a reduction in investment required; therefore, this savings should be deducted from the investment required for the N/C machine. The average tooling cost per job by conventional machining had been $1300; $600 was projected for the average N/C job. The engineer figured that 50 new jobs would load the new machine so an additional investment in tools of $35,000 was prevented in his view. The net installed cost of the N/C machine was then $115,000. In addition, he figured that there was an annual tool cost reduction which stemmed from two sources: the annual turnover of jobs for the machine, each new job requiring the smaller tool cost typical of N/C methods, and the annual reduction in the costs of storing, transporting, and repairing conventional tools. He found from company records that about 25 per cent of the jobs turned over each year, which would result in an annual tool cost reduction of $8750. On investigating the tool repair and carrying costs, the engineer found them to be 20 per cent of the value of tooling. He felt that legitimate cost reductions to include were the inventory carrying and repair costs on the one-time tool cost saving of $35,000, or an additional annual cost reduction of $7000.

Inventory Cost Reductions. The engineer reasoned that the combination of many operations into one, as indicated in Table II, eliminates the dead time between operations for handling and storage. This results in a shorter overall time that the job spends in process. In addition, the typically smaller setup time (cost) leads to shorter, more frequent runs which result in smaller finished goods inventories. Another factor leading to smaller finished goods inventories was the short lead time for N/C processes which would make possible a smaller safety or "buffer" stock requirement. Finally, typical inventory losses due to obsolescence should result from the shorter turn around or lead times. Because of the short lead times, parts formerly made to stock could be made to order, thus reducing substantially the risk of obsolescence.

On checking with the production control department, the engineer found that a typical job was in process for 3 months. Experience in plants where N/C had been tried seemed to average 2 months. In addition, the value of in-process inventory would be smaller because of the smaller direct costs indicated in Table II. Thus the amount of in-process inventory would be 33 per cent less and the value of an item in inventory would be 24 per cent less, assuming that valuation for inventory purposes would be average material cost of $5 per piece plus value added by manufacture. Thus the total value of in-process inventory should be reduced by 51 per cent. Calculating present equivalent in-process inventory levels, the engineer came up with a figure of $11,800 based on the average number of parts in process and their average value. The reduction of in-process inventory was therefore .51 × 11,800 = $6018. Previous studies had shown that the cost of carrying in-process inventory was 25 per cent, so the cost reduction was therefore $1505. The engineer did not attempt to appraise the cost reductions due to effects on finished goods inventories and risk of obsolescence.

Intraplant Material-Handling Cost Reductions.   The combining of operations due to N/C methods completely eliminates the usual material-handling activities normally required between operations. Previous studies in the Industrial Engineering Department indicated that the average material-handling trip cost $0.75. If we assume the part under study to be the typical one, five operations are combined into one. There will be about 500 lots per year, so 4 × 500 = 2000 trips per year saved. The annual cost reduction which results is 0.75 × 2000 = $1500. For some of the parts manufactured there was the possibility of considerable damage in transit; in some instances, special handling and packaging were used to avoid damage. A reduction in handling would, of course, also reflect itself in a reduction in these costs but no records existed to help estimate the magnitude of the saving. Besides, the engineer felt that he must be getting close to the needed total cost reduction to justify the new N/C machine. Before stopping, however, he investigated one more possibly fruitful area: inspection.

Inspection Cost Reduction.   The engineer reasoned that fewer inspections would be required if operations were combined, that less frequent inspection would be necessary, and that necessary inspection would often be less detailed. Since there is less human error involved in the operation of N/C machines, the inspector is in effect checking the correctness of the part program by checking carefully the first part produced. The result is that good control often can be maintained by first piece inspection only. Since in programming a part, all dimensions are in reference to some point, the inspection of the spacing of a series of holes may be accomplished by inspecting the first and last holes only. If these two holes are correctly positioned, those in between will be too. Not being sure how to estimate these savings, the engineer surveyed the N/C literature and found that a rule of thumb being used placed N/C inspection costs at one-half those for conventional machining. He estimated that approximately $3500 per year were being spent for inspection labor on a volume of parts approximately equivalent to what the N/C machine could handle. He, therefore, set the cost reduction due to inspection at $1750.

Summary of Cost Figures

On completing his survey the engineer summarized his cost study as shown in Table III. He completed a new report summarizing the advantages of N/C

TABLE III. Summary of Direct and Indirect Cost Reductions for an N/C Milling Machine Costing $150,000 Installed

Direct cost reduction:	
Labor	$20,618
Indirect cost reduction:	
Tool cost (annual turnover of jobs)	8,750
Carrying charges on one-time tool cost reduction	7,000
Inventory	1,505
Material handling	1,500
Inspection	1,750
Total annual cost reduction	$41,123
One-time reduction in tooling investment	$35,000

machines, together with his recommendation that the machine be purchased immediately. Then he presented it to the manufacturing manager.

(a) Evaluate the engineer's cost study.

(b) Should the manufacturing manager approve the recommendation?

REFERENCES

[1] Amber, G. H., and P. S. Amber. *Anatomy of Automation.* Prentice-Hall, Englewood Cliffs, N.J., 1962.

[2] Begeman, M. L., and B. H. Amstead. *Manufacturing Processes* (6th ed.). John Wiley, New York, 1969.

[3] Culliton, J. W. *Make or Buy.* Harvard University Graduate School of Business Administration, Soldiers Field, Boston, Mass., 1942.

[4] Eary, D. F., and G. E. Johnson. *Process Engineering for Manufacturing.* Prentice-Hall, Englewood Cliffs, N.J., 1962.

[5] Grabbe, E. M., editor. *Automation in Business and Industry.* John Wiley, New York, 1957.

[6] Hahir, J. P. "A Case Study on the Relationship Between Design Engineering and Production Engineering." *Proceedings, Fifth Annual Industrial Engineering Institute*, University of California, Berkeley–Los Angeles, 1953.

[7] Moore, H. D., and D. R. Kibbey. *Manufacturing Materials and Processes.* Richard D. Irwin, Homewood, Ill., 1965.

[8] Papen, G. W. "Minimizing Manufacturing Costs Through Effective Design." *Proceedings, Sixth Annual Industrial Engineering Institute*, University of California, Berkeley–Los Angeles, 1954.

[9] Schoderbek, P. P., editor. *Management Systems* (2nd ed.). John Wiley, New York, 1971.

[10] Starr, M. K. *Product Design and Decision Theory.* Prentice-Hall, Englewood Cliffs, N.J., 1963.

[11] Wilson, F. W., editor-in-chief. *Numerical Control in Manufacturing.* McGraw-Hill, New York, 1963.

10

Process Planning

Where does production design end and process planning begin? We have said that the basic process planning must begin during the product design stages where selections of materials and initial forms, such as casting, forgings, and die-castings, take place. The accepted end point for production design is manifested by the drawing release, which summarizes the exact specifications of what is to be made. Process planning takes over from this point and develops the broad plan of manufacture for the part or product. Thus we are using the term *process planning* in its organizational sense. In its functional sense, it includes the basic selection of processes necessitated in the design stage.

There is another important distinction that must be drawn, the relation of process planning to layout and facilities planning. Process planning necessarily blends with the layout of physical facilities. Some process planning takes place during the layout phases of the design of a production system. To accommodate physical and sequential limitations, to take advantage of available space, or to improve methods or sequence, modifications of the original process plans may be made. The division between process planning and layout is manifested by documents such as *route sheets* and *operation sheets* (which summarize the operations required, the preferred sequence of operations, auxiliary tools required, estimated operation times, etc.). We may regard the process plans as

251

inputs to the development of a layout. Figure 1 shows the overall conceptual framework of process planning in diagrammatic form.

Process planning takes as its input the drawings or other specifications which indicate *what* is to be made, and also the forecasts, orders, or contracts which indicate *how many* are to be made. The drawings are then analyzed to determine the overall scope of the project. If it is a complex assembled product, considerable effort may go into "exploding" the product into its components of parts and subassemblies. This overall planning may take the form of special drawings that show the relationship of parts, cutaway models, and assembly diagrams. Preliminary decisions about subassembly groupings to determine which parts to make and which to buy, as well as to determine the general level of tooling expenditure, may be made at this point. Then, for each part, a detailed routing is developed. Here technical knowledge of processes, machines and their capabilities is required, but of almost equal importance is a knowledge of production economics, as discussed in Chapters 5 and 6. Ordinarily the range of processing alternatives is considerable. The selection should be influenced strongly by the overall volume and projected stability of design. The concepts of breakeven volumes between basic alternatives come into play.

Product Analysis   Consider the problem of the initial setting up to manufacture the 12-part capacitor shown in Figure 2. It is an assembled product, although not complicated as assembled products go.

Assembly or "Gozinto" Charts.   Of what use are schematic models here? Particularly when the product is a complex one, they can help to visualize the flow of material and the relationships of parts: where they flow into the assembly process, which parts make up subassemblies, and where the purchased parts are used in the assembly sequence. Using the capacitor of Figure 2 as an example, a first step might be the preparation of an "assembly chart" or, as it is often called, a "Gozinto" chart (from the words "goes into"). Figure 3 is an assembly chart for the capacitor. Notice how clearly the chart shows the relationship of the parts, the sequence of assembly, and which groups of parts make up subassemblies. It is, in essence, a schematic model of the entire manufacturing process at one level of information and detail. Actually, the capacitor is simple enough so that the assembly chart could be eliminated; the operation process chart which follows also shows these relationships as well as additional information. However, for a really complex product such as an airplane or a missile, it would be difficult to compre-

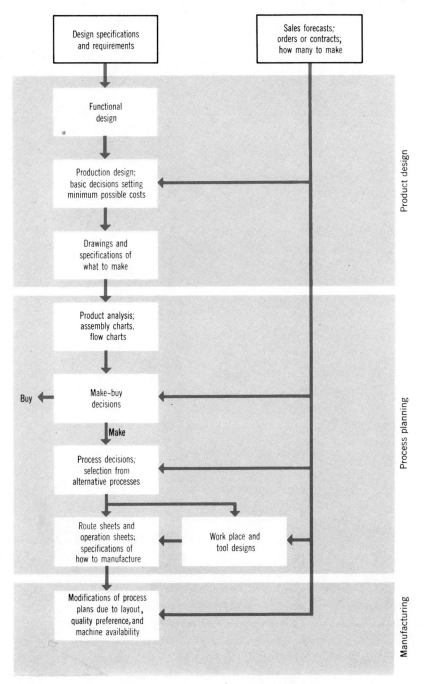

FIGURE 1. Diagram of the overall development of processing plans.

FIGURE 2. A capacitor, showing its several parts.

hend the grand plan for manufacture without an assembly chart. The assembly chart can be useful in making preliminary plans regarding probable subassemblies (alternatives usually exist; for instance, the cover subassembly could be assembled separately) and approprirate general methods of manufacture. For example, where do production lines fit in and where does process or functional layout seem appropriate? Final decisions depend on many factors. (See Chapter 12 on layout of physical facilities.)

FIGURE 3. Assembly or "Gozinto" chart for capacitor of Figure 2.

Operation Process Charts. Assuming that the product is already engineered, we have complete drawings and specifications of the parts and their dimensions, tolerances, and materials to be used. From the specifications and of "how many to manufacture" (contracts or sales forecasts), we can develop a plan of "how to manufacture." Decisions have to be made as to which parts to purchase and which to manufacture in our plant. The engineering drawings specify the locations, sizes, and tolerances for holes to be drilled, surfaces to be finished, etc., for each part. With this information and knowledge of the quantity to be produced and of manufacturing processes, the most economical equipment, processes, and sequences of processes can be specified.

The result of this work is a partial specification of "how to manufacture," usually summarized on a "route sheet" or "operation sheet," which specifies for each manufactured part the operations required in the preferred sequence, equipment to be used, special tools, fixtures, and gages. Estimates of the required setup time and run time are often added. All of this information can be summarized in the form of an operation process chart. Such a chart for the capacitor is shown in Figure 4. It is essentially a summary of all required operations and inspections for the capacitor. Symbols have been adopted: a large circle for an operation and a square for an inspection. This is all cast

Operation

Inspection

in the basic framework of the assembly chart so that now we have a schematic diagram of the basic flow of the parts from machine to machine, as well as the structure of how parts are related in the subassembly and assembly processes.

The operation process chart is of great value in the development of a layout plan. It shows clearly the operations to be performed, their sequence, and the equipment to be used. In the development of a layout, basic questions can be raised regarding the necessity of certain operations and possibilities for combining and rearranging the sequence of operations to improve physical flow.

Analysis of Existing Operations.   We have been discussing the operation process chart in terms of the development of a plan for manufacturing a new product and developing new facilities, but it is equally applicable to the analysis of existing operations. As time passes, changes creep into manufacturing plans because of redesign, the addition or elimination of products, and advances in manufacturing technology.

Sometimes operations are added to meet a temporary emergency; they then become permanent because no one takes action to delete them when the need passes. Reviews of existing operations are often very fruitful for eliminating duplication and illogical flow. The breakdown of the overall manufacturing process into its operations, and examination of the logical structure of the operation process chart form the basis for questioning the existence of every activity as well as the relationship of the activities.

Product Flow Process Charts. The flow process chart is similar in concept to the operation process chart, except that it adds more detail and has a slightly different field of application. The flow process chart adds transportation and storage activity to the information already recorded on an operation process chart. Thus, whereas the latter focuses only on the productive activity, the flow process chart focuses on the nonproductive activity as well.

The nonproductive activities of moving the material from place to place and storing it (while it waits for men and equipment to become available) actually represent by far the major amount of the total time spent in the manufacturing cycle for the common "job-shop" conditions which prevail in industry. These nonproductive activities require labor and equipment for transportation, loading, and unloading; capital investment for the plant storage space; and carrying charges on the inventory. Naturally, industrial management is strongly motivated to focus attention on these activities so that their expenditures can be minimized within the framework of minimum overall production cost. It is obvious that decreasing in-process inventories by reducing lot sizes to an extremely low level might result in much higher material-handling costs and idle direct labor at machines. In general, the operation process chart would be used at the broadest level dealing with entire complex products, and the flow process chart would be used with a smaller segment of the product. There is overlap, however, in the areas of their actual cost.

The flow process chart requires additional symbols in order to include nonproductive activities. There is some variation in the number and character of the symbols used, but it is of minor importance. For example, some analysts divide storage into temporary and permanent storage, using two different symbols; also, the symbol for transportation varies considerably. These are some of the symbols used: ● ⌂ ⇨.
For purposes of illustration, we shall use the symbols shown in Figure 5.

As an example, let us take the machining of the main frame for an

FIGURE 4.   Operation process chart for the capacitor of Figure 2. (Courtesy Westinghouse Electric Corporation.)

air breaker, as shown in Figure 6. The completed flow process chart was constructed by actually following the progress of the parts through the machine shop and gathering the required information. Armchair analysis is seldom accurate for these schematic charts. The resulting chart is shown in Figure 7. Notice how clearly each inverted triangle highlights the storages and each circle highlights the operations. Note the other information that the chart contains: distance moved in feet and required times.

It is often helpful to supplement the flow process chart by superimposing the flow chart on a floor plan of the work area in order that spatial relationships can be better visualized. The result is called a *flow diagram.*

Every detail of the process is questioned, first with the objective of completely eliminating steps that cannot be justified and then with the objective of combining operations. Let us see what sorts of questions might be raised about the air breaker flow process chart of Figure 7.

FLAT LEADS 5–32″ x 2″ x .003″
PDS. NO. 2428-1. IT. 6

| .0004 | O-7 | CUT OFF AND ROLL BURRS |
| D. W. | INS. 2 | INSPECT |

SECTION
172″ OF .00017″ x 1⅜″ AL. FOIL
348″ OF .0006″ x 1⅝″ PAPER NO. 7631-1
IT. 4

| .0371 | O-8 | WIND AND INSERT LEADS |
| D. W. | INS. 3 | INSPECT |

CAN 5″ x 5″ x .020″
PDS. NO. 1689, IT. 1

.00035	O-1	BLANK AND FIRST DRAW
.0009	O-2	2ND DRAW
.0009	O-3	3RD DRAW SHAPE BOTTOM AND CORNERS
.0020	O-4	TRIM
D. W.	O-5	DEGREASE

CELL BOTTOM AND SIDES–B. O.
IT. 3

D. W	INS. 1	INSPECT
.0010	O-6	ASSEMBLE CELL (BOTTOM & SIDES) TO CAN
.0060	O-9	ASSEMBLE SECTION IN CAN

WIRE LEADS –B. O
IT. 10

| .0065 | O-10 | SOLDER WIRE LEADS (2) |

TOP SECTION OF CELL
B. O. IT. 5

| .0007 | O-11 | ASSEMBLE TOP SECTION OF CELL TO CAN |

TERMINAL ⅞″ x ½″
OF 1–32″ PDS. NO. 2003–2.
IT. 11

| .00012 | O-26 | PIERCE AND BLANK |
| D. W. | INS. 10 | INSPECT |

.0080	O-22	ASSEMBLE COVER TO CAN
D. W.	INS. 9	DRY TEST
.0045	O-23	SOLDER
.0036	O-24	CLEAN

INERTEEN –B. O.

.0040	O-25	IMPREGNATE SPEC. NO. 61875
.0040	O-27	SOLDER TERMINALS AND VENT HOLE
.0010	O-28	CLEAN
D. W.	INS. 11	TEST FOR LEAKS
D. W.	INS. 12	ELECTRIC TEST
D W	INS. 13	FINAL INSPECTION

FIGURE 4.   (*continued*)

FIGURE 5. Flow process chart symbols.

First, note that O-1 calls for "straighten" (and grind). See Figure 8*a*. This straightening should be investigated to see if the reinforcing rib can be cast in such a way that warping is prevented. If the casting technique could be improved, the straightening operation could be eliminated.

Second, note in Figure 8*b* that our attention is focused on the fact that the casting is washed at O-8 in preparation for the painting operations. This is followed by O-9, which is a grinding and polishing operation. Does not O-9 produce some grinding dust and dirt on the casting and, therefore, is it not better to wash after grinding?

Third, in Figure 8*c* we see that considerable time is spent in baking, after the application of filler and also after the black enamel spray. Filler and paint materials should be investigated. Perhaps there is a

FIGURE 6. Main frame for a DA-50 air breaker. (Courtesy Westinghouse Electric Corporation.)

FIGURE 7. Flow process chart of main frame for a DA-50 air breaker. (Courtesy Westinghouse Electric Corporation.)

filler available that does not require baking. Would an "air dry" enamel be satisfactory?

Fourth, in Figure 8d we see that the casting goes to the milling section three times. This raises the question: Is it feasible to change sequence and perform all of the milling operations while the casting is in the department and thus eliminate backtracking?

Other questions could be raised, for example, the fact that holes are produced in three places. Can these operations be done at one time, perhaps on a radial drill? Finally, note that grinding is performed in O-1 and O-9 on the same surface, once as a rough grind and finally to produce a finished surface. Can the first grinding be postponed and the entire job be done in O-9? If it can, a transportation and a storage can be eliminated.

These questions and others were raised by Westinghouse industrial engineers in analyzing the manufacture of air breakers. We do not

FIGURE 8. Details of the process chart of Figure 7 are questioned to eliminate unnecessary steps, combine operations, or improve operation sequences.

mean to imply that all milling should always be done at one time, that air dry enamels should always be used, etc. But there should be good sound reasons for not doing these things, because manufacturing costs are drastically affected by the differences between the actual and proposed methods.

FIGURE 8. (*continued*)

When all unnecessary operations have been eliminated and all possible gains from combinations of operations and from sequence changes have been effected, the final question remains. Are necessary operations, transportations, and storages being accomplished in the best known way?

We then move to the next level of analysis which considers the individual operation as a unit. Here the definition of an operation does not necessarily coincide with that used by the operation and flow process charts, but includes any activity where a man is involved. It could be the activity of transporting materials or of placing them in storage, or any indirect labor that is ancillary to the direct flow of the product, or any of the direct labor operations defined as "operations" in the foregoing process charts. We refer to the types of analysis used to aid in the design or improvement of "jobs" as "man or man-machine analysis."

Make
or Buy

Every manufacturing concern must decide whether to use its production skill and effort to make each of a multitude of items or whether to buy them. The possibilities, of course, are tremendous when we consider all of the materials, supplies, and finished products with which a manufacturing concern deals. Fortunately, we need not consider manufacturing a very large share of these items. For such supply items as paper clips, pencils, and erasers, specialization makes their manufacture uneconomical to all concerns except those in that particular field. As a matter of fact, because of this pattern of buying many items which are out of the main line of effort, real opportunities are sometimes overlooked.

The product has been designed and its specifications are summarized on blueprints or drawings. Analysis of the product may reveal one, 10, 1000, or 10,000 parts that go into making it. A large transport aircraft is made up of over 50,000 parts. Which are to be made and which bought? What criteria are valid for making these decisions?

Economic Analysis. Most businessmen would agree that the major criterion for decision making in the make-buy area is cost. If a part can be bought cheaper than it can be made, buy it! When it comes to the kind of cost comparison needed, however, there is often much confusion because no standard cost comparison fits each case. Every situation must be analyzed in terms of the *incremental costs* involved, and the nature of these costs varies tremendously. Recall our discussion of incremental costs in Chapter 5. Many of the examples cited there were of a make-buy nature. The only real principles of make-buy economic analysis are those of incremental cost analysis. We must ask ourselves: If we buy this part instead of making it, what costs do we *actually* shed, and are these reductions in costs greater than the costs that we assume by buying the item? If so, we should buy. Conversely, if we are presently buying instead of making, what actual *added* costs will be involved in making and are these less than the reductions we shall experience by ceasing the purchase of the item? If so, we should make.

These statements sound simple enough, but the difficulties come in the interpretation of them. For example, if we already have idle capacity in the necessary equipment classifications, the cost of making will look relatively more attractive, because we cannot justify the allocation of overhead costs for equipment, floor space, supervision, etc., to the new product. On the other hand, if it is necessary to acquire equipment, floor space, and supervision, the analysis would have to reflect these facts. Conversely, if we consider buying an item for $2.00 which we now make for an average manufacturing cost of $2.25 each, we had better look closely at the overhead items in our manufacturing cost figure. It is likely that very few of these overhead cost items will actually be reduced by purchasing the part. The supervision, floor space, and general factory overhead will probably remain as continuing cost items. If the equipment involved is general purpose, we may retain it too. The incremental cost figure for comparison with the $2.00 per piece purchase cost may begin to look more like $1.50. The sunk costs of equipment and buildings and the realistic facts of idle capacity are strong economic pressures for making instead of buying.

The types of cost factors that can enter into a make-buy decision are often surprising. For example, one company found that they had not included extra material-handling costs for the buy situation; since it was a heavy and bulky part, this turned out to be important. The simple price per unit of purchased parts does not necessarily reflect the incremental costs for comparison of the alternative plans of make or buy. Another company failed to consider that there were incremental paperwork costs for its make program. Where previously they had bought a single assembled item and placed it in storage to await assembly into their final product, now they had to purchase several component parts plus the raw material for the parts made, as well as write shop orders, control inventories for the several parts, write assembly orders, etc. It turned out that some of these costs were measurable and significantly greater than the cost of buying the part. The important thing to remember is that the cost analysis must fit the particular case, and each case will be a little different.

We have been discussing this question as though we were either making or buying an item and considering a change of policy. Now, how about the new part or product? Is this situation any different? Not really, because we are faced with similar complicating factors that prohibit the assumption of traditional manufacturing cost figures compared with purchase prices. Purchase prices alone may not reflect accurately the comparative cost of buying. Similarly, we may have available idle equipment that could do the job so that incremental make costs are mainly the direct items. Perhaps the one best guiding comment for make-buy comparisons is that we must remember we are dealing with a *going concern*. A going concern carries with it conditions that are unique to itself alone. It has buildings, equipment, technical skill, and a supervisory and executive staff. Decide to buy a part instead of make it. How has the going concern changed? Reverse your decision. Did this fact require new equipment, floor space, or supervisors? For going concern X, perhaps not; but for going concern Y, it could affect all of these factors.

Noneconomic and Intangible Factors.   Other factors often influence a company to follow a given make-buy policy. Quality, reliability, and availability of supply; control of trade secrets; patents; research and development facilities; flexibility; and alternative supply sources are some of the factors entering into a make or buy decision in the face of apparent economic disadvantage. Companies dealing with large defense contracts often have imposed on them as a contract condition the subcontracting of a certain minimum proportion of the total contract.

Make-Buy Policies.   Most concerns wish to follow a basic policy that places the economic criterion in the driver's seat; they want to vary from this policy only in situations which they regard as limiting, such as when quality considerations, supply, patents, etc., seem to dictate a certain course of action. In these situations, the limiting noneconomic factor has been consciously or unconsciously equated to the cost disadvantage. Although make-buy policies commonly assume the outside purchase of the great bulk of standard items such as nuts, bolts, switches, and valves, they are likely to vary somewhat with overall plant load. It would be common practice to make parts for which basic processes are already available; but when the plant load requires overtime work, economic analysis may change considerably. Buying of parts formerly made increases almost automatically, reflecting a recognition of the effect of overtime premiums on cost, as well as the need to increase effective capacity to meet schedules.

It is realistic to recognize that businesses often buy when they could make for none of the reasons we have discussed but to retain goodwill of an important supplier and because of reciprocity arrangements with customers. Finally, make-buy decisions are often based on a company policy of specialization and the concentration of effort and skill in some one basic line rather than responding to economic pressures to move in many directions simultaneously.

The *decision rules* for make-buy situations used by process planners are based on a variety of reasons and logic. Any one of the following, or combinations of several, depending on the company, its policies, and the nature of the specific item under consideration, may be the basis for these decision rules: economic advantage, quality considerations, reliability of supply, need for alternative sources of supply, control of trade secrets, research and development facilities of a supplier, retention of goodwill; reciprocity, desire to specialize activities, and imposed subcontracting as with some government contracts.

Let us take the lathe family as an example of process selection. Assume that we have a part requiring turning operations. The operations can be performed on an engine lathe, a turret lathe, or an automatic lathe. These are the functional alternatives. The most economical selection depends on the volume that we contemplate and the relative magnitudes of the incremental costs for each alternative. To determine the most economical alternative, we must estimate the costs of setup and tooling, as well as the variable costs for the three alternatives. The estimates of labor cost might be based on standard data, reference to past costs of similar parts, or the skill of an experienced estimator.

Many organizations have developed standard data for various machine classes based on accumulated time studies. In the hands of an estimator who understands machine work, good estimates of setup and operation time can be developed. The bases and techniques for developing time standards are covered later in Chapter 14. Figure 9 shows an estimate built-up from these standard time data for the automatic lathe operations of an aluminum casting. It is obvious that a careful analysis of the part itself is needed in order to determine the cuts required and the sequence of the cuts. If manual operations are required which are not covered by the standard elements, time values for them can be synthesized by means of motion standard data such as MTM, Methods-Time Measurement, as discussed in Chapter 14.

By one or more of these approaches, estimates of labor cost can be made. Tooling costs, the costs of power and supplies, and other pertinent incremental costs can be estimated also. We assume illustrative figures shown in Table I for a part that can be machined equally well on an engine lathe, turret lathe, or an automatic lathe.

Figure 10 shows the range of volumes appropriate for each machine and specifies that range. Of course, the breakeven point between any two machines would change for different parts as the fixed and variable cost elements changed.

The appropriate decision rules are now obvious. If the lot quantity is less than 278, the engine lathe minimizes incremental cost; if the quantity is between 278 and 1000, the turret lathe yields minimum cost; in lots above 1000 parts, the automatic lathe yields the lowest cost. Note that this particular analysis assumes ownership of all three machines, so no capital costs enter the solution since these costs go on

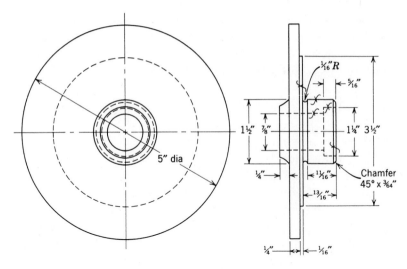

Estimate

Part. Cylinder head.

Material. Aluminum alloy casting.

Operation. Chuck on 5″ diameter. Face 5″ diameter to $\frac{1}{4}$″ dimension. Turn and face $3\frac{1}{2}$″ dimension. Form $\frac{1}{16}$-inch radius, 45° by $\frac{3}{64}$″ chamfer, and face end to $\frac{13}{16}$″ dimension. Bore $\frac{7}{8}$″ diameter through, and counterbore $1\frac{1}{4}$″ diameter $\frac{5}{16}$ inch deep.

		Minutes
1.	Pick up part, install casting in 3-jaw chuck. (Includes releasing of part and aside)	.200
2.	Position splash guard, adjust coolant, and start machine	.070
3.	Advance tool to work	.020
4.	Tool slide	
	(a) Back tool slide—face, counterface, form radius, and face end (500 rpm, .003 feed, 2″ length of cut)	1.334
	(b) Front tool slide—turn, bore, and counterbore	(.918)

Note: .918 is smaller than 1.334; therefore, use 1.334 time value

		Minutes
5.	Back tools from work	.020
6.	Stop coolant (automatic), stop machine (automatic), and position splash guard into clear	.040
7.	Release part and aside with part See element 1	
	Total time	1.684
8.	Allowances	
	(a) Check parts (this is done during element 4)	
	(b) Sharpen tools (10%)	.168
	(c) Personal (5%)	.084
	(d) Fatigue (10%)	.168
	Total estimate	2.104

FIGURE 9. Sample estimate for a machined part based on standard data. (Adapted by permission from [9].)

TABLE I.   Fixed and Variable Incremental Costs for Machining a Part on Three Alternative Machines

Machine	Fixed Costs, Setup Labor Plus Tooling	Variable Costs, Labor, Supplies, Power, Etc., per Unit
Engine lathe	$ 5.00	$00.19
Turret lathe	30.00	00.10
Automatic lathe	70.00	00.06

regardless of which of the three machines is selected. If it were necessary to purchase the automatic lathe, for example, the analysis would have to reflect this fact.

There are reasons, other than strictly economic ones, why one machine might be selected over another. Even though all alternatives meet functional requirements, a machine that holds closer tolerances might be selected for a "ticklish" job. For intermittent manufacture of custom-built parts and products, machine availability would be an overriding factor of importance. The most economical machine to use

Decision rules:
if $0 < n < 278$, select engine lathe
if $278 < n < 1000$, select turret lathe
if $1000 < n < \infty$, select automatic lathe

Engine lathe ($c = 0.19\,n + 5.00$)

Turret lathe ($c = 0.10\,n + 30.00$)

Automatic lathe ($c = 0.06\,n + 70$)

Breakeven between engine lathe and turret lathe = 278 parts

Breakeven between turret lathe and automatic lathe = 1000 parts

Incremental cost (c), dollars

Number of parts (n)

FIGURE 10.   Concept of process selection based upon marginal break-even analysis.

might be in use or broken down, thus, rather than hold up the order for long periods, the next most economical machine would be used. Therefore, while basic managerial philosophy of machine and process selection is one of using the most economical system, factors of expediency, quality, and functional preference may modify these selections.

Route Sheets and Operation Sheets.   At each stage of its processing, every part is analyzed in order to determine the operations required and to select and specify the processes that perform the functions required. Thus, the *routing* of the part is determined. This information is commonly summarized on *route sheets*. The route sheet (a) shows the operations required and the preferred sequence of these operations, (b) specifies the machine or equipment to be used, and (c) gives the estimated setup time and run time per piece. When a part is a standard part, which is run and rerun periodically to fill needs, the standard routing sheets are maintained as the accepted manufacturing methods. More precise specifications of manufacturing methods are often developed in the form of *operation sheets*, which tell in greater detail how the operation is to be accomplished; in other words, they give a standard method.

The route sheet, together with operation sheets, specifies how the part or product is to be manufactured. These documents are basic to the manufacturing organization and take the same relative position to the design of a production system as the blueprint or drawing does to the design of a part or product. The drawing specifies *what is to be made*; the route and operation sheets specify *how to make it*.

Process Planning for Continuous Industries.   The situation that we have been discussing is generally applicable to industrial process planning; however, those familiar with high-volume, continuous types of industries may comment on the lack of route sheets in such industries. This lack is common, but originally someone performed the equivalent task of process planning and routing. Once the process planning is done and the system installed, route sheets would serve no purpose because routes are either standardized or follow mechanical paths so operation sequence is not a problem. Similarly, although operation sheets often exist, they are maintained as records of job conditions and methods; they may be referred to only when it is necessary to train new personnel in the standard procedures of the job. Alterations to the standard routing are required only periodically to incorporate product design changes or to take advantage of some advance in production technology.

In the post-World War II era, there has been a recognition of the importance to our economy of the large-scale one-time project as a managerial problem. The massive scale and complexity of missile projects and the space programs demanded special methods for project planning as well as for scheduling and control. Thus there emerged the network planning methods known as PERT (Performance Evaluation and Review Technique) and CPM (Critical Path Methods). The technological fallout of these developments has provided new and important methodology for all sorts of large project-centered activities such as in the construction industry, research and development activities, the planning and execution of new product introductions, and new plant start-up and relocation of an existing plant. We discuss these network planning methods in Chapter 20.

PROCESS PLANNING IN NONMANUFACTURING ACTIVITIES

Process planning in nonmanufacturing activities is usually not so complex as in manufacturing but nevertheless follows a parallel conceptual framework. Make-buy considerations enter some systems. For example, data processing centers process payrolls, inventory records, etc., on a time-rental basis. This represents an alternative to internal manual or semimechanized processing. A building contractor must decide which parts of a structure he will subcontract and which parts he will do with his own crew.

Also, the specification of processes or methods and their sequences can have an important bearing on costs in many nonmanufacturing activities. Systems and procedures analysts perform these functions in office systems. The sequence of operations is very important in building construction in determining the costs incurred. For example, if the rough plumbing is not done until a house is framed and roofed, it is necessary to cut holes in the rough flooring and walls and to work in awkward positions in order to make the plumbing runs. Also, once a house is partially built, it is often impossible to get grading equipment to the back of the lot. Grading is then accomplished by the alternative means of sweat and muscle. Most people who have built homes have similar tales to tell of the poor planning of work sequences. Figure 11 is illustrative of this point.

"Aren't you jumping the gun a bit, Schultz?"

FIGURE 11.   Courtesy Pomona Tile Manufacturing Company.

SUMMARY

We have begun to deal with the design of *systems* of production with the subject matter of production design and process planning. Following in Chapters 11 to 14 we deal with components of the system. In Chapter 13 we emphasize man and the design of jobs for man, and in Chapter 14 we deal with production standards and work measurement. In the present chapter we have seen the importance of the processes we use in establishing the minimum possible production cost. Process planning in the organizational sense takes the drawings and specifications for the completed part or product and then specifies the remaining details of how to manufacture it. In performing this activity, decisions whether to make or buy parts must be made. For the manufactured parts, a specification of the required operations and their sequence must be made. The specification is commonly summarized on route sheets, supplemented by operation sheets, which give, in greater detail, instructions for the performance of each operation.

REVIEW QUESTIONS

1. What is process planning? Relate it to product design, production design, plant layout, and production control.
2. What is the nature of the economic analysis for a make versus buy decision? How does the "going concern" concept affect it?
3. Discuss the nature of noneconomic and intangible factors that may bear on the make-buy decision.
4. How does the breakeven concept apply in process selection?
5. Are there reasons for selecting a given process that are noneconomic?
6. What are route sheets and operation sheets? What information do they contain?
7. Does process planning in continuous industries follow the same general pattern as in intermittent industries?
8. Discuss production design and process planning as it applies in non-manufacturing industries.

PROBLEMS

1. Figure 12 shows a pipe valve with its various parts together with an assembled view.* Construct an assembly chart for this product.

2. Construct an operation process chart for the pipe valve based on the following additional information concerning processing requirements. The machines are available for use on the parts indicated as well as for other parts.

Assembly Operations	Operations	Machine	Output in Parts Per Hour
	1. Final assembly	Bench	30
	2. Clean	Solvent tank	100
	3. Inspect (pressure test)	Water test stand	50
	4. Pack in boxes	Bench	500

Fabrication Operations

Body, Part #1

Cast bronze	1. Cast	Bench mold	40
	2. Clean	Tumble barrel	150
	3. Machine—thread and face three surfaces	Turret lathe	25

*The pipe valve problems are reproduced from A. L. Roberts, *Production Management Workbook*, John Wiley, New York, 1962, p. 22.

Fabrication Operations	Operations	Machine	Output in Parts Per Hour
Bushing, Part #2			
	1. Cast	Bench mold	80
	2. Clean	Tumble barrel	300
	3. Machine all inside and outside diameters	Turret lathe	60
Stem, Part #3			
$\frac{3}{8}''$ bar stock	1. Machine all surfaces and cut off	Automatic screw machine	200
Cap, Part #5			
$\frac{3}{4}''$ hex bar stock	1. Machine all surfaces	Automatic screw machine	500
Handle, Part #6			
Cast bronze	1. Cast	Bench mold	50
	2. Clean	Tumble barrel	200
	3. Machine two surfaces	Turret lathe	80
	4. Broach square hole	Broach	80

Note: 100 per cent inspection required for all fabricated parts prior to delivery to final assembly.

3.   Develop a summary of equipment requirements for the production of 200 pipe valves per hour. How are the equipment requirements affected by an increase in production rate to 350 valves per hour?

4.   The Laudenbach Beer Company has for a number of years used pasteboard cases to pack six units of six-pack cans for shipment to wholesalers and retailers in its regional marketing area in eleven western states. The total volume of beer shipped from its two plants in Los Angeles and San Francisco was 36 million cans (1 million cases) last year, and this volume is expected to be maintained and probably increased by 15 per cent over the next five years.

The Laudenbach Company has always purchased its pasteboard cases in "knocked down" form imprinted with the company name and other information. At each of the two plants the company has box-folding equipment in its production lines which set up the box blanks. This requires a gluing operation for the bottom flaps as well as the forming of the case and is done automatically except for maintaining a supply of the case blanks in the machine supply hopper, maintaining glue supply, and a general surveillance of the machine and its operation.

Pipe valve

Body
Part #1

Bushing
Part #2

Stem
Part #3

Fiber packing
Part #4
(purchased)

Cap
Part #5

Handle
Part #6

Nut
Part #7
(purchased)

FIGURE 12.   Pipe valve, assembled and exploded views.

A new machine has come to the attention of the company's production analyst; it will perform the case-making operation, feeding case blanks to the case-forming machine. Printing requirements would be handled separately on sheets of paper to be glued to the case as a part of the case-making operation. The existence of the machine has raised the issue of whether the case blanks should be purchased or made in-plant, as well as some side issues regarding the company's general make-buy policies. The new machine costs $40,000 each, installed, and has a capacity considerably in excess of the needs at each of the two plants. Approximately 12 hours production per day from the case-making machine will satisfy two-shift requirements in the San Francisco plant. The alternatives being considered are the continuance of the current practice of purchasing case blanks, the installation of one case-making machine at the Los Angeles plant with trucking of the blanks to the San Francisco plant, and the installation of a case-making machine in each of the two plants. In the Los Angeles location, space for the new machine can be found by a minor relayout of the packaging area. This relayout is estimated to cost $500 for the relocation of one machine and rerouting of a small section of conveyor. Suitable space exists in the San Francisco location. Cost data are as shown in Table II.

The Laudenbach Company has a reputation in the community as a steady employer and with its vendors as a stable customer. Suppliers commonly quote a better price to Laudenbach than they would to customers whose future business might be uncertain because of business fluctuations. On being presented with the production analyst's report, Laudenbach executives were hesitant, fearing a breakdown in relations with suppliers because rapid obsolescence of the case-making machine was anticipated. A review of the history of such machines showed that the designs had changed radically in the last few years, although there was no indication that the present machine design was not reliable in performance. A final issue discussed at length by the company officials centered on the nature of the new operation. The Laudenbach Company has been exclusively a beer company, not a paper company. "Wasn't it smarter to stay out of case making and stick to beer making? We know beer making and our reputation rests on that fact. If we go into case making, perhaps we should also consider integrating back one more step and make the pasteboard too. If we are going to consider backward integration, there are probably other possibilities more closely allied to beer making which we should consider. Let the case makers have this business of ours. They are specialists and so are we."

In the light of all factors, what analysis would you make and what action do you recommend?

5. The International Electronics Corporation manufactures special-purpose electric motors for military use. The company has complete machine shop facilities with most types of equipment.

One part made by the company is part number A-12963, a flexible shaft coupling. A drawing of this part and a proposed operation sheet are shown in

TABLE II. Cost Data for the Laudenbach Company

	Cost per Hundred		
	Purchase Blanks	One Case, Machine in Los Angeles Plant	One Case, Machine in Each Plant
Purchased blanks	$22.39	—	—
Glue	0.70	$ 0.70	$ 0.70
Labor	3.02	3.90	3.90
Freight, blanks to plants	0.95	—	—
Insurance	0.09	0.15	0.15
Maintenance	0.12	0.15	0.15
Pasteboard (raw material)	—	8.20	8.20
Printed labels	—	0.30	0.30
Scrap	—	0.20	0.20
Floor space	0.30	0.40	0.75
Trucking blanks to San Francisco	—	1.50	—
Totals	$24.57	$15.50	$14.35

Other data:
Installed cost of case machines	$40,000 each
Expected economic life	8 years
Tax depreciation term (straight-line)	10 years
Incremental tax rate	50 per cent
Interest rate	15 per cent
Overhead factor at current output rates (25 per cent variable)	$10/1000
Cases required per year	1,000,000

Figures 13 and 14. The operation sheet is designed to be adequate for prototype production but is not appropriate for larger scale production. A list of proposed method changes has been prepared by the IEC engineers. The setup times and unit machine times have been estimated by the estimating department for the basic operation sheet and the proposed innovations.

The company has an average direct labor rate of $2.50 per hour, a burden rate of 200 per cent of direct labor, a general and administrative expense rate of 20 per cent of factory cost, and a government-allowed profit rate of 10 per cent of total cost. In addition, 10 per cent of the burden time is considered to be variable. The pay rate for the company tool maker is $3.00 per hour.

A.   Determine for the following list of alternative processes the production level at which each proposed innovation should be adopted.

(a) Operation 1 can be done in the turret lathe department. If run in the same

FIGURE 13. Drawing for flexible shaft coupling.

OPERATION SHEET

PART NO.	ISSUE	PART NAME
A-12963	A	FLEXIBLE SHAFT COUPLING

MODEL   Standard Part

MATERIAL   C-1018 Steel 1½ inch diameter

			Time	(hrs.)
OPER.	DEPT.	OPERATION	SETUP	MACHINE
1	engine lathe	Hold in three jaw chuck	.3	.8
		Centerdrill		
		Drill 15/32 X 7/8 in. deep		
		Bore .500 -.010 dia. X 5/8 in. deep (−.000)		
		Face end of part square		
		Turn .625 -.003 dia. X 1/2 in. long (−.000)		
		Cut off 29/32 long (7/8 1/32 extra)		
2	engine lathe	Hold in three jaw chuck on .625 dia.	.3	.6
		Face—Hold 7/8 in. dimension		
		Turn 1.000 -.001 dia. X 9/32 in. long (−.000)		
		Bore .8665 dia. to .855 -.003 X 9/32 deep (−.003)		
		Bore 3/4 dia. X 1/32 deep		
3	internal grinder	Hold in collet on .625 dia.	.5	.1
		Grind .8665 -.0004 dia. X 9/32 deep (−.0000)		
4	milling machine	Hold in dividing head on .625 dia.	.5	.2
		Mill 1 1/4 in. square (4 cuts)		
5	burring dept.	Deburr (milling burrs)	-	.03
6	jig boring	Hold in vise on 1 1/4 square	.5	.2
		Centerdrill and drill 4 #31 holes		
7	thread grinding	Hold on .8665 mandrel	1.5	.2
		Grind 5/8 -27 R.H. -3 thread X 3/8 long		
8	burring	Deburr (drilled holes and threads)	-	.02
9	outside processing	Cadmium plate costs $.15 ea.	-	-
10	inspection	Inspect	-	.01

FIGURE 14.   Operation sheet for flexible shaft coupling.

way as presently, the setup time would be 6 hours with a unit machine time of 0.3 hour.

(b) Operation 1 can be modified in the turret lathe to perform the function of operation 7 as well. To do this, a special thread rolling die head must be purchased, costing $350. The combined operation would then have a setup time of 8 hours with a unit machine time of 0.4 hour.

(c) Operation 2 can be done in the turret lathe department. If so, the setup time would be 5 hours and the unit machine time would be 0.4 hour.

(d) Operation 2 can be modified in the turret lathe to perform the function of operation 3 as well. To do this, a special type adjustable reamer called a Madison Bar is required. The cost of this tool is $150. The combined operation would then have a setup time of 6 hours and a unit machine time of 0.5 hour.

(e) Operation 4 can be done by straddle milling the part, thereby reducing the number of cuts from four to two. (Straddle milling is a method utilizing two milling cutters with a spacer of the desired length ($1\frac{1}{4}$ inches) between the cutters.) If operation 4 is done by straddle milling, the setup time will be 2 hours and the unit machine time will be 0.1 hour.

(f) Operation 6 can be simplified by the construction of a drill jig. It has been estimated that an appropriate drill jig would take 20 hours to construct. In addition, the company has a firm quotation from an outside company to construct the jig for $75. With such a jig, the setup time for operation 6 would be 0.2 hour and the unit machine time would be 0.1 hour.

B.　Should the company make, or buy, the drill jig discussed in item (f)?

C.　Under what conditions would your answer to B differ from the one you gave?

D.　Can you suggest any design or method changes in addition to the one given in the problem?

REFERENCES

[1] Begeman, M. L., and B. H. Amstead. *Manufacturing Processes* (6th ed.). John Wiley, New York, 1969.

[2] Culliton, J. W. *Make or Buy*. Harvard University Graduate School of Business Administration, Soldiers Field, Boston, Mass., 1942.

[3] DuMond, T. C. *Fabricated Materials and Parts*. Reinhold, New York, 1953.

[4] Eary, D. F., and G. E. Johnson. *Process Engineering for Manufacturing*. Prentice-Hall, Englewood Cliffs, N.J., 1962.

[5] Hahir, J. P. "A Case Study in the Relationship Between Design Engineering and Production Engineering." *Proceedings, Fifth Annual Industrial Engineering Institute*, University of California, Berkeley–Los Angeles, 1953.

[6] Knox, F. M. *Design and Control of Business Forms*. McGraw-Hill, New York, 1952.

[7] Moore, H. D., and D. R. Kibbey. *Manufacturing Materials and Processes.* Richard D. Irwin, Homewood, Ill., 1965.

[8] Niebel, B. W., and E. N. Baldwin. *Designing for Production* (Rev. ed.). Richard D. Irwin, Homewood, Ill., 1963.

[9] Nordhoff, W. A. *Machine-Shop Estimating.* McGraw-Hill, New York, 1947.

[10] Papen, G. W. "Minimizing Manufacturing Costs Through Effective Design." *Proceedings, Sixth Annual Industrial Engineering Institute,* Berkeley–Los Angeles, 1954, pp. 21–28.

11

Plant Location

The design of a production system is dependent on its location, because resulting physical factors influence layout and because the location partially determines operating and capital costs. In terms of the purely physical factors of plant design, location may determine whether or not power is purchased; the extent of heating and ventilating requirements; the necessary capacity for parts made, depending on the local availability of subcontractors; the amount of storage space needed to provide for raw materials, depending on reliability of supply; the types of carriers to provide for in shipping and receiving; etc. From the standpoint of operating and capital costs, ease of shipping raw materials and finished goods, costs of labor, taxes, land, construction, and fuel—all these factors and others in a complex interplay—contribute to the overall competitive position of an organization.

Location analysis for the multiplant situation is particularly interesting because of its dynamic character. The addition of a new plant is not a matter of determining a location independent of the location of existing plants. Rather, each location considered involves a new allocation of capacity to market areas, so a solution from the economic viewpoint is one that minimizes combined production and distribution costs for the network of plants rather than for the additional plants alone. Also, in the multiplant situation, locational factors continually influence the

283

extent of production in each plant to meet demand requirements and help determine which plants to operate and which to shut down if demand falls.

How Important Is a Plant's Location? The pressures to secure advantageous locations are continuous, especially for multiplant operations. There have been, for example, wholesale movements of industries, such as the textile industry, to the South in order to secure advantages of low labor costs. The industrialization of the South in recent years has been based partly on this attraction to industry. Currently, American producers of many lines of products are considering foreign locations in order to combat competition from Japanese and European manufacturers. The formation of the Common Market in Europe binds together 200 million people in a free trade area for participating countries. Many American producers feel that the only way they can compete with the Common Market producers, both in the United States and in foreign markets, is to establish plants within the Common Market area in order to secure the advantages of lower wages.

Within the United States we must recognize that our present industrial decentralization within industries means that many good locations exist for each industry. There is no such thing as a unique location that is clearly superior to all others. For example, television and radio plants are found in New England, the Middle Atlantic states, various parts of the Midwest, the South, and in the far West. Plastics raw material plants are located in Massachusetts, New York, New Jersey, Pennsylvania, Ohio, Michigan, and Tennessee. Plastics molding plants are dispersed throughout industrial America. Furniture is manufactured in North Carolina, New York, Illinois, Indiana, Virginia, Pennsylvania, California, Michigan, Ohio, Massachusetts, Wisconsin, Texas, and other states. The steel industry, which we tend to picture as being centralized, has plants in eighteen states that produce pig iron, plants in twenty-seven states that produce steel ingots, and plants in twenty-eight states that produce hot-rolled products.

Dynamic Nature of Plant Locations. We tend to think that the location problem occurs only once in a while and, as a conscious consideration by management officials, perhaps it does. We can all cite examples of companies that settled in a certain city and remained there twenty-five to fifty years and longer. This does not mean that the location problem was not considered during this period, especially if the organization expanded. The alternate choice of moving or staying put is always present, but it is emphasized when expansion is contemplated. The following alternate choices are available:

1. Instead of expanding physical facilities, expand subcontracting to achieve an overall expansion.
2. Expand the existing plant if possible.
3. Retain the existing plant and locate a second one elsewhere.
4. Junk the old plant and relocate everything in a new one.

Companies that stay put over the years always have these choices and continually elect either to expand their existing plant or to extend subcontracting to meet the demands for their products.

An initially good location does not necessarily remain so over the years. The center of gravity of market areas can change drastically. Changes in industry pricing policies can render an old location obsolete, as when the steel industry shifted from the basing point pricing system to f.o.b. plant. Some companies have moved in order to get away from what they considered an undesirable labor situation.

OBJECTIVE AND SUBJECTIVE FACTORS

The businessman's aim in location analysis is to minimize the sum of all costs affected by location. He recognizes that in the comparison of alternate locations, some cost items, such as freight, may be higher in Area 1 and lower in Area 2, whereas power costs, for example, may show the reverse pattern. He is seeking the location that minimizes costs on balance; however, he is thinking not only of cost today but of long-run costs, so he will be interested in some of the intangible factors that may influence future costs. Thus, factors such as the attitude of city officials and townspeople toward a company's location in their city may be an indication of future tax assessments. Poor local transportation facilities may mean future company expenditures to counterbalance this disadvantage. A short labor supply may cause labor rates to be bid up beyond rates measured during a location survey. The type of labor available may indicate future training expenditures. Thus, although a comparative cost analysis of various locations may point toward settling in one community, an appraisal of intangible factors may be the basis of a decision to select another.

This situation is brought out by Figure 1, which shows the results of one company's study of nine alternate locations. On the basis of cost comparisons only, City E is most favorable, with a difference of about

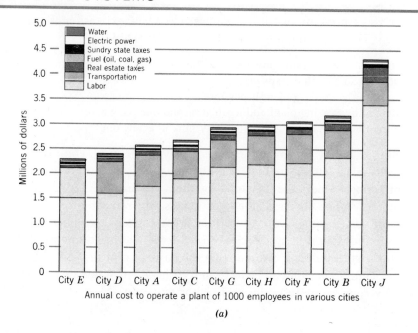

Annual cost to operate a plant of 1000 employees in various cities

(a)

COMPARISON OF OTHER FACTORS INFLUENCING CHOICE OF PLANT SITE

Factor	City E	City D	City A	City C	City G	City H	City F	City B	City J
Labor supply	adeq.	adeq.	plent.	plent.	adeq.	adeq.	plent.	plent.	plent.
Type of labor	good	good	excel.	excel.	excel.	excel.	excel.	excel.	excel.
Union activity	sign.	sign.	neg.	neg.	mod.	sign.	sign.	mod.	act.
Attitude	good	good	v.g.	v.g.	good	good	v.g.	v.g.	good
Appearance	fair	fair	good	good	excel.	fair	good	good	good
Transportation	good	good	v.g.	good	v.g.	good	v.g.	v.g.	v.g.
Recreation	good	v.g.	v.g.	v.g.	v.g.	good	v.g.	v.g.	v.g.

(b)

FIGURE 1. Summary of company *X*'s study of nine alternate locations. (Reprinted by special permission of National Industrial Conference Board, [14].)

$150,000 a year in annual operating expenses compared with City *D*, the next cheapest. However, in Figure 1*b*, seven intangible characteristics of the cities are rated. For each factor the cities are rated as excellent, plentiful, very good, good, adequate, or fair, except for the factor of union activity which carries the ratings active, significant, moderate, or negative. Both cities *A* and *C* rate higher than *E* on these characteristics. Does this mean that E's present cost advantage will vanish in the future? This is a question for individual management judgment. Note also in Figure 1a that the real estate taxes of City E are somewhat lower than for the other cities. This fact should raise the question: Is this condition likely to continue as an advantage?

Table I shows further general and specific information on the nine cities. Note that the bonded indebtedness of City E is over five times the per capita rate of City A and that City C has no bonded indebtedness. This may have future implications for tax loads. City E has no airport, nor does City C. Will this have any future implications in terms of both future tax load and of convenience of business transportation for company officials? The weighing of these intangible factors could be continued; however, the questions raised are typical.

SITE SELECTION

Although selecting the general area is the most important phase, the selection of the site is also important for both objective and subjective reasons. The area chosen must contain a site zoned for industrial use which meets the minimum needs of the company at reasonable development costs.

To choose a site that will meet minimum requirements, preliminary estimates of the building floor space requirements must be made. A site must then be obtained that is large enough to accommodate present floor space requirements, room for expansion, employee parking space, transportation facilities for receipt and shipment of material, extra space for trucks and rail cars waiting to be loaded or unloaded, etc. A site five times the actual contemplated plant area is considered minimum to allow for all of these things, including future expansion. If possible, open land adjacent to the site should be available to allow for future site expansion.

The site should also provide for necessary transportation facilities, utilities and sewage disposal. The soil structure must be sufficient to carry the bearing loads of building foundations. All of these factors are important in determining the development cost of the site.

Industrial districts are very often an excellent solution, since they are planned solely for factory site development. The needed utilities commonly are already provided and there is no problem of zoning or hostility from nearby residents.

Obviously the selection of an area and finally a site for a plant involves a careful study if a good job is to be done. A tremendous amount

TABLE I. Company X: Comparison of Proposed Plant Locations

City	Population 1940 Census	Est. 1949	Per Cent Colored	Bonded Indebtedness Total ×1000	Per Capita	Bank Deposits Total ×1000	Per Capita	For Plant (1)	Taxes State Personal Income	General Sales Taxes	Municipal Airports	Hospitals	No. of Beds	Churches	Schools	Hotels	No. of Rooms	Electric Power Cost (2)	Water Cost (3)	Gas Rate (4)	Coal Rate (5)	Oil Rate (6)	No. of Present Industries (7)	Per Cent Unionized	Unskilled M	Unskilled F	Semiskilled M	Semiskilled F	Skilled M	Skilled F
City A	14,585	20,000	12.5	$ 277	$13.86	$18,335	$ 916.74	$75,000	Yes	None	Yes	3	118	23	9	4	295	$2,287	$419.45	35¢	$4.11	9¢	4	25%	.50–.75	.45–.60	.75–1.00	.60–.75	1.00–1.50	.75–1.00
City B	20,129	27,600	8.0	1,677	60.75	24,911	902.60	111,430	None	Yes	Yes	1	106	30	8	2	50	3,695	603.06	55¢	10.44	10.5¢	5	80%	1.00–1.15	.60–.90	1.10–1.25	.96–1.22	1.25–1.75	.80
City C	6,734	10,500	15.0	None	0.00	10,000	925.50	46,100	Yes	None	No	1	75	10	5	1	120	4,066	484.60	32¢	5.68	9¢	1	0	.60–.80	.50–.65	.90–1.00	.65–.75	1.25–1.50	.80–1.00
City D	11,729	14,852	15.0	11	0.73	17,278	1,163.50	48,000	Yes	Yes	Yes	1	100	21	22	2	200	1,800	259.86	20¢	6.00 to 7.50	—	3	67%	.60	.60	.80	.70	1.60	—
City E	7,256	9,000	17.0	690	76.66	9,296	1,032.91	440	None	Yes	No	2	85	9	5	3	190	2,542	242.20	90¢	5.63	11.4¢	3	67%	.60–1.00	.45–.75	.75–1.10	.65–.90	1.00–1.30	.75–1.00
City F	62,693	76,800	5.4	1,431	18.64	82,456	1,073.65	96,822	None	None	Yes	2	433	99	37	14	1,163	5,000	396.20	62¢	5.00	10¢	30	87%	1.00–1.05	.75–.80	1.10–1.15	.90–.95	1.30–1.35	1.00–1.05
City G	21,940	25,100	7.8	373	14.86	20,009	797.19	110,880	None	Yes	No	1	192	28	8	3	167	3,925	605.00	35¢	6.00	12.5¢	8	100%	.80–1.00	.73–.96	.90–1.25	.85–1.05	1.25–1.80	.95–1.15
City H	12,514	16,087	1.0	40	2.49	14,472	900.00	81,180	None	None	No	1	70	21	10	3	161	5,000	978.00	55¢	4.35	10¢	8	88%	.75–.90	.60–.70	.90–1.30	.75–.90	1.60–1.80	None
City J	109,912	125,000	4.5	5,974	44.60	164,233	1,313.86	282,186	None	None	Yes	4	611	78	47	8	4,010	676.80	75¢	7.64	7.5¢	36	89%	1.434 av.* (incentive)		1.718 av.* (incentive)		1.475 / 1.945	

Reprinted by special permission of National Industrial Conference Board.

(1) Computed total tax on hypothetical plant.
(2) Per 200,000 kwh per month (1500 kw demand, 85% power factor).
(3) Cost for 3,000,000 gal (400,000 cu ft) per month.
(4) Per 1000 cu ft at lowest rate (1000 btu/cu ft).
(5) Per ton, stoker coal, delivered.
(6) Per gal. No. 2 fuel oil, delivered.
(7) Employing 100 people or more.
* Same rate for male and female.

of information needs to be obtained and correlated if any sense is to be made out of a complex problem.

CAPITAL EXPENDITURE—VOLUME EFFECTS

Another important variable between alternate locations is the necessary capital expenditure for land, building, and possible moving expenses. These fixed investment costs can differ considerably, depending on local construction and land costs and variations in the particular site selected, such as availability of railroad spurs into the property and adequacy of power and gas lines. Therefore, the concept of breakeven analysis could be used to contrast the objective cost factors of individual locations. Figure 2 shows such a contrast between the operating costs and assumed values of capital expenditure for the company and locations in Figure 1. Of course, such a breakeven analysis is valid only for volumes near the designed operating capacity, since large changes in volume would entail differences in capital investment, as well as possible differences in variable costs. Note that although City *J* offers attractive fixed costs, the operating costs make it the most expensive location for the volume contemplated. When viewed in this way, City *D* appears to be the most economical location.

MULTIPLANT LOCATION

As we mentioned earlier, multiplant location is influenced by existing locations as well as by the kinds of economic factors that we have already discussed. Each location considered must be placed in economic perspective with the existing plants and market areas. The objective is to select the new location that minimizes the total production-distribution cost. This aim is somewhat different from the location analysis for a single plant because each location requires a different allocation of capacity to markets from the several plants in order to minimize overall costs. The formal problem can be placed in a linear programming framework and solved in a distribution matrix according to the general methods of Chapter 7.

Let us examine the problem conditions of the Good-Wear Shoe Company case. *An Example*
The company manufactures a line of inexpensive women's shoes in two plants, Detroit and Chicago, and now distributes to five main distribution centers, Milwaukee, Cleveland, Cincinnati, Buffalo, and Atlanta, from which the shoes are shipped to retail shoe stores. The fifth center, Atlanta, has been added recently to serve the Southeast, an area in which the company has been expanding sales effort. To meet increased demand, the company has decided to

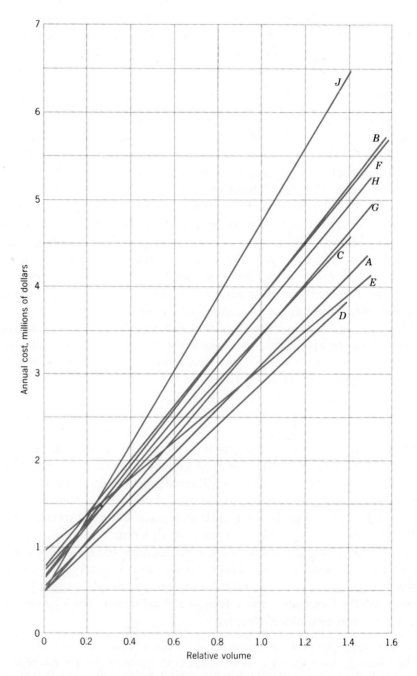

FIGURE 2. Fixed and variable cost relationships for the nine locations of Figure 1. Breakeven costs between pairs of alternatives occur where their cost-volume lines cross.

build a new plant with a capacity of 25,000 pairs per week. General surveys have narrowed the choice to three locations, Cincinnati, Cleveland, and Atlanta. (See Figure 3.) The production and distribution costs, as well as the plant capacities and distribution demands, are shown in Table II. The proposed plant capacity of 25,000 pairs weekly reflects average forecast demand in the several market areas and allows for some expected growth of sales. Distribution costs include freight, handling, and warehousing costs. As expected, the production costs would be low in the Atlanta plant, but distribution costs are relatively high compared to the other two locations. The important question now is: Which location will yield the lowest cost for the enterprise in combination with the existing plants and distribution centers? To determine this, we solve three distribution matrices, one for each combination. Capacities and demands are as given, and the costs in each cell are the production-plus-distribution costs for each factory-distribution center combination. Figure 4 shows the resulting three optimum matrices with the total cost for each.

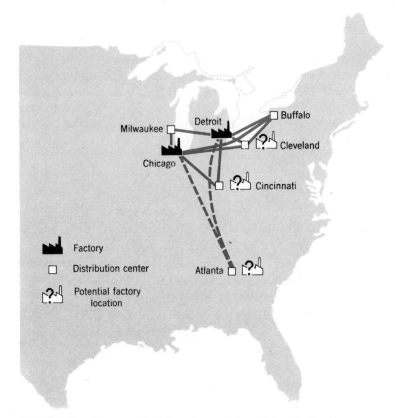

FIGURE 3. Geographical locations of factories, distribution centers, and potential new factory locations.

From plants To distribution centers	Distribution costs per pair, handling, warehousing, and freight					Forecast weekly market demand pairs
	Existing plants		Proposed plant locations			
	Detroit	Chicago	Cincinnati	Cleveland	Atlanta	
Milwaukee	$0.42	$0.32	$0.46	$0.44	$0.48	10,000
Cleveland	0.36	0.44	0.37	0.30	0.45	15,000
Cincinnati	0.41	0.42	0.30	0.37	0.43	16,000
Buffalo	0.38	0.48	0.42	0.38	0.46	19,000
Atlanta	0.50	0.49	0.43	0.45	0.27	12,000
Normal weekly plant capacity, pairs	27,000	20,000	25,000	25,000	25,000	
Unit production cost	$2.70	$2.68	$2.64	$2.69	$2.62	

TABLE II. Production Costs, Distribution Costs, Plant Capacities, and Market Demands for the Good-Wear Shoe Company

The solutions to the formal linear programming problems show the Atlanta plant to be a slightly better location in terms of variable costs. Atlanta is favored again by lower land and construction costs. Finally, if we consider future possible expansion of markets in the South, the Atlanta location seems to have an edge in terms of both present and future costs, without going into a discussion of other intangible factors. The problem solution as shown is a fairly simple one; however, other restricting conditions could have been added, such as inventory levels in the various locations as well as the location of future distribution centers.

Locational Dynamics for Multiplants. The decision to build the Atlanta plant was based on current costs, demand breakdowns, and an assessment of the future. But suppose that the balance of these factors changes. Then the allocation of capacity to markets should change also in order to yield a minimum total cost for whatever conditions exist. Thus, location analysis is continuous and necessary.

Suppose, for example, that after the Atlanta plant was built, our shoe company experienced a decline in demand because of increased competition from the low-cost Italian imports. Assume that instead of a total demand of 72,000 units per week as hoped and planned for, there is a demand of only 56,000 units divided among the market areas as follows: Milwaukee, 9,000; Cleveland, 13,000; Cincinnati, 11,000; Buffalo, 15,000; Atlanta, 8,000.

To distribution centers	From plants Detroit	Chicago	Cincinnati	Demand, 1000's
Milwaukee	3.12	3.00 (10)	3.10	10
Cleveland	3.06 (8)	3.12	3.01 (7)	15
Cincinnati	3.11	3.10	2.94 (16)	16
Buffalo	3.08 (19)	3.16	3.06	19
Atlanta	3.20	3.17 (10)	3.07 (2)	12
Capacity, 1000's	27	20	25	72

Production cost = $192,500
Distribution cost = 26,450
Total = $218,950

To distribution centers	From plants Detroit	Chicago	Cleveland	Demand, 1000's
Milwaukee	3.12	3.00 (10)	3.13	10
Cleveland	3.06	3.12 (15)	2.99	15
Cincinnati	3.11	3.10 (8)	3.06 (8)	16
Buffalo	3.08 (19)	3.16	3.07	19
Atlanta	3.20	3.17 (10)	3.14 (2)	12
Capacity, 1000's	27	20	25	72

Production cost = $193,750
Distribution cost = 26,960
Total = $220,710

To distribution centers	From plants Detroit	Chicago	Atlanta	Demand, 1000's
Milwaukee	3.12	3.00 (10)	3.10	10
Cleveland	3.06 (15)	3.12	3.07	15
Cincinnati	3.11 (10)	3.10	3.05 (6)	16
Buffalo	3.08 (12)	3.16 (7)	3.08	19
Atlanta	3.20	3.17	2.89 (12)	12
Capacity, 1000's	27	20	25	72

Production cost = $192,000
Distribution cost = 26,400
Total = $218,400

FIGURE 4. Optimum production-distribution solutions for three proposed locations for the added plant.

The Atlanta and Detroit plants can meet this demand without the Chicago plant by resorting to overtime work. In fact, any two of the three plants can meet the demand if overtime work is used. Therefore, we have these alternatives as well as the alternative of continuing to operate all three plants at partial capacities. Which alternative is best, and how much difference does it make? To determine the answers, we must know, in addition to the data that we have already, the cost of overtime work in each plant, the additional capacity available through overtime, and the cost reductions available by shutting down one plant. For each plant these data are as follows:

	Detroit	Chicago	Atlanta
Production cost at overtime	$ 3.37/unit	$ 3.33/unit	$ 3.27/unit
Additional overtime capacity, units	7,000/wk	5,000/wk	6,000/wk
Fixed costs:			
When operating	$12,000/wk	$9,000/wk	$13,000/wk
When shut down	5,000/wk	4,000/wk	6,000/wk

We can now set up a distribution matrix for each of the four alternatives and determine the total costs for each plan, as well as the appropriate fixed costs. This is done and the optimum distribution solution for each plan, including the appropriate fixed costs, is shown in Figure 5. Note that to keep the problem within the linear programming framework, we have regarded the overtime capacity as a separate source of supply. In actual shipment there would be no need to separate units produced on overtime. The results speak loudly. The most advantageous action is to shut down the Chicago plant and depend on the Detroit and Atlanta plants with 4000 units per week produced on overtime in the Atlanta plant. This alternative is $1500 per week better than the next best solution and $2250 per week better than the worst.

If the situation were even more serious, we might want to consider disposing of a plant. A similar analysis could be made to determine which plant. In such a case, all fixed costs attributed to the discarded plant would be eliminated and the capital recovered from the sale would have to be evaluated.

WAREHOUSE LOCATION

While plant location often involves the personal preferences of the owners and managers, especially if the location also dictates their residences, warehouse location more often yields to rational analysis.

A number of approaches are currently being taken to the problem including linear programming, simulation, heuristic procedures, and the branch and bound technique. For example, simulation models have been developed and used by the Nestle Company [8] and H. J. Heinz [13]. Heuristic models have been developed [9] and applied at the B. F. Goodrich Company [10]. Finally, the branch and bound technique has been applied at ESSO [6, 7].

Even with a single producing plant the problem is not simple, for the entire distribution system design is involved. If the organization is committed to the site of the production plant then it can be concerned with designing a distribution system to link its plant with its markets. Some of the remaining problems for resolution are:

1. Whether or not to use field warehouses and if so, how many and where to locate them.
2. What modes of transportation to use.
3. What inventories will be required to operate the system including those at the plant, in transit, and in the warehouses.

When markets are concentrated, then warehouse locations tend to be determined at or near the major points of concentration. Boundaries between warehouse territories are theoretically determined so that the distribution cost from either warehouse would be equal at the boundary. As a practical matter natural boundaries often occur in the form of rivers, mountains, state lines, etc.

The practical problems increase substantially when multiple plants producing multiple products are servicing multiple warehouses. The products produced by the several plants may be overlapping or independent. Should each plant supply customers (or warehouses) directly or should products not made in all plants be cross-shipped among plants so that orders can be filled as a unit? What territory should be served by a given plant for products made in more than one plant? For products made in more than one plant, how should production schedules be dovetailed to serve the entire market? The real problems are plant location, production system design, inventory control, production schedule, etc.

FOREIGN LOCATIONS

As noted in the introductory section, the lure of foreign countries as potential plant locations has become increasingly strong in the post-World War II era. Part of this lure is based upon the fear by United

To distribution centers \ From plants	Detroit	Chicago	Atlanta	Demand, 1000's
Milwaukee	3.12	3.00 (9)	3.10	9
Cleveland	3.06 (13)	3.12	3.07	13
Cincinnati	3.11	3.10 (11)	3.05	11
Buffalo	3.08 (14)	3.16 (1)	3.08	15
Atlanta	3.20	3.17 (8)	2.89	8
Unused capacity	0 (11)	0 (5)	0	16
Capacity, 1000's	27	20	25	72

Variable cost = $169,650
Fixed cost:
Detroit, 12,000
Chicago, 9,000
Atlanta, 13,000   34,000
Total = $203,650

(a) All plants operating

To distribution centers \ From plants	Chicago	Atlanta	Chic.-O.T.	At.-O.T.	Demand, 1000's
Milwaukee	3.00 (9)	3.10	3.65	3.75	9
Cleveland	3.12	3.07 (8)	3.77 (5)	3.72	13
Cincinnati	3.10 (11)	3.05	3.75	3.70	11
Buffalo	3.16 (9)	3.08	3.81 (6)	3.73	15
Atlanta	3.17	2.89 (8)	3.82	3.54	8
Capacity, 1000's	20	25	5	6	56

Variable cost = $177,730
Fixed cost:
Detroit, 5,000
Chicago, 9,000
Atlanta, 13,000   27,000
Total = $204,730

(b) Detroit plant shut down

FIGURE 5. Optimum production-distribution solutions for four alternatives of plant operations; (b), (c), and (d) have other equally optimal solutions.

States manufacturers of the growing competitive strength of foreign producers. Almost daily, articles expressing this fear and sounding a warning appear in newspapers and magazines. For example, one newspaper article headlined, "Security Danger Seen in Foreign Competition," told the story of a large turbogenerator to be purchased by a large city water and power department. The lowest bid for the unit was made by an overseas supplier and was nearly $3 million or 38 per cent below that of the lowest United States bidder. The reason for the price difference given by the article was that the European worker is paid approximately one-third the rate of an equivalently skilled worker in the United States.

Invariably, the wage advantage is cited as the reason for foreign competitive advantage. The most common solution to the problem offered

To distribution centers \ From plants	Detroit	Atlanta	Det.–O.T.	At.–O.T.	Demand, 1000's
Milwaukee	3.12	3.10 (6)	3.79	3.75 (3)	9
Cleveland	3.06 (13)	3.07	3.73	3.72	13
Cincinnati	3.11	3.05 (11)	3.78	3.70	11
Buffalo	3.08 (14)	3.08	3.75	3.73 (1)	15
Atlanta	3.20	2.89 (8)	3.87	3.54	8
Unused capacity	0	0	0 (7)	0 (2)	9
Capacity, 1000's	27	25	7	6	65

Variable cost = $173,150
Fixed cost:
  Detroit, 12,000
  Chicago, 4,000
  Atlanta, 13,000 29,000

    Total = $202,150

(c) Chicago plant shut down

To distribution centers \ From plants	Detroit	Chicago	Det.–O.T.	Chic.–O.T.	Demand, 1000's
Milwaukee	3.12	3.00 (9)	3.79	3.65	9
Cleveland	3.06 (9)	3.12	3.73 (4)	3.77	13
Cincinnati	3.11 (3)	3.10 (8)	3.78	3.75	11
Buffalo	3.08 (15)	3.16	3.75	3.81	15
Atlanta	3.20	3.17 (3)	3.87	3.82 (5)	8
Unused capacity	0	0	0 (3)	0	3
Capacity, 1000's	27	20	7	5	59

Variable cost = $178,400
Fixed cost:
  Detroit, 12,000
  Chicago, 9,000
  Atlanta, 6,000 27,000

    Total = $205,400

(d) Atlanta plant shut down

FIGURE 5. (continued)

is to establish manufacturing plants in these low-wage areas. Careful location analysis, however, dares not accept either low-wage rates as the reason, or the establishment of foreign plant locations as the panacea.

For a particular manufacturer, the important question is: *Is there a net advantage to him in a foreign location?* There are several important reasons why there may not be. The great attraction in establishing foreign manufacturing operations is, apparently, low wages. But, actually, wage levels themselves are not the important parameter; rather, *labor costs* will determine the advantage or disadvantage of foreign location. Indeed, the American manufacturer perhaps knows better than others that wages can be high and simultaneously labor costs can be low. The equating factor is *productivity*. The American worker is paid much more per hour, but through the relatively large capital investment behind him, his efforts are multiplied by tools, mechanization, and automation. The wages question, then, turns on the difference in labor costs, not on hourly wages.

Can a manufacturer couple the advantage in lower wages with high productivity by using the same levels of mechanization and managerial practice abroad as he does at home? Perhaps, but we must note the difference in basic production economics here and abroad. Since labor is cheap relative to equipment abroad, he may find it wise to use relatively more labor and less expensive machinery, with resulting productivity and final labor costs more in line with that achieved by his foreign counterpart. The most economical manufacturing methods and techniques are not necessarily always those with the greatest possible mechanization, but those which for a given situation strike a balance between the costs of labor and the costs of machinery.

Can a net advantage in labor costs be offset by a net disadvantage in other costs? Assume for a moment that a particular manufacturer will have a net labor cost advantage through foreign manufacture. Will items of costs, such as materials, fuel and power, equipment, and credit, partially or completely counterbalance the labor cost advantages? The answer is undoubtedly different for different organizations and product lines. There is no one answer. The components of labor, materials, and capital in different product lines vary considerably. In the petroleum industry, labor costs are low, perhaps 5 percent, but material and capital are very important. For the turbogenerator cited in the opening paragraph of this section, the proportion of the total that was labor cost was undoubtedly very high because this kind of equipment is custom-built to specifications.

The result of this discussion of net advantage or disadvantage of all costs indicates that a company could be burned badly by rushing to low-wage areas in foreign countries unless low wages translate into *low labor costs* for *their* products, and provided that this labor cost advantage will not be erased by higher material, energy, and equipment costs. On the other hand, companies with cost distributions that fit, might be missing a real opportunity if they do not manufacture abroad.

Wage Level Comparisons.　In making wage level comparisons with foreign countries, it is important to note that the wage paid in many European countries often drastically understates the costs to the employer for an hour of work. The reason is that the so-called social charges (social security, workmen's compensation, vacations, etc.) are somewhat larger proportionately than is usual in the United States. Particularly in countries such as Western Germany, France, and Italy, the social charges are very large, 41, 42, and 64 per cent, respectively [3].

Real Labor Costs. Good data on labor costs are very difficult to obtain for obvious reasons. Relative productivity figures, however, are available from special studies. Figure 6 shows the productivity in manufacturing for Canada, Western European countries, and the United States, all expressed as a per cent of the United States productivity figures. Figure 7 shows the comparison of the relative cost of an hour's work in the United States, Canada, and several Western European countries. Although we must still conclude that labor costs are lower in other countries in general, the differential is not as great as would be indicated by hourly wage rates. Indeed, on the average, in the case of France and Italy, labor costs may not be far different than in the United States. It would be dangerous to attach very strict interpretations to average country figures, however, because there are rather wide differences in productivity and wages paid by industry within each of these countries.

Other Manufacturing Costs. Material is usually the other component of costs that is direct and important in the final cost of the product. The National Industrial Conference Board made a special study [12] of

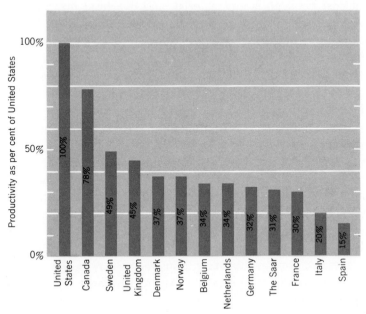

FIGURE 6. Relative productivity in several countries. (From Dresch [5].)

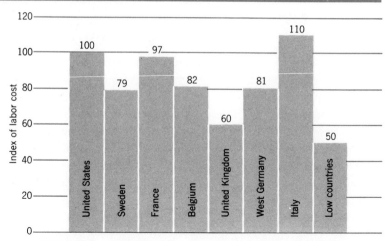

FIGURE 7. Relative cost of an hour's labor in several countries. (Adapted from [3].)

production costs among companies with both domestic and foreign operations.

The data were obtained by means of a questionnaire which asked for the percentage breakdown, for both domestic and foreign operations, of total unit cost between labor, material, and overhead on products that were basically similar. With these data, plus ratios of total unit costs, it was possible to tabulate relative figures on the three classifications of cost. Our interest is now in the material cost category of that study. It shows that only 29.9 per cent of the products were reported with material costs lower in foreign countries; 70.1 per cent were either equal or higher. This indicates a pattern that is somewhere the reverse of the labor cost picture. Thus, the company in an industry where the labor component is relatively large and the material component relatively small might find an advantageous balance of costs abroad. On the other hand, the reverse pattern might be true for a company in which material costs are large. Not only were material costs higher on the average in foreign countries, but, for *each* industry listed, higher material costs in foreign plants were reported with greater frequency.

In the general category of overhead costs, there is such a variety of items that generalizations are difficult. Some costs may be lower and some higher than would be typical for American plants. We would expect the labor component of overhead costs to be generally lower, in line with the generally lower wage rates. Capital costs in Europe are somewhat higher. The cost of the equipment itself may be higher or lower. Fuel and other sources of industrial energy are significant costs for some industries. Here again it appears that foreign costs are not attractive.

Overall Production Costs.   Of the products for which total unit cost ratios were given, 44.2 per cent were below United States costs, 19.3 per cent were equal to United States costs, and 36.5 per cent were greater than United States costs. When all costs are considered, there is no picture of either generally lower or generally higher costs abroad. On the other hand, what is indicated is considerable variability, with foreign costs ranging from less than 55 per cent to more than 145 per cent of domestic costs (see Figure 8). Apparently there are some products,

FIGURE 8.   Distribution of number of products by ratio of foreign to domestic unit costs. (Based on data from [12].)

industries, or companies that are favored by the structure of foreign costs; for others the conditions are unfavorable. Products in the industries that have relatively low labor content are predominant in the "Unit Cost Higher" column. Similarly, those industries that have the reverse pattern of labor and material costs, that is, chemicals, fabricating metal, and machinery, are predominant in the "Unit Cost Lower" column.

It does not appear logical that low-wage rates in foreign countries generally threaten the United States industry. It is true that foreign companies have an advantage in certain product lines. But, on the other hand, American companies have an advantage in other product lines. The most powerful defense against the low-wage rate appears to be the great advantage of high productivity enjoyed by America. The American lead here is significant, but not equally so in all industries. While European countries are increasing their productivity, so is the United States. Location studies in foreign countries need to take account of these differences in productivity, material, and other costs, as well as the differences in wage rates.

SUMMARY

There is a trend toward decentralization in plant location. This decentralization is taking place both on a nationwide scale and within industrial communities. Many small communities that have never had industry before have offered attractions, such as tax reductions, low-cost or even free land, and buildings, to lure industry to their communities. Within large industrial communities, decentralization has taken industry to the suburbs where land is cheaper and the more efficient one-story building is feasible. These suburban locations offer space for expansion and parking, as well as the opportunity to design plants of architectural beauty that fit into the landscape and in which employees are proud to work.

Location is of great importance because it fixes some of the physical factors of the overall plant design. In addition, location determines what investment costs must be incurred and the level of many operating costs. Although these factors are important, we must remember that there are normally a number of good locations. Although it is certainly possible to pick poor ones, careful analysis and planning ordinarily uncover good locations. The personal factor is a strong one in plant location. Owners of businesses often choose, or retain, plant locations because they prefer to live in those areas. This, too, speaks for the theory that many locations are acceptable, for many enterprises have survived over long periods even though location has been determined solely by the owner's personal preference.

REVIEW QUESTIONS

1. How important is a plant's location to its profitability?
2. How often does the question of plant location arise? What are the location alternatives that an organization faces?
3. What is the object of location analysis? What is the importance of subjective factors in appraising alternate choices for location?
4. What kinds of data are needed to perform an analysis of alternate sites within a given general location?
5. Can an advantage in projected operating costs be counterbalanced by capital expenditures required for a given location? What sort of analysis is called for?
6. How is the problem of locating a single plant different from locating an additional plant which manufactures the same items as existing plants? What sort of analytical technique is useful?
7. What do we mean by "locational dynamics" for multiple plants?
8. On what basis can foreign labor costs be compared with those in the United States? What are the general comparisons in labor costs between the United States and various European countries?
9. How do material costs compare between the United States and foreign countries?
10. On balance, are foreign locations attractive for U.S. manufacturers? In which kinds of industries?

PROBLEMS

1. A company with plants in Seattle, Chicago, and Louisville is considering the establishment of a manufacturing plant in a foreign location. The primary reasons are these: First and foremost is a steady decline in unit profit due to relatively higher manufacturing costs. Second is the growing popularity of the products in foreign countries. After a preliminary analysis, the list of possible locations has been narrowed down to the following countries: Japan, West Germany, and Puerto Rico.

    A. In any analysis of alternative plant locations, some assumptions are necessary for the degree of political stability, attitude toward foreign investors, currency fluctuations, etc. For each proposed alternative, assign a subjective value between one and ten (ten = best) and give your rationale for the values assigned.

(a) United States
(b) Japan
(c) West Germany
(d) Puerto Rico

B. Determine the best plant combination for the existing demand, using objective data (the comparison will basically narrow down to the alternatives of foreign locations versus overtime in existing plants). Data follows:

Present unit manufacturing costs:

	Seattle	Chicago	Louisville
Raw material	$0.02	$0.03	$0.02
Direct labor	0.04	0.03	C.05
Variable burden	0.02	0.02	0.01
Nonvariable burden	0.09	0.10	0.08
General and administrative	0.01	0.01	0.01
	$0.18	$0.19	$0.17

Annual present factory capacity; units:

	Seattle	Chicago	Louisville
(One-shift operation)	100,000	200,000	120,000

Additional production may be attained by using overtime (direct labor = 150 per cent of normal costs, all other costs constant). Maximum overtime capacity = 50 per cent of regular capacity.

Present annual demand; units:

Seattle	Chicago	Louisville	Japan	West Germany	Puerto Rico
90,000	150,000	100,000	30,000	40,000	20,000

Estimated foreign production costs:

	Japan	West Germany	Puerto Rico
Raw material	$0.018	$0.019	$0.017
Direct labor	0.037	0.040	0.022
Variable burden	0.005	0.011	0.011
Nonvariable burden	0.061	0.093	0.098
General and administrative	0.009	0.007	0.012
	$0.130	$0.170	$0.160

Estimated plant costs (50,000 annual capacity in units for one-shift operation, ignore the possibility of second-shift foreign operation):

Japan	West Germany	Puerto Rico
$10,000	$30,000	$20,000

Projected market growth per annum (not compounded):

United States	Japan	West Germany	Puerto Rico
5%	6%	7%	8%

Distribution costs, including import taxes, etc.:

To:

From:	Seattle	Chicago	Louisville	Japan	West Germany	Puerto Rico
Seattle	$0.02	$0.06	$0.08	$0.12	$0.16	$0.10
Chicago	0.06	0.04	0.05	0.15	0.15	0.09
Louisville	0.08	0.05	0.03	0.16	0.16	0.08
Japan	0.14	0.16	0.17	0.02	0.21	0.18
West Germany	0.17	0.16	0.17	0.20	0.03	0.19
Puerto Rico	0.11	0.10	0.09	0.22	0.20	0.01

C. Determine the optimal plant output combination for five years from the present. Include a 10-per-cent annual interest cost for proposed plants.

D. Based on your answers to problems A, B, and C and any other relevant information, what suggestions would you make to the company regarding foreign locations? Why?

2. The Good-Wear Shoe Company discussed as an example in the text installed the Atlanta plant discussed there. With the initial success of that producing location, and the incursion of imports in existing markets, management turned its attention to the exploration of new markets. They found ready opportunities by expanding their sales efforts westward and in the South and Southwest. They have been supplying these markets from existing distribution centers, but current volume in the new locations has raised the question of the advisability of a new warehouse location. Three possible locations are suggested because of market concentrations: Denver, Houston, and New Orleans. Data concerning capacities, demands, and costs are given in Table III. Based on these data which warehouse location should be chosen? What additional criteria might be invoked to help make a choice? How should they decide whether or not to build the new warehouse or continue to supply from the existing warehouses?

TABLE III. Production Costs, Distribution Costs, Plant Capacities, and Market Demands for the Good-Wear Shoe Company

To Distribution Center / From Plants	Distribution Costs per Pair, Handling, Warehousing, and Freight								Normal Weekly Capacity Pairs	Unit Production Cost
	Existing Warehouses					Proposed New Warehouses				
	Atlanta	Buffalo	Cincinnati	Cleveland	Milwaukee	Denver	Houston	New Orleans		
Atlanta	$0.27	$0.46	$0.43	$0.45	$0.48	$0.65	$0.58	$0.55	25,000	$2.62
Chicago	0.49	0.48	0.42	0.44	0.32	0.50	0.54	0.60	20,000	2.68
Detroit	0.50	0.38	0.41	0.36	0.42	0.55	0.60	0.65	27,000	2.70
Forecast weekly market demand, pairs	8,000	15,000	11,000	13,000	9,000	16,000	16,000	16,000		

REFERENCES

[1] *Basic Industrial Location Factors*. U.S. Department of Commerce, Washington, D.C., 1946.

[2] Brown, P. A., and D. F. Gibson. "A Quantified Model for Facility Site Selection—Application to a Multiplant Location Problem." *AIIE Transactions*, **4** (1), 1–10, March 1972.

[3] Buffa, E. S., and A. E. Bogardy. "When Should a Company Manufacture Abroad." *California Management Review*, **2** (2), 1960.

[4] Dillon, J. D. "The Geographical Distribution of Production in Multiple Plant Operations." *Management Science*, **2** (4), 353–365, July 1956.

[5] Dresch, F. W. *Productivity in Manufacturing*. Stanford Research Institute, Palo Alto, Ca., 1953.

[6] Effroymson, M. A., and T. L. Ray. "A Branch-Bound Algorithm for Plant Location." *Operations Research*, **14** (3), May–June 1966.

[7] Feldman, E., F. A. Lehrer, and T. L. Ray. "Warehouse Locations Under Continuous Economics of Scale." *Management Science*, **12** (5), May 1966.

[8] Gerson, M., and R. B. Maffei. "Technical Characteristics of Distribution Simulators." *Management Science*, **10**, 1968.

[9] Keuhn, A. A., and M. J. Hamburger. "A Heuristic Program for Locating Warehouses." *Management Science*, **9** (7), July 1963.

[10] Khumawala, B. M. "A Heuristic Simulation Approach to Warehouse Locations." *Proceedings of IBM's Third MS/OR Conference*, IBM Publication No. 320–2968, April 1969.

[11] Khumawala, B. M., and D. C. Whybark. "A Comparison of Some Recent Warehouse Location Techniques." *The Logistics Review*, **7** (31), 1971.

[12] "Production Costs Here and Abroad." *Studies in Business Economics*, National Industrial Conference Board, No. 61, New York, 1958.

[13] Shycon, H. N., and R. B. Maffei. "Simulation-Tool for Better Distribution." *Harvard Business Review*, Nov.–Dec. 1960.

[14] "Techniques for Plant Location." *Studies in Business Policy*, National Industrial Conference Board, No. 61, New York, 1953.

[15] Weston, F. C., Jr. "Quantitative Analysis of Plant Location." *Industrial Engineering*, **4** (4), 22–28, April 1972.

12

Layout of Physical Facilities

Plant layout is the integrating phase of the design of a production system. The basic objective of layout is to develop a production system that meets requirements of capacity and quality in the most economical way. Here the specifications of what to make (drawings and specifications), how it is to be made (route sheets and operation sheets), and how many to make (forecasts, orders, or contracts) become the basis for developing an integrated system of production. This integrated system must provide for: machines, workplaces, and storage in the capacities required so that feasible schedules can be determined for the various parts and products; a transportation system which moves the parts and products through the system; and auxiliary services for production, such as tool cribs and maintenance shops, and for personnel, such as medical facilities and cafeterias.

Because of the dynamic character of our economy, the design of this integrated production machine must retain an appropriate degree of flexibility to provide for future changes in product designs, product volumes, and mixes and for advancing production technology. Both the site and the building should make it possible to expand operations in a way that dovetails with existing operations. Certain financial and physical restrictions are a normal part of the layout problem. The physical restrictions may be due to the site: its size, shape, and orientation in relation to roads, railroads, and utilities. Or they may be due to local ordinances or state laws which specify building restrictions and safety codes. In redesign or relayout of facilities, the existing building imposes severe restrictions.

These general statements of the layout problem indicate something of its complexity. Almost all of the factors which enter the problem tend to interact. For example, providing flexibility affects the nature of processes and capacities, which, in turn, interact with short- and long-run costs. Material transportation methods affect not only transportation costs but also the amount of handling at machines and workplaces. The physical arrangement and relative location of work centers are important in determining transportation costs and direct labor costs. Storage locations and capacities interact with transportation costs and delay times.

We could continue for some time in describing the interdependent nature of the factors that enter into the layout problem, but our present point is that optimizing the design of such a system is largely an art. We have principles, rules, and guides which have been shown to be valuable in determining suboptimal solutions for components of the large problem. For example, queuing theory can provide a basis for optimal design capacities of service centers such as tool cribs and maintenance crews. Human engineering data can help in optimizing workplace design; operation sequence analysis can help to determine the best relative work center locations (discussed later in this chapter). And principles of production economics can aid in selecting the most economical processes, designs, handling systems, etc.

However, there is no overall general theory that makes it possible to relate the multitude of influencing factors in a composite optimal design. Rather, the development of a good plant layout is the result of a sequence of major decisions on such questions as location, design capacity, and general modes of manufacture. These decisions are followed by a multitude of less significant, but important, decisions related to the selection and placement of equipment, allocation of space, basic flow patterns, etc. Several components of plant design are discussed separately, because we have special knowledge about them and because they are important. Production processes, job and method design, production design, process planning, and plant location are examples.

These, however, tend to blend with the overall activity of layout during the actual development of a plant design.

THE CAPACITY DECISION

In contemplating a new plant design or the redesign or expansion of an existing system, a high-level decision on the design capacity is required. It is not enough simply to look at annual sales of various products, because the sales pattern may reveal seasonal fluctuations. Do we design for the peak or for some average level? If we choose to follow the sales curve, we shall minimize inventory risks, but we shall have a fluctuating labor force and our plant will have idle capacity except during peak production. If we adopt some intermediate level, we shall tend to stabilize employment levels and utilize plant facilities better, but it will be necessary to build inventories to meet the sales peak. Which plan will minimize the combined cost of inventories, plant investment costs, and labor turnover costs? We have here a problem in economic analysis that is of major significance. It can be approached as a programming problem where production capacity is allocated to operating periods, minimizing the combined plant investment costs, inventory costs, and turnover costs. Investment costs would be approximated by a nonlinear function of capacity.

Future Capacity.   Then there is the question of sales forecasts. Do we build for a capacity that matches our present sales experience or do we attempt to build for some forecast level of one, five, or ten years hence? Can we afford to build for more capacity than is needed now? We must remember that successive units of capacity are not equally expensive because capacity is bought in "chunks." Moreover, it is commonly true that at any one level there will be idle capacity in certain equipment classifications. Therefore, to move to the next level does not entail the purchase of equipment items where we already have idle capacity. Where capacity is built to match some forecast of future needs, it is common to buy equipment for current needs only and provide space in the building and layout for the additional equipment when it is needed. Thus, planning is for a future capacity, but extra overhead is carried for the building space only; as the capacity is needed, machines can be integrated into the system without need for relayout.

The question then really relates to the provision for extra space to match a future forecast. Some additional space can probably be justified when we consider that space added later is more expensive per square foot because existing walls must be removed, doors cut through to the new space, etc. More important than the cost of the additional space itself are relayout costs, which would be required to integrate the new space into the production system. If the new space is not integrated into the system but becomes a "thumb" stuck on to the existing layout, we would pay extra costs daily in the form of higher material-handling costs. These extra costs of adding future space must be balanced against the incremental costs of building more space now and carrying it as added overhead until it is needed.

Subcontracting and Multiple-Shift Effects on Capacity. Another aspect of the capacity problem is the question of how we shall meet our capacity needs. The investment-capacity ratio can be altered by the amount of subcontracting and by the intensity with which we use facilities, that is, one, two, or three shifts. The economics of make versus buy are especially significant where new capital equipment is involved, as it would be with the design of a new facility, for now we have no idle capacity behind which "make" can hide. Rather, we are setting the future pattern, so overall make-buy policies need to be reviewed.

The number of shifts appropriate for a given organization is not a simple question. If we use two shifts instead of one, investment costs are not halved because, as we noted before, increments of capacity are not equally expensive. Many other costs are also involved. Wage premiums of 10 to 15 per cent are common for second shifts, and many people question whether productivity and scrap ratios are as good on multiple shifts. Multiple shifts ordinarily increase supervision costs, also. There is no single answer to the question of shift operation, since the relative importance of building and equipment investment costs and labor costs varies from industry to industry. Economic analysis is required for each situation. In general, industries with very heavy investments in buildings and equipment per worker, such as steel, chemical, and oil refining industries, find multiple shifts more economical; those with moderate and low investments per worker find that wage premiums more than counterbalance the investment savings of multiple shifts.

Translating Capacity into Workable Units. What is the meaning of the term *capacity*? A steel man would think in terms of tons of steel per day, week, or month; an automobile manufacturer in terms of cars, etc. How about a job-shop machining company? Its products are so different that capacity in terms of the output of finished products is quite meaningless. Here capacity must be expressed in more universal terms. The units commonly used are *available hours* in various machine classifications per day, week, or month. This output potential is a good general measure of capacity for plant design because we can convert fairly easily to a physical capacity equivalent, the number of *machines* required. The number of machines required in various classifications is the data that we finally want to work with in developing a layout. We need to translate everything into physical units of capacity. In doing this, we must be careful to make allowances for two factors which reduce the utilization of equipment: the plant efficiency factor and the scrap factor.

Through the *plant efficiency factor* we recognize that because of scheduling delays, machine breakdowns, preventive maintenance, etc., a portion of the available hours cannot be used. Plant efficiency factors vary with the type of equipment and the company; they range generally from 0.50 to 0.95. Thus, if 100 outboard motors per week translated into the need for 550 milling machine-hours per week (summarized from data on route sheets, time studies, estimates, etc.), we need the equivalent of $550/0.80 = 688$ hours if our plant efficiency factor is 0.80, since we expect that about 138 machine-hours will be unavailable to us.

Through the *scrap factor* we recognize that for any real production process we shall produce some bad parts or products. When a decision was made to design a plant to build 100 outboard motors per week, we were obviously thinking of good motors, free of defective parts. But some of our milling capacity will be used up producing scrap, and so we must allow for this event too. If we expected 3 per cent scrap in our milling operations, 688 hours of available machine hours must be increased to $688/0.97 = 709$ hours. Now, if we expect to work 75 hours per week on two shifts, we need $709/75 = 9.45$ machines. As we noted, physical capacity comes in "chunks," so we must provide for either 9 or 10 milling machines. If we decide on 10 machines, we shall expect to have some idle capacity. If we decide to squeeze by with 9 machines, we should expect some bottlenecks now and then, which we may try to make up by overtime work. Thus, a capacity of 100 outboard motors translates into an equivalent milling machine capacity of 9 or 10 machines.

Summarizing, the capacity question involves important decisions that will determine total plant investment and future operating costs of the plant through: the selection of production levels in relation to seasonal sales levels, the determination of how many shifts are most economical, the decision of what proportion of the total effort to subcontract, and the determination of how much excess or "growth" capacity is economical. The financial strength and ability of the organization are always present as restrictions in determining how close we may approach ideal capacity conditions at a given time. A company with limited financial resources must constantly appraise alternative uses for available funds: for advertising and promotion, for product development programs, or for capital improvement.

BASIC LAYOUT TYPES

Which type of layout is appropriate? Do we have prerequisites for a streamlined production line layout such as we find in automobile assembly? During the development of a new plant design, these fundamental decisions plague production executives, and they should, for at this time they hold in balance the opportunity of the future on one side and miserable failure on the other. A shiny new plant housing an obsolete layout or an inappropriate layout would result in increased manufacturing costs. The appropriate type of layout may set the pattern for efficient manufacture for a long time to come.

In general, layouts can be classified as either process oriented or product oriented. In a *process layout,* equipment of the same functional type is grouped together, so we would have lathes grouped together, milling machines together, inspection in one place, all assembly in one place, etc., as shown in Figure 1. Process layout follows closely our model for intermittent production systems. Figure 2 shows the typical arrangement for product or line layout, which follows our model for continuous production systems. The name *product layout* comes from the fact that the basic organization of the layout is dictated by the part or product. Equipment is arranged according to the sequence in which it is used for a given part or product, following the route sheet sequences. If similar equipment is required for both parts A and B, it would normally be duplicated in the two lines of Figure 2, even though the equipment is not fully utilized for either part. Flow patterns for line layout are fixed by the nature of the layout and the type of transportation equipment commonly used.

Process layout is often called functional or job-lot layout. It is employed when the same facilities must be used to fabricate and assemble a wide variety of parts or when part and product designs are not stable. Quite often the volume of individual parts is low, and even though the total may be very large, as with aircraft parts fabrication, no single

FIGURE 1. Process or functional layout. Machines are arranged in functional groups. Parts take various routings as dictated by their design requirements. Illustrative routes for two parts, A and B, are shown. Parts are moved from operation to operation in batches or lots and stored temporarily at each work station to await their turn.

sequence of operations will accommodate very many parts. These are the general conditions that dictate the use of process layout. The prime requirement is flexibility: routing flexibility, part design flexibility, and volume flexibility.

In this missile age, many of us have been led to believe that process layout is used by inefficient manufacturers and line layout is used by "sharp" production men. Nothing could be further from the truth. Both types of layout can be inefficient if poorly designed, and both can be efficient. The important question is: Does the layout match the requirements imposed by the nature of the manufacturing problem? Actually, given the conditions described in the above paragraph, process layout would be more economical than line layout. This is because process layout leaves the equipment in flexible condition so it can be used on

FIGURE 2. Product or line layout. Machines and equipment are arranged according to the sequence of operations required to fabricate and assemble. Machines and workers are specialized in the performance of specific operations, and parts approach continuous movement.

various parts. Equipment utilization is thus very good, and total investment in equipment is low. If we attempted line layout under these conditions, the specialization of equipment for specific parts would result in very low utilization and a resulting high equipment investment in order to meet capacity requirements. If a machine breaks down in process layout, only that operation is affected. On a production line, however, breakdowns affect the entire sequence of operations and this affects overall utilization factors. If product designs change, line layouts become obsolete.

When the conditions for line layout are met, the result is very low-cost manufacture. We might summarize these requirements as follows:

1. Volume adequate for reasonable equipment utilization.
2. Reasonably stable product demand.
3. Product standardization.
4. Part interchangeability.
5. Continuous supply of material.

Each of these requirements needs to be qualified. There is no one volume that we can point to as being "adequate." Rather, economic analysis would determine the breakeven volume between process and line layout for a given part or product. Reasonably good equipment utilization is associated with high volume. Stable demand is required in terms of a minimum run which would at least cover the extra costs of tooling the line. Thus, stable demand is associated with product standardization. Engineering changes in product designs can be accommodated by production lines (witness automobile manufacture), but they cannot be too frequent. We must have an "economical run" to cover the costs of retooling and relayout which design changes may require. Part interchangeability is required so that no special reworking or fitting is needed on the line. If parts are not interchangeable at assembly, the flow of work is disrupted because of imbalance. Finally, where we have the high volume standardized product situation described by the foregoing requirements, continuous supply of material is crucial. The lack of supply of a single part or item of raw material can force the entire process to be stopped.

Line layout has found its great field of application in assembly rather than in fabrication. A moment's reflection will reveal why this is true. Machine tools commonly have fixed machine cycles while the cut is being made; this factor makes it difficult to achieve balance between successive operations. The result is poor equipment utilization and relatively high manufacturing costs. In assembly operations where the work is manual, balance is much easier to obtain because the total job can be fractionated into minute elements. If operation 10 is too short and 16 too long, a part of the work of 16 can probably be transferred to 10 (perhaps the tightening of a single bolt). Since very little equipment is involved at each operation anyway, utilization of equipment may not be too important.

Attempts to establish fabrication lines are sometimes premature. The general range of breakeven volumes is much higher for fabrication than for assembly. In one situation a plant actually had been laid out in a series of fabrication lines to serve major parts. However, an analysis of the utilization of the equipment by random sampling techniques revealed a shocking 21 per cent utilization figure. It was an obvious misapplication of line layout, and immediate steps were taken to relayout the shop.

When the conditions for line layout are met, it offers significant advantages. The production cycle is speeded up since materials approach continuous movement. And since very little manual handling is required, the cost of material handling is low. Since materials are not moved in batches or lots and because of the fast manufacturing cycle, in-process inventories are lower. Since aisles are not used for material movement and since in-process storage space is minimized, the total floor space required by a line layout is commonly less than for an equivalent process layout, even though more individual pieces of equipment may be required. Finally, the control of the flow of work (production control) is greatly simplified for a line layout because routes become direct and mechanical. No detailed scheduling of work to individual workplaces and machines is required; each operation is an integral part of the line. Scheduling the line as a whole automatically schedules the component operations.

Pure process or pure line layouts are rare. We are most apt to find fabrication shops arranged by process, with fabrication lines occurring sporadically where conditions permit. Assembly today is customarily accomplished on lines, except for very low volumes or for very large, bulky, heavy items such as locomotives, aircraft, and ships. For these items, fixed position assembly is common. A unique combination-type layout is possible where a product is made in various sizes and types. Since the sequence of operations is similar, machines can be arranged together in functional groups, as in process layout, but the process groupings can be arranged in a sequence that fits the various sizes and types fairly well.

PROCESS LAYOUT

The major problem of a strictly "layout" nature in process layout is the determination of the most economical relative location of the various process areas. The best arrangement is not immediately obvious, except for trivial cases. This fact is emphasized by the realization that for only six process areas arranged in a simple grid, as in Figure 3, there are 6! (six factorial) or $6 \cdot 5 \cdot 4 \cdot 3 \cdot 2 \cdot 1 = 720$ arrangements possible. Fortunately, only 45 of them are really different in terms of their effects on idealized measures of material-handling cost. The number of combinations goes up very rapidly as we increase the number of process areas.

Let us consider first the nature of our objective. The major criterion for selecting an arrangement is material-handling cost. Thus, we want an arrangement that places the process areas in locations relative to each other such that the material-handling cost for all parts is minimized. Therefore, if we examined the required material-handling activity be-

FIGURE 3.   There are 6! = 720 arrangements of the six process areas in the six locations of the grid.

tween Departments A and C of Figure 3 and found that it was heavy compared to AB, we would want to consider switching the locations of Departments B and C. But before jumping to the conclusion that this switch would be advantageous, we would want to see if this advantage would be wiped out by an increase in the relative material-handling activity between DB and DC. We might take as a measure of material-handling cost the product of the distance times the number of loads that must be moved in some period of time. For each combination of arrangements, then, we could simply add up the load-distance products between all combinations of departments. The combination with the smallest total is the basic arrangement that we are looking for. To formalize this statement of our objective, the measure of effectiveness, E, is:

$$E = \sum_i \sum_j A_{ij} X_{ij} = \text{minimum}$$

where

A_{ij} = number of loads per week, month, or period required to be transported between departments i and j

X_{ij} = distance between departments i and j

This measure of effectiveness closely approximates material-handling costs. Each material-handling operation requires certain fixed times associated with picking up the load, positioning it to set down, etc. These costs, mainly labor costs, would be about the same for large or small loads. The variable costs associated with a material-handling operation (mainly labor plus power) are related to distance.

Operation
Sequence
Analysis

The data that we need are the number of loads that must be transported between all combinations of work centers. This type of data can be summarized from route sheets and drawings. The route sheets indicate sequences; from the drawings of the parts themselves and the production rates, we can determine the number of parts transported at one time and, therefore, the number of loads. Table I shows a summary of the number of loads per month for all combinations of work centers for a typical small production situation.

In initial design we idealize our problem by assuming a structure similar to Figure 3, with circles representing the functional groupings of equipment. We regard departments as being adjacent if they are either next to each other, as are A and B, or diagonally across from each other, as are A and E. Nonadjacent locations are those which are more than one grid unit away from each other horizontally, vertically, or diagonally, represented by AC, AF, DC, and DF in Figure 3. We can see now that for our idealized layout, the measure of effectiveness reduces to minimizing the sum of the nonadjacent loads (unit distance) × (loads). For problems of reasonable size, the minimum nonadjacent (distance) × (load) solution is fairly readily seen by graphical methods.

This graphical approach to the solution is accomplished by placing the information contained in the load summary, Table I, in an equivalent schematic diagram in which circles represent work centers (functional groups of machines), and labeled connecting lines indicate the number of

TABLE I. Load Summary (Number of Loads per Month between All Combinations of Work Centers)

From		Rec. 1	Stores 2	Saw 3	Eng. Lathe 4	Turret Lathe 5	Drill 6	Mill 7	Grinder 8	Ass'y 9	F.G. 10	Ship 11
Departments							To					
Receiving	1		600									
Stores	2			400	100			100				
Saw	3				350	50						
Engine Lathe	4						100	450				
Turret Lathe	5							50				
Drill	6				100					150	100	
Mill	7						50		450	100		
Grinder	8						200			250		
Assembly	9										500	
Finished Goods	10											600
Shipping	11											

From Buffa [5].

loads transported between work centers. Figure 4 is a first solution obtained by merely placing the work centers on the grid, following the logic from the pattern indicated by Table I. When all connecting lines are on the diagram and labeled we have an initial solution which may be improved by inspecting the effect of changes in location. When an advantageous change is found, the diagram is altered. For example, in Figure 4 we see immediately that work center 4 has a total of 300 loads that are transported to or from work centers that are not adjacent, that is, 2 and 6. If 4 is moved to the location between 2 and 6, all loads to and from 4 become adjacent. Further inspection shows that 200 non-adjacent loads must be transported between work centers 6 and 8. Is an advantageous shift possible? Yes, by moving 9 down and placing 8 in the position vacated by 9, the number of nonadjacent loads is reduced from 200 to 100. Figure 5 shows the diagram with the changes incorporated.

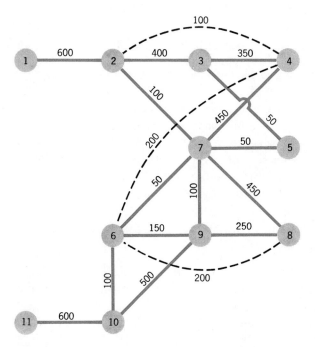

FIGURE 4. Initial graphic solution developed from load summary of Table I. It can be seen by inspection that 4 can be moved to the position between 2 and 6 to eliminate 300 nonadjacent loads. The positions of 8 and 9 are improved by replacing 9 by 8 and moving 9 to the position just below 8. (From Buffa [5].)

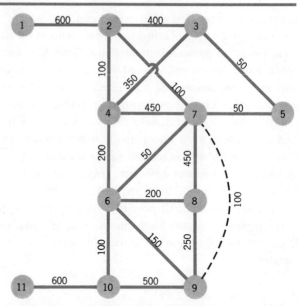

FIGURE 5. Ideal schematic diagram incorporating changes suggested by Figure 4. Solution is not necessarily optimal but no further location changes seem to yield improvement. (Based on Buffa [5].)

Further inspection reveals no further advantageous shifts of location, so we adopt Figure 5 as our ideal schematic layout which has a $2 \times 100 = 200$ load-distance rating. For larger problems the grid distance becomes an important part of the measure of effectiveness, because work centers might be separated by two, three, or four grid units. Figure 5 is not a provable optimum solution in the mathematical sense, because we have no test of optimality. The ideal schematic diagram is now the basis for developing a physical layout in which the work center or department locations are specified.

The Block Diagram   Now that we know how the work centers should be located in relation to each other in our idealized layout, we can use the ideal schematic diagram as a basis for developing a block diagram in which the physical areas required by the work centers take the same relative locations. Estimates of the areas required by each work center can be developed from the number of machines required in each center and the floor area required by each machine. Commonly, the machine areas are multiplied by a factor of 3 or 4 to obtain an estimate, or first approximation, of the total area required, including working space for the operator, material storage, and pro rata aisle space.

The block diagram itself is developed by substituting estimated areas for the small circles in the idealized schematic layout. Initially this can be done with block templates to find an arrangement that is compatible with both the flow pattern of the ideal schematic diagram and the various size requirements for work centers. Figure 6 shows such an initial block diagram for our example. We can see that the essential character of our ideal schematic diagram is retained. However, Figure 6 obviously does not represent a practical solution as yet. Slight variation of the shapes of work areas will make it possible to fit the system into a rectangular configuration and meet possible shape and dimension restrictions that may be imposed by the site or by an existing building if we are dealing with relayout. Figure 7 shows such a block diagram.

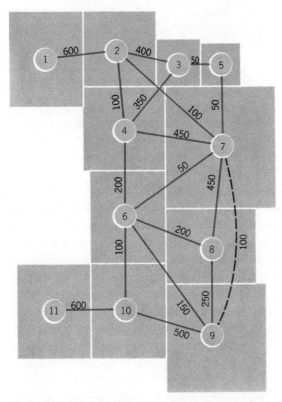

FIGURE 6.   Initial block diagram. Estimated work center areas are substituted for circles in the ideal schematic diagram of Figure 5. Block templates are used for estimated area requirements for the various work centers. (Based on Buffa, [5].)

FIGURE 7. Block diagram which takes account of rectangular building shape and other possible restrictions of shape and dimension imposed by site but still retains approximate work center area requirements and idealized flow pattern. (Based on Buffa [5].)

The final block diagram represented by Figure 7 marks the end point of general, overall layout. The block diagram presents a frame of reference for the development of the details of the layout. Now we can proceed with aisle layout, machine arrangement within work centers, workplace layout, design of plant and personnel service areas, selection of specific material-handling equipment, etc., knowing that the work centers are located relative to each other in the most economical way.

When the block diagram is complete, combinations of work centers can be made for practical departmentalization. These combinations can be based on work center sizes, the numbers of workers involved, similarity of work, and other criteria important to the particular application.

We should comment that our example was a simple one and that the solution to actual problems usually would involve many more non-adjacent loads. Therefore, the ideal schematic would not develop so easily.

The detailed layout phase undoubtedly requires minor shifts in space allocation and shape. Here, the templates and models discussed later in this chapter become valuable aids in visualizing the developing details. Standards for minimum machine spacing, aisle widths for different uses, and column spacings for different building designs all exist in handbook form. The allowances for in-process storage space and warehousing space and the design of material-handling systems depend on the specific conditions of the problem.

The graphical approach to the determination of the relative location of departments just discussed has obvious limitations. The technique depends on an individual analyst's insight to evolve better schematic diagrams; as the number of activity centers increases, the technique rapidly breaks down. Practical problems in facility location often involve 20 or more activity centers, and this number is already at the limit for feasible use of the operation sequence analysis technique. To overcome this limitation a Computerized Relative Allocation of Facilities Technique (CRAFT) was developed [2, 6] which easily handles up to 40 activity centers and has other important advantages. Before describing the structure and operation of the CRAFT program, let us state what were thought to be the basic requirements of such a program.

Computerized Relative Allocation of Facilities

1. It must take account of wide variations in flow paths.
2. It must allow for different material-handling systems to be used for different materials or parts, each handling system possibly having different costs in proportion to distance moved.
3. It must account for different floor area requirements for activity centers or departments.
4. It must meet the possible requirement that certain activity centers need an exact and specific location and cannot be moved.
5. It must incorporate a rigorous algorithm which minimizes material-handling costs jointly for the entire set of parts or products moved through the system.

Managers also are giving increased recognition to the needs of the "small group." The location of work groups in an existing facility may have developed working relationships that contribute to the overall effectiveness of operations. Will a new layout take this human problem into account? If management places a high value on this factor, we should be able to show how much extra material-handling cost is involved to retain a close physical relationship between two or more work groups, activities, or departments. Conversely, it may be desirable to separate two or more departments because of noise, vibration, dust, fumes, or other conditions which may call for isolation. If the data indicating the material-cost differentials which result from these requirements can be provided, a rational decision can be made.

Actually since there is such a large number of layouts possible, it is probable that several are quite good. It may easily be that one of them will accommodate the requirements of human relations or other constraints and still be a really excellent layout from the point of view of material-handling costs. What is needed then is a technique that can generate and evaluate a relatively large number of alternate layouts without a tremendous expenditure in time and money.

The basic problem is not trivial. With only 20 departments to consider, there are over 608,000,000,000,000 different combinations of layouts that could be generated. This makes it impossible to consider calculating the material-handling costs for all possible combinations to find the best one, even with rapid data processing equipment. The CRAFT program, a description of which follows, is governed by a rigorous heuristic algorithm which can provide answers that are excellent solutions to the problem.

The CRAFT Program. * The basic idea on which the computer program is based is similar in general concept to the method by which a linear programming algorithm converges on an optimal solution. The answers generated are not mathematically provable, unique optimums in the same sense as are the answers to linear programming problems, but rather represent solutions that cannot easily be improved. CRAFT takes as inputs data on interdepartmental flow and material-handling costs, together with a representation of a block layout. The block layout which is fed in may be the actual existing layout or any arbitrary starting solution if a new facility is being developed. The program calculates department centers and an estimate of total material-handling costs for the input layout. The governing heuristic algorithm then asks the following question: What change in material-handling costs would result if the locations of two departments were exchanged? Within the computer, the locations of the two departments or activity centers are exchanged and material-handling costs are recomputed. The result may be either an increase or decrease but the difference is recorded in the memory of the computer. The program then proceeds by asking the same question for other combinations of two departments, recording cost differences again. It proceeds in this way through all combinations of exchanges. When the number of departments is 20, the possible

---

*IBM SHARE LIBRARY No. SDA3391.

number of pair exchanges is computed as the number of combinations of 20 departments taken two at a time, or 190.

This number of computations is relatively small. When the cost differences for all such combinations have been computed, the program selects the exchange that would result in the largest reduction, makes the exchange in locations on the block diagram, and prints out the new block layout, the new total material-handling costs, the cost reduction just effected, and the departments involved in the exchange. The basic procedure is then repeated, generating a second, third, etc., improved block layout. Finally, when the procedure indicates that no exchanges in location which reduce material-handling cost can be made, the final block layout is printed out which becomes the basis for a detailed template layout of the facility.

As presently constructed, the program has the capacity for handling 40 departments or activity centers. Any departmental location can be fixed down by simply specifying in the instructions that the department or departments are not candidates for exchange. This feature is of great practical importance because existing layouts cannot be completely rearranged. Fixed locations may develop when costly heavy equipment has been installed, or the location of receiving or shipping facilities may be determined by the location of roads or railroad spurs. Finally, as mentioned previously, the locations of some work groups often make it desirable to treat them as fixed location points in the layout.

Whereas the explanation given previously indicates that the program considers the possible exchange of two departments at a time, the present construction of the program actually can consider the exchange in location of three departments simultaneously. When departments are exchanged three at a time, the number of computations required for each iteration is 1140. Whether the two- or three-way exchange is used is of small importance, however, since a trivial amount of computer time is required in either case. It turns out that the three-way exchange routine is somewhat more efficient than the two-way exchange routine, and the use of both routines together is still more efficient.

A Case Study Application. The computer program has been used widely in industrial and architectural practical situations. The application described here uses the program at its fully developed stage with the capability just described. The company was a precision manufacturer in the aerospace industry, and the plant involved was a general machine shop with about 42,000 square feet of floor area. The majority of shop orders were for small precision parts in low quantities, so most material handling was accomplished by the machinists themselves carrying orders to and from a central holding and dispatch area (Department K) in tote pans. The current layout had grown around the central holding and dispatch department. One important question which management wished to evaluate, in addition to the layout itself, was the validity of having material flow through the central holding area. Although the use of the central holding area had certain advantages of close control for a small plant, it was obvious that the physical flow of material to and from the holding area entailed incremental material-handling costs. The alternate policy was, of course, to dispatch orders directly from department to department, utilizing an information system for control.

Another operating policy which management wished to evaluate was the use of machinists to accomplish the majority of interdepartmental material handling. Originally, when the plant was small, the machinists had been used for this purpose because distances were short and it was felt that these short walks gave machinists a break from usual routines. The plant had been enlarged as time passed, however, and it was felt that the use of specialized material handlers should be evaluated. In summary then, there were four basic conditions for which it was desirable to determine the best layout and the material-handling costs associated.

1. Current practice: material flow through Department K—machinists used for handling.
2. Material flow through Department K—using material handlers.
3. Dispatch utilizing information system—machinists used for handling.
4. Dispatch utilizing information system—using specialized material handlers.

For purposes of analysis, there were 22 plant areas designated as department centers. Table II shows the department name, the letter code used for that department, and the approximate area requirement for each department. In the balance of our discussion, we shall use the letter codes for departments. Note that Departments U and V were the only ones fixed in location by the program. Department U, the washroom, was not a candidate for exchange because it was not feasible to relocate plumbing. Department V was actually not a real area but was included as a dummy department to fill out the need of the program for a rectangular configuration.

Input Data. As mentioned previously, three kinds of data are required for the program.

1. Interdepartmental flow per time unit—per week, per month, or some other time unit.

2. Unit load material-handling cost per unit distance such as per 100 feet of movement.

3. An initial block layout—in this application the existing plant layout.

To determine interdepartmental flow, it was necessary to analyze approximately 1600 shop orders (approximately an eight-week sample) which had indicated on them the routing required to fabricate the parts. Fortunately this data were available on punched cards so that it was relatively simple to develop a matrix which showed the number of loads flowing between all combinations of departments. This matrix

TABLE II. List of Departments with Letter Codes and Area Requirements

Letter Code	Department Name	Area, Square Feet
A	Electrical maintenance	1200
B	Drill presses	1800
C	Degrease	500
D	Milling machines	3900
E	Turret lathes and automatic screw machines	2000
F	Jig borers	1900
G	Boring mills	800
H	Hardinge and hand screw machines	400
I	Lathes	1500
J	Slabbing mills	600
K	Central holding and dispatching	1700
L	Grinding machines	2000
M	Saws	100
N	Gear hobbing machines	1700
O	Tool room	7500
P	Numerically controlled Fosdick jig borers	1400
Q	Numerically controlled Burgmasters	600
R	Deburring	600
S	Pantograph	1400
T	Inspection	3000
U	Washrooms (fixed location)	2400
V	Vacuous area not in building (fixed location)	5000
	Total area	42,000

From Buffa, Armour, and Vollmann [6].

is similar although not identical to that shown in Table I as the load summary for the operation sequence analysis graphical technique.

A similar matrix was developed to show the material-handling cost in dollars per 100 feet of movement for combinations of departments for which flow occurred. The existing block layout for the plant was reduced for input to the computer in the form shown by Figure 8 where the scale is 10 feet per character. Since there are 15 columns and 28 rows, we have represented an area 150 × 280 feet. Looking at Department T

```
      1  2  3  4  5  6  7  8  9 10 11 12 13 14 15
 1    T  T  T  T  T  V  V  V  V  V  V  V  V  V  V
 2    T           T  V                          V
 3    T           T  V                          V
 4    T           T  V                          V
 5    T           T  V  V  V  V  V  V  V  V  V  V
 6    T  T  T  T  T  N  N  N  N  N  B  B  B  A  A
 7    S  S  S  S  S  N        N     B     B  A  A
 8    S           S  N  N     N     B     B  A  A
 9    S  S  S  S  P  M  L  L  N  N  B     B  A  A
10    R  R  R  P  P  L        L  L  B     B  A  A
11    R  R  R  P  P  L           L  B  B  B  A  A
12    Q  Q  P     P  L        L  L  D  D  D  C  C
13    Q  Q  P     P  L  L  L  K  K  D     D  C  C
14    Q  Q  P  P  P  K  K  K     K  D     D  C  D
15    O  O  O  O  O  O  K        K  D        D  D
16    O              O  K  K  K  K  K  D        D
17    O              O  U  U  U  U  U  U  U  D  D
18    O              O  U                 U  D  D
19    O              O  U                 U  D  D
20    O              O  U  U  U  U  U  U  U  D  D  D  D
21    O                O  E  E  E  E  E  E  E  E  E
22    O                O  E  E  E  E  E  E  E     E
23    O                O  I  I  I  I  I  J  J  E  E
24    O                O  I                 I  J  J  J  J
25    O                O  I  I  I  I  I  I  F  F  F  F
26    O                O  H  H  H  H  F           F
27    O                O  G  G  G  G  F           F
28    O  O  O  O  O  O  O  G  G  G  G  F  F  F  F  F
```

TOTAL COST   3294.98   EST. COST REDUCTION   0.   MOVEA   MOVEB   MOVEC

FIGURE 8.   Existing block layout for a small aerospace precision manufacturer. (From [6].)

in the upper left-hand corner, for example, we can see that it has been allocated 50×60 feet or 3000 square feet in the existing layout, the equivalent of 30 characters. The computer output prints the outline of the area of each department for easy reading and recognition. Each department is represented in a similar way, and the total eight-week simulated material-handling cost for the existing layout with existing practices has been computed by the program as $3294.98, as shown at the bottom of Figure 8.

```
        1  2  3  4  5  6  7  8  9  10 11 12 13 14 15

 1      T  T  T  T  T  V  V  V  V  V  V  V  V  V  V
 2      T           T  V                          V
 3      T           T  V                          V
 4      T            T  V                         V
 5      T              T  V  V  V  V  V  V  V  V  V
 6      T  T  T  T  T  T  N  N  N  N  N  B  B  B  A  A
 7      P  P  P  P  P  P  N        N  B     B  A  A
 8      P              P  N  N  N  N  B     B  A  A
 9      P  P  P  P  P  S  M  L  L  N  N  B  B  A  A
10      R  R  R  S  S  L        L  L  B     B  A  A
11      R  R  R  S  S  L           L  B  B  B  A  A
12      Q  Q  S     S  L        L  L  D  D  D  C  C
13      Q  Q  S     S  L  L  L  L  K  K  D     D  C  C
14      Q  Q  S  S  S  S  K  K  K     K  D     D  C  D
15      O  O  O  O  O  O  K           K  D        D  D
16      O           O  K  K  K  K  K  K  D           D
17      O        O  U  U  U  U  U  U  U  D           D
18      O        O  U              U  D           D
19      O        O  U              U  D           D
20      O        O  U  U  U  U  U  U  U  D  D  D  D
21      O           O  E  E  E  E  E  E  E  E  E
22      O           O  E  E  E  E  E  E  E  E     E
23      O           O  I  I  I  I  I  I  J  J  E  E
24      O           O  I              I  J  J  J  J
25      O           O  I  I  I  I  I  I  F  F  F  F
26      O           O  H  H  H  H  H  F           F
27      O           O  G  G  G  G  G  F           F
28      O  O  O  O  O  O  O  G  G  G  G  F  F  F  F  F

TOTAL COST    3126.24    EST. COST REDUCTION    168.74    MOVEA P    MOVEB S    MOVE
```

FIGURE 9. Block layout following first exchange by CRAFT program involving departments P and S. (From [6].)

The program proceeded as described previously. It was found that the best first exchange involved Departments *P* and *S* which reduced material-handling costs by $168.74, as shown in Figure 9. For the particular conditions and policies of the current situation, the program went through 14 cycles or iterations. It finally produced the block layout shown in Figure 10, which represents a best layout for the restrictions of alternative 1, that is, existing policies and practices. At the time the program printed Figure 10, it could find no further improvements in location.

	1	2	3	4	5	6	7	8	9	10	11	12	13	14	15
1	P	P	P	P	P	V	V	V	V	V	V	V	V	V	V
2	P				P	V									V
3	T	P	P	P	P	V									V
4	T	T	T	T	T	V									V
5	T				T	V	V	V	V	V	V	V	V	V	V
6	T				T	B	B	B	B	B	B	D	D	H	H
7	T				T	B				B	D		D	H	H
8	T				T	B		B	B	B	D			D	D
9	T	T	T	T	M	B	B	K	K	K	D				D
10	S	S	S	L	L	L	L	K		K	D				D
11	S		S	L			L	K		K	D				D
12	S		S	L			L	K		K	D				D
13	S		S	L			L	K		K	D				D
14	R	S	S	L	L	L	L	I	K	K	D	D	D	D	N
15	R	R	R	C	I	I	I		I	I	I	N	N	N	N
16	R	R	C	C	I	I	I	I	I	I	I	N			N
17	Q	Q	Q	C	U	U	U	U	U	U	U	N	N		N
18	Q	Q	Q	C	U					U	G	G	N	N	N
19	F	F	F	F	U					U	G		G	J	J
20	F				F	U	U	U	U	U	U	G	G	G	J	J
21	F				F	E	E	E	E	E	E	A	A	A	J	J
22	F				F	E					E	A		A	A
23	F	F	F	F	E	E	E	E	E	E	E	E	A	A	A	A
24	O	O	O	O	O	O	O	O	O	O	O	O	O	O	O
25	O														O
26	O														O
27	O														O
28	O	O	O	O	O	O	O	O	O	O	O	O	O	O	O

TOTAL COST   2645.08   EST. COST REDUCTION   39.17   MOVEA R MOVEB S MOVEC

FIGURE 10. Best block layout for alternative 1, existing policies and practices. (From [6].)

Results for Four Alternatives.   The four conditions were computed, and the total material-handling costs per eight-week period were as shown in Table III, the far right column indicating the per cent reduction in cost of each alternative compared to the cost of the existing layout. Each alternative required less than one minute to compute. Alternative 4, by using an information system for control and specialized material handlers, resulted in a startling 73 per cent reduction. When the eight-week figures are placed on an annual basis, the cost reduction potential is approximately $15,500. If the company demands a 10 per cent return on plant investments of this kind and imposes a severe three-year payback period for capital recovery and return, it could afford to spend over $38,000 for the plant relocations and alterations necessary for relayout. The program has made it possible to compute improvement potential without attempting detailed template layouts of any alternative. When basic decisions are made concerning the course of action to be taken, a detailed template layout can be prepared for only one block layout.

Office Layout.   The same general concepts apply to the layout of large offices with functional groupings, though the measure of effective layout may change. As an example, a layout study was made in the

TABLE III.   Material-Handling Costs for Five Layouts

Alternatives	Total 8-Week Material-Handling Cost	Per Cent Reduction from Existing Layout
Existing layout—current policies	$3294.98	—
Cost for best layout under following conditions:		
1. Current practice: Material flow through Department *K*—machinists used for handling	2645.08	20%
2. Material flow through Department *K*— using material handlers	2402.97	27%
3. Dispatch utilizing information system— machinists used for handling	1186.89	64%
4. Dispatch utilizing information system— using specialized material handlers	900.93	73%

From [6].

engineering office of a large aerospace manufacturer. Initially, the study focused on the flow of work through the system, but it was difficult to generate meaningful cost data on this basis, since the flow of work involves the flow of paper and the material-handling cost is not a useful measure. The search for realistic measures of effectiveness finally narrowed to the relative location of people in the organization as required by their face-to-face contacts with others in the organization. It was decided to collect data on face-to-face contacts initiated by each person for a one-month period.

The entire office was divided into ten groups or areas as indicated in Figure 11 which represents the existing block layout. Table IV shows the data on face-to-face contacts in matrix form. Each cell value indicates the number of face-to-face contacts initiated by that group, for example, 15 from A to B. Table V summarizes the area requirements for each group as well as the average hourly wage paid in each group. The matrix of Table IV was then multiplied by the average hourly wage to obtain a cost matrix as an input to the CRAFT program. The existing block layout formed the basis for an initial starting solution and the

FIGURE 11. Existing block layout for ten groups within a large engineering office.

TABLE IV. Number of Face-to-Face Contacts per Month in an Engineering Office

From \ To	Filing (A)	Supervision (B)	Blueprint (C)	Product Support (D)	Structural Design (E)	Electrical Design (F)	Hydraulic Design (G)	Production Liaison (H)	Detailing and Checking (I)	Secretarial Pool (J)
(A) Filing		15				5		10		15
(B) Supervision	20		25	40	100	90	80	160	85	60
(C) Blueprint										
(D) Product Support	10	15					20	280		10
(E) Structural Design	50	20	600			40			340	50
(F) Electrical Design			475					160	270	60
(G) Hydraulic Design	10		460	20				140	320	45
(H) Production Liaison	20			200	160	190	240			680
(I) Detailing and Checking		210	690	40	190	240	80			20
(J) Secretarial Pool		25						15		

	Group	Area	Average Hourly Wage
A	Filing	20 × 15 = 300 sq. ft.	$1.80
B	Supervision	30 × 15 = 450 sq. ft.	5.00
C	Blueprinting	40 × 15 = 600 sq. ft.	2.10
D	Product support	25 × 20 = 500 sq. ft.	2.70
E	Structural design	65 × 25 = 1625 sq. ft.	4.50
F	Electrical design	25 × 35 = 875 sq. ft.	4.50
G	Hydraulic design	45 × 30 = 1350 sq. ft.	4.50
H	Production liaison	20 × 70 = 1400 sq. ft.	2.70
I	Detailing and checking	70 × 25 = 1750 sq. ft.	3.60
J	Secretarial pool	70 × 15 = 1050 sq. ft.	2.40
		90 × 110 = 9000 sq. ft.	

TABLE V. Area Requirements and Average Wage Rates for Ten Groups in a Large Engineering Office

final block layout generated by the CRAFT program is shown in Figure 12. The CRAFT computed cost of the existing layout was $2,524.68 which was reduced to $1,847.90 or a reduction of 27 per cent in this measure of the value of relative locations based on face-to-face contact.

Usefulness of CRAFT.   The CRAFT program is applicable for overall location of major activities as well as more detailed departmental locations within activities. For example, one project worked on was the relocation of major activities within a huge multibuilding complex in the aerospace industry. The complex of buildings and activities contained therein had grown and been added to piece by piece over a long period of time. The CRAFT program helped determine the best relative location of each major activity.

A similar kind of application has also been carried out to help determine the best relative location of major activities within a large integrated movie studio. Although it is not commonly thought of in this way, a

	1	2	3	4	5	6	7	8	9	10	11	12	13	14	15	16	17	18
1	A	A	A	A	B	B	B	B	B	B	E	E	E	D	D	D	D	D
2	A			A	B					B	E		E	D				D
3	A	A	A	A	B	B	B	B	B	B	E		E	D				D
4	I	I	I	I	I	I	E	E	E	E	E	E	E	D	D	D	D	D
5	I				I	E							E	G	G	G	G	G
6	I				I	E					E	E	G					G
7	I				I	E					E	G	G					G
8	I				I	E					E		G					G
9	I				I	E	E	E	E	E	E		G					G
10	I				I	C	C	C	C	C	E	E	E	G				G
11	I				I	C			C	C	E	E	G					G
12	I				I	C				C	E	E	G					G
13	I				I	C				C	E	E	G	G	G	G	G	G
14	I				I	C	C	C	C	C	E	E	G	G	H	H	H	H
15	I	I	I	I	I	I	I	I	I	I	I	I	I	I	H			H
16	I	F	F	F	F	F	F	F	F	F	H	H	H	H	H	H		H
17	F	F								F	H							H
18	F									F	H							H
19	F	F	F	F	F	F	F	F	F	F	H	H	H	H	H	H		H
20	J	J	J	J	J	J	J	J	J	J	J	J	J	J	J	H		H
21	J														J	H		H
22	J	J	J	J	J	J	J	J	J	J	J	J	J	J	H	H	H	H

TOTAL COST: 1847.90

FIGURE 12. Final CRAFT configuration for the engineering office layout.

movie studio can be conceived of as a very large job shop since each film sequence is a custom-made item. Material handling on the "lot" is much more expensive relatively than it would be in the average machine shop, so the relative location of major activity centers becomes a matter of extreme importance.

The CRAFT program is also applicable to a wide variety of other nonmanufacturing situations, such as hospital design and warehouse location, as well as certain equipment design problems where manufacturing costs may vary with component location.

The prime requirement of material-handling methods used in process layouts is flexibility: flexibility of path and flexibility of size, weight, and shape of load. The types of material-handling equipment that fit this requirement are, in general, mobile trucks, tractor trains, and cranes.

Material Handling in Process Layouts

Low *terminal time*, that is, the time required to set down or pick up a load, is an important characteristic of efficient material-handling equipment; therefore, quick pickup systems have developed around skids and pallets (see Figure 13). Material is loaded directly on a skid or pallet by the worker as he completes his operation on the part. Without further handling, a skid truck, pallet truck, or fork truck (Figure 13) can pick up the entire load very quickly and move it to its destination. Therefore, one important consideration in developing the details of a layout is to provide easy access to all operations by efficient material-handling equipment. The fork truck is designed specifically to stack loads so that storage floor area can be used efficiently. Pallets and skids, properly loaded, can be stacked four or five layers high. Overhead cranes

FIGURE 13. Typical methods of handling material for process layouts. (Courtesy Yale and Towne Manufacturing Company.)

are used to transport and position large, heavy pieces within a fixed area. Supplementary cranes are often required at workplaces to handle heavy pieces to and from machines.

Although it is not commonly done, material handling in process layouts can be accomplished by an overhead carrousel conveyor system when parts are small. The conveyor circulates to all work centers, so transportation between all combinations of work centers can be accomplished. Pans or boxes of parts may be placed on racks suspended from the chain conveyor with the destination work center indicated by some code. When the load arrives at its destination, the parts can be removed by assigned personnel and dispatched to the required machine, according to whatever assignment rules are in effect. If a shipment is not removed when it arrives, it merely recirculates in the system. Higher levels of mechanization could provide for automatic removal from the conveyor rather easily. Under such a material-handling system, the emphasis in the development of gross layout changes from one of minimizing the (distance) × (load) sum to one of minimizing the total length of the conveyor.

How much material-handling equipment is needed? This has always been a difficult question in process layouts because the demand for transporting capacity is on a random basis, and the material handling tasks vary in time somewhat. It is common even to find material-handling equipment idle a considerable share of the time and at the same time to hear complaints that the material can never be moved when it is wanted. The general problem situation has all of the characteristics of a waiting line model, as recognized by recent research [9]. Demand for transportation service can be analyzed and a distribution of equivalent *arrival rates*, or arrival times, can be constructed. Service time or handling time must be defined *as the interval from the moment a handling unit is assigned to move a certain load until it is available to be assigned to another load.* These service or handling times can then be formed into a distribution.

If the distribution fits a standard one for which mathematical models have been developed, as discussed in Chapter 8, direct mathematical solutions can be developed. If it does not fit the standard models, solutions can always be developed by simulation. The logic of economic analysis is to provide material-handling capacity to the extent that the combined costs of the handling capacity and incremental operating costs are minimized. These incremental operating costs are of three general types. First, if we add capacity, we add personnel to service that capacity, that is, a material handler. But, in addition, the added capacity will reduce delays and delay costs of two types: in-process inventory and idle labor at machines and workplaces. Additional capacity produces savings from reduced delay. The optimal capacity to provide is that which minimizes the combined costs that are affected. Optimal solutions will undoubtedly specify considerable idle time for material-handling equipment in order to reduce delay costs to reasonable levels. Table VI shows the relation of the delay times to truck idle time for a single truck and the indicated assumptions of distributions. To hold delays to an average of 15 minutes, the truck must be idle 50 per cent of the time.

PRODUCT OR LINE LAYOUT

Balance is the central problem in designing a production or assembly line. This is not to minimize the other problems of physical positioning of equipment, material-handling devices, design of special tools, and workplace layout, for in many instances solutions to these problems will contribute to the balance of the line. Balance refers to the equality of output of each successive operation in the sequence of a line. If they are all equal, we say that we have perfect balance and we expect smooth flow. If they are unequal, we know that the maximum possible output for the line as a whole will be dictated by the slowest operation in the sequence. This slow operation, often called the bottleneck operation, restricts the flow of parts in the line in much the same way that a half-closed valve restricts the flow of water, even though the pipes in the

TABLE VI.   Delays and Idle Time for a Single Unit with Various Loadings*

Loading, in Calls per 15 Minutes	Average Per Cent of Time Truck Is Idle	Average Delay in Hours, of Goods to Be Moved
0.1	90	0.03
0.5	50	0.25
0.8	20	1.0
0.9	10	2.25
0.95	5	4.75
0.99	1	24.75
1.00	0	Infinite!

*The assumptions underlying the table are Poisson call rates and negative exponential service times. From [9, p. 203].

system might be capable of carrying twice as much water. Thus, where imbalance exists in a line, we have wasted capacity in all operations, except the bottleneck operation.

First we shall consider procedures for *assembly* line balancing. Later we shall see what differences might exist if we were dealing with a fabrication line. To have the greatest ability to achieve balance, we need to know the performance times for the smallest possible whole units of activity, such as tightening a bolt or making a solder joint. We must also have a knowledge of the flexibility in the sequence of these tasks or activities. There are, of course, certain limitations on the sequence of the tasks. For example, a washer must go on before the nut, wires joined physically before they can be soldered, a hole drilled before it can be reamed and reamed before it can be tapped. On the other hand, the sequence may be irrelevant; for example, the order in which a series of nuts is put on. This sequence flexibility is important in helping us to specify the groups of elements making up operations, or stations, for the line which achieves the best balance.

Let us see the nature of the problem through an example. Figure 14 shows the cylinder subassembly for a typical small air compressor with the parts named and numbered. By examining the assembly we can readily see the sequence restrictions that we would have to observe. When assembling the cylinder head to the cylinder, the cylinder head

Balancing
Techniques

FIGURE 14.   Cylinder subassembly for a typical air compressor.

gasket (part No. 8) would have to be positioned first. Also, when assembling the discharge valve unit, the valve itself (part No. 3) must go in first, followed by a valve spring (part No. 6) and finally by a discharge valve fitting (part No. 4). A similar procedure for the suction valve unit would be followed, but the sequence of the valve and the spring would be reversed. These are the sequences that must be observed, because the cylinder subassembly cannot be assembled correctly any other way. On the other hand, it makes no difference whether the valve units are assembled to the cylinder head before or after the cylinder head is assembled to the cylinder. Similarly, which valve unit is assembled first is irrelevant. The cylinder head is joined to the cylinder by four screws. All four need not be assembled at the same time, and there is no required sequence for their assembly.

These task sequence restrictions are summarized in Table VII so we can use the result to advantage. The assembly tasks listed in Table VII are, in general, broken down into the smallest whole activity. Note, for example, that the screws and the valve fittings are first positioned and the threads engaged, so tightening can take place separately, perhaps as a part of the next station or some subsequent station. Also, for each task, we note in the far right-hand column the task or tasks which must precede it. Thus, tasks a, e, and i can take any sequence, because no tasks need precede them. However, task b, position cylinder head on cylinder, must be preceded by task a, position cylinder head gasket on cylinder. Task c-1 must be preceded by tasks a and b. The repetition of a is not absolutely necessary, since we know that b must be preceded by a. With this information, together with the task times also given in Table VII, we can construct the diagram in Figure 15.

Figure 15 merely reflects in a graphical way the sequence requirements that we have determined. The performance times are indicated beside the tasks for convenience. Now we can proceed with the grouping of tasks in order to obtain balance. But, balance at what level? What is to be the capacity of our line? This is an important point and one which makes a balancing problem difficult. With no restriction on capacity, the problem would be simple; we could take the lowest common multiple approach. For example, if we had three operations that required 3.2, 2.0, and 4.0 minutes, respectively, we could provide eight workplaces of the first, five of the second, and ten of the third, so that the capacity of the line would be 150 units per hour at each of the operations, all happily in balance. But capacity has been specified by balance rather than the considerations which we discussed previously.

TABLE VII. List of Assembly Tasks Showing Sequence Restrictions and Performance Times for the Cylinder Subassembly of Figure 14

Task	Performance Time, Seconds	Task Description	Task Must Follow Task Listed Below
a	1.5	Position cylinder head gasket (No. 8) on cylinder (No. 1)	—
b	2.0	Position cylinder head (No. 2) on cylinder (No. 1)	a
c-1	3.2	Position cylinder head screw (No. 7) in hole and engage threads	b
c-2	3.2	Repeat	b
c-3	3.2	Repeat	b
c-4	3.2	Repeat	b
d-1	1.5	Tighten cylinder head screw	c
d-2	1.5	Repeat	c
d-3	1.5	Repeat	c
d-4	1.5	Repeat	c
e	3.7	Position valve (No. 3) in bottom of discharge hole	—
f	2.6	Position valve spring (No. 6) on top of valve in discharge hole	e
g	3.2	Position discharge valve fitting (No. 4) in hole and engage threads	f
h	2.0	Tighten discharge valve fitting	g
i	3.1	Position second valve spring (No. 6) in bottom of suction hole	—
j	3.7	Position second valve (No. 3) on top of spring in suction hole	i
k	3.2	Position suction valve fitting (No. 5) in hole and engage threads	j
l	2.0	Tighten suction valve fitting	k

We must take the capacity of the line as given and develop good balance within that restriction. For illustrative purposes, let us assume that we must balance our line for a 10-second cycle. A completed unit would be produced by the line each 10 seconds; to meet this capacity requirement, no station could be assigned more than 10 seconds worth of the tasks shown on the diagram of Figure 15. Proceeding then, we could group the tasks into station assignments. The total of all task

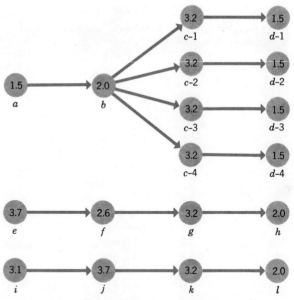

FIGURE 15. Diagrammatic representation of the sequence requirements shown in Table VII. Numbers indicate performance times of tasks.

times is 45.8 seconds. Therefore, with a 10-second cycle, five stations would be the minimum possible. Any solution that required more than five stations would increase direct labor costs. Figure 16 shows one solution that yields five stations. While this is a simple example, it illustrates the conceptual problems of line balancing.

Practical Balancing Methods. The general concepts of line balancing which we have discussed have been implemented through a number of practical methods for the large-scale problems in industry. These methods have ranged from linear programming models [3] and dynamic programming [10] to heuristic methods [11, 14, 24] and a computer-based biased sampling technique [1]. Perhaps of greatest interest for large-scale problems are the heuristic methods of Kilbridge and Wester [14, 30] and COMSOAL: a Computer Method for Sequencing Operations for Assembly Lines, developed by Arcus [1].

The heuristic methods involve the generation of a precedence diagram in a particular way which indicates the flexibility available for shifting tasks from column to column to achieve the desired balance. The heuristic rules are simple, but considerable individual ingenuity is required to obtain good solutions. The heuristic methods have been

FIGURE 16. A solution to the line balancing problem which requires no more than 10 seconds per station and does not violate the task sequence requirements.

applied to television assembly line problems with 45 and 133 tasks and have achieved excellent results [30]. COMSOAL methodology is based on the rapid generation of feasible solutions by a computer routine. The probability of generating either optimal, or very good, solutions is finite and dependent on the sample size of feasible solutions generated. The nature of the computer program biases the generation of feasible solutions toward the better ones in order to save computer time. COM-SOAL has already been implemented at Chrysler Corporation; Arcus has used it on a hypothetical line of 200 stations with 1000 tasks, achieving the known optimal solution of 0 idle time.

Mastor [17] evaluated a large number of different line balance models in a set of experiments involving a range of problem sizes (numbers of tasks to be assigned), line lengths (number of stations in the line), and order strengths (degree of sequence restriction imposed in the precedence relationships). He found that the dynamic programming formulation model [10] was consistently the best performer, with COMSOAL [1] a close second; however, the computer time requirements for the latter were very much smaller. For large problems (70, 92, and 111 tasks), the two techniques performed almost identically when the COMSOAL program was run for 999 sequences. Even for the large sample size on the 111-task problem, COMSOAL required only 56 seconds of computer time compared to 94.3 for the dynamic programming model.

Auxiliary Balancing Techniques. Other techniques are available to obtain balance in both the design and operation stages. If one station requires greater time than the others, a careful study of the activities, as well as the psychophysiological aspects of the tasks, may result in a reduction of time. The material discussed in Chapter 13 would be applicable. Compensations for imbalance can be accomplished by assigning fast operators to the limiting operations. When there are some very fast operations which cannot be combined into a single station, as might be true with machine operations, material banking before and after the fast operations may be required. These fast operations would be operated only a small portion of the day; the machine, the operator, or both, could be used for other purposes.

Balancing Fabrication Lines. Conceptually, there is no difference in the balancing procedures for assembly and fabrication lines. However, the fixed machine cycles found in fabrication operations considerably limit freedom in achieving balance. It is often impractical to divide a machine operation into two or more suboperations in order to level out the time requirements at each station. This situation partially accounts for the fact that fabrication lines are generally economical only for very high volumes, since good balance is likely to be achieved only at high levels of output. Otherwise, equipment utilization is very low. If we try to use the idle capacity to machine other parts, material-handling costs increase because the equipment has been located to minimize handling costs for the line product. The process layout, which minimizes overall handling costs, is usually more economical under these conditions.

Material Handling in Line Layouts

Material-handling methods and equipment, like the layout itself, tend to be special purpose in nature for line layouts. There is often considerable confusion about the relation of conveyors and line layout. The mere existence of conveyors does not make a line layout, nor does it guarantee the efficiency of any kind of a layout. The nature of line layout does, however, require some direct means of transportation between operations. This may be accomplished in some instances by simply arranging flow so that each operator places the unit down in such a position that it can be picked up by the succeeding worker. Where the nature of the product permits it, gravity chutes can be used effectively. Finally, where these cheaper means are impractical, conveyors to fit all types of applications of size, shape, and weight of parts are available commercially. Figure 17 shows a selection of applications of material-handling equipment used in production lines.

Although standard sizes and types of conveying equipment are available commercially, they ordinarily require a considerable amount of special design work to fit them into an effective overall design of a line layout. The best systems of internal transportation for lines integrate the functions of transportation with those of processing and storage, so it is not necessary to perform supplementary handling to and from the line. This means a careful allowance for the size of banks needed at various stages. Many processes, such as painting and drying, may take place while the material moves. The special-purpose nature of line layout design often makes it worthwhile to design special handling equipment that is integrated with the processing so completely that the entire line functions as a single integrated machine. Much of the actual material handling performed in industry occurs as a part of the pro-

FIGURE 17.   Typical methods of handling materials in line layouts. (Courtesy Lamson Corporation.)

ductive operations, such as moving parts to and from machines. When integrated handling systems are designed, much of this type of handling can be eliminated.

SERVICE FACILITIES

Plant Services

Many plant services must fit into the overall layout. The fact that many of these activities are not a part of the direct production activity of the enterprise has often tended to promote the idea that whatever space is left over is good enough for them. Actually, some of these activities, such as receiving, shipping, and warehousing, are in the direct material flow and they process the product as do the production departments. Others, such as maintenance facilities and tool cribs, do not work on the product but interact with production costs so that their physical location and capacity deserve careful thought. The overall material flow patterns should be the major factors in determining the relative locations of receiving, shipping, storage, and warehousing areas. Our discussion of operation sequence analysis for process layouts included these functional areas. For line layouts the material flow is more obvious, so the proper location for these areas is fairly well determined.

The capacity question for receiving areas does not have an obvious answer. In general, the problem is such that we do not have control over the rate at which materials come in. Since receipts of shipments from suppliers occur in a somewhat random pattern, a good design provides capacity that meets the reasonably expected peak loads for truck and rail docks, unloading crews, and temporary setdown areas for materials. Here again, waiting line theory may provide a guide for determining what these capacities should be. Of course, many other factors influence the details of the layout of receiving areas, such as climate, safety codes, handling equipment, dock heights, and the necessity to accommodate a variety of vehicles.

The location of tool cribs is important because of the travel time of high-priced mechanics to and from the area. Therefore, a study of the use frequency in relation to the physical layout of the production areas should determine a good location or locations. The tool storage problem is comparable to the material and part storage problem in using space efficiently while making items available quickly and conveniently. The number of attendants required to serve the tool crib is another waiting line problem, as indicated in our example on pages 203–207.

Maintenance facilities are commonly provided for buildings and grounds, plant utilities, and machinery and equipment. The capacity of maintenance for machinery and equipment again poses the problem of balancing the idle time of maintenance crews against the idle time of production workers, as well as losses of output capacity. Ordinarily, a considerable amount of idle capacity in equipment and crews is justifiable, as would be shown by solutions to waiting line models of these types of problems.

Present-day personnel services cover a broad spectrum including parking, cafeterias, medical services, credit unions, locker rooms, toilets and lavatories, and, quite often, recreational facilities. Obviously, providing for these services presents layout problems. In many instances, the location of these services does not have an effect on production costs since the services are used after hours. In these instances, the layout problem is to provide the space designed to perform the services in the amounts required. The activities must be studied to determine what must be done and facilities provided accordingly.

Employee Services

For those services used during working hours, such as medical facilities, toilet facilities, and drinking fountains, the size of the facility and its location in relation to the users become important. Studies of travel distances to and from the service facility should be made in order to determine reasonable locations. Waiting line models are again useful in determining a balance between waiting times of employees and service capacity costs. In one large company which offered a broad medical service, the question of whether or not an additional doctor on the staff was warranted was answered by a waiting time study. The results of the study indicated that there was an average of 15 employees in the waiting room during the 8-hour work day; assuming a 2000 working-hour year and a modest average hourly wage of $2, this translates into $60,000 of waiting time per year. The study led to both an enlargement and decentralization of medical services.

PLANT BUILDINGS

As a layout develops, many of the specifications for and characteristics of the building develop simultaneously. For example, the location of equipment specifies minimum floor loadings, requirements for electrical distribution system, plumbing, etc. The size and shape of the building are outgrowths of the layout. The location and spacing of columns to support the roof must be determined during the layout phase so that a subsequent building design does not invalidate the layout work. Factory building design today tends to stress architectural beauty and landscaping, and employees have reacted by an expression of pride in working in these types of plants.

Single versus Multistory Buildings.   The trend in factory building design for some time has been toward the single-story building. The reasons for this are numerous; the cheaper construction possible with single-story buildings tells only part of the story. The net usable area of a multistory building is much smaller because of the space required by columns, stairwells, and elevators, so building costs per net usable unit areas are actually *much* cheaper for the single-story buildings. In central industrial areas where land costs are very high, the balance may be tipped in favor of multistory construction, however.

In addition to the usual net construction cost advantage, the single-story building offers wide unobstructed bays (100-foot bays are common) that free the layout and make for greater flexibility of the original layout as well as for subsequent relayouts. Floor loads are unrestricted and ventilation is easier to obtain. Also, greatest advantage can be taken of natural illumination through sawtooth roof designs. The operating advantage of a single-story building is probably most important of all. Material-handling costs for most products are lower in the horizontal plane than in the vertical. However, there are exceptions. In meat packing, for example, a multistory building seems to offer handling cost advantages because drop chutes can be used to transfer the product from station to station and from floor to floor as it is processed.

Building Shapes and Roof Designs.   The basic building shape is the rectangle, and logical patterns of combinations of rectangles are numerous. Some of these variations can be likened to the shapes of block letters such as I, C, U, L, F, E, and H.

The selection of roof type depends on the bay size wanted and on the overhead clearance required for operations. During the layout phase, standards of this type would be used in making decisions which become specifications for the building itself. Wider column spacings, of course, have a higher construction cost than small bays, but this must be balanced against layout flexibility and assumed (but difficult to measure) operating cost advantages.

GRAPHIC LAYOUT TECHNIQUE

Layouts and models using two- and three-dimensional templates have a wide area of application in the development and planning of new facilities, as well as in the relayout of existing facilities which is a continual process to accommodate changes in products, manufacturing methods, and technology. These graphic aids are important in visualizing the development of the design of the complex machine which we call a manufacturing plant. The resulting layout expresses the designer's specifications of the location of all equipment, storage areas, aisle space, utilities, etc., and the relationships between machines and departments. It is important, however, not to mistake the activity of preparing and locating templates on a layout board for the broader activity of plant layout. The templates themselves are tools. Our purpose here is to make known the kinds of materials available for templates and layout boards.

Two-Dimensional Templates. These are by far the most commonly used. They can successfully represent the plan view of a layout and can show floor utilization fairly well. Figure 18 shows two types of templates. The "block" template shows the outline of the maximum projected area of a machine; that is, if tables or other parts move, the outline shows the maximum movement in the horizontal plane. The two-dimensional template gives additional detail, showing the outline of the machine itself, with dotted lines indicating maximum table movements.

The important characteristics of these kinds of templates are dimensional accuracy and flexibility in use. Flexibility in use means that the template can be fixed in place firmly enough so that it will not be moved by jarring or air movement, but not be fixed permanently because it may be necessary to make changes. Various alternatives meet these requirements in varying degrees. Some of the most satisfactory materials are the plastic templates, which already have an adhesive backing, used in conjunction with a cross-sectioned plastic sheet as a backing material.

Dial-type vertical milling machine

Tool No.

Two-dimensional template

Dial-type vertical milling machine

Block template

FIGURE 18.   Two types of machine templates.

The cross sectioning provides the measurement scale; consequently, very little actual measurement is required. This type of template is available commercially for virtually all standard machines as well as for many kinds of auxiliary equipment. Colored adhesive tapes are used for walls, aisle lines, etc. Figure 19 is an example of a layout using this media. Figure 20 shows the ease with which the templates are cut out and applied.

Three-Dimensional Templates. These templates or scale models add an element of realism which can sometimes be justified if the visualizing of height is of considerable importance and also if people not acquainted with layout practice must pass judgment on the result. Anything that can be done to help these people visualize the proposals may be worth the extra expense. While these models can be made in a woodworking shop to specifications, it is seldom practical to do so, especially for standard machines, since die cast models are available commercially for virtually all standard equipment. These models are made in considerable detail which would be very expensive to duplicate in wood or cardboard. Practically all kinds of items are available, that is, columns, wall

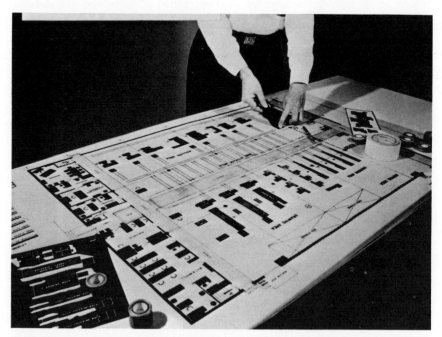

FIGURE 19. A layout using plastic templates and backing with colored tapes for wall sections. (Courtesy General Electric Company.)

FIGURE 20. (*a*) Plastic templates may be cut from strip without following closely the outline of the template. (*b*) After backing is tripped off, template adheres to plastic grid and may be moved at will. (Courtesy General Electric Company.)

sections, waste barrels, skids, pallets, etc. A heavy cross-sectioned plastic sheet is commonly used for the base, and this provides the scale to minimize measuring.

LAYOUT IN NONMANUFACTURING ACTIVITIES

There are counterparts of the major types of layouts that we have discussed in nonmanufacturing activities. The equivalent of line layouts occur in cafeterias and many large offices. Process layouts are common in offices, but the basis of departmentation is less likely to revolve around equipment types than in manufacturing. Rather, we find functional divisions, such as billing departments, accounts receivable, and accounts payable, where all of the processing dealing with these functions is performed.

In contrast to manufacturing, layout in nonmanufacturing is not necessarily measured in terms of material-handling cost. In offices, for example, the cost of handling the pieces of paper from one location to the next is not usually significant, especially where the interoffice mail system is used. It could be an important cost if a highly paid executive regularly carried an important document to its destination. In offices, one major concern of layout is to provide work conditions and suitable separation of activities so that people can perform their tasks and functions effectively and accurately. The layout of a supermarket will be designed to let the customer see as many items as possible, in the hope that this may suggest their purchase, and to eliminate annoying congestion in the traffic patterns, rather than attempt to minimize the store's cost of handling the merchandise to the display racks.

SUMMARY

In discussing layout, we have assumed as inputs the data concerning the thing being processed, how many items we expect to process, and how we shall process. In manufacturing activity these data take the form of drawings of the products; forecasts, contracts, or orders which indicate how many should be made; and route sheets and operations sheets which indicate what processes are appropriate and their sequence. Layout, then, requires a sequence of important decisions concerning capacity, type of layout, equipment, building types, bay widths, etc. The difficulty with layout is the interaction of the various aspects of the problem, and the fact that no unified theoretical framework makes it possible to see the dynamic effects of all variables working together. Layout furnishes a basic specification for the building to house the physical facilities; it also represents the integration of the several aspects of the design of a production system. It is here that the topics we have studied separately, and will study in Chapters 13 and 14, are integrated into a unified design.

REVIEW QUESTIONS

1. Discuss the broad framework for the development of solutions to layout problems.
2. For what capacity should a new layout be designed? What is the effect of a seasonal sales pattern on the capacity decision? Should excess capacity be included? Discuss the effect of multiple shifts, subcontracting, and make-buy policy.
3. How can capacity be translated into workable units? What is the significance of plant efficiency and scrap factors?
4. What is the distinction between a process and a product layout?
5. What are the conditions for which each type of layout is appropriate?
6. What is a basic measure of effectiveness for process layouts?
7. What measure of effectiveness is used in operation sequence analysis? Is it the same as the answer to question 6?
8. How is a block diagram developed from the data given by a load summary?
9. What kinds of material-handling equipment are appropriate for process layouts? When can a carrousel conveyor be used?
10. Since some material-handling needs in a process layout do not occur by any fixed schedule, how can we determine how much material-handling equipment is needed?
11. How is assembly line balancing different from fabrication line balancing?
12. What is the effect of a change in capacity requirements on the balance of an assembly line?
13. Should a production line utilize rigid pacing, i.e., have a fixed time cycle for the performance of all activities?
14. What is the function of banks between operations on a production line? Ideally, what should be the maximum size of these banks?
15. What kinds of material-handling equipment are appropriate for line layouts?
16. What should be the relationship of plant services, such as receiving, storage, and shipping, to the production departments in a layout?
17. Are the locations of employee service facilities important to a layout?
18. What are the advantages of single-story buildings? Of multistory buildings?

PROBLEMS

1.   The Stamped Metal Products Company (StaMPCo) makes among other things a *V*-belt pulley of the design specifications shown in Figure 21. StaMPCo is currently considering a relayout of its entire facility and is projecting man-machine needs for the pulley. The pulley sales forecasts indicate a capacity need for 9000 pulleys per week for the coming year and 11,000 per week for two years hence. The average plant efficiency factor is 85 per cent. Based on the data in Table VIII, calculate the number of fractional men and machines needed for each of the two forecast levels of output. Assuming men can be moved freely between job assignments, how many men and machines are needed in round numbers?

2.   What type of layout do you think might be appropriate for the manufacture of the *V*-belt pulley?

3.   Consider the ideal schematic diagram shown in Figure 5. Can you improve it?

4.   Given the load summary in Table IX for a plant, develop an ideal schematic diagram for the relative locations of departments.

Tolerance on wobble ±0.010 from center. Tolerance on concentricity ±0.010 from center. Fractional tolerances ±$\frac{1}{64}$. Angular tolerances ±$\frac{1}{2}$°. Finish: Cadmium plated all over 0.0003 ±0.0001. *Notes:* 1. Press fit flanges to hub. 2. Spotweld flanges to hub, two spots each side. 3. Spotweld flanges together—four spots. 4. Flange material: SAE #1010 deep-drawn steel: 5. Hub material: SAE #X1112 cold-finished screw stock.

FIGURE 21.   Drawing of a *V*-belt pulley.

TABLE VIII. StaMPCo Data for Processes, Output, and Scrap Factors

Operation	Machine Used	Standard Output (pieces/hour)	Scrap Factor (per cent)
Machine hub	Turret lathe	66.7	3
Form flange	Punch press	4800	5
Drill and tap hub	Drill press	240	2
Assemble flange to hub	Arbor press	600	1
Weld flanges together	Small spot welder	300	3
Weld flanges to hub	Large spot welder	350	5
Ream and chamfer	Drill press	300	2
Deburr flange	Polishing lathe	200	—
Inspect	Inspection k	400	—
Insert set screw	—	1200	—

5. Given the estimated space requirements in Table X, develop a block diagram based on the ideal schematic diagram determined in problem 4.

6. Block out a single-story building with 20-foot bays, utilizing the block diagram developed in problem 5, on the company site diagrammed in Figure 22.

7. Pro rata space for washrooms, cafeteria, tool crib, etc., were included in

TABLE IX. Load Summary, Loads per Month

From \ To	1	2	3	4	5	6	7	8	9	10	11	12	13	14	15	16	17
1		2000							•								
2			500	450	600	125		300							75		
3											400	100					
4						200	100				100						
5						100	200		150	100					50		
6							175		90	60	70	30			625		
7						25			50		200	150			400		
8											300	200	100	150	175		
9							50		40	100		155					
10						45	55				50	60					
11						50					600	500	150	20			
12						480	300		50	100		100	50	100			
13						40							305	600			
14							20						655				
15															3500		
16																3500	
17																	

TABLE X. Space Requirements		
Department Number	Name	Required Square Feet
1	Receiving	500
2	Raw material storage	1,000
3	Shearing	200
4	Sawing	200
5	Automatic screw	4,000
6	Turret lathe	2,000
7	Engine lathe	500
8	Punch press	1,000
9	Hobbing	300
10	Broaching	200
11	Milling	3,000
12	Drilling	1,100
13	Heat treating	500
14	Plating	300
15	Assembly	700
16	Finished goods storage	1,000
17	Shipping	500
		17,000 sq. ft.
	Offices	2,200
	Total	19,200 sq. ft.

the space requirements given in problem 5. What would you consider to be the best location for the tool crib? Why?

8. How do you propose to expand manufacturing facilities for the plant design resulting in problem 6?

9. Given the following assumptions and data shown in Table XI, determine the theoretical minimum number of stations if a line is to be designed for an output of 8400 units per week:

(a) The company works an 8-hour day for 5 days per week.

(b) The line will be operated 7 hours per day to allow for personal needs such as rest and delay.

(c) The line workers receive $2.50 per hour.

(d) Overtime is paid at time and a half.

(e) Assume actual performance times are equal to the given task times unless otherwise stated.

10. Determine the actual number of stations by means of a schematic diagram, showing the time available at each station and the station number for the data of problem 9.

11. Given the data of problem 9, if 5040 units per week are needed:

A Street

200'

350'

B Street

Mainline R.R.

FIGURE 22   Site layout for problem 6.

(a) How many actual stations are required?

(b) Is the number of stations proportional to the answer to problem 10 for this different output?

(c) How much idle time is there?

(d) How could banking be used to reduce the number of stations and idle time?

12.   After 2 months of operation the company is spending 4 hours per week in overtime to meet their requirements of 8400 units per week using your solution for problem 10. It has now been determined that the actual performance times have distributions with a maximum standard deviation of 0.5 second. The mean times are the given element times. Does this fact call for a change in design for the line? What is the lowest cost alternative?

13.   It appears that the time for operation i in Table XI could be decreased by method study. What action should be taken?

14.   Table XII is a list of assembly tasks showing sequence restrictions and performance times. Develop a diagram showing the sequence requirements and determine a task grouping that minimizes the number of stations (groups of tasks), does not violate sequence restrictions, and produces 10 units per hour.

TABLE XI. Tasks, Estimated Times, and Precedence Restrictions for Work on an Assembly Line

Task	Given Task Times (seconds)	Task Must Follow Task Listed Below
a	14	—
b-1	5	a
b-2	5	a
c	30	b
d	3	—
e	5	d
f	13	e
g	9	e
h	14	e
i	6	fgh
j	7	i
k	3	j
l	4	k
m	7	l

Total = 125 seconds

TABLE XII

Task	Performance Time, Minutes	Task Must Follow Task Listed Below
a	4	—
b	3	a
c	5	ab
d	2	—
e	4	abc
f	6	abcd
g	2	—
h	3	dg
j	5	dgh
k	2	—
l	3	k
m	4	kl

15. An organization does job machining and assembly and wishes to relay-out its production facilities so that the relative location of departments better reflects the average flow of parts through the plant. In Table XIII is shown an operation sequence summary for a sample of seven parts, with approximate area requirements for each of the thirteen machine or work centers. The numbers in the columns headed by each of the parts indicate the number of the work center to which the part goes next. Just below the sequence summary is shown a summary of production per month and the number of pieces handled at one time through the shop for each part.

(a) Develop a load summary showing the number of loads per month going between all combinations of work centers.

(b) Develop an ideal schematic layout.

(c) Develop a block diagram that reflects the approximate area requirements given and results in an overall rectangular shape.

16. A private industrial clinic performs service under contract to a number of business and industrial firms. These services include medical examinations for new employees as well as annual physical examinations. The clinic performs eight types of examination sequences depending on the details of the individual contracts.

TABLE XIII

Machine or Work Center	Area, Square Feet	Work Center Number	Part A	B	C	D	E	F	G
Saw	50	1		2	2				2
Centering	100	2		4	3				3
Milling machines	500	3	5	9	5	5		4	4
Lathes	600	4		5, 7	7		5	10	5
Drills	300	5	8	3	4	11	7		6
Arbor press	100	6					11		7
Grinders	200	7		12	12		6		8
Shapers	200	8	9			3			9
Heat treat	150	9	11	4					10
Paint	100	10						11	11
Assembly bench	100	11	12	13	13	13	13	13	12
Inspection	50	12	13	11	11				13
Pack	100	13							

Production Summary

Pieces per month			500	500	1600	1200	400	800	400
Pieces per load			3	100	40	40	100	100	2
Loads per month			250	5	40	30	4	8	200

Table XIV gives the number of examinations per year of each type together with the sequence of activities required for each. Table XV indicates the space requirements for each of the major activities.

Many complaints have been received concerning the excessive walking required by those being examined because of the layout of the clinic. Figure 23 shows the present layout. Propose an improved layout.

TABLE XIV. Summary of Examination Load and Activity Sequence

Type of Exami- nation	Exami- nations per Year	Activity											
		A	B	C	D	E	F	G	H	I	J	K	L
1	200	X	X	X	X	X	X	X	X	X	X		X
2	1,200	X			X	X			X				X
3	1,950	X	X	X	X			X	X				X
4	700	X	X	X	X			X	X		X		X
5	400	X		X	X			X		X			X
6	1,800	X	X	X	X	X						X	X
7	650	X			X	X					X		X
8	250	X			X					X		X	X

TABLE XV. Space Requirements for Major Activities

Code and Activity	Square Feet Required
A. Initial processing	400
B. Height and weight measurement and general external examination	200
C. Eye examination	300
D. Ear, nose, and throat	100
E. X-ray and fluoroscope	300
F. Blood tests	100
G. Blood pressure check	100
H. Respiratory check	100
I. Electrocardiographic and electroencephalographic examination	100
J. Laboratory tests	400
K. Dental examination	200
L. Final processing	100
Total	2,400

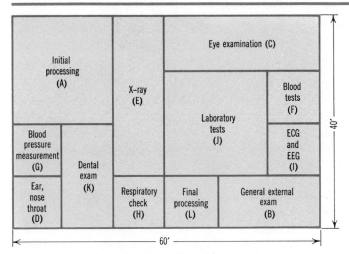

FIGURE 23. Present layout of clinic.

REFERENCES

[1] Arcus, A. L. "COMSOAL: A Computer Method for Sequencing Operation for Assembly Lines." In: *Readings in Production and Operations Management*. E. S. Buffa, editor. John Wiley, New York, 1966.

[2] Armour, G. C., and E. S. Buffa. "A Heuristic Algorithm and Computer Simulation Approach to the Relative Location of Facilities." *Management Science*, **9** (2), Jan. 1963.

[3] Bowman, E. H. "Assembly-Line Balancing By Linear Programming." *Operations Research*, **8** (3), 1960.

[4] Buffa, E. S. "Pacing Effects in Production Lines." *Journal of Industrial Engineering*, **12** (6), Nov.–Dec. 1961.

[5] Buffa, E. S. "Sequence Analysis for Functional Layouts." *Journal of Industrial Engineering*, **6** (2), Mar.–Apr. 1955.

[6] Buffa, E. S., G. C. Armour, and T. E. Vollmann. "Allocating Facilities with CRAFT." *Harvard Business Review*, Mar.–Apr. 1964.

[7] Buffa, E. S., and W. H. Taubert. *Production-Inventory Systems: Planning and Control* (Rev. ed.). Richard D. Irwin, Homewood, Ill., 1972.

[8] Denholm, D. H., and G. H. Brooks, "A Comparison of Three Computer Assisted Plant Layout Techniques." *Proceedings of Technical Papers*, AIIE Convention, May 1970.

[9] Fetter, R. B., and H. T. Galliher. "Waiting-Line Models in Material Handling." *Journal of Industrial Engineering*, **9** (3), 202–208, May–June 1958.

[10] Held, M., R. M. Karp, and R. Sharesian. "Assembly-Line Balancing— Dynamic Programming with Precedence Constraints." *Operations Research*, **11** (3), May–June 1963.

[11] Helgeson, W. B., and D. P. Birnie. "Assembly Line Balancing Using the Ranked Position Weight Technique." *Journal of Industrial Engineering*, **12** (6), Nov.–Dec. 1961.

[12] Hoffman, T. F. "Assembly Line Balancing with a Precedence Matrix." *Management Science*, **9** (4), July 1963.

[13] Jackson, J. R. "A Computing Procedure for a Line-Balancing Problem." *Management Science*, **2** (3), 251–272, Apr. 1956.

[14] Kilbridge, M. D., and L. Wester. "A Heuristic Method of Assembly-Line Balancing." *Journal of Industrial Engineering*, **12** (4), July–Aug. 1961.

[15] Kilbridge, M. D., and L. Wester. "The Balance Delay Problem." *Management Science*, **8** (1), Oct. 1961.

[16] Mallick, R. W., and A. P. Gaudreau. *Plant Layout: Planning and Practice.* John Wiley, New York, 1951.

[17] Mastor, A. A. *An Experimental Investigation and Comparative Evaluation of Production Line Balancing Techniques.* Unpublished Ph.D. Dissertation, UCLA, 1966. Also: *Management Science*, **16** (11), 728–746, July 1970.

[18] Moore, J. M. *Plant Layout and Design.* Macmillan, New York, 1962.

[19] Muther, R. *Practical Plant Layout.* McGraw-Hill, New York, 1955.

[20] Nugent, C. E., T. E. Vollmann, and J. Ruml. "An Experimental Comparison of Facilities to Locations." *Operations Research*, Jan.–Feb. 1968.

[21] Reed, R. *Plant Layout.* Richard D. Irwin, Homewood, Ill., 1961.

[22] Ritzman, L. P. "The Efficiency of Computer Algorithms for Plant Layout." *Management Science*, **18** (5), 240–248, Jan. 1972.

[23] Smith, S. P. "Travel Charting." *Journal of Industrial Engineering*, **6** (1), 13, Jan. 1955.

[24] Tonge, F. M. "Summary of a Heuristic Line-Balancing Procedure." *Management Science*, **7** (1), 21, Oct. 1960.

[25] Vazsonyi, A. *Scientific Programming in Business and Industry.* John Wiley, New York, 1958.

[26] Vergin, R. C., and J. D. Rogers. "An Algorithm and Computational Procedure for Locating Economic Facilities." *Management Science*, **13** (6), 240–254, Feb. 1967.

[27] Volgyesi, A. S. "Space-Age Approach to Space Allocation." *Computer Decisions*, May 1970, pp. 32–35.

[28] Vollmann, T. E., and E. S. Buffa. "The Facilities Layout Problem in Perspective." *Management Science*, **12** (10), 450–468, June 1966.

[29] Vollmann, T. E., C. E. Nugent, and R. L. Zartier. "A Computerized Model for Office Layout." *Journal of Industrial Engineering*, **19** (7), July 1968.

[30] Wester, L., and M. D. Kilbridge. "Heuristic Line Balancing: A Case." *Journal of Industrial Engineering*, **13** (3), May–June 1962.

13

Job Design & Man-Machine Systems

The materials of Chapter 12 on layout of physical facilities provide the basis for an overall integrated design of productive systems. Implicit in the layout process is an extremely important decision about the basic organization of the work to be done. For example, whether the system is organized around the principles of a functional or product layout will have great impact on the definition of jobs and their content. Within each of these physical configurations there would be a number of possible ways to divide up the work to be done as a basis for the design of jobs.

Unless there is a conscious effort to consider alternatives of overall organization of the work, job content will be determined by the process, existing machine designs, the physical layout, time requirements, or simply traditional patterns.

Thus, in a typical case, we may take an entire complex assembly process and break it down into a series of operations so that the product can be produced on an assembly line. The line is designed to meet certain capacity requirements, such as an output of 480 units per eight-hour shift or 1 unit per minute. Output then dictates the maximum content of each operation, which can take no longer than one minute. What is more, there is a certain required sequence of assembly; operation 1 takes the tasks that come first which require one minute or less, operation 2 the second one-minute group, etc. Of course, there is usually some flexibility as to sequence; by rearranging the sequence we end up with the job content in each operation that seems to make the most sense. (Recall the methods of line balancing discussed in Chapter 12.)

In other situations, the process, the machine, the physical layout, or other considerations are likely to play a dominant role in determining job content. Each resulting job or operation can be analyzed as a separate man-machine system by the methods and data of this chapter in order to produce the best job design. *But how would this design compare with other basic alternatives of job content*? If we were to consider as part of the problem all possible alternatives of job content, there might be a baffling number. Unfortunately, there is very little information available to guide us here. The result, in practice, is that such considerations as the machines, layouts, production quotas, and machine and conveyor pacing often dictate job content.

MEASURES OF EFFECTIVENESS IN JOB DESIGN

Over the years since Adam Smith, the main guide for determining job content has been *division of labor*. We have accepted this idea almost completely. Adam Smith specified no limit to the division of labor and the principle has been applied as a one-way mechanism to achieve the maximum benefits of job design. Jobs have been broken down to the point where the worker finds little satisfaction in performing his tasks. In recent years there has been a reaction against excessive job breakdown; a few investigators have found that combinations of operations to create jobs of greater scope recaptured the worker's interest; increases in productivity, quality level, etc., were reported. A new term, *job enlargement*, appeared. Practical applications of job enlargement that were written up in the literature tended to verify the findings of the investigators. Unfortunately, although exponents of job enlargement recognize that division of labor can be carried too far, they have not been able to specify any principles or guides on how far to go in the other direction. Job enlargement is also a one-way mechanism. It does, however, provide a balancing force through the inclusion of job satisfaction as a major criterion of successful job design. The ultimate answer lies in research attempts to isolate the factors that determine an optimal combination of tasks to make up jobs. This effort has been called job design.

The past and present viewpoint of American business and industry emphasizes the economic criterion as the controlling factor in determining job content and considers other criteria as effective mainly in so far as they meet economic requirements. Thus, a quality criterion often reduces to an economic one when the job design that improves quality levels also improves productivity. For example, removing fatiguing elements of a job commonly improves productivity; eliminating hazards may reduce insurance premium rates as well as improve productivity; designing tasks that increase employee satisfaction often also improves productivity.

However, there certainly are instances where the various subcriteria do not correlate with the economic criterion. To obtain higher quality levels often demands increased costs, and the value of the reduced scrap may not counterbalance the higher labor costs. The employee satisfaction criterion would not necessarily decrease costs. To reduce the risks of hazards to extremely low levels might be very costly.

In Taylor's time the noneconomic criteria would have been shrugged off. Today jobs and methods are frequently designed or altered to meet noneconomic needs. It is true that the economic criterion is dominant, and job and method designs are seldom set or altered without reference to the effects on costs. Most often, costs are regarded as the "quantitative" measure, with noneconomic criteria being considered in the list of "intangible" advantages or disadvantages. Figure 1 shows in schematic form the relationship of constraints, criteria, and other pressures in determining job content. The inputs to the determination of job methods then become job content plus a host of other inputs related to man-machine systems.

In industrial organizations the professional designer of jobs and work methods is the industrial engineer. In many less formalized organizations, however, foremen and managers at various levels design jobs. In most nonmanufacturing organizations, managers and supervisors are responsible for determining job content and method design. The wide variety of organizations and of people holding responsibility for job design makes dissemination of the known data a difficult problem.

Who Designs Jobs and Work Methods?

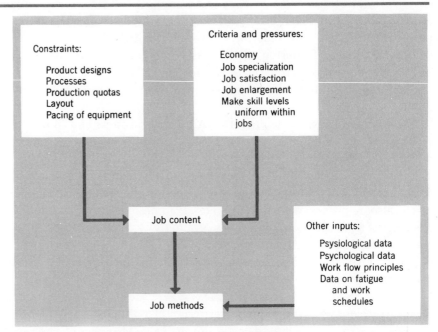

FIGURE 1. Relationship of constraints, criteria, and other pressures in determining job content. Inputs to job methods design.

Since, for most of these people, job design is only a part of their responsibility, they tend to rely on existing standard workplace designs and on basic equipment (such as office desks, typewriters, benches, and standard machine tools) to fix many of the characteristics of the job; actual details of method are often left to the workers themselves. In fact, worker participation in job design has been experimented with for some time.

In discussing job design we shall concentrate our attention on man-machine systems, focusing on the job methods component of job design. We will see that man's great potential is not in the repetitive mechanical activities at all, but rather in situations requiring improvisation, reasoning, and judgment. From a human point of view we have been misusing man's capabilities. In the current era of highly organized and expensive labor, it is becoming obvious that we may also be misusing man's capabilities from an economic point of view.

MAN-MACHINE SYSTEMS

The great advances in computers and automation technology has changed the conceptual framework for man in productive systems. While there is still a great deal of manual labor in business and industry today, most work involves the use of at least some kind of mechanical aid, and, therefore, the conceptual framework of man-machine systems is appropriate for the entire spectrum of systems involving the human operator.

Even in an automated system, labor is necessary in a surveillance capacity. In such situations, an operator may be seated in front of a control board which continually flashes information about the progress of the manufacturing process. It is important that these display panels be designed to transmit the essential information with minimum error.

Perhaps the majority of business and industrial manual jobs today consist of some combination of man and machine. Where there is a fixed machine cycle as in most machine tool processes, the design of the machine in relation to the operator is of great importance. The location and design of controls, working heights, information displays, the flow of work, safety features, and the utilization of both the man and the machine in the cycle are all important determinants of quality, productivity, and worker acceptance of the job situation.

Many jobs are strictly manual, such as assembly, maintenance, and heavy labor. Here mechanical aids or tools are common, and we need to consider the design of these tools from the viewpoint of the user. In addition, we must consider the layout of the workplace, the flow of work, and physical and mental fatigue produced in the worker by his physical environment. In some situations, environmental factors of heat, humidity, light, noise, and hazards can seriously affect fatigue, productivity, quality, health, and worker acceptance of the job. Thus, in studying man-machine systems we assume that the questions of job content have fairly well been settled, and we concentrate attention on the detailed design of jobs.

Man has certain physiological, psychological, and sociological characteristics which define both his capabilities and his limitations in the work situation. These characteristics are not fixed quantities but vary from individual to individual. This does not mean, however, that we cannot make predictions about human behavior. Rather, it means that predictive models of human behavior must reflect this variation. To take a physical factor as an example, the distribution of the arm strengths of men indicates the per cent of the male population that can exert a given force. This distribution also indicates the limitations in demand for arm strength. The average man can exert a right-hand pull of 120 pounds. If we design a machine lever that requires the operator to exert this force, approximately half of the male population would be unable to operate the machine. On the other hand, the distribution also tells us that about 95 per cent of the male population can exert a right-hand pull

Man versus Machines

of 52 pounds. A lever designed to take this fact into account will accommodate a large proportion of the male population.

In performing work, man's functions fall into three general classifications:

1. Receiving information through the various sense organs, that is, eyes, ears, touch, etc.

2. Making decisions based on information received and information stored in the memory of the individual.

3. Taking action based on decisions. In some instances, the decision phase may be virtually automatic because of learned responses as in a highly repetitive task. In others, the decision may involve an order of reasoning and the result may be complex.

Note that the general structure of a closed-loop automated system is parallel in concept. (See Figure 9, Chapter 9.) Wherein lies the difference? Are automated machines like men? Yes, they are in certain important respects. Both have sensors, stored information, comparators, decision makers, effectors, and feedback loops. The differences are in man's tremendous range of capabilities and in the limitations imposed on him by his psychological and sociological characteristics. Thus, machines are much more specialized in the kinds and range of tasks they can perform. Machines perform tasks as faithful servants, reacting mainly to physical factors; for example, bearings may wear out because of a dusty environment. But man reacts to his psychological and sociological environment as well as to his physical environment. The latter fact requires that one measure of effectiveness of job design must be worker acceptance or job satisfaction.

Although there are few really objective guides to the allocation of tasks to men and machines on other than an economic basis, a subjective list of the kinds of tasks most appropriate for men and for machines is given by McCormick [21].

Human beings appear to surpass existing machines in their ability to:

1. Detect small amounts of light and sound.

2. Receive and organize patterns of light and sound.

3. Improvise and use flexible procedures.

4. Store large amounts of information for long periods and recall relevant facts at the appropriate time.

5. Reason inductively.

6. Exercise judgment.

7. Develop concepts and create methods.

Existing machines appear to surpass humans in their ability to:

1. Respond quickly to control signals.
2. Apply great force smoothly and precisely.
3. Perform repetitive and routine tasks.
4. Store information briefly and then erase it completely.
5. Perform rapid computations.
6. Perform many different functions simultaneously.

Such lists raise a question. Why do business, industry, and government not use men and machines according to these guides? We have all observed that man is used extensively for tasks given in the list for machines. The answer lies in the balance of costs for a given situation. Both labor and machines cost money; when the balance of costs favors machines, conversions are normally made. In many foreign countries extremely low-cost labor, in relation to the cost of capital, dictates an economic decision to use manual labor in many tasks in which man is not well suited. Because of relatively high wages in the United States, machines are used much more extensively.

As we noted previously, men and machines perform similar functions in accomplishing work tasks though they each have comparative advantages. The functions they perform are represented in Figure 2; these functions are generally comparable to those of the closed-loop feedback diagram of Figure 9 in Chapter 9. The four basic classes of functions are sensing, information storage, information processing, and action. Information storage interacts with all three of the other functions; however, sensing, information processing, and action functions occurs in sequence.

Conceptual Framework for Man-Machine Systems

FIGURE 2. Functions performed by man or machine components of man-machine systems.

Information is received by the *sensing function*. If by a man, sensing is accomplished through the various sense organs of eyes, ears, sense of touch, etc. Machine sensing can parallel human sensing through electronic or mechanical devices. Machine sensing is usually much more specific or single purpose in nature than the broadly capable human senses.

Information storage for man is in the human memory or by access to records. Machine information storage can be by magnetic tape or drum, punched cards, cams and templates, etc.

The function of *information processing and decision* takes sensed and/or stored information and produces a decision by some simple or complex process. The processing could be as simple as a choice between two alternatives, depending on input data, or very complex, involving deduction, analysis, or computing to produce a decision for which a command is issued to the effector.

The effector or *action function* occurs as a result of decisions and command, and may involve the triggering of control mechanisms by man or machine, or a communication of decisions. Control mechanisms would in turn cause something physical to happen such as moving the hands or arms, starting a motor, increasing or decreasing the depth of a cut on a machine tool, etc.

Input and output is related to the raw material, or the thing being processed. The output represents some transformation of the input in line with our discussion of processes in Chapter 9. The processes themselves may be of any type, that is, chemical, processes to change shape or form, assembly, transport, clerical, and so on.

Information feedback concerning the output states is an essential ingredient for it provides the basis for control. Feedback operates to control the simplest hand motion through the senses and the nervous system. For machines, feedback concerning the output states provides the basis for machine adjustment. As we discussed in Chapter 9, automatic machines couple the feedback information directly so that adjustments are automatic (closed-loop automation). When machine adjustments are only periodic based on information feedback, the loop is still closed, but not on a continuous and automatic basis.

Types of Man-Machine Systems

We shall use the module of the functions performed by man or machine shown in Figure 2 to discuss the basic structure for three typical systems: manual, semiautomatic, or mechanical and automatic systems. Figure 3 uses the module of Figure 2 to show the structure of the three types of systems in schematic form.

FIGURE 3. Schematic diagram of man and machine functions in three types of systems. (From *Human Factors Engineering* by E. J. McCormick. Copyright 1970. Used with permission of McGraw-Hill Book Company.)

Manual systems involve man with only mechanical aids or hand tools. Man supplies the power required and acts as controller of the process; the tools and mechanical aids help multiply his efforts. The basic module of Figure 2 describes the functions where the man directly transforms input to output as shown in Figure 3(*a*). In addition we must envision the manual system as operating in some working environment which may have an impact on the man and the output.

Semiautomatic systems involve man mainly as a controller of the process as indicated in Figure 3(*b*). He interacts with the machine by sensing information about the process, interpreting it and using a set of controls which may start and stop the machine and possibly make intermediate adjustments. Power is normally supplied by the machine. Figure 4 shows the general cycle of activity of a man-machine system of the semiautomatic type imbedded in the working environment. Of course, there are combinations of the manual and semiautomatic systems where the man is also supplying some of the system power, perhaps in loading the machine or in some activities in which he may be involved while the machine goes through its cycle. Common examples of semi-

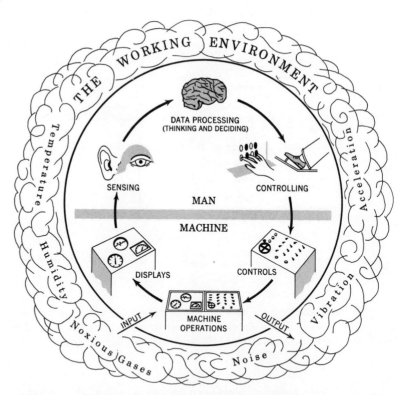

FIGURE 4. Simplified model of a man-machine system for semi-automatic operations. (From A. Chapanis, *Man-Machine Engineering*, Copyright © 1965 by Wadsworth Publishing Company, Belmont, California. Reprinted by permission of the publisher, Brooks/Cole Publishing Company, Monterey, California.)

automatic systems are the machine tools commonly used in the mechanical industries.

Automatic systems presumably do not need a man since all of the functions of sensing, information processing and decision, and action are performed by the machine. Such a system would need to be fully programmed to sense and take required action for all possible contingencies. Automation at such a level is not economically justified even if the machines could be designed. Figure 3(*c*), therefore, indicates man's role as a monitor to help control the process. In this role the man periodically or continuously maintains surveillance over the process through displays which indicate the state of the crucial parameters of the process. Figure 5 shows such a situation where the man is monitoring an automated engine block production line by a fairly complicated display panel.

In discussing man-machine system analysis and design in the balance of the chapter, we will organize the material in terms of information input, focusing particularly on visual displays; human control of man-machine systems including human motor activities, human control of

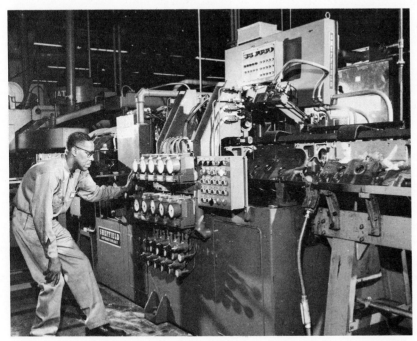

FIGURE 5. Display panel in an automated engine block production line. (Courtesy Ford Motor Company.)

systems, man-machine relationships, analysis of hand motions, applied anthropometry and the analysis of man and man-machine cycles; and, the working environment and its impact on output. Throughout the discussion our emphasis is really on man and his relationship to machines.

Figure 4, representing the general cycle of activity for semiautomatic operations, is of central value for it involves all of the relationships which we will want to discuss. In Figure 4 man is receiving and interpreting information about the process from information displays, and manipulating mechanisms which control the processes. He is also maintaining a general surveillance over the process. The machine responds to these control actions to convert input to output. Thus we have represented all of the kinds of functions for man for the three types of man-machine systems just discussed. For example, the manipulative activity is representative of the dominant features of manual systems; the information input, sensing, and controlling activities are representative of both semiautomatic and automatic systems; and the information input and general monitoring or surveillance activities are representative of automatic systems. The impact of environment and the physical relationships of the man to work flow and workplace arrangements are, of course, applicable to all man-machine systems.

INFORMATION INPUT

Modern technology has made it possible to present vital information concerning the process which humans cannot sense directly, or at least cannot sense precisely in a direct way. Thus, the man in Figure 5 is sensing indirectly such measurements as bore diameter, surface smoothness, etc. On the other hand some sensing may result from direct observation, for example, if the transfer mechanisms were jammed in Figure 5. The pathways of information from original source to human sensory receptors is shown schematically in Figure 6.

Figure 6 indicates immediately some marriage between man and machine in indirect sensing which involves an intermediate sensing by mechanisms and a coding or conversion to some new form which is then presented and sensed by the human. Therefore, in man-machine systems, human sensing can be direct, but increasingly is indirect, placing emphasis on encoding and information display systems. The design of these systems of display for information input to man is important if operations are to be effective.

Figure 6 implies the full range of possible human sensory receptors. The most common business and industrial applications focus on the use of

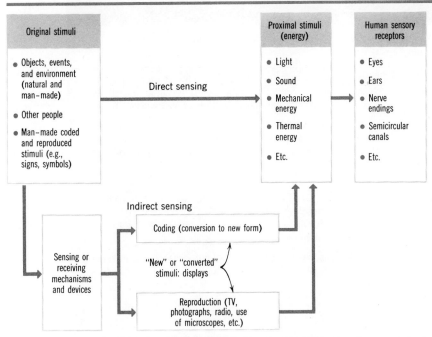

FIGURE 6. Schematic illustration of pathways of information from original sources to sensory receptors. (Although typically the original, basic source is an object, event, condition, the environment, etc., in some situations the effective original source to an individual consists of some man-made coded or reproduced stimuli; office personnel, for example, usually deal with recorded symbols which, for practical purposes, are their "original" stimuli.) (From *Human Factors Engineering* by E. J. McCormick. Copyright 1970. Used with permission of McGraw-Hill Book Company.)

the eyes, ears, and nerve endings, in that order, with visual display being by far the most common. Table I shows a summary of visual and auditory coding methods which indicate a range for both visual and auditory channels which may be a bit surprising. Table I summarizes some general guides for each coding method such as the number of levels which can be discriminated and some general comments on uses.

Much of the postwar effort of experimental psychologists has been directed toward improving visual displays. Questions such as these have been raised: Which dial shapes are most legible? What scale units should be used and how should they be marked on dials? Do people have number preference patterns that affect their interpretation of dial readings? What characteristics of numbers and letters make them most legible? Are black numbers on a white background superior to white on

Visual Displays

TABLE I. Summary of Certain Visual and Auditory Coding Methods

(Numbers refer to number of levels which can be discriminated on an absolute basis under optimum conditions.)

Alphanumeric	Single numerals, 10; single letters, 26; combinations, unlimited. Good; especially useful for identification; uses little space if there is good contrast. Certain items easily confused with each other.
Color	Hues, 9; hue, saturation, and brightness combinations 15–24. Particularly good for searching and counting tasks; poorer for identification tasks; trained observers can use many codes (up to 24). Affected by some lights; problem with color-defective individuals.
Geometric shapes	15 or more. Generally useful coding system, particularly in symbolic representation; good for CRTs. Shapes used together need to be discriminable; some sets of shapes more difficult to discriminate than others.
Visual angle	24. Generally satisfactory for special purposes such as indicating direction, angle, or position on round instruments like clocks, CRTs, etc.
Size of forms (such as squares)	5. Takes considerable space. Use only when specifically appropriate; preferably use less than 5.
Visual number	6. Use only when specifically appropriate, such as to represent numbers of items. Takes considerable space; may be confused with other symbols.
Brightness of lights	3–4. Use only when specifically appropriate. Preferably limit to two levels; weaker signals may be masked.
Flash rate of lights	4. Limited applicability. Preferably limit to two levels; combination of individual flashes and controlled time intervals may have special application, such as lighthouse signals and naval communications.
Sound frequency	5. For untrained listeners, use less than 5 levels; space widely apart, but avoid multiples and low and high frequencies; intensity should be 30 dB above threshold. Frequency changes easier to detect than single frequencies; combinations usually require training except for clearly distinguishable sounds such as bells, buzzers, and sirens.
Sound intensity	4. Preferably use less than 4. Intensity changes easier to detect than single intensities; for pure tones restrict to 1000–4000 Hz, but preferably use wide band.
Sound duration	Use clear-cut differences, preferably 2 or 3.
Sound direction	Difference in intensity to two ears should be distinct; particularly useful for directional information (i.e., right versus left).

black? How big should letters and numerals be and what proportions of line thickness, height, and width are best? How should systems of dials be arranged? Experimental work has been carried out on these and many other questions.

Sleight [27] experimented with the shape of dials. He constructed an experiment around five types of dials and had sixty subjects read seventeen settings from each dial in a random sequence. Figure 7 shows the results in terms of the percentage of errors recorded. A multitude of studies, of which the Sleight study is typical, has indicated the following general guides on dial design, as summarized by Chapanis, Garner and Morgan [8].

1. A dial about 2.75 or 3 inches in diameter is probably the best all-around size if we are going to read it at a distance of 30 inches or less.

2. Marks should be located at the 0, 5, 10, 15, 20, etc. (or 0, 50, 100, 150, 200, etc.) positions. The marks at the 9, 10, 20, . . . (or 0, 100, 200, . . .) positions should be longer than those at the 5, 15, 25, . . . (or 50, 150, 250, . . .) positions. Only the marks at 0, 10, 20, . . . should be numbered.

3. The distance between the numbered markers should be about a half inch as measured around the circumference of the dial.

4. The separation between scale markers should be the same all around the dial.

5. There should be a gap between the beginning and end of the scale.

6. Values on the scale should increase in a clockwise direction.

FIGURE 7. Five different dial shapes and the percentage of incorrect readings recorded for each. (From [27].)

When there is a bank of dials to be read, it helps to orient them in a pattern so that normal readings are in the nine o'clock or twelve o'clock positions. (See Figure 8). This makes it possible to tell at a glance if an

Unpatterned dial display

Patterned dial display

FIGURE 8. The dials in the upper diagram are unpatterned; those below are patterned. Patterning helps us see at a glance which ones are not indicating "normal" readings. (From [8].)

abnormal reading is among the group instead of reading each dial individually. As a matter of fact, we often find that the operator is presented with too much information. He may not need to *read* the dial at all. Perhaps all that is required is simple recognition of whether the reading is in the normal operating region or not. Or perhaps the real need is to know only if something is functioning or not. Simple on-off lights may be satisfactory in such situations.

There is also the question of the letters and numbers that are used on visual displays. Studies have indicated that capital letters and numbers are read most accurately when the stroke width to height ratio is between 1:6 and 1:8 and when the overall width to height ratio is about 2:3.

Auditory and Tactual Displays

While auditory displays are not as commonly used as visual, they have particular value as warning devices or to attract attention. There are, of course, other opportunities for using the auditory channel, for example, when vision is impaired, or at night, or in photographic darkrooms, when vision cannot be used. Some of the common devices are bells, buzzers, horns, sirens, chimes, and whistles.

Tactual displays are even less common than auditory in business and industry. Yet there are applications when vision cannot be used such as in photographic darkrooms, or the shape coding of control knobs so they can be identified by touch (discussed in the following section).

HUMAN CONTROL OF MAN-MACHINE SYSTEMS

Given information input by direct or indirect means the human operator of a man-machine system responds by performing work in the physical sense. He may be assembling objects, manipulating controls, and in general using his body to accomplish the required tasks to fit in with the objectives of the system. The analysis of the hand and body motions and how they contribute to effective operation is important.

Manipulative activity in handling controls has been studied with considerable care and this knowledge can be used to design effective systems.

Finally, workplace layout can be based on a knowledge of anthropometry so that manual motions can take place within a prescribed area and chair and table heights can be set at levels appropriate to human body sizes.

Analysis of Manual Activity

Table II is a summary of the areas of application of different manual activity methods of analysis. Before any method of analysis described here is used, the need for performing the activity at all should already have been established through overall studies of the sequence and

TABLE II. Summary of Areas of Application of Different Man and Man-Machine Analysis Methods

Nature of Activity	Analysis Method
Repetitive short-cycle task, low- to moderate-production volume	Operation chart or operation chart supplemented by motion-time standard data
Repetitive short-cycle task, high-production volume	Micromotion analysis chart, motion-time standard data
Repetitive long-cycle tasks	Man flow process charts, activity charts
Repetitive tasks involving a crew and/or a machine	Activity charts
Jobs involving tasks occurring at irregular intervals	Activity classification

relationship of operations performed in producing a part or processing a paperwork form. The product analysis methods of Chapter 9 are appropriate for these overall studies.

Repetitive Short-Cycle Tasks. *Operation charts* are appropriate when the task has a fairly short cycle and the production volume is low to moderate. The operation chart analyzes the motions of the right and left hands into components of reach, grasp, transport, position, assemble, etc., and places the activities for each hand in parallel columns so that it can readily be seen how the two hands work together. Sometimes symbols are added, as in Figure 9, usually with large circles to indicate manipulative activity, small circles to indicate reaches and transports of material, and a simple connective line to indicate the idle hand. With the symbols, Figure 9 shows a complete operation chart for the assembly of a bolt and three washers.

Sometimes the data of the operation chart are displayed against a time scale so that the relative value of the activities can be appraised. These time data may come from standard time values for motions such as reach, grasp, move, and position, or from detailed time studies of the operation being analyzed. Motion-time-standard data (discussed in the next chapter) may be helpful particularly in evaluating the estimated effect of proposed changes.

Principles of Motion Economy. Over the years, industrial engineers have developed a set of general statements, called principles of motion

LEFT HAND

Carries finished assembly to bin 1.......
Releases assembly into bin 1...........
Reaches for bolt in bin 2..............
Grasps bolt from bin 2................
Carries bolt to central position.........

Holds bolt............................

Carries finished assembly to bin 1.......

RIGHT HAND

Reaches for lock washer in bin **3.**
Grasps lock washer from bin 3.
Carries lock washer to central position.

Positions lock washer.

Assembles lock washer onto bolt.
Reaches for plain steel washer in bin 4.
Grasps steel washer from bin **4.**
Carries steel washer to bolt.
Positions steel washer.
Assembles steel washer.
Reaches for rubber washer in bin **5.**
Grasps rubber washer from bin **5.**
Carries rubber washer to bolt.
Positions rubber washer.
Assembles rubber washer.
Releases finished assembly.

FIGURE 9. Operation chart of bolt and washer assembly—old method. (From Barnes [1].)

economy, which concern work arrangement, the use of the human hands and body, and the design and use of tools. Table III summarizes the most widely circulated statement of these ideas. These guides to job design have general applicability and are supplemented, and in some cases corroborated, by some of the research into the speed and accuracy of motor activities discussed later in this chapter.

Let us look at the operation chart of the bolt and washer assembly

TABLE III.   Principles of Motion Economy—A Check Sheet for Motion Economy and Fatigue Reduction

These twenty-two rules or principles of motion economy may be profitably applied to shop and office work alike. Although not all are applicable to every operation, they do form a basis or a code for improving the efficiency and reducing fatigue in manual work.

Use of the Human Body

1. The two hands should begin as well as complete their motions at the same time.
2. The two hands should not be idle at the same time except during rest periods.
3. Motions of the arms should be made in opposite and symmetrical directions and should be made simultaneously.
4. Hand motions should be confined to the lowest classification with which it is possible to perform the work satisfactorily.
5. Momentum should be employed to assist the worker wherever possible, and it should be reduced to a minimum if it must be overcome by muscular effort.
6. Smooth continuous motions of the hands are preferable to zigzag motions or straight-line motions involving sudden and sharp changes in direction.
7. Ballistic movements are faster, easier, and more accurate than restricted (fixation) or "controlled" movements.
8. Rhythm is essential to the smooth and automatic performance of an operation, and the work should be arranged to permit easy and natural rhythm wherever possible.

Arrangement of the Work Place

9. There should be a definite and fixed place for all tools and materials.
10. Tools, materials, and controls should be located close in and directly in front of the operator.
11. Gravity feedbins and containers should be used to deliver materials close to the point of use.
12. Drop deliveries should be used wherever possible.
13. Materials and tools should be located to permit the best sequence of motions.
14. Provisions should be made for adequate conditions for seeing. Good illumination is the first requirement for satisfactory visual perception.
15. The height of the workplace and the chair should preferably be arranged so that alternate sitting and standing at work are easily possible.
16. A chair of the type and height to permit good posture should be provided for every worker.

Design of Tools and Equipment

17. The hands should be relieved of all work that can be done more advantageously by a jig, a fixture, or a foot-operated device.
18. Two or more tools should be combined whenever possible.
19. Tools and materials should be prepositioned whenever possible.
20. Where each finger performs some specific movement, such as in typewriting, the load should be distributed in accordance with the inherent capacities of the fingers.
21. Handles, such as those used on cranks and large screwdrivers, should be designed to permit as much of the surface of the hand to come in contact with the handle as possible. This is particularly true when considerable force is exerted in using the handle. For light assembly work the screwdriver handle should be so shaped that it is smaller at the bottom than at the top.
22. Levers, crossbars, and handwheels should be located in such positions that the operator can manipulate them with the least change in body position and with the greatest mechanical advantage.

From [1].

shown in Figure 9 from the viewpoint of the principles of motion economy. An examination shows that the left hand holds the bolt for a considerable part of the cycle while the right hand assembles parts on the bolt. This suggests the possibility of a fixture to relieve the left hand for useful work (Number 17, Table III). When the left hand is free, the possibility of making duplicate assemblies is suggested by numbers 1, 2, and 3. In addition, numbers 4, 8, 9, 11, 12, 13, 15, and 16 all contribute to the improved method for performing the bolt and washer assembly which is shown in the operation chart of Figure 10.

Micromotion Analysis. This analysis breaks down an operation into elements, called therbligs, which represent a finer breakdown than do the elements for the operation chart. The results are plotted against a time scale so that the exact simultaneity of the two hands working together can be examined. The resulting chart is often called a "simo chart" because it shows this relationship. The data for the chart are gathered by means of motion pictures taken of a qualified operator.

Owing to the extra time and cost required to use micromotion analysis, its area of use is commonly limited to situations where many workers perform the same repetitive task. Thus, the total saving may be great, even though the per cent reduction might be fairly small. It has also been found valuable in the design and development of new special equipment. A motion analyst and a machine designer working together often produce a superior design.

Repetitive Tasks Involving Long Cycles. *Man flow process charts* are commonly used to analyze long-cycle tasks in which the worker moves about considerably from place to place in the performance of his work. The same general type of analysis of the product flow process chart (discussed under "product analysis" in Chapter 9) is used, except that the analyst follows the worker, instead of a part, and classifies his activities sequentially into operations, transports (walking as well as transporting material), storages (idleness), and inspections. Analysis of the resulting chart parallels product flow process charts; activities are examined with the objectives of (a) elimination, (b) combination, (c) improved sequence, etc. Gang process charts are used where activities of a crew are studied; one column of symbols is used for each man in the crew.

Activity charts are used to analyze operations into the time required to perform major manual and machine elements, or activities, and to plot the elements on a time scale. Relationships between man and machine or between crew members can then be examined. Let us take the milling

LEFT HAND	RIGHT HAND
Reaches for rubber washer in bin 1......	Reaches for rubber washer in bin 1.
Grasps rubber washer from bin 1.......	Grasps rubber washer from bin 1.
Slides rubber washer to countersunk hole	Slides rubber washer to countersunk hole.
Positions rubber washer in countersunk hole 5...........................	Positions rubber washer in countersunk hole 5.
Reaches for plain steel washer in bin 2..	Reaches for plain steel washer in bin 2.
Grasps steel washer from bin 2........	Grasps steel washer from bin 2.
Slides steel washer to countersunk hole..	Slides steel washer to countersunk hole.
Positions steel washer in countersunk hole 5.......................	Positions steel washer in countersunk hole 5.
Reaches for lock washer in bin 3.......	Reaches for lock washer in bin 3.
Grasps lock washer from bin 3........	Grasps lock washer from bin 3.
Slides lock washer to countersunk hole..	Slides lock washer to countersunk hole.
Positions lock washer in countersunk hole 5...........................	Positions lock washer in countersunk hole 5.
Reaches for bolt in bin 4..............	Reaches for bolt in bin 4.
Grasps bolt from bin 4...............	Grasps bolt from bin 4.
Carries bolt to washers at 5...........	Carries bolt to washers at 5.
Positions bolt preparatory to inserting it into washers at 5................	Positions bolt preparatory to inserting it into washers at 5.
Assembles bolt and washers...........	Assembles bolt and washers.
Lifts bolt and washers, carries to left and releases into top of chute 6.......	Lifts bolt and washers, carries to RIGHT and releases into top of chute 6.

FIGURE 10. Operation chart of bolt and washer assembly—improved method. (From Barnes [1].)

of a slot in a bracket as an example. Figure 11 shows the bracket and the activity chart for the milling of the slot. Here the major elements of the repetitive work of the man and the machine have been plotted side by

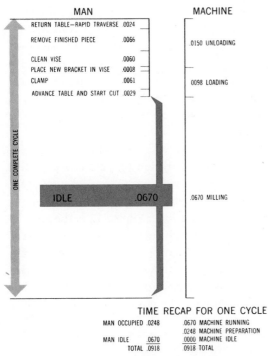

FIGURE 11. Activity chart of "mill slot in bracket." (Courtesy Westinghouse Electric Corporation.)

side on a time scale. In this instance the times are recorded in decimal hours. In this type of analysis, the major objective commonly is to maximize man and machine utilization. In the example of the milling of the bracket slot, we see that the machine is 100 per cent utilized, since it is always either being loaded, unloaded, or actually taking a cut, and at no time is it idle. Nevertheless, machine effectiveness could be increased by improving the manual methods of loading and unloading, thus improving machine output per unit of time. The techniques for accomplishing this require a detailed study of the manual activity by means of the operation chart, etc., already discussed. On the other hand, the man is idle 73 per cent of the cycle while he waits for the milling machine to complete its cut. This general situation is common in many kinds of machine and process operations.

The question is what to do with the man's idle time in such a situation. Perhaps the first consideration is whether the operator is really idle: some types of machine operations require operator vigilance and surveillance during the machine cycle, and an attempt to utilize such time could affect quality adversely. But it is often true that this is purely idle time. When such is the case on repetitive operations of considerable volume, it may be possible to have the man operate two or more machines. For the bracket slot milling operation, the operator could handle three machines doing the identical operation without introducing any idle machine time. Beyond that number, idle machine time develops, and an economy study would be required to determine whether idle man or machine time would be preferable.

Where the volume of the activity in question does not justify multiple-machine operation, examination of the operation process chart for that part might reveal other elements which could be performed during the idle time. As an example, the operation which followed the slot milling on the bracket happened to be milling the lugs. Figure 12 is the activity chart for lug milling. Figure 13 is the resulting composite operation of milling both the slot and the lugs. Note that the man's idle time has now been reduced to about 40 per cent of the total cycle, but in so structuring the job, idle machine time has been introduced into the lug milling machine, amounting to about 45 per cent. The question again comes up

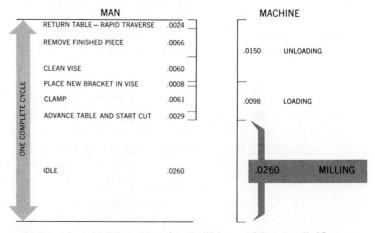

FIGURE 12. Activity chart for "mill lugs of bracket." (Courtesy Westinghouse Electric Corporation.)

MAN		MACHINE NO. 1 MILL BRACKET SLOT		MACHINE NO. 2 MILL BRACKET LUGS	
RETURN TABLE OF NO. 1 MACHINE	.0024				
REMOVE FINISHED BRACKET	.0066	.0150	UNLOADING		
CLEAN VISE	.0060			.0268	IDLE
PLACE NEW BRACKET IN VISE	.0008				
CLAMP	.0061	.0098	LOADING		
ADVANCE TABLE AND START CUT	.0029				
WALK TO NO. 2 MACHINE	.0020				
RETURN TABLE OF NO. 2 MACHINE	.0024				
REMOVE FINISHED BRACKET	.0066			.0150	UNLOADING
CLEAN VISE	.0060				
PLACE NEW BRACKET IN VISE	.0008			.0098	LOADING
CLAMP	.0061				
ADVANCE TABLE AND START CUT	.0029				
WALK TO NO. 1 MACHINE	.0020	.0670	MILLING	.0260	MILLING
IDLE	.0382				
				.0142	IDLE

TIME RECAP FOR ONE CYCLE

	.0670 MACHINE RUNNING	.0280 MACHINE RUNNING
MAN OCCUPIED .0536	.0248 MACHINE PREPARATION	.0248 MACHINE PREPARATION
MAN IDLE .0382	.0000 MACHINE IDLE	.0410 MACHINE IDLE
TOTAL .0918	.0918 TOTAL	.0918 TOTAL

FIGURE 13. Activity chart for the composite operation, "mill slot and lugs of bracket." (Courtesy Westinghouse Electric Corporation.)

whether idle man or idle machine time is preferable. Note that if milling capacity were greater than demand, there would be incremental labor costs to do the two activities separately. On the other hand, if milling demand were at capacity or exceeded it, there would be created additional demand equal to the new machine idle time and there would be incremental labor costs equal to the extra hours at overtime rates. But since the two operations are being performed in the labor time of the slot milling operation, there is still a net gain from combining the two operations.

Where it is impractical to combine two or more machining operations, other kinds of activity may be incorporated to reduce the idle time for example, the removal of burrs produced by machining, or stacking otherwise jumbled parts so that they may be procured more easily in the following operation. Any useful work that can be accomplished during such idle times, of course, incurs no incremental labor cost.

Sometimes there are objections made by skilled workers to running more than one machine, but where idle times are long, workers often become bored and may welcome a more even distribution of load. It is common that other workers, such as inspectors, assemblers, and many who operate machines that do not have automatic or semiautomatic cycles, are loaded fairly steadily throughout the workday.

Crew or team activities, which often appear complex to the observer, are considerably simplified by activity charts. Because of the difficulty in observing the simultaneity of the operations, the motion picture camera is an excellent means for gathering the basic data. Figure 14 is an example of such a chart for a team of three women who are wrapping eight pints of ice cream in a package. Work is fed to the team at a constant rate by a machine. Here is an instance where partial improvements only serve to increase operator idle time unless and until one entire operator can be eliminated.

Analysis of Tasks Occurring at Irregular Intervals. *Activity classification* often provides valuable data for the analysis of jobs that have tasks (usually of wide variety) which occur at irregular intervals. An initial step in analysis is to determine the average proportion of time spent in each of several categories of activity. There are two valuable methods for gathering pertinent data for activity classification: work sampling and time-lapse movie camera techniques.

Work sampling involves a random sampling of activities so that the proportion of time spent in each activity can be estimated; it will be discussed in greater detail in the chapter on standards and work measurement. Time-lapse movie cameras also can be used to obtain similar data. The camera, which takes pictures at slow-speed intervals, one per second or slower, is set to view the field of activity. It is driven by a synchronous motor so that each film frame represents a definite time unit. Since camera speeds are slow, it is possible to obtain half-day or full-day records with a fairly modest film consumption.

ANALYSIS OF CONTROL ACTIVITY

The design of controls and control systems has an important impact on the effectiveness of a man-machine system. A knowledge of the forces that man can exert may be of importance in some systems so that these capabilities are not exceeded in the design of controls. Positioning activities are commonly required in operating controls and control coding is sometimes important so that controls are not confused.

Strength and Forces of Body Movements. Data on the forces that can be exerted by most of the working population is important for designing machines and tools which do not require operators with

ACTIVITY CHART

SUBJECT	Pack 8 pints of Ice Cream				Date 3/30/54		

Present X / Proposed — Dept. Ice Cream (Time in thousandths of mins.) — Sheet 1 of 1 — Chart by ESB

Supplier		Packer #1		Packer #2	
Elements	Time	Elements	Time	Elements	Time
Get and position 4 pints	47	Get and position 8 pints-wrap	89	continued Get tape-seal	37
				Dispose to right	8
Wait for machine	11			Idle	74
Get and position second 4 pints	34				
Release 8 pints to Packer #2	16	Get tape-seal	14		
		Dispose to left	14		
Get and position 4 pints	33	Meter and cut tape	21	Get and position 8 pints-wrap	81
Wait for machine	11	Idle	62		
Get and position second 4 pints					
Release 8 pints to Packer #1	14			Get tape-seal; cont. at top	

20, 40, 60, 80, 100, 120, 140, 160, 180, 200

FIGURE 14. Activity chart of a team of three women wrapping eight pints of ice cream in a package.

unusual physical strength. Rather exhaustive population measurements have been made for arm strength (in various directions and different starting positions), grip strength, turning strength (such as turning a door knob), elbow and shoulder strength, and back and leg strength.*

---

*A good summary of the results of these studies can be found in [21].

Typical of such data is that developed for the USAF at Wright Air Development Center for arm strength in a seated position. Subjects were measured for maximum push, pull, upward force, and downward force for various angular positions. See Figure 15. Table IV summarizes the results for the maximum forces exerted by the fifth percentile of the measured group. These figures, then, represent forces that nearly all males can equal or exceed. Jobs designed so that required arm forces do not exceed these values can draw on almost anyone in the male population. In general, from Table IV we can see that left-hand strength is consistently less than that for the right hand, and that pushes and pulls are weaker when the arm is down at the side. With upward and downward movements, however, greater force can be exerted when the arm is down at the side. Pull is slightly better than push, down slightly better than up, and in better than out.

Speed and Accuracy of Motor Responses

A motor response is one that involves physical movement and/or control of body parts. It is a muscular activity. Since man's hands are his most important asset for the performance of muscular tasks, we

FIGURE 15. Subject positions for arm strength study. Data are shown in Table IV. (*a*) Side view of subject showing various angular positions of upper arm. For each position, maximum strength was determined for pull, push, up, and down movements shown in (*b*). (*b*) Top view of subject showing in-and-out movements made at each of the arm positions shown in (*a*). (Adapted from [15].)

TABLE IV. Arm Strength, in Pounds, of Movements in Various Directions for Different Angular Positions of Upper Arm

Angle of Arm (degrees)	Fifth Percentile			
	Left	Right	Left	Right
	Pull		Push	
180	50	52	42	50
150	42	56	30	42
120	34	42	26	36
90	32	37	22	36
60	26	24	22	34
	Up		Down	
180	9	14	13	17
150	15	18	18	20
120	17	24	21	26
90	17	20	21	26
60	15	20	18	20
	In		Out	
180	13	20	8	14
150	15	20	8	15
120	20	22	10	15
90	16	18	10	16
60	17	20	12	17

Adapted from [15].

find that most of the available data pertain to the hands. Thus, in designing tasks that involve positioning elements, for example, a knowledge of where in the work area positioning can be accomplished most accurately may affect the workplace layout.

Positioning Elements. Much experimental effort has gone on to determine how positioning elements of various types can be best accomplished. A number of interesting results have been found, some expected and some unusual. For example, Barnes [1] showed that positioning elements that require visual control take somewhat longer to accomplish (about 17 per cent) than where some sort of mechanical guide or stop is used to establish the exact final desired position of the part or hand. The implications of this fact tend to corroborate the idea of a fixed and definite location for everything. The rapid typing speeds attained by the touch system are based partially on this fact since key locations are fixed. Conceptually, it is the difference between finding something in a carefully indexed and maintained file or in a stack of papers.

Briggs [5] performed a set of positioning experiments where *speed and accuracy* were the criteria. The task required subjects to move back and forth between a buzzer and a target with a metal stylus. When the stylus was pressed against a 3-inch square or circle, the buzzer was actuated. The stylus was then moved 14 inches to a paper target through which it was punched. The measure used was the number of punch marks on the target in a 20-second trial. The target size and the angular position of the buzzer were varied, as in Figure 16. In a second experiment the positions of the buzzer and target were reversed, so the buzzer was immediately in front of the subject and the target was placed at various angular positions. Figure 16 shows the results. Speed and accuracy were consistently greater for the second experiment when the target was away from the subject. Not only that, but the angular position of about 60° optimized the scores. In a third set of experiments,

FIGURE 16. General experimental setup and results of positioning experiments. Optimal angle was near 60°. (Adapted from [5].)

the distance of movement was also varied, and angles to both the right and left of the subject were used. In general, scores were better when movement was to the right instead of to the left, and short distances were better than long.

When the right and left hands work in simultaneous and symmetrical patterns, Barnes and Mundel [3] showed that the accuracy of positioning is optimum when both hands are directly in front of the subject.

Positioning through Settings of Dials, Cranks, and Handwheels. Movements to position dials, knobs, cranks, and handwheels are common means by which the human operator controls processes and machines. Several studies have been made to determine factors that optimize the design of such devices. For example, when knob settings must be accomplished without visual control (blind), Chapanis [7] showed that average errors and variability of settings are minimized at the "twelve o'clock" position of the dial. Jenkins and Connor [17] showed that there is a large difference in the time needed to make a setting, depending on the ratio between knob movement and the movement of the pointer on the dial. Low ratios tend to minimize the time to make final adjustments, but the time to bring the pointer to the approximate setting is fairly long. The reverse is true for high ratios. The optimum ratio turned out to be about 2 inches of pointer movement to each turn of the knob, as shown in Figure 17. Friction added to the system increased the travel time but had no effect on the final adjustment time.

Davis [9] performed a set of experiments to determine optimal sizes of cranks and handwheels under various conditions of frictional torque, position and height. These types of cranks and handwheels are common devices used to move carriages and cutting tools to desired settings. Davis measured the time taken to make required settings for the various conditions. He found that for zero or very low frictional torque, the small handwheels and cranks were best (3 to 6 inches in diameter). When it was necessary to crank against some frictional load, however, the larger diameters were better (10 to 16 inches). Cranks were superior to handwheels. Davis varied the height from the floor and the angular position of the wheel, because in practice these types of mechanisms might be found in various relative positions. The interesting general result was that location was not a serious factor for zero or low loads but, when heavy frictional load was encountered, the $-45°$ and $+45°$ positions were significantly better than the horizontal or vertical positions.

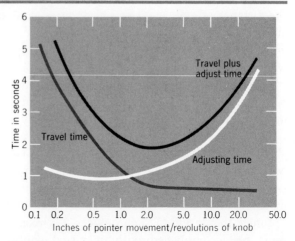

FIGURE 17. The time for setting indicators with different control ratios. Times are divided into two parts: the time of travel to get the pointer in the vicinity of the target and the time for adjusting the pointer accurately on the target. Note that there is an optimum at about 2 inches of pointer movement for each revolution of the knob. (Adapted from [17].)

Coding Controls. In complex operations where a number of controls are used, coding by color, size, shape, or location helps to distinguish between them so that mistakes are minimized. Hunt [16] found that round knobs could be distinguished from each other when the smaller was five-sixths the size of the larger. The location of controls can be used to distinguish them from each other. For example, the clutch, brake, and accelerator pedals of automobiles are normally used without looking to see where they are. Here again, the Hunt study provides basic information. He found that when toggle switches were arranged in vertical columns, the errors in blind reaching to specified switches were lower than when the switches were arranged horizontally in rows. For switches arranged vertically, Hunt's results indicated that a 5-inch difference in location was desirable, but for horizontal arrangements this difference was about 8 inches.

Hunt also investigated knob shapes that could be distinguished solely by touch. He classified the designs into three groups: multiple rotation knobs, fractional rotation knobs, and detent positioning (that is, where knob position is critical as, for example, a television channel selector dial where each position "clicks" into place). The sixteen knob designs developed are shown in Figure 18.

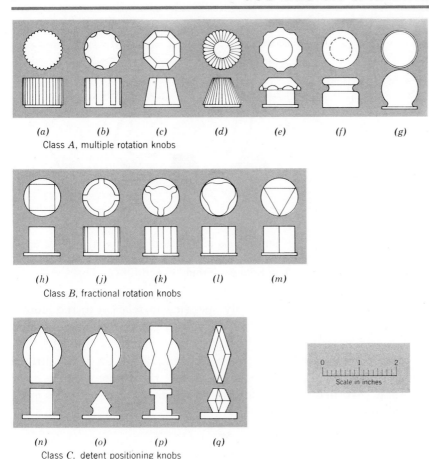

(a)   (b)   (c)   (d)   (e)   (f)   (g)

Class A, multiple rotation knobs

(h)   (j)   (k)   (l)   (m)

Class B, fractional rotation knobs

(n)   (o)   (p)   (q)

Class C, detent positioning knobs

FIGURE 18.   Knob designs of three classes that are seldom confused by touch. (Adapted from [16].)

Work Area Limits.   Many tasks, such as assembly work, the operation of many types of machines, and much clerical work, are performed while the worker is seated or standing at a bench, table, or desk. Figure 19 shows maximum and normal work areas based on the actual measurement of people. Movements beyond the maximum work area require that the trunk of the body be moved. For repetitive operations, these trunk movements are fatiguing. Similar measurements have been made for the vertical plane; guides for locating materials, supplies, tools, and controls are available in three dimensions.

Chair and Table Heights.   Since there is so much manual and clerical activity, the height of chairs and tables is important. The two are closely

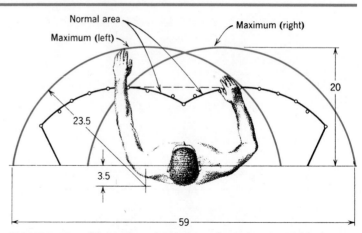

FIGURE 19.   Dimensions in inches of maximum working areas in horizontal plane as proposed by Barnes, with normal work area proposed by Squires. (From [1] and [29].)

related. Table height is commonly specified in relation to the elbow, so that adjustments in either chair or table height from the floor can be made to give greatest comfort to individual workers. A study by Ellis [11] corroborates earlier estimates by Barnes [1] that the work surface height should be about three inches below the elbow. Actual work table and chair heights then depend on whether the setup is designed for sitting-standing or sitting only.

THE WORKING ENVIRONMENT

The working environment, which includes such factors as temperature, humidity, noise, and light, can produce marked effects on productivity, errors, quality levels, and employee acceptance, as well as on physiological well-being. Therefore, we cannot measure the effectiveness of a job design without a knowledge of the working environment in which it will be placed. It is a part of the total picture.

Temperature, Humidity, and Air Flow

We have all experienced the fact that our feeling of comfort is not determined solely by the thermometer reading. If there is a breeze we feel cooler, even though the temperature has not changed. On a stifling day we have all heard the comment, "it isn't the heat, it's the humidity." The sensation of warmth or cold is affected by each of these factors, which have been combined into a single psychological scale called *effective temperature*. Effective temperature is the temperature of still, saturated (100 per cent humidity) air, which gives the identical sensation of warmth or cold as the various combinations of air temperature, humidity, and air movement would. The American Society of Heating, Refrigerating and Air Conditioning Engineers (ASHRAE) Laboratory performed the experiments that led to the effective temperature scale. There is one factor that the effective temperature scale does not take into account. This is the temperature of objects in the environment which could radiate directly to the workers, such as furnaces.

The human body has automatic heat regulatory mechanisms that allow compensation for the environment over a certain effective temperature range. This compensation, of course, is also dependent on the activity level. Thus, a higher activity level can produce body comfort at a lower effective temperature.

Temperature and Humidity Effects on Performance.   Atmospheric conditions can have important effects on performance in both mental and physical tasks. Figure 20 shows, in summary form, the effects of various levels of effective temperature on performance for Morse code receiving and for weight lifting. For Morse code receiving, Figure 20a, the average number of errors goes up sharply as effective temperature goes beyond 90° F. For heavy work, represented by weight lifting in Figure 20b, the total accomplished work in foot-pounds begins to fall off rapidly above 80° F effective temperature.

FIGURE 20.   (a) Relationship of effective temperature and average number of mistakes per man-hour in receiving Morse code. (From Mackworth [20].) (b) Foot-pounds of work performed by men under various effective temperatures. (From McCormick [21].)

Control of the Thermal Atmosphere.   Dr. L. A. Brouha, working at E. I. du Pont de Nemours, experimented with protective clothing for workers who must operate in very hot atmospheres such as near industrial furnaces. He found that simple protective clothing actually increased the heat stress. However, a ventilated suit, through which a continuous air flow was maintained, reduced the heat stress considerably.

Control for workers adjacent to hot areas such as furnaces, where heat radiation is the main problem, can be accomplished with shielding and by isolating the hot spot. General thermal control is accomplished through air conditioning but is not universally practiced. For most United States climates and working conditions, the zones of physiological compensation are effective, except for a few hot summer days. The most frequent use of air conditioning to date has been in offices to provide attractive working conditions and to help control clerical errors in warm weather. Of course, winter heating has long been accepted as necessary by business and industry for inside tasks.

Noise
Unwanted sound is commonly called noise. There is growing evidence that it can produce damaging effects, especially when workers are exposed to it over a period of years. Sounds of all kinds, including noise, consist of variations in atmospheric pressure that are propagated in waves similar to ripples on water. These variations in pressure are called *sound pressure*. We measure sound in decibels (db), but that measurement is not a measure of the pressure of sound. Rather, it is related to the ratio of the sound pressure of the source being measured to some reference sound pressure. Considerable confusion is possible here since more than one reference base is commonly used. Figure 21 helps to relate typical noise levels to the db scale. Another thing to note about noise measurements is that we must know something about the distribution of the sound energy over the range of tones, or frequencies, in order to know what will be the effects on man. Therefore, it is common to indicate the db levels in the various octave bands of frequencies.

Hearing Loss Due to Noise Exposure.   Some recent work in this general area has been done by the Research Center, Subcommittee on Noise in Industry, Los Angeles, California. Figure 22 shows comparative data for a container manufacturer and typical industrial exposure, plus data for the general population and a group termed *nonexposed* because the noise levels of their typical surroundings were very low. Here we see that hearing loss is characteristic of the general population, even of the nonexposed group, but the severity of loss depends on the intensity of exposure.

FIGURE 21. Decibel sound pressure levels of some typical noises.

Noise Effects on Work Performance. Industry, of course, has been interested in the possible direct effects that high noise levels may have on performance measures such as output, errors, and quality levels. In a number of studies on this subject, the general result was that if the injection of noise into the environment had any bad effects, they were temporary. We should note that good experimental design is difficult in such situations because the experiments usually must go on over a period of time; it is difficult to know whether the results are attributable to noise effects or due to other changes which may have taken place

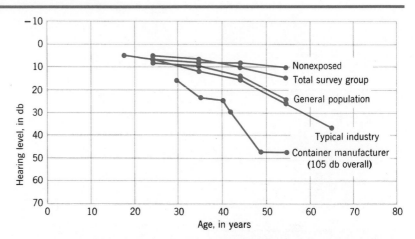

FIGURE 22. Comparative hearing loss in relation to age for different groups. Zero is a reference base of average normal hearing. Readings show the power level required to reach the average level. Readings were taken at 2000 cycles (speech range). (Data courtesy of Research Center, Subcommittee on Noise in Industry, Los Angeles.)

during the same time interval. The one sure reaction is that higher noise levels are annoying, but human beings seem able to adapt to them.

Noise Control. Noise control can be accomplished in different ways, depending on the nature of the problem. Acoustical engineers often control noise at its source, by redesigning the noise producing parts, by using vibration isolation mountings of equipment, or sometimes by isolating the source of noise through the construction of proper enclosures so that the amount of noise transmitted beyond the enclosures is reduced. In the latter method, a knowledge of the physics of sound transmission is important. The wrong enclosure design might transmit the noise with little or no loss or might even amplify it.

Other forms of control are baffles, sound absorbers, and acoustical wall materials. Sound absorbers can be installed near or above noise sources to help reduce noise levels. Acoustical wall materials can be used to reduce noise levels within a room by reducing reverberation, the reflection of the sound waves back and forth in the room. Of course, these wall materials have no effect on the original sound waves emanating from the source.

In severe noise situations, a properly fitted earplug can be effective. The maximum possible attenuation from earplugs is limited to about 50 db, because there are alternate paths to the eardrum through bone conduction. The more usual expected protection from earplugs would be an attenuation of 20 to 30 db.

The conditions for seeing are important aspects of the working environment. However, no universally accepted standard for lighting is available, although there are recommended levels from many sources. Experimental data on illumination levels compared to some given criterion seem to indicate that many recommended standards are based on the view that "if 50 footcandles are good, then 100 footcandles of illumination are better." Part of the difficulty lies in the fact that various criteria have been used, such as visual acuity, blink rate, preference ratings, and critical illumination levels. From a business and industrial viewpoint, critical illumination levels make the most sense, since they are essentially performance types of criteria. The critical level of illumination for a given task is that level beyond which there is practically no increase in performance for increases in illumination intensity. Thus, increases in intensity beyond these critical levels are assumed to be of no value. M. A. Tinker has constructed a table of recommended standards for different tasks based on the critical level criterion. Table V summarizes his recommendations.

Light

TABLE V. Levels of Illumination Recommended or Accepted by Tinker Based on Critical Levels as a Criterion

Task or Situation	Recommended or Accepted Illumination Level (footcandles)
Halls and stairways	5
Reception rooms and washrooms	10
Reading good-sized print (9 to 11 point) on good quality paper	10–15
School class rooms, shops, and offices	15
Typical home tasks	15
Reading newsprint	15–20
Reading handwriting and comparable tasks	20–30
School sewing and drafting rooms	25
General office work, private office work and mail rooms	25
Most severe visual tasks in home	25–30
Tasks comparable to discrimination of 6-point type	30–40
Most severe tasks encountered in workday situations	40–50
Accounting, bookkeeping, and drafting	50

From [30].

Illumination Effects on Work Performance.   There have been many laboratory studies of the effect of illumination level on some measure of performance of a task. In general, there is a rapid improvement in performance as illumination levels increase to the critical level, at which point performance measures level off and further increases in illumination produce little or no improvement in performance.

In many actual work situations where illumination levels have been increased, records of output and quality before and after the changes have indicated substantial improvements. Some studies report that output went up 4 to 35 per cent.* We should be wary of this type of support data, however. In the complex set of conditions existing in a business or industrial environment, variables other than just the illumination level could very well have changed, such as work methods, product designs, control procedures, supervision, the weather, and the psychological climate. For example, in the famous Hawthorne studies at the Hawthorne Works, Western Electric Company, lighting values were increased for an experimental work group and performance went up. Someone thought to check on the result by lowering intensities. The employees cooperated again by lowering performance. But performance increased again when employees were told that the light intensity had been increased when actually it had been lowered, and then the smiles drained. It was finally realized that the employees were reacting to the psychological situation. They were experimental subjects, set aside from ''ordinary'' employees, and unconsciously were simply being very cooperative for those ''nice experimenters.'' When the situation was understood, the direction of the study changed to an evaluation of factors in morale. Very little concerning illumination was learned.

Glare Effects.   Glare can reduce the effectiveness of the illumination provided. Glare is produced by some bright spot in the visual field, such as a bright light or reflected light from a polished surface, and can cause discomfort as well as reduce visual effectiveness. This reduction in visual effectiveness is summarized by Figure 23. Figure 23, based on experimental results, shows that the effects of glare become acute when the sources are close to the line of sight.

Glare effects can be reduced by moving light sources where possible,

---

*For a summary of these studies, see [21].

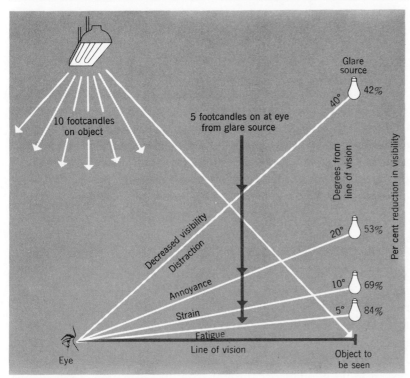

FIGURE 23. Glare becomes worse as it comes closer to the direct line of vision. (From Luckiesh [19].)

by diffusing light sources that cannot be moved, or by increasing the general illumination level of the surroundings so that the brightness contrast between the glare source and the surroundings is reduced. Reflection surfaces may sometimes be moved in relation to workplaces or changed so that the surface diffuses light.

Criteria for the Lighting Environment. There is little doubt that it is worthwhile to provide at least the general critical levels of illumination. Although there is little evidence of any changes in performance above the critical levels, these levels may be exceeded without any known bad effects in order to allow for a margin of error. This idea seems to represent current practical philosophies. General illumination levels that are more than adequate are provided and the problem is forgotten. Often missed, however, is the need for special lights for fine detailed work and the elimination of glare.

A large number of fumes, dusts, gases, liquids, and solids have proved harmful to workers. These, together with the general mechanical hazards from machine moving parts, traffic from material, transportation, falling objects, etc., from a part of the working environment.

Noxious Substances. The number of industrial poisons is tremendous. Fortunately, however, in most situations only a few would be present and potentially dangerous. Industrial medicine is a special field which concerns itself with the diagnosis, treatment, and control of the noxious substances. Maximum allowable concentrations (MAC) have been determined for most of these substances as a basis for proper control.

Control Procedures. Control procedures vary greatly because of the great variation of possible contaminants and their characteristics. In general, the control of the emissions of these substances in manufacturing processes poses engineering problems. Protection of workmen may require exhaust systems to collect dusts, gases, and vapors in order to maintain concentrations below MAC. Personal protective gear, such as respirators and gas masks, supplement exhaust systems. Other protective clothing, such as rubber aprons, coats, gloves, boots, and goggles, is available for various jobs which involve the handling of chemicals and where the unprotected skin may leave the employee exposed to injury. In addition, vigilance through careful explanation of safe operating procedures and safety programs is common.

SUMMARY

Men and machines perform similar basic functions in accomplishing work; however, their abilities are sharply divergent in the nature of tasks each can do well. The essence of man's great advantage lies in his flexibility, whereas machines can perform consistently. In general, man's role in man-machine systems falls into three main classes: as a power source and controller in manual systems, as a controller of semiautomatic systems, and as a monitor of automatic systems.

Figure 4 is an excellent general representation of the man-machine cycle representing information input, data processing and decision, manual activity and control functions and action, all imbedded in the working environment. Experimentalists have amassed a great deal of data concerning man in relation to machines which has value in designing man-machine systems. These data and modes of analysis become important inputs to the job methods phase of job design.

REVIEW QUESTIONS

1. What kinds of functions can man perform in the work situation?
2. Compare man's capabilities with those of known machines.
3. Differentiate man's role in the three typical man-machine systems.
4. Describe the man-machine cycle for semiautomatic operations.
5. What is the difference between direct and indirect sensing?
6. What are the various ways that visual and auditory information can be coded?
7. Which dial shape is easiest to read?
8. Summarize the general guides for dial design in terms of size, position of markers, distance between markers, etc.
9. When there is a bank of dials to read how should they be oriented?
10. Can a flow process chart be made for the activities of a man as well as the processing of a part or product?
11. What sort of analytical tool might be used to show working relationships between an operator and the machine he is using? What information is necessary for the development of such a tool?
12. What information is contained in an operation chart?
13. Under what conditions would micromotion analysis be justified?
14. What is an activity chart and what is its field of application?
15. Is it always best to have one worker operating more than one machine?
16. What are the principles of motion economy and how are they used in the design of manual activities?
17. What modes of analysis are appropriate for activities which have no set repetitive pattern? How can the data be gathered?
18. How can the data shown in Table IV be useful in the design of levers as control mechanisms?
19. What sort of information is available concerning the speed and accuracy of positioning elements?
20. What is the optimum ratio of pointer movement to each turn of the knob when making a setting?
21. What kinds of guides to design are available for the coding of controls by color, size, shape, or location?
22. What is effective temperature?
23. Does elevated effective temperature have an effect on good performance for heavy work? For very light work?
24. What kinds of control measures are available for the thermal environment?
25. What effects on work performance are produced by noise? What health effects?
26. How can noise be controlled?
27. What is the critical illumination for a given task?
28. What are glare effects and how can they be controlled?

29. What is MAC?
30. What kinds of control procedures are used for industrial poisons and contaminants?

PROBLEMS

1. Construct an operation chart for the assembly of some simple device such as a ball-point pen, a chair caster, or a pair of scissors.

2. A custom machining company has received an order for a lot of 10,000 parts which requires a simple milling operation for which the company has available capacity. Plans are now being made for the method of operation to be used. Work will begin next week, the promised delivery date being 13 weeks from the first of next week. The plant works one shift, 40 hours per week, with up to 20 per cent overtime possible. The company normally attempts to obtain better labor utilization on relatively large orders like this one by having one worker operate more than one machine when it is feasible with the established layout and by investing in special jigs and fixtures to speed up unloading and loading of the machine.

The layout of the milling machine area and the automatic machining cycle for the required operation permit an operator to unload and load a machine, start the machine on its automatic cycle, and then proceed to the next machine, giving it the required attention when it has completed its machining cycle, and so on. The machines will automatically turn off when the normal machining cycle has been completed. From previous records of similar orders and from standard data on machining times for specified materials and lengths of cut, the following estimates of times for the job elements have been assembled:

Load part in machine	1.00 minute
Machine part (automatic)	5.00 minutes
Unload part from machine	0.50 minute
Inspect part	0.75 minute
Walk from machine to machine	0.25 minute

After feasible man-machine cycles have been assembled using the foregoing data, the company follows the practice of adding 10 per cent to the total cycle to obtain a standard time for the job to be used in cost calculations. The 10 per cent allowance is for rest, delay, and other personal needs. The following cost data have also been assembled:

Milling machine operator's rate	$3.00/hour
Machine variable cost (power, cutting fluids, etc.)	1.00/hour
Material	1.50/piece
Tooling (special holding fixtures)	300/setup
Labor cost to set up machine	100/setup

There are up to four machines available; the department supervisor says that he could assign as many as three men to the job.

(a) Determine the method of operation which would minimize costs by developing a table of pertinent costs for the lot of 10,000 parts for systems where a worker operates one, two, three, and four machines. Which mode of operation would you choose and why?

(b) What kinds of costs do you think may have been ignored in the statement of the problem? Are any of the costs given as irrelevant data?

3. A young couple has started a launderette. Their business, The Blue Monday Launderette, offers the following services:

(a) Washers for use by customers.
(b) Drying service for customers' washes.
(c) Dry cleaning and finished laundry.
(d) Washing and fluff drying.

The husband performs the "fluff dry" work (washing, extracting, and fluff drying). The wife handles all other matters such as dealing with customers and aiding people who do their own washing. She also folds and bundles the "fluff dry" work during slack periods in the day.

The "fluff dry" business has been unusually heavy and the couple has been forced to work evenings to get work out on time. It is their contention that five washers, if kept busy, can do the "fluff dry" work. But there are so many other things to be done, such as semidrying the wet clothes in the extractor and loading and unloading the dryer, that one person simply cannot keep the washers loaded. The wife does not have time to assist the husband during normal working hours.

The following times are required to perform the various tasks:

	Time (minutes)
Washer (five available for "fluff dry")	
Load soiled clothes and soap, set water temperature, start machine	2
Running time (automatically stops)	40
Unload wet clothes into cart	2
Extractor (one available for "fluff dry"; each holds only one washer load)	
Load wet clothes, start machine	2
Running time (automatically stops)	5
Unload semidry clothes into cart	2
Dryer (two available for "fluff dry" each holds only one washer load)	
Untangle and load clothes, start machine	3
Running time (automatically stops)	20
Unload dry clothes into cart	2
Miscellaneous	
Travel times between equipment	Negligible

(a) With the data given, construct an activity chart for the best method of co-ordinating the work of one man, five washers, one extractor, and two dryers.
(b) What is the overall cycle time (time difference between identical points in the process) such as loading washer No. 1 on consecutive loads?

4.   A company is constructing a parking lot for which dump trucks and a power shovel are the primary equipment being used. Time studies reveal the following average times:

Time to load a truck	7.50 minutes
Travel time to dump point	9.00 minutes
Dumping time	2.00 minutes
Return time	7.00 minutes

(a) How many trucks are required to move dirt as rapidly as possible?
(b) If it cost $19 per hour for the shovel and operator and $12 per hour for each truck and driver, what number of trucks will minimize idle equipment cost?
(c) Construct a multiple-activity chart for the answer to (b).

5.   A company has decided to plate its own bushings rather than have them done elsewhere. Under their newly developed process, a single operator performs the entire process:
(1) A tumbler to remove burrs, etc.
(2) A degreasing tank to remove oil.
(3) Two plating tanks.
Loads consist of 250 bushings each with all equipment starting by the operator's push of a button and shutting off automatically. Therefore, the equipment does not require the operator's attention while running. The times required to perform the various operations are as follows:

Load tumbler	5 minutes
Running time for tumbler	24 minutes
Unload tumbler	6 minutes
Load degreaser	3 minutes
Degreaser running time	36 minutes
Unload degreaser	6 minutes
Load plating tank	6 minutes
Plating process time	60 minutes
Unload plating tank	6 minutes

(a) How many minutes does it take to complete one full cycle?
(b) How much of the total idle time of each plating tank is unnecessary?
(c) If the running time of the limiting process is reduced 25 per cent by equip-ment redesign, what is the new cycle time in minutes?

6.   A moonshine company utilizes one man and several pieces of automated equipment (blender, ager, and bottler) to produce their product. The process and associated times are as follows:

Blending:

Put in ingredients	6 minutes
Blending cycle	25 minutes
Remove blend, put in crock	4 minutes

Aging:

Put blend in aging tank	2 minutes
Aging cycle	26 minutes
Remove and filter into crock	10 minutes

Bottling:

Filter blend into bottling machine	7 minutes
Bottling cycle	15 minutes
Remove cans, pack in case	12 minutes

(a) What is the cycle time?

(b) What percentage of the time is the blender idle?

7. A one-man washing operation consists of the following process:

Washing cycle:

Load clothes, soak	2 minutes
Run (automatic)	25 minutes
Unload	2 minutes

Extracting cycle:

Load clothes into extractor	1 minute
Run (automatic)	6 minutes
Unload	1 minute

Drying cycle:

Load clothes into dryer	2 minutes
Run (automatic)	40 minutes
Unload, fold clothes	12 minutes

The present setup utilizes one washer, one extractor, and two dryers.

(a) What is the cycle time?

(b) What reduction in the extractor unnecessary idle time would occur if a second washing machine were purchased?

8. For the following example, recommend production equipment design changes and improved work methods based on principles of motion economy, anthropometric data, and common sense.

Job description of printed circuit tester: Inspects printed circuits for resistance, impedance, and heat emission rate by inserting the printed circuits in a testing device and reading the different indicator scales.

Sequence of operations (see workplace layout, Figure 24):

(1) The right hand picks up an untested circuit from the table on the right.

(2) Both hands insert the printed circuit in the testing device. (This requires 25 pounds of force to put it in.)

(3) Right foot applies power to the testing device with the foot pedal. (Average pedal time is 1.5 seconds.)

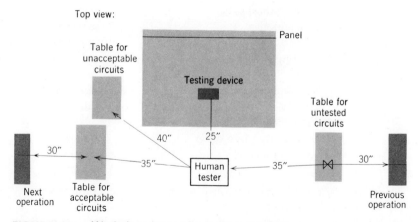

FIGURE 24. Workplace layout for testing circuits.

(4) The eyes read the three indicators to determine if all dials indicate the proper amount. (See diagram of dial panel, Figure 25.)

(5) Both hands remove the circuit from the device. (This requires 25 pounds of force to disengage the circuit board.)

(6) The left hand places the circuit either on the acceptable or unacceptable table to the left.

(7) Cycle starts over again.

Miscellaneous data:

(1) A minimum vertical insertion force of 15 pounds is required for placing the circuit in the testing device. This is required to simulate a closed circuit after the printed circuit is in place.

Indicator Display Panel

→ Readings for an acceptable circuit

FIGURE 25. Indicator display panel.

(2) Power must be applied gradually to the testing device with a power pedal. The minimum time allowed for this power application is 0.9 second.

(3) The footcandle reading at the indicator panel is 10.

(4) Occasionally a small shock is felt by the tester when the printed circuit is removed from the testing device.

(5) The printed circuits weigh 0.5 pound.

REFERENCES

[1] Barnes, R. M. *Motion and Time Study: Design and Measurement of Work* (6th ed.). John Wiley, New York, 1968.

[2] Barnes, R. M., H. Hardaway, and O. Podalsky. "Which Pedal Is Best?" *Factory Management and Maintenance*, **100**, 98–99, Jan. 1942.

[3] Barnes, R. M., and M. E. Mundel. *A Study of Simultaneous Symmetrical Hand Motions.* University of Iowa Studies in Engineering, Bulletin 17, 1939.

[4] Bennett, E., J. Degan, and J. Spiegel. *Human Factors in Technology.* McGraw-Hill, New York, 1963.

[5] Briggs, S. J. "A Study in the Design of Work Areas." Unpublished Ph.D. Dissertation, Purdue University, Lafayette, Ind., Aug. 1955.

[6] Chapanis, A., *Man-Machine Engineering.* Wadsworth, Belmont, Ca., 1965.

[7] Chapanis, A. "Studies of Manual Rotary Positioning Movements: I. The Precision of Setting an Indicator Knob to Various Angular Positions." *Journal of Psychology*, **31**, 51–64, 1951.

[8] Chapanis, A., W. R. Garner, and C. T. Morgan. *Applied Experimental Psychology.* John Wiley, New York, 1949.

[9] Davis, L. E. "Human Factors in Design of Manual Machine Controls." *Mechanical Engineering*, **71**, 811–816, Oct. 1949.

[10] Davis, L. E., "Toward a Theory of Job Design, *Journal of Industrial Engineering,* **8** (5), 305–309, Sept.–Oct. 1957.

[11] Ellis, D. S. "Speed of Manipulative Performance as a Function of Work-Surface Height." *Journal of Applied Psychology,* **35,** 289–296, 1951.

[12] Fitts, T. M. "A Study of Location Discrimination Ability." In: *Psychological Research on Equipment Design.* T. M. Fitts, editor. Army Air Force Psychology Program, Research Report 19, 1947.

[13] Fogel, L. J. *Biotechnology: Concepts and Applications.* Prentice-Hall, Englewood Cliffs, N.J., 1963.

[14] Gagné, R. M. *Psychological Principles in System Development.* Holt, Rinehart, and Winston, New York, 1963.

[15] Hunsicker, P. A. *Arm Strength at Selected Degrees of Elbow Flexion.* USAF, Wright Air Development Center, Technical Report 54–548, Aug. 1955.

[16] Hunt, D. P. *The Coding of Aircraft Controls.* USAF, Wright Air Development Center, Technical Report 53–221, Aug. 1953.

[17] Jenkins, W. L., and N. B. Connor. "Some Design Factors in Making Settings on a Linear Scale." *Journal of Applied Psychology,* **33,** 395–409, 1949.

[18] Karpovich, P. U. *Physiology of Muscular Activity.* Saunders, Philadelphia, 1953.

[19] Luckiesh, M. *Light, Vision, and Seeing.* D. Van Nostrand, Princeton, N.J., 1944.

[20] Mackworth, N. H. "Effects of Heat on Wireless Telegraphy Operators Hearing and Recording Morse Messages." *British Journal of Industrial Medicine,* **3,** 143–158, 1946.

[21] McCormick, E. J. *Human Factors Engineering* (3rd ed.). McGraw-Hill, New York, 1970.

[22] Meister, D., and G. F. Rabideau. *Human Factors Evaluation in System Development.* John Wiley, New York, 1965.

[23] Morgan, C. T., J. S. Cook, A. Chapanis, and M. W. Lund. *Human Engineering Guide to Equipment Design.* McGraw-Hill, New York, 1963.

[24] Müller, E. A. "The Physiological Basis of Rest Pauses in Heavy Work." *Quarterly Journal of Experimental Physiology,* **38** (4), 1953.

[25] Mundel, M. E. *Motion and Time Study* (3rd ed.). Prentice-Hall, Englewood Cliffs, N.J., 1960.

[26] Nadler, G. *Work Design* (Rev. ed.). Richard D. Irwin, Homewood, Ill., 1970.

[27] Sleight, R. B. "The Effect of Instrument Dial Shape on Legibility." *Journal of Applied Psychology,* **32,** 170–188, 1948.

[28] Spector, W. L., editor. WADC Technical Report 56/273, ASTIA Document No. AD. 110501, Wright Air Development Center, 1957.

[29] Squires, P. C. *The Shape of the Normal Work Area.* Navy Department, Bureau of Medicine and Surgery, Medical Research Laboratory, New London, Conn., Report 275, July 23, 1956.

[30] Tinker, M. A. "Trends in Illumination Standards." *Transactions of the American Academy of Opthalmology and Otolaryngology*, 382–394, Mar.–Apr. 1949.

[31] Woodson, W. E. *Human Engineering Guide for Equipment Designers* (2nd ed.). University of California Press, Berkeley, 1966.

14

Production Standards & Work Measurement

What is a "fair day's work"? A production standard is an answer to the question, and the field of work measurement provides methodology and a rationale for determining a fair day's work for different jobs. Production standards state how many parts, assemblies, etc., should be produced per minute, hour, or day, or they indicate the amount of time allowed as standard for producing a unit of work. Whether standards are expressed in terms of pieces per unit or time per piece is quite irrelevant; however, they are often called "time standards" when expressed in time units. Although production standards are designed to determine how much output is expected of an employee, they include more than just work. Actually, production standards include standard allowances for rest, delays that occur as part of the job, time for personal needs, and, where the work is heavy, an allowance for physical fatigue. You can see that the problems of measuring work and setting up good standards of performance that are consistent from job to job are difficult. So why go to the trouble of setting them up? Why are standards important?

PRODUCTION STANDARDS

Data Provided

Production standards provide data that are basic to many decision-making problems in production. The production standard is of critical importance because labor cost is a predominant factor, influencing many decisions that must be made. For example, decisions to make or buy, to replace equipment, or to select certain manufacturing processes require estimates of labor costs, as well as estimates of other costs. These decisions necessarily require an estimate of how much output can be expected per unit of time.

Production standards also provide basic data used in the day-to-day operation of a plant. For example, scheduling or loading machines demands a knowledge of the projected time requirements for the various orders. For custom manufacture, we must be able to give potential customers a bid price and delivery date. The bid price is ordinarily based on expected costs for labor, materials, and overhead, plus profit. Labor cost is commonly the largest single component in such situations. To estimate labor cost requires an estimate of how long it will take to perform the various operations.

Finally, production standards provide the basis for labor cost control. By measuring worker performance in comparison to standard performance, indexes can be computed for individual workers, whole departments, divisions, or even plants. These indexes make it possible to compare performance on completely different kinds of jobs. Standard labor-costing systems and incentive wage payment systems are based on production standards. Production standards are useful in so many ways in both the design and the operation and control of production systems that we must regard them as truly basic data.

Informal Standards

The plain fact is that every organization has production standards of sorts. Even when they seem not to exist formally, foremen and supervisors have standards in mind for the various jobs that come under their supervision based on their knowledge of the work and past performances. These types of standards are informal. They can be formalized merely by writing them down and recognizing them as the standards of performance expected. Standards based on foremen's estimates and past performance data have weaknesses, however. First of all, in almost all such situations, methods of work performance have not been standardized. Therefore it is difficult to state what production rate, based on past records, is appropriate, because past performance may have been based on various methods. Since it has been demonstrated that production rates depend heavily on job methods, standards based on past performance records might not be too dependable. A second major defect in standards based on estimates and past performance records is that they are likely to be too strongly influenced by the working speeds of the individuals who held the jobs during the periods of the available records. Were those workers high or low performers?

We wish to set up production standards that are applicable to the industrial population, not just to a few selected people within that population. Our production standards problem is comparable in some ways to that of designing a lever with the proper mechanical advantage to match the capabilities of man. But not just any man; the force required to pull the lever should accommodate perhaps 95 to 99 per cent of the population, so that anyone who comes to the job will have the necessary arm strength. If the lever requires a man with superhuman strength, we would have to seek out only these people for the job. Recall from Chapter 13 that the section on strength and forces of body movements dealt with this problem.

The Core of the Work Measurement Problem

The production standard that we wish to set up actually requires a knowledge of the distribution of performance times (or production rates) for the entire working population doing the job for which we are setting up a standard. Suppose that we have 500 people all doing an identical task, make sample studies on all of them, and plot the data. Figure 1 shows the results of just such a study. The distribution shows that average performance time varies from 0.28 minute to 0.63 minute per piece. Obviously, if our past records reflected data from one or more individuals taken at random from our population of 500, a standard based on their performance might not fit the whole population very well. On the other hand, if we know the entire distribution, as in Figure 1, we can set up standards that probably would accommodate everyone who might come to the job. One way to do this is to follow a procedure similar to that used in job design when drawing on anthropometric data. Set the standard so that it accommodates about 95 per cent of the population. For Figure 1, a standard performance time of about 0.48 minute is one which about 95 per cent of the individuals exceeded. If we pegged the standard at this level, we would expect that practically

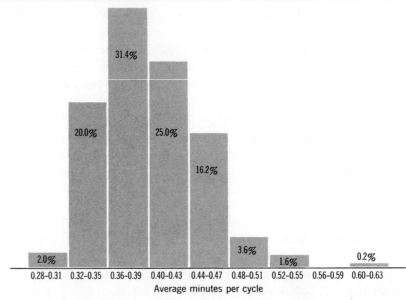

FIGURE 1. Percentage distribution of the performance of 500 people performing a wood block positioning task. About 5.4 per cent of the people averaged 0.48 minute per cycle or longer. (Adapted from Barnes [3].)

all employees on the job should be able to meet or exceed the standard.

Some industrial managers feel that it is not good to quote minimum performance standards such as these for fear that they will encourage relatively poor performance as acceptable. These people prefer to say that the standard performance is about the average of the distribution (0.395 minute for Figure 1) and expect that most workers will produce about standard, that some will fall below, and that some will exceed standard. Both systems of quoting standards are used, although the practice of quoting *minimum acceptable values* is more common than that of quoting average values.

To this point we have been discussing only the work time. The distribution of Figure 1 shows how long it took on the average to perform the task. Using the minimum acceptable level as our basic standard of performance, we shall call the actual work time at that level the *normal time*. The normal time for the data of Figure 1 is 0.48 minute; the total standard time is then:

Normal time + standard allowance for personal time
          + allowance for measured delays normal to the job
          + fatigue allowance

We shall discuss the several allowances later, but the central question now is: "How do we determine normal time in the usual situation when only one or a few workers are on the job?" Seldom would we find a large number of workers doing the same job, so usually we cannot build up a distribution. Without knowledge of the distribution, how can we pick out the level which about 95 per cent of the workers could meet or exceed, that is, normal time? The approach to this problem used in industry is called performance rating.

Performance rating is a critically important part of any formal means of work measurement. To be able to rate accurately requires considerable experience. It works something like this. A pace or performance level is selected as standard. An analyst observes this pace, compares it with various other paces, and learns to judge pace level in per cent of the standard pace. For Figure 1 we called the cycle time of 0.48 minute "normal," and the pace or rate of output associated with this time is normal pace. A pace of work that is 25 per cent faster would require proportionately less time per cycle, or $0.48/1.26 = 0.381$ minute. If a skilled analyst observed a worker performing the task on which Figure 1 is based and he rated performance at 125 per cent of normal while simultaneously measuring the actual average performance time as 0.381 minute, he would have to add 25 per cent to his observed time to adjust it to the normal level. In this instance, his performance rating is perfect, according to our distribution, since $0.381 \times 1.25 = 0.48$. Other perfect combinations of rating and actual observed time are 150 per cent and 0.32 minute, 175 per cent and 0.274 minute, 90 per cent and 0.533 minute, etc.

Performance Rating

In an actual work measurement situation, of course, the analyst does not have the answer beforehand, so he simultaneously observes the actual time taken to do the task and rates the performance. The normal time is then computed as:

$$\text{Normal time} = \text{Actual observed time} \times \frac{\text{Performance rating}}{100}$$

All of the formal work measurement systems involve this rating or judgment of working pace or some equivalent procedure. Alternate methods of actually measuring time and determining normal time will be considered later in the chapter.

Rating as a System of Measurement. What do we need in order to be able to measure something, whether it be the length of a line the pressure inside a vessel, or the pace at which a man is working? It is really quite simple. We need basically two things:

1. A standard for comparison which is accepted.
2. A unit of measurement or a scale.

Both may be set arbitrarily. For example, in linear measurement (the measurement of length) our basic standard has been a platinum-iridium bar held in the Bureau of Standards in Washington, D. C., which, in turn, is based on the international standard. Two scales are commonly used, based on two different ways of dividing up the bar. One is the English system (yards, feet, inches) and the other the metric system (meters, centimeters, millimeters). Any number of other scales could be based on the same basic standard. Also, any number of other bar lengths could serve as basic standards of length on which to base the scales. The thing that makes our present basic standard and the two common scales valuable measurement systems is that they have received general acceptance.

Does the use of these systems of measure then involve judgment? Yes, even the use of the best precision measuring instruments involves some judgment. (See Chapter 22, "Control of Quality," for a study of inspectors' use of various precision measuring instruments.) In using a micrometer, for example, one must judge how tightly to turn down the spindle, and the importance of this "feel" cannot be minimized.

Let us consider performance rating in the same general light. Are there basic standards of reference that have general acceptance? Yes, there are motion picture films of operations in many types of occupations which show "normal paces" for those tasks as well as faster and slower paces. One set of such films was made by the Society for Advancement of Management (SAM) and consists of 24 factory and clerical operations which were rated by thousands of experienced time study analysts throughout the country. Walking at 3 miles per hour has been selected as "normal pace." Many organizations, such as Deere and Company, General Motors, and Caterpillar Tractor Company, have their own standards in the forms of films of various operations throughout their plants, which exhibit normal and other paces of work. These film standards do not enjoy the same degree of acceptance as do the physical standards of weights and measures, but they exist. Analysts can use them to recalibrate their judgment and to train people in performance rating.

Now to the question of scales. There are, unfortunately, three scales in common use, and this fact is often the source of some confusion. Figure 2

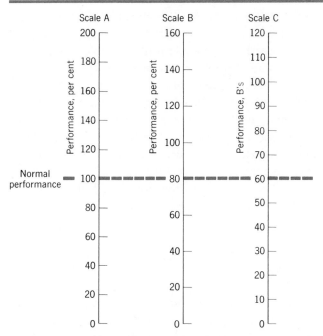

FIGURE 2. Three alternate performance rating scales in relation to normal performance.

shows these scales in relation to the basic standards of walking at 3 miles per hour, etc. Scale A, the most common, is the scale which we shall assume throughout this book where work standards are mentioned. It labels "normal pace" as 100 per cent. Scale B provides maximum confusion by labeling a much higher level of performance as 100 per cent. We can convert easily between the two scales by recognizing that 125 per cent on scale A is the same performance level as 100 percent on scale B. Scale B is used by organizations who wish to quote standards at a higher level. (See our discussion on pages 419–421 of performance distributions.) Scale C is in points instead of per cent, and it is often called the Bedaux scale. On the Bedaux scale, 60 points are equivalent to 100 per cent performance on scale A.

How Accurate Is Performance Rating? In the actual work measurement situation, it is necessary to compare our mental image of "normal performance" with what is observed and to record our rating of the performance. This rating enters the computation of production standards as a factor and the final standard can be no more accurate than the rating. How accurately can experienced people rate? Commonly accepted figures would be ± 5 per cent. Controlled studies in which films have been rated indicate a standard deviation of 7 to 10 per cent [11, 15]. In other words, experienced people probably hold these limits about 68 per cent of the time. Therefore, the effect of the element of judgment in current work measurement practice is considerable. This fact is important in all of the uses of production standards which we discussed at the beginning of this chapter. Nonetheless, standards developed by measurement (including the rating) are better than standards based simply on past records, because they specify a given work method and they correct for the working pace of the employee observed. A standard based on past records only could easily be off 200 to 300 per cent for these reasons, and ± 7 to 10 per cent is modest by comparison.

WORK MEASUREMENT SYSTEMS

All practical work measurement systems involve: (a) the measurement of actual observed time and (b) the adjustment of observed time to obtain "normal time" by means of performance rating. The alternate systems which we shall discuss combine these factors in somewhat different ways.

Stopwatch Methods
By far the most prevalent approach to work measurement currently used involves a stopwatch time study and simultaneous performance rating of the operation to determine normal time. The general procedure is as follows:

1. Standardize methods for the operation; that is, determine the standard method, specifying workplace layout, tools, sequence of elements, etc. Record the resulting standard practice.

2. Select the operator for study, experienced and trained in the standard methods.

3. Determine elemental structure of operation for timing purposes. This may involve a breakdown of the operation into elements and the separation of the elements that occur each cycle from those that occur only periodically or randomly. For example, tool sharpening might be required each 100 cycles to maintain quality limits. Machine adjustments might occur at random intervals.

4. Observe and record the actual time required for the elements, making simultaneous performance ratings.

5. Determine the number of observations required to yield the desired precision of the result based on the sample data obtained in step 4. Obtain more data as required.

6. Compute normal time = averaged observed actual time × average rating factor/100.

7. Determine allowances for personal time, delays, and fatigue.

8. Determine standard time = normal times for elements + time for allowances.

Breakdown of Elements. Common practice is to divide the total operation into elements rather than to observe the entire cycle as a whole. There are several reasons why this practice is followed:

1. The element breakdown helps to describe the operation in some detail indicating the step-by-step procedure followed during the study.

2. More information is obtained which may have valuable use for comparing times for like elements on different jobs and for building up a handbook of standard data times for common elements in job families. With standard data for elements, cycle times for new sizes can be forecast without additional study.

3. A worker's performance level may vary in different parts of the cycle. With an element breakdown, different performance ratings can be assigned to different elements where the overall cycle is long enough to permit separate evaluation of performance.

In breaking an operation into elements, it is common practice to make elements a logical component of the overall cycle, as illustrated in Figure 3. For example, element 1, "pick up piece and place in jig," is a fairly homogeneous task. Note that element 4, "drill $\frac{1}{4}$-inch hole," is the machining element, following the general practice to separate machining time from handling time. Finally, constant elements usually are separated from elements that might vary with size, weight, or some other parameter.

Taking and Recording Data. Figure 3 is a sample study where 20 cycles were timed by the continuous method; that is, the stopwatch is allowed to run continuously, being read at the breakpoints between elements. Elapsed times for elements are then obtained by successive subtraction. *Repetitive* or "snap-back" methods of reading the watch are also common. In repetitive timing, the observer reads the watch at the end of each element and snaps the hand back to zero so that each reading gives the actual time without the necessity of subtraction. Comparative studies indicate that the two methods are equally accurate.

Note the other data recorded in Figure 3 that identify the part, operation, operator, material, etc., as well as check data of elapsed time of the study, and the number of completed units. The "selected times" repre-

OBSERVATION SHEET

SHEET 1 OF 1 SHEETS   DATE

OPERATION   Drill ¼″ Hole   OP. NO.   D-20

PART NAME   Motor Shaft   PART NO.   MS-267

MACHINE NAME   Avey   MACH. NO.   2174

MALE [√]   FEMALE [ ]

OPERATOR'S NAME & NO.   S.K. Adams 1347

EXPERIENCE ON JOB   18 Mo. on Sens. Drill   MATERIAL   S.A.E. 2315

FOREMAN   H. Miller   DEPT. NO.   DL 21

BEGIN 10:15	FINISH 10:38	ELAPSED 23	UNITS FINISHED 20	ACTUAL TIME PER 100 115	NO. MACHINES OPERATED 1

ELEMENTS	SPEED	FEED		1	2	3	4	5	6	7	8	9	10	SELECTED TIME
1. Pick Up Piece and Place in Jig			T	.12	.11	.12	.13	.12	.10	.12	.12	.14	.12	
			R	.12	.29	.39	.54	.66	.77	.92	8.01	14	.32	
2. Tighten Set Screw			T	.13	.12	.12	.14	.11	.12	.12	.13	.12	.11	
			R	.25	.41	.51	.68	.77	.89	7.04	.14	.26	.43	
3. Advance Drill to Work			T	.05	.04	.04	.04	.05	.04	.04	.04	.03	.04	
			R	.30	.45	.55	.72	.82	.93	.08	.18	.29	.47	
4. DRILL ¼″ HOLE	980	H	T	.57	.54	.56	.51	.54	.58	.52	.53	.59	.56	
			R	.87	.99	3.11	4.23	5.36	6.51	.60	.71	.88	11.03	
5. Raise Drill from Hole			T	.04	.03	.03	.03	.03	.03	.03	.03	.04	.03	
			R	.91	2.02	.14	.26	.39	.54	.63	.74	.92	.06	
6. Loosen Set Screw			T	.06	.06	.07	.06	.06	.06	.06	.06	.07	.08	
			R	.97	.08	.21	.32	.45	.60	.69	.80	.99	.14	
7. Remove Piece from Jig			T	.08	.09	.08	.08	.09	.08	.07	.08	.09	.07	
			R	1.05	.17	.29	.40	.54	.68	.76	.88	10.08	.21	
8. Blow Out Chips			T	.13	.10	.12	.14	.13	.12	.13	.12	.12	.11	
			R	.18	.27	.41	.54	.67	.80	.89	9.00	.20	.32	
9.			T											
			R											
10. (1)			T	.12	.11	.13	.14	.12	.12	.11	.13	.12	.12	.12
			R	11.44	.56	.69	.82	.87	1701	18.09	.21	.31	.42	
11. (2)			T	.12	.14	.12	.11	.12	.10	.13	.15	.12	.11	.12
			R	.56	.70	.81	.93	.99	.11	.22	.36	.43	.53	
12. (3)			T	.04	.04	.04	.03	.04	.04	.04	.04	.04	.04	.04
			R	.60	.74	.85	.96	16.03	.15	.26	.40	.47	.57	
13. (4)			T	.54	.53	.55	.52	.57	.54	.50	.53	.55	.54	.54
			R	12.14	13.27	14.40	15.48	.60	.69	.76	.93	21 02	22.11	
14. (5)			T	.03	.03	.03	.03	.03	.03	.03	.03	.03	.03	.03
			R	.17	.30	.43	.51	.63	.72	.79	.96	.05	.14	
15. (6)			T	.06	.06	.06	.07	.06	.05	.06	.06	.05	.06	.06
			R	.23	.36	.49	.58	.69	.77	.85	20.02	.10	.20	
16. (7)			T	.08	.08	.09	.08	.08	.07	.08	.06	.08	.08	.08
			R	.31	.44	.58	.66	.77	.84	.93	.08	.18	.28	
17. (8)			T	.14	.12	.10	.09	.12	.14	.15	.11	.12	12	.12
			R	.45	.56	.68	.75	.89	.98	19.08	.19	.30	22.40	
18.			T											1.11
			R											

SELECTED TIME	1.11	RATING	100%	NORMAL TIME	1.11	TOTAL ALLOWANCES	5%	STANDARD TIME	1.17

Overall Length 12″   Drill ¼″ Hole   1″   ¾″   1″

TOOLS, JIGS, GAUGES: Jig No. D-12-33
Use H.S. Drill ¼″ Diam.
Hand Feed
Use Oil - S4

TIMED BY   J.B.M.

FIGURE 3.   Stopwatch time study of a drilling operation made by the continuous method. (From Barnes [3].)

sent averages of the element times; the cycle "selected time" is merely the sum of the element averages. A single performance rating of 100 per cent was made for the study and a 5 per cent allowance added to obtain the standard time of 1.17 minutes per piece.

Adequacy of Sample Size. Considering the work measurement problem from the viewpoint of statistics, we are attempting to estimate, from the sample times and performance ratings observed, a normal time of performance. The precision desired will determine how many observations will be required. For example, if we wanted to be 95 per cent sure that the resulting answer, based on the sample, was within ± 5 per cent, we would calculate the sample size n required from a knowledge of the mean and standard deviation of our sample data. If we wanted greater confidence or closer precision, the sample size would have to be larger.

Figure 4 is a convenient chart for estimating required sample sizes to maintain a ± 5 per cent precision in the answer for 95 and 99 per cent confidence levels. To use the chart, we merely calculate the mean value $\bar{x}$ and the standard deviation based on the sample data. The "coefficient of variation" is simply the percentage variation, $100(s_x/\bar{x})$. The chart is entered with the calculated coefficient of variation, and the sample size is read off for the confidence level desired. The most common confidence level is 95 per cent in work measurement.

Let us test the adequacy of the sample taken in the study of Figure 3. First, was $n = 20$ adequate for estimating the overall cycle within a precision of ± 5 per cent and a confidence level of 95 per cent? Table I shows the calculation of the coefficient of variation for the cycle times as about 5 per cent; that is, the standard deviation 0.057 minute is about 5 per cent of the mean cycle time of 1.12 minutes. From Figure 4 we see that a sample of $n = 4$ would be adequate to maintain a precision within ± 5 per cent of the correct mean cycle time, 95 per cent of the time, or $n = 10$ for a confidence level of 99 per cent. Our actual sample of 20 was more than adequate.

The reason that the small sample size was adequate is easy to see. The variability of the readings is small in relation to the mean cycle time, so a good estimate of cycle time is obtained by only a few observations. Incidentally, this is commonly true of operations dominated by a machine cycle. In this case, the actual drill time is almost half of the total cycle and the machining time itself does not vary much.

If all we wanted was an estimate of cycle time, we could stop at this point. Let us suppose, however, that we want our estimates of each of the

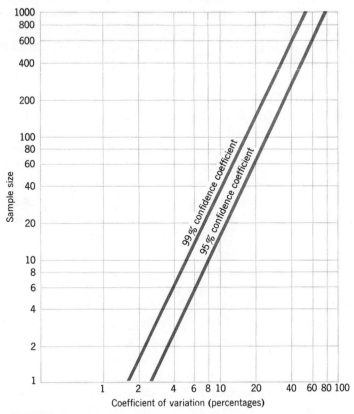

FIGURE 4. Chart for estimating the sample size required to obtain maximum confidence intervals of ±5 per cent for given coefficient of variation values. (From Abruzzi [1].)

average element times to be adequate for future use as elemental standard data. Was the sample size of $n = 20$ adequate for each of these elements? Let us take element 1 as an example. The mean element time is $\bar{x} = 0.121$ minute, the standard deviation is $s = 0.0097$ minute, and the coefficient of variation is 8 per cent. From Figure 4 we see that we should have taken a sample of $n = 10$ for a 95 per cent confidence level and $n = 20$ for a 99 per cent confidence level. The reason why a larger sample is needed for element 1 than for the entire cycle is that element 1 is somewhat more variable than is the total cycle (coefficient of variation of 8 per cent compared with only 5 per cent for the cycle). Therefore, if data on each of the elements are needed, the element for which the largest sample size is indicated, from Figure 4, dictates the minimum sample size for the study. This procedure insures the precision and confidence requirements for the limiting element and yields better results than this on all other elements.

TABLE I.   Cycle Times from Figure 3, and Calculated Mean Value, Standard Deviation, Coefficient of Variation and Required Sample Sizes from Figure 4

Cycle Number	Cycle Time (minutes)	Cycle Time (squared)	Cycle Number	Cycle Time (minutes)	Cycle Time (squared)
1	1.18	1.395	11	1.13	1.280
2	1.09	1.190	12	1.11	1.235
3	1.14	1.300	13	1.12	1.255
4	1.13	1.280	14	1.07	1.145
5	1.13	1.280	15	1.14	1.300
6	1.13	1.280	16	1.09	1.190
7	1.09	1.190	17	1.10	1.215
8	1.11	1.235	18	1.11	1.235
9	1.20	1.440	19	1.11	1.235
10	1.12	1.255	20	1.10	1.215
			Sum	22.40	25.150

$$\bar{x} = \frac{22.40}{20} = 1.12$$

$$s = \sqrt{\frac{\Sigma x_i{}^2 - \frac{(\Sigma x_i)^2}{n}}{n-1}} = \sqrt{\frac{25.150 - \frac{(22.40)^2}{20}}{19}} = 0.057$$

$$\text{Coefficient of variation} = \frac{0.057 \times 100}{1.12} = 5.09\%$$

From Figure 4 :

$$n \approx = \ 4 \ @ \ 95\% \text{ confidence level.}$$

$$n \approx = 10 \ @ \ 99\% \text{ confidence level.}$$

Procedures for Ensuring Consistency of Sample Data.   A single study always leaves open the question: "Were the data representative of usual operating conditions?" If a similar study were made on some other day of the week or some other hour of the day, would the results be different? This question suggests the possibility of dividing the total sample into smaller subsamples taken at random times. Then, by setting up control limits based on an initial sample, we can determine if the subsequent data taken are consistent. That is, did all of the data come from a common universe?

This situation is comparable to that found in quality control. If a point falls outside of the $\pm 3s$ control limits, we know that the probability is high that some assignable cause of variation is present which has resulted in an abnormally high or low set of sample readings. These assignable causes could be anything that could have an effect on the time of production such as material variations from standard; changes in tools, workplace, or methods of work; and in the working environment. As with quality control, we would attempt to determine the nature of these assignable causes and eliminate data where abnormal readings have an explanation.

The general procedure is as follows:*

1. Standardize methods, select operator, and determine elemental breakdown as before.

2. Take an initial sample study. (a) Compute preliminary estimates of $\bar{x}$ and s. (b) Determine estimate of total sample needed from Figure 4. (c) Set up control limits for balance of study based on preliminary estimates of $\bar{x}$ and s.

3. Program and execute balance of study. (a) Divide total sample by subsample size to find the number of separate subsamples to obtain. Subsample sizes are commonly 4 to 5. (b) Randomize the time when these subsamples will be taken. A random number table is useful. (c) At the random times indicated, obtain subsample readings and plot points on control chart. If points fall outside limits, investigate immediately to determine the cause. Eliminate data from computations for standards where causes can be assigned. (d) When study is complete, make final check to be sure that the precision and confidence level of the result are at least as good as desired.

4. Compute normal time, determine allowances, and compute standard time as before.

Work Sampling The unique thing about work sampling is that it accomplishes the results of stopwatch study without the need for a stopwatch. Although this statement does not summarize, by any means, the net advantage or disadvantage of work sampling, it indicates that there is something startlingly different about work sampling, and indeed there is.

Work sampling was first introduced to industry by L. H. C. Tippett in 1934. However, it has been in common use only since about 1950. We can illustrate the basic idea of work sampling by a simple example. Suppose we wish to estimate the proportion of time that a worker, or a group of workers, spends working and the proportion of time spent not working. We can do this by long-term stopwatch studies in which we measure the work time, the idle time, or both. This would probably take a day or longer, and after measuring we would not be sure that the term of the study covered representative periods of work and idleness.

Instead, suppose that we make a large number of *random* observations

---

*For detailed procedures with appropriate charts for estimating sample sizes, precision limits, and control limits, see [2] and [3].

	Tally	Number	Per cent
Working	THL THL THL THL THL THL THL THL THL THL THL THL THL THL THL THL THL THL THL THL THL I	96	88.9
Idle	THL THL II	12	11.1
Total		108	100.0

FIGURE 5. Work sampling tally of working and idle time. When observations occur at random times, the percentages estimate the per cent of time that the worker was in the working or idle state. The accuracy of the estimate increases with the number of observations.

in which we simply determine whether the operator is working or idle and tally the result (see Figure 5). The percentages of the tallies that are recorded in the "working" and "idle" classifications are estimates of the actual per cent of time that the worker was working and idle. Herein lies the fundamental principle behind work sampling: *the number of observations is proportional to the amount of time spent in the working or idle state*. The accuracy of the estimate depends on the number of observations, and we can preset precision limits and confidence levels.

Number of Observations Required. The statistical methods of work sampling depend on the distributions for proportions, as do control charts and sampling by attributes in quality control. Recall that

$$\bar{p} = \frac{x}{n} = \frac{\text{number observed in classification}}{\text{total number of observations}}$$

and

$$s_p = \sqrt{\frac{\bar{p}(1 - \bar{p})}{n}}$$

From these simple formulas for mean proportion and the standard deviation of a proportion, charts and tables have been developed which give directly the number of observations required for a given value of $\bar{p}$, precision limits, and the 95% confidence level. Estimates of sample sizes can be obtained from Figure 6.*

Note that the number of observations required is fairly large. For example, to maintain a precision in the estimate of $\bar{p}$ of ± 1.0 percentage point at 95 per cent confidence, 10,000 observations are required if $\bar{p}$ is in the neighborhood of 50 per cent, that is, to be 95 per cent sure that an estimate of $\bar{p} = 50$ per cent is between 49 and 51 per cent. About 3600 observations are required to hold that an estimated $\bar{p} = 10$ per cent

---

*More complete information on sample sizes is available in [4].

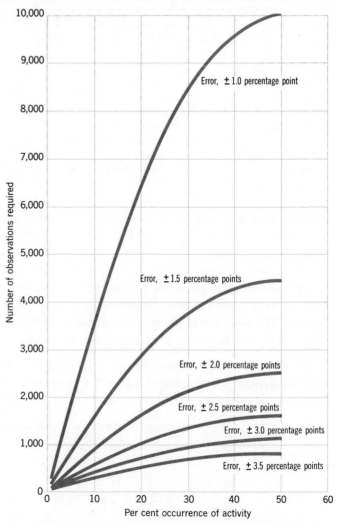

FIGURE 6. Curves for determining the number of observations required to maintain precision within the percentage points indicated at the 95 per cent confidence level.

between 9 and 11 per cent. Smaller samples are required for looser limits. Although these numbers of observations seem huge, we must remember that the nature of the observation required is merely a recognition of whether or not the employee is working, or possibly a classification of his activity into various reasons for idleness.

Measuring Delays and Allowances. One common use of work sampling is to determine the per cent of time that workers are actually spending for personal time and delays that are a part of the job. The resulting information could then be used as the basis for the percentage allowances that enter into the calculation of standard time.

Let us consider, as an example, the determination of delay and personal allowances in a lathe department of a machine shop. There are ten workers involved. The delays of which we are speaking are a part of the job such as waiting for tools, materials, and instructions; machine cleanup; securing an inspector's approval; change of jobs; and minor mechanical difficulties. We wish to determine the extent of the delays and to determine how much time workers are spending for personal time. Our procedure is as follows:

1. *Design work sampling study.*
   (a) Estimate preliminary values for the per cent of time spent in the three categories of work, delay, and personal time from past knowledge, studies, foremen's estimates, or a preliminary study of the jobs. These preliminary estimates are necessary to gauge the magnitude of the data-taking phase. Based on a composite of past information and foremen's estimates, our best guesses are:

Work	85 per cent
Delay	10 per cent
Personal time	5 per cent

   (b) Set desired precision limits of estimates to be obtained. We decide that ± 1.0 percentage point at 95 per cent confidence on our delay estimate will be controlling. Thus, if the estimate for delays is actually 10 per cent, we want to be 95 per cent sure that it is not less than 9 per cent or more than 11 per cent, with 10 per cent being the most probable value.
   (c) Estimate total number of readings from Figure 6. For $\bar{p} = 10$ per cent, $N = 3600$ for ± 1.0 percentage point error. Note from Figure 6 that our precision for personal time of 5 per cent would then be slightly better than ± 1.0 percentage point and for working time slightly worse.
   (d) Program total number of readings over desired time span of study. We decide that 3600 readings over a 2-week period (10 working days) will cover a representative period. Therefore, we propose to obtain $\frac{3600}{10} = 360$ observations per day. Since there are 10 workers involved, we shall obtain 10 observations each time we sample. So we need to program $\frac{360}{10} = 36$ random sampling times each day for 10 days to obtain the total of 3600 readings. The easiest way to select 36 random sampling times is to use a random number table.

(e) Plan the physical aspects of the study. This includes an appropriate data sheet, as well as a determination of the physical path, observation points, etc., so that the results are not biased because workers see the observer coming and change activities accordingly.

2. *Take the data as planned.* Table II shows a summary of the actual data taken in this instance with a breakdown between morning and afternoon observations. The percentages for "work," "delay," and "personal time" have been computed for each half-day and for the total sample.

3. *Recheck precision of results and consistency of data.* A final check of the delay percentage of 9.97 per cent shows that the number of readings taken was adequate to maintain the ± 1.0 percentage point precision on the delay time. The consistency of the data could be checked by setting up a control chart for proportions to see if any subsample points fell outside the limits. Other statistical tests comparing A.M. observations with P.M. observations could also be carried through.

TABLE II.   Summary of Work Sampling Data for Lathe Department Study

Date		Total Obser- vations	Work		Delay		Personal	
			Obs.	Per Cent	Obs.	Per Cent	Obs.	Per Cent
10–2	a.m.	190	152	80.0	24	12.6	14	7.4
	p.m.	170	145	85.3	14	8.2	11	6.5
10–3	a.m.	160	144	90.0	10	6.3	6	3.7
	p.m.	200	158	79.0	19	9.5	23	11.5
10–4	a.m.	150	127	84.7	15	10.0	8	5.3
	p.m.	210	182	86.6	23	11.0	5	2.4
10–5	a.m.	180	142	78.9	24	13.3	14	7.8
	p.m.	180	148	82.2	20	11.1	12	6.7
10–6	a.m.	220	189	85.9	24	10.9	7	3.2
	p.m.	140	114	81.4	17	12.1	9	6.5
10–9	a.m.	210	185	88.2	14	6.6	11	5.2
	p.m.	150	135	90.0	9	6.0	6	4.0
10–10	a.m.	190	155	81.6	25	13.2	10	5.2
	p.m.	170	146	85.9	14	8.2	10	5.9
10–11	a.m.	200	166	83.0	22	11.0	12	6.0
	p.m.	160	136	85.0	14	8.8	10	6.2
10–12	a.m.	140	118	84.3	15	10.7	7	5.0
	p.m.	220	185	84.1	25	11.4	10	4.5
10–13	a.m.	210	181	86.2	19	9.1	10	4.7
	p.m.	150	130	86.7	12	8.0	8	5.3
		3600	3038	84.4	359	9.97	203	5.63

Based on the work sampling study, we could then conclude that the delay part of the work in the lathe department was about 10 per cent. We are 95 per cent sure that the sampling error has been held to no more than ± 1.0 percentage point and it is probable that it is less. We have based these conclusions on a study which covered 2 weeks of time, with any time of the day being equally likely as a sampling time. The personal time of 5.6 per cent is slightly greater than the company standard practice of allowing 5 per cent; however, 5 per cent is within the probable range of error of estimate.

Determining Production Standards. The previous example showed the use of work sampling to determine percentage allowances for noncyclical elements such as delays and for personal time. Why not carry the idea forward one more step and utilize the observations on per cent work time to establish production standards? What additional data do we need? If we knew (a) how many pieces were produced during the total time of the study and (b) the performance rating for each observation of work time, we could compute normal time as follows:

$$\text{Normal time} = \frac{\left(\begin{array}{c}\text{total}\\\text{time of}\\\text{study in}\\\text{minutes}\end{array}\right) \times \left(\begin{array}{c}\text{work time}\\\text{in decimals}\\\text{from work}\\\text{sampling study}\end{array}\right) \times \left(\begin{array}{c}\text{average}\\\text{performance}\\\text{rating in}\\\text{decimals}\end{array}\right)}{\text{total number of pieces produced}}$$

Standard time is then computed as before:

Standard time =

normal time + allowances for delays, fatigue, and personal time

We have already seen how the allowances for delays and personal time can be determined from work sampling. Here we see the complete determination of a production standard without the use of a precise timing device. All that was needed was a rather ordinary calendar from which we might calculate the total available time.

Although work sampling approaches to work measurement can be used in most situations, its most outstanding field of application is in the measurement of noncyclical types of work where many different tasks are performed but where there is no set pattern of cycle or regularity. In many jobs, the frequency of tasks within the job is based on a random demand function. For example, a storeroom clerk may fill requisitions, unpack and put away stock, deliver material to production departments, clean up the storeroom, etc. The frequency and time requirements of some of these tasks depend on things outside the control of the clerk himself. To determine production standards by stopwatch methods would be difficult or impossible. Work sampling fits this situation ideally because, through its random sampling approach, reliable estimates of time and performance for these randomly occurring tasks can be obtained.

An Example

As an example, let us consider the determination of standards for a warehouse handling group, reported by George H. Gustat of Eastman Kodak Company.* In this study thirty people were engaged in the following nine groups of activities: packing, shipping, receiving, small orders, reoperating (opening and repacking for tests, etc.), sort and stack, inventory, wait for equipment, personal and lost time.

Two separate work sampling studies were made in which the observer classified the activities of the workers and rated their performance using IBM cards and mark-sensing lead so that computations could be carried out on card-tabulating equipment. The combined overall results of these studies, which involved 6601 observations, are shown in Table III. Here we see the distribution of time spent by the thirty men. Figures 7 and 8 show the summary of data for the packing operation only and the control chart for the operation, both being based on the second of the two work sampling studies. Figure 9 shows sample calculations of standard time for the packing operation. (Allow-

TABLE III.   Combined Results of Two Work Sampling Studies of Warehouse Handling Group Covering a Total of 14 Days and 6601 Observations

Operation	Number of Observations	Per Cent of Total
Packing	2223	33.7
Shipping	1141	17.3
Receiving	912	13.8
Small orders	462	7.0
Reoperating	213	3.2
Sort and stack	361	5.5
Inventory	246	3.7
Wait for equipment	194	2.9
Personal and lost time	849	12.9
	6601	100.0

Adapted from [8, 9].

*See [4, pp. 151–161], [8, pp. 130–143], and [9, pp. 80–86].

Packing operation, summary			
Day	Total observations	Total packing observations	Daily per cent p
M	450	142	31
T	467	152	32
W	477	125	26
T	470	160	34
F	470	177	38
M	464	155	33
T	465	159	34
W	475	142	30
T	470	153	33
F	466	169	36
	4674	1534	327

Average subsample size = 4674 ÷ 10 = 467

$\bar{p} = 33\%$

FIGURE 7.   Daily summary of sampling data for the packing operation. (From [8, 9].)

ances were added to the total of all operations.)

Before the study was made, there were few sound data on which to base estimates of labor needs to perform the tasks in the warehouse. Based on the work sampling standards, a wage incentive payment plan was established which increased output per man to the extent that sixteen men could perform

FIGURE 8.   Work sampling control chart. (From [8, 9].)

Packing operation—calculation of standard time				
Employee:	J. Green	R. Smith	M. O'Riley	_ _ _ _ _ _ _etc.
a. Total hours	78	80	65	_ _ _ _ _ _ _ _ _
b. Total observations	134	157	142	_ _ _ _ _ _ _ _ _
Packing operation:				
c. Observations	42	53	61	_ _ _ _ _ _ _ _ _
d. Per cent of total *(c ÷ b)*	31.3	33.8	43.0	_ _ _ _ _ _ _ _ _
e. Packing time, hours *(d × a)*	24.4	27.1	28.0	_ _ _ _ _ _ _ _ _
f. Average rating	105	90	95	_ _ _ _ _ _ _ _ _
g. Standard time packing, hours *(f × e)*	25.6 +	24.4 +	26.6 +	_ _ _ _ _ _= 386 Total standard packing hours
h. Total footage of film shipped = 11,309,529				
i. Standard unit time = 386 ÷ 11,309,529				
j. Standard hours per 1000 feet = 0.034				

FIGURE 9. Calculation of the standard time for the packing operation. (From [8, 9].)

all of the work formerly done by thirty men. It is unlikely that such a program could have been attempted in the absence of work sampling.

Stopwatch Study and Work Sampling Compared

Perhaps the final major question to be raised is: "Are stopwatch study and work sampling interchangeable?" So far as general accuracy of results is concerned, apparently they are. Figure 10 shows the results of a comparative study in which both stopwatch and work sampling studies were made on fourteen different operations to estimate normal time. The differences between the two techniques are within the limits of rating error. This does not mean that both techniques have the same field of application, however. We cannot overestimate the importance of the work sampling advantage of not requiring the use of a stopwatch. The psychological impact of using a stopwatch on personnel being measured has never been determined, but many people feel that it is significant. If for no other reason than this, it is likely that the practical use of work sampling will grow.

Standard Data Work Measurement Systems

We have already had occasion to refer to standard data systems in connection with job design and process planning. Two kinds of standard data are used: universal data based on minute elements of motion (often called microdata) and standard data for families of jobs (often called macrodata or element standard data).

Universal Standard Data. Universal standard data give time values for fundamental types of motions, so complete cycle times can be synthesized by analyzing the motions required to perform the task. Funda-

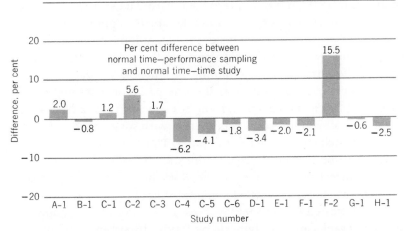

FIGURE 10. Results of a comparison between work sampling and stopwatch study on fourteen operations. Bars indicate positive and negative deviations from work sampling. (From: R. M. Barnes and R. B. Andrews, "Performance Sampling in Work Measurement," *Journal of Industrial Engineering*, **6** (6), 8–18, Nov.–Dec. 1955.)

mental time values of this nature can be used as building blocks to forecast the all-important time criterion, provided that the time values are properly gathered and that the various minute motion elements required by the tasks are analyzed perfectly. Taylor envisioned something comparable to this, and many alternative proposals have been made by management consultants who sell services consisting of installing systems based on their data and training client personnel in the use of these data. Some of these alternate time value systems are known by trade names: Methods-Time-Measurement (MTM) [12], Work Factor [17], and Basic Motion Time Study [5].

The result provided by these synthetic standards is an estimate of normal time for the task. Standard time is then determined as before by adding allowances for delay, fatigue, and personal time. Does performance rating enter into standards developed from universal data? Not for each standard developed because the analyst simply uses the time value from the table for a given motion without adjustment. However, performance rating was used to develop the time values that are in the tables. So the rating factor enters the system, but not for each occasion that the data are used.

Many people feel that universal standard data lead to greater consistency of standards, since analysts are not called on to judge working pace in order to develop a standard. This does not mean that judgment is eliminated from the use of universal standard data systems, however. A great deal of judgment is required in selecting the appropriate classifications of motion to use in analyzing an operation; an inexperienced person ordinarily will not be able to perform these selections accurately enough for the purpose of determining production standards.

Using universal standard data as the sole basis for determining production standards is not common. In most cases where data of this kind are used, they are employed in conjunction with some other technique, such as stopwatch study or work sampling. The reason for this methodology seems to be that most organizations feel more comfortable when some actual direct measurement of the work involved has been made.

How good are these systems of standard times? Do they show up the differences indicated by our sample of research studies? For example, in the study of cranks and handwheels by Davis, discussed in Chapter 13, would standard data time values have signaled the fact that the $-45°$ and $+45°$ positions are superior for cranks and handwheels under conditions of heavy resistance? Would the system have indicated that cranks are generally a little faster than handwheels? The answers are no. These differences are too subtle for the standard data systems as presently constructed. In designing jobs it is necessary that research data be used as a background of knowledge for selecting certain kinds of mechanisms (such as cranks in preference to handwheels), for judging arm strength required, for using positioning stops and guides, and for arranging the workplace so that positioning elements occur in the best positions. In other words, the principles of motion economy serve as guides. Standard data systems cannot substitute for this knowledge, but they can be used to compare and evaluate gross differences in methods which represent alternatives to the job designer. These alternatives might represent manual labor versus degrees of mechanization; alternative machines; one-handed versus two-handed approaches to the task, etc. The degree of difference which can be distinguished is surprisingly great, however, especially by a trained man. It may be that a carefully planned standard data system, based on good experimental design and technique, will be able to reflect some of the more subtle differences based on the known results of present research.

Although we have discussed standard time data systems as a means of helping to develop job designs, they also serve to forecast expected output while the employee is working. This forecast is of considerable importance; business and industrial management are always interested in the labor content of a given job design and, therefore, an estimate of the work standard is desirable. These work standards, however, usually involve appraisals of work time, rest time, delay allowances, and allowances for personal time. The standard time data discussed give estimates for the *work time* only.

Standard Data for Job Families.   Standard data for job families give normal time values for major elements of jobs (macrostandard data). Also, time values for machine setup and for different manual elements are given, so a normal time for an entirely new job can be constructed by an analysis of blueprints to see what materials are specified, what cuts must be made, how the work piece can be held in the machine, etc. Unlike the universal standard data discussed previously, however, the time values for these elements have been based on actual previous stopwatch or other measurement of work within the job family.

In these previous studies, the operations were consistently broken down into common elements until finally a system of data emerged that showed how "normal element time" varied with size, depth of cut, material used, the way the work piece was held in the machine, etc. At that point the data themselves could be used to estimate production standards without a separate study actually being performed on every different part. Again, although individual performance rating does not enter each application of the standard data, it was used in constructing the data originally. As before, final production standards are determined by adding allowances for delays, fatigue, and personal time to the normal cycle time derived from the standard data.

Macrostandard data are in common use, especially in machine shops where distinct job families have a long-standing tradition. However, the occurrence of this kind of standard data is by no means limited to machine shops. It is likely to exist wherever job families exist or when parts or products occur in many sizes and types. Macrostandard data have a large field of application where short runs of custom parts and products occur. In these instances, if we attempt to determine production standards by actual measurement, the order may be completed by the time the production standard has been determined; the result will be of no value unless the identical part is reordered.

ALLOWANCES IN PRODUCTION STANDARDS

As we noted previously, allowances are commonly added to the computed normal time for delay, fatigue, and personal time. Allowances for delay and fatigue depend on the nature of the operation. They may not exist for some activities. The usual approach is to express allowances in per cent of the total available time. Thus, a 10 per cent allowance over an 8-hour (480-minute) day is the equivalent of 48 minutes.

Delay Allowances.   Delay allowances must be based on actual measurement of the magnitude of the delays. Although stopwatch study can be used, work sampling provides a much more efficient means of obtaining accurate data because delays often occur randomly. Work sampling expresses its measurement of delays directly in terms of per cent of the total available time.

Fatigue and Personal Allowances.   For some very heavy industrial jobs, a man might work 20 minutes and rest 20 minutes. This was the case for the "shake out" of poured iron castings at a well-known automotive foundry. It was a continuous operation which required the worker to break open the iron molding box containing the solidified but very hot casting. This was done over a vibrating grate, so that the molding sand could drop through to a recirulating conveyor; the casting was then conveyed to subsequent cleaning operations. The worker then placed the top half of the molding box on one overhead chain conveyor hook and the bottom half on another; each half weighed 50 pounds. The work was done under conditions of high temperature, of dust from the molding sand, and of high-noise intensity. The schedule of 20 minutes of work and 20 minutes of rest was probably none too generous. This type of very heavy work is not common today, but it occurs often enough so that there is a continuing interest in the subject of physical fatigue and rest allowances.

Unfortunately, we still lack an accepted framework for the establishment of rest allowances based on any rational or scientific measurements. In most instances, schedules of *fatigue allowances* for various types of work are used based on general acceptability and are often the subject of agreements between labor and management.

A Physiological Basis for Rest Pauses

Recent research has indicated that physiological methods of measurement hold considerable promise for the determination of workloads and optimal environmental design. One application of physiological methods that goes to the heart of the long-standing question of fatigue allowances is the work of E. A. Müller in Germany [13].

Based on his studies, Müller proposes an energy expenditure standard of 4 large calories (kcal) per minute as the maximum that the average man can expend continuously without rest. (This is an expenditure above the basal metabolism rate which Müller takes as 1 kcal per minute.) This level of energy expenditure he calls the endurance limit (EL). If the task demands more than the EL, the man must tap his energy reserve; therefore, he must take a rest pause so that his muscles can recover. Müller suggests a standard energy reserve of 24 kcal. The rest or recovery time following work is necessary if the energy reserve of 24 kcal is used up. He further relates work time and rest, or recovery time, by the statement that the average expenditure rate cannot exceed 4 large calories during the work plus resting time if the effects of fatigue are not to accumulate. For example, a task that demands 6 kcal per minute would require an average of 20 minutes of rest in an hour, or a fatigue allowance of $33\frac{1}{3}$ per cent of the total work plus resting time.

Figure 11 shows how this would work out for different levels of energy expenditure. Up to the 4-kcal rate, a man would be expected to work continuously without needing rest owing to physical fatigue. At the 6-kcal rate, however, he could work for a maximum of 12 minutes, at which time he would have used up his 24-kcal energy reserve. In order to continue work, Müller suggests that he would have to have at least 6 minutes of rest, so that the average energy expenditure for the work plus rest time, or $12 + 6 = 18$ minutes does not exceed an average of 4 kcal per minute (72 kcal $\div$ 18 = 4 kcal per minute).

Other energy expenditure levels are shown in Figure 11. For example, according to Müller's standards, a man could be expected to work at the 12-kcal rate for 3 minutes at which point he would be exhausted since his energy reserve would be used up. To keep the energy expenditure

FIGURE 11. Various patterns of energy expenditure within the endurance limit or within the energy reserve limit. (Adapted from [13].)

level from exceeding 4 kcal, he would have to rest 6 minutes following the 3 minutes of work at 12 kcal per minute. This pattern of work 3 minutes, rest 6 minutes would be required by the high energy expenditure level.

Physiologists have measured the energy costs of a large number of different activities, many of which are industrial tasks. Table IV lists, for a few of these tasks, the energy costs and the fatigue allowances (per cent of total time that is rest), using Müller's concept. This list is not meant to be a recommendation for allowances of similar job titles in business and industry, since local job conditions and duties may vary considerably from plant to plant. However, it does give an idea of how the Müller standard would operate for various widely known *types* of work. From Table IV we see that the majority of activities listed require no fatigue allowance at all, which does not mean that these activities require no personal rest allowances of any kind. It merely means that no rest allowances are necessary in order to recover from *physical* fatigue. There may be psychological factors of boredom and work monotony that would make rest allowances desirable.

The tasks that have energy costs above the EL require rest allowances for the recovery from physical fatigue or exertion beyond the EL. Thus, we see that jobs such as shoveling, various coal mining tasks, and general industrial labor require fatigue allowances according to Müller's standard. However, all types of office work, light assembly, and light machine shop work would require no allowances for fatigue.

At present, determinations of fatigue allowances are not based on measurements of energy expenditure as implied by the discussion of Müller's work, partly because suitable measurement devices for the practical business and industrial situations do not exist and partly because there has been no acceptance of Müller's or anyone else's concept of the fatigue problem.

Allowances for *personal time* provide at least a minimum of time that the worker can be away from the job. This personal time allows a break from both the physical and psychological stresses that a job may contain and is, in a sense, a minimum fatigue allowance. The minimum allowance is normally 5 per cent of the total available time.

Application of Allowances in Production Standards

The usual interpretation of the meaning of percentages allowances is that they allow a per cent of the total available time. A personal time allowance of 5 per cent translates into $0.05 \times 480 = 24$ minutes of personal time in a normal 8-hour day. If the normal time has been measured as 1.20

TABLE IV. Energy Cost and Fatigue Allowances for Various Tasks

Activity	Energy Cost,* Kcal/min, Above Basal Level	Fatigue Allowance, (per cent)
Men's activities:		
Miscellaneous office work, sitting	0.6	0
Miscellaneous office work, standing	0.8	0
Armature winding	1.2	0
Light assembly line work	0.8	0
Medium assembly line work	1.7	0
Sheet metal worker	2.0	0
Light machine work	1.4	0
Machinist	2.1	0
Plastic molding	2.3	0
Tool room worker	2.9	0
Loading chemicals into mixer	5.0	20.0
Shoveling 8-kg load, 1 m lift, 12/min	6.5	38.5
Push wheelbarrow, 57-kg load, 4.5 km/hr	4.0	0
Bricklaying	3.0	0
Mixing cement	3.7	0
Plaster lathing	2.1	0
Plastering walls	3.1	0
Coal mining:		
Hewing	6.0	33.3
Loading	6.1	34.4
Timbering	4.7	14.9
Drilling	4.8	16.7
Pushing tubs	7.0	42.8
Women's activities:		
Machine sewing, foot operated	0.43	0
Typing, electric, 40 words/min	0.31	0
Typing, mechanical, 40 words/min	0.48	0
Tool setting	2.4	0
Gaging	3.0	0
General industrial labor	4.1	2.4

*Handbook figures were adjusted to energy cost above basal level by subtracting 1 kcal/min from each rate given to conform to Muller's formulation.

Source of activities and energy cost data: William S. Spector, Editor, *Handbook of Biological Data*, WADC Technical Report 56–273, ASTIA Document No. AD 110501, Wright Air Development Center.

minutes per piece, then the personal time must be prorated properly to the normal time in computing standard time per piece:

$$\text{Standard time} = \text{normal time} \times \frac{100}{100 - \text{percentage allowance}}$$

$$= 1.20 \times \frac{100}{95} = 1.263 \text{ minutes per piece}$$

If all the allowances for delay, fatigue, and personal time are expressed as percentages of total available time, they can be added together to obtain a single total percentage allowance figure. Then standard time can be computed from normal time by a single calculation using the preceding formula.

NONMANUFACTURING APPLICATIONS

Work measurement is advancing into many nonmanufacturing activities today. Barnes [3, 4] reports examples in agriculture, education, hospitals, warehouses, and trucking; and in the larger offices it is already in common use. In fact, a system of universal standard times for office operations has been constructed. Work measurement is applicable in any situation where an appraisal of labor content needs to be made. Work sampling as a technique makes it possible to measure work in many situations where it was impractical to do so before.

SUMMARY

Work measurement methods are the formal basis for establishing standards of output for labor. These standards are of great importance in both the design and operating phases of production systems. In the design phases, performance standards are important in estimating labor costs of products and of alternative methods and in estimating required capacities for layouts. In the operation and control of production systems, labor performance standards are needed in programming and scheduling production, evaluating performance, and controlling labor costs, as well as in helping to evaluate countless operating alternatives such as make-buy and equipment replacement.

We need to face up realistically to the probable final accuracy of production standards. This accuracy cannot be better than about ± 10 per cent when we consider the precision with which trained people can rate performance. Where heavy physical work is involved, the limits of accuracy are probably greater, because there are no presently available practical means of measuring the allowance for fatigue which should be made. Recognition of the limitations of work measurement accuracy is not to damn work measurement methods but simply to recognize that the limitations exist.

REVIEW QUESTIONS

1. Why are labor standards important? How are they used?
2. Appraise standards based on foreman's estimates or past performance data.
3. Relate the problem of the determination of production standards to the problem of designing a lever that requires arm strength available in 95 per cent of the working population.
4. Define these terms: normal time, performance rating, allowances, and standard time.
5. Discuss the function of performance rating in the determination of production standards.
6. Discuss performance rating as a system of measurement. How accurate is performance rating?
7. What is the general procedure for determining standards by stopwatch methods?
8. Why is it general practice to divide a job into elements for a stopwatch study?
9. Discuss the problem of determining the adequacy of sample sizes for various elements in a stopwatch time study.
10. Outline the procedures necessary for ensuring that sample data are consistent and representative of usual operating conditions.
11. What is the fundamental principle on which work sampling is based?
12. Outline the general procedure for a work sampling study to determine the extent of delays and personal time.
13. What additional information is necessary to determine production standards completely by work sampling?
14. Compare stopwatch study and work sampling in terms of the cost to make studies, representativeness of samples taken, field of application, and comparative accuracy.
15. What is the difference between "micro" and "macro" standard data?
16. Where is judgment required in the use of standard data to determine production standards?
17. What is the current basis for fatigue allowances used in work measurement?
18. Allowances are normally expressed as a per cent of the total time available. How are they properly prorated to normal times to obtain standard time?

19. Discuss the possible range of application of work measurement techniques in manufacturing and nonmanufacturing activities.

PROBLEMS

1. Determine an elemental breakdown which might be used for a stopwatch time study of the old method of assembling bolts and washers shown in Figure 9 of Chapter 13. Justify the elemental breakdown made.

2. Select a simple assembled product for which parts can be obtained. Determine a time study elemental breakdown for the assembly of the product and time 12 cycles. Determine the adequacy of this sample size.

3. Lay out a 100-foot walking course in such a way that the total time for walking the course can be measured. Using the standard 3 mile per hour pace as 100 per cent performance, one should walk the course in 0.2785 minute. Figure 12 shows a chart that relates measured time for walking 100 feet versus per cent performance using the 3 mile per hour pace as a standard. Working in groups, have subjects walk the 100-foot course while one individual measures elapsed time. Others in the group should rate the walking pace in per cent. After observing several different walking paces, compare actual pace (from Figure 12) with rated pace. Plot the results on a graph of actual pace in per cent versus rated pace.

FIGURE 12. Actual time for walking 100 feet versus performance in per cent with 3 miles per hour used as a standard walking pace.

4. A department store manager wishes to make a work sampling study to estimate the per cent time that clerks are busy waiting on customers and the per cent time that they are idle. The current best guess is that clerks are idle 25 per cent of the time. Determine the number of observations required if we wish to be 95 per cent confident that the result is within ±1.5 percentage points.

5. You have obtained the following work sample from a study during 40-hour work week:

Idle time	20 per cent
Performance rating	135 per cent
Total parts produced	280

The allowance for this particular type of work is 10 per cent. Determine the standard time per part.

6. A time study is made of a punch-press operator, the results of which yield an average actual time per piece of 0.30 minute. The punch-press operator's performance during the study was rated at 120 per cent. If total allowances are 10 per cent of standard time, what is the standard time in minutes for this operation?

7. A continuous time study was made on a collating job in an office with the following results:

Element	Cycle (minutes)						Performance Rating (per cent)
	1	2	3	4	5	6	
Apply glycerin to fingers	0.04	—	0.46	—	3.10	—	120
Get four pages with each hand	0.16	0.35	0.63	2.99	3.24	3.45	105
Jog eight sheets	0.19	0.39	2.83*	3.04	3.28	3.49	110
Staple and put aside	0.22	0.41	2.86	3.07	3.30	3.52	90

*Operator dropped the eight sheets on the floor.

(a) Calculate the normal time per collated set.
(b) If allowances for this type of work total 15 per cent, what would be the standard time per set?
(c) Should the set of papers dropped be considered as a part of the study or should this data be thrown out? What are the implications of not considering this data in the study?

REFERENCES

[1] Abruzzi, A. *Work Measurement*. Columbia University Press, New York, 1952.

[2] Allderige, J. M. "Statistical Procedures in Stop-Watch Work Measurement." *Journal of Industrial Engineering*, **7** (4), 154–163, July–Aug. 1956.

[3] Barnes, R. M. *Motion and Time Study: Design and Measurement of Work* (6th ed.). John Wiley, New York, 1968.

[4] Barnes, R. M. *Work Sampling* (2nd ed.). John Wiley, New York, 1957.

[5] Bailey, G. B., and R. Presgrave. *Basic Motion Time-Study*. McGraw-Hill, New York, 1957.

[6] Buffa, E. S. "Time Study Rating as Measurement." *Advanced Management*, **18** (3), 1953.

[7] Buffa, E. S., and J. Lyman. "The Addivity of the Times for Human Motor Response Elements in a Simulated Industrial Assembly Task." *Journal of Applied Psychology*, **42** (2), 1958.

[8] Gustat, G. H. "Applications of Work Sampling Analysis." *Proceedings of Tenth Time Study and Methods Conference*, SAM–ASME, New York, Apr. 1955.

[9] Gustat, G. H. "Incentives for Indirect Labor." *Proceedings, Fifth Industrial Engineering Institute*, University of California, Berkeley–Los Angeles, 1953.

[10] Heiland, R. E., and W. J. Richardson. *Work Sampling*. McGraw-Hill, New York, 1957.

[11] Lifson, K. A. "A Psychological Approach to Pace Rating." Unpublished Ph.D. Dissertation, Purdue University, Lafayette, Ind., 1951.

[12] Maynard, H. B., G. J. Stegemerten, and J. L. Schwab. *Methods—Time Measurement*. McGraw-Hill, New York, 1948.

[13] Müller, E. A. "The Physiological Basis of Rest Pauses in Heavy Work." *Quarterly Journal of Experimental Physiology*, **38** (4), 1953.

[14] Mundel, M. E. *Motion and Time Study* (3rd ed.). Prentice-Hall, Englewood Cliffs, N.J., 1960.

[15] Nadler, G. *Work Design A Systems Concept* (Rev. ed.). Richard D. Irwin, Homewood, Ill., 1970.

[16] Niebel, B. W. *Motion and Time Study* (5th ed.). Richard D. Irwin, Homewood, Ill., 1972.

[17] Quick, J. H., J. H. Duncan, and J. A. Malcolm. *Work Factor Time Standards*. McGraw-Hill, New York, 1962.

part four

Operations Planning & Control

Production-Inventory Systems

The several chapters of Part 3 dealt with the design of productive systems. When such a system has been designed, we may presume that there has been a careful specification of the product or whatever it is that is being processed, a specification of the nature and sequence of the processes, and a physical design or layout that relates the processes into a unified physical system. As a part of the system, jobs must be designed to fit into the needs of the processes and flow of work, and consideration must be given to the question of the location of the system.

Now, however, we shall concern ourselves with the design of information systems, policies, and control procedures necessary to operate the system. Thus Part 4 is concerned with such questions as these: What policies and procedures will guide us in setting basic production rates? Should we hire or layoff personnel and in what numbers? When is the use of overtime justified instead of increasing the size of the work force? When should we take the risk of accumulating seasonal inventories to stabilize employment? How big should inventories be to sustain the production-distribution process? What policies and procedures are appropriate for the control of inventories and the reordering of materials? What policies and procedures are necessary to schedule men and machines for effective operations? Should the utilization of men and machines be maximized or is there a value to idleness? How do we maintain the reliability of the productive system so that specified quantity and quality are produced? When is a preventive maintenance policy justified? What policies and procedures can be effective in controlling labor and other costs? Is it possible to control *costs*, or is it really the activities that must be controlled?

These and other important questions are the focus of Part 4. In some instances there are rigorous models to help guide decisions and policies such as in aggregate planning and scheduling, inventories, maintenance, and quality control. In other situations, policies and procedures are systematic but thus far not accessible by the newer analytical methods such as in labor and cost control programs.

Before proceeding, let us again recognize that there are extremely important problems in the operation and control of most productive systems, related to human values, supervision of personnel, selection of personnel, and organizational behavior, which are not covered in this book. Although we recognize these behaviorally oriented problems, in this book we have established a more limited definition of operating problems. Students should seek other books and courses for the behavioral orientation.

A SYSTEMS POINT OF VIEW

Let us begin our analysis of operating problems by returning to the basic schematic diagram for the generalized model of operational systems shown in Figure 1. Figure 1 is identical to Figure 4 in Chapter 3, and a general review of the discussion on pages 51–57 is appropriate at this point. Figure 1 shows general relationships between the operations function and six crucial flows: information, orders, materials or energy, cash, populations, and capital equipment. The major reason for focusing our attention on Figure 1 again is to begin our discussion of operating problems in a "systems" context. While we shall discuss the several major topics of Chapters 16–22 separately, it is important that we see some of the interrelationships between them.

Interdependence
of Functions

Of course, the operations phase of the organization is our focus, yet we must maintain a systems viewpoint with regard to the interdependence of operations functions and other functions such as marketing, finance, personnel, purchasing, and the professional or service function. Note in Figure 1 the existence of pools of labor, materials and energy, equipment, external services, and financing. These pools exist in the environment and there is, of course, interaction between our enterprise and competitive enterprises in drawing on these pools of supply.

When we attempt to structure the problems of operations management, reality demands that we consider not only the complex interactions of the factors internal to the operations phase but, where appropriate, the interactions between the operations phase and other functions as well as their interactions with the environment systems. Thus, the planning of production rates, size of work force, use of overtime, and planned inventories (commonly called aggregate planning and scheduling) demands a model that accounts for some of these "between subsystems" interactions in setting production rates and employment levels for the upcoming period. The first, and perhaps most obvious,

FIGURE 1. General model for operational systems—basic schematic diagram. (From Reisman and Buffa [6].)

environment factor is consumer demand where we are in direct competition with other enterprises. Part of the aggregate planning model must include a forecast as well as the feedback of information on our actual orders flow. The production rate and employment level decisions are also dependent on interactions with the labor pool (since the decisions may call for either hiring or layoff), on the raw material and equipment pools to facilitate the production rate decisions, and on the financing pool (since the decision may call for the accumulation or drawing down of inventories). The coordination with other functional subsystems is parallel; that is, marketing in the forecast problem, purchasing in the equipment and raw material problem, personnel in the manpower problem, and finance in the inventory, payroll, and purchasing problems.

The power of system analysis is in the development of the structure of interactions between a number of elements in a system. To develop an effective model for aggregate planning, for example, we do not have to develop a detailed model for all coordinating subfunctions. We need only to represent the resulting interacting effects. Thus we do not need a detailed model of the personnel-manpower pool complex to reflect its effects on the aggregate planning problem just because we may hire or layoff personnel. We can abstract just the parts that are meaningful to the problem at hand. For example, because of union agreements the layoff rate may be limited to a certain number of men or a certain per cent of the work force. Or, because of the competition for labor in the pool, wages may have gone up. This fact needs to be reflected in the aggregate planning model because that model will be attempting to balance certain kinds of costs. As long as we relate the interdependencies of the various organizational functions, we shall be utilizing a true systems point of view. Retaining this viewpoint is difficult in complex organizational problems, but it is important to attempt to do so to the greatest extent possible.

If it were possible we might like to construct a single model of the operational system within the framework of Figure 1 which would forecast the operation of any production system, given the characteristics of the system and the various related subsystems. This is much too ambitious at the present stage of development of the analysis operational systems. Currently, we must be satisfied with models that usually account for only small parts of the problem. Maintaining the systems point of view helps to minimize the effects of *suboptimization*; that is, the best solution viewed from within the subsystem but not the best solution when viewed within the system as a whole. In general, our present capability does not permit the strict adherence to this systems point of view. In attempting to approach it, however, we shall endeavor to apply this principle: models of operations should be as broad as practicable, taking into account (insofar as is feasible by means of existing techniques) interactions between various subsystems. The result is that whenever such a model has been reasonably validated and indicates incremental gains which exceed incremental costs, we shall assume that the systems point of view has been approached.

Because of its importance, let us expand somewhat on suboptimization. It can and does occur in many ways. We could easily suboptimize by taking a short-range view of maximizing profits or an organizational narrow gage view. A short-range view might cause a production manager to produce according to the rise and fall of the sales curve. With a broader horizon he would look for trends and seasonal variations and develop a production program to meet requirements over the longer term. The latter view might stabilize production levels, causing higher total inventory costs but substantially lower hiring and layoff costs. The short-range view would be a suboptimization, since it focuses only on the payroll cost but ignores the long-time effects and costs of production fluctuation and inventories.

Suboptimization

Organizational suboptimization is common where the production function and the distribution function are operated essentially as two separate businesses. The factory, then, will try to minimize its costs independently, as will the sales and distribution function. Thus sales and distribution will be faced mainly with inventory management, shipping, and customer service problems and will try to minimize the associated costs. On the other hand, the factory will be faced with minimizing production cost. Each suborganization, optimizing separately, probably will result in a combined cost somewhat larger than if the attempt were made to optimize the combined system as a whole. The reasons are fairly obvious. In minimizing the costs of inventories, the sales function will transmit directly to the factory most of the effects of sales fluctuation instead of absorbing these fluctuations through buffer inventories; suboptimization is the result. By coordinating their plans and efforts, however, it may be possible to achieve some balance between inventory costs and production fluctuation costs.

SYSTEM CONTROL

The elements of the control of a productive system are shown in Figure 2. While there may be many different aspects of operation to consider, the general control process is the same regardless of which particular factor is being controlled. Figure 2 is generalized in terms of a measure-

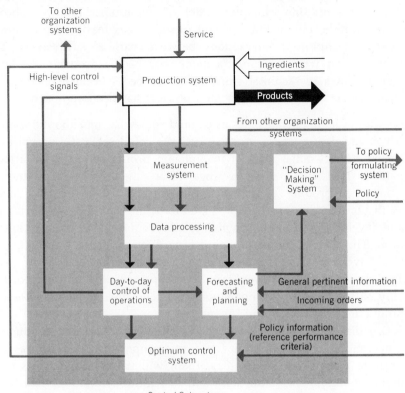

FIGURE 2. General structure of control systems in relation to a production system. (From [1].)

ment system, data processing, day-to-day control, forecasting and planning, and so on. While Figure 2 is generalized in structure, let us discuss it in terms of an example, the control of inventories.

Our objective is to control the level of finished goods inventories. To do this we must set standards for inventory levels and procedures for maintaining them. This is represented in Figure 2 by the block "day-to-day control of operations." These standards for inventory control involve some kind of model for relating reordering or replenishment procedures, relevant costs, and policies regarding the desired level of customer service, that is, a desired level of risk of stock runout. Control models for inventories are discussed in Chapter 16. Day-to-day control is based on measurements concerning the actual level of inventories which are channeled through data processing for any required computing or transformation and compared to the standards in the model. The standards in the model may signal reordering a standard quantity if inventories have fallen below a preset order point, or the model may call for the computation of the amount to be ordered each period based on actual demand and other factors. Thus we have a basic day-to-day feedback control loop which takes action to readjust inventories.

On a longer time base, however, "forecasting and planning" is assessing the changing level of demand to determine if the standards for control should be changed. Based on new information concerning demand, the ordering rules may be changed as well as the amount of reserve or safety stock. Thus the day-to-day control model and the new information from forecasting and planning are inputs to the "optimum control system." The optimum control system then automatically responds to both day-to-day needs and longer time shifts in demand. Other policy information may be pertinent to the adjustment of the optimum control system. For example, a policy to establish a stabilized work force will allow relatively large inventory accumulations in slack demand periods and their reduction to near minimum levels in high demand periods. Control of other aspects of the system follows the same pattern. In general the controls of interest to us are those associated with the control over the amounts produced or quantity control, control over quality, and cost control.

Quantity Control

The control over quantities produced is not exercised by simply setting production rates. There is a complex interaction between actual demand and its forecasted pattern, production rates, and the size of the work force. The amount to produce in the upcoming planning period depends on the use of the most economical combination of equivalent capacities (such as existing inventories, regular production, overtime production, and additional production due to an increased work force size) in relation to some reasonable time horizon for demand. If we see ahead in the planning time horizon an annual seasonal demand slump, then the comparative costs of laying off some workers must be balanced against carrying excess inventories into the seasonal slump. Production rates and layoff decisions depend on the combination of equivalent capacities which minimizes these combined costs. Similarly, if we see ahead in the planning time horizon the seasonal demand peak, then the comparative costs of hiring workers and using overtime must be balanced against the costs of back-ordering and lost sales. Production rate and hiring decisions depend on the combination of capacities that minimizes these costs. Basic production rate and employment level decisions are of great importance; we shall consider them in greater detail in Chapter 17. The existence of inventories in the system, of course, has an impact on production rate and employment decisions; inventory models and policies are the subjects of Chapter 16.

The effective implementation of basic aggregate plans for production largely depends on how men and machines are actually utilized; that is, how these resources are scheduled and controlled. In continuous production systems, changes in basic production rate and employment levels called for by the aggregate plan require a rebalancing of facilities and assembly lines to adjust to the new employment level and match the new output rates. In intermittent production systems the detailed scheduling problem is much more complex since materials are moved through the facility in lots. General-purpose equipment is usually used in intermittent systems, and many different orders compete for and share the time available on such equipment. Thus, for each lot or order, machines must be set up especially and workers assigned to operate them. In addition to the scheduling problem, an information system must be established to feed back current information on the status of orders so that operations can be controlled. For large-scale projects the activities required may be planned, scheduled, and controlled as a network of activities. These scheduling and control problems are covered in Chapters 18, 19, and 20.

Finally, in terms of quantity control, the designs of both maintenance and quality control procedures are important. Both sets of procedures have an impact on the control of output levels since both are concerned with maintaining the reliability of the physical system. If equipment is not maintained in good working order, there will be interference with attaining the planned production quotas. If machines break down, they cause idle labor costs, sometimes for an entire production line. Thus preventive maintenance programs are often economical. Quality control procedures also have an effect on the attainment of production quotas. When production quotas are planned they are, of course, for output that meets quality standards, not scrap. The special problems of maintenance and quality control are the subjects of Chapters 21 and 22, respectively.

Quality Control   The control of quality is based originally on the design of processes and the selection of equipment. The basic quality capabilities must be designed into the system. But, given these basic capabilities, the desired quality levels are controlled by selecting and training personnel, maintaining the physical plant and its equipment, controlling the quality requirements of incoming raw materials, and controlling the quality characteristics of the output of individual processes and of the system as a whole. As just discussed under quantity control, machine breakdown can have important effects on schedules and idle labor costs. But, one cause of breakdowns can be failure to produce according to the established quality standards, so maintenance of the reliability of the system refers both to quantity and quality of output.

The techniques of quality control are largely centered in inspection methods and statistical control methods. The statistical control methods are of particular interest since they have broad application for probabilistic controls generally. The statistical methods fall into two main groups, acceptance sampling and process control. Acceptance sampling can determine the probability that the entire batch or lot of materials meets quality standards on the basis of a sample. Process control involves a continuous or periodic sampling of the output of a process to check if quality standards are within limits. The established control limits are based on probabilities. Therefore, when a sample falls outside of control limits, the probability is high that action is needed. Conversely, as long as samples fall within control limits, the probability is low that poor quality is being produced in any meaningful amount. Process control is truly management by the exception principle. Quality control as a general subject and acceptance sampling and process control in particular are discussed in Chapter 22.

Cost Control

As we noted previously the currency given the term *cost control* is in a sense not justified. Costs are a result and a function of the activities involved. If the activities are properly controlled, then the resulting costs are controlled. The simple reason for this is that most of the models of managerial systems discussed throughout this book have cost-related criterion functions. When we establish control of the activities on the basis of these criterion functions, we control costs. Nevertheless, the term *cost control* has a more specific meaning which has to do with the periodic generation of important cost figures and their organization to provide data on which many important decisions can be made to control activities and therefore costs.

CLASSIFICATION OF PRODUCTION-INVENTORY SYSTEMS

It is useful to establish a general classification of production-inventory systems at this point rather than to continue discussing such systems in general. The reason for wishing to be more specific about particular kinds of production-inventory systems is that the nature of the most important operating problems is quite different for different systems. We shall establish two bases of calssification: (a) continuous versus intermittent systems, and (b) the production of inventoriable versus noninventoriable items.

Continuous
versus
Intermittent
Systems

The continuous-intermittent basis of classification was used in discussing models of production systems in Chapter 2. Continuous systems were typified there by the production lines, continuous chemical processes, and, in general, by production systems of enterprises that produce the high-volume standardized products for which our society is noted. The basis for the term *continuous*, however, is that the physical flow of material in production is either continuous or approaches continuous movement. On the other hand, intermittent production systems are those where the physical facilities must be flexible enough to handle a wide variety of products and sizes, or where the basic nature of the activity imposes changes of product design from time to time. In such instances, no single sequence pattern of processes is appropriate so the relative location of the operations must be a compromise that is best for all products. The emphasis is on flexibility of product design, processes, flow paths through the system, and so on. The system is termed "intermittent" because the flow is intermittent. Intermittent systems are characterized by custom or job order-type machine shops, batch-type chemical operations, general offices, large-scale one-time projects, etc.

The basis of the continuous-intermittent classification is then the basic nature of the physical layout of facilities in the *production system*. We now wish to broaden our conception of what constitutes the system to include the supply of raw materials at the head end and the distribution of finished goods at the output end of the manufacturing phase. Thus, the term *production-inventory system* for the expanded concept includes the inventories throughout and suggests the second basis for classification.

Systems for
Inventoriable
versus
Noninventoriable
Items

Figure 3 is a diagram of a production-inventory system for an inventoriable product. It emphasizes the broad flow characteristics of the system as a whole. In Figure 3, the manufacturing phase could be either continuous or intermittent. Of course, many intermittent manufacturing systems produce to inventory. Such plants may be physically arranged and scheduled internally like job shops. Common situations where this is true are the machine shops of the large automotive companies. Such shops are closed to job order from outside the organization

FIGURE 3. Supply-production-distribution system for an inventoriable product. Time lags are characteristic between and within each stage, and inventories serve vital functions at each stage.

and may produce a set of products repetitively in cycles. Equipment is time-shared between many different products, and the products are produced to inventory because they are of standard designs for which there are predictable markets. Such intermittent shops are called closed job shops because they are closed to job order.

Thus, we may have production-inventory systems in the inventoriable classification whose physical configuration may be of the continuous as well as the intermittent types. Now if we refer again to Figure 3, we may find a commonly occurring enterprise specialization in the distribution of products. These enterprises specialize in the distribution of products and are called simply "distributors." The portion of Figure 3 under managerial control for distribution systems focuses attention mainly on inventories. The operations phase of such enterprises has to do with the replenishment of inventories, the control of inventory levels, and shipment. Service rendered may be judged in terms of frequency of stockout or inability to supply the demands for products from inventories. Distribution systems are nearly pure inventory systems from an operations management viewpoint and are of interest simply because they are common in society. Chapter 16 is devoted to inventories and inventory models. Thus, production-inventory systems for inventoriable items include systems where production is continuous, systems where production may be intermittent, and systems involving only distribution. Grouping systems involving inventoriable items together is of importance because we can use inventories effectively in aggregate planning and programming as discussed in Chapter 17.

Custom products and services require production-inventory systems that have no finished goods inventories. They may still be characterized by the term production-inventory system, however, because they have raw material and in-process inventories which are subject to control in some measure. Open job shops and large-scale one-time projects are the most prominent examples. The open job shop produces to job order or contract. These orders or contracts may never be repeated so the requirement for flexibility is an overriding one. The focus of managerial attention is on the scheduling and utilization of men and machines to meet agreed due dates and quality standards. The difference between the open job shop and the large-scale project in our classification is largely one of scale and complexity. There is no clear dividing line between the two systems, except that when a contract is large enough and complex enough to justify the special PERT-type planning and scheduling techniques discussed in Chapter 20, it is called a large-scale project.

A Comparison
To summarize, the continuous-intermittent classification results in the following:

Continuous Systems	Intermittent Systems
Production-inventory systems for high-volume standardized products Distribution systems	Job shops (open and closed) Large-scale projects

This classification is most useful for designing the layout of physical facilities and for indicating the nature of detailed scheduling of both men and machines.

The inventoriable-noninventoriable item classification results in the following:

Systems for Inventoriable Items	Systems for Noninventoriable Items
Continuous high-volume standardized product systems Closed job shop systems Distribution systems	Open job shop systems Large-scale projects

This classification is most useful in determining the nature of aggregate planning and programming that is appropriate. The production-inventory system concept is also useful in focussing on the system as a whole to avoid the organization suboptimization to which we referred earlier. When one takes an integrated view of materials flow, it is possible to see more clearly which alternatives for organizing enterprise functions might be most effective.

ORGANIZING FOR INTEGRATED MATERIAL FLOW

It is often difficult to conceive of the overall flow of material and information that directly or indirectly affects total system costs. In most instances, the system extends at least to the immediate supplier of raw materials, and it is entirely feasible that it could extend further upstream than the immediate supplier. Suppliers' modes of distribution may well affect costs for the overall system being considered. Similarly, the total system extends downstream through production phases to and including finished product distribution as indicated by Figure 3. Such a total systemic view may well involve many separate organizations. It is undoubtedly fair to say that a total integrated analysis of such tremendously complex systems is still not really practical for day-to-day operation, although the computer simulation of such large-scale systems holds considerable promise.

The long-run trend in job specialization commented on in Chapter 13 on job design has had a parallel in overall enterprise organization. As organizations have grown, the multitude of functions which must be performed tends to split off into various divisions, departments, and groups. With this fragmentation comes an apparent need for specialists within the organization. Each specialist tends to assume his role and become more proficient in carrying out his duties. The larger the organization the greater is the degree of specialization and the greater the tendency to lose track of the overall organization objectives and to concentrate on strengthening the individual function. Since the specialist's functions are limited in scope, he drives for success through suboptimization, for example, minimizing his own costs on a local basis. Since his performance is judged on a local basis, he finds it to his advantage to attempt to influence policies and practices wherever possible which will make his own local unit look good. The defect is not in the psychology of an individual who reacts this way to his environment, but in the organization structure which constrains him. The point is that an overall system view would encourage just the opposite effect.

It would encourage a balancing of interdepartmental advantage and disadvantage to seek a system optimum. While it may be true that overall system analysis may still not be capable of handling this problem, organization structures can be designed to help minimize suboptimization. Following is a brief report of a case study in reorganization to achieve better integrated control.

The *Purex Corporation* [2] had the basic organization structure illustrated by Figure 4 prior to a study which had the objective of reorganization to obtain a more integrated control. Many of the material flow functions were fragmented and responsibility was divided between several major departments. In the old organization a traffic manager was responsible for arranging transportation of outbound products from major production plants to warehouses and other distribution points. The production planning function was handled by informal committees with members from sales, manufacturing, and finance. The warehousing function was handled by the sales department as was the inventory control function. Managers of some smaller plants reported to the financial function.

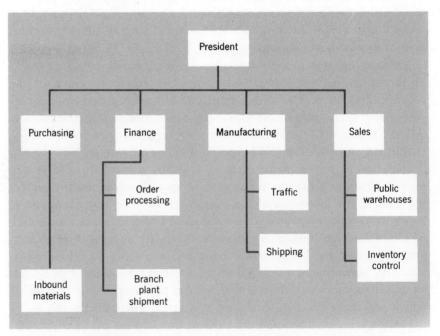

FIGURE 4. Organization of Purex Corporation prior to adoption of an integrated material flow concept. (From [2].)

These plants produced liquid bleach throughout the country and handled some warehousing of finished products produced at other major production facilities. Shipping of finished products from these plants was the responsibility of the plant manager and, as a result, the lines of authority for these functions emanated from the vice-president for finance. Some functional authority was exercised by the traffic manager because it was his duty to furnish routing guides and transportation rates. Inasmuch as the sales department was responsible for inventory control and maintenance of inventories at regional public warehouses, it also exercised some control over shipments from these facilities. The purchasing function was responsible for control of all procurement of raw material and supplies; however, order processing was a function of finance. There was no attempt to exercise overall control of the material flow process.

A reorganization of the activities and functions resulted in the structure shown in Figure 5. A number of important functions governing the flow of materials are placed under the jurisdiction of a director of distribution and materials flow. He has direct line authority over traffic, overall production planning, inventory control, and distribution services. Regional traffic managers report directly to him; in addition, he has functional control over the distribution function at the various branch plants. Since these branch plants now report directly to the

FIGURE 5. Organization of Purex Corporation for control of material flows after adoption of the integrated concept. (Adapted from [2].)

director of production, who in turn reports to the vice-president of manufacturing and research, this functional authority achieves line status because the distribution and materials flow director can exercise a great deal of control over all activities affecting material movement at the branch plant level. Direct line authority over inventory control now gives him the power he needs to control movement both into and out of public warehouses located throughout the country. Although it is not shown on the chart of Figure 5, the director of distribution and materials flow also works closely with the director of purchasing in controlling inbound shipments of raw materials and supplies.

It is reported that the new organizational structure has effected many benefits to the company, resulting in estimated cost reductions of several hundred thousand dollars. Public warehouses have been reduced in number from 65 to 35. More efficient management controls are now exercised over inventories and production planning, and integrated management of many functions related to the flow process is being exercised.

It may be interesting to contrast the material flow process in rather different kinds of organizations. The Purex Corporation is primarily concerned with outbound movements of finished goods. It has more than 200 finished products that must be distributed from several plants and warehouses to wholesalers and retailers throughout the country. The inbound materials are few in number and consist primarily of bulk shipments of chemicals, oils, etc. A contrasting situation would be one involving a complex assembled product with relatively few customers; for example, the Boeing Airplane Company [2]. In the Boeing Company, the primary concern is inbound and internal movement of more than 100,000 different parts and the raw materials required for the production of each airplane. The inbound materials and parts are drawn from nearly every state in the country and, in general, each individual shipment is small. The end product is normally flown away by the customer. Distribution activities are normally concerned with spare parts which must be moved to a limited number of airline companies and military organizations. The Boeing Company is in general production-oriented; however, sales is an important activity. Purex, however, might be considered sales-oriented with production playing a vital role.

The general orientation of these two companies is indeed quite opposite. Transportation costs alone in the Purex Company amount to more than $8,000,000 per year, or approximately 10 per cent of the sales dollar. In the Boeing Company, on the other hand, transportation costs are a fraction of 1 per cent of sales. Traffic and distribution in the

Purex Corporation are of extreme importance, whereas in the Boeing Company, traffic plays a minor role. Nevertheless, the overall material-control problems in the two organizations are very great. In both instances, an organization structure which accommodates an integrated view of the material flow from supplier to ultimate consumer would contribute to a system optimum.

SUMMARY

The term *production-inventory system* places emphasis on the fact that we are dealing with the total supply-production-distribution system, not just the physical production system. There are interfunctional dependencies in the organization which must be taken into account, such as interactions between production, marketing, finance, procurement, and so on. There are also time lags in the overall flow process which place emphasis on the dynamic nature of the system. While we may most easily think in terms of the physical flow, Figure 1 traces six different flows of importance. Information flow is of crucial value in setting managerial controls over quantity, quality, and costs.

We have established two bases of classifying production-inventory systems: (a) continuous versus intermittent systems and (b) systems that produce for inventories versus those that do not. The continuous-intermittent basis is most useful when considering the problems of physical layout and detailed scheduling of activities. The inventoriable-noninventoriable basis of classification is most useful when considering the problems of aggregate planning and programming.

An operations management point of view requires us not only to look at the inventory and the material flow of processes within the manufacturing phase, but to examine the overall system of flow from suppliers of raw material through manufacturing and distribution and ultimate delivery to users. When the total system is not viewed as an integrated whole, organizational fragmentation can occur which is likely to lead to each organizational unit establishing policies and practices which may not be the best ones for the system as a whole. The Purex study indicates that basic organization structure can help promote an integrated system viewpoint. The concepts of "integrated material flow management" also require that we look at not just the production unit separately or the distribution of products separately but also the combined production-distribution system which is in effect. The objective in such a situation is to minimize total system costs rather than certain costs taken separately.

REVIEW QUESTIONS

1. Using Figure 1 as a frame of reference, discuss the interdependence of functions in the context of some particular control problem of your choice.

2. What is meant by the term "suboptimization"? What is organizational suboptimization?

3. Discuss the generalized structure of control subsystems using quality control as an example.

4. What is the value of classifying production-inventory systems on the basis of continuous versus intermittent flow?

5. What is the value of classifying production-inventory systems on the basis of whether or not the system is producing for inventory?

6. What is a closed job shop system? Open job system?

7. Discuss the supply-production-distribution system diagrammed in Figure 3. What problems of supply tend to interact with production and distribution? What problems of production tend to interact with problems of supply and distribution? What problems of distribution tend to interact with problems of supply and production?

8. Compare the concepts of job specialization with those of managerial specialization as indicated in the original organization of the Purex Corporation.

9. Compare the new organization of the Purex Corporation with the generalized supply-production-distribution system diagrammed in Figure 3. Has the new organization structure made it possible to take a more integrated point of view for the system as a whole?

10. Figure 6 shows an organization chart of the transport division of the Boeing Airplane Company. More than 100,000 different parts, pieces, and raw materials go into the production of each airplane. When completed, the plane is flown away by the customer. Spare parts supply is an important function for both the military and for airlines. Propose and justify an organization plan directed at integrated planning and control where a total system viewpoint is in effect.

11. Select some organization, for example, a company known to you, and classify it according to the five classes of production-inventory systems discussed in the chapter. It would be preferable to select a system which might not be the pure form of any of the five discussed in the text. Develop a flow diagram similar to Figure 3 identifying the major raw-material, in-process, and finished-good stock points. Estimate the order and delivery times for the major links in the system. Describe the inventory replenishment rules used at each point. What portion of the overall system is under managerial control? Indicate by drawing a boundary around the system. If management could extend control up- and downstream in terms of ordering and replenishment of inventories, what would be accomplished?

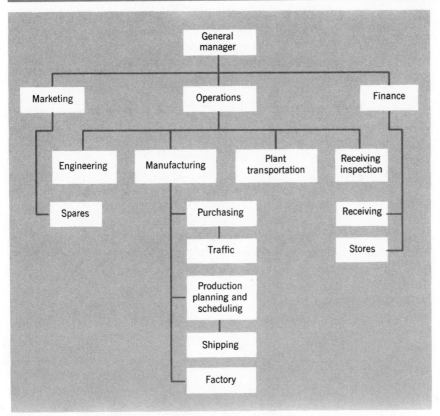

FIGURE 6. Present organization of transport division, Boeing Airplane Company. (From [2].)

12. Assume the following classifications of inventories: raw materials, in process, and finished goods. Compare the magnitude of each of these subinventory problems with respect to each of the five production-inventory systems discussed in the text.

13. Broaden the definition of the term of *inventory* to mean any productive resource which is stored for later use. Now reconsider each of the five production-inventory systems discussed in the text and discuss which productive resources might be stored and under what conditions.

REFERENCES

[1] *Alcalay, J. A., and E. S. Buffa. "A Proposal for a General Model of a Production System." *International Journal of Production Research*, Mar. 1963.

*The starred items are also reprinted in their entirety in: *Readings in Production and Operations Management*. E. S. Buffa, editor. John Wiley, New York, 1966.

[2] Brewer, S. H., and J. Rosenzweig. "Rhochrematics and Organization." *California Management Review*, **3** (3), Spring 1961.

[3] Buffa, E. S., and W. H. Taubert. *Production—Inventory Systems: Planning and Control* (Rev. ed.). Richard D. Irwin, Homewood, Ill., 1972.

[4] Fey, W. R. "An Industrial Dynamics Case Study." *Industrial Management Review*, **4** (1), Fall 1962.

[5] Forrester, J. *Industrial Dynamics*. MIT Press, Cambridge, Mass., 1961.

[6] *Reisman, A., and E. S. Buffa. "A General Model for Production and Operations Systems." *Management Science*, **11** (1), Sept. 1964.

[7] Schoderbek, P. P. *Management Systems* (2nd ed.). John Wiley, New York, 1971.

[8] *Starr, M. K. "Evolving Concepts in Production Management." In: *Evolving Concepts in Management*. E. Flippo, editor. Academy of Management Proceedings, 24th Annual Meeting, Dec. 1964.

[9] Symkay, E. W. "Physical—Distribution Management: Concepts, Methods, and Organizational Approaches." In: *New Concepts in Manufacturing Management*, AMA Management Report No. 60, New York, 1961.

16

Forecasting & Inventories

Which production plan will meet sales requirements? What effect will the plan have on inventory levels? On manpower levels? On capacity requirements? What sort of service must we provide for? Do we dare run out of stock? What level of stock runout protection should we provide for? How should we control these inventories? Should we buy raw materials hand-to-mouth or in large lots? How big should the manufacturing lots be; that is, should we make 10, 50, 100, or 1000 at a time? Given an overall plan for production, how should we adjust production levels when actual sales patterns deviate from forecasts? How about detailed scheduling of departments and machines? How can we schedule to get the best utilization from men and machines without risk of tons of in-process inventories? How can we schedule to get orders through the production system on time? Are there common answers to all of these questions for both the intermittent and continuous models of production systems? An organization that has good answers to all of these questions is probably doing a good job in planning and controlling inventories and production.

Production plans occur at several levels and we should take a moment to distinguish between them. The broadest level of production plans deals with the initial design of the entire system. Here we are making plans that may set basic patterns for years to come in terms of location and general modes of production as well as more detailed methods, equipment, and layout. We have dealt with these problems in Part 3, and we have referred to that section as the *Design of the Production System* to distinguish it from the day-to-day, month-to-month, and even year-to-year planning for production to meet the immediate, shorter-term objectives and goals. We shall use the term *planning* to refer to the activities required for operation of the system. Of course, redesign of the system may be required periodically to keep up with production technology and changes in product design and product mixes.

Within the scope of planning for production, we may have relatively long-term plans concerning how we shall employ facilities. These plans, based on anticipated demands, may include the addition of capacity in the future. But in the shorter term, we must plan master schedules and inventory levels. In the shortest term, we must plan the material needs for individual parts and products, determine how each item will be processed, and schedule equipment and manpower for all parts and products in a manner which dovetails so that men, material, and machines are available at the right time and in the amounts needed.

INVENTORIES

The Functions of Inventories

In a sense, inventories make possible a rational production system. Without them we could not achieve smooth production flow, obtain reasonable utilization of machines and reasonable material handling costs, or expect to give reasonable service to customers on hundreds of items regarded as "stock" items. At each stage of both manufacturing and distribution, inventories serve the vital function of *decoupling* the various operations in the sequence beginning with raw materials, extending through all of the manufacturing operations and into finished goods storage, and continuing to warehouses and retail stores. Between each pair of activities in this sequence, inventories make the required operations independent enough of each other that low-cost operations can be carried out. Thus, when raw materials are ordered, a supply is ordered that is large enough to justify the out-of-pocket cost of putting through the order and transporting it to the plant. When production orders to manufacture parts and products are released, we try to make them big enough to justify the cost of writing the orders and setting up machines to perform the required operations. Otherwise, order writing and setup costs could easily become prohibitive. Running parts through the system in lots also tends to reduce handling costs because parts can be handled in groups. Similarly, in distributing finished products to warehouses and other stock points, freight and handling costs per unit go down if we can ship in quantity. Inventories are not only desirable, they are vital to low-cost manufacture.

These advantages are partially lost when we are dealing with custom manufacture. Because the lot size is dictated by the customer's order and the order may never be repeated, we cannot risk making extras. Thus, order writing, material-handling, and machine setup costs are just as high for the custom-sized lot as for an economically sized lot. Similarly, when the custom job is shipped to the customer, we cannot take advantage of carload or truckload freight rates. If the custom order were for only one part, all of these charges must be absorbed by the single part. It is easy to see why low-volume special orders are exceedingly expensive.

Unfortunately, the inventory question is not a one-sided one, which is precisely why inventories are a problem in the operation of a production system. If there were not an optimal level to shoot for, there would be no problem. Anyone could follow the simple rule: "make inventories as big as possible." Inventories require that invested capital be tied up and, therefore, there is an appropriate opportunity cost associated with their value. Not only that, they require valuable space and absorb insurance and taxation charges. It is not uncommon for a manufacturing concern to have 25 per cent of its total invested capital tied up in inventories. Table I shows figures for a sample of companies where we see that inventories were as low as 9 per cent for Interstate Bakeries and as high as 55 per cent for Pillsbury Mills.

TABLE I. Inventories in Relation to Total Assets for Several Companies

Company	Date	Total Assets	Inventories	Inventories as a Per cent of Assets
Abbott Laboratories	Dec. 31, 1969	$345,382,000	$77,540,000	23
Allied Supermarkets	June 28, 1969	221,313,276	61,062,034	28
Eastman Kodak	Dec. 27, 1970	3,042,793,000	577,514,000	19
Interstate Bakeries	Dec. 27, 1969	78,203,372	7,263,890	9
Lockheed Aircraft	Dec. 29, 1968	936,783,000	285,707,000	31
Merck & Co.	Dec. 31, 1970	634,378,334	92,376,367	15
Pillsbury Mills	May 31, 1969	139,117,657	76,079,744	55
U.S. Steel	Dec. 31, 1970	3,450,149,776	923,458,156	27
John Wiley & Sons	Apr. 30, 1971	29,549,028	12,201,665	41

The significance of the inventory problem is indicated by the inventory changes of Eastman Kodak and U.S. Steel between 1966 and 1970. In 1966 Kodak had 25 per cent of its assets in inventories which had declined to 19 per cent by 1970, representing a $36 million cost saving at a carrying cost of 20 per cent. In the same period U.S. Steel's inventories increased from 23 to 27 per cent resulting in an increased cost of carrying inventories of almost $26 million if carrying costs are computed at 20 per cent of inventory value.

Thus, we have one set of costs that are fixed by the purchase or production order size and another set of costs that increase with the level of inventory. The first set of costs exerts pressure toward large purchase and production lots to reduce unit order writing and setup costs to a reasonable level. The second set of costs exerts pressure toward small lots in order to maintain inventory costs at reasonable levels. We are dealing with another problem which requires that good management find policies and decision rules which have the effect of balancing the various opposing costs for the system being considered.

Kinds of
Inventories

To see the various kinds of inventories that might be appropriate for analytical purposes, let us take as an example the simple factory-warehouse system shown in Figure 1. The factory manufactures a number of products, but we shall consider only one. For this particular product, there is an average demand at the warehouse of 200 units per week. Normal warehousing procedures are to prepare a procurement order to the factory when the warehouse inventory falls to a critical

FIGURE 1. Simple factory-warehouse system.

level called the *order point*. It takes one week to prepare the order, get it approved and mailed, and finally received at the factory. Once the order is received at the factory, it takes two weeks for loading, trucking, and unloading at the warehouse.

Pipeline Inventories.   The warehouse must, at a minimum, carry enough stock on hand to meet demand during the transit time. Figure 2 shows an idealized graph of the inventories required at the warehouse just to cover trucking time from the factory. The average transit inventory is the product of the truck time and the demand rate, or 2 × 200 = 400 units. At all times, then, 400 units are in motion from the factory to the warehouse or, in an equivalent sense, the warehouse must maintain an inventory that takes account of this fact. The order time delay of one week has the effect of a transit time, since the warehouse must also carry inventories to cover this delay. This point is a general one. Every lag in the system generates the need for inventory to fill the pipeline. Inside a production system we call it in-process inventory.

Lot Size or "Cycle" Inventories.   Let us return to our example. Since the truck is to make the trip from the factory to the warehouse, a logical question is how many to truck at one time. Most costs of trucking will occur anyway, and this is true of the costs of preparing the requisition and the other clerical costs involved. We shall not attempt to answer the question of what the lot size should be in this instance, but the general question will be discussed at a later point. Let us assume

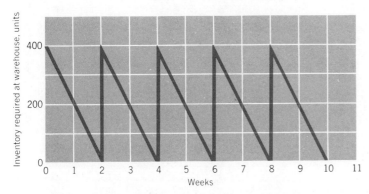

FIGURE 2.   Idealized graph of inventories required at the warehouse to cover trucking time from the factory. The average transit inventory is the product of truck time and demand rate, or 2 × 200 = 400 units. Average inventory at the warehouse is 400/2 = 200 units.

that orders are placed for a truckload of 800 units, equivalent to a four-week supply. Figure 3 shows an idealized graph of inventories required at the warehouse when orders are placed for a truckload. We see that the average inventory at the warehouse must necessarily increase.

Buffer Inventories. Figure 3 is, of course, completely unrealistic because it assumes that demand rate, truck time, and order time are all constant. We know, however, that these factors are not ordinarily constant, so a buffer stock is normally required to protect against unpredictable variations in demand and supply time. Figure 4 shows the contrast in inventory levels at the warehouse which might occur if the maximum demand of 300 units per week occurred during the supply time of three weeks. In order to not run out of stock, a buffer inventory of 300 units would be required. As we shall see, techniques for taking account of uncertainty are of great importance in inventory models.

Decoupling Inventories. Previously we referred to the decoupling function of inventories. Inventories make the required operations independent enough of each other so that low-cost operations can be carried out. For example, with inventories the warehousing operation in Figure 1 can proceed relatively independently of manufacturing. Similarly the existence of inventories at the retail level makes it possible to carry on that function relatively independently; replenishment stocks are ordered only periodically. No extra inventories over and above those for the other functions we have discussed are necessary to provide

FIGURE 3. Idealized graph of inventories required at the warehouse when orders are placed for a truckload, 800 units. Average inventory is now 800/2 = 400 units. Transit inventories are unchanged.

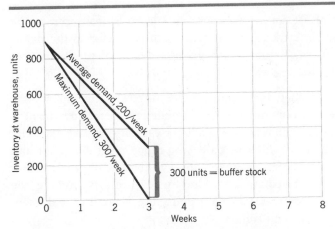

FIGURE 4. Contrast of idealized inventory levels required for average demand and maximum demand. The difference, 300 units, represents a minimum inventory or "buffer stock" required to protect against the occurrence of shortages resulting from random fluctuations in demand.

for the decoupling function. But the existence of inventories provides the needed independence between stages.

Seasonal Inventories. Many products have a fairly predictable but seasonal pattern through the year. Where this is true, management has the choice of changing production rates over the year to absorb the fluctuation in demand or of absorbing some or all of the fluctuation in demand with inventories. If we attempt to follow the demand curve through the seasons by changing production rates, the capital investment for the system must provide for the peak capacity and we must absorb costs for hiring, training, and separating labor, as well as overtime costs. The use of inventories often can strike a better balance of these costs. The concepts and methods for handling this seasonal problem are covered in Chapter 17.

Before considering the models and methodologies which have been developed for inventory control, we shall discuss the question of forecasts. To decide on what risks we can justify for investing in inventories, we must have a means of estimating demand.

FORECASTING

The demand forecast is a critical input for some of the most important decision models in production and operations management, particularly those related to inventories, aggregate planning and scheduling, and production control. Of course, forecasts are also a critical input to the design of productive systems for they are a direct factor in the determination of the most economical production design of products, processes, equipment, tooling, capacities, and layouts.

Time Horizons Forecasts may be needed for roughly three different time spans: the immediate future on which to base plans for current operations, the next three to five years on which to base plans for capacity adjustments, and long-range forecasts on which to base long-range plans for plant and warehouse locations, capacities, and changes in the mix of product lines or services. The intermediate and long-range forecasts involve the study of consumer preferences and trends, the economy, and technological developments and trends.

FIGURE 5. Reprinted through the courtesy of Helipot Division of Beckman Instruments, Inc.

Our interest is in forecasting for current operations and for a reasonable planning horizon time into the future. A reasonable horizon time depends on the incremental value of additional periods of forecast information. Ordinarily, if there is a seasonal aspect to demand, a reasonable planning horizon would include one full season.

The forecasting methodology which we shall discuss is applicable to the needs for guiding current operations for inventoriable items. The guidance of these current operations is closely tied in not only with the question of inventories but with the production planning and scheduling functions discussed in Chapters 17, 18, and 19.

Patterns of demand for specific products or services might vary widely but in general can be reduced to five components: average demand, trends in the average, seasonal effects, cyclic effects, and random variations. Figure 6 shows a portion of the record of monthly sales of a cooking utensil manufactured by Wearever, Inc. This figure shows the general situation where at least four of the five components are operating simultaneously (cyclic variations are beyond our scope). We need to be able to state a forecast for the upcoming period which takes account of the four components: average demand, trend, seasonal effects, and random variations.

Average Demand.   When we look at the actual sales (colored line) in Figure 6, the average demand for the entire three and one-half years is

Forecasting
Methodology

FIGURE 6.   Actual sales and an exponentially smoothed forecast for a cooking utensil at Wearever, Inc. (Adapted from [15].)

meaningless since the trend is an important factor. Therefore, some kind of moving average is needed which emphasizes the recent experience and estimates the trend effect. Furthermore, the estimate of demand for the upcoming period must take account of the expected seasonal variation. Finally, we wish not to be influenced by the random variations in demand when making an estimate for the upcoming period, or preferably we may wish to state the expected demand with probable limits of variation from the expected value due to random causes.

The common way of smoothing the effects of random variations in demand is to estimate average demand by some kind of *moving average*. Table II gives some sample demand data taken from the actual sales of Figure 6 for the first eleven periods. Note from Figure 6 and Table II that actual demand is quite variable. The three-month moving average, however, is much more stable because the demand for any one month receives only a one-third weight. Extreme values are discounted; if they are simply random variations in demand, we are not strongly influenced by them if we gage demand by the three-month moving average. Greater smoothing effect is obtained by averaging over a longer period, as is shown by the five-month moving average in Table II. Extreme values are discounted even more since each period demand carries only a one-fifth weight in the moving average.

TABLE II. Actual Demand and a Three-Month and a Five-Month Moving Average*

Period	Actual Demand	Three-Month Moving Average	Five-Month Moving Average
42	2000	—	—
43	1350	1767	—
44	1950	1758	2075
45	1975	2342	2025
46	3100	2275	2065
47	1750	2133	1935
48	1550	1533	1980
49	1300	1683	1915
50	2200	2092	2035
51	2775	2442	—
52	2350	—	—

*Data From Figure 6 on the demand for a cooking utensil.

Simple moving averages provide a smoothing effect, but we may have greater interest in the most recent data and wish to emphasize it more in the estimate of demand. Weighted averages can achieve this objective. One convenient and easy to use method of accomplishing differential weighting and smoothing is by *exponentially weighted moving averages.*

The simplest exponential smoothing model estimates average forecast demand for the upcoming period $\bar{F}_t$ by adding or subtracting a fraction (α) of the difference between actual current demand D_t and the last forecast average $\bar{F}_{t-1}$. The new forecast average $\bar{F}_t$ is then:

New smoothed average = old average
$$+ \alpha(\text{new demand} - \text{old average})$$

or stated symbolically,

$$\bar{F}_t = \bar{F}_{t-1} + \alpha(D_t - \bar{F}_{t-1}) \tag{1}$$

The smoothing constant α is between 0 and 1 with commonly used values of 0.01 to 0.30. Equation 1 can be rearranged in a more convenient and possibly more understandable form as follows:

New smoothed average = α(new demand)
$$+ (1 - \alpha) \text{ (old average)}$$

or stated symbolically,

$$\bar{F}_t = \alpha D_t + (1 - \alpha)\bar{F}_{t-1} \tag{2}$$

If $\alpha = 0.10$, then Equation 2 says that the forecast average in the upcoming period $\bar{F}_t$ will be determined by adding 10 per cent of the new actual demand information D_t and 90 per cent of the last forecast average $\bar{F}_{t-1}$. Since the new demand figure D_t includes possible random variation, we are discounting 90 per cent of those variations. Obviously, then, small values of α will have a stronger smoothing effect than large values. Conversely, large values of α will react more quickly to real changes (as well as random variations) in actual demand. The choice of α is normally guided by judgment, though studies could produce economically best or near best values of α.

It is important to place the time periods for $\bar{F}_t$, D_t, and $\bar{F}_{t-1}$ in perspective and to recognize that the so-called new forecast average $\bar{F}_t$ is not an extrapolation beyond known demand data. Rather, it is the most current smoothed average used to help guide current operations. In a sense then it is not a forecast but a statement of current demand. As a parallel, consider driving a car under three conditions of guiding the car: (1) based on a view out the windshield, (2) with the windshield covered but with a view out the side windows, and (3) with the windshield and side windows covered and a view out the back window, using the rear view mirror. Our situation is roughly comparable to being able to look out the side windows to see where we actually are. However, since there must be some time lag in compiling information on actual demand D_t, we are really looking out the *rear* side windows. But, there are no guesses, projections, or extrapolations involved. Each updated figure is based only on past actual demand data weighted to emphasize the most recent experience.

Extrapolation and Forecast. Since no trend or seasonality is expected in the model, direct extrapolation from $\bar{F}_t$ to infer a forecast is justified. Therefore, the forecast for the upcoming period $\bar{F}^*_{t+1}$ is taken directly as the computed value of $\bar{F}_t$. (Starred symbols, *, will represent extrapolated or forecasted values.)

Equation 2 actually gives weight to all past actual demand data, though this is not obvious. This occurs through the chain of periodic calculations to produce forecast averages each period. In Equation 2, for example, the term $\bar{F}_{t-1}$ was previously computed from

$$\bar{F}_{t-1} = \alpha D_{t-1} + (1 - \alpha)\bar{F}_{t-2}$$

which includes the previous actual demand D_{t-1}. The $\bar{F}_{t-2}$ term was calculated in a similar way which included D_{t-2} and so on back to the beginning of the series. Therefore, the forecasts are based on a sequential process representing all previous actual demands.

Trend Effects. If there were a trend present in the data, Equation 2 would respond to it but with a lag. But the apparent trend each period is simply the difference between the last two forecast averages $\bar{F}_t - \bar{F}_{t-1}$. This difference represents another series which can be estimated and smoothed by exponentially weighted averages just as with average demand. Therefore, the new average trend adjustment $\bar{T}_t$ is

$$\bar{T}_t = \alpha(\bar{F}_t - \bar{F}_{t-1}) + (1 - \alpha)\bar{T}_{t-1} \qquad (3)$$

The expected demand $E(D_t)$ for the upcoming period including trend adjustment is the forecast average $\bar{F}_t$ computed in Equation 2 plus a fraction of the new average trend adjustment $\bar{T}_t$ computed in Equation 3:

$$E(D_t) = \bar{F}_t + \frac{(1 - \alpha)\bar{T}_t}{\alpha} \qquad (4)$$

The term $(1 - \alpha)/\alpha$ corrects for lag in the trend adjustment $\bar{T}_t$. Note that the only facts and figures required to update a forecast are α, D_t, $\bar{F}_{t-1}$, and $\bar{T}_{t-1}$, yet all past actual demand data are weighted in the model but with rapidly decreasing weights as we proceed backward in time. If a large number of items were to be forecast, as is commonly true, the entire process could be computerized requiring minimum computer storage for each item, and the only new data to be supplied the computing program each period would be the current actual demand D_t.

Extrapolation and Forecast. As with the no-trend model, Equation 4 involves no extrapolation beyond known demand data. To extrapolate from Equation 4 to forecast D_{t+1}^* requires that we add $\bar{T}_t$, the most recent average trend adjustment,

$$D_{t+1}^* = E(D_t) + \bar{T}_t \tag{5}$$

Seasonal Adjustments. The basis for including a seasonal adjustment to an exponentially smoothed forecast model is to develop a *base series* which represents the seasonal cycle. A demand ratio of actual to base series demand is then computed for each period. This ratio is then smoothed, correcting for trend effects, resulting in an expected demand ratio. Finally, the expected demand $E(D_t)$ is computed through a period by period multiplication of actual period demand D_t by the smoothed ratio, resulting in the final forecasted demand with trend and seasonal effects included. See references [3] and [6] for computed examples involving the simplest exponential model represented by Equation 2, the inclusion of trend effects represented by Equation 4, as well as examples including seasonal effects.

The exponential smoothing methodology is a competent and efficient way of forecasting demand for current operations. The forecast (black line) in Figure 6 is a record of actual sales and forecast sales for the cooking utensil at Wearever, Inc. The exponentially smoothed forecast tracks the average, trend, and seasonal effects, but discounts the most extreme demand variations as being simply random effects.

Of course, there is an entirely equivalent statistical methodology involving ordinarily moving averages, trend estimation by regression analysis, and so on, but the numerical work required is greater and it is not as well adapted to automatic computation since considerably more computer memory space is required for each item to be forecast.

SIZE OF PURCHASE AND PRODUCTION ORDERS

Purchase Order Quantities

The opposing pressures of the various inventory related costs produce a situation calling for policies and practices that strike a balance between these costs. The age-old question of how many units to buy at one time may be conceptualized by observing the behavior of the costs affected by changes in lot sizes.

First, let us define the system with which we are dealing. Figure 7 diagrams what happens to inventory levels for a particular item. If we assume an annual requirement of $R = 2400$ units, or an average of 200 per month, the inventory levels would fluctuate as in Figure 7a if we were to order in lots of $Q = 200$. The average inventory level for the idealized situation shown is one-half the number ordered at one time or $Q/2 = 100$ units. If the item is ordered more often in smaller quantities

$Q = 200$ units

Average inventory level

Jan.   Feb.   Mar.   Apr.   May

$Q = 200$, the lot size or number manufactured at one time
$R = 2400$, the total requirement for one year
Average inventory $= \dfrac{Q}{2} = 100$ units

(a)

$Q = 150$ units

Average inventory level

Jan.   Feb.   Mar.   Apr.   May

$Q = 150$
$R = 2400$
Average inventory $= \dfrac{Q}{2} = 75$ units

(b)

FIGURE 7. Simplified model of the effect of lot size on inventory levels.

as shown in Figure 7b, we can see that the inventory level will fall in proportion to the number of units ordered at one time. Inventory level will, of course, affect the incremental costs of holding inventory, so we may say in effect that these costs of carrying inventory are proportional to the lot size Q, the number ordered at one time. From Figure 7 we also see that the total annual cost of placing orders increases as the number of units ordered at one time decreases. Therefore, we have isolated two types of incremental costs that represent the measures of effectiveness for the system we are developing. They are the costs associated with inventory level, *holding costs*, and with the number of orders placed, *preparation costs*.

In further defining the system with which we are dealing, let us attempt to construct a graph that shows the general relation between Q (lot size) and the incremental costs which we have isolated. We noted in Figure 7 that if Q were doubled, average inventory level was doubled. It costs, perhaps, $c_H = 0.60 per year to carry a unit of inventory (interest costs, insurance, taxes, etc.). Since the average inventory level is Q/2 and the inventory cost per unit per year is $c_H = 0.60, then the annual incremental costs associated with inventory are:

$$\frac{Q}{2} c_H = \frac{Q}{2} (0.60) = 0.30Q \tag{6}$$

Substituting different values for Q, we can plot the result as in Figure 8, curve (a).

We can plot the costs of ordering in a similar way. Let us use the symbol c_P to represent the costs of preparing and following up on an order. We calculate the number of orders by $R/Q = 2400/Q$. If each order preparation costs $c_P = 20, then the total annual incremental cost due to ordering is:

$$\frac{R}{Q} c_P = \frac{2400 \times 20}{Q} = \frac{48,000}{Q} \tag{7}$$

Therefore, as Q increases, the annual incremental cost due to ordering decreases. This makes good sense since as Q increases, the number of order preparations decreases and therefore the incremental cost decreases. This relationship is plotted in Figure 8, curve (b), by substituting different values of Q in 48,000/Q.

Figure 8, curve (c), shows the resulting total incremental cost curve, determined simply by adding the two previous curves. Thus we have a model that expresses the effectiveness E as a function of the variables which define the system. The equation for the total cost curve is also

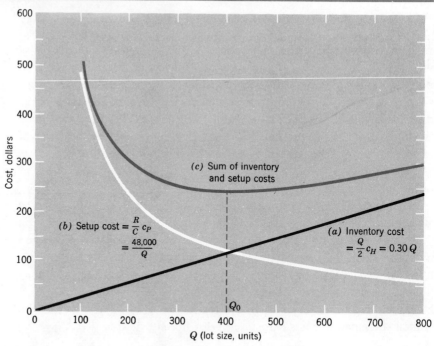

FIGURE 8.　Graphical model of simple inventory problem.

determined by adding the equations for the two separate cost functions and we have

$$E = \frac{Q}{2} c_H + \frac{R}{Q} c_P \qquad (8)$$

$$\begin{matrix} \text{Total} \\ \text{incremental} = \\ \text{cost} \end{matrix} \begin{pmatrix} \text{average} \\ \text{inventory} \end{pmatrix} \begin{pmatrix} \text{unit inven-} \\ \text{tory cost} \\ \text{per year} \end{pmatrix} + \begin{pmatrix} \text{number} \\ \text{of orders} \\ \text{per year} \end{pmatrix} \begin{pmatrix} \text{cost} \\ \text{of an} \\ \text{order} \end{pmatrix}$$

Looking at this equation we might now ask which variables are controllable and which are uncontrollable. Recall that controllable variables are those which may be manipulated pretty much at the will of management. In our example the controllable variable is Q (lot size). Uncontrollable variables are those which management cannot control, at least not within the limitations of the problem. For example, consumer demand, taxes, and insurance rates would fall in this category. For our example, uncontrollable variables are c_H (inventory costs per unit), R (demand or requirements), and c_P (order preparation costs). We might argue that management can influence c_H by bringing pressure to bear to have taxes or insurance rates reduced. Nevertheless, management cannot change taxes and insurance rates at will. In general, tax rate changes would be reflected in E, and management would respond by adjusting Q to minimize E again. The new policy would be the best policy, given the new tax rate.

A General Solution.   For our simplified inventory model we can pick off the minimum point from the total incremental cost curve of Figure 8, curve (c). It is a minimum for $Q_0 = 400$ units. (The symbol Q_0 denotes the optimal value of Q.) This is a solution to the specific problem with the given values of c_H, R, and c_P. The important thing about this model, however, is that we can obtain a general solution which will give us the minimum point directly for any values of c_H, R, and c_P. From the equation for the total incremental cost, we may derive a formula for the minimum point on the curve by use of differential calculus. The formula that represents the general solution for the model is

$$Q_0 = \sqrt{2Rc_P/c_H} \qquad (9)$$

This formula gives directly the value of Q_0, which yields the minimum total incremental cost for the model. Substituting the values of our example, we have

$$Q_0 = \sqrt{\frac{2 \times 2400 \times 20}{0.60}} = \sqrt{160,000} = 400 \text{ units}$$

In using the formula, if it is desired to express the economic quantity in dollars, the requirements must also be expressed in dollars. Similarly, if the requirements are expressed in monthly rates, the inventory costs must be expressed as a monthly rate. These and other changes in the units lead to apparent modifications of the formula used in practice, although the end result in terms of the size of the order is the same. In practice, the formula itself is not used often; rather, charts, graphs, and tables based on the formula are used to minimize computations.

The Effect of Quantity Discounts.   The basic economic lot size formula assumes a fixed purchase price. When quantity discounts enter the picture, additional simple calculations determine if there is a net advantage. As an illustration, assume that a manufacturer's requirement for an item is 2000 per year. The purchase price is quoted as $2 per unit in quantities below 1000 and $1.90 per unit in quantities above 1000. Ordering costs are $20 per order, and inventory costs are 16 per cent per year per unit of average inventory value, or $0.32 per unit per year at the $2 unit price. Our formula indicates the economic order quantity to be

$$Q_0 = \sqrt{\frac{2 \times 2000 \times 20}{0.32}} = \sqrt{250,000} = 500 \text{ units}$$

If we buy in lots of 1000, we save $200 per year on the purchase price plus $40 on order costs, since only two orders need be placed per year to satisfy the annual needs. This saving of $240 per year must be greater than the additional inventory costs that would be incurred if the price discount is to be attractive. Under the 500 unit order size, average inventory is 250 units and inventory costs are $250 \times 2.0 \times 0.16 = \$80$. If orders of 1000 units are placed, the inventory costs would be $500 \times 1.90 \times 0.16 = \$152$. There is a net gain of $240 - (152 - 80) = \$168$ by ordering in lots of 1000 instead of 500. If the vendor had a second price break of $1.86 per unit for lots of 2000 or more, a similar analysis shows that the incremental inventory costs outweigh the incremental price and order savings, so there is no net advantage in purchasing lots of 2000. Table III summarizes the calculations for all three cases. Obviously, no generalization can be drawn from this for purchase lots other than the fact that an incremental cost analysis of this sort would be required for each individual case.

Purchase Order Quantities

Production order quantities are based on the same general concepts as purchase order quantities, as we have noted, and Equation 9 can be applied. (Preparation costs are costs related to machine setups and

TABLE III.   Incremental Cost Analysis to Determine Net Advantage or Disadvantage When Price Discounts Are Offered

	Lots of 500 Units Price = $2.00 per Unit	Lots of 1000 Units Price = $1.90 per Unit	Lots of 2000 Units Price = $1.86 per Unit
Purchase of a year's supply (2000 units)	$4000	$3800	$3720
Ordering cost	80	40	20
Inventory cost (average inventory × unit price adjustment × 0.16)	80	152	298
Total	$4160	$3992	$4038

incremental paperwork costs to write production orders and control the flow of orders through the shop; inventory costs are costs associated with holding in-process inventory.) However, the assumption that the order is received and placed into inventory all at one time is often not true in manufacturing runs. The basic formula assumes the general inventory pattern shown in Figure 9a, where the order quantity Q is received into inventory. The inventory then is drawn down at the usage rate, subsequent orders being placed with sufficient lead time so that their receipt coincides with zero (or minimum stock) inventory.

For many manufacturing situations the production of the total order quantity Q takes place over a period of time and the parts go into inventory, not in one large batch but in smaller quantities, as production continues. This results in an inventory pattern similar to Figure 9b. The maximum and average inventory levels are reduced. The minimum cost production quantity formula becomes

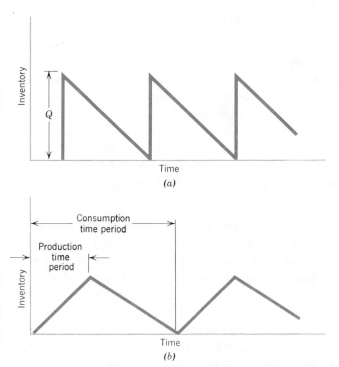

FIGURE 9. Comparison of inventory balance: (a) when the order quantity, Q, is received all at one time, and (b) when Q is received over a period of time, as would be true in many production situations.

$$Q_p = \sqrt{\frac{2Rc_P}{c_H\left(1 - \dfrac{r}{p}\right)}} \qquad (10)$$

where

r = requirements or usage rate (short term, perhaps daily or weekly)
p = production rate (on same time base as for r)
c_p = ordering and setup cost
c_H = unit inventory cost
Q_p = minimum cost production order quantity
R = annual requirements

The Q_p which results is, of course, larger than that which would result from the basic formula. Average inventory is smaller for a given Q_p and so balance between setup costs and inventory costs takes place at a higher value of the order quantity Q_p. By dividing the annual requirement by Q_p, we have the number of production cycles for the part or product which should be produced in a year.

Production Runs for Several Parts or Products. The more general problem is not to determine the economical length of a production run for a single part or product but jointly to determine the runs for an entire group of products which share the use of the same facilities. If each part or product run is set independently, it is highly likely that some conflicts of equipment needs would result, unless the operating level is somewhat below capacity and considerable idle equipment time is available. The formal problem is similar to the one product case, but the objective is to minimize combined setup and inventory costs for the entire set (see [5, 6, 11]).

Variability of Demand To this point we have been idealizing the structure of the inventory problem beyond reasonable limits of reality in order to discuss the formal solutions for optimum lot sizes. We have assumed a constant demand, constant lead times, and constant production rates. Actually, of course, none of these assumptions describes the real situation. Although average demand may be for 2500 units per year, daily demand may not be very well represented by 2500/250 = 10 units per working day. We may have no orders today, but tomorrow we may receive orders for 100, then none for the next week, and then on three successive days orders for 20, 50, and 5, respectively.

Customer demand controls this rate, and no one has devised a way to dictate to the customer when he should place his order. Similarly, supply times are not constant. It could take longer than usual for the supplier to fill the order because he himself is out of stock, because of equipment breakdowns, labor troubles, or a host of other delays. The shipment time from the supplier is also subject to variability. The result is that no practical system can depend on a plan based on the inventory balance structures of Figures 7 and 9.

Safety Stocks. The variations in demand and supply time are commonly absorbed by the provision of safety (buffer) stocks. The size of these planned extra inventories depends on the stability of demand and supply in relation to our willingness to run out of stock. If we are determined almost never to run out of stock, these planned minimum balances have to be very high. If service requirements permit stock run-outs and back-ordering, the safety stocks can be moderate. Figure 10 shows the general structure of inventory balance with a fixed-order quantity system. The safety stock level is set so that inventory balances would be drawn down to zero during the lead time, if we should experience near maximum demand.

The determination of safety stocks therefore turns on a knowledge of the demand distribution during lead time together with a decision regarding the risk of stock run-out that we are willing to accept. This

FIGURE 10. Structure of inventory balance for a fixed-order quantity system, with safety stocks to absorb fluctuations in demand and in supply time. The safety stock level is set so that a reasonable figure for maximum usage would draw down the inventory to zero during the lead time.

is shown by the distribution of demand in Figure 11. Approximate average monthly usage is about 460 units (corresponding to 50 per cent from Figure 11). If normal lead time is a month on the item, and if we wish to be 90 per cent sure of not running out of stock, we must have 620 on hand when the replenishment order is placed. The safety stock is then 620 − 460 = 160 units. If we wish to be 95 per cent sure of no run-outs, the safety stock must be 670 − 460 = 210 units. It is easy to see from the shape of the demand curve that, for high levels of assurance, the safety stock required goes up disproportionately and, therefore, the cost of providing this protection goes up.

Practical Methods for Setting Safety Stocks. In practice, the generalized methodology for determining safety stocks which we have just discussed is much too cumbersome. Instead of gathering data for individual demand distributions such as Figure 11, studies are made to validate the mathematical form of distributions for entire classes of items. Computations are then simplified considerably if we can justify the assumption that the demand distribution follows some particular

FIGURE 11. Distribution showing the per cent of months that demand exceeded a given level.

mathematical function such as the normal, Poisson, or negative exponential distributions. These three distributions have been found to be applicable in many situations at different stages in the supply-production-distribution system. For example, the normal distribution has been found to describe adequately many demand functions at the factory level, the Poisson distribution at the retail level, and the negative exponential distribution at the wholesale and retail levels [4]. The general procedure is the same for all distributions.

1. Determine the applicability of the normal, Poisson, or negative exponential distribution of demand during lead time.
2. Establish a service level based on managerial policy or an assessment of the balance of costs.
3. Define the maximum demand during lead time, D_{max}, based on the appropriate distribution and the service level. For example, if we select a service level of 5 per cent, then maximum demand is 670 units in Figure 11.
4. Compute the required safety stock from $I_{min} = D_{max} - \overline{D}$ where $\overline{D}$ is average demand and both D_{max} and $\overline{D}$ are based on the demand distribution over the lead time.

Basic Control Systems for Handling Demand Variability. To control inventories to meet requirements, we can manipulate the size and frequency of orders for replenishment, the frequency of review of usage levels, and the method of information feedback on which reviews are based.

The *fixed-order quantity* system is diagrammed in Figure 10. In this system, a reorder point is set which allows the inventory level to be drawn down to the safety stock level within the lead time if average usage is experienced during the lead time. Replenishment orders are placed in a fixed predetermined amount (the economic quantity or some other fixed quantity) timed to be received at the end of the lead time. Maximum inventory levels average the order quantity Q plus the safety stock I_{min}. The average inventory is $I_{min} + Q/2$. Review of the usage rates is periodic, at which times the order quantity and safety stock levels may be changed.

Demand for an item is ordinarily taken from the subsequent operations; that is, if the item were a standard screw used in several end products, assembly departments would issue requisitions for the screw according to their needs to produce. The demand for the end products may, in turn, be based on orders placed by warehouses which, in turn, may be based on salesmen's actual customer orders. The chain of demand, therefore, is reflected back through a series of stock points, each point maintaining inventories and placing orders for replenishment. Fixed-order quantity systems are common with low-value items, such as nuts and bolts, where the inventory level is under rather continuous surveillance so that notice can be given when the reorder level is reached.

Fixed-reorder cycle systems operate by placing orders for replenishment at regular intervals. The size of the order is varied to absorb the variations in usage, so the maximum inventory is maintained at a given level. Again, periodic review of usage rates would set the inventory levels and, therefore, determine the average size of an order. The periodic system offers tighter control through more frequent replenishment, compared to the fixed-order quantity system, since it is responding directly to changes in demand with each replenishment order. Its use is common with items of higher value and where a large number of items are regularly ordered from a single source. These multiple-item orders can then be grouped together for shipment to gain freight cost advantages.

Just as optimum order quantities can be derived for the fixed quantity system, so can optimum reorder cycles be derived for the fixed cycle system. However, since one main objective in the fixed cycle system is to order for all (or a group) of items at one time, the individual optimum cycles are not computed in practice. It would be appropriate, of course, to compute optimum cycles for individual items and classify them into appropriate groups. Then one group might be reviewed weekly, another each two weeks, a third each month, and so on.

The *base stock* system [11] is a blend of the fixed-order quantity and fixed-reorder cycle systems. It uses an information feedback system that establishes demand at each stock point directly with information regarding customer orders rather than through a chain of operations and stock points. In the base stock system, stock levels are reviewed on a periodic basis, but orders are placed only when inventories have fallen to a predetermined "reorder level." Then an order is placed to replenish inventories to the "base stock" level, which is sufficient for buffer stock plus a fixed quantity calculated to cover current usage needs. Periodic reviews of current usage rates can result in an upward or downward revision in the base stock level. The base stock system has the advantages of close control associated with the fixed-reorder cycle system, which makes it possible to carry minimum buffer stocks. On the other hand, since replenishment orders are placed only when the reorder point has been reached, fewer orders, on the average, are placed, so order costs are comparable to those associated with the fixed quantity systems.

The contrast in information feedback systems is illustrated in Figure 12. The disadvantage of the chain information flow system shown in Figure 12*a* is that, although actual customer orders may be received frequently in smaller quantities, replenishment orders to operations in the chain become larger and less frequent. Therefore, *variability* in demand at stock point 1 is amplified by the time it is reflected at stock point 3, resulting in an increase in safety stocks to prevent run-out. (Refer to Figure 11 and note the effect of increased variability in the demand distribution on the need for safety stocks for a given service level.) Under the general scheme of Figure 12*b*, each link in the production chain works against actual customer demand, so no amplification of demand *variability* takes place. Since all stock points are working against consumer demand so that amplification of demand variability does not take place, buffer stocks can be reduced even further because

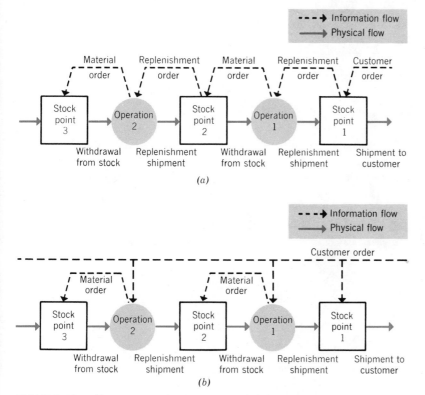

FIGURE 12. Two contrasting systems of information feedback for inventory control systems. (By permission from [11, p. 89].)

the extreme levels of maximum demand are not experienced. In addition, there is a reduction in the cost of production fluctuations (hiring, separation, and training), since the magnitude of production fluctuations is also associated with the type of information feedback system used.

SUMMARY

We have been discussing inventory controls as if they could be set up independently of the production system, inferring criteria or measures of effectiveness that do not reflect the effect of inventories on production programs and on the control of general levels of production. This independence is unrealistic because there are interactions between these problems. Inventory policy must fit in with schedules to produce a *combined* minimum cost of operation rather than a minimum for inventories alone. Greater inventories may make it possible to reduce hiring, training, and severance costs, as well as to reduce investments in plant and equipment. It may be economical at times to utilize overtime work at higher wage rates instead of to build inventories to meet demand. In the following chapter on planning master programs and controlling production and employment levels, we shall attempt to relate these problems.

REVIEW QUESTIONS

1. Distinguish between production plans and the design of production systems.
2. Distinguish between transit, cycle, safety, and seasonal inventories. Which of these types of inventories might be termed "pipeline" inventories?
3. Discuss the *decoupling* function of inventories.
4. In what ways can inventories serve to reduce costs? To increase costs?
5. What is planning time horizon?
6. What components of demand are involved in a forecast?
7. Why do moving averages discount random effects?
8. Compare the results of simple moving average forecasts and exponential moving average forecasts.
9. Explain why exponential moving averages contain effects from all past actual demands.
10. Outline the rationale behind the derivation of the minimum cost purchase quantity formula.
11. In the minimum cost purchase quantity formulation, why does the total incremental cost curve have a minimum point in it?
12. If we are dealing with production lot size decisions instead of purchase

quantity decisions, what comparable factors enter the formula? Can the same formula be used if the production lot enters inventory all at one time?

13. What type of analysis is required to take account of quantity discounts in determining optimal order sizes?

14. When production of a lot takes place over a period of time, what modification in inventory pattern and economic lot size formulation takes place? Is the resulting economic lot size larger or smaller than that which would result from the usual formula? Why?

15. What is the general problem of production runs for several parts or products? What may happen if production runs are determined independently? Under what conditions is it usually safe to determine them independently?

16. How do practical inventory control systems take account of variability in demand, lead times, production rates, etc.?

17. How can the size of safety stocks be determined in a rational way? Why not follow a policy which states that we want never to run out of stock?

18. Contrast the three basic control systems discussed for handling the problems of variability. Under what conditions would they be used?

19. What difference does the type of information feedback make in an inventory control system?

20. How sensitive are lot size decisions and costs to changes in c_p, c_H, R, r/p?

21. If management is attempting to adhere reasonably closely to an economic order quantity purchase policy, which parameters (variables) should it monitor most closely? Why?

22. A company manufactures a line of four detergents which are processed on common equipment through a cycling schedule. The aggregate demand for each of the four detergents is growing and is forecastable within reasonably close limits, though demand for various sizes of boxes and special promotions are much more erratic. Based on new forecasts of demand for the coming year, production lots and product sequencing are being revised. The plant works 8 hours per day, 240 days per year. Preliminary calculations indicated production runs for each product in the following case lots: (1) Wave, 25,000 cases; (2) O-Zone, 13,000 cases; (3) Tornado, 8,000 cases; and, (4) Zap, 9,000 cases. A case is a standard measure involving the same amount of detergent regardless of individual box sizes. These case lot sizes would require twelve production runs of Wave per year, ten of O-Zone, eight of Tornado, and two of Zap to meet the overall requirements for each product. The scheduler had developed a cycling sequence that met aggregate sales requirements as follows, coding the products by the numbers listed previously: 1234, 123, 123, 13, 12, 12, 14, 12, 123, 123, 123, 123. Each changeover requires four hours of cleaning and other preparations for the next product. Production was started according to the plan, but before the end of the first cycle the inventory of Wave (product 1) had been exhausted by

sales requirements. More trouble developed as the schedule developed into the second cycle—the inventory for O-Zone was also exhausted. The production foreman urged larger lots to build up larger cycle inventories. The scheduler stated that this would only magnify the problem and that his lot sizes were close to economic quantities and the system should work if given a chance. Why is the scheduler's plan not working? Discuss.

23. Taking the broad view of the enterprise as a whole and thinking in terms of the various functions of inventories, discuss how inventories could reduce overall costs. Increase overall costs.

24. Consider the various functions of inventories discussed in the text in relation to service industries. What functions do inventories perform in these kinds of organizations? Analyze, for example, operations such as a barber shop, a restaurant, a movie theater.

25. If you were the manager of a supermarket, would you be likely to reorder stock periodically, such as in the fixed reorder cycle system, or when inventories declined to certain levels, such as in the fixed reorder quantity system? Why?

PROBLEMS

1. Given the following five-year record of monthly demand for a product:
(a) Compute a three-month moving average forecast for the series.
(b) Compute an exponentially weighted forecast $\bar{F}^*_{t+1}$ for the series using only Equation 2 and $\alpha = 0.1$.
(c) Compute an exponentially weighted forecast D^*_{t+1} which takes account of trend effects, $\alpha = 0.1$.
(d) Plot the demand data and the three forecasts and compare results.

| Monthly Demand Data | | | | |
Month	1965	1966	1967	1968	1969
Jan.	47	22	41	68	82
Feb.	42	44	28	52	62
Mar.	16	42	53	77	63
Apr.	47	29	48	55	64
May	38	46	64	52	44
June	34	45	54	58	71
July	45	56	39	41	71
Aug.	50	50	50	62	45
Sept.	47	39	39	59	81
Oct.	54	44	48	37	77
Nov.	40	24	54	73	86
Dec.	43	46	28	65	69

2.   Given the following data, compute the minimum cost order quantity.

Annual requirements in units	5200
Cost of order writing and setup	$9
Annual cost of holding one unit	$0.03
Weekly production rate	200 units
Weekly demand rate	100 units
Unit production cost	$10

3.   A company buys 30,000 parts per year at a unit price of $10. If it costs $20 to process a purchase order, and interest and storage charges total 20 per cent, what is the approximate economic order quantity?

4.   The Stamped Metal Products Company (StaMPCo) has recently received an order from an automobile water pump manufacturer for 500,000 V-belt pulleys. The specifications and other details are shown in Figure 21 of Chapter 12. Although StaMPCo has the order, it finds that it will have to "farm out" the manufacture of the pulley hubs to a machine shop because of the close tolerances required by the customer. The machine shop will make the hubs while StaMPCo will make the flanges, assemble the pulleys, plate them, and ship the finished product.

The production level has been set at 28,500 good pulleys per month. Each month has an average of twenty working days.

Because of the close coordination required between the two companies to fulfill the StaMPCo contract successfully, you have been hired as a consultant to resolve any inventory problems. Your investigation has produced the following information.

(a) It normally requires three days from the time that a purchase requisition is initiated until the purchase order is mailed out.

(b) The mail time to the steel supply company is one day.

(c) The steel supplier requires two working days to process the order.

(d) Delivery time after the order is processed by the steel supplier is normally five days.

(e) The average rejection rate for inferior quality pulleys is about 5 per cent.

(f) Material data: (1) The bar stock for making the 1-inch long hubs has a diameter of $\frac{7}{8}$ inch and comes in 11-foot 9-inch lengths. The tool for cutting off the hubs from the bar stock is $\frac{1}{8}$ inch wide and produces an equal shrinkage loss for each hub. In addition, a 6-inch butt remains in each bar after the last hub has been cut off. (2) The steel strip for making flanges comes in 245-foot rolls and is $3\frac{1}{4}$ inches wide and 0.050 inch thick. The distance between centers of the flanges in the blanking operations is $3\frac{1}{4}$ inches. Approximately 15 inches are left in the automatic feeding mechanism at the end of each roll.

(1) Determine the total amount of material (in terms of bars and strip rolls) required for one month's production (round off to next larger whole number).

(2) How many working days after a material requisition is initiated could delivery be expected in the routine procurement procedure?

(3) If a minimum supply of fifteen days is to be maintained of all raw materials

to prevent interruption in production owing to external uncertainties, what is the reserve quantity and what is the reorder point for strip stock in whole rolls? Include a graphic sketch.

5. Your client is interested in applying the concept of "economic lot size" to the purchasing of raw materials. He has provided you with the following additional information:

(a) The cost (purchasing department expenses, receiving, etc.) of procuring 1500 individual line items last year was $12,555.

(b) As steel is the only raw material used in the company's processing, all inventories are assumed to have the same value to bulk or weight ratio. The total raw material storage costs (storekeeper wages, storage space, taxes and insurance on inventory, etc.) last year were $7650 on an average raw material inventory valued at $45,000.

(c) The valuation of inventories is on a standard cost method. The standard cost of strip steel rolls for 3-inch pulley flanges is $12 per roll.

(d) The company earns an average of 10 per cent on its invested capital.

(1) Calculate: (1) the unit cost of processing a purchase order and (2) the raw material storage cost as a percentage of the average raw material inventory value.

(2) Complete the following table using your problem calculations.

Order Quantity, No. of Rolls	Minimum Inventory	Average Inventory	Standard Roll Cost	Average Value of Inventory @ Std.
10			$12.00	
25			$12.00	
50			$12.00	
75			$12.00	
100			$12.00	
200			$12.00	

6. The company's steel supplier has the following price discount schedule on 245-foot rolls of $3\frac{1}{4}$ inches wide by 0.050 inch thick steel for 3-inch pulley flanges.

No. of Rolls Ordered	Price per Roll
0–24	$12.00
25–74	11.95
75–199	11.90
200 and over	11.875

Complete the following table (per year basis):

Lots of	10	25	50	75	100	200
Purchase price for one year's supply of rolls						
Purchase expense						
Total purchase costs						
Storage costs						
Capital costs						
Total cost per year						

What is the optimum quantity to purchase per order?

7. Plot the total purchasing costs from the table (Problem 5) on a graph. Plot the total costs (purchasing plus carrying) from the table on the graph.

8. Utilizing the economic lot size formula, determine the optimum number of rolls per order.

9. Does your answer in Problem 8 agree with the answer determined in Problem 7? If not, how do you explain the difference?

10. From the graph in Problem 6, what would be the approximate yearly cost using the order quantity obtained? What is the significance of the difference between this figure and the total yearly cost at the economic order quantity in Problem 8?

11. StaMPCo is anxious to apply inventory control concepts to its factory lot sizes to gain further economies of production. You are asked to devise the economic lot sizes. The following information is available for 3-inch V-belt pulley production.

Production: 28,500 good units are produced per month.
Setup costs:

Machine	No. Machines Needed	Costs/Machine
Turret lathe	3	$4.00
Punch press	1	2.50
Drillpress	1	negligible
Arbor press	1	1.00
Small spot welder	1	0.50
Large spot welder	1	0.50
Polishing	1	negligible

Direct labor costs: $24,375 per year.

Material costs: Bar stock (120 hubs/bar) $13.30/bar
               Steel strip (900 flanges/roll)   23.75/roll
               Set screw   0.01/each
               Cadmium plating   0.05/unit

Fixed overhead: $26,000 per year (amount apportioned to pulley production).

Variable overhead: $0.45 per dollar of direct labor.

The company earns an average of 10 per cent on its invested capital. Determine for 3-inch *V*-belt pulleys:

(a) Units per year.
(b) Setup cost per run.
(c) Direct labor cost per unit.
(d) Direct material cost per unit.
(e) Overhead cost per unit.
(f) Economic lot run quantity.
(g) Number of lots to be run per year.

12.   How accurate should economic production lot size determinations be?

13.   Why does the economic production lot size formula not yield the exact answer in practice?

14.   Another category of inventories is work in process. It is important that these inventories also be managed in a manner that results in low costs. Assuming

FIGURE 13.   Distribution representing expected random variation in weekly sales, exclusive of seasonal and trend variations.

job lot type production, "economic lot size" is analogous to "economic order quantity" in material and parts inventories.

(a) What cost factor associated with a production lot run is analogous to the procurement cost of materials?

(b) What cost factors associated with a production lot run are analogous to the purchase price of materials?

(c) What costs should be balanced in the economic production lot size formula?

15. Weekly demand for a product, exclusive of seasonal and trend variations, is represented by the empirical distribution shown in Figure 13. What safety or buffer stock would be required for the item to insure that one would not run out of stock more than 15 per cent of the time? Five per cent of the time? One per cent of the time? (Normal lead time is one week.)

16. If the product for which data are given in Problem 15 has a unit value of $50, shortage costs of $10 each, and an annual inventory carrying cost of 25 per cent of the average inventory value, which of the three levels of service would be most appropriate?

REFERENCES

[1] Brown, R. G. *Decision Rules for Inventory Management*. Holt, Rinehart, and Winston, New York, 1967.

[2] Brown, R. G. *Smoothing, Forecasting and Prediction*. Prentice-Hall, Englewood Cliffs, N.J., 1963.

[3] Brown, R. G. *Statistical Forecasting for Inventory Control*. McGraw-Hill, New York, 1959.

[4] Buchan, J., and E. Koenigsberg. *Scientific Inventory Control*. Prentice-Hall, Englewood Cliffs, N.J., 1963.

[5] Buffa, E. S. *Operations Management: Problems and Models* (3rd ed.). John Wiley, New York, 1972.

[6] Buffa, E. S., and W. H. Taubert, *Production-Inventory Systems: Planning and Control* (Rev. ed.). Richard D. Irwin, Homewood, Ill., 1972.

[7] Churchman, C. W., R. L. Ackoff, and E. L. Arnoff. *Introduction to Operations Research*. John Wiley, New York, 1957.

[8] Fetter, R. B., and W. C. Dalleck. *Decision Models for Inventory Management*. Richard D. Irwin, Homewood, Ill., 1961.

[9] Hadley, G., and T. M. Whitin. *Analysis of Inventory Systems*. Prentice-Hall, Englewood Cliffs, N.J., 1963.

[10] Harris, F. *Operations and Cost* (Factory Management Series). A. W. Shaw, Chicago, 1915, pp. 48–52.

[11] Magee, J. F., and D. M. Boodman. *Production Planning and Inventory Control* (2nd ed.). McGraw-Hill, New York, 1967.

[12] Raymond, F. E. *Quantity and Economy in Manufacture*. D. Van Nostrand, Princeton, N.J., 1931.

[13] Starr, M. K., and D. W. Miller. *Inventory Control: Theory and Practice.* Prentice-Hall, Englewood Cliffs, N.J., 1962.

[14] Wagner, H. M. *Statistical Management of Inventory Systems.* John Wiley, New York, 1962.

[15] Winters, P. R. "Forecasting Sales by Exponentially Weighted Moving Averages." *Management Science,* **6** (3), 324–342, Apr. 1960.

Aggregate Plans & Programs

Most managers want to plan and control operations at the broadest level through some kind of aggregate planning that bypasses the details of individual products and the detailed scheduling of facilities and men. Management would rather deal with the basic relevant decisions of programming the use of resources by reviewing projected employment and subcontracting levels and by setting production rates which can be varied within a given employment level by varying hours worked (working overtime or undertime). Once these basic decisions have been made for the upcoming period in the planning horizon, detailed scheduling can proceed at a lower level within the constraints of the broad plan. Finally, last-minute changes in production levels need to be made with the realization of their possible effects on the costs to change levels and on inventory costs.

What is needed first for aggregate plans is to develop some logical overall unit of measuring sales and output, for example, gallons in the paint industry, cases (representing an equal quantity regardless of package style) in the beer industry, or perhaps equivalent machine

507

hours in some mechanical industries. Second, management must be able to forecast for some reasonable planning period, perhaps a year, in these aggregate terms. Finally, management must be able to isolate and measure the relevant costs that we shall discuss in this chapter and, depending on the methods used, reconstruct these costs in the form of a model that will permit near optimal decisions for the sequence of planning periods in the planning horizon. The sequential nature of the decisions should be kept in mind; a decision on employment levels and production rates made for an upcoming period cannot be termed either right or wrong, good or bad. Decisions will also be made two periods hence based on the decisions just made, on new information about the actual progress of sales, and on the forecasts for the balance of the planning horizon. The result is that all decisions are right or wrong only in terms of the sequence of decisions over a period of time.

Most of our discussion deals with systems that produce inventoriable items, where the existence of finished goods inventories can make possible a cost trade-off for the costs of changes in employment level. Near the end of this chapter, however, we shall discuss aggregate planning for noninventoriable items as well.

To place our discussion in context, let us visualize the various plans for production in terms of their time horizons. Figure 1 shows five bands of plans. The implementation of the present plans in the shortest time horizon operates under the constraints of the established firm aggregate plans already made and is the subject of Chapters 18 and 19. The intermediate- and long-range plans shown in Figure 1 are involved in the broad strategic planning for the enterprise. The plans and decisions related to the upcoming and immediate future periods, however, are what we are calling aggregate planning and scheduling.

NATURE OF AGGREGATE PLANNING

Aggregate planning increases the range of alternatives for capacity use that must be considered by management. The term *aggregate planning* includes scheduling in the sense of a program; the terms *aggregate planning* and *aggregate planning and scheduling* are used almost interchangeably. The economic significance of these ideas is by no means minor. The concepts raise such broad basic questions as: To what extent should inventory be used to absorb the fluctuations in demand that will occur over the next six to twelve months? Why not absorb these fluctuations by simply varying the size of the work force? Why not maintain a fairly stable work force size and absorb fluctuations

Planning Time Horizon

Present period—implementation of firm plans already made	Firm plans for upcoming period	Tentative plans for immediate future periods	Intermediate-range plans for products and capacity	Long-range plans for products, markets, and capacities
Detailed plans and schedules for the use of the existing work force and equipment	Based on forecasts of demand for this and future periods, make plans for immediate capacity needs. This may involve hiring or laying off personnel, the setting of production rates, and plans for the use of overtime and inventories.	Size of work force Production rates Subcontracting Overtime Inventories	Changes in product mix Projected capacity needs for equipment and manpower	Studies of markets and their locations Studies of the size and location of facilities

FIGURE 1. Relationship of plans for various time horizons.

by changing production rates through varying work hours? Why not maintain a fairly stable work force and production rate and let subcontractors wrestle with the problem of fluctuating order rates? Should the firm purposely not meet all demands? In most instances it is probably true that any one of these pure strategies would not be as effective as a balance among them. Each strategy has associated costs and, therefore, we seek an astute combination of the alternatives.

If inventories are used to absorb seasonal changes in demand, then capital and obsolescence costs, as well as the costs associated with storage, insurance, and handling, tend to increase. Beyond the question of seasonal factors, the use of inventories to absorb short-term fluctuations incurs increases in these same costs compared to some ideal or minimum inventory level necessary to maintain the production process. When inventories fall below this ideal or minimum level, stockout costs and all costs associated with short runs increase.

Changes in the size of the work force affect the total costs of labor turnover. When new workers are hired, costs arise from selection, training, and lower production effectiveness. The separation of workers may involve unemployment compensation or other separation costs, as well as an intangible effect on public relations and public image. Large changes in the size of the work force may mean adding or eliminating an entire shift; the incremental costs involved are shift premium as well as incremental supervision costs and other overhead.

If fluctuations are absorbed through changes in the production rate, overtime premium costs for increases and probably idle labor costs (higher average labor cost per unit) for decreases also will be absorbed. Usually, however, managers try to maintain the same average labor costs by reducing hours worked to somewhat below normal levels. When undertime schedules persist, labor turnover and the attendant costs are likely to increase.

Many costs affected by aggregate planning and scheduling decisions are difficult to measure and are not segregated in accounting records. Some, such as interest costs on inventory investment, are alternative costs of opportunity. Other costs, such as those associated with public relations and public image, are not measurable directly. However, all of the costs are real and bear on aggregate planning decisions.

PROBLEM STRUCTURE

The simplest structure of the aggregate planning problem is represented by the single-stage system shown in Figure 2. In Figure 2 the planning horizon is only one period ahead; therefore we call Figure 2 a single-stage system. The state of the system at the end of the last period (which becomes the initial conditions for the upcoming period)

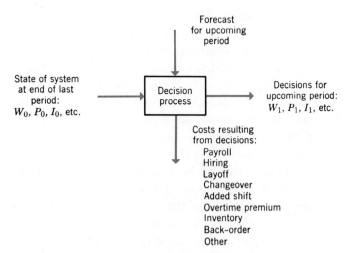

FIGURE 2.   Single-stage aggregate planning decision system where planning horizon is only one period. W = size of work force, P = production rate, and I = inventory level.

is defined by W_0, P_0, and I_0, the aggregate work force size, production rate, and inventory level, respectively. We have a forecast of the requirements for the upcoming period; through some decision process, decisions are made which set the size of the work force and production rate for the upcoming period. Projected ending inventory I_1 is then determined as the excess of the sum of the inventory carried forward from the previous period plus production during the period over forecasted sales during the period; that is, $I_1 = I_0 + P_1 - F_1$, where F_1 is forecasted sales.

The decisions made may call for hiring or laying off personnel, thus expanding or contracting the effective capacity of the production system. The work force size together with the decision on production rate during the period then determines the required amount of overtime, inventory levels or back-ordering, whether or not a shift must be added or deleted, and other possible changes in operating procedure. The comparative costs which result from alternate decisions on work force size and production rate are, of course, of great interest in judging the effectiveness of the decisions made and the decision process used. The comparative cost of a sequence of such alternate decisions is also of interest in judging the applicability of the single-stage model.

Let us suppose that we make a sequence of decisions by the structure of the single-stage model of Figure 2. Suppose that the forecasts for each period for the first four periods are progressively decreasing. Our decision process responds by decreasing both the work force size and the production rate in some combination, incurring layoff and changeover costs. Then, for the fifth through tenth periods we find the period forecasts are progressively increasing, and each period the decision process calls for hiring personnel and increased production rates, incurring hiring and more changeover costs. The single-period planning horizon has made each independent decision seem internally logical but has resulted in first the layoff of workers only to hire them back again, incurring costs for both actions plus changeover costs due to changing production rates.

Had we been able to look ahead for several periods with an appropriate decision process, we might have decided to stabilize the work force size at least to some extent and absorb the fluctuations in demand in some other way, perhaps solely with changes in production rate through the use of overtime and undertime or by carrying extra inventories through the trough in the demand curve. It appears that broadening the planning horizon can improve the effectiveness of the aggregate planning system.

Figure 3 shows a multistage aggregate planning system where the horizon has been expanded with forecasts for each period. Our objective is the same as before: to make decisions concerning the work force size and production rate for the upcoming period. In doing so, however, we consider the sequence of projected decisions in relation to forecasts and their cost effects. The decision for the upcoming period is to be affected by the future period forecasts and the decision process must consider the cost effects of the sequence of decisions. The connecting links between the several stages are the W, P, and I values which are, in effect, at the end of one period and the beginning of the next. The feedback loop from the "decision process" box to the stage boxes indicates that the decision process may involve some iterative or trial-and-error process to obtain a solution.

DECISION PROCESSES FOR AGGREGATE PLANNING

Given the structure of Figure 3 as a general statement of the problem, our interest now is drawn to the decision processes. What are the decision processes used and proposed for use? There are several and they may be classified as graphic, mathematical, heuristic, and computer search methods. We might classify them further as static versus dynamic as well as single stage versus multistage models. We shall discuss the graphic, mathematical, and computer search methods.

FIGURE 3. Multistage aggregate planning decision system for planning horizon of N periods.

Table I shows a forecast of expected production requirements for a product, together with the required safety stocks for each projected month. The available production days for each month emphasize that although the monthly seasonal requirement swing is expected to be 13,000/3,000 = 4.33 (peak in September, 13,000; low in March, 3,000), the production rates required to follow the sales pattern would be much greater since the plant shuts down for two weeks in July for vacations. The resulting swing in requirements per production day is from 143 units per day in March to 917 units per day in July, or a ratio 917/143 = 6.41. The dashed line of Figure 4 shows the projected requirements in terms of rates per working day, with the peak occurring in July instead of September because of the restriction on production time available in July.

Normal production capacity is 500 units per day, and up to 600 units per day can be produced by resorting to overtime at an extra cost of $10 per unit. To exceed the 600 units per day limit, subcontracting is required, which costs an extra $15 per unit compared to in-plant normal production.

Figure 4 shows three alternate production programs for meeting the requirements. Plan 1, level production, is in many ways the simplest,

TABLE I.   Forecast of Sales and Safety Stocks

Month	Expected Production Requirements	Required Safety Stocks	Production Days	Cumulative Production Days
Jan.	6,000	3,000	22	22
Feb.	4,000	2.500	19	41
Mar.	3,000	2,100	21	62
Apr.	4,000	2,500	21	83
May	6,000	3,000	22	105
June	9,000	3,500	20	125
July	11,000	4,000	12	137
Aug.	12,000	4,200	22	159
Sept.	13,000	4,400	20	179
Oct.	12,000	4,200	23	202
Nov.	11,000	4,000	19	221
Dec.	9,000	3,500	21	242
	100,000	40,900		

Average safety stock = $\dfrac{40,900}{12}$ = 3400.

FIGURE 4. Comparison of three alternate production programs that meet requirements.

since employment levels are stable. No overtime or subcontracting is required because the rate of 413 units per day is well within normal plant capacity. The inventory costs of this plan are high, however. At an inventory carrying cost of $40 per unit, the average seasonal stock of 9600 units costs $384,000. The seasonal inventory is that required to meet projected seasonal sales peaks, over and above the amounts being produced, and is simply total monthly inventory less safety stock in that month for the particular production plan. See Table II for a comparative summary.

Plan 2 attempts to minimize inventory costs by following the requirement curve fairly closely. It accomplishes this very well since average seasonal inventories are held to about 1150 units at a cost of only $46,000 per year, a saving of $338,000 per year. However, labor turnover costs are high, since the plant labor force must roughly be doubled to build the production rate from the low of 250 units per day to the normal plant capacity of 500 per day. These turnover costs are assessed at $164,300 per year. (No extra labor is employed above the normal plant capacity level.) (See Table II.) In addition, we must engage in both over-

TABLE II. Comparison of the Three Alternate Production Programs of Figure 4

	Plan 1	Plan 2	Plan 3
Average seasonal inventory	9,600	1,150	2,275
Average safety stock	3,400	3,400	3,400
Average total inventory	13,000	4,550	5,675
Peak capacity required (No. 1 = 100)	100	181	133
Incremental costs:			
Seasonal inventory cost*	$384,000	$ 46,000	$ 91,000
Labor turnover costs†	0	164,300	164,300
Overtime premium‡	0	60,000	52,820
Extra subcontracting**	0	60,000	0
Total	$384,000	$330,300	$308,120

*Inventory carrying cost is $40 per year per unit.
†Assuming that a change in the rate of output of 35 units per day requires the employment or release of 100 men and the cost of hiring and training an employee is $230.
‡At $10 per unit produced at overtime.
**Extra cost is $15 per unit subcontracted.

time and subcontracting to meet peak loads. The overtime bill is $60,000 and the extra subcontracting costs are $60,000. The total incremental costs compared to plan 1 are $330,300, a definite improvement over plan 1, although the turnover and excess capacity costs are quite high.

Plan 3 attempts to steer a path between plans 1 and 2 by holding the labor employed over a longer period in order to eliminate the need for extra subcontracting. This involves a higher inventory cost than plan 2, but eliminates the $60,000 extra subcontracting cost. Labor turnover costs are the same as in plan 2, because in both instances the labor force fluctuation is based on a minimum level of 250 units per day and a maximum level of 500 per day, which is normal plant capacity. (No extra labor is employed above the normal plant capacity level.) The total incremental cost of plan 3 is $308,120, the lowest of the three plans.

Whether either plan 2 or 3 is acceptable is another question. They both involve a great labor force fluctuation (about 713 employees). If these employees have relatively high skills and are difficult to find, this approach might be impractical and the effect on employee and community relationships would not be good. Other combinations involving less severe labor force fluctuation could be examined in the same way.

While Figure 4 shows the effects of the production rate changes quite clearly, it is actually somewhat easier to work with a set of cumulative curves as shown in Figure 5. The procedure is to plot first the cumulative production requirements. The cumulative maximum requirement curve is then simply the former curve with the required buffer stocks added for each period. The cumulative graph of maximum requirements can then be used as a basis for generating alternate program proposals. Any production program that is feasible in the sense that it meets requirements while providing the desired buffer stock protection must fall entirely above the cumulative maximum requirement line. The vertical distances between the program proposal curves and the cumulative maximum requirement curve represent seasonal inventory accumulation for the plan in question.

The graphic methods are simple and have the advantage of visualizing

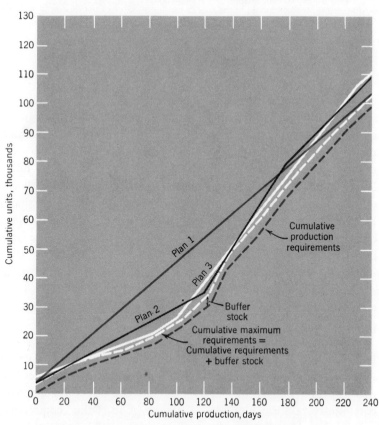

FIGURE 5. Cumulative graphs of requirements and alternate programs.

alternate programs over a broad planning horizon. The difficulties with graphic methods, however, are the static nature of the graphic model and the fact that the process is in no sense optimizing. In addition, the process does not generate good programs itself but simply compares proposals made.

We shall discuss three mathematical optimization methods: the optimum reaction rate method, the Linear Decision Rule, and linear programming. All three have a basis for optimizing the model developed so our interest is particularly in appraising how closely the three models represent reality.

Mathematical
Optimization
Methods

Optimum Reaction Rate Methods.   These methods were developed by Magee [19] with a focus on two main variables under managerial control: the frequency of adjustments in production levels and the reaction rate of adjustment to changes in forecasted sales in the immediate period ahead.

The reaction rate of adjustment of production levels determines how much of an adjustment is made for a given fluctuation in demand. If we adjust planned production levels by the full amount that sales vary from forecasts, we would have a 100 per cent reaction rate, and fluctuations in sales would be transmitted directly to production. The 100 per cent reaction rate leads to the most severe problems in hiring, training, and laying off of personnel, with the attendant costs of this instability. If we adjust production levels by only one-half of the change indicated by demand fluctuation, we would have a 50 per cent reaction rate. Obviously these reaction rates could take on any value from zero to 100 per cent. Low reaction rates would lead to stable production but higher inventories, and high reaction rates would lead to the reverse conditions.

The frequency of review also has an effect. Short review periods lead to small production fluctuations and smaller inventories for a given reaction rate. Figure 6 shows the relationship of control numbers (reaction rate/100) and review periods to the size of production fluctuation and the size of reserve or buffer inventories.

The selection of a reaction rate and review period for a given case then would depend on the balance of inventory carrying costs in relation to the costs of production fluctuation; a mathematical analysis leads to the optimum combination for a given application. In general, high reaction rates and long review periods tend to overcontrol.

Since much of the fluctuation in sales demand is from random causes, there is no need to react quickly. Lower reaction rates and short review

FIGURE 6. (a) Magnitude of production fluctuations versus control number and length of review period. (b) Reserve inventory required versus control number and length of review period. (By permission from [19].)

periods tend to create a "wait-and-see" attitude by bringing about small adjustments fairly often. Essentially they create a stalling action to see if the sales fluctuation is actually a true increase or decrease rather than a random fluctuation. The wait-and-see policy requires greater inventories but results in lower turnover costs. The optimal amount of control minimizes the sum of the two types of costs, rather than minimizing one at the expense of the other.

A Comparative Example

Magee [19] relates a hypothetical case which compares operations and costs for different basic systems of production and inventory control. The example considers a company that manufactures and sells about 5000 small machines per year for $100 each. The factory supplies four warehouses located in strategic areas around the country, which in turn supply the customer. We shall show the calculated results for three alternate systems of control: an economical order quantity system, a two-week fixed-reorder cycle system, and a base stock system with a reaction rate of 5 per cent and a review period of one week. Table III summarizes the comparative incremental costs of the three systems, and Figure 7 graphically shows typical effects on production levels. Obviously, we cannot draw the conclusion that all organizations would find these precise comparative effects, because there are differences in cost characteristics for inventories and volume fluctuation between different companies. What we can see is that the idea of economic order quantities is not a valid concept for the organization as a whole because it produces a sub-optimum solution which does not account for the cost of production fluctuations. For the example which we have used, these costs were of extreme importance. They could be of less importance in other situations, but they are always factors to be considered in the design of production and inventory control systems.

The reaction rate methods provide automatic decision rules which are dynamic and simple to apply, but like the graphic methods they lump the two relatively independent decisions of work force size and production rate into the single variable of production level. Given the production level, one must still decide what is the best way to meet the production objective, that is, hiring versus layoff, overtime versus undertime, basic production rate, and so on. In addition the model is only a single-stage one since it looks ahead just one period. For this

TABLE III. Comparative Incremental Costs for Three Inventory Control Systems

	Economical Order Quantity System	Two-Week Fixed-Cycle Reorder System	Base Stock System with 5% Reaction Rate
Inventory costs:			
Factory	$ 1,750	$ 515	$ 648
4 Branches	2,340	2,020	2,300
Reorder costs:			
Factory	350	350	350
4 Branches	990	1,980	2,081
Cost of production fluctuations	8,500	2,250	256
Total incremental costs	$13,930	$7,115	$5,635

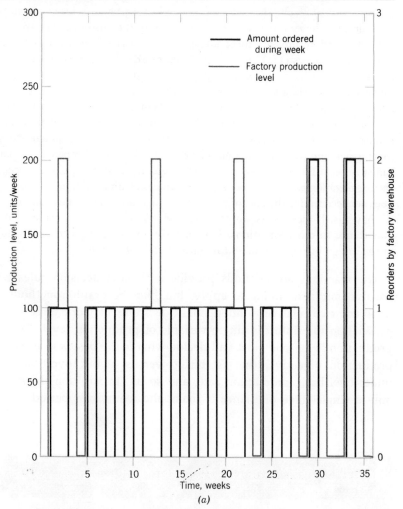

FIGURE 7. (a) Factory orders and production level, economical order quantity system. (b) Production level, fixed-reorder cycle system. (c) Production level, base stock system; reaction rate = 5 per cent. (Adapted by permission from [19].)

reason it would not handle seasonal effects as well as other methods which we shall discuss.

The Linear Decision Rule. The Linear Decision Rule (LDR) was developed in 1955 by Holt, Modigliani, Muth, and Simon [13, 14, 15] as a quadratic programming approach for making aggregate employment and production rate decisions. The LDR is based on the develop-

FIGURE 7.   (*continued*)

ment of a quadratic cost function for the company in question with cost components of: (1) regular payroll, (2) hiring and layoff, (3) overtime, and (3) inventory holding, back-ordering, and machine setup costs. The quadratic cost function is then used to derive two linear decision rules for computing work force levels and production rate for the upcoming period based on forecasts of aggregate sales for a preset planning horizon. The two linear decision rules are optimum for the model.

Figure 8 shows the form of the four components of the cost function.

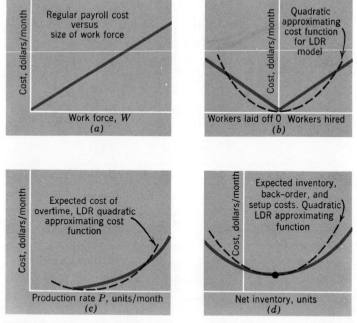

FIGURE 8. Approximating linear and quadratic cost functions used by the Linear Decision Rule (LDR) model. Colored lines represent presumed actual cost functions and dashed lines represent the LDR approximating functions.

The work force size is adjusted in the model once per period with the implied commitment to pay employees at least their regular time wages for that period. This is indicated in Figure 8a. Hiring and layoff costs are shown in Figure 8b, and the LDR model approximates these costs with a quadratic function as shown. If the work force size is held constant for the period in question, then changes in production rate can be absorbed by the use of overtime and undertime. Undertime is the cost of idle labor at regular payroll rates. The overtime cost depends on the size of the work force, W, and on the aggregate production rate, P.

The form of the overtime-undertime cost function in relation to production rate is shown in Figure 8c, being approximated by a quadratic function. Whether overtime or undertime costs will occur for a given decision depends on the balance of costs defined by the horizon time. For example, in responding to the need for increased output, the costs of hiring and training must be balanced against the overtime costs. Or conversely, the response to a decreased production rate would require the balancing of layoff costs against the costs of undertime.

The general shape of the net inventory cost curve is shown in Figure 8d. When inventories deviate from ideal levels, either extra inventory costs must be absorbed if inventory levels are too high, or costs of back-ordering or lost sales will occur if inventory levels are too low. Again, these costs are approximated by a quadratic function in the LDR model.

The total incremental cost function is then simply the sum of the four component cost functions for a particular example. The mathematical problem is to minimize the sum of the monthly combined cost function over the planning horizon time of N periods. The result of this mathematical development is the specification of two linear decision rules to be used to compute the aggregate size of the work force and the production rate for the upcoming period. These two rules require as inputs the forecast for each period of the planning horizon in aggregate terms, the ending size of work force, and inventory level in the last period. Once the two rules have been developed for a specific application, the computations required to produce the decisions recommended by the model require only ten to fifteen minutes by manual methods.

An LDR model was developed for a paint company and applied to a six-year record of known decisions in the company. Two kinds of forecasts were used as inputs: a perfect forecast and a moving average forecast. The actual order pattern was extremely variable, involving both the 1949 recession and the Korean War. The graphical record of actual factory performance compared with the simulated performance of the LDR is shown in Figures 9 and 10 for production rates and work force levels. Additional graphical results of over-time hours, inventories, and back-orders are contained in references [5, 14, 15]. Costs were reconstructed for the six-year period of actual operation and projected for the decision rules based on the non-quadratic cost structure originally estimated from paint company data. The cost difference between actual company performance and performance with the LDR with the moving average forecast was $173,000 per year in favor of the LDR.

An Example

LDR has many important advantages. First, the model is optimizing and the two decision rules, once derived, are simple to apply. In addition, the model is dynamic and representative of the multistage kind of system which we discussed in connection with Figure 3. On the other hand, the quadratic cost structure may have severe limitations and probably does not adequately represent the cost structure of any organization. Also, since there are no constraints on the size of workforce, overtime, inventory, and capital, it may be possible to generate decisions that are not feasible from some points of view.

FIGURE 9. Comparative performance of the Linear Decision Rule (LDR) with actual factory performance for production rates. (From [15].)

Linear Programming Methods. The aggregate planning problem has been developed in the context of both simplex and distribution models of linear programming. Bowman [2] proposed the *distribution model* of linear programming as a format for aggregate planning. This model focused on the objective of assigning units of productive capacity so that production plus storage costs were minimized and sales demand was met within the constraints of available capacity. The rim conditions in the distribution matrix form the constraints that sales requirements must be met on the one hand and that capacity limitations in the form of initial inventory, regular time production capacity, and over-time production capacity must be met on the other hand. Both beginning and ending inventories must be specified for the program developed over the N periods in the planning horizon. The matrix elements are costs.

The criterion function to be minimized is the combined regular production, overtime production, and inventory cost. The output of the process is a program that specifies the amount of regular and over-time production in each period of the planning horizon. The basic

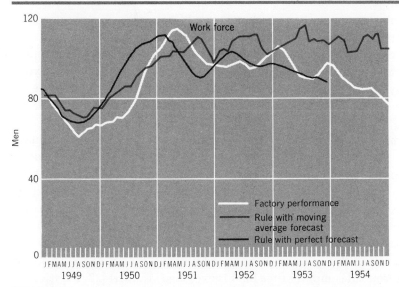

FIGURE 10. Comparative performance of the Linear Decision Rule (LDR) with actual factory performance for work force size. (From [15].)

matrix can be extended to more than one product by establishing a separate column in each period for each product.

Distribution methods of linear programming have serious limitations when applied to the aggregate planning problem. First, the distribution model does not account for production change costs such as hiring and layoff of personnel, and there is no cost penalty for back-ordering or lost sales. Thus, resulting programs may call for changes in production levels in one period, requiring an expanded work force, only to call for the layoff of these workers in the future periods. Also, the linearity requirement often is too severe.

The *simplex method* of linear programming makes it possible to include production level change costs and inventory shortage costs in the model [12, 20]. Hanssmann and Hess [12] developed a simplex model which is entirely parallel with the linear decision rule in terms of using work force and production rate as independent decision variables, and in terms of the components of the cost model and inclusion of a preset planning horizon. The main difference between the Hanssmann-Hess linear programming model and the LDR is that all cost functions must be linear rather than quadratic and that linear programming is used as a solution mode. Therefore, the advantages and disadvantages of the Hanssmann-Hess model are roughly the same as for the LDR. One's preference between the two models would depend on a preference for either the linear or quadratic cost model in a given application.

Industrial applications of linear programming to aggregate planning problems are reported by Eisemann and Young [7] in a study of a textile mill, by Fabian [8] in a study of blast furnace production, and by Greene, Chatto, Hicks, and Cox [11] in a study of the packing industry.

Search Decision Rule (SDR)

A computer optimum-seeking procedure may be used to evaluate systematically the cost criterion function at trial points. In the procedure it is hoped that an optimum value will be eventually found, but there is no guarantee. In direct search methods of computer optimum seeking, the cost criterion function is evaluated at a point, the result compared to previous trial results, and a move determined on the basis of a set of heuristics. The new point is then evaluated and the procedure repeated until either a better value of the function cannot be found or the predetermined computer time limit is exceeded. Taubert [23, 24] selected the Hooke-Jeeves [16] pattern search program as a vehicle for experimenting with the aggregate planning and scheduling problem. To test the feasibility of using such a program, he selected the paint company example used to test the LDR.

In general terms the cost criterion function represents the costs to be minimized over the planning horizon time; it can be expressed as a function of production rates and work force levels in each period of the planning horizon. Therefore, each period included in the planning horizon requires the addition of two dimensions to the criterion function, one for production rate and one for work force level. The particular pattern search program used was written to handle a maximum of twenty independent variables and, therefore, the planning horizon time was limited to ten months in Taubert's analysis of the paint company. The search program was set to end whenever the decrease in the objective cost function found by SDR's exploration of the response surface was less than $\$0.5 \times 10^{-6}$.

Table IV shows a sample of the computer output for the first month of factory operation of the paint company. The computer output gives the first month's decision as well as an entire program for the planning horizon of 10 months. In the lower half of the table the program prints out for the entire planning horizon the component costs of payroll, hiring and firing, overtime, inventory, and the total of these discretionary costs. Thus a production manager is provided not only with the immediate decisions for the upcoming month but also with the

TABLE IV. SDR Output for the First Month of Factory Operation (Perfect Forecast)

A. SDR Decisions and Projections

Month	Sales (gallons)	Production (gallons)	Inventory (gallons)	Work Force (men)
0			263.00	81.00
1	430	471.89	304.89	77.60
2	447	444.85	302.74	74.10
3	440	416.79	279.54	70.60
4	316	380.90	344.44	67.32
5	397	374.64	322.08	64.51
6	375	363.67	310.75	62.07
7	292	348.79	367.54	60.22
8	458	358.63	268.17	58.68
9	400	329.83	198.00	57.05
10	350	270.60	118.60	55.75

B. Cost Analysis of Decisions and Projections (dollars)

Month	Payroll	Hiring and Firing	Overtime	Inventory	Total
1	26,384.04	743.25	2,558.82	18.33	29,704.94
2	25,195.60	785.62	2,074.76	24.57	28,080.54
3	24,004.00	789.79	1,555.68	135.06	26,484.53
4	22,888.86	691.69	585.21	49.27	24,215.03
5	21,932.79	508.43	1,070.48	0.36	23,512.06
6	21,102.86	383.13	1,206.90	7.06	22,699.93
7	20,473.22	220.51	948.13	186.43	21,828.29
8	19,950.99	151.70	2,007.33	221.64	22,331.66
9	19,395.30	171.76	865.74	1,227.99	21,660.79
10	18,954.76	107.95	−1,396.80	3,346.46	21,012.37
					241,530.14

From Taubert [23].

projected decisions based on monthly forecasts for the planning horizon time and the economic consequences of each month's decisions.

Table V gives a month-by-month comparison for the first twenty-four months of the results obtained by the SDR program and those obtained by the two optimum decision rules for the LDR. The month-by-month decisions are not identical, but they are very close to each

		Production (gallons)		Work Force (men)*		Inventory (gallons)		Monthly Cost (dollars)	
Month	Monthly Sales (gallons)	LDR	SDR	LDR	SDR	LDR	SDR	LDR	SDR
0				81	81	263	263		
1	430	468	472	78	78	301	305	29,348	29,705
2	447	442	443	75	74	296	301	27,797	27,930
3	440	416	418	72	71	272	279	26,294	26,460
4	316	382	385	69	68	337	348	24,094	24,415
5	397	377	376	67	66	317	327	23,504	23,436
6	375	368	366	66	64	311	318	22,879	22,672
7	292	360	360	65	63	379	386	22,614	22,539
8	458	382	382	65	63	303	309	23,485	23,322
9	400	377	379	66	64	280	288	23,367	23,331
10	350	366	366	67	64	296	304	22,846	22,569
11	284	365	359	69	67	377	379	23,408	23,004
12	400	404	401	72	70	381	380	25,750	25,654
13	483	447	447	75	74	345	344	28,266	28,367
14	509	477	479	79	78	313	314	30,180	30,408
15	500	495	498	83	81	307	312	31,310	31,479
16	475	511	510	87	86	343	348	32,422	32,481
17	500	543	547	91	90	386	394	34,858	35,074
18	600	595	592	96	94	380	387	38,118	38,216
19	700	641	642	100	98	321	328	40,849	41,110
20	700	661	659	103	101	282	287	41,848	41,898
21	725	659	658	105	103	216	220	41,945	41,981
22	600	627	624	106	105	244	245	39,074	38,940
23	432	605	601	107	106	417	413	38,134	37,928
24	615	653	655	109	108	455	454	41,785	42,003
Totals		11,621	11,619	1,972	1,936	7,859	7,970	734,176	734,982

TABLE V.   A Comparison of Linear Decision Rule and Search Decision Rule for the First 24 Months of Operation with Paint Company Data (Perfect Forecast)

*Rounded to the next larger number of men.
From Taubert [23].

other; the twenty-four-month production totals differ by only two gallons. The total cost of the SDR program exceeds the LDR total by only $806 or 0.11 per cent. This difference may be accounted for by the fact that the SDR used a planning horizon of only ten months as compared to the twelve-month horizon used by the LDR.

With the encouraging results in virtually duplicating the performance of LDR in the paint company, it was decided to test SDR in more demanding situations. Thus, models were developed for three rather different situations: (1) the Search Company [4, 5, 6], a hypothetical organization involving a much more complex cost model including the possibility of using a second shift when needed; (2) the Search Mill [4, 21], based on disguised data obtained from a major American integrated steel mill; and, (3) the Search Laboratory [4, 5, 24], a fictitious name for a division of a large aerospace research and development laboratory. All three situations represent significant extensions beyond the paint company application with highly complex cost models and other factors to challenge the SDR methodology. We select the Search Laboratory model for further discussion because it involved the most varied cost components and because it occurs in a nonmanufacturing environment, thus demonstrating the pervasiveness of aggregate planning concepts.

Search Laboratory Application of SDR. Taubert [24] developed an aggregate planning cost model for the Search Laboratory in 1968. The laboratory is housed in a 100,000 square feet facility employing a staff of 400. Approximately 300 of the staff are classified as direct technical employees and the balance are indirect administrative support for the operations of the laboratory.

The laboratory offers a capability through its scientific staff and facilities, and widely fluctuating employment could severely impair this capability. The research programs of the laboratory are funded by both the government and by the corporation, and an important part of the operating environment is wide fluctuations in government sales and rapid shifts in technology. Thus, the operations planning problem is defined by the need for employment stability on the one hand and wide fluctuations in government sales on the other.

Specifically, the operations planning problem is centered in a monthly decision by the director to determine the size of the scientific staff and administrative staff as well as the allocation of the scientific staff to government contracts, corporate research programs, and overhead. Overhead charges arise when there are no contracts or corporate research programs available for scientists. This charge is in addition to the charges normally made to overhead for the usual indirect costs. In effect, then, overhead is used as a buffer to absorb fluctuations in the demand for scientific manpower. The four independent decision variables incorporated in the aggregate planning model are as follows:

1. The size of the scientific staff:
   (a) WS_t, manpower allocated to government contracts.
   (b) WR_t, manpower allocated to corporate research programs.
   (c) WO_t, manpower allocated to overhead.
2. WI_t, the size of the administrative support staff.

Cost Model.   Figure 11 shows the twelve cost relations which form the components for the cost model of the Search Laboratory. Note that a variety of mathematical relationships are included, such as linear, piecewise linear, constraints, and nonlinear forms. Taubert also built into the model a complete set of equations representing the overhead cost structure used to compute the overhead rate for any given set of decision variables. The resulting overhead rate is then used to compute the monthly government sales volume which in turn is compared to a cumulative sales target. The inputs to the decision system are monthly forecasts of contract manpower, research manpower, overhead manpower, and a cumulative sales target which represents the financial plan of the laboratory. The total manpower forecast must be met and it is a part of the director's operations planning problem to determine the best combination of decision variables which will accomplish the

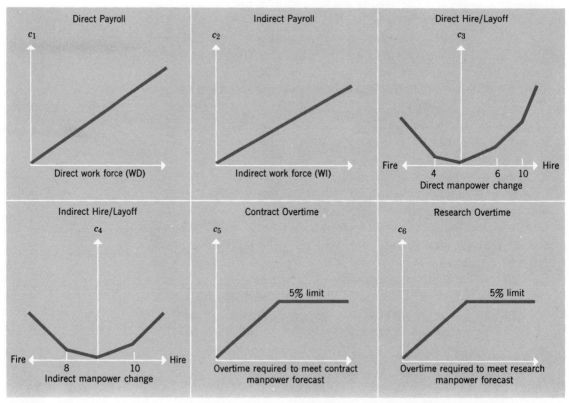

FIGURE 11.   The twelve cost relationships entering the Search Laboratory cost model. (From Taubert [24].)

objective. Failure to meet the manpower requirements increases costs, and this effect is also implemented in the cost model.

Results. Taubert validated the cost model against the financial record of the laboratory over a 5.5 year period. Following the validation, the decision system was operated for each month in the 5.5 year test period. A six-month planning horizon was used which required SDR to optimize a 24-dimensional response surface (four decisions per month for a six-month planning horizon). Figure 12 summarizes the comparative results, Figure 12*a* showing the contrast between SDR decisions on contract and research manpower compared with forecasts, and Figure 12*b* showing a similar comparison of actual management decisions compared with forecasts. Note that the SDR decisions respond much more smoothly to fluctuating manpower forecasts than did actual management decisions.

The costs resulting from SDR decisions compared to actual management decisions indicated that SDR would have produced cost savings.

FIGURE 11.   (*continued*)

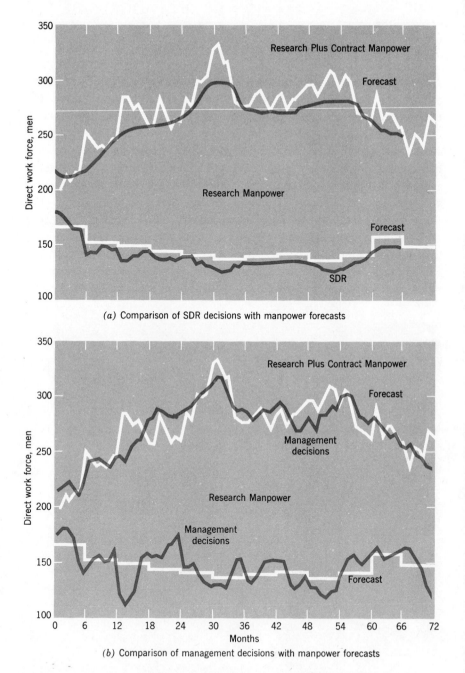

(a) Comparison of SDR decisions with manpower forecasts

(b) Comparison of management decisions with manpower forecasts

FIGURE 12. Results of SDR decisions for Search Laboratory I compared to forecasts and actual management decisions. (From Taubert [24].)

Over the 5.5 year test period, the SDR advantage ranged from a high of 19.7 per cent to a low of 5.2 per cent, averaging 11.9 per cent over the entire test period. The SDR decisions produced lower overhead rates and significant cost reductions in direct payroll, research program staffing, sales target penalties and rewards, and direct hiring costs. It achieved these results largely through the more extensive use of overtime.

Following the successful application of SDR to the aggregate planning problem of the Search Laboratory, Taubert subsequently disaggregated the decision variables for the size of the scientific staff in six departments. In effect, each department was considered as a miniature laboratory with its own contract and research manpower forecast as a cumulative sales target. Thus, the allocation of scientific staff had to be made in each of the six departments. While some transferring of personnel between departments was allowed, this practice was limited to represent the fact that, in general, scientists are not interchangeable and cannot be readily shifted from one department or technical expertise to another simply to meet fluctuating manpower requirements. Residual departmental manpower adjustments then had to be handled by hiring and layoff decisions. Again, it appeared that SDR continued to be able to produce logical and realistic decisions. The SDR decisions followed the forecast with a smooth response, carrying members of the scientific staff in overhead for short periods of time when faced with downturns in manpower forecasts [5].

AGGREGATE PLANNING FOR JOB SHOPS AND LARGE-SCALE PROJECTS

Aggregate planning for noninventoriable items need not take account of the risk of carrying inventories; but it also eliminates inventories as one of the managerial degrees of freedom—they cannot be used as a trade-off for the cost of fluctuating production. We have classified two kinds of systems as producing noninventoriable items, the custom job shop and the large-scale one-time project.

If we are producing a good or service to order, how can we anticipate and plan employment and operating levels? Forecasting the demand for unique items at first seems impossible, but the demand must be related to something in the economy as a whole or in our particular industry. It is commonly true that custom shops are not open to job

Job Shops

order from just any source but rather operate within a field, for example the aerospace industry, or operate locally. Thus, demand may be related to demand within the industry, for example the gross value of aerospace contracts, or employment levels in the community. At any rate, demand forecasting probably cannot be as simple as the exponential forecasting models we discussed in Chapter 16. Forecasting must be tailored to the situation, but it can be done.

It is commonly true in custom organizations that the demand for flexibility of the design of the item is transmitted into a demand for relatively highly skilled personnel. For example, the most highly skilled machinists are required in custom job shops, prototype shops, and so on. Personnel at these skill levels are the most scarce, are paid at the highest levels, and are the best organized into trade unions. The fact that such personnel are generally scarce places a premium on holding a good man even when shop loads decline. As a matter of fact, we can view the custom organization as holding an inventory of capacity and skills to produce in a field, available on demand, rather than holding an inventory of goods. The result is that hiring and layoff costs tend to be high, producing a pressure toward employment stability within custom organizations for all of the reasons discussed. We must recognize that part of the high cost of turnover is an opportunity cost of maintaining the "going concern" value of the organization. If the organization disintegrates through layoffs to the extent that it is no longer viewed as a going concern, then a decline in demand will be accentuated.

Good managers of custom organizations are very sensitive to these factors that argue for relative employment stability, even to the extent of altering price policies to maintain the integrity of the organization in slack times. It is not uncommon for managers to price at cost or below in hard times in order to keep their staffs busy and/or to absorb the cost of idle labor time. In general, managers of custom organizations tend to indulge somewhat less in hiring and layoff to absorb demand fluctuations. By maintaining a seemingly small staff relative to average demand, fluctuations in demand can be absorbed largely through changes in hours worked, resorting to overtime for increases in demand and to undertime and price policy adjustments for decreases. As an observation it is noteworthy that custom shops do use overtime at premium rates as a regular part of their employment policy.

Large Projects　　Much of what we have said about aggregate planning in job shops is applicable to the large-scale, one-time project system. However, there is a substantial difference in that large-project managers can forecast load in the near term because of the scale of projects. Project planning and scheduling are, in a sense, aggregate planning and scheduling. The entire project and all of its activities are planned at one time. Such programs may call for projecting loads one to two years in advance. These loads are not forecasts of demand but actual demands for contracted work.

The techniques for smoothing loads in network schedules to be discussed under "Deployment of Resources" in Chapter 20, are in fact attempts to reduce the cost effects of load fluctuation, or what we have termed the costs of production fluctuations in the aggregate planning models of this chapter.

SUMMARY

Aggregate plans and programs are of the greatest importance to production and operations management, since through these plans management deploys the major resources at their command. These resources can be deployed effectively or ineffectively. Top management's interest is focused on the most important aspects of this deployment process such as employment levels, production rates, and inventory levels. If basic plans can be based on decisions in these areas which establish operating constraints, then detailed planning and scheduling of operations can go forward.

We have discussed the structure of the aggregate planning problem and a number of decision processes designed to meet the needs of aggregate planning. At this point the graphic methods are probably used most. The mathematical and computer search methods have been developed in an effort to improve on the traditional methods by making the process dynamic, optimum seeking, and representative of the usual multistage nature of the problem. Several models have been of value, mainly as stepping stones to more useful models that represent reality more accurately. The most important single stepping stone undoubtedly has been the LDR. Presently, the computer search methods seem to offer the most promise because of their greater flexibility in representing costs that really occur in organizations. Although some of the mathematical methods do produce optimum solutions, we must remember that it is the model that is optimized. The real-world counterpart of the model is also optimized only if the mathematical model duplicates reality. The computer search methods are only optimum seeking by their nature, but do not suffer from the need to adhere to strict mathematical forms in the model and can therefore more nearly duplicate reality in cost models. It is, after all, the real-world situation that we wish to optimize, not the model. See [18] for a comparative study.

The extension of the SDR methodology to the nonmanufacturing setting of the Search Laboratories is encouraging in the development of the generality of the production and operations management field. The great complexity of the cost model in the Search Laboratories and the extension of the number of independent decision variables to nineteen indicate the developing power of the computer search methodology in representing realistic managerial situations.

REVIEW QUESTIONS

1. Characterize the term "aggregate plan." What is implied by the term "aggregate"? What are the objectives of aggregate plans? What are the required inputs?

2. Place aggregate planning in context with the term "planning horizon." What is the appropriate planning horizon for aggregate planning?

3. Discuss the relevant cost components involved in aggregate planning decisions.

4. Describe a single-stage aggregate planning decision system. Under what conditions would such a system be appropriate?

5. Describe a multistage aggregate planning decision system. Under what conditions would such a system be appropriate?

6. Describe graphic methods for aggregate planning. How would they be used for multiple products?

7. Appraise graphic aggregate planning methods.

8. Describe optimum reaction rate methods of aggregate planning. What are the main variables under managerial control in reaction rate methods?

9. Describe how optimization is obtained in reaction rate methods. What costs are being minimized?

10. Appraise reaction rate methods of aggregate planning.

11. Describe the LDR. What cost components are being minimized in this model?

12. Characterize the results of the paint company application of the LDR.

13. Appraise the LDR as an aggregate planning decision system.

14. Appraise distribution and simplex methods of linear programming as decision models for aggregate planning.

15. As a decision system, contrast the SDR with the LDR. What are the advantages and disadvantages of each?

16. What is the value of aggregate planning with disaggregate output of results as described in the projected Search Laboratories application of the SDR?

17. Appraise the SDR as a decision process for aggregate planning.
18. Describe aggregate planning in organizations which produce a custom product or service. Would you expect fluctuating or stable employment to meet varying demand in these kinds of organizations? Why?
19. Why is a network plan the equivalent of an aggregate plan for large-scale one-time projects?
20. Conceivably, a production-oriented organization has at its disposal a number of possible responses to anticipated changes in demand when developing an aggregate plan. Among the possible responses are production rate changes, inventory fluctuations, changes in employment level, the use of overtime or undertime, back-ordering or the absorption of lost sales, and subcontracting. Why then is it relatively difficult for organizations to develop rational modes for aggregate production scheduling? Referring to Figure 8:
    (a) Rationalize why the cost of overtime should increase at an increasing rate as production rate increases.
    (b) If inventory varies from the optimal level (minimum cost level) why should the incremental costs increase at an increasing rate as represented in Figure 8d?
21. Criticize the usefulness and validity of the strict aggregate planning concept, that is, making decisions solely in aggregate terms of size of work force and production rate.
22. What is the meaning of the term *capacity* in aggregate planning models? How does a decision to hire, fire, or subcontract affect capacity? How does physical or limiting capacity affect these decisions?
23. Cost comparisons between the result of actual managerial decisions and those produced by solving decision rule models are typically made by running both sets of decisions through the cost model and then comparing the results. Does this methodology seem valid? If not, what other approach might be followed?

PROBLEMS

1. Given a control number of 0.6, a decreased demand fluctuation of 600 units in the first period, and a forecasted production level of 15,000 units in the third period, what would be the revised production quantity set for period three? (Owing to lead times, it is not possible to adjust the production level for the second period.)

2. A company manufactures a single product for which the following table represents a schedule of forecasted and actual demand in units for one year.

Month	Forecasted Demand	Actual Demand
Jan.	23,000	23,000
Feb.	24,000	25,000
Mar.	21,000	20,000
Apr.	23,000	22,000
May	20,000	22,000
June	19,000	24,000
July	17,000	22,000
Aug.	14,000	15,000
Sept.	8,000	6,000
Oct.	10,000	13,000
Nov.	9,000	10,000
Dec.	10,000	14,000
Total	198,000	216,000
Average	16,500	18,000

The initial inventory is 15,000 units. The desired ending inventory is 20,000 units. The cost of storage is $1 per unit per month. It costs $1000 to change production from zero to 3000 units and $3000 to change production from 3000 to 6000 units. No change larger than 6000 units is possible in one period. Back orders are permitted at a cost of $5 per unit per period.

(a) What is the best production plan for the forecasted demand if one wishes to minimize pertinent costs?

(b) Assuming that the year is over, what is the best production plan for the actual demand utilizing the benefit of hindsight?

(c) To correct for deviations in actual demand as compared to forecasted demand, evaluate the choice of a control number of 0.25 versus one of 0.75. Assume that at the end of a month sufficient time exists to alter the planned production for the next month.

(d) What would be the cost impact of these two control numbers if the following additional rules were formulated.

(1) Determine the planned production change.

(2) Add or subtract the additional change due to the forecast error modified by the appropriate control number factor.

(3) If the total change is less than or equal to 1500, do not change production levels.

(4) If the total change is greater than 1500 but less than or equal to 4500, change production level by 3000 units.

(5) If the total change is greater than 4500, change production levels by 6000 units.

(6) Subtract the production change as per rules (3), (4), and (5) from the total change indicated by rule (2) and add or subtract the result to the planned production change for two months hence.

3. The following data show projected requirements for the production of a middle-priced camera together with buffer stock requirements and available production days in each month. Develop a chart of *cumulative* requirements and *cumulative* maximum requirements for the year, plotting cumulative production days on the horizontal axis and cumulative requirements in units on the vertical axis.

Month	Production Requirements	Required Buffer Stocks	Production Days
Jan.	3,000	600	22
Feb.	2,500	500	18
Mar.	4,000	800	22
Apr.	6,000	1,200	21
May	8,000	1,600	22
June	12,000	2,400	21
July	15,000	3,000	21
Aug.	12,000	2,400	13
Sept.	10,000	2,000	20
Oct.	8,000	1,600	23
Nov.	4,000	800	21
Dec.	3,000	600	20
	87,500	17,500	244

4. Using the data of problem 3, compare the total incremental costs involved in level production, in a plan which follows maximum requirements quite closely, and in some intermediate plan. Normal plant capacity is 400 units per working day. An additional 20 per cent can be obtained through overtime but at an additional cost of $10 per unit. Inventory carrying cost is $30 per unit per year. Changes in production level cost $5000 per 10 units in production rate. Extra capacity may be obtained from subcontracting certain parts at an extra cost of $15 per unit. Beginning inventory is 4000 units.

5.* Consider a situation where the organization wishes to look back over the last twenty-four periods to see what would have been the effects of a level production policy with the smallest possible production rate. Assume that all production is available only at the end of the period at which it is produced. Also, determine the total storage cost if $c_H = \$1$ per unit per period, assuming that there is no storage cost on units produced within the period and that units sold within the period are stored for one-half of the period. In essence, the problem is one of determining the minimum level production rate per

---

*Problem developed by Professors J. Baker and J. W. Gotcher, Department of Management Sciences, California State College, Hayward, California.

period and reduces to finding the period during which inventories would be exhausted. Actual demands for the twenty-four periods are:

5,000	4,600	5,600	5,200
5,100	4,900	5,500	4,800
4,900	5,100	4,900	5,000
4,700	5,600	4,300	5,100
4,600	5,700	4,400	4,400
4,800	5,400	5,000	5,000

6. An organization is nearing the end of the year, and is making plans for the coming year. It can, through minor adjustments in production rate, end the year with any final inventory between 150 and 1,500 units. The minimum buffer stock is 150 units. What combination of ending inventory (beginning inventory for the new year) and level daily production rate should be used if the criterion for good performance is to minimize the weighted seasonal inventory cost, where c_H = $100 per unit per year? Suggested procedure: Plot cumulative maximum requirements in relation to production days and compute for two alternate plans which seem logical to you. Cumulative maximum requirements by months is as follows:

Month	Production Days	Cumulative Maximum Requirements
Jan.	22	550
Feb.	18	1,075
Mar.	22	1,575
Apr.	21	2,075
May	22	2,700
June	21	3,530
July	13	4,450
Aug.	21	5,100
Sept.	20	5,700
Oct.	23	6,175
Nov.	21	6,550
Dec.	20	6,950

7. An organization has forecasted maximum production requirements for the coming year as follows:

Jan.	400	July	580
Feb.	510	Aug.	600
Mar.	400	Sept.	300
Apr.	405	Oct.	280
May	460	Nov.	440
June	675	Dec.	500

The present labor force can produce 470 units per month. An employee added or subtracted from the labor force affects the production rate by 20 units per month. The average salary of employees is $660 per month and overtime can be used at the usual premium of time and one-half pay up to 10 per cent of time for each employee. Therefore, an employee, working the maximum overtime, could produce the equivalent of an additional two units per month. Hiring and training costs are $100 per man, and layoff costs are $200 per man. Inventory holding costs are $10 per month per unit, and shortages cost $50 per unit short. Changeover costs for any increase or decrease in production rate are $3,000 per changeover over and above pertinent hiring and layoff costs. These costs include replanning and rebalancing of production lines and so on. No change cost is appropriate when added production is achieved through the use of overtime. What plan do you recommend? What is the incremental cost of your plan?

8. Given the data in Table II.
(a) What value of c_H would make Plans 1 and 2 equally desirable?
(b) What hiring-layoff cost makes Plans 1 and 2 equally desirable?
(c) What subcontracting extra cost makes Plans 1 and 2 equally desirable?

9. *Production control game.* You are the production manager of a company making a single product. Your plant has unlimited capacity within the potential sales range. Orders for your product vary from period to period, and it is your job to devise a production plan that will fill shipping orders each period from available inventory. The goal of the plan should be to minimize the total annual costs for holding inventories, failing to meet orders on time, and changing the current production rate.

Since it takes time to change the production rate, there is a one-period interval between the time that you make a decision and the time that the change goes into effect. Thus a decision made at the end of the first period goes into effect during the second period. Any change in the output level must be in thousand-case lots and may not be less than 5000 cases nor more than 10,000 cases. Excess production is stored in plant warehouses up to a total capacity of 240,000 cases. Inventory above this amount may be stored in outside facilities at extra cost.

At the beginning of the year, the following rules and conditions apply:
(a) Opening inventory—to be furnished by game referee.
(b) Current shipments average 100,000 cases per period with the following approximate distribution: (1) 76 per cent of the time shipments will be between 70,000 and 130,000 cases per period, and (2) 96 per cent of the time shipments will be between 50,000 and 150,000 cases per period.
(c) To change the production rate costs $5000 per change, regardless of the magnitude of the change.
(d) There is an inventory holding charge of $200 per year for each 1000 cases of average inventory. In addition, each 1000 cases stored in outside facilities costs $500 per year.

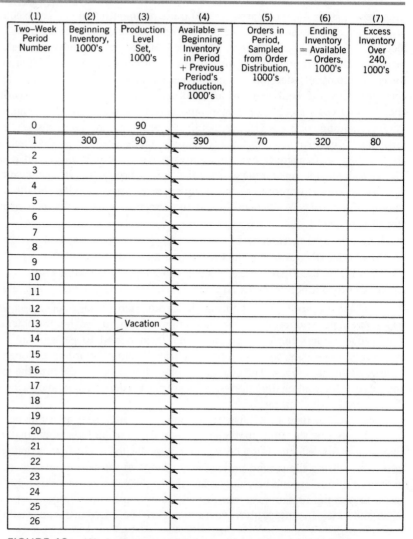

(1)	(2)	(3)	(4)	(5)	(6)	(7)
Two–Week Period Number	Beginning Inventory, 1000's	Production Level Set, 1000's	Available = Beginning Inventory in Period + Previous Period's Production, 1000's	Orders in Period, Sampled from Order Distribution, 1000's	Ending Inventory = Available – Orders, 1000's	Excess Inventory Over 240, 1000's
0		90				
1	300	90	390	70	320	80
2						
3						
4						
5						
6						
7						
8						
9						
10						
11						
12						
13		Vacation				
14						
15						
16						
17						
18						
19						
20						
21						
22						
23						
24						
25						
26						

FIGURE 13.   Work sheet, production and inventory control game.

(e) There is a charge of $750 per period for each 1000 cases ordered which cannot be shipped because of insufficient inventory (100 per cent back-order rate).

(f) The plant shuts down for vacation during the thirteenth period. Orders continue to be shipped, although production is zero.

Procedure. Figure 13 shows the work sheet used. Beginning inventory at the time play starts in period one will be furnished by the game referee.

(a) Enter the figure for beginning inventory furnished by the game referee on line 1 under column 2.

(b) Set the initial production level for period zero and period one and enter in column 3.

(c) Calculate "available" (column 4), the sum of beginning inventory (column 2) for the period, plus "production" (column 3) for the previous period.

(d) Decide on production levels for the next period by entering the amount in column 3 for period two.

(e) Record "orders" for period one in column 5. This figure will be read by the game referee and represents a Monte Carlo sampling from the order distribution. As an example, the orders for period one are shown as 70 in Figure 13.

(f) Calculate "ending inventory" (column 6) by subtracting orders for the period from the total available for the period.

(g) Calculate "excess inventory" (column 6) by subtracting 240 from the ending inventory for the period. For the example shown in Figure 13, the excess inventory which must be stored at extra cost in outside facilities is 80.

(h) Transfer the figure for ending inventory to column 2, "beginning inventory," for the next period.

(i) Repeat for 26 periods, making sure to account for the vacation in the thirteenth period during which no production will occur but during which orders will be delivered. If during any period, orders exceed the amounts available, simply record negative ending inventory and beginning inventory for the next period. This takes account of the 100 per cent back-order rule.

(j) Compute incremental costs. Using the form shown in Figure 14, calculate

Cost Calculations	Condition 1	Condition 2
1. Production changes. Multiply the number of changes made in the year by $5000 per change.	_____	_____
2. Inventory-holding cost. Total ending inventories for each 2-week period, divide by 26 and multiply the number of 1000 cases resulting by $200. (Do not deduct shortages.)	_____	_____
3. Outside storage facilities. Total excess inventory (over 240,000 for each 2-week period, divide by 26, and multiply by $500.	_____	_____
4. Stock shortage cost. Determine the number of 1000-case shortages and multiply by $750.	_____	_____
5. Total yearly cost.	$_____	$_____

FIGURE 14. Form for calculating costs.

costs for production changes, inventory costs, excess inventory costs, and stock shortage costs. The total of these four costs represents a measure of the effectiveness of the sequence of decisions made.

(k) Based on the experience gained in the first run, attempt to reduce annual incremental costs in a second run.

(l) Summarize the decision rules that you feel might be appropriate to obtain the lowest total annual incremental costs.

REFERENCES

[1] Bowman, E. H. "Consistency and Optimality in Managerial Decision Making." *Management Science*, **4** (1), 100–103, Jan. 1963.

[2] Bowman, E. H. "Production Scheduling by the Transportation Method of Linear Programming." *Operations Research*, **4** (1), 100–103, Feb. 1956.

[3] Buffa, E. S. "Aggregate Planning for Production." *Business Horizons*, Fall 1967.

[4] Buffa, E. S. *Operations Management: Problems and Models*, (3rd ed.). John Wiley, New York, 1972, Chapter 13.

[5] Buffa, E. S., and W. H. Taubert. *Production-Inventory Systems: Planning and Control* (Rev. ed.). Richard D. Irwin, Homewood, Ill., 1972, Chapters 5, 6, and 7.

[6] Buffa, E. S., and W. H. Taubert. "Evaluation of Direct Computer Search Methods for the Aggregate Planning Problem." *Industrial Management Review*, Fall 1967.

[7] Eisemann, K., and W. M. Young. "Study of a Textile Mill with the Aid of Linear Programming." *Management Technology* (1), 52–63, Jan. 1960.

[8] Fabian, T. "Blast Furnace Production—A Linear Programming Example." *Management Science*, **14** (2), Oct. 1967.

[9] Fetter, R. B. "A Linear Programming Model for Long-Range Capacity Planning." *Management Science*, **7** (4), 372–378, July 1961.

[10] Gordon, J. R. M. *A Multi-Model Analysis of an Aggregate Scheduling Decision*. Unpublished Ph.D. Dissertation, Sloan School of Management, Massachusetts Institute of Technology, 1966.

[11] Greene, J. H., K. Chatto, C. R. Hicks, and C. B. Cox. "Linear Programming in the Packing Industry." *Journal of Industrial Engineering*, **10** (5), 364–372, 1959.

[12] Hanssmann, F., and S. W. Hess. "A Linear Programming Approach to Production and Employment Scheduling." *Management Technology* (1), 46–52, Jan. 1960.

[13] Holt, C. C., F. Modigliani, and J. F. Muth. "Derivation of a Linear Decision Rule for Production and Employment." *Management Science*, **2** (2), 159–177, Jan. 1956.

[14] Holt, C. C., F. Modigliani, J. F. Muth, and H. A. Simon. *Planning Production, Inventories and Work Force*. Prentice-Hall, Englewood Cliffs, N.J., 1960.

[15] Holt, C. C., F. Modigliani, and H. A. Simon. "A Linear Decision Rule for Production and Employment Scheduling." *Management Science*, **2** (2), 1–30, Oct. 1955.

[16] Hooke, R., and T. A. Jeeves. "A 'Direct Search' Solution of Numerical Statistical Problems." *Journal of the Association for Computing Machinery*, Apr. 1961.

[17] Jones, C. H. "Parametric Production Planning." *Management Science*, **13** (11), 843–866, July 1967.

[18] Lee, W. B. "A Comparison of Aggregate Production Planning Rules Using A Corporate Simulation Model," Presented at XIX International Meeting, The Institute of Management Sciences, Houston, Texas, April 1972.

[19] Magee, J. F., and D. M. Boodman. *Production Planning and Inventory Control* (2nd ed.). McGraw-Hill, New York, 1967.

[20] McGarrah, R. E. *Production and Logistics Management: Text and Cases.* John Wiley, New York, 1963, Chapter 5.

[21] Redwine, C. N. *A Mathematical Programming Approach to Production Scheduling in a Steel Mill.* Unpublished Ph.D. Dissertation, UCLA, 1971.

[22] Silver, E. A. "A Tutorial on Production Smoothing and Work Force Balancing." *Operations Research*, **15** (6), Nov.–Dec. 1967.

[23] Taubert, W. H. "Search Decision Rule for the Aggregate Scheduling Problem." *Management Science*, **14** (6), Feb. 1968.

[24] Taubert, W. H. *The Search Decision Rule Approach to Operations Planning.* Unpublished Ph.D. Dissertation, UCLA, 1968.

[25] Vergin, R. C. "Production Scheduling Under Seasonal Demand." *Journal of Industrial Engineering*, **17** (5), May 1966.

Scheduling & Control for High-Volume Systems

For high-volume continuous systems it appears on the surface perhaps that when the aggregate plan has been developed the system has already been scheduled. After all, continuous systems are typified by production lines and continuous chemical processes where the production rate has been set and the sequence of individual operations and their interrelationships are already fairly well determined by the design of the physical system. The system operates as a giant machine. If the production rate is set, then the dovetailing and sequencing of operations are already taken care of by the system design. Isn't the detailed scheduling problem already accomplished by the system design? In a sense this is true. But, given aggregate planning decisions setting employment levels and production rates, the remaining problems are still significant.

First, how can we determine the amounts of each product to be produced? The aggregate plan has specified an overall production rate, but, in fact, this overall total must be allocated to the various sizes and types of items produced. Second, the aggregate plan may have called for a change in the size of the work force. A change in manpower level must be translated into a rebalancing of facilities with modified work assignments for the crew. Therefore, while the aggregate plan has specified the quantitative change in work force size, there still

FIGURE 1. Reprinted through the courtesy of Helipot Division, Beckman Instruments, Inc.

remains the implementation of this change in a way that makes the most sense. In other words, which workers and what kinds of skills are involved? If the aggregate plan has called for a decrease in employment, union agreements may specify who will be laid off. Third, the combined work force size and production rate decisions determine the aggregate amount of overtime or undertime to be worked. How will the overtime or undertime be allocated to products and manpower? And, fourth, do the projected inventory levels that result from a proposed detailed schedule of items agree with the aggregate planning level and with the policies and procedures developed for individual items?

NATURE OF THE PRODUCTION-DISTRIBUTION SYSTEM

In order to understand the nature of the scheduling and control problems for high volume continuous systems we need to understand the overall flow, appreciate the importance of system inventories, and understand the system dynamics. One of the crucially important factors to keep in mind is that the scheduling of the factory output is very dependent on the behavior of distributors and retailers downstream in the flow system and that these elements of the system are normally outside the control of management.

Let us begin by examining the production-distribution system diagrammed in Figure 2. Assume that the system represents the manufacture and distribution of a small appliance. Figure 2 shows the major functions performed in the production and distribution of the appliance, beginning with raw material procurement, extending through manufacture and thence through the sequence of distribution steps to the ultimate consumer. There are 500 independent retailers, 50 independent distributors, and a single factory in the system. Each of the distribution steps involves a stock point for the finished product. Therefore, one way of looking at the system downstream from the factory is to envision it as a *multistage* inventory system.

Note also that Figure 2 indicates basic elements of the ordering procedure for replenishing the finished goods inventory at each stage. Thus each retailer has a replenishment cycle which involves the review of his demand and inventory status, transmission of orders to his supplying distributor, and the filling and shipping of the order by the distributor. Similarly, each distributor has an equivalent replenishment cycle, based on the assessment of demand from retailers, the transmission of orders to the factory warehouse followed by the filling and shipping of the orders. Similar cycles are required for the factory warehouse in ordering from the factory and for the factory itself ordering raw materials from vendors.

We are interested in some aspects of all of these steps, keeping in mind that our key interest will be in scheduling the factory to produce. Before concerning ourselves with the scheduling of the factory, however, let us make some rough calculations to get some idea of how much inventory will be required to make the system function.

SYSTEM INVENTORIES

Recall from Chapter 16 the discussion of the several functions of inventories. Some inventory is required just to fill the flow pipelines of the system, another component to take account of the periodic nature of the ordering cycles, and a third component to absorb fluctuations in demand. Depending on the nature of the policies for factory scheduling, additional seasonal inventories might also be required.

FIGURE 2. Production-distribution system for high-volume continuous system showing broad flow of materials and information, transit times, and order processing delays. (System volume averages 2000 units per week.)

Pipeline Inventories. If the average system volume is 2000 units per week and it takes one day to transport from the factory to the factory warehouse, then there are 2000 (1/7th) units in motion at all times. If the order processing delay at the factory warehouse is five days, then there are 2000 (5/7ths) units tied up at all times because of the delay. Table I summarizes the pipeline inventory requirements for finished goods for the entire system, indicating a minimum of 7,144 units required just to fill the pipelines. These inventories cannot be reduced unless transit times, delays, and handling times can be reduced. The inventories are proportional to the system volume and the physical flow times. If system volume increases then this component of inventories must increase to keep the pipelines full and keep the system functioning.

Cycle Inventories. We will assume that the fixed reorder cycle system of inventory replenishment is being used at the factory warehouse, distributor, and retailer levels. The average order size is then set by the ordering frequency at each stage. For example, the average retailer orders once each two weeks following a review of sales (the information and physical flow cycle is shown in Figure 2). Therefore, when a retailer orders it must be for a 2-week supply, just to meet average demand. The average retailer sells 2000/500 = 4 units per week, or 8 units during the 2-week ordering cycle. He must, therefore have no less than 8 units on hand to service sales during the replenishment period, and the average inventory for this purpose is half this amount or 4 units. The cycle inventory for the entire system of 500 retailers is then

TABLE I. Summary of Pipeline Inventory Requirements for Finished Goods (Average system volume is 2000 units per week.)

	Average Transistor Delay Time, Days	Average Pipeline Inventory, Units (Days/7) × 2000
Factory to factory warehouse	1	286
Delays at factory warehouse	5	1,429
Warehouse to distributors	10	2,857
Delays at distributors	2	571
Distributors to retailers	5	1,429
Delays at retailers	1	286
Retailers to customers	1	286
Totals	25	7,144

TABLE II. Summary of Cycle Inventory Requirements for Finished Goods (Average system volume is 2000 units per week.)

	Recorder Cycle Time, Weeks	Average Cycle Inventory Units
500 Retailers	2	2,000
50 Distributors	4	4,000
Factory warehouse	6	6,000
Total		12,000

$4 \times 500 = 2000$ units. Table II summarizes the cycle stock requirements of the system showing that 12,000 units are required in average inventory because of the periodic nature of ordering.

Buffer Inventories. Recall from our discussion in Chapter 16 that buffer inventories are designed to absorb random variation in demand and that the size of buffer inventories depends on the nature of the distribution of demand and the service levels which we wish to maintain. Table III shows the computation of buffer stocks for the system. For example, the buffer stock required for each retailer is the difference between the estimated maximum demand over the 17-day review plus supply lead time and the average demand, or $18 - 9.7 = 8.3$ units. The average system buffer stock for 500 retailers is then $8.3 \times 500 = 4,150$ units. The buffer stock requirements for the entire system are 13,864 units.

Summarizing, the inventories in the system needed to accommodate all three functions are as follows:

Pipeline inventories	7,144
Cycle inventories	12,000
Buffer inventories	13,864
Total	33,008

These are inventories required by the structure of the system and the ordering rules and service levels used. These inventories represent the minimum possible amounts necessary to operate the system. Overall inventories might be larger than this minimum if controls were not effective or if seasonal inventories were also accumulated in the system.

The impact of inventories on the problem of scheduling the factory is underlined when one notes that management has control over only

TABLE III. Summary of Buffer Inventory Requirements for Finished Goods (Average system volume is 2000 units per week.)

	Average Demand per Week	Lead Time, Days	Average Demand over Lead Time	Maximum Demand over Lead Time	Average System Buffer Stock
500 Retailers	4	17	9.7	18	4,150
50 Distributors	40	35	200.0	300	5,000
Factory Warehouse	2,000	36	10,285.7	15,000	4,714
Total					13,864

approximately one-third of these inventories, the balance being held by distributors and retailers. Also, management does not have control over the ordering policies and procedures of the retailers and distributors.

SCHEDULING AND AGGREGATE PLANNING

The broad outlines of the scheduling process for the multistage production-distribution system in relation to the aggregate planning process is shown in Figure 3. Within the "Company System under Managerial Control" and above the dashed line in Figure 3 we see the activities which are directly related to scheduling.

Forecasts of demand based on information concerning the progress of sales at the retail-consumer level, as well as order rates at the factory warehouse, are fed into the forecasting model. The forecasting model produces period forecasts over the planning horizon for the aggregate planning process which in turn produces basic decisions on production rate and work force levels for the upcoming period. From the basic decisions produced by the aggregate planning process we can either compute the overtime and subcontracting required, as well as the projected end of period inventory, or these data will be produced as a part of the output of the aggregate planning procedure, depending on the aggregate planning model used. Translating these aggregate plans into detailed working schedules is then the next task.

The Product Mix Problem.   The effect of an aggregate planning decision on employment levels and production rates is the adjustment of the effective capacity of the system for the upcoming period. In other words, capacity limits have been set, creating a set of capacity constraints which must be observed in the detailed schedule which is generated. Thus the allocation of the limited capacity to product types and sizes becomes an important economic problem.

The product mix problem may be most complex in chemical industries such as oil refining where there are also interdependencies in the quantities of different products which can be produced. If more of one product, such as aviation gasoline, is to be produced, then less of some other product must be produced by the very nature of the refining

FIGURE 3. Relationship of forecasts, aggregate scheduling, and detailed scheduling to production-distribution system.

process. The profitability of various products may be different, and there are limits to the markets for each. The result is a complex programming problem to determine the best product mix. The interdependencies always exist in oil refining, for example, because the basic raw material, crude oil, can be processed into many different products and an increase or decrease in one product always means a change in the quantities of some other products.

In the mechanical industries the interdependencies between products are more likely to stem only from the capacity limits proposed by the aggregate planning decisions and, in some instances, by the capacity of time-shared facilities which are used to produce a variety of types and sizes. In all instances, however, we face an allocation problem of how best to use available limited capacity. These problems of product mix have been approached through linear programming as discussed in Chapter 7. In present day practice it is common to ignore the allocation problem and determine the product mix by applying percentage sales figures with modifications based on personal judgment.

At any rate, a result of the allocation to types and sizes gives basic information for detailed scheduling, detailed hiring and layoff instructions, and material procurement schedules as shown in Figure 3. Conflicts in detail schedules may occur at this point because of capacity limitations for either labor or facilities since detailed scheduling involves setting individual type and size production rates and manpower schedules.

In setting the individual type and size production rates and manpower schedules the scheduler may be faced with either great rigidity or reasonable flexibility depending on the nature of the processes and the design of the production system. Production lines are quite rigid in their nature in that once designed and set up the line produces assembled units at a fairly fixed hourly rate since all operations have been balanced to coordinate with the preset hourly rate. What flexibility does the scheduler have to obtain a certain target weekly or monthly rate of output? He has basically two alternatives. He can schedule the work force on the line to work shorter or longer hours (including overtime), or he can rebalance the entire line to achieve a somewhat higher or lower hourly rate or output. Obviously, he would use the latter to achieve more drastic changes in output rate since it involves hiring or laying off workers while simply changing hours worked is cheaply done unless overtime must be scheduled. Here, however, the scheduler will be following the basic instructions given him by the aggregate plan, which presumably has taken into account the relative costliness of changing production rates through changing hours, using overtime, and re-balancing (hiring and laying off).

The aggregate plan establishes the constraints under which the scheduler must perform. Thus we see that assembly line balance is a subject for concern not only for original design of production systems but for continued operation, since it is through rebalancing that the scheduler can change the basic hourly production rate of the system. For example, the use of rebalancing in automotive assembly lines to achieve different hourly rates of output is common.

If the line is completely rigid in design, being mechanically paced at a fixed rate, then the scheduler can change total output for the period only by changing the number of hours per period that the man-machine system is operated. The rigid system is, of course, often used.

The Detailed Scheduling Process. Since the broadly based optimization has already taken place in the development of the aggregate plan, the main problems of detailed scheduling are to devise ways of following out the aggregate plan as far as possible. Following the allocation of aggregate production to product types and sizes, an iterative process begins which develops a tentative plan and checks back to see if the details of the plan fit the stated constraints of the aggregate plan and other possible company policies.

The first question raised in the schematic diagram of Figure 4 involves possible changes in employment levels called for by the aggregate plan. These changes will call for a rebalancing of manpower to facilities. In the case of complex assembly lines the methods and procedures of Chapter 12 may be used. In many instances, alternate manning plans probably exist for various output rates of facilities based on previous careful studies. In any case, the result of rebalancing will be to hire or layoff personnel in specific skill categories, checking to see if the result is within the aggregate plan. If the aggregate planning model has been carefully constructed to reflect the relationship between productivity and manpower, it should be possible to adjust manning assignments within the constraints of the plan. Recall from our study of line balancing, however, that balance solutions must deal with the assignment of whole manned units so that cost and capacity increase or decrease in step fashion rather than in a continuous relationship to manpower.

When the hiring-layoff question has been answered with resultant rebalancing, this information is an input to the initial attempt to generate a detailed schedule of products to facilities. Using the aggregate plan,

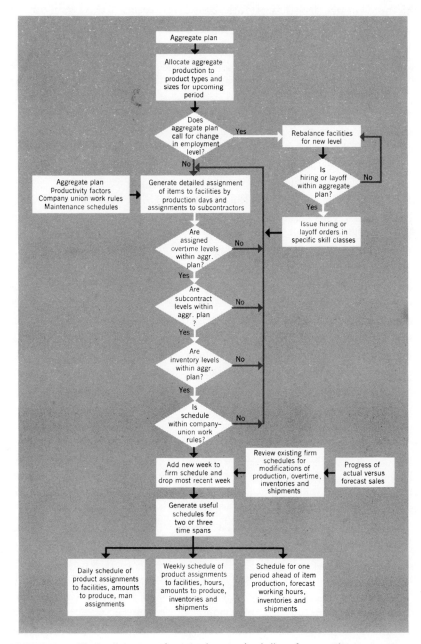

FIGURE 4. Flow diagram of operations scheduling for continuous systems. (From [4, p. 316].)

the new basic production rate based on rebalancing, productivity factors, company-union work rules, and a knowledge of existing maintenance schedules, the scheduler generates a detailed assignment of product items to facilities by production days as well as assignments to subcontractors if that is appropriate. He then checks the result in an iterative fashion to see if assigned overtime levels, subcontracting levels, and inventories meet the requirements of the aggregate plan, as well as other constraints such as maintenance schedules and agreed company-union work rules. The result is a feasible daily schedule which will add an additional period, perhaps a week, to the firm schedule (see Figure 4).

In a parallel way, the existing firm schedules are reviewed for possible modification based on new information dealing with the progress of actual sales versus forecasted sales. The schedules of production commitments is then updated by adding the newest information and dropping off the most recent week or period.

Based on the resultant information the scheduler may then develop full schedules for two or three time spans such as those shown at the bottom of Figure 4. For some specific company situations most of the process could possibly be computerized. We assume also that at some point our technical capability will improve to the point that aggregate and detailed scheduling can be largely combined into one "optimum seeking" model, perhaps by the SDR methodology discussed in Chapter 17.

SYSTEM DYNAMICS

Now let us attempt to understand the impact of activities downstream in the production-distribution system on the scheduling of factory operations. To do this, let us focus our attention again on the multistage system diagrammed in Figure 2. Though highly idealized and simplified in many respects, this model is sufficient to represent for us some of the important material and information flow asked of the system.

We are already familiar with the significance of the time lags in relation to inventories needed for replenishment and to fill the distribution pipelines. Now, however, it will be of value to look more closely at the behavior of the system and examine its significance for factory scheduling. The general behavior of the system is dependent on the periodic review of inventory needs and on the preparation and transmission of orders for replenishment to the next stage upstream.

Now suppose that consumer demand falls by 10 per cent from its previous rate. During his next review of inventory needs, the retailer reflects this decrease in orders for replenishment sent to the distributor, but ten days had elapsed. Similarly, the distributor reflects the decrease in his next orders for replenishment to the factory warehouse, but an additional twenty days have elapsed before the factory warehouse will feel the fall in sales. Thus, adding up all of the time delays in the information system the factory will not learn of the 10 per cent fall in demand until thirty-five days have passed. Meanwhile, the factory has been producing 1.00/0.90 or 111 per cent of the new consumer requirement. An excess of 11 per cent would have accumulated each day in the inventory at the various stock points. This system inventory will have increased to $11 \times 35 = 385$ per cent of the usual normal day's supply.

In order to react to the change, retailers, distributors, and the factory warehouse decrease the quantities ordered, and to take account of the excess inventory, the factory will now have to cut back by substantially more than the 10 per cent. We can see now that the effect of the time lags in the system is to amplify the original 10 per cent change at the consumer level to a much greater change in production levels than would have seemed justified by the simple 10 per cent decrease in consumer demand, and we see that inventories have increased instead of decreased. Obviously, a more direct communication of changes in demand can reduce the magnitude of this amplification.

Figure 5 is identical to Figure 2 with the exception that a more direct information feedback loop has been added in the form of a system for assessing actual demand and forecasting demand in the immediate period ahead. The ten-day delay in assembling the actual demand and forecasting information reduces the total delay by twenty-five days. A 10 per cent decrease in sales under this sytem would mean an excess inventory of only $11 \times 10 = 110$ per cent of the normal levels would accumulate before the factory was aware of the change. Obviously, the forecast combined with the aggregate scheduling system shown in Figure 3 would stabilize the effects even more.

A Dynamic Simulation.   We can demonstrate the dynamic effects of the time lags and changes in the system structure more dramatically through the mechanism of a simulation study. Figure 6 shows the structure of a production-distribution system which is similar to that in Figure 2, but which involves different time values for overall flow of goods and information. In this structure the solid lines represent physical flow and the lines with small circle dots represent information flow. Forrester [5] developed a dynamic computer simulation model of this system and used it to test a variety of changes in parameters and system organization structure. We will look only at what happens to inventory levels at various points in the system and to factory output when retail sales increase by 10 per cent. Figure 7 indicates results similar to those shown in connection with our discussion of Figure 2; the response in inventory and production levels is not simply 10 per cent. Note that there is an amplification of the effect of each stage back through the system and that actual factory production finally increased to a peak of 45 per cent above its original level with a time lag of five months. The amplification and oscillating response are the result of the time lags in the information system.

What happens if we are able to reduce these time lags through more efficient procedures or by changing the structure of the system? Figure 8 shows the result when the entire distributor stage is eliminated. Note that the system response is similar but that the peak values of inventories are considerably reduced. The peak factory output rises to only 26 per cent instead of 45 per cent. (The curve of factory output based on the original distribution system from Figure 7 is included in Figure 8 for comparison).

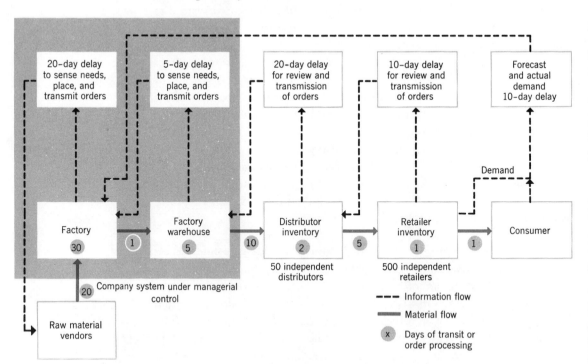

FIGURE 5. Production-distribution system with information feedback loop provided by forecasts and up-to-date information concerning actual consumer demand.

FIGURE 6.   Organization of production-distribution system. (From [5].)

Forrester also tested the effect of simply improving the speed with which information was handled back through the system by reducing purchasing time to one-third of these values. The effect, however, was only minor. This tends to indicate that improvements in structure, such as those discussed in connection with Figures 7 and 8 are likely to yield much better results than simply doing what is already being done but doing it faster.

System Dynamics of Scheduling.   It seems evident that a system for tracking the progress of sales at the retail-consumer level is essential, feeding back this information to factory scheduling. This would short-circuit the system of time lags inherent in a multistage production-distribution system. Just this tracking and information feedback in Forrester's results shown in Figure 7 would have stabilized the wild oscillations considerably. Second, a forecast based on some smoothing and anticipation of changes in demand would have had a very important effect in stabilizing Forrester's system. Finally, the incorporation of some aggregate planning system in combination with a presumably

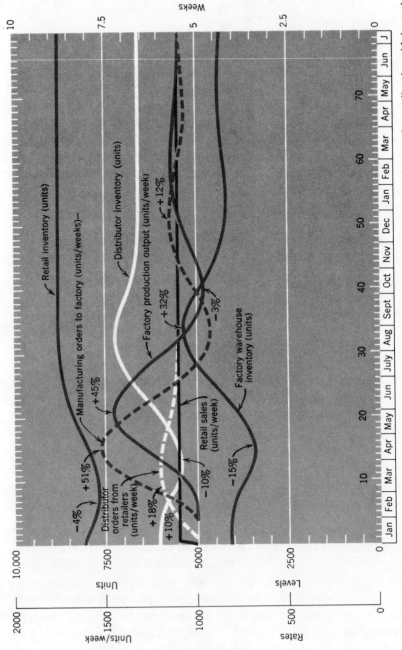

FIGURE 7. Response of production-distribution system to a sudden 10 per cent increase in retail sales. (Adapted from [5, Figure 2-2].)

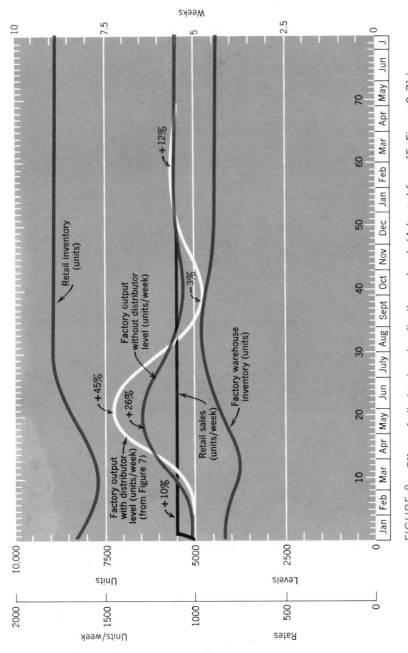

FIGURE 8.   Effect of eliminating the distributor level. (Adapted from [5, Figure 2-7].)

smoothed forecast, as shown in Figure 3, combines all of the features of tracking the progress of sales to provide information feedback, a smoothed forecast, and the stabilizing effect of anticipation and longer-range planning.

PRODUCTION CONTROL

Given the schedules produced by the kind of process envisioned in Figure 4, it is relatively simple to design an information system which feeds back to managerial personnel rapidly and accurately the actual quantities produced in comparison to plans. When serious deviations from plans occur, management can react through daily adjustment of hours worked. Large deviations from plan ordinarily cannot be adjusted in the short term but must be an input to the next aggregate planning period as a carryover of too much or too little inventory.

SUMMARY

Operations scheduling and control focus attention on the shortest planning horizon. How should projected aggregate output be allocated to individual items? How should the resources of men and machines be deployed to meet requirements? How will individual work assignments be determined?

For continuous systems where aggregate planning is the most direct and easiest, the detailed scheduling process involves a rebalancing of the manning of facilities to implement the decision to change work force size and to match the requirements of the new production rate decision. Otherwise the process is one of cut-and-try solutions which stay within the constraints of the aggregate plan. While this two-stage process of attempting to optimize at the aggregate level and developing detailed schedules within the constraints of the aggregate plan is suboptimal, present research holds promise of an aggregate planning model capable of specifying more detail in the aggregate plan.

The scheduling problem for high-volume continuous systems needs to be thought of in relation to the system as a whole and designed to be a part of the information flow of that system. Forrester shows that the production facility would be affected most by a change in demand because it is furthest upstream, and there is progressive amplification of variation in demand as we proceed upstream in the system. Yet the costs of variations in level of activity are most expensive at the production facility, involving the heavy costs of hiring, training, and laying off employees. Thus, information feedback loops short-circuiting the ordinary chain of demand are essential to stabilize the otherwise oscillatory behavior of the system. Also, forecasts and aggregate planning are essential to anticipate seasonal and trend effects in demand rather than simply to respond after the demand changes happen.

Control of operations in continuous systems is relatively simple by providing information feedback on actual output in relation to plan. Control action can affect only minor changes in output within a given period, however, leaving larger changes to be put into effect for the next planning period.

REVIEW QUESTIONS

1. Discuss the aggregate plan as a constraint to operations scheduling.
2. Given the aggregate plan as a constraint to operations scheduling in continuous systems, what flexibility is left to planners in developing detailed schedules?
3. Under what circumstances is rebalancing of production lines necessary when adjusting to a new aggregate plan?
4. Discuss the allocation problem involved in the determination of the breakdown of an aggregate plan into the quantities of types and sizes of products to be produced.
5. Criticize the flow diagram of Figure 4 as an overall process for developing optimal schedules.
6. What flexibility is left to management in continuous systems for adjusting to deviations in actual output from planned levels within a given period?
7. Note in the model of the production-inventory system of Figure 5 that information concerning demand at the retail level is fed back directly to the factory and that, as a result, there is a considerable reduction in the magnitude of oscillations in orders and production activity. What are the implications of this result for organizing and establishing lines of authority and responsibility for a multistage production-distribution system?

PROBLEMS

1. Field study: Locate a case study in the field involving the scheduling of a high-volume system.
(a) Analyze the planning and scheduling system used and describe it in detail with the aid of flow diagrams and other illustrative charts.
(b) Relate the scheduling process found in (a) to the generalized diagram of Figure 3:

(1) What is the source of forecasts, that is, from which point in the distribution process is the information generated?

(2) What is the time lag between demand generation and the availability of forecasts for use?

(3) How is aggregate planning accomplished? What modes of absorbing demand fluctuations are used?

(4) How is product mix in the upcoming production schedule determined?

(5) What degrees of freedom are open to the scheduler, that is, changes in hours worked, hiring and layoff, rebalancing of facilities, expansion or contraction of physical capacity, use of inventory, etc.?

(6) Under what constraints does the scheduler work?

(c) What techniques are used to rebalance the man and machine assignments if the size of the work force changes?

(d) Relate the activities of the schedules to the schematic diagram of Figure 4.

(e) What kinds of schedules are developed, that is, to cover which time spans into the future and at what level of detail?

2.   Considering the field study work in question 1, generate the data needed to produce a diagram comparable to Figure 3 for your particular project.

(a) Given whatever feedback of demand data structure which exists in the organization, compute the reaction at the factory level of a sudden 10 per cent decrease in demand.

(b) Consider what improvements in the information feedback structure might be effective.

3.   Considering all forecasting, and aggregate and detailed scheduling aspects of the production-distribution system of the field study in questions 1 and 2, draft a management report with recommendations for improvement.

4.   Consider a supply-production-distribution system for a high-volume standardized product, perhaps a small appliance, which has the physical flow, transit, and handling time as indicated in Figure 9. The total system volume is 2,000 units per day. Compute the equivalent pipeline inventory required for the system.

5.   Referring to the system shown in Figure 9 and discussed in problem 4, consider the effects of the ordering behavior of the retailers, distributors, and the factory warehouse.

(a) The system volume of 2,000 units per day is not of course equally distributed among the 1,000 retailers or is their ordering behavior identical. Three-fourths of the retailers carry no inventory, depending on the distributor to supply their needs when sales occur. These retailers account for 25 per cent of the total sales volume. The other 250 retailers account for 1,500 sales units per day and carry inventories to give customers immediate service. A study of their average sales volumes and ordering behavior shows that the largest 10 retailers sell 50 per day, the next largest 40 sell 10 per day, and the remaining group of 200 sell 2 per day. The 50 largest retailers place orders each ten days to cover sales. The 200 remaining retailers who carry inventories order each twenty days to cover sales. The total supply lead time is five days.

(b) The 10 distributors each have approximately equal volume of 200 units per day. The ordering behavior of the 5 company-owned distributors is somewhat different than that of the independent distributors. Since the company-owned distributors are not charged with their inventories, they seem to order less often and in larger quantities to make sure that excellent service is always given the retailers. They review needs monthly and order a month's (thirty days) supply. It takes them approximately sixteen days to review sales records and prepare orders, two days to transmit these orders to the factory warehouse, and it requires ten days for shipment plus transit to the distributor. The distributor then takes two days to receive, unload, and store the merchandise in order to make it available for future shipment to retailers. The company-owned distributors therefore have a replenishment cycle of $16 + 2 + 10 + 2 = 30$ days.

The independent distributors review needs twice each month (fifteen days) and order fifteen days' supply. It takes them six days to review needs and prepare orders, and the remaining replenishment times are the same as for the company-owned distributors resulting in a replenishment cycle of $6 + 2 + 10 + 2 = 20$ days.

Compute the cycle inventories required at the retail and distributor stages of the system.

6. Referring again to the system shown in Figure 9 and discussed in problems 4 and 5, consider the problems faced by the factory warehouse, distributors, and retailers, in trying to give good delivery service. All of the usage levels we have stated previously were average rates. The various units have ex-

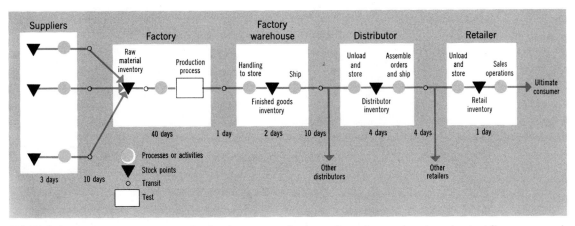

FIGURE 9. Supply-production-distribution system for a small appliance showing physical flow, assumed handling and transit times, and major stock points (five company-owned and five independent distributors, one thousand retailers).

perienced extreme demand levels which would result in their running out of stock (stock-out) if they carried no buffer stock. The reasonable maximum demand rates expected are as follows:

	Maximum Expected Demand during Supply Lead Time
Largest 10 retailers	350 per 5 days per retailer
Next largest 40 retailers	70 per 5 days per retailer
Next largest 200 retailers	15 per 5 days per retailer
Five company-owned distributors	6,800 per 30 days per distributor
Five independent distributors	4,400 per 20 days per distributor

The factory warehouse carries a buffer inventory of ten days' supply to ensure that extreme demand from distributors can be accommodated. Compute the system finished goods buffer inventory requirement.

7. Referring again to the system shown in Figure 9 and discussed in problems 4, 5, and 6, compute the total system inventory for finished goods. How could this finished goods system inventory be reduced? Since 5 of the distributors and all of the 1,000 retailers are outside managerial control, and own their own inventory, should the management of the enterprise (factory, factory warehouse, and 5 distributors) be at all concerned about how the rest of the system operates, i.e., does the behavior of the independent distributors and retailers affect them and if so, how?

8. If sales are seasonal, what are the alternatives available to management as a means of absorbing these seasonal variations in demand? What is the nature of the criterion function which might be appropriate to measure the alternatives for scheduling production in the face of seasonal demand?

REFERENCES

[1] Allen, M. "The Efficient Utilization of Labor Under Conditions of Fluctuating Demand." Chapter 16 in: *Industrial Scheduling*. J. F. Muth and G. L. Thompson, editors. Prentice-Hall, Englewood Cliffs, N.J., 1963.

[2] Bock, R. H., and W. K. Holstein. *Production Planning and Control*. Charles E. Merrill, Columbus, Ohio, 1963.

[3] Buffa, E. S. *Operations Management: Problems and Models* (3rd ed.). John Wiley, New York, 1972.

[4] Buffa, E. S., and W. H. Taubert. *Production-Inventory Systems: Planning and Control* (Rev. ed.). Richard D. Irwin, Homewood, Ill., 1972.

[5] Forrester, J. *Industrial Dynamics*. MIT Press, Cambridge, Mass., 1961.

[6] Greene, J. H. *Production Control: Systems and Decisions*. Richard D. Irwin, Homewood, Ill., 1965.

[7] Magee, J. F., and D. M. Boodman. *Production Planning and Inventory Control*. McGraw-Hill, New York, 1967.

[8] Moore, F. G., and R. Jablonski. *Production Control* (3rd ed.). McGraw-Hill, New York, 1969.

[9] Voris, W. *Production Control* (3rd ed.). Richard D. Irwin, Homewood, Ill., 1966.

Scheduling & Control for Intermittent Systems

As we discussed in Chapter 15 there are three common types of intermittent systems: the closed job shop which produces inventoriable items, the open job shop which produces custom items, and the large-scale one-time project. The two types of job shops can be considered together insofar as detailed scheduling and control of operations are concerned, since the physical flow and control problem is the same for both. The special problems associated with planning, scheduling, and control for large-scale projects are considered separately in the next chapter.

The job shop scheduling problem is commonly recognized as the most complex scheduling problem in existence. The complexity stems from the fact that the nature of the system requires that virtually everything is left flexible: part or product designs, routes through the system, processes to be used, processing times, etc. Progress in understanding the nature of the system was made when it was characterized as a network of queues with arrivals and departures at each work center described by probability distributions. The usual system, however, is so complex that analytical approaches of waiting line theory are useless. Thus, while the general concepts of waiting line analysis described in Chapter 8 are useful in understanding the nature of the flow process in a job shop, the formulas themselves make no contribution toward problem solving. With the availability of large-scale computers, however, a complex network of queues can be simulated. The general concepts of Monte Carlo simulation discussed in Chapter 4 apply, and simulation has been the dominant technique used in studying job shop scheduling.

ORDER CONTROL

Since each individual order must be segregated and treated as a unit, scheduling and control systems for job shops are often termed *order control systems*. The problem is to develop planning, scheduling, and control procedures appropriate for the situation, where each order in house at a given moment may have a unique sequence of processing with unique processing times and uniquely determined due dates. To control the flow of work in an order control system, we must make some detailed plans, schedule the order, dispatch it to the various operations according to some set of decision rules, and finally track the progress of the order to be sure that the schedule is being met.

Plans and Shop Papers
New orders for parts or products which have never been made before must be processed to determine what the manufacturing plan will be; that is, what operations will be performed, operation sequences, special tooling requirements, and method designs. We have already covered the details of this activity in Chapters 9, 10, 12, 13 and 14. If the part or product has been made before, standard route sheets should be available for reuse. But this is only part of the preparation required. It is customary to prepare shop orders, material requisitions, part drawings, shop travel orders, identification tags, tool requisitions, move tickets, scrap tickets, labor tickets and job progress cards. One example of the flow of these various plans and shop papers is shown in Figure 1.

Order Scheduling
While individual orders may call for different products, standardization of parts and component designs often makes economies possible by combining orders for identical parts and subassemblies. Cross classification charts, "Gozinto" charts and mathematical techniques can reveal the

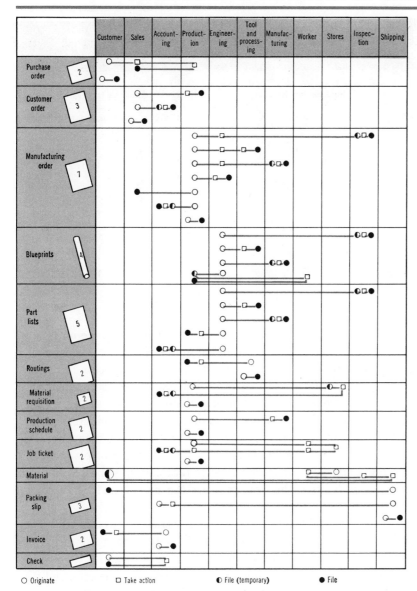

FIGURE 1. Flow of paperwork in a production control procedure. (Courtesy Professor John G. Carlson, University of Southern California.)

structure of these part and component families. Table I is a cross classification chart showing the number of parts and subassemblies that go into subassemblies and end products. Requirements of parts and subassemblies can then be summed for all end products and advantage can be taken of economical manufacturing and purchase lot sizes.

TABLE I. Cross Classification Table Showing the Number of Common Parts and Subassemblies That Go into Subassemblies and Final Assemblies

Part or Sub-assembly Number	Subassembly Number								Assembly Number							
	SA-1	SA-2	SA-3	SA-4	SA-5	SA-6	SA-7	SA-8	A-1	A-2	A-3	A-4	A-5	A-6	A-7	A-8
1	1	1			1				1							
2	1		1						1							
3				1		1	1	2					1			
4			4								1					
5	1		1		1										1	2
SA-1									1		1					1
SA-2											1					
SA-3												2				
SA-4													1			
SA-5													1			
SA-6										1			1			1
SA-7													1			
SA-8												1		1		

In constructing a schedule for an assembled product, we must work backward from the required completion dates of the end product, using the general concept of the schedule diagram. The *schedule diagram* takes the basic structure of assembly, subassemblies, part fabrication, material procurement, etc., and relates them to a time scale. Figure 2 is an example of a schedule diagram for an assembled product. Beginning with the receipt of the customer's order, the schedule diagram shows the time schedules that must be met at the various stages of planning and scheduling, material procurement, parts fabrication, subassembly, and assembly in order that the final product can be shipped by the target date.

For a complex product, such as an airplane, a missile, or a complicated electronic component, such charts are necessary. For a complex engineered product, time also would have to be allowed for the product engineering design to be completed. By determining the required time for final assembly, we determine the due dates for the subassemblies. The time to produce subassemblies in turn establishes due dates for manufactured and purchased parts, etc. In each instance these estimates of time requirements must allow for process time, move time, and time between operations. These set-back times determine when production must start and when purchase orders for needed raw material and purchased parts must be placed to meet schedules completion dates. The actual schedule of parts, subassemblies, and final products is the due date for each stage of manufacture and assembly.

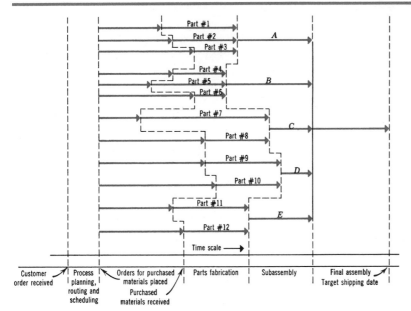

FIGURE 2. Schedule diagram for an assembled product. *A, B, C, D,* and *E* are subassemblies comprised of the parts indicated to the left of each subassembly.

Gantt Charts.   Gantt charts and their modern counterparts help provide information about the production schedule. They measure progress against the schedule, the load on departments or individual machines, and the availability of equipment or manpower. The plans and progress against plans are plotted in relation to time.

Several kinds of Gantt charts may be used. Figure 3 shows an example of the *Gantt project planning chart* which may be used to map out a detailed plan to accomplish target objectives. Figure 3 represents a plan to manufacture an assemmbled product so that the availability of parts for assembly dovetails with the fabrication and the assembly time required, as shown by the schedule diagram of Figure 2. Note that final assembly is scheduled to begin during the week of March 26th, before all of the subassembly units have been completed. As subsequent subassemblies are completed, they will be taken to the final assembly area. The schedule in this case could undoubtedly be compressed further by applying the same overlapping scheduling to the subassemblies in relation to the parts fabrication.

The overall scheduling of this project depends in part on the availability of men, machines, and materials. Therefore, the same basic concepts of the Gantt chart can be applied. Figure 4 shows a *Gantt load chart* for some of the machines that might be used in fabricating the

Activity Description	Dec. 1972	Jan. 1973	Feb. 1973	Mar. 1973	Apr. 1973	May 19
	4 11 18 25	2 8 15 22 29	5 12 19 26	5 12 19 26	2 9 16 23	7 14 21
Process planning, routing, & scheduling						
Materials procurement						
Parts fabrication						
Part #1						
#2						
#3						
#4						
#5						
#6						
#7						
#8				M		
#9				M		
#10				M		
#11						
#12						
Subassemblies						
A						
B						
C						
D						
E						
Final assembly						

FIGURE 3. Gantt project planning chart based on schedule diagram of Figure 2. At the beginning of the week of March 5, material procurement is one week behind schedule so the fabrication of parts 8, 9, and 10 has been held up.

various parts in our assembled product. It shows the overall projected load on these machines month by month, together with the accumulated backlog of work. Figure 5 shows greater detail; for each machine it shows the orders schedule with the total time reserved for each order. This is called a *Gantt layout chart* or a *Gantt reserved time planning chart*. It shows at a glance the status of a given order. Similar charts could be constructed for materials or men.

The charts must be maintained in order to be of any value as tools for planning, scheduling, and control. If we use paper and pencil charts similar to those illustrated in Figures 3, 4, and 5, the task of maintenance can be considerable. If, for example, the Gantt layout chart has to be modified to accommodate the fabrication of a new rush order, the entire sequence might have to be rescheduled. This is one reason why mechanical boards have been developed. They allow changes to be made rather quickly by the shifting of pegs or cards.

Even with the mechanical boards, the problem of maintenance is considerable, especially in large complex installations; this often results in discarding any attempt at the close control implied by the charts. The role of the electronic computer and modern programming methods looms large in the future. If we use the hand methods of developing the best schedule represented by the charts, the number of alternatives will often be very large, and selecting the best schedule becomes a trial-and-error process. A high-speed computer can be set up to make the trials quickly.

The need to maintain records of loads depends on how close to full capacity we are operating. At less than capacity levels, load records usually can be ignored because there is a great deal of slack in the system anyway; if the master schedule is followed, no great difficulties should be encountered. Under these conditions, orders are simply scheduled sequentially by assigning start dates and due dates. This, of course, offers no assurance that some machines will not be overscheduled by simple chance occurrence.

Load records of critical machines or known bottleneck operations are often kept instead of records on all machines. The assumption is that any schedule that fits within the load limits of the critical or bottleneck machine will probably work out all right for the rest of the machines.

The start date or the due date at each operation often serves as a simple priority decision rule to departmental foremen in getting the work out on time. The work load for each machine class is represented by the waiting line of jobs or shop orders. If the priority system were to take as the subsequent order on which to work the one with the earliest due date, there would be a constant reshuffling of the sequence of jobs to accommodate orders just received from other work centers which may have earlier due dates. This reshuffling is not particularly difficult, but nagging questions remain. Does this priority decision rule work better than some other rule? Are any decision rules significantly better than the simplest of all, first come–first served?

We might state the overall problem of the operation of a job shop as one of balancing the costs of carrying in-process inventory, labor, and the capital costs of capacity, together with the costs associated with meeting specified order completion dates. To have a high degree of

Dispatching
Decision Rules

Turret Lathe Dept.	Mach. No.	March	April	May
Gisholt #2	321			
Gisholt #4	422			
Warner and Swasey #2	729			
Warner and Swasey #2	730			
Warner and Swasey #5	810			
Bullard vert. turret #1	769			

FIGURE 4. Gantt load chart. Light lines show per cent of month that machines have scheduled work. Heavy lines show cumulative load.

labor and machine utilization it would be necessary to have a large number of orders waiting so that labor and equipment are very seldom idle. The result is relatively high in-process inventory carrying costs and poor schedule performance.

If we strive to meet order completion dates without fail, however, we need a very large equipment and labor capacity so that orders ordinarily would not have to wait. This would result in relatively low in-process inventory costs but poor machine and labor utilization. The problem of balancing these costs in a complex system is at best a difficult one. Thus there has been a focus on system simulation as a technique for testing alternate decision rules. To test various priority decision rules in the factory would be time consuming and would also disrupt factory operations by continual shifting from one decision rule to the next.

Early work in the simulation of dispatching decision rules was done by Rowe [23] at the General Electric Company. In conjunction with Rowe's work, the IBM Corporation developed a generalized simulation program which they called "the job shop simulator." This program is flexible in terms of the input characteristics of the system to be simulated and has been used effectively by the General Electric Company, Hughes Aircraft Company, Westinghouse Electric Corporation, and others. The general characteristics of the job shop simulator are shown in Figure 6.

June	July	August				

FIGURE 4. (*continued*)

Hughes Aircraft Company's application of the IBM job shop simulator represents an adaptation of the program to the company's El Segundo plant operations. The adaptation made it possible to take order input data directly from random access files, transposed to the form required for simulation, together with other input data supplied to the simulator. LeGrande [15] made a study testing six dispatch decision rules with the El Segundo job shop simulation process. By operating the simulated shop according to each of the six decision rules and measuring results by certain criteria which we shall discuss, it was possible to compare the effectiveness of the six different rules. The rules used in the study were as follows:

1. *Minimum Processing Time per Operation* or, Shortest Operation Time, (SOT): Of the jobs waiting in line at a machine group, this rule assigns the next job to be worked on by choosing the one with the shortest processing time (setup plus machining time).

2. *Minimum Slack Time per Operation* or, Dynamic Slack per Remaining Operation, (DS/RO): The next order to be worked on is determined by subtracting the remaining processing time for the order from the total time remaining (due date minus present time), and dividing the result by the number of remaining operations. The order for which this amount is smallest will be assigned to be processed next.

3. *First Come—First Served*, (FCFS): This rule places orders in line as

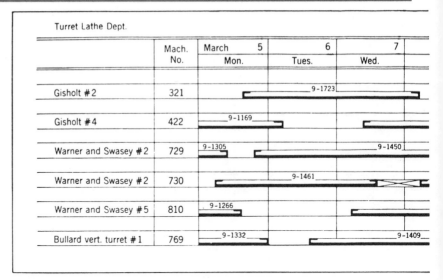

Turret Lathe Dept.

FIGURE 5.   Gantt layout or reserved time planning chart.

they arrive at a machine group, choosing the next order to be processed from the front of the line.

4. *Minimum Planned Start Date per Operation,* (MINSD): In this rule the order assigned next is the order with the earliest planned start date for the current operation. This is the theoretical operations start date which has been calculated previously by the scheduling procedure.

5. *Minimum Due Date per Order* or, First in System, First Served, (FISFS): This rule is based on the due dates for orders waiting in line. The order that has the earliest planned due date will be assigned first.

6. (*Random Selection,* (RAND): This rule has no special priorities. The order to be assigned next is selected at random from all of the orders waiting in line at the machine group.

The criteria by which the various simulation runs were evaluated are as follows:

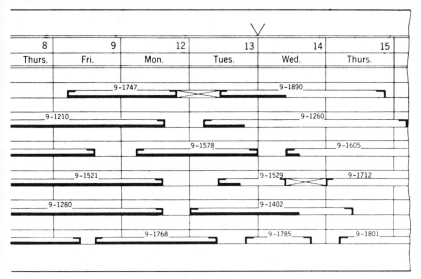

8	9	12	13	14	15
Thurs.	Fri.	Mon.	Tues.	Wed.	Thurs.

FIGURE 5. *(continued)*

1. Number of orders completed.
2. Per cent of orders completed late.
3. Mean of the distribution of completions.
4. Standard deviation of the distribution of completions.
5. Average number of orders waiting in the shop.
6. Average wait time of orders.
7. Yearly cost of carrying orders in queue.
8. Ratio of inventory carrying cost while waiting to inventory cost while on the machine.
9. Per cent of labor utilized.
10. Per cent of machine capacity utilized.

Figure 7 shows the distributions of order completions for the six decision rules. On the basis of an equal weighting of the criteria, the minimum processing time per operation rule (SOT) gives the best results. As LeGrande points out, a different weighting with perhaps emphasis on getting orders out on time would tend to favor minimum slack time per operation (DS/RO) as a decision rule. If management places a premium on getting orders out on time, then some kind of due-oriented rule, should give superior results. Carroll [6] experimented with a family of rules which sequenced orders according to the largest ratio of downstream waiting-time cost to operation process time or c/t (called c over t, or COVERT). In comparison with five rules tested, the COVERT rule was extremely effective in meeting due dates as shown in Figure 8.

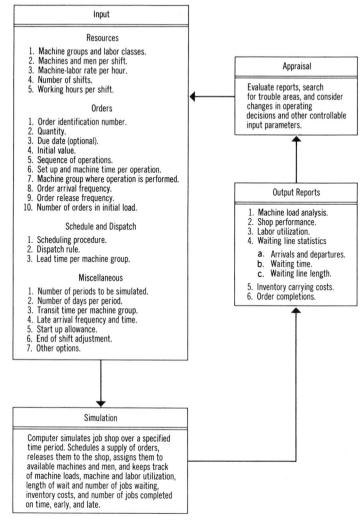

FIGURE 6. Overall characteristics of the job shop simulator. (From LeGrande [15].)

Tracking the Progress of Orders

Unfortunately, we cannot predict the flaws in our original plans. Machines may break down, work may pile up behind some critical machine, and dozens of other unexpected production troubles may occur that interfere with original schedules. With hundreds or even thousands of current orders in a shop, the only way to be sure that orders ultimately will meet schedules is to provide information feedback and a system of corrective action that can compensate for delays. Returned job tickets, move orders, and inspection reports can provide

Dispatch Rule	MINSD	FCFS	FISFS	DS/RO	RAND	SOT
Per cent orders early	54	57	63	68	65	71
Per cent orders on due date	6	5	5	12	5	5
Per cent orders late	44	38	32	20	30	24
Mean of completions (days)	3.0	3.6	4.2	4.2	5.2	6.6
Standard deviation (days)	9.2	10	8.2	8.2	10.4	9.9
Total number of orders completed	3118	3190	3484	3217	3117	3708

FIGURE 7. Distributions for the time of order completions. (From LeGrande [15].)

formal information which can be compared with schedules. But to be of value, this information flow must be rapid so that action can be taken on up-to-date reports. Usual company mail systems are much too slow to serve the needs of production control systems. Therefore, special communication systems are in common use, such as special mail services, intercommunication systems, teletype writers interconnected to central offices, pneumatic tube systems, and remote data collection centers tied directly in with automatic computing systems. These systems in combination with rapid data processing can grind out current reports which can be used as a basis for expediting and rescheduling orders.

FIGURE 8. Lateness distribution for six rules, pure job shop single-component order (3072 orders, utilization = 0.80). (From Carroll [6].)

Computerized Planning, Scheduling, and Control Systems

As mentioned earlier the complexities of job shop planning, scheduling, and control, together with the difficulties of maintaining graphic methods such as Gantt charts, have led to the use of computer-based systems [5, 9, 15, 17, 22, 24]. One such system, installed at the Hughes Aircraft Company, is of particular interest since it combines shop load forecasting, daily simulation scheduling, remote data collection, and a series of important reports, all in a computer-based system [5, 15, 24].

The Hughes Job Shop Control System. The Hughes plant in which the system is installed has approximately 1000 machines and/or work centers which are grouped into 120 functional machine or work centers.

The work centers are manned by 400 direct workers. Approximately 2000 to 3000 orders are in process at any one time with an average of seven operations per order. The average total processing time for an order is 2.5 hours, and the average order cycle time is three to four weeks.

The broad outlines of the entire system are shown in Figure 9. Operational process planning is developed from engineering blueprints to yield the critical data of processes to be performed, standard process times, and

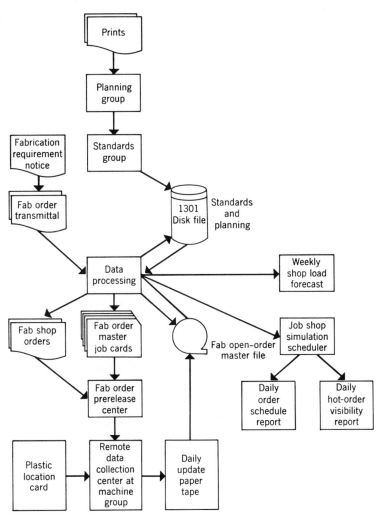

FIGURE 9. Hughes Aircraft Company's production, planning, and control system. (Adapted from LeGrande [15].)

standard flow allowances through the shop. These data are placed in the disk file of the computing system. When a fabrication requirement notice is received from one of the assembly product line departments, a fabrication order is transmitted to data processing which initiates the preparation of a fabrication shop order and establishes an open order in the fabrication open-order master file. A deck of master job cards also is produced which accompanies the order through the shop. These papers are then sent to a fabrication order control prerelease center from which orders are dispatched to the shop. After release to the shop, the master job cards are used in conjunction with plastic location cards at machine groups to actuate the remote data collection devices. At the end of the day, a paper tape containing all order moves transacted during the day is used to update current order locations and to code completed operations in the fabrication open-order file. The fabrication open-order master file contains, on a daily updated basis, the information on every open order. It is the heart of the system which produces the three documents: the *weekly shop load forecast*, the *daily order schedule report*, and the *daily hot-order visibility report*.

The *daily order schedule report* and the *hot-order visibility report* are developed by the job shop simulation scheduler. These documents are used by shop foremen and expediters in the daily sequencing of orders at the machine groups in the shop. The simulation scheduler is a separate computing routine used to simulate one shift of shop activity and to generate the two daily reports. Involved in the simulation scheduling process is the use of a priority dispatch decision rule related to slack time in the schedule.

The reports of the performance of the Hughes system given in [15] indicate that the computer-based integrated system has yielded substantial improvements. For example, in the first six months of operation there was a 10 per cent increase in the number of orders completed on time. The average order cycle time was reduced by one week, thus reducing in-process inventory and increasing man and machine utilization significantly. The new system seemed to relieve what we might term organizational stress and pressure, as indicated by a 60 per cent reduction in expediting effort. Expediting effort occurs with hot orders when special personnel are assigned to these hot orders to make sure that they receive special attention at each stage.

Western Electric Interactive System. An interesting development which uses the capabilities of time-shared computing has promise for the job shop scheduling problem. Godin and Jones [10] developed interactive scheduling systems which use either typewriter or display terminals and thereby place the production supervisor, or a scheduler, in a loop with a computer program. By interacting with the computer program the scheduler develops and/or alters a schedule. Schedules are generated by making choices from among sets of decision rules, for example, rules for the acceptance or rejection of orders, rules for sequencing orders, and rules for allocating the use of overtime. A schedule is developed by testing the effects of various combinations of possibilities, simulating various alternate assignments and their effects.

Godin and Jones developed a small-scale application of the interactive scheduling concept in one of the coil winding shops of the Western Electric Company. Of the 200 types of coils manufactured, approximately 65 are active at any point in time and each type is usually being produced for three or four different orders. There are twenty of one type winding machine and two of the second type, and the work force consists of from twenty to thirty-five machine operators working on two or three shifts depending on shop load.

Because of differences in skills, not all operators can wind all types of coils, and performance against standard varies considerably for various combinations of operators and coil types. Similarly, some machines cannot be used to wind some types of coils. The production supervisor must assign workers and machines to each other in a way which balances pressures for on-time deliveries against the other factors which make for production effectiveness.

The system functions through a main program and twenty-three subroutines. To communicate with the program through the typewriter terminal, a simple conversational language was developed. A single key stroke indicates a whole series of commands. For example, when the key marked "Load" is depressed, the computer understands it as a request to print the winding shop load on the printer.

The system allows for the production supervisor to consider seven variables in constructing schedules:

1. Skill levels of workers.
2. Skill needs of products.
3. Capability of machines.
4. Availability of workers, machines, and materials.
5. Quantities required.
6. Completion dates.
7. Existing machine set ups.

The computer program can carry out simulations of shop schedules so that the supervisor can test various alternate assignments and try to anticipate future problems. Various reports can be called for at any time that the system is in operation such as shop status, a history of work by operator or by machine, load summarized by standard hours, etc.

SUMMARY

Operations scheduling and control focus attention on the shortest planning horizon. How should projected aggregate output be allocated to individual items? How should the resources of men and machines be deployed to meet requirements? How will individual work assignments be determined?

Operations scheduling and control for intermittent systems are very complex, since individual orders must flow through a sequence of unique operations. Cross classification tables, schedule diagrams, and Gantt charts are tools which help one visualize and simplify the great complexities of the scheduling problem.

Sequencing orders at work centers has been a subject of considerable research; given certain managerial objectives, superior priority dispatching decision rules can be specified. The LeGrande study of priority dispatching decision rules indicates that the weighting of various criteria will make an important difference in terms of which decision rule seems superior. When a heavier weighting is placed on criteria which emphasize on-time delivery, some sort of due date oriented decision rule provides superior performance.

Computer-based integrated systems of planning, scheduling, and control, such as the Hughes system, makes possible the effective management of large job shops. Computer-based systems have also been developed for the smaller shop situation, however, since the nature and complexity of small-shop problems seemed to be nearly identical with the larger-shop problems in terms of the information, scheduling, and control systems needed. The required differences in the capabilities of such systems for the small versus the large shop seemed to be largely in terms of the scale of the system needed. Finally, the availability of time-shared computing and the development of the concepts of interactive scheduling systems similar to the Western Electric system seem ideally suited for the small shop.

REVIEW QUESTIONS

1. In order scheduling, of what value are cross classification charts?
2. How does the concept of the schedule diagram help in order scheduling of a complex assembled product?

3. What is a dispatching decision rule?

4. If management's objectives place a high value on low in-process inventories, what kind of priority dispatching rule seems best?

5. If management's objectives place a high value on on-time delivery of orders, what kind of priority dispatching decision rule seems best?

6. What are Gantt charts? Discuss the functions of the Gantt project planning chart, the Gantt load chart, and the Gantt layout or reserved time planning chart.

7. Evaluate the Gantt chart as a representation of the schedule problem in job shops.

PROBLEMS

1. Consider the pipe valve assembly shown in Figure 12 of Chapter 10 and discussed in problem 1 on page 275. Based on the following data, construct a schedule diagram for the production of an order of 500 valves.

(a) All designing and planning for the production of the pipe valve have been completed.

(b) Patterns for the various cast parts can be obtained in four working days.

(c) Two days are required for the production of castings, body, bushing, and handle, i.e., parts 1, 2, and 6. (Castings cannot be produced in the foundry until the patterns are received.)

(d) Bar stock for the stem and cap (parts 3 and 5) can be obtained from a local metal supply house within three days after orders have been placed.

(e) Nuts, screws, packing, etc. can be obtained in three days.

(f) The machine shop estimates fabrication and assembly times for a lot of 500 parts as follows: body, three days; bushing, three days; stem, one day; cap, one day; handle, three days; and assembly, three days.

2. You are production scheduler in the plumbing supplies company which makes the valves discussed in the previous problem and are scheduling the use of four machines for next week. A colleague in the scheduling department reviews the situation and sees a solution which produces a combined operating plus setup cost of $1395. He challenges you to beat it. The plant works eight hours per day, five days per week, and does not work overtime. Using a Gantt chart, schedule the work orders and calculate the total incremental cost for your schedule. Data are as follows:

Orders Due Next Week	Quantity	Material Available	Completion Time
1. Valve bodies	1400	Mon., 8:00 A.M.	Thurs., 5:00 P.M.
2. Handles	700	Mon., 8:00 A.M.	Fri. 5:00 P.M.
3. Valve guides	300	Mon., 8:00 A.M.	Thurs., 5:00 P.M.
4. Stems	1200	Tues., 8:00 P.M.	Fri., 5:00 P.M.
5. Cap	1500	Mon., 8:00 P.M.	Fri., 11:00 A.M.

Setup and Operating Times

Order	Engine Lathe	Vertical Turret Lathe	Screw Machine	Turret Lathe
		Machines		
1; Setup, hrs	—	2.00	1.00	4.00
Opr. time, hrs/pc	—	0.01	0.02	0.02
2; Setup, hrs	3.00	4.00	—	1.00
Opr. time, hrs/pc	0.05	0.07	—	0.05
3; Setup, hrs	1.00	—	1.00	—
Opr. time, hrs/pc	0.18	—	0.10	—
4; Setup, hrs	2.00	2.00	2.00	—
Opr. time, hrs/pc	0.12	0.04	0.04	—
5; Setup, hrs	—	2.50	2.00	4.00
Opr. time, hrs/pc	—	0.05	0.03	0.02
Number machines available	2	1	2	2
Operating cost/hr	$9.50	$8.00	$4.00	$4.00
Setup costs:				
1	—	$325.00	$90.00	$30.00
2	$25.00	170.00	—	75.00
3	13.00	—	10.00	—
4	50.00	380.00	25.00	—
5	—	400.00	200.00	50.00

3. Job orders are received at a work center with the characteristics indicated by the following data. In what sequence should the orders be processed at the work center if the priority dispatch decision rule is:

(a) FCFS (first come–first served).
(b) SOT (shortest operation time).
(c) SS (static slack, that is, due date less time of arrival at work center).
(d) FISFS (due date system, first in system–first served).
(e) SS/RO (static slack/remaining number of operations).

Which decision rule do you prefer? Why?

Compute priorities for each rule and list the sequence in which orders would be processed.

Order Number	Due Date	Date and Time Received at Center	Operation Time, Hours	Remaining Operations
1	May 1	Apr. 18, 9 A.M.	6	3
2	Apr. 20	Apr. 21, 10 A.M.	3	1
3	June 1	Apr. 19, 5 P.M.	7	2
4	June 15	Apr. 21, 3 P.M.	9	4
5	May 15	Apr. 20, 5 P.M.	4	5
6	May 20	Apr. 21, 5 P.M.	8	7

REFERENCES

[1] Berry, W. L. "Labor Assignments In Job Shops: An Application of Work Flow Analysis." Unpublished Ph.D. Dissertation, Harvard Business School, 1968.

[2] Bock, R. H., and W. K. Holstein. *Production Planning and Control.* Charles E. Merrill, Columbus, Ohio, 1963.

[3] Buffa, E. S. *Operations Management: Problems and Models* (3rd ed.) John Wiley, New York, 1972.

[4] Buffa, E. S., and W. H. Taubert. *Production-Inventory Systems: Planning and Control* (Rev. ed.). Richard D. Irwin, Homewood, Ill., 1972.

[5] Bulkin, M. H., J. L. Colley, and H. W. Steinhoff, Jr. "Load Forecasting, Priority Sequencing, and Simulation in a Job Shop Control System." Chapter 11 in: *Readings in Production and Operations Management*, E. S. Buffa, editor. John Wiley, New York, 1966. Also published in similar form in: *Management Science*, **13** (2), 29–51, Oct. 1966.

[6] Carroll, D. C. "Heuristic Sequencing of Single and Multiple Component Jobs. Unpublished Ph.D. Dissertation, Sloan School of Management, MIT, 1965.

[7] Conway, R. W., and W. L. Maxwell. "Network Scheduling by the Shortest Operation Discipline." *Operations Research*, **10** (1), 51–73, 1962. Also reprinted as Chapter 17 in: *Industrial Scheduling*. J. F. Muth and G. L. Thompson, editors. Prentice Hall, Englewood Cliffs, New Jersey, 1963.

[8] Conway, R. W., W. L. Maxwell, and L. W. Miller. *The Theory of Scheduling.* Addison-Wesley, Reading, Mass., 1967.

[9] Elmaghraby, S. E., and R. T. Cole. "On the Control of Production in Small Job-Shops." *Journal of Industrial Engineering*, **14** (4), 186–196, July–Aug. 1963.

[10] Godin, V., and C. H. Jones. "The Interactive Shop Supervisor." *Industrial Engineering*, Nov. 1969, pp. 16–22.

[11] Groff, G. K., and J. F. Muth. *Operations Management: Analysis for Decisions.* Richard D. Irwin, Homewood, Ill., 1972.

[12] Holstein, W. K. "Production Planning and Control Integrated." *Harvard Harvard Business Review*, **46** (3), 121–140, May–June 1968.

[13] Holstein, W. K., and W. L. Berry. "The Labor Assignment Decision: An Application of Work Flow Structure." *Management Science*, **16** (6), 324–336, Feb. 1970.

[14] Kusnick, A. A. "Management and Engineering Information Systems." *Industrial Management Review*, 3–16, Spring 1966.

[15] LeGrande, E. "The Development of a Factory Simulation System Using Actual Operating Data." *Management Technology*, **3** (1), May 1963. Also reprinted as Chapter 9 in: *Readings in Production and Operations Management*. E. S. Buffa, editor. John Wiley, New York, 1966.

[16] Magee, J. F., and D. M. Boodman. *Production Planning and Inventory Control* (2nd ed.). McGraw-Hill, New York, 1967.

[17] Moodie, C. L., and D. J. Novotny. "Computer Scheduling and Control Systems for Discrete Part Production." *Journal of Industrial Engineering*. **19** (7), 336–341, July 1968.

[18] Moore, F. G., and R. Jablonski. *Production Control* (3rd ed.). McGraw-Hill, New York, 1969.

[19] Nanot, Y. R. "An Experimental Investigation and Comparative Evaluation of Priority Disciplines in Job Shop-Like Queuing Networks." Unpublished Ph.D. Dissertation, UCLA, 1963. Also printed as *Management Sciences Research Project, Research Report No. 87*, UCLA, 1963.

[20] Nelson, R. T. "Labor and Machine Limited Production Systems." *Management Science*, **13** (9), 648–671, May 1967.

[21] O'Malley, R. L., S. E. Elmaghraby, and J. W. Jeske, Jr. "An Operational System for Smoothing Batch-Type Production." *Management Science*, **12** (10), 433–449, June 1966.

[22] Reiter, S. "A System for Managing Job Shop Production." *Journal of Businrss*, **34** (3), 371–393, July 1966.

[23] Rowe, A. J. "Sequential Decision Rules in Production Scheduling." Unpublished Ph.D. Dissertation, UCLA, Aug. 1958.

[24] Steinhoff, H. W., Jr. "Daily System for Sequencing Orders in a Large-Scale Job Shop." Chapter 10 in: *Readings in Production and Operations Management*. E. S. Buffa, editor. John Wiley, New York, 1966.

[25] Voris, W. *Production Control* (3rd ed.). Richard D. Irwin, Homewood, Ill., 1966.

20

Planning, Scheduling, & Control for Large-Scale Projects

With the relatively recent emphasis on research and development and on very large-scale one-time projects in the aerospace and construction industries, the planning methods described in Chapter 10 are not adequate. While assembly and operation process charts are still valid mechanisms for more detailed studies, they implicitly presume that we are dealing with substantial numbers of items which would justify careful analysis of minute details. But for the large-scale project, an entirely different level of planning becomes necessary. For example,

593

the entire manufacturing process represented by the operation process chart for the capacitor in Figure 4 of Chapter 10 becomes condensed into a broader question: "When must these capacitors be available to dovetail with the assembly of the guidance computer component?" Or the production of the capacitor may be completely submerged in another question: "When must the guidance computer component be available for test and assembly into the guidance system as a whole?" The fabrication of the capacitor component is not considered at all in this question since it probably would be subcontracted, and the detailed plans for its manufacture are for someone else's consideration.

The central focus for the project as a whole then is in planning the important activities in larger blocks and giving close attention to how they must dovetail to achieve the total end result. Which activities depend for their execution on the completion of other activities? Which activities can proceed relatively independently or in parallel with other activities? As we shall see, these kinds of plans are intimately bound up in the basic sequencing required and in the schedule.

The very nature of the one-time large project demands that planning of *what* has to be done and the *schedule* for performance must be done together. They are interdependent, and the planning for large projects, involves a plan for deployment of resources to the total project. To accomplish this, we must determine the activities required, the timing and interdependencies, the requirements of various possible schedules for manpower and other resources, and the relationship of all the foregoing to a project completion date. The project completion date is most often a part of a contract with penalties for nonperformance. Therefore, the complexities and the one-time nature of the project require a coordinated plan which involves activities required, schedule, and deployment of resources. The great complexity of such projects calls for special methods; network planning techniques have been developed to meet this need.

Network planning techniques go under a confusion of acronyms with variations. The two original names, PERT (Performance Evaluation and Review Technique) and CPM (Critical Path Methods), have been differentiated into a variety of brand names applied essentially to the same basic methodology. Some of the alternate names used are: CPS (Critical Path Scheduling), LES (Least-cost Estimating and Scheduling), Micro-PERT, 1-time-PERT, PERT/COST, and PEP. These various names for PERT/CPM techniques are at least a measure of the degree of interest that has developed.

ORIGIN OF NETWORK PLANNING

Network planning methods seem to have been developed by two different groups independently. As an internal project of the DuPont Company, critical path methods were developed to plan and control the maintenance of chemical plants and were subsequently widely used by DuPont for many engineering functions. Parallel efforts were undertaken by the U.S. Navy at about the same time to develop methods for planning and controlling the Polaris missile project. The magnitude of the task may be envisioned when one realizes that approximately 3000 separate contracting organizations were involved. The result was the development of the PERT methodology. The immediate success of both the CPM and PERT methodologies may be gauged by the following facts. DuPont's application of their technique to a maintenance project in their Louisville works resulted in reducing down time for maintenance from 125 to 78 hours; the PERT technique was widely credited with helping to shorten by two years the time originally estimated for the completion of the engineering and development program for the Polaris missile.

PERT and CPM are based on substantially the same concepts, although there are some differences in details. First, as originally developed, the PERT methods were based on probabilistic estimates of activity times which resulted in a probabilistic path through a network of activities (such as that shown in Figure 1) and a probabilistic project completion time. The CPM methods, however, assumed constant or deterministic activity times. Actually, either the probabilistic or deterministic model is equally applicable to and usable by either technique. As a matter of fact, most present-day applications of PERT methods have dropped the use of the probabilistic activity times and use the slightly simpler deterministic time estimates. The second difference between the two techniques is in the details of how the arrow diagram is prepared. In the discussion that follows, we shall point out more clearly both the probabilistic-deterministic and the arrow diagram differences.

In the following sections we shall first develop PERT planning methods and then show the differences between PERT and CPM methods.

PERT PLANNING METHODS

The essence of PERT planning is based on the development of a network representation of the required activities, as indicated by Figure 1b. In

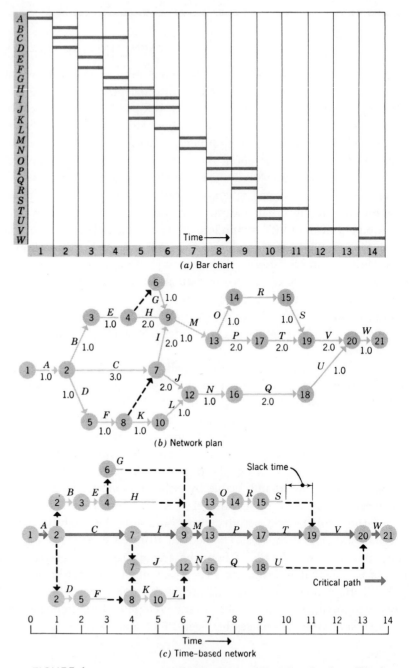

FIGURE 1. Comparison of bar chart with network plan. The heavy colored line indicates the critical path; the horizontal dashed lines indicate slack time. (From Archibald and Villoria [1, p. 4].)

Figure 1b, the arrows represent the required activities coded by the letters, with estimated performance times shown near the arrows. In network planning, the length of the arrows ordinarily has no significance for reasons which we shall comment on later. The numbered circles define the beginning and end points of activities and are called *events* or *nodes*. The direction of arrows indicate flow in the sense that node 2 marks the end of activity *A* and the beginning of activities *B*, *C*, and *D*; node 3 marks the end of activity *B*. The network then also represents the required precedence relationships of all activities. For example, activities *B*, *C*, and *D* cannot start until activity *A* has been completed, but activities *B*, *C*, and *D* can all proceed simultaneously.

Figures 1a, b, and c all represent the same plan. It is undoubtedly easier to visualize the fixed time relations in the bar chart of Figure 1a, but actually the bar chart does not contain all of the crucial information about precedence requirements. The bar chart does show the earliest time that each activity can begin and end, but it does not show the latest time that each activity can begin in order that its completion time does not interfere with the beginning of following activities.

Note, however, that the "time-based network" in Figure 1c shows this information. Here the length of the solid lines represents the estimated activity times, and the dashed lines represent slack in the schedule. Note, for example, that activity *S* requires 1 time unit and can begin as early as time $t = 9$ but need not begin before $t = 10$ in order to be completed by its latest finish time, $t = 11$. If activity *S* is completed any time between $t = 10$ and $t = 11$, activity *V* which follows can begin on time. Note also that activity *V*, which depends on the completion of both *S* and *T* by $t = 11$ for its start time, has no slack in its schedule.

We see from Figure 1c that only activities *G*, *F*, *H*, *S*, and *U* have slack. Note, however, that some other activities can use some or all of the slack shown. For example, if activity *J* is delayed by 1 time unit, it is not serious because *N*, *Q* and *U* can all be set back by 1 time unit, using up 1 unit of the slack shown associated with *U*. If any one of them uses up as much as 3 units of slack, however, all of the following activities become *critical*; that is, they must begin and end by their latest event times or the entire project will be held up and the project completion date cannot be met.

Now let us focus attention on the sequence of activities *A-C-I-M-P-T-V-W* in the time based network of Figure 1c. They are connected by the heavy colored line labeled as the *critical path*. There is no slack in the schedules of any of these activities, nor can any of them borrow slack from another activity such as was possible with activities *J*, *N*, and *Q* using some or all of the slack associated with *U*. This set of activities defines a critical path through the network. Each of these critical path activities must begin and end on time if the project completion time of *t* = 14 is to be met. The critical path is the longest time path through the network.

The network plan summarizes, in compact form, a great deal of important information: the activities required, their precedence relationships, and slack in the schedule. From the basic network plan, we can easily calculate crucial information regarding the earliest and latest start and finish times, available slack in the schedules of activities, and the critical path. Ordinarily, it is the network plan similar to Figure 1*b* that is used rather than the time-based network plan. The reason is simply that the entire system is normally computer based; given the activities and their precedence relationships, standard computer programs will provide all of the schedule information for each activity (the earliest and latest start and finish times and available slack), indicating which activities are on the critical path. Thus, as we noted previously, the length of arrows in the network plan need not have significance since the network itself is only an input to the computation of the other important schedule data. Of course, the time-based network can be constructed from the data given by the computer output if it is felt that there is significant value in visualizing the schedule through graphic means.

Let us note again that the interdependent nature of the set of activities, the importance of a project completion date, and the one-time nature of projects require that the planning for what must be done and the schedule considerations must be intimately bound up together. The equally important related plan for the use of manpower and other resources will be discussed later in this chapter, after we have developed more fully the network planning methods.

With the generalities of PERT methods just discussed in mind, let us utilize a relatively simple example, house construction, to develop the methods used in generating the network representation of a project. The phases of development may be divided into (a) activity analysis, (b) arrow diagramming, and (c) node numbering.

Activity Analysis. This is comparable functionally to what a production engineer or production planner does when specifying operations, work methods, and tooling for fabricated parts and products. For large projects, however, there is imposed a degree of complexity due to the extremely large number of components and required activities such that it is possible to overlook the need for some activities. Therefore, while professional planning personnel are commonly used, the generation of the activity list is often partially done in meetings and round table discussions which include managerial and operating personnel. The result of the entire process is a list of required activities such, as the one shown in Table I, showing the basic activities required to construct a house.

Arrow Diagramming. This requires a consideration of the precedence relationships among activities and must be based on a complete, veri-

TABLE I. Precedence Chart Showing Sequence of Activities and Required Times to Finish a House			
Job No.	Description	Immediate Predecessors	Time (days)
a	Start		0
b	Excavate and pour footings	a	4
c	Pour concrete foundation	b	2
d	Erect wooden frame including rough roof	c	4
e	Lay brickwork	d	6
f	Install basement drains and plumbing	c	1
g	Pour basement floor	f	2
h	Install rough plumbing	f	3
i	Install rough wiring	d	2
j	Install heating and ventilating	d, g	4
k	Fasten plaster board and plaster (including drying)	i, j, h	10
l	Lay finishing flooring	k	3
m	Install kitchen fixtures	l	1
n	Install finish plumbing	l	2
o	Finish carpentry	l	3
p	Finish roofing and flashing	e	2
q	Fasten gutters and downspouts	p	1
r	Lay storm drains for rain water	c	1
s	Sand and varnish flooring	o, t	2
t	Paint	m, n	3
u	Finish electrical work	t	1
v	Finish grading	q, r	2
w	Pour walks and complete landscaping	v	5
x	Finish	s, u, w	0

From [12].

fied, and approved activity list. The important information required for the arrow diagram is generated by the following three questions:

1. Which activities must be completed *before* each given activity can be started?
2. Which activities can be carried out in *parallel*?
3. Which activities immediately succeed other given activities?

The common practice is simply to work backwards through the activity list, generating the immediate predecessors for each activity listed as shown in Table I for the house construction project. The estimated normal time for each activity is also shown in the table, although it is not necessary at this point. The arrow diagram may then be constructed to represent the logical precedence requirements shown in Table I.

Dummy Activities. Care must be taken in correctly representing the actual precedence requirements in the arrow diagram. For example, look at the immediate predecessor activities for activity *s*, sand and varnish flooring, and activity *u*, finish electrical work. Activity *s* has as immediate predecessors *o* and *t*, finish carpentry and painting, respectively, while *u* has a predecessor of only activity *t*. The relationship shown in Figure 2a does not correctly represent this situation because it specifies that the beginning of *u* is dependent on both *o* and *t* and this is not true. To represent the situation correctly, we must resort to the use of a dummy activity which requires zero performance time. Figure 2b now represents the stated requirement. The finish electrical work, *u*, now depends only on the completion of painting, *t*. Through the dummy activity, however, both finish carpentry and painting must be completed before activity *s*, sand and varnish flooring, can be started. The

(a)   *(b)*

FIGURE 2.   (*a*) Diagram does not properly reflect precedence requirements since *u* seems to be dependent on the completion of both *o* and *t* but actually depends only on *t*. (*b*) Creating two nodes with dummy activity between provides the proper predecessors for both activities *s* and *u*.

dummy activity provides the logical sequencing relationship; but since it is assigned zero performance time, it does not alter any scheduling relationships which will be developed later.

Another use of the dummy activity is to provide a specific and separate beginning and ending event or node for each activity which cannot be confused. In Table I, for example, note the relationship between activities *l*, *m* and *n*, and *t*. The activity *l*, lay finish flooring, must precede both *m* and *n*, install kitchen fixtures and install finish plumbing, respectively. But *m* and *n* are the predecessors of *t*, paint. Therefore, the functionally correct relationship is represented by Figure 3*a*. But if Figure 3*a* were used, it would not be possible to identify each activity by its predecessor and successor events because both activities *m* and *n* would begin and end with the same node numbers. This is particularly important in larger networks employing computer programs for network diagram generation. The computer is always programmed to identify each activity by a pair of event numbers; the problem is solved through the insertion of a dummy activity as shown in Figure 3*b*. The functional relationship is identical since the dummy activity requires zero time but now both *m* and *n* are identified by different combinations of node numbers.

Figure 4 shows the completed arrow diagram for the house construction project. Activities are identified with their required times in days, all of the nodes are numbered, and the critical path is shown. The activity times were, of course, not used to this point and were not necessary for the construction of the diagram; we have not yet shown how to determine the critical path. However, the activity times will have great significance in the generation of schedule data, the critical path determination, and the generation of alternatives for the deployment of resources.

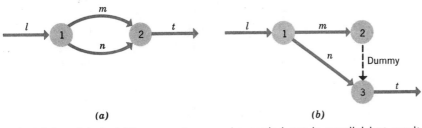

(a)   (b)

FIGURE 3. (*a*) Activities *m* and *n* may be carried out in parallel but result in identical beginning and end events. (*b*) Use of dummy activity makes possible separate ending event numbers, thus making activity identification by pairs of event or node numbers unambiguous.

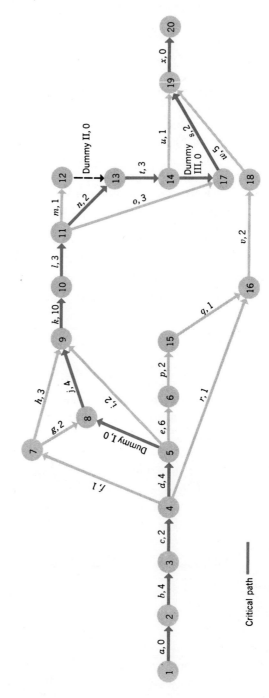

FIGURE 4. PERT network diagram for the house construction project.

Node Numbering. The *node numbering* shown in Figure 4 has been done in a particular way. If we identify each activity by its tail (i) and head (j) numbers, the nodes have been numbered so that for each activity i is always less than j, $i < j$. The numbers for every arrow are progressive, and no backtracking through the network is allowed. This convention in node numbering is effective in computing programs to develop the logical network relationships and to prevent the occurrence of cycling or closed loops.

A closed loop would occur if an activity were represented as going back in time. This is shown in Figure 5 which is simply the structure of Figure 3b with the activity n reversed in direction. Cycling in a network can result through a simple error or if, when developing the activity plans, one tries to show the repetition of an activity before beginning the next activity. A repetition of an activity must be represented with additional separate activities defined by their own unique node numbers. A closed loop would produce an endless cycle in computer programs, without a built-in routine for detection and identification of the cycle. Thus one property of a correctly constructed network diagram is that it is *noncyclical*.

With a properly constructed arrow diagram, it is a simple matter to develop the important schedule data for each activity and for the project as a whole. The data of interest to us are the earliest and latest start and finish times and available slack for all activities, as well as the critical path through the network.

Critical Path Scheduling

Earliest Start and Finish Times. If we take zero as the starting time for the project, then for each activity there is an earliest starting time (*ES*) relative to the project starting time, which is the earliest possible time that the activity can begin, assuming that all of the predecessors also are started at their *ES*. Then, for that activity, its earliest finish (*EF*) is simply *ES* + activity time.

This activity results in cycling

FIGURE 5.   Example of a closed loop or cycling in a network diagram.

Latest Start and Finish Times. Now let us assume that we have a target time for completing the project which, for the house construction example, is three days after the *EF* time possible or thirty-seven days. This is called the latest finish time (*LF*) of the project and of the final activity *x*. The latest start time (*LS*) is the latest time at which an activity can start if the target or schedule is to be maintained. Thus *LS* for the final activity *x* is *LF* − activity time. Since the finish activity requires zero time units, *LS* = *LF*.

Existing computer programs may be used to compute these schedule data automatically, requiring as inputs the activities, their performance time requirements, and the precedence relationships established by the *ij* numbers of the tails and heads of arrows. The computer output might be similar to Figure 6, which shows the schedule statistics for all activities when three days of slack has been allowed in the overall project completion time. Note then that all critical activities, marked with an asterisk (*), have slack in their schedules of three days. All other activities have greater schedule slack. Dummy activities I and III are on the critical path but their effect is only to establish correct precedence relationships since their activity times are zero. The schedule slack is simply the difference between computed early and late start times (*LS* − *ES*) or between early and late finish times (*LF* − *EF*).

Actually, there are twenty-two different paths from start to finish through the network. The shortest path requires fourteen days by the sequence *a-b-c-r-v-w-x* and the longest or limiting path requires thirty-four days by the critical sequence *a-b-c-d-j-k-l-n-t-s-x*. In a small problem such as this one, we could enumerate all of the alternate paths to find the longest path but there is no advantage in doing so since the critical path is easily determined from the schedule statistics, which are themselves useful.

Manual Computation of Schedule Statistics. This is appropriate for smaller networks and helps to convey the significance of the schedule statistics. To compute *ES* and *EF* manually from the network, we proceed as follows, referring to Figure 7:

1. Place the value of the project start time in both the *ES* and *EF* positions near the start activity arrow. See the legend for Figure 7. We shall assume relative values, as we did in the computer output of Figure 6, so the number 0 is placed in the *ES* and *EF* positions for the start activity. (Note that it is not necessary in PERT to include the start activity with zero activity duration. It has been included to make this example parallel in its activity list with the comparable CPM

Critical Path	Sequence i	j	Activity	Activity Description	Activity Time (days)	Start Early	Start Late	Finish Early	Finish Late	Slack
*	1	2	a,	Start	0	0	0	0	3	3
*	2	3	b,	Excavate and pour footings	4	0	3	4	7	3
*	3	4	c,	Pour concrete foundation	2	4	7	6	9	3
*	4	5	d,	Erect frame including rough roof	4	6	9	10	13	3
	5	6	e,	Lay brickwork	6	10	21	16	27	11
	4	7	f,	Install basement drains and plumbing	1	6	10	7	11	4
	7	8	g,	Pour basement floor	2	7	11	9	13	4
	7	9	h,	Install rough plumbing	3	7	14	10	17	7
	5	9	i,	Install rough wiring	2	10	15	12	17	5
*	5	8		Dummy I	0	10	13	10	13	3
*	8	9	j,	Install heating and ventilating	4	10	13	14	17	3
*	9	10	k,	Fasten plaster board and plaster, including drying	10	14	17	24	27	3
*	10	11	l,	Lay finish flooring	3	24	27	27	30	3
	11	12	m,	Install kitchen fixtures	1	27	31	28	32	4
	12	13		Dummy II	0	28	32	28	32	4
*	11	13	n,	Install finish plumbing	2	27	30	29	32	3
	11	17	o,	Finish carpentry	3	27	32	30	35	5
	6	15	p,	Finish roofing and flashing	2	16	27	18	29	11
	15	16	q,	Fasten gutters and downspouts	1	18	29	19	30	11
	4	16	r,	Lay storm drains for rain water	1	6	29	7	30	23
*	14	17		Dummy III	0	32	35	32	35	3
*	17	19	s,	Sand and varnish flooring	2	32	35	34	37	3
*	13	14	t,	Paint	3	29	32	32	35	3
	14	19	u,	Finish electrical work	1	32	36	33	37	4
	16	18	v,	Finish grading	2	19	30	21	32	11
	18	19	w,	Pour walks and complete landscaping	5	21	32	26	37	11
*	19	20	x,	Finish	0	34	37	34	37	3

FIGURE 6. Sample computer output of schedule statistics and critical path for the house construction project. Slack in project completion and for all critical activities is three days.

example of Figure 9. The start and finish activities are often necessary in CPM.)

2. Consider any new unmarked activity, *all of whose predecessors have been marked* in their *ES* and *EF* positions, and mark in the *ES* position of the new activity the *largest* number marked in the *EF* position of any of its immediate predecessors. This number is the *ES* time of the new activity. For activity *b* in Figure 7, the *ES* time is 0 since that is the *EF* time of the preceding activity.

3. Add to this number the activity time, and mark the resulting *EF* time in its proper position. For activity *b*, *ES* + 4 = 4.

4. Continue through the entire network until the "finish" activity has been reached. As we showed in Figure 6, the critical path time is thirty-four days so *ES* = *EF* = 34 for the finish activity.

To compute the *LS* and *LF*, we work backwards through the network, beginning with the finish activity. We have already stated that the target time for completing the project is three days after the *EF* time or thirty-seven days. Therefore, *LF* = 37 for the finish activity without delaying the total project beyond its target date. Similarly, the *LS* time for the finish activity is *LF* minus activity time. Since the finish

FIGURE 7. Flow of calculations for early start (*ES*) and early finish (*EF*) times.

activity requires 0 time units, $LS = LF$. To compute LS and LF for each activity, we proceed as follows, referring to Figure 8:

1. Mark the value of LS and LF in their respective positions near the finish activity according to the information in Figure 7.

2. Consider any new unmarked activity, all of whose successors have been marked, and mark in the LF position for the new activity the smallest LS time marked for any of its immediate successors. In other words, LF for an activity equals the earliest LS of the immediate successors for that activity.

3. Subtract from this number the activity time which becomes the LS for the activity.

4. Continue backwards through the chart until all LS and LF times have been entered in their proper positions on the network diagram. Figure 8 shows the flow of calculations, beginning with the finish activity backward through several activities.

As discussed previously, the schedule slack for an activity represents the maximum amount of time that it can be delayed beyond its ES

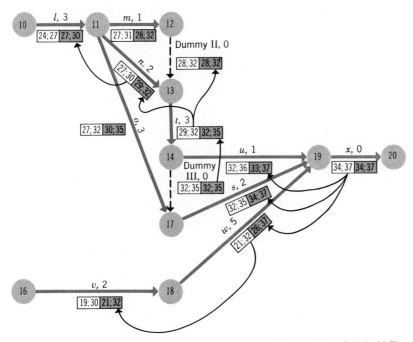

FIGURE 8. Flow of calculations for late start (LS) and late finish (LF) times.

without delaying the project completion time. Since critical activities are those in the sequence of the longest time path, it follows that the activities will have the minimum possible slack. If the project target date coincides with the LF for the finish activity, all critical activities will have 0 slack. If, however, the project date is later than the EF of the finish activity, as it is in the house project example (three days), all critical activities will have slack equal to this time-phasing difference. The manual computation of slack is simply $LS - ES$ or, alternately, $LF - EF$.

PERT/CPM— Arrow Diagram Differences

To this point we have been using the PERT arrow diagramming procedure to illustrate network methods. The CPM procedure results in a slightly simpler network system by representing activities as occurring at the nodes with the arrows showing the sequences of activities required for the project. The advantage in the CPM methodology is that it is not necessary to invoke the use of dummy activities in order to represent the proper sequencing. Figure 9 shows the CPM network for the house construction project which may be compared with the comparable PERT network shown in Figure 4. The analysis developing the early and late start and finish times and slack times is identical with the procedure previously outlined. The net results of both systems are the schedule statistics which are computed. Since these are the data of interest, and since the entire procedure is normally computerized for both methodologies, the choice between the two may fall to other criteria such as the availability and adaptability of existing computer routines or may be simply a matter of taste.

PROBABILISTIC NETWORK METHODS

The network methods which we have discussed so far may be termed deterministic since estimated activity times are assumed to be the expected values. But no recognition is given to the fact that the mean or expected activity time is the mean of a distribution of possible values which could occur. Deterministic methods assume that the expected time is actually the time taken.

Probabilistic network methods assume the reverse, more realistic, situation where activity times are represented by a probability distribution. With such a basic model of the network of activities, it is possible to develop additional data important to managerial decisions. Such data help in assessing planning decisions which might revolve around questions such as: What is the probability that the completion of

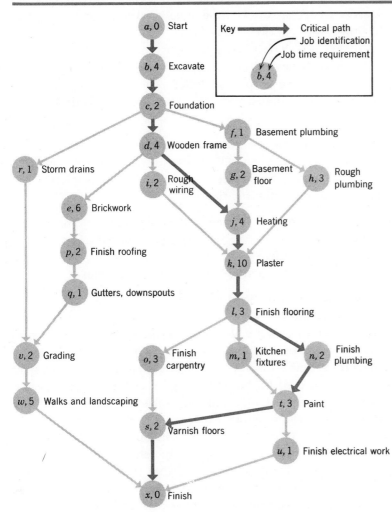

FIGURE 9. CPM project graph of activities for a house building project. (From Levy, Thompson, and Wiest [12].)

activity A will be later than January 10? What is the probability that the activity will become critical and affect the project completion date? What is the probability of meeting a given target completion date for the project? What is the risk of incurring cost penalties for not meeting the contract date? The nature of the planning decisions based on such questions might involve the allocation or reallocation of manpower or other resources to the various activities in order to derive a more satisfactory plan. Thus, a "crash" schedule with extra resources might be justified to insure the on-time completion of certain activities. The extra resources needed are drawn from noncritical activities or activities where the probability of criticality is small.

The discussion which follows is equally applicable to either the PERT or CPM basic format, although the probabilistic methods were in fact originally developed as part of PERT. The probability distribution of activity times is based on three time estimates made for each activity.

Optimistic Time. Optimistic time, *a,* is the shortest possible time to complete the activity if all goes well. It is based on the assumption that there is no more than one chance in a hundred of completing the activity in less than the optimistic time.

Pessimistic Time. Pessimistic time, *b,* is the longest time for an activity under adverse conditions but barring acts of nature. It is based on the assumption that there would be no more than one chance in a hundred of completing the activity in a time greater than *b.*

Most Likely Time. Most likely time, *m,* is the modal value of the activity time distribution.

The three time estimates are shown in relation to an activity completion time distribution in Figure 10. The computational algorithm reduces these three time estimates to a single average or expected value, t_e, which is actually used in the computing procedure.* The expected value is also the one used in computing schedule statistics for the deterministic model. The example distribution in Figure 10 represents only one possibility. Actually, the time distributions could be symmetrical, or skewed to either the right or the left.

With a probabilistic model, we can see that there is a probability that seemingly noncritical activities could become critical. This could happen either by the occurrence of a long performance time for the activity in question or of short performance times for activities already on the critical path. This is a signal that the schedule plans developed are likely to change. As actual data on the progress of operations come in, it may be necessary to make changes in the allocation of resources

---

*The usual model assumes that t_e is the mean of a beta distribution. The estimates of the mean and variance of the distribution may be computed as follows:

$$\bar{x} = \tfrac{1}{6}[A + 4M + B]$$

$$s^2 = [\tfrac{1}{6}(B - A)]^2$$

where *A, B,* and *M* are estimates of the values of *a, b,* and *m,* respectively, and $\bar{x}$ and s^2 are estimates of the mean and variance, t_e and σ_t^2.

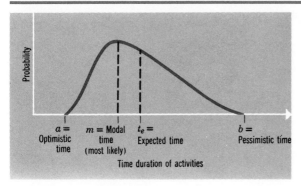

FIGURE 10   Time values in relation to a distribution of activity time.

in order to cope with the latest set of critical activities. Thus, an effective set of original plans requires a rapid feedback of information and the reissue of corrected schedules during the performance and control phases of a project.

DEPLOYMENT OF RESOURCES

Given the activity network, the critical path, and the computed schedule statistics, we have a plan for the project. But, is it a good plan? We can abstract from our data some additional data on the demand for resources of the early start schedule. By using the schedule flexibility available through slack in certain activities and/or slack in the project completion date, we can generate alternate schedules, comparing the use of important resources with the objective of *load leveling*.

Another way to look at the initial or raw plan is in terms of activity costs. Note that the initial activity duration estimates are based on an assumed level of resource allocation. Is it possible to alter activity times by pouring in more or less resources? Activity times for some activities can be directly affected in this way. For example, adding carpenters will usually shorten the time to frame a house, and this was a critical activity in our house construction example. Would it be worthwhile to pour in more manpower on the critical framing and allocate less to the noncritical brickwork which has eleven days of slack? Would the alternate plan be more or less expensive? Would shortening the critical path be advantageous? *Least costing* considerations are worth examining.

Finally, in some situations we may be faced with a demand for some critical resource which is limited in supply. The raw plan may in fact not be feasible if it schedules the use of the only available power shovel in two places at the same time. The raw plan must be examined with the objective of the feasible scheduling of *limited resources*, again using available slack time where possible or even lengthening the project in order to generate a feasible plan.

Load Leveling

Why level loading? What are the costs of not attempting to level loads in an already feasible schedule? Some factors which enter the problem occur in the following example of a major oil refinery repair and overhaul project [1, pp. 269–280]. After a raw plan was developed, a series of computer runs was made to examine manpower requirements for the refinery project. In the first run it was found that the schedule required 50 boilermakers for the first 4 hours, 20 for the next 6 hours, and 35 for the immediately following period. Similar fluctuations in requirements were found for other crafts. In terms of costs associated with this fluctuation, there is first the possible cost of idle labor.

For example, in the first 10 hours of the refinery project the peak requirement of 50 boilermakers will probably mean productive work of 50×4 hours $+ 20 \times 6$ hours $= 320$ man-hours. But the likelihood is that it will be difficult to assign the extra 30 men for the balance of the 8-hour day, so in the first 10 hours of the project the payroll may reflect $50 \times 8 + 20 \times 2 = 440$ man-hours, 120 of which are idle labor. Figure 11 shows the deployment of manpower *after* leveling; we see that some of these same kinds of problems remain. Other costs that may be implicit in manpower fluctuation are hiring and separation costs in projects that extend over long periods. Load leveling has the objective of reducing idle labor costs, hiring and separation costs, or the cost of any resource, such as an equipment rental, which may be affected by fluctuations in the demand for its use.

For very large and complex projects, a computer-based leveling model may be required. Simulation methodology commonly is used to generate alternate solutions. The starting solution might be the early start schedule, and a first attempt at leveling could then set a maximum of the resource in question just below the highest peak level recorded in the raw plan. The simulation program would then proceed as indicated by the arrow diagram, beginning all activities leaving node 1, keeping track of the amount of resources used and available. As the calendar is advanced and as activities are completed, resources are returned to the "available" pool; as new activities are started, resources are drawn from the pool. Simulation then proceeds until an activity requires resources from a temporarily exhausted pool. Depending on the decision

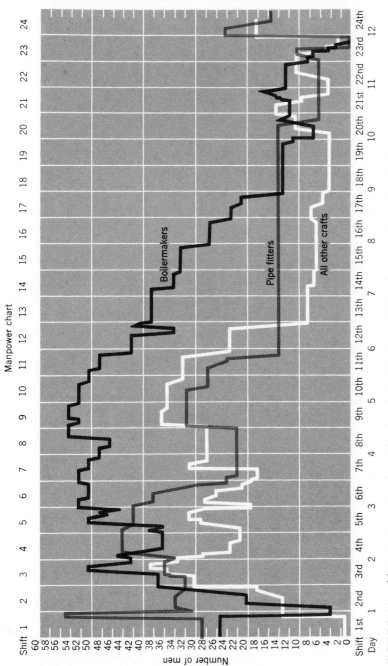

FIGURE 11.   Manpower usage chart after leveling. (From Archibald and Villoria [1, p. 274].)

criteria used by the simulator, the activity may be delayed, even past its latest starting time, until resources are available. Other decision criteria "bump" noncritical jobs and reassign resources to the delayed job when the latest starting time has been reached. By a progressive lowering of the resource limits in such a simulation program, the leveling effect takes place until a satisfactory deployment of resources is achieved. A survey of rigorous methods of resource allocation in project network models has been developed by Davis [4]; specific resource leveling models have been developed by Dewitte [5] and by Levy, Thompson, and Wiest [11].

Least Costing

Least costing concepts are based on cost versus activity time curves such as in Figure 12. Different activities respond differently to changes in the application of resources, and some of the activities may not be responsive to changes in resources. Figure 12a may be typical of an activity like house framing, as we discussed previously, where crash, normal, and slow schedules are progressively less costly. A curve similar to Figure 12b, where the slow schedule is more costly than the normal schedule, could be typical where the meager resources associated with a slow schedule might enforce the use of inefficient methods. The cost trade-offs are possible partially because of the differential cost-time characteristics of different activities. Formal methodologies for least costing have been developed by Fulkerson [7] and Kelly [9] in the form of linear programming models which idealize the cost-time functions by assuming a straight-line connecting the crash and normal points. The total project cost is taken as the sum of the linear activity cost functions; this total project cost function is minimized by the linear programming algorithm.

Limited Resources

A limited resource model called SPAR (Scheduling Program for Allocation of Resources) has been developed by Wiest [17]. SPAR is a heuristic

FIGURE 12. Typical activity time-cost curves.

scheduling model for limited resources designed to handle a project with 1200 single resource activities, 500 nodes, and twelve shops over a span of 300 days. The model focuses on available resources which it allocates, period by period, to activities listed in order of their early start times. The most critical jobs have the highest probability of being scheduled first, and as many jobs are initially scheduled as available resources permit. If an available activity fails to be scheduled in one period, an attempt is made to schedule it in the next period. Finally, all jobs that have been postponed become critical and move to the top of the priority list of available activities.

Wiest applied the SPAR program to a space vehicle project which required large block engineering activities with up to five different types of engineers and involving 300 activities. Figure 13 shows an overall manpower loading chart for the program. The unlimited resources line resulted from a conventional PERT schedule with all activities at their early start times. The limited resources line results from the SPAR schedule where peak manpower requirements were considerably reduced. The total length of the project was shortened by five months and the number of gross hirings of personnel was reduced by 30 per cent as a result of the SPAR schedule.

DIFFICULTIES IN USING NETWORK METHODS

There have been problems in the managerial use of network methods. First, the difficulty in making the three time estimates has often produced mere guesses or the arbitrary addition and subtraction of time

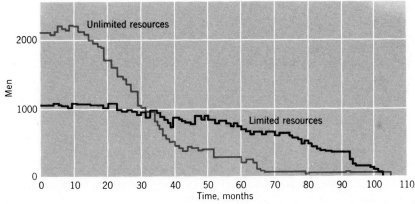

FIGURE 13.   Manpower loading schedule for the space vehicle project. (From Wiest [17].)

from the most likely time to determine the pessimistic and optimistic time estimates. The result of such practices has been that the Department of Defense has abandoned probabilistic methods for most contracts.

Other difficulties have been apparent when time lags have been too great in the reporting of activity status and the recomputing of up-to-date schedules. The result has been, of course, that managers tend to ignore the schedules that exist because they have lost faith in them. The ultimate solutions to these kinds of difficulties are in computer-based reporting and control systems.

SUMMARY

Network planning techniques are unique in the form they have taken, especially the concepts of critical path. The associated concepts of load leveling, least costing, and limited resource scheduling have provided a rational base for project management resting on carefully laid, broad plans. The plans can be said to be derived from analyses of some prominent alternatives, are computer based and thus applicable to very large systems, and are flexible so that they can be changed as actual experience with them develops.

It is interesting that the independent development of PERT and CPM in two different environments produced essentially equivalent methodologies but with the stamps of their spawning grounds. CPM developed in engineering maintenance operations where a great deal of experience existed and activity times were relatively well known. Thus, CPM developed as a deterministic model. PERT, however, developed in an environment of research and development where great uncertainty of activity times exists. The result was the probabilistic model.

REVIEW QUESTIONS

1. What are the unique factors in the nature of large-scale one-time projects that require special planning methods? Why are the general methods of Chapter 10 inadequate?
2. Why is it necessary that the planning of what must be done and schedule planning should be performed together for large projects?
3. Discuss the origin of network planning methods.
4. In the context of network planning methods, define the following terms: activity, event, node, and critical path.
5. For PERT planning methods, discuss and interrelate the three phases: (a) activity analysis, (b) arrow diagramming, and (c) node numbering.
6. What are the functions of dummy activities in PERT network diagrams?

TABLE II. Activities, Sequence Requirements, and Times for the Renewal of a Pipeline.

Activity	Letter Code	Code of Immediate Predecessor	Activity Time Require- ment, (days)	Crew Require- ments per Day
Assemble crew for job	A	—	10	—
Use old line to build inventory	B	—	28	—
Measure and sketch old line	C	A	2	—
Develop materials list	D	C	1	—
Erect scaffold	E	D	2	10
Procure pipe	F	D	30	—
Procure valves	G	D	45	—
Deactivate old line	H	B, D	1	6
Remove old line	I	E, H	6	3
Prefabricate new pipe	J	F	5	20
Place valves	K	E, G, H	1	6
Place new pipe	L	I, J	6	25
Weld pipe	M	L	2	1
Connect valves	N	K, M	1	6
Insulate	O	K, M	4	5
Pressure test	P	N	1	3
Remove scaffold	Q	N, O	1	6
Clean up and turn over to operating crew	R	P, Q	1	6

7. What is the convention for numbering nodes in a PERT network? Why is this convention used?
8. Why must activity networks be noncyclical?
9. Define the following terms: early start (*ES*), early finish (*EF*), latest start (*LS*), latest finish (*LF*), and slack.
10. Outline the procedure for manual computation of schedule statistics.
11. What are the differences in the construction of the arrow diagram between the PERT and CPM methodologies? How can the probabilistic network model provide additional data helpful for managerial decisions?
12. Define the terms optimistic time, pessimistic time, most likely time, and expected time in probabilistic PERT networks.
13. What is meant by load leveling? How may it be accomplished?
14. Discuss the concepts of least costing in relation to crash, normal, and slow schedules.
15. What is the nature of the SPAR limited resource model?
16. Account for the differences between PERT and CPM as they were originally developed.

	Optimistic	Most Likely	Pessimistic	Expected
Activity Code	Time Estimate of, *a*	Time Estimate of, *m*	Time Estimate of, *b*	Time Estimate of, t_e
A	8	10	12	10
B	26	26.5	36	28
C	1	2	3	2
D	0.5	1	1.5	1
E	1.5	1.63	4	2
F	28	28	40	30
G	40	42.5	60	45
H	1	1	1	1
I	4	6	8	6
J	4	4.5	8	5
K	0.5	0.9	2	1
L	5	5.25	10	6
M	1	2	3	2
N	0.5	1	1.5	1
O	3	3.75	6	4
P	1	1	1	1
Q	1	1	1	1
R	1	1	1	1

TABLE III.   Time Estimates for the Pipeline Renewal Project.

PROBLEMS

1.   Listed in Table II is a set of activities, sequence requirements, and estimated activity times required for the renewal of a pipeline. Prepare both a PERT and CPM project diagram.

2.   For the data of problem 1 and the arrow diagram generated there:
(a) Compute *ES*, *EF*, *LS*, and *LF* for each of the activities.
(b) For the data generated in (a), compute slack for the system. Which activities can be delayed beyond their respective *ES* without delaying the project completion time of 65 days? Which activities can be delayed, and by how many days, without delaying the *ES* of any other activity?
(c) Determine the critical path for the pipeline renewal project.

3.   In Table III there is additional information in the form of optimistic, most likely, and pessimistic time estimates for the pipeline renewal project. Compute variances for the activities. Which activities have the greatest uncertainty in their completion schedules?

4.   Suppose that, due to penalties in the contract, each day the pipeline renewal project can be shortened is worth $100. Which of the following possibilities would you follow and why?

(a) Shorten t_e of activity B by 4 days at a cost of $100.

(b) Shorten b of activity G by 5 days at a cost of $50.

(c) Shorten t_e of activity O by 2 days at a cost of $150.

(d) Shorten t_e of activity O by 2 days by drawing resources from activity N, thereby lengthening its t_e by 2 days.

5.   Table II indicated the crew requirements *per day* for each activity in the pipeline renewal project.

(a) Prepare a crew size versus time chart representing the deployment of manpower for the *ES* schedule generated in problem 2. Assume that men on all crews are completely interchangeable, that is, any man can do any task.

(b) Now assume that the man-days allocated for each activity can be deployed in any way you wish. For example, activity L has a crew requirement of 25 men per day for 6 days from Table II or 150 man-days. These 150 man-days may be allocated over any chosen activity time; for example, 10 men per day for 15 days or vice versa. To try to achieve load leveling of the total crew, re-allocate the man-days required for each activity so that no activity has a labor rate greater than a crew size of 10 men per day. This will require extending the activity times of some activities. (1) Compute the schedule statistics and new critical path. (2) Prepare a new crew size versus time chart representing the deployment of manpower, but with the restriction that maximum total crew size per day is 10, using available slack as necessary. Also, use available slack to make this labor schedule as compact as possible; that is, the fewest number of fluctuations in overall crew size and condensed in time span.

REFERENCES

[1] Archibald, R. D., and R. L. Villoria. *Network-Based Management Systems.* John Wiley, New York, 1967.

[2] Buffa, E. S., and W. H. Taubert. *Production-Inventory Systems: Planning and Control* (Rev. ed.). Richard D. Irwin, Homewood, Ill., 1972, Chapters 13 and 14.

[3] Burgess, A. R., and J. B. Killebrew. "Variation in Activity Level on a Cyclical Arrow Diagram." *Journal of Industrial Engineering.* 13 (2), 76–83, Mar.–Apr. 1962.

[4] Davis, E. W. "Resource Allocation in Project Network Models—A Survey." *Journal of Industrial Engineering,* 17 (4), 177–188, Apr. 1966.

[5] Dewitte, L. "Manpower Leveling in PERT Networks." *Data Processing Science/Engineering,* Mar.–Apr. 1964.

[6] Elmaghraby, S. E. "On Generalized Activity Networks." *Journal of Industrial Engineering,* 17 (11), 621–631, Nov. 1966.

[7] Fulkerson, D. R. "A Network Flow Computation for Project Cost Curves." *Management Science,* 7, 1961.

[8] Johnson, R. A., F. E. Kast, and J. E. Rosenzweig. *The Theory and Management of Systems* (2nd ed.). McGraw-Hill, New York, 1967.

[9] Kelly, J. E. "Critical Path Planning and Scheduling: Mathematical Basis." *Operations Research,* **9** (3), 1961.

[10] Levin, R. I., and C. A. Kirkpatrick. *Planning and Control with PERT/CPM.* McGraw-Hill, New York, 1966.

[11] Levy, F. K., G. L. Thompson, and J. D. Wiest. "Multi-Shop Work Load Smoothing Program." *Naval Research Logistics Quarterly,* Mar. 1963.

[12] Levy, F. K., G. L. Thompson, and J. D. Wiest. "The ABCs of the Critical Path Method." *Harvard Business Review,* Sept.–Oct. 1963, pp. 98–108.

[13] MacCrimmon, K. R., and C. A. Ryavec. "An Analytical Study of the PERT Assumptions." *Operations Research,* Jan.–Feb. 1964. Also reprinted as Chapter 30 in: *Readings in Production and Operations Management.* E. S. Buffa, editor. John Wiley, New York, 1966.

[14] Malcolm, D. G., J. H. Roseboom, C. E. Clark, and W. Fazar. "Application of a Technique for Research and Development Program Evaluation." *Operations Research,* **7** (5), Sept.–Oct. 1959. Also reprinted as Chapter 29 in: *Readings in Production and Operations Management.* E. S. Buffa, editor. John Wiley, New York, 1966.

[15] Moder, J. J., and C. R. Phillips. *Project Management with CPM and PERT.* Reinhold, New York, 1964.

[16] Shaffer, L. R., J. B. Ritter, and W. L. Meyer. *The Critical Path Method.* McGraw-Hill, New York, 1965.

[17] Wiest, J. D. "A Heuristic Model for Scheduling Large Projects with Limited Resources." *Management Science,* **13,** (6), 359–377, Feb. 1967.

[18] Wiest, J. D. "Heuristic Programs for Decision-Making." *Harvard Business Review,* Sept.–Oct. 1966, pp. 129–143.

[19] Wiest, J. D. "Some Properties of Schedules for Large Projects with Limited Resources." *Operations Research,* **12** (3), May–June 1964. Also reprinted as Chapter 31 in: *Readings in Production and Operations Management.* E. S. Buffa, editor. John Wiley, New York, 1966.

[20] Wiest, J. D., and F. K. Levy. *A Management Guide to PERT/CPM.* Prentice-Hall, Inc., Englewood Cliffs, N.J., 1969.

Maintenance

Let's face it, machines break down! Production management must provide for this eventuality in a way that maintains the reliability of the production system at reasonable levels without "going broke" just keeping machines running. We are faced with another problem of attempting to strike a balance between cost factors. When machines break down, these kinds of costs occur: machine down time and possible loss of potential sales, idle direct and indirect labor, delays in other processes that may depend for material supply on the machine that is down, increased scrap, customer dissatisfaction from possible delays in deliveries, and the actual cost of repairing the machine.

We can view the problem as one of maintaining the reliability of the entire production system. In general, this reliability can be maintained and improved by:

1. Increasing the size of repair facilities and crews so that average machine down time is reduced because maintenance crews are less likely to be busy when a breakdown occurs.

2. Utilizing preventive maintenance where practical so that critical parts are replaced before they fail. It is often possible to do this on second and third shifts and, thereby, not interfere with normal production schedules. Whether preventive maintenance is worthwhile or not depends on the distribution of breakdowns and the relation of preventive maintenance time to repair time, as we shall see.

3. Providing for slack in the system at critical stages so that we have parallel paths available. This means excess capacity so some ma-

chines can be down without affecting the delay costs to any great degree.

4. Making individual components within a machine or the machines within the system more reliable through improvements in engineering design. For example, special lubrication systems may be used that may extend the life of working parts.

5. Decoupling successive stages of the production system by inventories between operations. The resulting independence of operations localizes the effect of a breakdown, so operations preceding and following the machine that is down are less likely to be affected.

To accomplish increased reliability by any of these means is costly; therefore, we can justify it only insofar as the costs of attaining it are offset by cost reductions in idle labor, scrap, lost business, etc. Number 4 may be regarded as an engineering design problem coupled with economic analysis. Number 5 interacts with problems of layout and inventory control, which we have discussed in previous chapters. Numbers 1, 2, and 3, however, represent ideas not previously discussed. We shall devote the bulk of this chapter to a consideration of approaches to these problems which can guide maintenance policy.

Before launching into the maintenance problem itself, however, let us consider some simple facts which help explain why complex equipment seems unreliable and may break down often, even though the equipment itself may have been designed and manufactured to the highest standards. Machines can be viewed as being made up of a sequence of components each of which performs a function. For example, when one strikes a key on an electric typewriter an electric switch is closed which actuates a solenoid which causes the mechanical action of the type to strike the ribbon which in turn transfers carbon to the paper. The type linkage returns to its normal position and the carriage indexes one space to make ready for the next cycle. The number of individual mechanical and electrical components required to perform correctly in sequence (series) is larger than one might think. If anyone of them fails to function correctly due to either breakdown or faulty adjustment, the system as a whole fails to function correctly. How does this affect system reliability?

Figure 1 tells the story. Note that if we are dealing with a machine made up of $n = 50$ components in series, each with an average reliability of 99.5 per cent, the reliability of the machine as a whole is only about 80 per cent. Translating this statement, if the average probability of breakdown of each of the 50 components were $100 - 99.5 = 0.5$ per

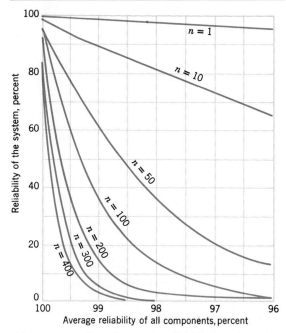

FIGURE 1. Overall system reliability as a function of complexity (number of components) and component reliability with components in series. (From Lusser [5].)

cent, then the probability that the machine might break down because of the breakdown on any one of the components is 20 per cent. Depending on how long it takes to repair the machine it is easy to see that machine down time might be prohibitive.

From Figure 1 we see that as complexity increases in terms of the numbers of components in series, the reliability of the system as a whole declines very rapidly.

The reliability of a system in which the components are in parallel is entirely different. With parallel components there are two or more components which in some way are performing the same function. Thus for the system to fail both components in parallel must fail, increasing the reliability of the system. Increasing reliability through parallel components and systems is of course expensive, but when the possible losses are great it may be justified. In space vehicle systems, for example, parallel systems are often used because of the potential costs of system failure. In production systems, as we noted in Item 3 on page 621 we may provide parallel paths by having more than one machine which is capable of performing the same operation.

BREAKDOWN TIME DISTRIBUTIONS

Breakdown time distribution data are basic if we hope to be able to formulate any general policies concerning maintenance. Breakdown time distributions show the frequency with which machines have maintenance-free performance for a given number of operating hours, and are ordinarily shown as distributions of the fraction of breakdowns that exceed a given run time. Breakdown time distributions are developed from distributions of run time free of breakdowns, such as Figure 2. Figure 3 shows three breakdown time distributions. These distributions take different shapes, depending on the nature of the equipment with which we are dealing. For example, a simple machine with few moving parts would tend to break down at nearly constant intervals following the last repair. That is, it exhibits minimum variability in breakdown time distributions. Curve *a* of Figure 2 would be fairly typical of such a

T_a = average free run time

Run time free of breakdowns ⟶

FIGURE 2. Frequency distribution of run time free of breakdowns representing three degrees of variability in free run time.

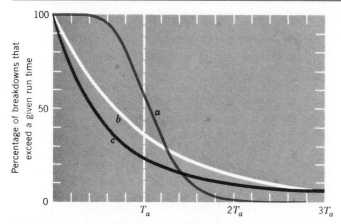

FIGURE 3.   Breakdown time distributions. Curve *a* exhibits low variability from the average breakdown time T_a. Curve *b* is the negative exponential distribution and exhibits medium variability. Curve *c* exhibits high variability; dashed line shows constant breakdown times. (Adapted from Morse [7].)

situation. A large per cent of the breakdowns occur near the average breakdown time, T_a, and only a few occur at the extremes.

If a machine were more complex, having many parts, each part would have a failure distribution. When all of these were grouped together in a single distribution of the breakdown time of the machine for any cause, we would expect to find greater variability because the machine could break down for any one of a number of reasons. Some breakdowns could occur shortly after the last repair or anytime. Therefore, for the same average breakdown time T_a, we would find much wider variability of breakdown time as in curve *b* of Figure 2.

To complete the picture of representative breakdown time distributions, curve *c* is representative of distributions with the same average breakdown time T_a, but with wider variability. A large proportion of the breakdowns with a distribution such as curve *c* occur just after repair; on the other hand, a large number of machines have a long running life after repair. Curve *c* may be typical of machines that require "ticklish" adjustments. If the adjustments are made just right, the machinery may run for a long time; but if not, readjustment and repair may be necessary almost immediately.

In models for maintenance, we normally deal with distributions of the percentage of breakdowns that exceed a given run time, such as in Figure 3. They are merely transformations of the distributions of free run time typified by those in Figure 2. Taking curve *a* of Figure 2 as an example, we may convert it to the breakdown time distribution of curve *a* in Figure 3 in the following way. If the vertical scale of Figure 2 is converted to the percentage of breakdowns that occur instead of the frequency of breakdowns, we can then easily plot the percentage of breakdowns that exceed a given run time. First, we know that all the breakdowns, or 100 per cent, exceed an average run time of zero. To obtain curve *a* in Figure 3, we simply subtract successively the percentages that occur at different free run times. We can see by examination of Figure 3 that almost 60 per cent of the breakdowns exceeded the average breakdown time T_a and that very few of the breakdowns occurred after $2T_a$.

In practice, actual breakdown time distributions can often be approximated by standard distributions, three of which are shown in Figure 3. Curve *b* is actually the negative exponential distribution which we discussed in connection with waiting line theory. From this point on, our reference will be to the breakdown time distributions plotted in Figure 3, recognizing that the basic data for breakdown time distributions would be accumulated as a distribution of the frequency of free run time as in Figure 2.

Preventive Maintenance versus Repair (Single Machine)

Let us assume a preventive maintenance policy which provides for an inspection and perhaps replacement of certain critical parts after the machine has been running for a fixed time, called the preventive maintenance period. The maintenance crew takes an average time, T_m, to accomplish the preventive maintenance. This is the preventive maintenance cycle. A certain proportion of the breakdowns will occur before the fixed cycle has been completed. For these cases the maintenance crew will repair the machine, taking an average time, T_s, for the repair. This is the repair cycle. These two patterns of maintenance are diagrammed in Figure 4. The probability of occurrence of the two

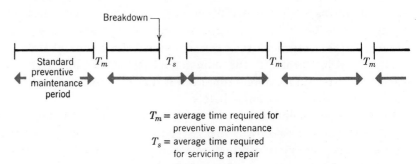

T_m = average time required for preventive maintenance

T_s = average time required for servicing a repair

FIGURE 4. Illustrative record of machine run time, preventive maintenance time T_m, and service time for actual repairs T_s.

different cycles depends on the specific breakdown time distribution of the machine and the length of the standard preventive maintenance period. If the distribution has low variability and the standard period is perhaps only 80 per cent of the average run time without breakdowns, T_a, actual breakdown would occur rather infrequently and most cycles would be preventive maintenance cycles. If the distribution were more variable, for the same standard preventive maintenance period, more actual breakdowns would occur before the end of the standard period. Obviously, shortening the standard period would result in fewer actual breakdowns and lengthening it would have the opposite effect for any distribution.

Assuming that either a preventive maintenance or a repair puts the machine in shape for a running time of equal probable length, Morse [7] has shown that the per cent of machine running time depends on the ratio of the standard maintenance period and the average run time, T_a, for the breakdown time distribution. Figure 5 shows the relation

FIGURE 5.   Per cent of time a machine is working for the three distributions of breakdown time shown in Figure 3. Preventive maintenance time, T_m, is 20 per cent of T_a; repair time is 50 per cent of T_a. (Adapted from Morse [7].)

of the per cent of time that the machine is working and the ratio of the standard period to average run time, T_a, for the three distributions of breakdown times shown in Figure 3. Note that, in general, when the standard period is short, say less than 50 per cent of T_a, the machine is working only a small fraction of the time. This is because the machine is down so often owing to preventive maintenance. As the standard period is lengthened, more actual breakdowns occur which require repair. For curves b and c, this improves the fraction of time the machine is running because the combination of preventive maintenance time and repair time produces a smaller total down time.

Curve a, however, has a peak in it, or an optimum preventive maintenance period which maximizes the per cent of machine working time. What is different about curve a? It is based on the low variability breakdown time distribution from Figure 3. For curve a, lengthening the maintenance period beyond about 70 per cent of T_a reduces the fraction of machine working time because actual machine breakdowns are more likely. For the more variable distributions of curves b and c, this is not true because breakdowns are more likely throughout their distributions than they are in curve a. Comparable curves can be constructed showing the per cent of time that the machine is in a state of preventive maintenance and the per cent of time the machine is being repaired because of breakdown.

Guides to a Preventive Maintenance Policy

Some generalizations about preventive maintenance policy can be made through the concepts we have developed. First, preventive maintenance is generally applicable to machines with breakdown time distributions that have low variability, exemplified by curve a of Figure 3. In general, distributions with less variability than the exponential, curve b, are in this category. The reason is that low variability means that we can predict with fair precision when the majority of breakdowns will occur. A standard preventive maintenance period can then be set which anticipates breakdowns fairly well.

Equally important, however, is the relation of preventive maintenance time to repair time. If it takes just as long to perform a preventive maintenance as it does to repair the machine, there is no advantage in preventive maintenance, which has the effect of reducing the amount of time that the machine can work. In this situation, the machine spends a minimum amount of time being down for maintenance if we simply wait until it breaks down. This is shown by Figure 6 where we compare the per cent of the time a machine is working when repair time is greater than preventive maintenance time and when the two times are equal.

FIGURE 6. Comparison of per cent of machine working time when preventive maintenance time is less than repair time, curve *d*, and when they are equal, curve *e*. Curve *d* is identical with curve *a*, Figure 5. T_m and T_s are expressed as per cents of the average breakdown time, T_a.

Both curves are based on the low-variability distribution of curve *a*, Figure 3. Note that curve *d* exhibits an optimum, but curve *e* does not. For curve *e*, the per cent of time that the machine works continues to increase as the standard maintenance period is lengthened, which results in more repairs and fewer preventive maintenance cycles. Clearly, there is no advantage in preventive maintenance when $T_m = T_s$ from the viewpoint of maximum machine working time. To sum it up at this point, preventive maintenance is useful when breakdown time distributions exhibit low variability and when the average time for preventive maintenance is less than the average time for repair after breakdown.

The effect of down-time costs can modify the conclusions just stated, however. Suppose that we are dealing with a machine in a production line. If the machine breaks down, the entire line may be shut down, with very high idle labor costs resulting. In this situation, preventive maintenance is more desirable than repair *if* the preventive maintenance can take place during second or third shifts, vacations, or lunch hours when the line is normally down anyway. This is true even when $T_m = T_s$. The determination of the standard preventive maintenance period would require a different, but similar analysis in which the per cent of machine working time is expressed as a function of repair time only, since preventive maintenance takes place outside of normal work time.

An optimal solution would be one that minimized the total of down-time costs, preventive maintenance costs, plus repair costs. The effect of the down-time costs would be to justify shorter standard preventive maintenance periods and to justify making repairs more quickly (at higher cost) when they do occur. There are many situations, however, where extra manpower on a repair job would not speed it up. In such cases, total down time might be shortened by overtime on multiple shifts and weekends, with attendant higher costs. Optimal solutions would specify the standard preventive maintenance period, the machine idle time, and the repair crew idle time, striking a balance between down-time costs and maintenance costs.

A special case exists when sales are such that the plant must operate at full capacity to meet demand. Under these circumstances, reduced machine working time due to repair and preventive maintenance reduces the number of units that can be sold and, therefore, affects income. Optimal maintenance policy is then even more heavily weighted in favor of shortening standard preventive maintenance periods and pouring in more effort to repair machines quickly when breakdowns occur. Morse [7, pp. 165–166] has developed basic models which fit this special case in which an income-less-maintenance cost function is maximized.

MAINTAINING SEVERAL MACHINES

The single-machine situation which we have been discussing contains basic elements of general policy which can be carried over into the multimachine case. However, when several machines must be serviced, our problem more closely resembles the usual waiting line model. If we assume that all machines have the same breakdown time distribution, breakdowns are comparable to arrivals in the waiting line model, and the repair crew is the service station. As machines break down, the repair crew services them in the average time, T_s, as before. If the crew is already working on a machine, successive machines that break down must wait for service and the costs associated with down time grow with the delay. We can reduce the chance that this will happen by increasing the size of the crew, but this solution also costs money and increases the amount of time that the crew will be idle, waiting for breakdowns to occur. The problem, then, is one of striking a balance between the down-time costs of the machines and the idle-time costs of the maintenance crew [2, 7].

SIMULATION OF ALTERNATE PRACTICES

When maintenance is being performed anyway, it is a fairly common practice to replace parts that have not yet failed in order to prevent a future breakdown. The incremental cost of replacing these parts is often small since the machine is already partially disassembled. For example, if an automobile engine is disassembled to replace piston rings, other parts, such as the connecting rod bearings, also can be replaced for little more than the cost of the parts. If these parts are not replaced and fail later, the cost to replace them will be high because the engine must be disassembled again. Whether such practices are economical or not for individual cases depends on the distribution of part lives and the relative magnitudes of maintenance labor, part costs, and down-time costs. Because of the complexity of interacting probable lives of parts, simulation is often a practical way of evaluating alternate practices.

A Preventive Maintenance Example

Let us take, for example, the case of a company that maintained a bank of machines which were exposed to severe service, causing bearing failure to be a common maintenance problem. There were three bearings in the machines that caused trouble. The general practice had been to replace bearings at the time that they failed. However, excessive down-time costs raised the question of whether or not a preventive policy was worthwhile. The company wished to evaluate three alternative possible practices.

1. The current practice of replacing bearings that fail.
2. When a bearing fails, replace all three.
3. When a bearing fails, replace that bearing plus other bearings that have been in use 1700 hours or more.

To simulate operation under the three alternate policies, data on bearing lives were needed, together with cost data. Figure 7 shows the cumulative distribution of bearing lives; Table I summarizes pertinent time and cost data.

To simulate the alternative maintenance operations, we follow the procedures outlined in Chapter 4, establishing a percentage or probability scale, as in Figure 7. We can now use Figure 7 to select bearing lives at random from

FIGURE 7. Cumulative distribution of bearing lives.

the distribution. By using a random number table, or some other system for selecting numbers at random between 0 and 100, we can proceed to select bearing lives and simulate operation. For example, the random number 32 selects a bearing with a life of 1500 hours, as shown in Figure 7. To simulate the first alternate practice, bearings are selected serially for the three positions and costs can be calculated according to the maintenance time, bearing cost, and down time that results. To simulate the second practice, three bearing lives are drawn at random, the shortest of the three determining when they will be replaced, etc. Figure 8 shows the resulting graphical representation of 20,000 hours of simulated operation for the three plans.

TABLE I. Maintenance Time and Cost Data for Bearing Replacement	
Maintenance mechanic's time:	
Replace one bearing	5 hours
Replace two bearings	6 hours
Replace three bearings	7 hours
Maintenance mechanic's wage rate	$3/hour
Bearing cost	$5 each
Down-time costs	$2/hour

FIGURE 8. Graphical result of simulation of three alternate maintenance procedures.

Table II summarizes the comparative results. Plan 2 is somewhat cheaper than the other two. Although bearing cost is higher, the time demand for maintenance mechanics is lower and, therefore, down-time costs are lower. Plan 3 is next best. Other plans between 2 and 3 could be tested as well, shortening the permitted running life of bearings below 1700 hours, etc. We should note that a change in the structure of costs could easily change results. For example, if the value of the new bearing is $100 instead of $5, Plan I is cheapest, the new totals being, respectively, $4250, $4690, and $4420.

SIMULATION OF OPTIMAL SIZE OF REPAIR CREWS

Feorene [3] reports a study made at the Eastman Kodak Company of the size of a repair crew. The problem deals with the maintenance of twenty automatic machines which had been maintained by a crew of six mechanics. Production forecasts indicated the need for two more machines to meet capacity needs. This raised the question of whether or not the size of the repair crew should be enlarged. After careful study, the following data were gathered to simulate the maintenance operation.

TABLE II. Results of 20,000 Hours of Simulated Operation under Three Alternate Maintenance Plans

	Plan 1— Replace bearings when they fail	Plan 2— When a bearing fails, replace all three	Plan 3— Replace bearing that fails plus others if they have had 1700 hours of service or more
Number of single replacements	34	—	28
Number of double replacements	—	—	4
Number of triple replacements	—	14	—
Total number of bearings replaced	34	42	36
Down time, hours	170	98	164
Costs :			
Maintenance mechanics	$ 510	$294	$ 492
Cost of bearings	170	215	180
Down time	340	196	328
Total	$1020	$705	$1000

1. A breakdown time distribution which showed the length of time that the machines would run before requiring service.

2. A distribution of the length of time a machine was down while being serviced by a mechanic.

3. A distribution of the time spent by the mechanic with the machine, after it had been started again, to make final adjustments and insure that it was ready for service. This is the mechanic's "run-in-time."

4. A distribution of mechanic's service time when the machine could be serviced while it was still operating.

5. A distribution of the time for a mechanic to become available to work on the machine.

6. A determination of the per cent of cases where the machine could be serviced while running, and the per cent where the machine had to be shut down for adjustments and repairs. Studies showed that two-thirds of the cases were those in which the machine could continue to produce (a run call) and one-third required the machine to be shut down (a down-time call).

Figure 9 shows the structure of the computer simulation model that was used. The computer was programmed to follow this structure,

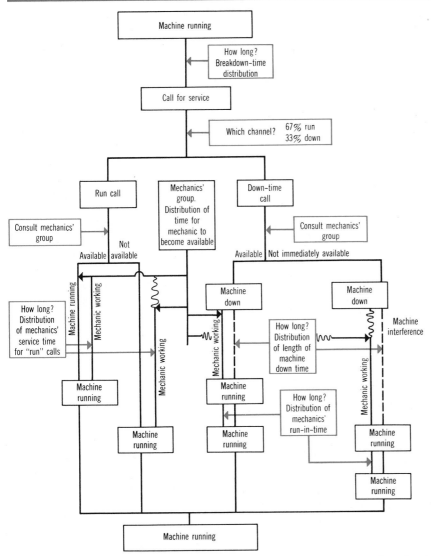

FIGURE 9. Structure of simulation model for the determination of optimal repair crew size. (Adapted from [3].)

selecting at random from the appropriate distributions to provide data for the simulation of specific run and down-time calls.

Figure 10 shows the cost curve in relation to crew size for twenty-two machines in service. The cost factors included were maintenance labor cost and machine down-time costs. Figure 10 is one of a number of such curves prepared for various numbers of machines in service. The

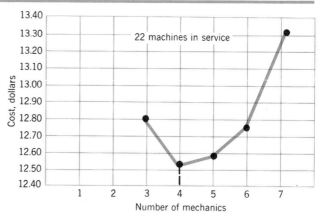

FIGURE 10. Curve of cost versus number of mechanics in repair crew for twenty-two machines in service. (Adapted from [3].)

simulation model could now furnish information quickly regarding the optimal number of machines and repair crew size for a given production level.

MAINTENANCE DEPARTMENTS

The maintenance function extends beyond machine and equipment maintenance to include plant maintenance as well. Plant maintenance includes the building, grounds, plant services such as power plants, heating and ventilating systems, plumbing system, and general house-keeping. Personnel in the plant maintenance function frequently do minor remodeling and relocation of partitions and machines to accommodate changing layout needs. Maintenance departments usually include a general machine shop in which needed repair parts can be fabricated.

Busy Work between Emergencies.   What makes machine maintenance expensive are the down-time costs. As we have discussed previously, an optimal balance of costs requires a sizable percentage of idle time for the maintenance-crew. From the viewpoint of machine maintenance, this time is idle because the crew must be ready to answer service calls. However, the idle time can be used to some extent with fill-in work that is not particularly pressing. We must recognize that anything useful that can be accomplished by maintenance crews during these idle times is achieved at *zero* incremental labor cost since the total maintenance crew cost is essentially fixed. The amount of this type of "rainy day" work is not usually great enough to soak up idle time. Even where work is available, highly skilled maintenance men avoid it by appearing to be busy at some other tasks, because much fill-in work requires low skills.

Records. Maintenance records are of critical importance if any rational analysis of maintenance problems is to be possible. What is the distribution of breakdowns? Which parts are critical and what are their expected lives? Without records we can only guess or project experience from other machines into the problem. Should we attempt a preventive maintenance program for a particular machine? If its breakdown time distribution exhibits great variability, or if the parts that fail are extremely expensive, it may not be worthwhile. Records are needed to establish sound policies and to adjust practices. Records of maintenance costs are important also when replacement studies are made.

SUMMARY

General concepts of probability, of waiting line theory, and of incremental cost analysis have provided a rational basis for designing preventive maintenance programs, determining optimal crew sizes, and determining capacity requirements so that the reliability of production systems can be maintained. The continued development of line production and automatic systems places an emphasis on general maintenance policy and preventive maintenance in particular, because of the heavy down-time costs associated with these systems. We cannot assume, however, that a preventive maintenance policy should always be used; the utility of such a policy depends on the structure of the pertinent costs.

An entirely parallel situation to that of a repair crew servicing a bank of machines is the problem of assigning operators to keep a bank of automatic machines running. In problems of this type, the operator usually goes through some loading and unloading sequence and then starts the machine. The machine proceeds automatically until service is needed again. In some situations, as in tending automatic looms, the occurrence of broken threads or other difficulties may require service at random intervals. These problems of the assignment of operators to service automatic machines are treated in reference [4].

REVIEW QUESTIONS

1. What kinds of costs are associated with machine breakdown?
2. Discuss the general methods by which the reliability of production systems can be maintained.
3. What is a breakdown time distribution?

4. Discuss the types of situations of machine breakdown which are typified by curves *a*, *b*, and *c*, respectively, in Figure 2.

5. What are the general conditions for which preventive maintenance is appropriate for a *single* machine?

6. If it takes just as long to perform a preventive maintenance as it does a repair, is there an advantage to preventive maintenance? How can high down-time costs modify this?

7. Compare the problem of maintenance of a bank of machines to the general waiting line model discussed in Chapter 8.

8. How can the technique of simulation help in evaluating alternate maintenance practices?

9. In the simulation example given in this chapter, what would be the effect of making the cost of bearings very high, say $100 each? Why?

10. What are the general responsibilities of maintenance departments?

11. What is the incremental labor cost to the organization of "rainy day" work for maintenance crews?

PROBLEMS

1. Assume we are considering alternate production line configurations for the cylinder subassembly given as an example in Chapter 12. Figure 16 in that chapter represents a solution which would produce 360 cylinders per hour with a line composed of five stations. Trial runs with this line structure indicate a large number of defectives are introduced at each of the five stations and management is beginning to question the reliability of the system. In fact the number of defects traceable to each of the five stations averages 4 per cent. What per cent defects would you expect from the line as a whole?

2. As a solution to the basic difficulty posed in Problem 1, management has proposed rebalancing the line for ten stations at a somewhat higher production rate, running the line only part-time to match the demand needs. There are some obvious disadvantages to this scheme, but management wants to know if such a setup would solve the problem of system unreliability. Their basic assumption was that each station would have a more restricted work content, and, therefore, the defects produced at each station should be reduced. New trial runs were made with the ten station lines and defects traceable to each of the ten stations now average only 3 per cent. What is the projected reliability of the new line?

3. Data concerning the breakdown of free performance of all of the electric typewriters in the general offices of a firm are given in Table III. Generate the breakdown time distribution.

4. The text describes a preventive maintenance example involving bearing failure in a bank of machines exposed to severe service (summarized on pp. 631–633). Following the establishment of Plan 2, "when a bearing fails, replace all

TABLE III. Distribution of Hours of Operation Free of Breakdowns

Frequency of Breakdown	Hours of Operation Free of Breakdown
2	100
6	200
18	250
15	300
13	350
7	400
3	500
1	550

three," a bearing made of more durable material has been proposed for use in the machines, and inflation has caused all relevant costs to increase. Simulate 20,000 hours of service for the same three alternate plans, that is:

(a) Plan 1—replace bearings when they fail.

(b) Plan 2—when a bearing fails replace all three.

(c) Plan 3—replace bearing that fails plus others if they have had 2,000 hours of service or more.

Tables IV and V give new data concerning the distribution of bearing lives and maintenance time and costs.

TABLE IV. Distribution of Bearing Lives

Number of Bearings	Bearing Life, Hours
3	1400
9	1500
13	1600
19	1700
25	1800
32	1900
35	2000
30	2100
20	2200
10	2300
3	2400
1	2500
Total 200	

TABLE V. Maintenance Time and Cost Data for Bearing Replacement	
Maintenance mechanic's time:	
Replace one bearing	6 hours
Replace two bearings	7 hours
Replace three bearings	7 hours
Maintenance mechanic's wage rate:	$5.00/hour
Bearing cost	$10.00 each
Down-time costs	$3.00/hour

5. A company is reorganizing its maintenance activities by assigning maintenance mechanics to specific departments as their primary assignments. When these mechanics are idle, that is, not being called on for service from their primary department, they do fill-in maintenance activities as needed. In one particular department there is a bank of thirty machines which must be kept in operation. Excellent data is available on the time between breakdowns and on repair time based on previous records maintained. We now wish to determine whether or not it is feasible for one man to service these machines. The distributions for breakdown and repair times are shown in Table VI. Using the flow chart shown in Figure 11, estimate the percent of time that the mechanic is idle based upon the simulated breakdown and repair for twenty breakdowns.

TABLE VI. Cumulative Distributions of Breakdown and Repair Times

Breakdown Times			Repair Times		
Cumulative Frequency	Cum. Per Cent	Time between Breakdowns, Hours	Cumulative Frequency	Cum. Per Cent	Repair Time, Hours
4	5.48	10	2	2.74	8
14	19.18	11	5	6.85	9
28	38.36	12	13	17.81	10
44	60.27	13	29	39.73	11
56	76.71	14	43	58.90	12
62	84.93	15	55	75.34	13
66	90.41	16	63	86.30	14
69	94.52	17	68	93.15	15
72	98.63	18	71	97.26	16
73	100.00	19	72	98.63	17
			73	100.00	18

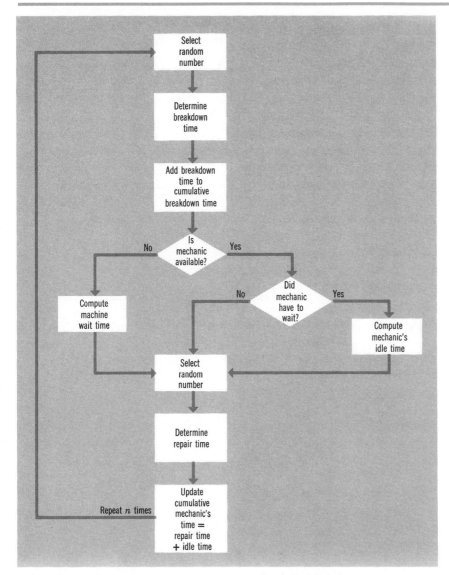

FIGURE 11. Flow chart showing structure of repair simulation.

REFERENCES

[1] Bowman, E. H., and R. B. Fetter. *Analysis for Production and Operations Management* (3rd ed.). Richard D. Irwin, Homewood, Ill., 1967.

[2] Buffa, E. S. *Operations Management: Problems and Models* (3rd ed.). John Wiley, New York, 1972, Chapters 14 and 15.

[3] Feorene, O. J. "The Gentle Art of Simulation." *Proceedings, Twelfth Annual Industrial Engineering Institute*, University of California, Berkeley–Los Angeles, 1960, pp. 15–21.

[4] Fetter, R. B. "The Assignment of Operators to Service Automatic Machines." *Journal of Industrial Engineering*, Sept.–Oct. 1955, pp. 22–29.

[5] Lusser, R. "The Notorious Unreliability of Complex Equipment," *Astronautics*, 3(2), 74–78, Feb. 1958.

[6] Malcolm, D. G. "Queuing Theory in Organization Design." *Journal of Industrial Engineering*, Nov.–Dec. 1955, pp. 19–27.

[7] Morse, P. M. *Queues, Inventories, and Maintenance*. John Wiley, New York, 1958.

[8] Turban, E. "The Use of Mathematical Models in Plant Maintenance." *Management Science*, 13 (6), 342–358, Feb. 1967.

Control of Quality

What do we mean by quality? To a manufacturer it does not carry the connotation implied by "mink" or "Rolls Royce," but rather a specified quality. The establishment, maintenance, and control of quality then deal with the determination of quality standards and the measurement and control necessary to see that the established standards are maintained and practiced. These standards may be specified dimensions, chemical composition of raw materials, hardness, strength, surface finish, or more subjective factors such as dimples in a painted service, scratches, or other possible defects which may detract from physical appearance. The established standards may very well be standards for low-quality merchandise.

FOUR PHASES OF QUALITY CONTROL

Quality control is involved at: (a) policy levels in determining desired market level of quality, (b) the engineering design stage during which quality levels are specified to achieve the market target levels, (c) the producing stage when control over incoming raw materials and productive operations is necessary to implement the policies and design specifications, and (d) the use stage in the field where installation can affect final quality and where the guarantee of quality and performance

643

must be made effective. These four general phases are shown schematically in Figure 1 together with some of the interrelationships that exist.

Product Policy and Quality. The basic policies regarding quality must necessarily emanate from top levels of the organization because they are so interrelated with the most basic decisions regarding the purpose, direction, and focus of the enterprise. These policy determinations are necessarily based on an assessment of markets and their potential at various quality levels. These policies involve questions of

FIGURE 1. Schematic representation of the role of quality control throughout the planning, production, and distribution of a product.

how quality in the product is really measured by consumers. Is it measured by appearance and esthetic design, ruggedness, dependability, long life, or what? How sensitive is the production cost and needed plant investment to these quality measures of a particular product? Therefore, in relation to the market potentials, what "return on investment" can be projected for various quality levels which could be produced? What is the competitive situation at various quality levels within the particular industry? These and other considerations may determine which sector of the market an organization shoots for. At any rate, the organization's objectives become the base points for the quality levels to be designed into the product and for the capability to be designed into the production system.

Quality and Product Design.   The detailed specifications of quality to be produced are set by the product designer when he determines materials to be used and their specifications, dimensions, tolerances, product capability, and service requirements. Here, of course, there is an interaction between what can be specified, what can be produced, and the cost of production. Thus there is a complex process of design for quality, production design of the product, and the design of the production system itself, each one affecting the other to some degree as indicated in Figure 1. (Recall our discussion of "production design" in Chapter 9.) These standards become the basis for the control of quality through manufacturing and distribution phases.

Quality Control in Manufacture.   Quality control in manufacture is, in fact, what is brought to mind to most people by the term *quality control*. In actuality, we have three important subphases which describe quality control in manufacture. These three subphases are centered around (a) the inspection and control of the quality of incoming *raw materials*, (b) the product inspection and control of *processes*, and (c) the inspection and testing for product *performance*. It is in these subphases that the well-known techniques for inspection and statistical quality control find their greatest application. We shall discuss these techniques in some detail later in the chapter.

At this point, however, let us recognize that the objective of quality control in manufacture is to implement the quality standards by measuring characteristics of the raw materials, parts, and products and comparing these measurements with established standards so that we may (a) accept or reject and (b) correct performance through information feedback. Thus the techniques of acceptance inspection and sampling provide control by filtering out items that do not, or probably do not, meet standards. Process control techniques, on the other hand, are directed toward determining when the process which generates the measurements is probably out of control. These techniques provide for corrective action to be taken before scrap losses become prohibitive. Finally, information feedback from the various inspection and production operations provides data for possible revision of quality standards and of product designs as indicated in Figure 1.

Quality Control in Distribution, Installation, and Use. A total concept of the control of quality in an organization cannot stop with the setting of broad policies, with the engineering of quality standards into the product, or with the controls established for manufacture. Quality control must extend into distribution, installation, and use phases. To the ultimate user, quality is not what was directed by policy, designed by engineers, or produced, but total performance of the product in his hands. A perfectly conceived and produced item may be damaged in distribution or be improperly installed. Therefore, for many types of products, control procedures need to extend through these phases and be regarded almost a part of the production process.

In reality, if we take the broad operations management point of view adopted by this book, we must certainly view these "after-production" processes of distribution and installation as a part of the total process requiring controls over quality. Finally, the best-conceived designs and optimally controlled production processes will pass some defective items. Thus policies and practices with regard to guarantees of quality may, in the final analysis, determine whether or not the ultimate user is satisfied with the quality of the product.

Organizing for Quality. Our discussion so far has pointed up the fact that the commonly stated slogan, "quality is everyone's job," is just about true. All levels of an organization are somehow concerned with product quality, whether it be in terms of policy setting, conception of product designs, design of the producing system, production itself, or distribution. Figure 1, in its schematic relationships of the major segments of quality control, attempts to focus our attention on the pervasive nature of the quality function. In attempting to organize for quality, it is apparent that some total coordination of a quality program is necessary. Someone in an organization needs to have a total responsibility for quality in order to coordinate quality objectives throughout the various phases indicated by Figure 1 and our discussion so far. This means that the responsible individual needs to be attached fairly high in the organization structure. His exact location in the organization and his power and influence necessarily vary from one organization to the next, since the importance of the quality function is not the same for all products and for all organizations.

However, the integrated view of the quality function is probably important for all organizations. In an organization where quality may be a dominating factor, we may find a quality control manager reporting to a vice-president of manufacturing. In organizations where the quality function may be of lesser importance because of the nature of the products, markets, and the industry, the coordination for quality may be vested in some line organization officer. In both instances, however, the total conception of the quality functions needs to be recognized for effective control within the enterprise objectives and policies.

CONTROL OF QUALITY IN PRODUCTION

We must draw a distinction between inspection and quality control. Inspection involves setting up a way of measuring quality characteristics and comparing them to quality standards. Obviously, the good parts are separated from the bad parts in this way, but no corrective action is implied. Control raises questions of when and how often to inspect and how many units to inspect. When defective units occur, control determines the cause and corrects it so that more defective units are not produced. Probability concepts play a dominant role in the control phases by setting up sampling plans which can control outgoing quality and through control chart procedures which continually track critical machines or processes.

Variation is not an exception but is characteristic of measurements in the production field. What we must recognize now is that part of the variation that we actually observe is the error of measurement and that judgment plays a strong role in the measuring process. Many experiments have been run that demonstrate this in various ways. For example, to check on the consistency of inspectors, one company mixed fifty known defective parts with a group of known good parts and sent them through the normal inspection procedure. The unsuspecting inspectors caught only thirty-nine defective parts. With the remaining eleven defectives still included, the lot was sent through again but only nine were found. A third pass found one more. Successive passes never turned up the last one—it was found by a customer.

How could this happen? The inspectors had high-quality precision measuring instruments and were trained to use them. The answer is that

The Element
of Judgment

the use of these precision instruments involves some judgment, particularly for borderline cases. Skilled mechanics call the judgment element in using precision micrometers and gages the "feel." For example, in using a precision micrometer, feel determines how tightly the operator turns down the spindle on the piece. Widely different readings can result, depending on how this is done.

To document the importance of this judgment element, Lawshe and Tiffin conducted controlled performance tests with 245 experienced inspectors. Each man was tested on the instruments that he normally used, with standard work pieces of known dimensions. Each instrument used had accepted limits of measurement. For example, with a 1-inch vernier micrometer, it is possible to measure within plus or minus 1/10,000 of an inch. Figure 2 shows the percent of the inspectors who failed to meet the accepted standards for the instrument used. The results are rather startling. Averaging over the entire experiment, a large majority of the inspectors could not use the instruments to the

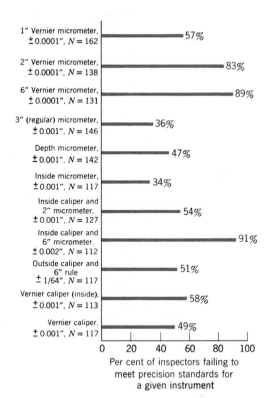

FIGURE 2.   Results of study on the accuracy of precision measurement. (Adpated from[10].)

standard levels of precision. For individual instruments, the results are much worse. Significantly, reading accuracy did not correlate with age, amount of experience with the company, or the length of time on the present job. Apparently the amount of judgment demanded in these types of measurement is somewhat greater than is generally suspected.

We generally can establish control over quality in two ways. First, we can control the actual processes that make the parts, so adjustments and corrections can be made immediately when needed in order that bad parts in any quantity are never produced. This procedure, of course, is a direct application of the statistical control chart.

Kinds of Control

Second, we can control the level of outgoing quality from an inspection point to ensure that, on the average, no more than some specified per cent of defective items will pass. This procedure assumes that the parts or products are already made and we want to set up procedures and decision rules that ensure outgoing quality will be as specified or better. This general set of methods is known as *acceptance sampling*.

In the simplest case of acceptance sampling, we draw a random sample of size n from the total lot N and decide whether or not to accept the entire lot based upon the sample. If the sample signals a decision to reject the lot, it may then either be subjected to 100 per cent inspection, sorting out bad parts, or be returned to the original supplier, which may be a vendor or another department within the organization. Parallel acceptance sampling procedures are available for the situation where we simply classify parts as good or bad (sampling by attributes) or where we make an actual measurement of some kind which indicates how good or bad a part is (sampling by variables).

Control charts attempt to control the quality produced. Acceptance sampling attempts to control the quality that passes an inspection point after production.

In general, acceptance sampling is appropriate when:

1. Possible losses by passing defective items are not great and the cost of inspection is relatively high. In the limiting situation, this can mean no inspection at all.

2. Inspection requires the destruction of the product; for example, when it is necessary to determine the strength of parts by pulling them apart. Inferring the acceptability of an entire lot from a sample is necessary in these instances.

3. Further handling of any kind is likely to induce defects, or when mental or physical fatigue is an important factor in inspection. In

either instance, a sampling plan may actually pass fewer defective items than would 100 per cent inspection, and it also costs less.

ACCEPTANCE SAMPLING BY ATTRIBUTES

The inspection procedure for attribute sampling results in the simple classification of parts as good or not good. For part dimensions, this often can be accomplished by the use of snap or plug gages that incorporate a go-not-go feature, as indicated in Figure 3. If the inspection is for surface paint defects or some other attribute of appearance, again the two-part classification of good or not good would be made. In all instances, then, attribute sampling inspection uses some criteria to grade products as acceptable or not acceptable; the statistical methods used are based on distributions, such as the binomial distribution or the Poisson distribution. (The appropriateness of these and other distributions in specific situations is beyond our scope.)

Operating
Characteristic
(*OC*) Curves

To specify a particular sampling plan, we indicate the random sample size n and the number of defectives in the sample c (acceptance number) permitted before the entire lot from which the sample was drawn is to be rejected. The *OC* curve for a particular combination of n and c shows how well the plan discriminates between good and bad lots. Figure 4 is an *OC* curve for a sampling plan, with sample size $n = 50$ and acceptance number $c = 1$. Figure 4 shows the probability of acceptance of a lot for various values of per cent defectives in the lot. For example, if the actual lot quality were 2 per cent, samples of $n = 50$ would accept the lot as

FIGURE 3. A part measured by a snap gauge. No actual part measurement is recorded, but classification of parts is made as simply good or defective.

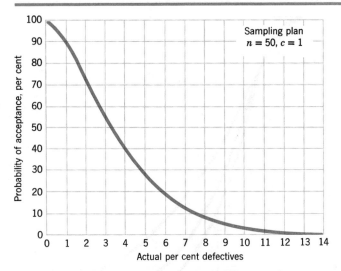

FIGURE 4.   Operating characteristic (*OC*) curve for a sampling plan with $n = 50$ and $c = 1$. (Adapted from [2].)

satisfactory about 73 per cent of the time and reject it about 27 per cent of the time. In other words, the probability of finding zero or one defective in random samples from such a lot is 73 per cent, whereas the probability of finding more than one defective is only 27 per cent. Note, however, that if the actual quality of the lot were somewhat worse than 2 per cent defective, say 5 per cent, the probability of accepting these lots falls drastically to about 27 per cent. This is the situation that we would like in a sampling plan. If the actual quality is good, we want there to be a high probability of acceptance, but if the actual quality is poor, we want the probability of acceptance to be low. Thus the *OC* curve shows how well a given plan discriminates.

The discriminating power of a sampling plan depends heavily on the size of the sample, as we might expect. Figure 5 shows the *OC* curves for sample sizes of 100, 200, and 300, with the acceptance number remaining in proportion to the sample size. Note that the *OC* curve becomes somewhat steeper as the sample size goes up. If we compare the discrimination power of the three plans represented in Figure 5, we see that all three would accept lots of about 0.7 per cent defectives about 83 per cent of the time (the approximate crossover point of the three curves). However, if actual quality falls to 3.0 per cent defectives, the plan with $n = 100$ accepts lots about 20 per cent of the time, $n = 200$, about 6 per cent of the time, and $n = 300$, less than 1 per cent of the time. Plans with large sample sizes are definitely more effective.

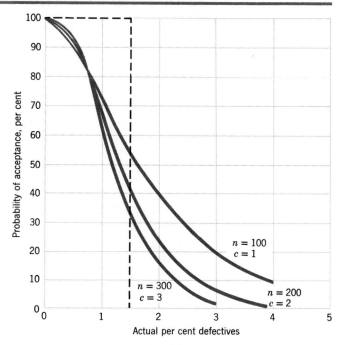

FIGURE 5.   *OC* curves for different sample sizes with acceptance numbers in proportion to sample sizes. (Adapted from [2].)

What happens to the *OC* curve if only the acceptance number changes? Figure 6 shows *OC* curves for a sample of $n = 50$ and acceptance numbers of $c = 0$, 1, 2, and 3. Note that the effect is mainly to change the level of the *OC* curve, so that lower acceptance numbers make the plan "tighter," that is, hold outgoing quality to lower per cents.

A sampling plan that discriminated perfectly between good and bad lots would have a vertical *OC* curve; that is, it would follow the dashed line of Figure 5. For all lots having per cent defectives to the left of the dashed line, the probability of acceptance is 100 per cent. For all lots having per cent defectives to the right of the line, the probability of acceptance is zero. Unfortunately, the only plan that could achieve this discrimination is one requiring 100 per cent inspection. Therefore, the justification of acceptance sampling turns on a balance between inspection costs and the probable cost of passing bad parts.

By making sampling plans more discriminating (increasing sample sizes) or tighter (decreasing acceptance numbers), we can approach any desired level of outgoing quality that we please, but at increasing

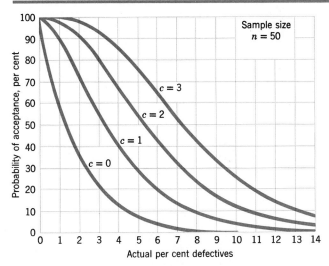

FIGURE 6. *OC* curves with different acceptance numbers for a sample size of *n* = 50. (Adapted from [2].)

inspection costs. This increased inspection effort would result in lower probable costs of passing defective parts; at some point the combination of these incremental costs is a minimum. This minimum point defines the most economical sampling plan for a given situation.

Stated simply, then, to justify a 100 per cent sample, the probable losses due to the passing of bad products would have to be large in relation to inspection costs, perhaps resulting in the loss of contracts and customers. On the other hand, to justify no inspection at all, inspection costs would have to be very large in relation to probable losses due to passing bad parts. The most usual situation is between these extremes, where there exists a risk of not accepting lots that are actually good and a risk of accepting lots that are bad. The first risk is called the producer's risk and the second, the consumer's risk.

Producer's and Consumer's Risks. We can be very specific about producer's and consumer's risks by referring to a typical *OC* curve. Figure 7 shows graphically the following four definitions.

AQL = acceptable quality level. Lots at this level of quality are regarded as good, and we wish to have a high probability of acceptance.

α = producer's risk—the probability that lots of the quality level AQL will *not* be accepted. Usually α = 5 per cent.

FIGURE 7.   Complete specifications of a sampling plan. An *OC* curve which goes through points *a* and *b* meets the requirements stated by α and *AQL* and β and *LTPD*, thus specifying a sampling plan with a given *n* and *c*. (*AQL* = acceptable quality level; *LTPD* = lot tolerance per cent defectives.)

LTPD = lot tolerance per cent defective—the dividing line selected between good and bad lots. Lots at this level of quality are regarded as poor and we wish to have a low probability for their acceptance.

β = consumer's risk—the probability that lots of the quality level *LTPD* will be accepted. Usually β = 10 per cent.

When we set levels for each of these four values, we are determining two critical points on the *OC* curve that we desire, points *a* and *b* in Figure 7.

Specification of a Specific Sampling Plan.   To specify a plan that meets the requirements for *AQL*, α, *LTPD*, and β, we must find a combination of *n* and *c* with an *OC* curve which passes through points *a* and *b* of Figure 7. The mechanics of actually finding specific plans that fit can be accomplished by using standard tables, charts, or formulas, all of which result in the specification of a combination of sample size and acceptance number which closely approximates the requirements for AQL, α, LTPD, and β.*

If we assume that when a sampling plan rejects a lot, the lot is then subjected to 100 per cent inspection, the sampling plan gives definite assurance that the average outgoing quality will not exceed certain limits. We now can develop a curve for any given sampling plan which shows the AOQ for any level of incoming quality. Such a curve can be plotted by assuming different values of actual incoming quality, determining from the OC curve the probability of acceptance for that incoming quality P_a. These figures can then be substituted in a formula to compute AOQ. Each calculation for different incoming quality levels determines a point on the AOQ curve, as indicated in Figure 8. The AOQ curve of Figure 8 is based on a sampling plan with $n = 50$, $c = 1$, and $N = 1000$, the OC curve of which is shown in Figure 4.

Note the interesting characteristics of the AOQ curve. First, there is a maximum or limiting quality which can be passed on the average. This peak of the curve is called the average outgoing quality limit (AOQL). There is an AOQL for every sampling plan which depends on the characteristics of the plan. We can reason why the AOQ curve takes the shape illustrated. When good quality is presented to the sampling plan, for example, 0 to 3 per cent, the probability of acceptance is relatively high, so most defectives will be passed. As we go beyond 3 per cent incoming quality, however, the probability of acceptance is declining. Therefore, the probability of 100 per cent inspection is increasing, so a larger share of defectives is screened out. This accounts for the fact that the outgoing quality improves as incoming quality becomes worse.

The essence of the characteristics of the sampling plan represented by the AOQ curve of Figure 8 is simply that average outgoing quality will never exceed approximately 1.6 per cent, regardless of the incoming quality. The amount of inspection required to maintain quality standards automatically adjusts to the situation. If incoming quality is very poor, perhaps 10 per cent, the sampling plan reacts by rejecting lots much more frequently, calling for 100 per cent inspection, so average outgoing quality is about 0.3 per cent. On the other hand, if incoming quality is excellent, perhaps 4 per cent, the sampling plan more frequently passes the lots and the amount of inspection required

Average Outgoing Quality (AOQ) Curves

---

*For example, see [2], [3], and [11].

FIGURE 8. Average outgoing quality (AOQ) curve for a sampling plan with $n = 50$, $c = 1$, and lot size $N = 1000$; OC curve shown in Figure 4.

is small. Inspectors usually will be spending their time screening bad lots and not wasting their time going over good lots.

The level of $AOQL$ which should be selected for a given situation depends on the consequences of bad quality. If subsequent operations can catch further defectives without disrupting production, $AOQL$ can be fairly loose. These probability controls over outgoing quality are ideal, especially since we first can specify the level of quality demanded by technical and economic considerations and then set up controls which guarantee the average performance needed, using inspection labor heavily when bad lots occur and only slightly when good lots occur.

Double Sampling In double sampling an initial sample is taken and the number of defectives found is compared to two acceptance numbers, c_1 and c_2. If the number of defectives is less than c_1, the lot is accepted. If it exceeds the large acceptance number c_2, the lot is rejected and inspected 100 per cent. If, however, the number of defectives is between c_1 and c_2, a second sample is taken. If the total number of defectives found in the *combined* *sample* exceeds c_2, the lot is rejected and inspected 100 per cent. If it is less than c_2, the lot is accepted.

The advantages of double sampling lie in possible reductions in the total amount of inspection required. This occurs because the initial sample is smaller than that required by a comparable single sampling plan. If the lot can be accepted on the basis of the first sample, there will be a saving in total inspection. This saving in inspection is greatest for large lot sizes and when incoming quality is quite good.

With double sampling there also is an appeal to the layman of the idea of "giving it a second chance." Actually this psychological advantage is illusory. The probability of acceptance is determined by the *OC* curve for any plan, and a single sampling plan can be designed which yields greater discrimination between good and bad lots than a given double sampling plan. The disadvantage of double sampling is that the inspection load varies considerably. As before, plans are specified by the four requirements of *AQL*, α, *LTPD*, and β. Tables, graphs, and formulas can then be used to select a double sampling plan that has the desired *OC* curve [2].

Sequential Sampling Plans

Double sampling has the advantage of lower inspection costs for a given level of protection, accomplished by taking a smaller sample initially from which the lot is either accepted or rejected, or a second sample is taken. Why not carry this basic idea further? This is essentially what happens with sequential sampling. Samples are drawn at random, as before. But after each sample is inspected, the cumulated results are analyzed and a decision made to (a) accept the lot, (b) reject the lot, or (c) take another sample. The sequential sample sizes can be as small as $n = 1$.

Figure 9 shows the graphical structure of a sequential sampling plan. The main advantage of sequential sampling is a further reduction in the total amount of inspection required to maintain a given level of protection, as compared to double sampling. In the plan shown in Figure 9, a minimum of fifteen items must be inspected in order to accept a lot. If the number of rejects on the graph rises such that the point falls on or above the upper line, the lot is rejected. If the point should fall on or below the lower line, the lot is accepted. Until one of these events happens, sampling is continued. As with double·sampling, the disadvantage is that inspection loads vary considerably. As with the single and double sampling plans, a sequential plan is specified by the four requirements: *AQL*, α, *LTPD*, and β. In turn, these requirements deter-

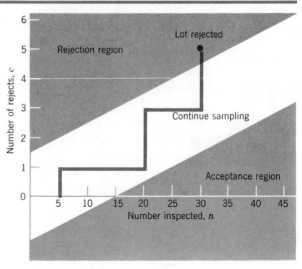

FIGURE 9. Sequential sampling plan.

mine OC curves of sequential plans which meet the functional requirements.

ACCEPTANCE SAMPLING BY VARIABLES

In acceptance sampling by variables, we make and record actual measurements instead of simply classifying items as good or bad as in attributes sampling. This difference in procedure changes the details of determining a plan that meets our specifications of acceptable quality, producer's risk, minimum acceptable quality, and consumer's risk, because the appropriate statistical distribution is now the *normal* distribution instead of distributions for proportions. In addition, inspection methods must change. Conceptually, however, the basic ideas on which the control of outgoing quality is maintained remain the same. The discriminating power of a plan still is represented by an OC curve, which shows the probability of acceptance for different levels of actual quality presented to the plan. To specify a plan that gives the desired protection requires basically the same procedure.

Upper and lower tolerance levels are often specified on measurements of part dimensions, chemical content, etc., as part of variables sampling plan specifications. In these instances, the variables sampling must provide two-sided protection from defectives occurring because the measured characteristic may be too small or too large to be useful. A sampling plan then would specify a sample size, an upper acceptance average, and a lower acceptance average.

Criteria for acceptance can be expressed in per cent defective, as with attributes sampling, even though actual measurements are made. This merely requires a conversion of units within the plan. Also, *double sampling* is as applicable to acceptance sampling by variables as to sampling by attributes.

Obviously, inspection, recording, and computing costs per unit will normally be higher with variables sampling inspection plans than with attributes plans. Then why use variables plans? The most important reason is that, for a given level of protection, variables plans require smaller samples and less total inspection than do attributes plans. From an economic viewpoint, then, variables inspection should be used where the smaller sample size tips the balance of costs of inspection, recording, and computing. In addition to the possible cost advantages, the data generated by variables inspection (mean and standard deviation) provide more valuable diagnostic information for controlling production processes.

CONTROL CHARTS

In general, variations that occur in an industrial process fall in two broad categories: *chance* variations and those due to *assignable causes*. The chance variations may be due to a complex of minor actual causes, none of which can account for any significant part of the total variation. The result is that these variations occur in a random manner, and there is very little that we can do about them, given the process. On the other hand, variations due to assignable causes are relatively large and can be traced. In general, assignable causes are:

1. Differences among workers.
2. Differences among machines.
3. Differences among materials.
4. Differences due to the interaction between any two or all three of these factors.

When a process is in a state of statistical control, variations that occur in the number of defects, the size of a dimension, chemical composition, weight, etc., are due to chance variation only. With the control chart, we set up standards of expected normal variation due to chance causes. Thus, when variations due to one or more of the assignable causes are superimposed, they "stick out like a sore thumb" and tell us that something basic has changed. The *natural tolerance* of a process is commonly taken as $\bar{x} \pm 3s$.

Control Charts for Attributes

p-Charts. Control charts for the proportion or fraction of defectives (p-charts) occurring are based on the binomial distribution. Recall that:

$$\bar{p} = \frac{x}{n} = \frac{\text{number of defectives}}{\text{total number observed}}$$

$$s_p = \sqrt{\frac{\bar{p}(1 - \bar{p})}{n}}$$

where n = the size of the subsample.

When we follow the general ideas for control charts, the control limits are normally set at the process average of defectives plus and minus three standard deviations, that is, they are set at $\bar{p} \pm 3s_p$.

Table I shows a set of data covering twenty-four consecutive production days on the number of defectives found in daily samples of 200. We wish to determine first if the data exhibit statistical control and to set up a control chart. The daily fraction defective is calculated by dividing each daily figure by the sample size, $n = 200$. Preliminary

TABLE I. Record of Number of Defectives and Calculated Fraction Defective in Daily Samples of $n = 200$

Production Day	Number of Defectives	Fraction Defective	Production Day	Number of Defectives	Fraction Defective
1	10	0.05	14	14	0.07
2	5	0.025	15	4	0.02
3	10	0.05	16	10	0.05
4	12	0.06	17	11	0.055
5	11	0.055	18	11	0.055
6	9	0.045	19	26	0.13
7	22	0.11	20	13	0.065
8	4	0.02	21	10	0.05
9	12	0.06	22	9	0.045
10	24	0.12	23	11	0.055
11	21	0.105	24	12	0.06
12	15	0.075	Total	294	
13	8	0.04			

$$\bar{p} = \frac{294}{24 \times 200} = 0.061 \qquad 3s_p = 0.051$$

$$UCL = \bar{p} + 3s_p = 0.061 + 0.051 = 0.112$$

$$s_p = \sqrt{\frac{0.061 \times 0.939}{200}} = 0.017 \qquad LCL = \bar{p} - 3s_p = 0.061 - 0.051 = 0.010$$

figures for $\bar{p}$, s_p, and the upper and lower control limits, *UCL* and *LCL*, are calculated in Table I also. These preliminary figures are used to determine if the data are in control. Figure 10 shows the resulting plot of the daily fraction defective in relation to the preliminary control limits. Two points are outside of limits and the point for day 7 is nearly outside the upper limit. Investigation shows nothing unusual for the first point, day 7. For the second point, it appears that a logical explanation is that three new men were taken on that day. The foreman contends that the following day's defectives were also affected by the breaking in of these men. The last was explained by the fact that the die had worn and finally actually fractured that day.

To set up standards for normal variation, we eliminate the data for days on which we have established assignable causes (days 10 and 19), and recompute $\bar{p}$, *UCL*, and *LCL* as follows:

$$\bar{p} = \frac{244}{200 \times 21} = 0.055$$

$$UCL = 0.055 + 3\sqrt{\frac{0.055 \times 0.945}{200}} = 0.104$$

$$LCL = 0.055 - 3\sqrt{\frac{0.055 \times 0.945}{200}} = 0.008$$

These revised values reflect the variation due to chance causes. We now use them as standards by which we judge future samples of fraction

FIGURE 10.   A *p*-chart for examining past data and establishing preliminary and revised control limits.

defective. If any future samples fall outside these limits, our immediate reaction is that it is highly probable that there is an assignable cause for the unusual observation of fraction defective. We then attempt to determine the cause and correct it before more scrap has been produced.

When the p-chart is based upon a 100 per cent sample, we may expect that the total number inspected will vary from day to day. Therefore, each successive point on the control chart will have different control limits. Under these conditions, we use the same process average fraction defective in calculating the control limits. But since n varies from day to day, s_p also varies, thus affecting the control limits.

Another control chart for attributes is based on the number of defects per unit of product. On a painted surface these might be dimples, paint runs, etc. A measure of the quality might then be the number of these blemishes per unit or per unit area sampled. Control charts set up on this basis are called c-charts.

Control Charts for Variables

Control charts could be constructed for individual measurements. Usually, however, control charts are constructed for sample means rather than for individual measurements. One important reason for this is that *although a universe distribution may depart radically from normality, the sampling distribution of means of random samples will be approximately normal if the sample size is large enough.* This statement is very important for it gives us some assurance that the probabilities associated with the $3s$ limits will apply. Figure 11 demonstrates that the deviation from normality can be fairly great and yet, with the sampling distribution of the means of samples as small as 5, follow the normal distribution quite closely.

If we take samples of four from the shaft data distribution of individual measurements in Figure 12 and determine an average for each sample, we have a new distribution. We regard each sample mean as an observation; if we plot a frequency distribution of the sample means, it will have a mean and a variance of its own. This distribution is called *a sampling distribution of means of $n = 4$.* To distinguish the *statistics* from those of the distribution of individual observations, we use the notation $\bar{x}$ for the grand mean of the sampling distribution and $s_{\bar{x}}$ for the standard deviation. We expect that $\bar{x}$ and $\bar{\bar{x}}$ will be very nearly the same and that they will be equal in the limit as the number of subsamples increases. The variance and standard deviation will be much smaller for the sampling distribution of means, however, since the variation is reduced by the averaging process within each sample. The resulting relationship be-

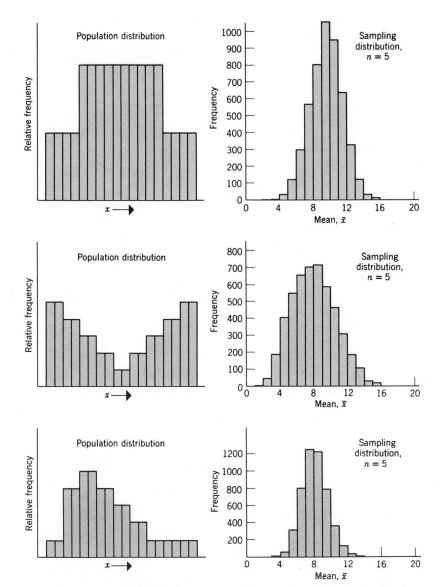

FIGURE 11.　Normality of sampling distributions. The three distributions on the left are populations from which 5000 samples of $n = 5$ were drawn at random. The resulting sampling distributions are shown on the right.

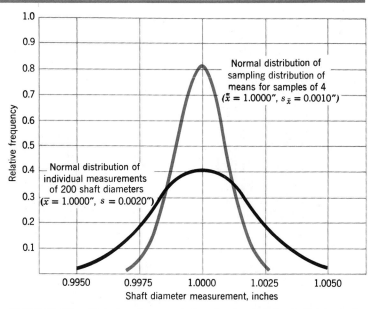

FIGURE 12. Relation between the distribution for individual observations and the sampling distribution of samples of 4 for shaft diameter data.

tween the two distributions for the shaft data is shown in Figure 12. Actually the relationship between s and $s_{\bar{x}}$ is given by

$$s_{\bar{x}} = \sqrt{s^2/n}$$

where n is the size of the subsample.

Now to construct a control chart for the means ($\bar{X}$-charts), we first need to establish standard values for $\bar{\bar{x}}$ and $s_{\bar{x}}$, which are based on the normal conditions of whatever it is that we wish to control. The upper and lower control limits are established at $\bar{\bar{x}} \pm 3s_{\bar{x}}$. Means of subsequent samples are plotted; again, action would be called for if a sample mean should fall outside the control limits.

The reasons why sample means may fall outside the control limits are, of course, related to the technology of the processes being controlled. For example, if parts were being produced on a lathe, they would tend to become oversized as the cutting tool became worn. Changes of this general nature tend to reflect themselves in the mean of the sampling distribution. If, however, the bearings of the lathe spindle had worn, this situation would be reflected by an increase in variability of the sampling distribution, and we would expect points to go outside of both control limits. The control chart can show up changes in the mean of the distribution actually being generated, changes in the variance, standard deviation, or range, and combinations of changes in the mean and changes in variability. Where changes in variability are particularly important, a special control chart on a measure of variability can be constructed.

Control Charts on Measures of Variability. When developing the control chart for means, we used the sampling distributions of means and calculated control limits based on the means as the statistic of main interest. We can as well take some measure of variability as the statistic, for example, the variance. For each subsample of size n, we can calculate a sample variance s^2. If we made a frequency distribution of these variances, we would have a distribution which approximated the normal distribution. This distribution of sample variances would itself have a mean and a standard deviation. We could, therefore, use this distribution of sample variances to establish a control chart which would tell us when the variability of the thing being controlled is greater or less than normal.

In quality control work, the statistic chosen is usually the *range* instead of the variance, because of the ease with which it can be computed for the successive samples. For each subsample, the difference between the highest and lowest measurement is plotted on a control chart for ranges. The control chart for ranges represents a distribution of ranges for samples of size n. This distribution has an average, $\bar{R}$, and a standard deviation s_R. The $3s_R$ limits have the same general significance as before. The probability that a sample range will fall outside the limits is only 0.27 per cent if it comes from the original universe. Therefore, when sample ranges do fall outside the control limits, we can presume that something has happened to cause greater than expected variability. Convenient tables and charts exist which make it very easy to establish the $3s_R$ control limits.

SUMMARY

The control of quality in an organization requires a broad integrated view of the responsibility for quality, not just a focus on the control of quality levels of incoming raw materials and the control over manufacturing processes. The chain of enterprise policies, engineering design decisions, production system design, and control over the operations phases, including distribution and use, requires dovetailing and coordination if the total enterprise objectives with regard to quality are to be achieved.

The development of the use of probability controls in industry has reached its greatest height in quality control. Acceptance sampling gears the amount of inspection to probable incoming quality levels and calls for 100 per cent inspection when there is a strong probability that incoming quality is poor. On the other hand, when samples indicate that incoming quality is probably fairly good, the entire lot is accepted without further inspection. Control charts attempt to prevent the production of poor quality in the first place by indicating, when the probability is high, that there is some assignable cause for defective parts being produced. By running up the distress signal at the first sign of trouble, we prevent the production of more scrap and save the cost of subsequent inspection to screen out the bad parts.

Although the concepts of acceptance sampling and statistical control have been presented in a background of industrial quality control, we should recognize that these ideas have very general application. Decisions in all functional areas are commonly based on sample data. Why not assess the risks involved as is done in acceptance sampling? The concepts of statistical control are finding a widening field of application outside manufacturing today. Control charts have been used for labor turnover, costs, accident rates, etc.

REVIEW QUESTIONS

1. What is the meaning of the term *quality* in the manufacturing sense?
2. Differentiate between inspection and quality control.
3. Discuss the role of judgment in the use of precision measurement devices and in inspection.
4. What kind of control can be exercised in maintaining quality standards?
5. What conditions make acceptance sampling appropriate?
6. What is an *OC* curve and what information does it convey?
7. What is the effect of increasing sample size on the *OC* curve? What practical result does it achieve in terms of the discriminating power of a sampling plan?
8. What is the effect of decreasing acceptance numbers on the *OC* curve? What practical result does it achieve in terms of outgoing quality levels?
9. Define *AQL*, α, *LTPD*, and β. Relate these definitions to a typical *OC* curve.
10. Discuss the significance of the shape of the average outgoing quality (*AOQ*) curve. Relate this to the amount of inspection required at various levels of incoming quality.

11. What is the general structure for double sampling? What are its advantages and disadvantages?

12. What is the general structure for sequential sampling? What are its advantages and disadvantages?

13. Contrast the differences in concept and statistical technique for sampling by attributes and by variables.

14. What conditions favor the use of sampling by variables?

15. What are the sources of assignable causes of variation in quality control?

16. Discuss the procedure for setting up a p-chart.

17. What is the significance of the fact that the sampling distribution of means can be normal even though the distribution of individual measurements departs radically from normality?

18. What is the relationship between s and $s_{\bar{x}}$?

19. Why is the range usually used as the measure of variability in quality control?

PROBLEMS

1. StaMPCo, who makes the V-belt pulley shown in Figure 21 on page 356, has decided to employ certain statistical control techniques to reduce the cost of inspection and to improve quality control. StaMPCo buys 0.875-inch diameter rolled bar stock on a contract basis from a large, dependable supplier. Shipments are made in lots of 400 as required. At the present production rate of pulleys having 0.875-inch diameter hubs, 400 bars roughly correspond to six to seven days' usage.

To properly match the pulley flanges produced on punch presses, the bar stock cannot vary more than 0.002 inch from the nominal diameter. Therefore, the specification for bar stock diameter is 0.875 inch $\pm$ 0.002 inch. If the bar diameter exceeds the upper specification limit, the flanges tend to split excessively when forced onto the hub by the arbor press. If the diameter is smaller than specified, the flange-hub fit is loose and the spot-welding operation tends to pull the flanges off the axis of rotation. As a result, a large number of pulleys must be rejected because of excessive "wobble."

(a) The company's contract with the steel supplier specifies that 95 per cent of the bars are to meet the diameter specification of 0.875 inch $\pm$ 0.002 inch.

(b) The production manager and purchasing agent have decided that the company should not accept an individual shipment in which more than 17.5 per cent of the bars are oversized or undersized. What are the values of the parameters which would define an acceptance sampling plan?

2. After several months the production manager feels that the receiving inspection department has been accepting too many lots in which the actual number of defective bars exceeds 17.5 per cent. He therefore recommends reducing the probability of accepting lots which have more than 17.5 per cent

defectives by one-half. How must the plan discussed in problem 1 be modified to carry out this recommendation?

3.   StaMPCo has been experiencing a large number of rejects among its smaller V-belt pulleys because of hub defects. Since the pulley hub is largely fabricated on the turret lathe, the production manager has requested a complete study of the turret lathe pulley hub operations.

To test the quality capability of the turret lathes, ten samples of four pulley hubs each were taken when the lathes were operating in a "typical" manner. The results for hub lengths are given below; $n = 4$.

Sample Number	Sample Average $\bar{X}$	Sample Range R
1	1.007 inch	0.013 inch
2	1.008	0.022
3	0.991	0.018
4	0.993	0.014
5	0.998	0.019
6	1.008	0.026
7	0.996	0.024
8	0.995	0.011
9	0.999	0.021
10	0.995	0.024
Totals	9.990 inch	0.192 inch

Determine the natural tolerance of the lathes for cut-off operations.

4.   If the design specification for small pulley hub lengths is 1.000 ± 0.040 inch, are the turret lathes inherently capable of meeting these specifications? Why?

5.   Based on the design specifications for the pulley hub length of 1.000 ± 0.040 inch and the natural tolerance interval, at what basic dimension (average hub length) should the turret lathe be set whenever a tool change or adjustment is made? (Assume that tool wear is the only predictable variable in process changes.) Sketch this situation and explain.

6.   With the quality capability information which you have developed, determine the control limits and set up the control charts for the control of the cut-off operation on turret lathes. A sample of four pulleys is to be taken every half hour.

(a) Control chart for sample means $\bar{X}$. Under normal conditions the width of the cut-off tool is known to wear at the rate of 0.001 inch per hour of use. The shop works from 8:00 A.M. to 12:00 noon and 12:30 P.M. to 4:30 P.M. (The lunch period is 12:00 to 12:30 P.M.) It is shop practice to replace the cut-off tool at the beginning of the work day in accordance with the procedure which you established in problem 3.

(1) Determine the appropriate control limits for the sample mean so as to reflect the known rate of cut-off tool wear.

(2) Plot the $\bar{X}$ control limits and the predicted trend line of average hub length on the control chart.

(b) Control chart for sample ranges R.

(1) Determine the appropriate control limits for the sample range. (Show all calculations.)

(2) Plot the R control limits and the average range $\bar{R}$ on the control chart.

REFERENCES

[1] Bowker, A. H., and H. P. Goode. *Sampling Inspection by Variables*. McGraw-Hill, New York, 1952.

[2] Dodge, H. F., and H. G. Romig. *Sampling Inspection Tables* (2nd ed.). John Wiléy, New York, 1959.

[3] Duncan, A. J. *Quality Control and Industrial Statistics* (3rd ed.). Richard D. Irwin, Homewood, Ill., 1965.

[4] Feigenbaum, A. V. *Total Quality Control*. McGraw-Hill, New York, 1961.

[5] Grant, E. L., and R. S. Leavenworth. *Statistical Quality Control* (4th ed.). McGraw-Hill, New York, 1972.

[6] Hansen, B. L. *Quality Control*. Prentice-Hall, Englewood Cliffs, N.J., 1963.

[7] Harris, D. H., and F. B. Chaney. *Human Factors in Quality Assurance*. John Wiley, New York, 1969.

[8] Hoel, P. G., and R. J. Jessen. *Elementary Statistics for Business and Economics*. John Wiley, New York, 1971.

[9] Kirkpatrick, E. G. *Quality Control for Managers and Engineers*. John Wiley, New York, 1970.

[10] Lawshe, C. H., and J. Tiffin. "The Accuracy of Precision Instrument Measurement in Industrial Production." *Journal of Applied Psychology*, Dec. 1945, pp. 413–419.

[11] MIL-STD-105C. *Military Standard Sampling Procedures and Tables for Inspection by Attributes*, July 18, 1961.

[12] MIL-STD-414. *Military Standard Sampling Procedures and Tables for Inspection by Variables for Per Cent Defective*, June 11, 1957.

[13] Vance, L. L., and J. Neter. *Statistical Sampling for Auditors and Accountants*. John Wiley, New York, 1956.

part five

Synthesis

Production & Operations Management— Summary

Times are changing, and in no place is this fact any more evident than in the field of production and operations management. The field is in a state of flux from several viewpoints. The meaning of the word *production* today reflects a broader view than formerly. It deals with the *operations* side of any enterprise, and we may find production systems in offices, stores, hospitals, etc., as well as in factories. In all these systems, there are inputs, some kind of processing, and outputs. Production and operations management deals with decision making within the system. One of the recent conceptual changes is that waste in the system and its possible effect on pollution has come to be regarded as a part of the processing system.

The organization of this book has been around the problems encountered in the design and operation of productive systems, given a background of applicable analytical methods. In general, we discussed within each problem area how that problem was affected by the special conditions of different kinds of productive systems. As a basis for summation let us now try to integrate our knowledge in terms of each of the major kinds of systems: distribution systems, production-distribution systems for high-volume products, job shops (both closed and open), and large-scale projects.

DISTRIBUTION SYSTEMS

In essence, the management of distribution systems is centered in the management of an inventory system, usually a multistage inventory system. The design of the physical distribution system is concerned with the strategic location of inventory points in relation to markets in order to provide the required service at reasonable transportation cost. Logistics dominates the system design in determining whether or not to use intermediate warehouses and, if so, where to locate them.

The operating problems of distribution systems are centered in inventory management. What is the distribution of demand? How do we forecast requirements? When should we replenish inventories? How much inventory should be ordered at one time? What buffer stocks should be maintained to offer the service needed? How do we determine the appropriate service level?

Though the problems are similar for each of the levels in the system, they have a somewhat different emphasis. For example, the problem of determining distribution of demand and forecasting demand is local for the retailer, whereas at the factory warehouse it may be national or international in scope. On the other hand, the factory warehouse may need a data processing system for a relatively few sizes, types, and styles, whereas the distributor and retailer are likely to be dealing with a very much larger number of items. Also, the concept of service and service systems is physical in terms of the inventories required at each level, however, at the retail level service systems must include not only the availability of inventory, but the design of a service system around the concepts of waiting line analysis.

The major production and operations management problems which confront distribution kinds of organizations are as follows:

1. Determination of the nature of the distribution of demand.
2. Forecasting demand.
3. Determination of how much to order at one time.
4. Determination of when to reorder.

5. Determination of service levels and the size of buffer stocks.

6. Design of data processing systems.

HIGH-VOLUME PRODUCTION-DISTRIBUTION SYSTEMS

Adding a production system to the head end of a distribution system. changes the focus and adds enormous complexity to the managerial problems. The system under managerial control centers around the production system and extends downstream into the distribution system to some extent, depending on the particular organization. In some instances, it may include the entire distribution system. One of the great advantages in coupling the production and distribution systems is that inventories become an important tradeoff to other means of absorbing fluctuations in demand, and the kinds of aggregate planning models discussed in Chapter 17 take on considerable significance.

Forecasting consumer demand is extremely important both in the short and long run. In the short run, forecasts are the basis for raw material procurement, and aggregate planning and scheduling of facilities and labor in order to combine the various sources of capacity in the most economical way. Longer-range forecasts, however, are also of great significance in planning long-range aggregate capacity and its location and layout, as well as the size and location of distribution warehouses.

The process of generating day-to-day schedules for high-volume systems is one of working within the constraints of the aggregate plan, taking advantage of whatever flexibility may be left to "cut and try" for a practical schedule. This may include rebalancing of lines, inventory adjustments, the use of overtime and subcontracting, etc. The nature and design of the information and data processing system which couples measurement of actual demand, forecasting, inventory control, and production control is of extreme importance.

Though no one would say that the design, planning, scheduling, and control problems of high-volume production-distribution systems are simple, they are, nonetheless, simpler than for intermittent systems.

The major production and operations management problems which confront organizations producing and distributing high-volume standardized products are as follows:

1. Forecasting demand and the behavior of multistage inventory systems.
2. Long-range aggregate planning for facilities—plant capability, sizes and location, and warehouse sizes and location.
3. Production facility design.

4. Aggregate planning and scheduling for facilities and manpower.
5. Raw materials procurement.
6. Day-to-day scheduling and adjustment of production levels as demand becomes known.
7. Design of data processing systems.

INTERMITTENT SYSTEMS

In contrast to the high-volume system, intermittent systems key everything to the basic requirement of holding facilities and manpower "in inventory" to supply the needs of a demand that varies in terms of its design, style, and technological requirements. Thus, the jobbing printer holds in readiness equipment and trained personnel capable of performing a wide variety of operations to reproduce the printed word. Jobbing machine shops hold in readiness equipment and trained mechanics capable of performing a wide variety of operations on various metals of different sizes, types, and designs. If the number of orders falls temporarily, such an organization does not sell its equipment nor fire its skilled mechanics for it is this capability that it has for sale. Similarly, and perhaps even more essential to organizational survival, aerospace and other research and developmental organizations may stockpile engineering and scientific brains because it is this kind of capability which is crucial in obtaining contracts.

Though most often the relationships with the ultimate consumer may be direct, the internal complications are tremendous. These complications arise from the custom nature of the fabrication process, where each order, or item, will require individual planning and scheduling and will follow a unique processing sequence. The typical time delays in the information system are in the bid and order procedure, the special production planning and scheduling requirements, and the special ordering of materials. The physical flow time involved in actual fabrication and assembly is usually relatively long because of the intermittent nature of physical flow. The inventory problems are largely for raw material and in-process inventories, and the scheduling problem is focused more on the use of individual pieces of equipment rather than the factory as a whole as with high-volume systems.

The most complex of job shop systems is the open shop, which is open to job orders from virtually anyone. Under such circumstances one must forecast, design the physical facility, make aggregate plans, schedule, procure materials, and bid with the greatest uncertainty.

The closed job shop is the captive shop of some concern and manufactures for its own internal use in its own product line. Its product line usually has a degree of predictability, although the captive shops may also receive internal one-time orders. Closed job shops in fact produce a largely forecastable line of parts, components, and products, and this is an important distinction because, if we know in advance what our product line mix will be, then the problems can take on a considerably different hue.

The major production and operations management problems which confront job shop kinds of organizations may be summarized as follows:

1. Design and layout of a system to minimize aggregate handling cost.
2. Forecasting demand.
3. Aggregate planning for the use of facilities.
4. Scheduling orders to meet promised delivery dates.
5. Scheduling labor and equipment to minimize combined costs of machine setup, machine down time, labor overtime and undertime, and in-process inventories.
6. Scheduling equipment to utilize most efficient processes.
7. Procuring materials in economical quantities to mesh with the production schedule.
8. Developing bidding policy and procedure to obtain orders at margins that will achieve a balance between use of labor and facilities, and desire for profit.

LARGE-SCALE PROJECTS

A structural model for large-scale projects is not far different from a job shop model. The differences are in terms of the immense complexity and the extensive time delays and coordination required within the system. In planning the activities of what must be done, the very complexity of the project makes process sequences of extreme importance, for operations performed out of sequence can cause delays and extra costs. Thus, the development of the production plan as a network of operations is the key to managerial control of the project. Given the network of required operations, a second focus of problems centers on scheduling and the effective use of available resources. The generation of the critical path schedule is an important input to the scheduling and control processs and may be regarded as a first feasible schedule. The knowledge of permissible slack or schedule slippage of certain operations gives management flexibility in achieving a practical schedule. This flexibility can also be used to level the labor requirements over the entire project or make it possible to use limited equipment for several operations in a way that does not conflict and still does not extend the project time.

The inventory problem at first seems simple and direct, yet there are important inventory problems. Inventory cost is in general directly related to overall project time. To minimize the investment in inventories during the project, material receipt schedules must be carefully coordinated with the schedule of operations. If orders for raw material supply are released in a block at the beginning of the project, a large fraction of inventories would be held for a much larger period than necessary and would probably also create a physical storage problem. If material is wasted or scrapped so that a certain operation cannot be completed, then the entire project may be delayed if the activity is on the critical path schedule. Thus, an important inventory decision problem centers on the quantity of material to be ordered in the first place. A relatively inexpensive item of material could cause idle labor costs, or possible penalties for not meeting project delivery dates.

In summary, the major production and operations management problems of large-scale projects are:

1. Planning a network of operations to accomplish the desired end result.
2. Developing schedules of the network of operations such that the critical path schedule of the network meets promised delivery dates.
3. Allocating the use of limited resources of equipment and/or labor in ways that will not interfere with the critical path schedule.
4. Procuring materials by a schedule that minimizes total inventory costs but meets the needs of the critical path schedule.
5. Developing bidding policy and procedures to obtain contracts at margins that will achieve a balance between the use and maintenance of the stockpile of critical resources (engineers, scientists, skilled labor, key facilities, etc.) and the desire for profit.

The four major kinds of systems which we have discussed do not represent rigid classifications, since systems in practice tend to be combinations of job shop and line or job shop and project, etc. The classifications, however, have provided a basis for developing concepts and techniques for the typical production line, distribution system, job shop, or project. Analytical methods have grown around the concepts of the pure system and combination systems may then be analyzed by analyzing the components and merging the results.

SIGNIFICANCE OF NEWER ANALYTICAL METHODS

Perhaps the thing that has shaken traditional production management in both teaching and practice more than anything else is the rapid development of mathematical and simulation models of production systems and subsystems during the post-World War II period, together with rapid data-processing techniques. These developments are the prelude to the recognition of a new applied science. Many areas have yielded to formal analysis. A true "systems" approach is being taken in many instances where previously each problem was considered by itself. System simulation with the aid of high-speed computers promises to create a laboratory for production management which could not otherwise exist.

Of what importance are these tools to personnel, present and future? People already in business and industry must consider their backgrounds incomplete without a knowledge of them. As time passes, they will be considered more and more "old foggies" unless they attempt to acquire a basic understanding of the new methods and concepts. They will find themselves obsolete before their careers are ended and, perhaps, even sidetracked into less desirable "dead-end" positions. For the young men and women who are just now getting their educational backgrounds, there is a basic choice. Will they prepare themselves adequately or will they dodge the issue only to face it later? It is true that no one can prepare himself completely for the next forty years, but he can provide himself with a basic education which will help him to grow with the times. In a field that is developing rapidly, it is important to start in the right direction.

The fact that there is a rapid development of the use of the newer analytical methods is shown clearly by Table I. Table I summarizes the results of three surveys taken successively in 1957, 1958, and 1964. These surveys were directed toward the determination of the extensiveness of the use of operations research techniques in the various fields listed. The trends in the areas of production and operations management are unmistakable. In the applications in production, generally 24 per cent of responding companies said they used such techniques in the 1957 survey, but this figure jumped to 32 per cent a year later and to 68 per cent in the 1964 survey. Similar trends are shown in the areas of long-range planning, inventories, and transportation. Though less dramatic by comparison, substantial progress is evident in the applica-

TABLE I.   A Comparative Table of Areas of Application of Operations Research Techniques (in per cent of *n*)*

	Survey†		
	AMA Report 1957 *n* = 631	Hovey and Wagner 1958 *n* = 90	Schumacher and Smith 1964 *n* = 65
Production	24	32	68
Long-range planning	23	39	55
Advertising, sales, and marketing	25	14	20
Inventory	21	31	68
Transportation	15	18	41
Top management	15	n.a.	n.a.
Research	14	n.a.	n.a.
Finance	13	n.a.	n.a.
Accounting	11	11	13
Purchasing	8	n.a.	n.a.
Personnel	8	n.a.	n.a.
Quality control	n.a.	22	38
Maintenance	n.a.	11	24
Plant location	n.a.	10	24
Equipment replacement	n.a.	10	20
Packaging	n.a.	9	5
Capital budgeting	n.a.	7	29
Average per area	15	18	34

*Comparative table in this form from E. Turban, "The Use of Mathematical Models in Plant Maintenance Decision Making," *Management Science,* **13** (6), B 346, Feb. 1967.
†n.a.—data not available.
n = total number of firms participating in the survey.
The Schumacher and Smith survey is a follow-up of the Hovey and Wagner survey.
Source: [1, 3, 4].

tion of these techniques to quality control, plant location, equipment replacement, and capital budgeting.

With the new availability of time-shared computing, simulation can take on a new and conceptually important characteristic, that is, the decision maker can be included in the loop. Given the simulation model, the decision maker can raise a host of "what if" questions about his operations and get back immediate answers showing the impact of the proposed operational change on the important indices of performance. Of course, through a series of computer runs one can assess the impact of these kinds of questions in batch mode computing also. The key difference, however, is the interactive capability of time-shared systems where the immediacy of results prompts new questions to be raised.

Thus, the decision maker takes on a mental set of problem solving, working in concert with the power of large-scale computing. Such models have now been applied in a wide variety of enterprises. Those with a particular emphasis in production systems have been at Inland Steel Company [2, 3], Potlatch Forests Incorporated [3, 5], and Van den Berghs & Jurgens, Ltd., a subsidiary of Unilever, Ltd. [5].

HOW GOOD IS JUDGMENT?

People, especially in higher positions, often try to ignore the problem of becoming obsolete to their organizations by saying: "I am paid for my expert judgment. If I need brains I can hire them." Well and good. Business judgment probably always will be a major asset. But how valuable is judgment alone in complex situations and does it warrant the self-assurance so commonly expressed? Obviously, there is no complete answer to this question, but we have some indications. We constructed problems requiring decisions that could be made by business judgment but which also could be subjected to formal analysis and a "right answer" determined. These problems were given to groups of executives who were asked to make the required decisions using any methods they chose. The results indicated that formal analysis had it all over judgment. Figure 1 summarizes the results for one of these problems (summarized on pages 23–29) that was given to members of the UCLA Executive Program. The fifty-two participants were all successful executives of the level of president, vice-president, head of major division, etc.

Recall that the decision involved bidding on two government contracts where the probability of receiving the contracts depended on the bid price in one case and the amount of capital invested in test equipment in the second case. The decision was complicated by the threat of a strike. This strike threat could be settled by giving in to the union, but at an increase in production costs due to demanded wage increases. If the company refused to settle on union terms, a direct strike loss would be involved, as well as the fact that it would be impossible to bid on one of the contracts. These conditions formed twenty strategies of bidding on the two contracts. Executives chose one of the courses of action which are coded as ADH, ACH, etc., in Figure 1. The desirability of each strategy is indicated by the left scale; the per cent of the executives who elected the various alternatives is shown to the right. Only 10 per cent of the executives made the best possible decision and, significantly, all of these men worked out the solution mathematically. Intuition, good judgment, and emotion all proved poor seconds. What

FIGURE 1. Distribution of decisions made by fifty-two members of the UCLA Executive Program on a bidding problem containing twenty alternatives. (From [4].)

does it mean? This problem, although complex, did not approach the complexity of modern systems. It must mean that business judgment is falling short of ideal results in the real situations.

Another comparison between human decisions and mathematical models was carried out by Pegels [7]. He developed mathematical models for production and work force decisions for a firm manufacturing prefabricated houses on an assembly line. These models were similar to the Linear Decision Rule models for aggregate planning discussed in Chapter 17. An experiment was then carried out to see how well decision makers could make decisions in the face of fluctuating demand when optimal decisions could be computed by the model. In appraising the comparative results Pegels states, "The experiment clearly points out that some decisions will be more effective from a cost point of view if they are based on a mathematical model."

How can we deal with the argument of the "big boy" who says: "If I need brains, I can hire them"? For one thing, he needs to know something about the new concepts and techniques to know where he can use talent and where it will be wasted. Secondly, the executive needs to be able to evaluate the work of these "brains" that he has hired. If he is going to accept without further ado whatever they tell him, his function becomes uncertain. Finally, a person in this unfortunate position is bound to be insecure in both the economic and psychological sense. He must live with himself!

A SUMMARY VIEWPOINT

Throughout this book we noted that most production problems involve a balance of costs for an optimum solution. Invariably, cost factors affected by a given decision follow different patterns, so the best solution never involves minimizing one cost factor at the expense of others. This means that we *do* produce some scrap, we *do* have some late orders, we *do* run out of stock sometimes, etc. Otherwise, we are controlling some factors too tightly and not operating in an optimal fashion.

We must remember that many of the quantitative methods we have studied were more than simply problem-solving techniques. Perhaps their most important function has been to help us to understand the nature of the system with which we are dealing. For example, waiting line theory gives insight into the probabilistic nature of the flow problem. If we understand something of waiting line theory, we may be able to make excellent judgments about staffing of activities where arrivals of the item being processed are controlled by random processes.

When we understand that a jobbing machine shop may be described as a network of waiting lines, we may gain some insight into why it seemingly takes an order so long to get through such a system.

Linear programming is a formal means of allocating scarce resources to competing demands. But there are many kinds of allocation problems in an enterprise, most of which we may not be able to solve formally. However, the structure of the problems and answers to the formal problems have a transfer to all kinds of allocation problems. For one thing we know that there are probably alternate optimal solutions and that there may be many more solutions which are almost as good as the optimal ones. The result is that we know we have considerable flexibility, and this makes it easier to accommodate to a variety of side conditions.

As noted previously, we have not attempted to deal with many of the human behavior problems that obviously do occur in production systems. Perhaps it is important to point out, however, that formal models and analysis can often take account of human problems even though human "variables" may not enter directly into the models constructed. A good example is the computer model for layout, CRAFT, discussed in Chapter 12. A manager may feel that it is important that two work groups not be separated in a new layout. Before concluding that this should be the answer, however, let us appraise this requirement. It may be that an excellent solution exists which accommodates this constraint. It may also be true that this constraint will be very costly. Let us make the analysis, however, rather than specify conditions without analysis or appraisal.

Finally, the broader the viewpoint that we can take, the more likely it is that we can avoid suboptimization. Thus, we found that it was not valid for us to consider inventory problems in isolation because inventory levels were partially dependent on production fluctuations. As knowledge of production management grows, we shall determine the effects of the interactions of many other variables in the system. We shall be able to take a true "systems" viewpoint.

REFERENCES

[1] AMA Management Report No. 10. *Operations Research Reconsidered*. American Management Association, Inc., New York, 1958.

[2] Barkdoll, G. "Models—New Management Decision Aid." *Industrial Engineering*, 31–40, Dec. 1970.

[3] Boulden, J. B., and E. S. Buffa. "Corporate Models: On-Line, Real-Time Systems." *Harvard Business Review*, July–Aug. 1970, pp. 65–83.

[4] Boulden, J. B., and E. S. Buffa. "The Strategy of Interdependent Decisions." *California Management Review*, **1** (4), 94–98, 1959.

[5] Buffa, E. S. *Operations Management: Problems and Models*. (3rd ed.). John Wiley, New York, 1972, Chapter 21.

[6] Hovey, R. W., and H. M. Wagner. "A Sample Survey of Industrial Operations Research Activities." *Operations Research*, **6** (6), 876–881, Nov.–Dec. 1958.

[7] Pegels, C. "Human Decision vs. Math Model: An Experiment." *Industrial Engineering*, Dec. 1970, pp. 41–44.

[8] Schumacher, C. C., and B. E. Smith. "A Sample Survey of Industrial Operations Research Activities, II." *Operations Research*, **13** (6), 1023–1027, Dec. 1965.

[9] Starr, M. K. "Evolving Concepts in Production Management." In: *Evolving Concepts in Management*. E. Flippo, editor. Academy of Management Proceedings, 24th Annual Meeting, Dec. 1964. Also reprinted in: *Readings in Production and Operations Management*. E. S. Buffa, editor. John Wiley, New York, 1966.

[10] Turban, E. "The Use of Mathematical Models in Plant Maintenance Decision Making." *Management Science*, **13** (6), Feb. 1967.

part six

Appendix – Tables

TABLE I. PV_{sp}, Present Value Factors for Future Single Payments

Years Hence	1%	2%	4%	6%	8%	10%	12%	14%	15%	16%	18%	20%
1	0.990	0.980	0.962	0.943	0.926	0.909	0.893	0.877	0.870	0.862	0.847	0.833
2	0.980	0.961	0.925	0.890	0.857	0.826	0.797	0.769	0.756	0.743	0.718	0.694
3	0.971	0.942	0.889	0.840	0.794	0.751	0.712	0.675	0.658	0.641	0.609	0.579
4	0.691	0.924	0.855	0.792	0.735	0.683	0.636	0.592	0.572	0.552	0.516	0.482
5	0.951	0.906	0.822	0.747	0.681	0.621	0.567	0.519	0.497	0.476	0.437	0.402
6	0.942	0.888	0.790	0.705	0.630	0.564	0.507	0.456	0.432	0.410	0.370	0.335
7	0.933	0.871	0.760	0.665	0.583	0.513	0.452	0.400	0.376	0.354	0.314	0.279
8	0.923	0.853	0.731	0.627	0.540	0.467	0.404	0.351	0.327	0.305	0.266	0.233
9	0.914	0.837	0.703	0.592	0.500	0.424	0.361	0.308	0.284	0.263	0.225	0.194
10	0.905	0.820	0.676	0.558	0.463	0.386	0.322	0.270	0.247	0.227	0.191	0.162
11	0.896	0.804	0.650	0.527	0.429	0.350	0.287	0.237	0.215	0.195	0.162	0.135
12	0.887	0.788	0.625	0.497	0.397	0.319	0.257	0.208	0.187	0.168	0.137	0.112
13	0.879	0.773	0.601	0.469	0.368	0.290	0.229	0.182	0.163	0.145	0.116	0.093
14	0.870	0.758	0.577	0.442	0.340	0.263	0.205	0.160	0.141	0.125	0.099	0.078
15	0.861	0.743	0.555	0.417	0.315	0.239	0.183	0.140	0.123	0.108	0.084	0.065
16	0.853	0.728	0.534	0.394	0.292	0.218	0.163	0.123	0.107	0.093	0.071	0.054
17	0.844	0.714	0.513	0.371	0.270	0.198	0.146	0.108	0.093	0.080	0.060	0.045
18	0.836	0.700	0.494	0.350	0.250	0.180	0.130	0.095	0.081	0.069	0.051	0.038
19	0.828	0.686	0.475	0.331	0.232	0.164	0.116	0.083	0.070	0.060	0.043	0.031
20	0.820	0.673	0.456	0.312	0.215	0.149	0.104	0.073	0.061	0.051	0.037	0.026
21	0.811	0.660	0.439	0.294	0.199	0.135	0.093	0.064	0.053	0.044	0.031	0.022
22	0.803	0.647	0.422	0.278	0.184	0.123	0.083	0.056	0.046	0.038	0.026	0.018
23	0.795	0.634	0.406	0.262	0.170	0.112	0.074	0.049	0.040	0.033	0.022	0.015
24	0.788	0.622	0.390	0.247	0.158	0.102	0.066	0.043	0.035	0.028	0.019	0.013
25	0.780	0.610	0.375	0.233	0.146	0.092	0.059	0.038	0.030	0.024	0.016	0.010

TABLE II. PV_a, Present Value Factors for Annuities

Years (n)	1%	2%	4%	6%	8%	10%	12%	14%	15%	16%	18%	20%
1	0.990	0.980	0.962	0.943	0.926	0.909	0.893	0.877	0.870	0.862	0.847	0.833
2	1.970	1.942	1.886	1.833	1.783	1.736	1.690	1.647	1.626	1.605	1.566	1.528
3	2.941	2.884	2.775	2.673	2.577	2.487	2.402	2.322	2.283	2.246	2.174	2.106
4	3.902	3.808	3.630	3.465	3.312	3.170	3.037	2.914	2.855	2.798	2.690	2.589
5	4.853	4.713	4.452	4.212	3.993	3.791	3.605	3.433	3.352	3.274	3.127	2.991
6	5.795	5.601	5.242	4.917	4.623	4.355	4.111	3.889	3.784	3.685	3.498	3.326
7	6.728	6.472	6.002	5.582	5.206	4.868	4.564	4.288	4.160	4.039	3.812	3.605
8	7.652	7.325	6.733	6.210	5.747	5.335	4.968	4.639	4.487	4.344	4.078	3.837
9	8.566	8.162	7.435	6.802	6.247	5.759	5.328	4.946	4.772	4.607	4.303	4.031
10	9.471	8.983	8.111	7.360	6.710	6.145	5.650	5.216	5.019	4.833	4.494	4.192
11	10.368	9.787	8.760	7.887	7.139	6.495	5.988	5.453	5.234	5.029	4.656	4.327
12	11.255	10.575	9.385	8.384	7.536	6.814	6.194	5.660	5.421	5.197	4.793	4.439
13	12.134	11.343	9.986	8.853	7.904	7.103	6.424	5.842	5.583	5.342	4.910	4.533
14	13.004	12.106	10.563	9.295	8.244	7.367	6.628	6.002	5.724	5.468	5.008	4.611
15	13.865	12.849	11.118	9.712	8.559	7.606	6.811	6.142	5.847	5.575	5.092	4.675
16	14.718	13.578	11.652	10.106	8.851	7.824	6.974	6.265	5.954	5.669	5.162	4.730
17	15.562	14.292	12.166	10.477	9.122	8.022	7.120	6.373	6.047	5.749	5.222	4.775
18	16.398	14.992	12.659	10.828	9.372	8.201	7.250	6.467	6.128	5.818	5.273	4.812
19	17.226	15.678	13.134	11.158	9.604	8.365	7.366	6.550	6.198	5.877	5.316	4.844
20	18.046	16.351	13.590	11.470	9.818	8.514	7.469	6.623	6.259	5.929	5.353	4.870
21	18.857	17.011	14.029	11.764	10.017	8.649	7.562	6.687	6.312	5.973	5.384	4.891
22	19.660	17.658	14.451	12.042	10.201	8.772	7.645	6.743	6.359	6.011	5.410	4.909
23	20.456	18.292	14.857	12.303	10.371	8.883	7.718	6.792	6.399	6.044	5.432	4.925
24	21.243	18.914	15.247	12.550	10.529	8.985	7.784	6.835	6.434	6.073	5.451	4.937
25	22.023	19.523	15.622	12.783	10.675	9.077	7.843	6.873	6.464	6.097	5.467	4.948

TABLE III. Factors Useful in the Construction of Control Charts*

Number of Observations in Sample, n	Chart for Averages — Factors for Control Limits			Chart for Standard Deviations — Factors for Central Line		Factors for Control Limits				Chart for Ranges — Factors for Central Line		Factors for Control Limits				
	A	A_1	A_2	c_2	$1/c_2$	B_1	B_2	B_3	B_4	d_2	$1/d_2$	d_3	D_1	D_2	D_3	D_4
2	2.121	3.760	1.880	0.5642	1.7725	0	1.843	0	3.267	1.128	0.8865	0.853	0	3.686	0	3.267
3	1.732	2.394	1.023	0.7236	1.3820	0	1.858	0	2.568	1.693	0.5907	0.888	0	4.358	0	2.575
4	1.500	1.880	0.729	0.7979	1.2533	0	1.808	0	2.266	2.059	0.4857	0.880	0	4.698	0	2.282
5	1.342	1.596	0.577	0.8407	1.1894	0	1.756	0	2.089	2.326	0.4299	0.864	0	4.918	0	2.115
6	1.225	1.410	0.483	0.8686	1.1512	0.026	1.711	0.030	1.970	2.534	0.3946	0.848	0	5.078	0	2.004
7	1.134	1.277	0.419	0.8882	1.1259	0.105	1.672	0.118	1.882	2.704	0.3698	0.833	0.205	5.203	0.076	1.294
8	1.061	1.175	0.373	0.9027	1.1078	0.167	1.638	0.185	1.815	2.847	0.3512	0.820	0.387	5.307	0.136	1.864
9	1.000	1.094	0.337	0.9139	1.0942	0.219	1.609	0.239	1.761	2.970	0.3367	0.808	0.546	5.394	0.184	1.816
10	0.949	1.028	0.308	0.9227	1.0837	0.262	1.584	0.284	1.716	3.078	0.3249	0.797	0.687	5.469	0.223	1.777
11	0.905	0.973	0.285	0.9300	1.0753	0.299	1.561	0.321	1.679	3.173	0.3152	0.787	0.812	5.534	0.256	1.744
12	0.866	0.925	0.266	0.9359	1.0684	0.331	1.541	0.354	1.646	3.258	0.3069	0.778	0.924	5.592	0.284	1.716
13	0.832	0.884	0.249	0.9410	1.0627	0.359	1.523	0.382	1.618	3.336	0.2998	0.770	1.026	5.646	0.308	1.692
14	0.802	0.848	0.235	0.9453	1.0579	0.384	1.507	0.406	1.594	3.407	0.2935	0.762	1.121	5.693	0.329	1.671
15	0.775	0.816	0.223	0.9490	1.0537	0.406	1.492	0.428	1.572	3.472	0.2880	0.755	1.207	5.737	0.348	1.652
16	0.750	0.788	0.212	0.9523	1.0501	0.427	1.478	0.448	1.552	3.532	0.2831	0.749	1.285	5.779	0.364	1.636
17	0.728	0.762	0.203	0.9551	1.0470	0.445	1.465	0.466	1.534	3.588	0.2787	0.743	1.359	5.817	0.379	1.621
18	0.707	0.738	0.194	0.9576	1.0442	0.461	1.454	0.482	1.518	3.640	0.2747	0.738	1.426	5.854	0.392	1.608
19	0.688	0.717	0.187	0.9599	1.0418	0.477	1.443	0.497	1.503	3.689	0.2711	0.733	1.490	5.888	0.404	1.596
20	0.671	0.697	0.180	0.9619	1.0396	0.491	1.433	0.510	1.490	3.735	0.2677	0.729	1.548	5.922	0.414	1.586
21	0.655	0.679	0.173	0.9638	1.0376	0.504	1.424	0.523	1.477	3.778	0.2647	0.724	1.605	5.950	0.425	1.575
22	0.640	0.662	0.167	0.9655	1.0358	0.516	1.415	0.534	1.466	3.819	0.2618	0.720	1.659	5.979	0.434	1.566
23	0.626	0.647	0.162	0.9670	1.0342	0.527	1.407	0.545	1.455	3.858	0.2592	0.716	1.710	6.006	0.443	1.557
24	0.612	0.632	0.157	0.9684	1.0327	0.538	1.399	0.555	1.445	3.895	0.2567	0.712	1.759	6.031	0.452	1.548
25	0.600	0.619	0.153	0.9696	1.0313	0.548	1.392	0.565	1.435	3.931	0.2544	0.709	1.804	6.058	0.459	1.541
Over 25	$\dfrac{3}{\sqrt{n}}$	$\dfrac{3}{\sqrt{n}}$	—	—	—	†	‡	†	‡	—	—	—	—	—	—	—

$$\dagger\; 1 - \frac{3}{\sqrt{2n}} \qquad \ddagger\; 1 + \frac{3}{\sqrt{2n}}$$

Chart	Central Line	3σ Control Limits
$\overline{X}$	$\bar{\bar{x}}$	$\bar{\bar{x}} \pm A_1 s_x$ or
		$\bar{\bar{x}} \pm A_2 \bar{R}$
	μ_x	$\mu_x \pm A\sigma_x$
R	$\bar{R}$	$D_3 \bar{R}$ and $D_4 \bar{R}$
	$d_2 \sigma_x$	$D_1 \sigma_x$ and $D_2 \sigma_x$
σ_x	s_x	$B_3 s_x$ and $B_4 s_x$
	σ_x	$B_1 \sigma_x$ and $B_2 \sigma_x$

Definitions: $A = 3/\sqrt{n},\; A_1 = \dfrac{3}{c_2\sqrt{n}},\; A_2 = \dfrac{3}{d_2\sqrt{n}},\; B_1 = c_2 - K,\; B_2 = c_2 + K,\; B_3 = 1 - \dfrac{K}{c_2},\; B_4 = 1 + \dfrac{K}{c_2},\; D_1 = d_2 - 3d_3,$

$D_2 = d_2 + 3d_3,\; D_3 = 1 - 3\dfrac{d_3}{d_2},$ and $D_4 = 1 + 3\dfrac{d_3}{d_2},$ where $K = 3\sqrt{\dfrac{(n-1)}{n} - c_2{}^2}.$

Warning: The fourth significant figures for D_1, D_2, D_3, and D_4 are in doubt for n greater than 5.

*From *Economics Control of Manufactured Products* © 1931 by Litton Educational Publishing, Inc. Reprinted by permission of Van Nostrand Reinhold Company.

TABLE IV. Table of Random Digits*

78466	83326	96589	88727	72655	49682	82338	28583	01522	11248
78722	47603	03477	29528	63956	01255	29840	32370	18032	82051
06401	87397	72898	32441	88861	71803	55626	77847	29925	76106
04754	14489	39420	94211	58042	43184	60977	74801	05931	73822
97118	06774	87743	60156	38037	16201	35137	54513	68023	34380
71923	49313	59713	95710	05975	64982	79253	93876	33707	84956
78870	77328	09637	67080	49168	75290	50175	34312	82593	76606
61208	17172	33187	92523	69895	28284	77956	45877	08044	58292
05033	24214	74232	33769	06304	54676	70026	41957	40112	66451
95983	13391	30369	51035	17042	11729	88647	70541	36026	23113
19946	55448	75049	24541	43007	11975	31797	05373	45893	25665
03580	67206	09635	84612	62611	86724	77411	99415	58901	86160
56823	49819	20283	22272	00114	92007	24369	00543	05417	92251
87633	31761	99865	31488	49947	06060	32083	47944	00449	06550
95152	10433	52693	22480	50336	49502	06296	76414	18358	05313
05639	24175	79438	92151	57602	03590	25465	54780	79098	73594
65927	55525	67270	22907	55097	63177	34119	94216	84861	10457
59005	29000	38395	80367	34112	41866	30170	84658	84441	03926
06626	42682	91522	45955	23263	09764	26824	82936	16813	13878
11306	02732	34189	04228	58541	72573	89071	58066	67159	29633
45143	56545	94617	42752	31209	14380	81477	36952	44934	97435
97612	87175	22613	84175	96413	83336	12408	89318	41713	90669
97035	62442	06940	45719	39918	60274	54353	54497	29789	82928
62498	00257	19179	06313	07900	46733	21413	63627	48734	92174
80306	19257	18690	54653	07263	19894	89909	76415	57246	02621
84114	84884	50129	68942	93264	72344	98794	16791	83861	32007
58437	88807	92141	88677	02864	02052	62843	21692	21373	29408
15702	53457	54258	47485	23399	71692	56806	70801	41548	94809
59966	41287	87001	26462	94000	28457	09469	80416	05897	87970
43641	05920	81346	02507	25349	93370	02064	62719	45740	62080
25501	50113	44600	87433	00683	79107	22315	42162	25516	98434
98294	08491	25251	26737	00071	45090	68628	64390	42684	94956
52582	89985	37863	60788	27412	47502	71577	13542	31077	13353
26510	83622	12546	00489	89304	15550	09482	07504	64588	92562
24755	71543	31667	83624	27085	65905	32386	30775	19689	41437
38399	88796	58856	18220	51016	04976	54062	49109	95563	48244
18889	87814	52232	58244	95206	05947	26622	01381	28744	38374
51774	89694	02654	63161	54622	31113	51160	29015	64730	07750
88375	37710	61619	69820	13131	90406	45206	06386	06398	68652
10416	70345	93307	87360	53452	61179	46845	91521	32430	74795
99258	03778	54674	51499	13659	36434	84760	76446	64026	97534
58923	18319	95092	11840	87646	85330	58143	42023	28972	30657
39407	41126	44469	78889	54462	38609	58555	69793	27258	11296
29372	70781	19554	95559	63088	35845	60162	21228	48296	05006
07287	76846	92658	21985	00872	11513	24443	44320	37737	97360
07089	02948	03699	71255	13944	86597	89052	88899	03553	42145
35757	37447	29860	04546	28742	27773	10215	09774	43426	22961
58797	70878	78167	91942	15108	37441	99254	27121	92358	94254
32281	97860	23029	61409	81887	02050	63060	45246	46312	30378
93531	08514	30244	34641	29820	72126	62419	93233	26537	21179

*Reproduced with permission from The Rand Corp., *A Million Random Digits with 100,000 Normal Deviates*. Copyright, The Free Press, Glencoe, Ill., 1955, pp. 180–183.

Abruzzi, A., 428, 449
Acceptable quality level (AQL), definition, 653
Acceptance sampling, by attributes, 650
    average outgoing quality curves (AOQ), 655
    double sampling, 65
    operating characteristic curves, 650
    sequential sampling, 657
    specification of a plan, 654
  by variables, 658
    field of application, 658
  when appropriate, 649
Ackoff, R. L., 18, 211, 505
Activity analysis, in PERT networks, 598
Activity charts, man-machine charts, 385–389
    multiple activities, 391
Aggregate plans and programs, 507–545
    decision processes for, graphic methods, 513
        Linear Decision Rule, 521
        linear programming, 524
        reaction rate model, 517
        Search Decision Rule, 526–533
    for job shops, 534
    for large projects, 535
    for noninventoriable items, 533
    multistage model, 512
    nature of, 508
    plans for various horizons, 509
    single stage model, 510
Albers, H. A., 43
Alcalay, J. A., 43, 63, 471
Allderige, J. M., 450
Allen, M., 568
Allowances, in work measurement, 441
    application of, 444
    for delays, 442
    for fatigue and personal time, 442
AMA, 684
Amber, G. H., 249
Amber, P. S., 249
Amstead, B. H., 249, 280
Analysis, process of, 68–74

Analytical methods, kinds of, breakeven
        analysis, 75
    cost analysis, 74, 109–126, 127–146
    heuristic methods, 99–102
    linear programming, 76–83
    schematic and graphic, 103–105
    search methods, 102
    simulation models, 88–97
    statistical analysis, 97–99
    waiting line or queuing models, 83–88
  significance of, 679
Andrews, R. B., 439
Anthony, R. N., 108, 125
Anthropometric data, chair and table
        heights, 397
    strength and forces of body movements, 393
    work area limits, 398
Applied science, production management as, 15
Archibald, R. D., 613, 619
Arcus, 344, 363
Armour, G. C., 325, 363
Arnoff, E. L., 211, 505
Arrow diagramming, 599
Assembly chart, 252
Automation, 229–238
    closed loop, 230
    feedback, 230
    numerical control, 234
    open loop, 230
    open loop applications, 231
    sensing, comparison, decision making,
        and effector functions, 231
    social and economic effects, 229
Average investment criterion for comparing
        economic alternatives, 137
Average outgoing quality (AOQ), calculation
        of, 655

Babbage, Charles, 7, 18
Bailey, G. B., 450
Balancing techniques in production lines, 341–346

693

Baldwin, E. N., 281

Barish, N, N., 146

Barkdoll, G., 684

Barnes, R. M., 108, 383, 384, 386, 398, 413, 420, 426, 439, 450

Barth, Carl, 10

Base stock system of inventory control, 496

Basic Motion Time study (BMT), 439

Beer, S., 63

Begeman, M. L., 249, 280

Bennett, E., 413

Berry, W. L., 591, 592

Bertoletti, M. E., 190

Bidding, example of, 23

Biotechnology, see Human engineering; Job design

Birnie, D. P., 364

Blast furnace, 220

Bock, R. H., 568, 591

Boeing Airplane Co., 468, 471

Bogardy, A. E., 307

Boodman, D. M., 505, 545, 568, 592

Book value, 128

Boulden, J. B., 43, 63, 684, 685

Bowker, A. H., 669

Bowman, E. H., 108, 190, 363, 524, 544, 641

Breakdown-time distributions, 624

Breakeven analysis, breakeven chart, 112
  breakeven point, 112
  causes of changes in breakeven point, 114
  construction of breakeven charts from cost data, 112
  construction of breakeven charts from scatter plots, 113
  contribution, 111
  effect of managerial decisions on breakeven point, 114
  in multiproduct organizations, 115
  in process selection, 269
  usefulness of, 115

Brech, E. S. L., 18

Brewer, S. H., 472

Briggs, S. J., 413

Brigham, F., 211

Brooks, G. H., 363

Bross, I. D. F., 43

Brouha, L. A., 400

Brown, P. A., 307

Brown, R. G., 505

Buchan, J., 505

Buffa, E. S., 18, 43, 63, 64, 108, 146, 190, 211, 307, 320–324, 363, 364, 450, 471, 472, 505, 544, 568, 591, 619, 641, 648, 685

Buffer stocks, 478

Buildings, plant, 349

Bulkin, M. H., 591

Burgess, A. R., 619

Capacity decision for facility design, 311
  future capacity, 311
  multiple shifts, 312
  subcontracting, 312
  workable units of capacity, 312

Capital additions, as a component of capital costs, 132

Capital costs, 127, 130–133

Carlson, J. G., 573

Carroll, D. C., 581, 584, 591

Chair and table heights, 397

Chaney, F. B., 669

Chapanis, A., 374, 379, 413, 414

Chapiro, J., 190

Charnes, A., 190

Chatto, K., 191, 544

Chrysler Corp., 345

Churchman, C. W., 211, 505

Clark, C. E., 620

Cleland, D. I., 63

Close, G., 102, 108

Closed loop automation, 230

Closed system, 47

Cole, R. T., 591

Colley, J. L., 591

Computer search methods, 102

COMSOAL, 344

Connor, N. B., 414

Consumer's risk (α), definition, 654

Contaminants and hazards in the working environment, 406

Contour control in numerical control of machine tools, 236

Contribution, 111

Control, costs, see Cost control

Control, production levels, 507–545
  control numbers and reaction rates, 517

Control charts, 659–665
  by attributes, 660
    calculation of control limits, 661
    example of a p-chart, 661
    other types of attributes control charts, 662

Control charts (*continued*)
  by variables, 662
    normality of sampling distributions of
      small samples, 663
  on measures of variability, 665
Control knob coding, 396, 397
Control subsystems, 57
Conway, R. W., 591
Cook, J. S., 414
Cooper, W. W., 190
Cost control, 461
COVERT, 581, 584
Cox, C. B., 191, 544
CRAFT, 325
Critical Path Methods, 608
Critical path scheduling, 603
Cross classification charts, 574
Culiton, J. W., 249, 280
Cycle inventories, 477

Dalleck, W. C., 505
Davis, E. W., 614, 619
Davis, L. E., 413, 414
Dean, J., 146
Decision making, function of models in, 29, 33
  nature of, 19, 20
  relation to models, 29, 33
  structure of, 20
  system, 20
  under certainty, 22
  under conflict, 22
  under risk, 23
  under uncertainty, 22
Decision theory, 21
Decisions, cost data for, 109–126
  kinds of, 21–29
  long run, 39
  probability of attainment, 21
  related to control of systems, 39
  related to design of systems, 40
Decoupling function of inventories, 478
Degan, E. J., 413
Denholm, D. H., 363
Dewitte, 614, 619
Differential costs, *see* Incremental costs
Dillon, J. D., 307
Dispatch decision rules, 577
Displays, visual, 377–380
  banks of dials, 380
  coding of controls, 396

Displays, visual (*continued*)
  dial design, 379
  dial shapes, 379
Distribution methods—linear programming,
    degeneracy, 155–157
  distribution matrix, 149
  improvement of feasible solutions, 151
  Northwest initial solution, 150
  optimal solutions, 154
  techniques for simplifying solution, 157
  unequal supply and demand, 156
  uses for, 158
Division of labor, advantages of, 6
Dixon, W. J., 108
Dodge, H. F., 669
Double sampling by attributes, 656
Dresch, F. W., 307
Dummy activities, in PERT networks, 600
DuMond, T. C., 280
Duncan, A. J., 669
Duncan, J. H., 450
Dynamic programming, 184

Early finish time, definition and computation
    of, 604
Early start time, definition and computation
    of, 603
Eary, D. F., 249, 280
Eastman Kodak Co., 436–438, 633–636
Economic life, 133
Economic lot sizes, 485–492
Effective temperature, 398
  effect on performance, 399
Effroymson, M. A., 307
Eisemann, K., 191, 544
Ellis, D. S., 414
Elmaghraby, S. E., 591, 592, 619
Emerson, H., 10
Erlang, A. K., 193
Estimating costs, 268
Events in PERT networks, 597, 603
Expense classification, 109, 110
Exponential service times, 198–200

Fabian, T., 191, 544
Fabrycky, W. J., 146
Fatigue, 442–445
Fazar, W., 620
Feedback control, 47, 230
  time-lag effects, 49

Feigenbaum, A. V., 669
Feldman, E., 307
Feorene, O. J., 211, 633–636, 642
Ferguson, R. O., 191
Ferrara, W. L., 126
Fetter, R. B., 108, 190, 191, 363, 505, 544, 641, 642
Fey, W. R., 472
Fillipetti, G., 18
Fitts, T. M., 414
Fixed costs for breakeven analysis, 110
  definition of, 110
Fixed order quantity system of inventory control, 495
Fixed reorder cycle system of inventory control, 496
Flow diagram, 258
Flow process charts, analysis of,
  man, 385
  product, 257
Fogel, L. J., 414
Forecasting, 479–485
  methodology, 481–485
    exponential, 483
    moving averages, 482
  time horizon, 480
Foreign plant locations, 295–302
  labor cost comparisons, 299
  other costs, 299
  overall comparative costs, U.S. versus abroad, 301
  wage level comparisons, 298
Forming processes of metal, 220
  comparison of forming processes, 222
Forrester, J., 43, 63, 472, 559–563, 568
Friden, 226
Friedman, L., 212
Fulkerson, D. R., 614, 619
Functional layout, see Process layout

Gagné, R. M., 414
Galliher, H. T., 363
Gantt, H. L., 10
Gantt charts, as a graphic model, 576–581
Garner, W. R., 413
Garrett, L. J., 64
Gaudreau, A. P., 364
General Electric Co., 216, 352, 353
General-purpose machines, 228
Gerson, M., 307

Gibson, D. F., 307
Gilbreth, Frank and Lillian, 10
Godin, V., 586, 591
Goetz, B. E., 125
Gonzales, R. F., 64
Goode, H. P., 669
Gordon, J. R. M., 544
Grabbe, E. M., 249
Grant, E. L., 126, 146, 669
Greene, J. H., 191, 544, 568
Groff, G. K., 43, 591
Grosse, R. A., 18, 108, 191
Gustat, G. H., 436–438, 450

Hadley, G., 505
Hahir, J. P., 249, 280
Hamburger, M. J., 307
Hannsmann, F., 191, 544
Hansen, B. L., 669
Hardaway, H., 413
Hare, V. C., Jr., 63
Harris, D. H., 669
Harris, F. W., 11, 505
Hawthorne studies, 404
Hazelwood, R. N., 212
Heiland, R. E., 450
Held, M., 363
Helgeson, W. B., 364
Helipot Division of Beckman Instruments, 480, 548
Hess, S. W., 191, 544
Heuristic methods, 99
Hicks, C. R., 191, 544
Hodge, B. J., 18
Hoel, P. G., 108, 669
Hoffman, T. R., 364
Holstein, W. K., 568, 591, 592
Holt, C. C., 520, 544, 545
Hooke, R., 526, 545
Hovey, R. W., 685
Hughes Aircraft Co., 579, 585
Human engineering, 14
  see also Job design
Human factors, see Human engineering; Job design
Hunsicker, P. A., 414
Hunt, D. P., 414

IBM, 572
Incremental costs, above breakeven points, 118

Incremental costs (*continued*)
  for an assembly line, 116
  in make-buy decisions, 116
  in selecting processes, 267–269
  leasing costs, 119
  when direct labor is fixed, 117
Infinite waiting line models, 200
Inland Steel Co., 59
Interest factors, compound, 134
  present worth tables, 689, 690
Inventories, effect of variability, 493–495
    basic control systems for handling, 495
    safety stocks, 493–495
  functions of, 474–479
  information feedback systems in
      controlling, 497
  lot sizes, 485–490
    production, 490
    production runs for several products, 492
    purchase, 485
    with quantity discounts, 489
Inventory and production control, controlling
      production levels, 507–545
  forecasts, 479–485
  inventories, 474–479, 485–498
  lot sizes, 485–490
    production, 490
    production runs for several products, 492
  with quantity discounts, 489
  master programs, 507–545
  production plans for seasonal sales, 507–545
  safety stocks, 493–495
Investment criteria for comparing economic
      alternatives, average investment, 137
  payoff periods, 139
  present values, 135, 137
  rate of return, 138
Ireson, W. G., 126, 146
Irregular tasks, analysis of, 390

Jablonski, R., 569, 592
Jackson, J. R., 364
Jeeves, T. A., 526, 545
Jenkins, W. L., 414
Jeske, J. W., 592
Jessen, R. J., 108, 669
Job design, 365–415
  anthropometric data, 393
  arrangement and flow of work, 398
  conceptual framework, 368, 371

Job design (*continued*)
  fatigue and work schedules, 442
  information displays, 376
  man as an element in, 370
  man-machine systems, 368
  measures of effectiveness, 366
  principles of motion economy, 384
  relationship of factors determining job
      content and job methods, 368
  rest pauses, 442
  speed and accuracy of motor responses, 392
  where man surpasses machines, 370
  who designs jobs, 367
Job enlargement, 367
Johnson, G. E., 249
Johnson, H. J., 18
Johnson, R. A., 64, 619
Jones, C. H., 545, 586, 591
Judgment as a factor in measurement, in
      performance rating, 421–424
  in quality control, 646
  in use of precision gages, 648
Judgment in business, how good, 681

Karp, R. M., 363
Karpovich, P. U., 414
Kast, F. E., 64, 619
Keller, I. W., 126
Kelley, J. E., 614, 620
Keuhn, A. A., 307
Khumawala, B. M., 307
Kibbey, D. R., 249, 280
Kilbridge, M. D., 344, 364
Killebrew, J. B., 619
King, W. R., 63
Kirkpatrick, C. A., 620
Kirkpatrick, E. G., 669
Knox, F. M., 280
Koenigsberg, E., 505
Kusnick, A. A., 592

Lamson Co., 346
Lane, Kenneth, 216
Large project planning and control, *see* PERT
Large-scale systems, 58
Latest finish time, definition and computation
      of, 604
Latest start time, definition and computation
      of, 603
Lawshe, C. H., 669

Layout of physical facilities, 309–364
  capacity decision, 311
  CRAFT, 325
  graphic layout technique, 350
  layout types, 314
    combinations, 318
    process, 318–340
    product, 340–348
  line balancing techniques, 341–346
  material handling, in process layouts,
    337–340
    in product layouts, 346
  nonmanufacturing activity, 354
  office layout, 333
  operation sequence analysis, 320
  plant buildings, 349
  service facilities, 348
    employee, 349
    plant, 348
Least costing of PERT networks, 614
Leavenworth, R. S., 669
Lee, W. B., 545
LeGrand, E., 582–585, 592
Lehrer, F. A., 307
Levin, R. I., 620
Levy, F. K., 609, 614, 620
Lifson, K. A., 450
Lighting, 403
  criteria for environment of, 403
  critical levels of, 403
  effects of performance, 404
  glare effects, 404
Limited resources model for PERT, 614
Line layout, see Product layout
Line speeds for production lines, 337
Linear Decision Rule, 521
Linear programming, 147–191
  applications, 158
  distribution matrix, 149
  distribution methods, 147–159
  simplex methods, 159–191
Litterer, J. A., 18, 43
Load leveling in PERT, 612
Lockheed Aircraft Corp., 217, 218
Lot tolerance per cent defective (LTPD),
  definition, 654
Luckiesh, M., 405, 414
Lusser, R., 623, 642
Lyman, J., 450

MacCrimmon, K. R., 620
Mackworth, N. H., 414
Maffei, R. B., 307
Magee, J. F., 505, 517, 518, 545, 568, 592
Maintenance, breakdown time distributions,
  624
  maintenance departments, 636
  preventive for several machines, 630
  preventive for single machine, 626
    effect of down-time costs, 629
    effect of relation of preventive maintenace
      time to repair time, 628
    guides to preventive maintenance
      policy, 628
    per cent of time machine works for
      three different breakdown-time
      distributions, 629
  reliability, 621, 622
  simulation of alternate practices,
    an example, 631–636
Make-buy decisions, 264
  economic analysis for, 264
  make-buy policies, 266
  noneconomic and intangible factors in, 266
Malcolm, D. G., 212, 620, 642
Malcolm, J. A., 450
Mallick, R. W., 364
Man-machine chart (activity chart), 385–390
  analysis of, 387–390
  examples of, 387–390
Man-machine systems, 368–376
  automatic systems, 375
  conceptual framework, 371
  control, 381
  functions performed, 371, 373
  information input, 376
  man versus machines, 370
  man's functions in performing work, 370
  manual systems, 373
  semiautomatic systems, 374
  simplified model of, 374
  working environment, 398
Marginal costs, see Incremental costs
Massey, F. J., Jr., 108
Master programs in production planning,
  507–545
  cost of alternate programs, 515
  functions of forecasts in, 508–510
  graphic methods, 513

Master programs in production planning
(*continued*)
  Linear Decision Rule, 521
  linear programming methods, 524
  nature of problem, 508
  reaction rate model, 517
  Search Decision Rule, 526–533
Mastor, A. A., 345, 364
Material handling, in process layouts, 337
  in product layouts, 346
Maxwell, W. L., 591
Maynard, H. B., 450
McCormick, E. J., 373, 377, 378, 399, 414
McDonough, A. M., 64
McGarrah, R. E., 545
McMillan, C., 64
Meister, D., 414
Methods-Time Measurement (MTM), 439
Metzger, R. W., 191
Micromotion study, 385
Miller, D. W., 43, 506
Miller, L. W., 591
MIL-STD-105C, 669
MIL-STD-414, 669
Models—mathematical, construction of, 70–74
  controllable variables, 71
  definition of systems under study, 68–70
  measures of effectiveness, 71
  related to decisions, 29
  uncontrollable variables, 71
Moder, J. J., 620
Modigliani, F., 520, 544, 545
Monte Carlo methods, 89–97
Moodie, C. L., 592
Moore, F. G., 569, 592
Moore, H. D., 249, 280
Moore, J. M., 364
Morgan, C. T., 413, 414
Morse, P. M., 212, 625, 627, 630, 642
Most likely time in PERT, 610
Motion economy, principles of, *see* Principles of
  motion economy
Müller, E. A., 414, 450
Mundel, M. E., 413, 414, 450
Muth, J. F., 43, 520, 544, 591
Muther, R., 364

Nadler, G., 108, 414, 450
Nanot, Y. R., 592

National Industrial Conference Board,
  307
Nelson, R. T., 195, 212, 592
Neter, J., 669
Network planning, *see* PERT
Niebel, B. W., 281, 450
Nodes, in PERT networks, 603
  numbering of, 603
Noise, 400–403
  control of, 402
  db levels of, 401
  effects on performance, 401
  hearing loss due to, 402
Nordhoff, W. A., 281
Normal time in work measurement, 421
Novotny, D. J., 592
Nugent, C. E., 364
Numerical control, 234–239
  contour control, 236
  economics of, 237, 239
  position control, 234
  position controlled drill press, 235
  programming systems, 236

Obsolescence, 133
Office layout, 333
O'Malley, R. L., 592
Open systems, 47
Open loop automation, 230
Operation chart, 383
Operation process chart, 255
Operation sheet, 270
Operations planning and control, aggregate
  plans, 507–545
  classification of systems, 462–464
  forecasting, 479–485
  interdependence of functions, 454
  inventories, functions of, 474–479
  lot sizes, 485–490
  organizing for, 465
  production-inventory systems, 453–472
  suboptimization, 457
  system control, 457
Operations sequence analysis, 320–325
  block diagrams, 323, 324
  ideal schematic solution, 322
  load summary, 320
Opportunity costs, 131
  see also Capital costs

Optimistic time in PERT, 610
Organizing for material flow, 465
Out-of-pocket costs, *see* Incremental costs

Papen, G. W., 249, 281
Payoff periods as criteria for comparing
    economic alternatives, 139
Peck, L. G., 212
Pegels, C., 683, 685
Performance rating, 421
    accuracy of, 423
    as a system of measurement, 421
    scales, 423
PERT, 593–620
    activity analysis, 598
    arrow diagramming, 599
    critical path scheduling, 603
    deployment of resources, 611
    difficulties with, 615
    dummy activities, 600
    manual computation of schedule statistics, 604
    node numbering, 603
    origin of, 595
    PERT/CPM differences, 608
    probabilistic model, 608
Pessimistic time in PERT, 610
Phillips, C. R., 620
Pin manufacture, 7
Pipeline inventories, 476
Plant efficiency factor, 313
Plant location, 283–307
    capital expenditure—volume effects, 289
    dynamic nature of, 284
    example of a location study, 285
    foreign locations, 295
    how important, 284
    location of the steel industry, 284
    locational dynamics of multiplants, 292
    multiplant location, 289
    objective and subjective factors, 285–288
    site selection, 287
    warehouse location, 294
Podalsky, O., 413
Poisson arrival rates, 195
Pollution, 6
Pomona Tile Manufacturing Co., 272
Position control, 234
Positioning elements, speed and accuracy of, 393

Positioning through settings of dials, cranks,
    and handwheels, 395
Potlatch Forests, Inc., 58
Present values, 134
    as criteria for comparing economic
        alternatives, 135, 137
    tables, 689, 690
Preventive maintenance, *see* Maintenance,
    preventive
Principles of motion economy, 384
Process layout, 318–340
    CRAFT, 325
    material handling in, 337–340
    measure of effectiveness for, 319
    operation sequence analysis, 320
    requirements for, 314
Process planning, 251–281
    analysis existing operations, 256
    conceptual framework, 252
    continuous industries, 270
    estimating and process selection, 267
    make versus buy, 264
    network planning, 271
    nonmanufacturing, 271
    product analysis, 252
    route and operation sheets, 270
Processes, 219–228
    assembly, 223
    chemical, 219
    clerical, 224
    shape or form, 220
    transport, 224
Producer's risk (β), definition, 653
Product analysis, analysis methods, 252–258
Product layout, 340–348
    banks and line speeds, 346
    line balancing techniques, 341–346
    material handling in, 346
    requirements for, 315, 316
Production, definition of, 33
Production design, 215–218
    basic alternatives of, 237
    effect of parts joining methods on, 240
    effect on indirect costs, 218
    range of costs affected by, 218
    reduced machining, 242
    simplified designs, 242
    tolerances, 240

Production economics, 5
Production-inventory systems, 453–472
  classification of, continuous versus
      intermittent, 462, 464
    inventoriable verus noninventoriable,
      462, 464
  organizing for, 465
  role in society, 4
  suboptimization, 457
  system control, 457
  system view in, 454
Production levels, control numbers and
    reaction rates, 517
  objective defined, 508
Production processes, 219–237
  metal, classification of, 220–223
Production runs for several products, 492
Production standards, allowances, 441–446
  based on work measurement, 424
  informal standards, 418
  need for, 418
  performance rating, 421
  standard data methods, 438–441
  stopwatch methods, 424
  work sampling, 430
Purex Corp., 466–468

Quadratic programming, 184
Quality control, acceptance sampling, by
    attributes, 650
  by variables, 658
  when appropriate, 649
  control charts, by attributes, 660
  by variables, 662
  on measures of variability, 665
  element of judgment, 647
  in distribution, installation, and use, 646
  in manufacture, 645
  in product design, 645
  organizing for, 640
  product policy and quality, 644
Queuing models, see Waiting line models
Quick, J. H., 450

Rabideau, G. F., 414
Random numbers, 692
Rate of return criterion for comparing economic
    alternatives, 138

Ray, T. L., 307
Raymond, F. E., 11, 505
Redwine, C. N., 545
Reed, R., 364
Reisman, A., 43, 64, 108, 146, 472
Reiter, S., 592
Reliability of production systems, methods
    of maintaining, 621, 622
Replacement, criteria for, average
    investment, 137
  payoff periods, 139
  present values, 135, 137
  rate of return, 138
Research Center, Sub-Committee on Noise, 402
Rest pauses, a physiological basis, 442
Richardson, W. J., 450
Rieznik, H. R., 190
Ritter, J. B., 620
Ritzman, L. P., 364
Rogers, J. D., 364
Romig, H. G., 669
Roseboom, J. H., 620
Rosenzweig, J., 64, 472, 619
Route sheet, 270
Rowe, A. J., 592
Ruml, J., 364
Ryavec, C. A., 620

Saaty, T. L., 212
Safety stocks, 493–495
    see also Buffer stocks
Salvage values, fall in, 132
Sargent, L. F., 191
Sasieni, M., 18, 212
Schedule, analysis by graphic means, 576–581
Schedule diagram, 575
Scheduling and control—high volume
    systems, 547–569
  detailed scheduling process, 556
  nature of, 549
  production control, 564
  scheduling and aggregate planning, 553
    product mix problem, 553
  scheduling system dynamics, 561
  system dynamics of, 558
  system inventories for, 550
Scheduling and control—intermittent
    systems, 571–592

Scheduling and control—intermittent systems
   (*continued*)
   COVERT, 581, 584
   cross classification charts, 574
   dispatching decision rules, 577
   Gantt charts, 576–581
   Hughes' production, planning and control
      system, 585
   Job Shop simulator, 582
   order control, 572
   order scheduling, 572
   plans and shop papers, 572
   schedule diagram, 575
   tracking order progress, 582
   Western Electric interactive planning and
      control system, 586
Schematic and graphic analysis, flow process
      charts, 257, 385
   for product analysis, 385
   Gantt charts, 576–581
   man or man-machine charts, 257, 385–389
   schedule diagram, 575
   templates, 350
Schoderbek, P. P., 43, 64, 249, 472
Schumacher, C. C., 685
Schwab, J. L., 450
Schwarzbek, R., 191
Scientific management, Taylor's four
      principles of, 9
Scrap factor, 313
Search Decision Rule, 526–533
   compared to the Linear Decision Rule, 528
   evaluation of, 535, 536
   Search Labs application, 529
Sequential sampling, by attributes, 657
Shaffer, L. R., 620
Sharesian, R., 363
Shewhart, Walter, 12
Shycon, H. N., 307
Silver, E. A., 545
Simon, H. A., 520, 544, 545
Simplex methods of linear programming,
      algebraic formulation, 164–170
   calculation of coefficients in succeeding
      tables, 176
   checking work, 180
   degeneracy in simplex solutions, 180
   development of main row, 176
   general applicability of, 170, 182

Simplex methods of linear programming
   (*continued*)
   graphic interpretation of, 159–164
   identifying key row, column, and key
      number, 174, 175
   improving initial solution, 174–179
   initial solution, 173
   kinds of objective functions, 170
   nomenclature of simplex matrix, 174
   procedure summary, 179
   symbolic formulation for, 165
Simulation, of alternate maintenance
      policies, 631
   of optimal repair crew size, 633
   of PERT networks, 612
Slack in PERT and CPM networks, 597, 604
Sleight, R. B., 379, 414
Smith, A., 6, 7
Smith, B. E., 685
Smith, W. P., 364
Special-purpose machines, 228
Spector, W. S., 414
Spiegel, J., 413
Squires, P. C., 398, 414
Stanbus, G. J., 126
Standard time data systems, 438–441
   for job families, 441
   universal, 438
Standard time in work measurement, 420
Starr, M. K., 43, 250, 472, 506, 685
Stegmerten, G. J., 450
Steinhoff, H. W., 591, 592
Stopwatch methods of work measurement,
      breakdown of elements, 425
   consistency of sample data, 429
   general procedure, 424
   sample sizes, 427
   chart for estimating, 428
   taking and recording data, 425
Sunk costs, 130
Symkay, E. W., 472
Systems, closed, 47
   control subsystems, 57
   definition, 46
   feedback control, 47
      time lag effects, 49
   general model of operational, 53
   large-scale, 58
   managerial, 50

Systems (*continued*)
  open, 47
  subsystem modules, 49
Systems viewpoint, 45–66, 454

Taubert, W. H., 63, 108, 363, 472, 505,
    526–533, 544, 545, 568, 591, 619
Taylor, F. W., 8, 18
Templates, layout, block, 350–354
  plastic, 352
  three-dimensional, 352
  two-dimensional, 351
Terborgh, G., 146
Thierauf, R. J., 18, 108, 191
Thompson, G. L., 609, 614, 620
Thuesen, H. G., 146
Tiffin, J., 669
Tinker, M. A., 414
Tippett, L. H. C., 12
Tonge, F. M., 364
Turban, E., 642, 680, 685

UCLA Executive Program, 682
Uncertainty in inventory control, 493–495
  basic control systems for, 495
Unilever, Ltd., 59
Urwick, L., 18

Vajda, S., 191
Vance, L. L., 669
Variable costs, definition of, 110
Vazsonyi, A., 364
Vergin, R. C., 364, 545
Villoria, R. L., 613, 619
VISUAL Plant Layouts, 347
Volgyesi, A. S., 364
Vollmann, T. E., 363, 364
Voris, W., 569, 592

Wagner, H. M., 506, 685
Waiting line models, 83–88, 193–211
  effect of increasing number of channels, 206
  effect of pooling facilities, 207
  finite, 200
  infinite, 200
  multiple-channel, single-phase, 204
  Poisson arrival and service rates, 87, 195–200
  Poisson arrivals, 87, 195

Wearever, Inc., 481
Wester, L., 344, 364
Western Electric Co., 586
Westinghouse Electric Corp., 239–243,
    387–389
Weston, F. C., 307
White, M., 7
Whitin, T. M., 505
Whybark, D. C., 307
Wiest, J. D., 100, 102, 108, 609, 614, 620
Wilson, F. W., 250
Winters, P. R., 506
Woodson, W. E., 414
Work area limits, 398
Work environment, contaminants and
    hazards in, 406
  control of the thermal atmosphere, 400
  criteria for lighting environments, 403
  critical levels of illumination, 403
  db levels of typical noises, 401
  effective temperature, 399
  effective temperature and performance, 398
  glare effects, 405
  hearing loss due to noise, 402
  lighting, 403
  noise, 400
  noise effects on performance, 401
Work factor, 439
Work measurement, allowances, 441–446
    application of, 444
    for delay, 442
    for fatigue and personal time, 442
  conceptual framework of, 418–424
  normal time, 421
  performance rating, 421
    accuracy of, 423
    as a system of measurement, 421
    scales, 423
  standard data systems, 438–441
    for job families, 441
    universal, 438
  standard time, 420
  stopwatch methods, breakdown of
    elements, 425
    consistency of sample data, 429
    general procedure, 424
    sample sizes, 427
      chart for estimating, 428
    taking and recording data, 425

Work measurement (*continued*)
   systems, 424–441
Work sampling, 430–441
   advantages and disadvantages, 439
   compared to stopwatch study, 438
   for delays and allowances, 432
      example, 434
      procedure, 433
   for production standards, 435
      example, 436

Work sampling (*continued*)
   number of observations, 431
      chart for estimating, 432

Yale and Towne Manufacturing Co., 338
Yaspan, A., 212
Young, W. M., 191, 544

Zartier, R. L., 364